The Juvenile Justice System
Delinquency, Processing, and the Law

Sixth Edition

Dean John Champion
Texas A & M International University

Prentice Hall

Upper Saddle River, New Jersey
Columbus, Ohio

Library of Congress Cataloging-in-Publication Data

Champion, Dean J.
    The juvenile justice system : delinquency, processing, and the law / Dean
John Champion. — 6th ed.
        p. cm.
    Includes bibliographical references and index.
    ISBN 0-13-500805-0 (alk. paper)
    1. Juvenile justice, Administration of—United States.   2. Juvenile courts—United States.   I. Title.
    KF9779.C425 2010
    345.73′08—dc22

                                                                                    2008047542

Editor-in-Chief: Vernon Anthony
Acquisitions Editor: Tim Peyton
Editorial Assistant: Alicia Kelly
Project Manager: Jessica Sykes
Senior Operations Supervisor: Pat Tonneman
Art Director: Diane Ernsberger
Cover Designer: Rokusek Design
Cover Photo: Photoshot
Director of Marketing: David Gesell
Marketing Manager: Adam Kloza
Senior Marketing Coordinator: Alicia Wozniak
Manager, Rights and Permission: Zina Arabia
Image Permission Coordinator: Debbie Hewitson

This book was set in Minion by TexTech International and was printed and bound by R.R. Donnelley/Willard. The cover was printed by Lehigh-Phoenix Color.

Pearson Education Ltd., London
Pearson Education Singapore Pte. Ltd.
Pearson Education Canada, Inc.
Pearson Education—Japan

Pearson Education Australia Pty. Limited
Pearson Education North Asia Ltd., Hong Kong
Pearson Educación de Mexico, S.A. de C.V.
Pearson Education Malaysia Pte. Ltd.

Prentice Hall
is an imprint of

www.pearsonhighered.com

10 9 8 7 6 5 4 3 2 1

ISBN-13: 978-0-13-500805-8
ISBN-10:   0-13-500805-0

Brief Contents

Contents

Chapter 3

Theories of Delinquency and Intervention Programs   79

Chapter 4

The Legal Rights of Juveniles   115

Chapter 5

Juveniles and the Police   155

Chapter 8

Classification and Preliminary Treatment: Waivers and Other Alternatives

Chapter 9

The Adjudicatory Process: Dispositional Alternatives   265

Chapter 10

Nominal Sanctions: Warnings, Diversion, and Alternative Dispute Resolution   305

Chapter 11

Juvenile Probation and Community-Based Corrections   349

Chapter 12

Juvenile Corrections: Custodial Sanctions and Parole   389

The Juvenile Justice System: Delinquency, Processing, and the Law, Sixth Edition, is a complete examination of the juvenile justice system. It examines how juvenile offenders are defined and classified and draws on current literature to depict significant stages of juvenile processing.

Current juvenile cases are used to illustrate the legal bases for decisions about juveniles. Landmark Supreme Court cases are included, although persuasive decisions from various state courts are presented to show juvenile justice trends. A legalistic perspective is used, therefore, to highlight the different rights juveniles have acquired and how different components of the juvenile justice system relate to them. An integral feature of this book is the distinction between status offenses and delinquent offenses. This difference has significant consequences for all juveniles affected.

The history of juvenile courts is described, including crucial events that have influenced the course of juvenile justice. Increasingly, juveniles are extended rights commensurate with the rights of adults. An indication of this trend is the growing use of waivers (certifications or transfers) to criminal court. This option is intended to expose more serious juvenile offenders to more severe punishment forms compared with the possible punishments that juvenile judges may impose. However, the spreading use of waivers has not always achieved the intended result of more severe penalties for juveniles, since many juveniles who are waived to criminal courts receive minimal punishments, if punished at all.

One explanation is that most juveniles who are transferred to criminal courts are not necessarily the most serious, dangerous, or violent offenders. A majority of those transferred continue to be property offenders, drug users, or public order and status offenders. Once juveniles are waived to the jurisdiction of criminal courts, their age becomes a mitigating factor. Quite often, this factor trivializes the seriousness of their offending and lessens the punishments imposed. Many cases against juveniles are dropped or reduced to less serious charges. Thus, many juveniles who are tried as adults receive sentences that are comparatively less severe than those that would otherwise be contemplated and imposed by juvenile judges. However, one potential penalty that receives increasing attention is the death penalty applied to juveniles. Current case law about imposing the death penalty as a punishment for juveniles is examined, and several juvenile death penalty cases are described.

Juveniles are not only classified according to type of offense, but they are also tracked according to the nature of offenses committed across years. Delinquency is defined and measured according to several popular indices, such as the *Uniform Crime Reports* and the *National Crime Victimization Survey*. The fact is that no single resource discloses the true amount of delinquency in the United States.

Organization of the Book

The major components of the juvenile justice system are featured, including law enforcement, prosecution and the courts, and corrections. Corrections is presented in a broad context, with each correctional component described. Correctional strategies ranging from diversion to full-fledged incarceration are featured, together with a discussion of the favorable and unfavorable dimensions of such programs. One interesting feature is a section devoted to recidivism among juveniles, depending upon the nature of the treatment program described. Thus, community-based correctional programs are assessed, together with probation and parole alternatives for managing a growing juvenile offender aggregate. Electronic monitoring and home confinement are described as strategic and technological means of coping with growing numbers of juvenile offenders.

Each chapter contains career snapshots of people who work with juvenile offenders in different capacities. Some are juvenile court judges, while others are juvenile probation and parole officers and counselors. These profiles are intended to show why juvenile justice professionals have chosen their careers and what they find rewarding about them. At the same time, they set forth what they believe are requirements and characteristics people should possess who plan to enter the field of juvenile justice. Not just anyone can work with juvenile offenders effectively. Special training, preparation, and education are required. On-the-job experiences with juveniles are described by most of these professionals, and such experiences help students understand some of the situational difficulties these people experience. Their work is often frustrating, but at the same time, it is rewarding in various ways. More than a few successful experiences are reported, as these professionals relate how some of their juvenile clients have gone on to lead law-abiding, productive lives.

Every effort has been made to include the most up-to-date sources, references, and other materials. Thus, at the time this book went into production, the most current material was used as the base for tables, figures, and juvenile justice statistics. The most current material is not always that current, however. For instance, government documents about juvenile justice statistics are published 12 to 18 months after the time the information is actually collected and analyzed. Therefore, it is not unusual for a government document published in 2009 to report "recent" juvenile delinquency statistics for 2007 or earlier. This situation is common, since governmental compilation and reporting of such information is a slow and tedious process. It is not possible, therefore, for the government to report 2009 information in 2009. The historical factual information about juveniles and the juvenile justice system does not change, however. Also, there are few changes in juvenile laws from year to year. Of course, new information is constantly being generated by researchers and government agencies. As a textbook ages, therefore, those seeking more current information about juvenile delinquency trends and other statistical information can obtain these data from several sites on the Internet. But the reader should be assured that most textbooks are replete with rather constant or consistent information about the juvenile justice system. I have sought to provide the reader with the best and most recent information available at the time this manuscript was prepared.

Features

There are several important features that have been prepared for this book. First, there are chapter objectives that outline what each chapter is designed to accomplish. Key terms that are fundamental to understanding the juvenile justice system, the criminal justice system, and various programs and processes are highlighted in color. A complete glossary of these terms is provided. Each chapter contains a summary, highlighting the chapter's main points.

Also included at chapter ends are questions for review. Students are encouraged to study these questions and learn to answer them based on chapter information provided. These questions may also be used in preparation for semester or quarter examinations. At chapter ends, Internet sites are listed that will prove to be useful in looking up significant historical events or factual information relevant to juvenile justice and its many organizations and agencies. As is the case with just about every information source, the Internet is constantly changing. New sites are being added, almost daily, while older, even established, sites are discontinued or changed. Again, every effort has been made to include relevant Internet sites that were functional and up and running at the time of this book's publication. In the event some of these Internet sites are no longer in existence, various Internet search engines can be used to locate most topics of student interest.

For instructors, a Test Bank (TestGen) and PowerPoint illustrations are provided. An Instructor's Manual includes chapter outlines and summary information. It also includes short-answer essay questions that can be used for examination purposes. To access supplementary materials online, instructors need to request an instructor access code. Go to **www.pearsonhighered.com/irc,** where you can register for an instructor access code. Within 48 hours after registering, you will receive a confirming e-mail, including an instructor access code. Once you have received your code, go to the site and log on for full instructions on downloading the materials you wish to use.

Any questions about the text or factual information, as well as any inadvertent inaccuracies, may be sent directly to the author through the contact information below:

Dean J. Champion
Department of Behavioral, Applied
    Sciences, and Criminal Justice
Texas A & M International University
5201 University Blvd.
Laredo, TX 78041
(956) 326-2611 (O)
E-mail: dchampion@tamiu.edu

Reviewers

Elaine Cohen
Broward Community College

Myrna Cintron
Prairie View A & M University

Craig Laker
Tri-State University

Christian Vaccaro
Florida State University

Dana Markiewitz
Bakersfield College

Fredric Oddone
Salt Lake Community College

Norma Sullivan
College of Dupage

Carl Russell
Scottsdale Community College

Acknowledgments

Any textbook is the result of the hard work of many persons. First, I wish to acknowledge the reviewers who took the time to examine the previous editions of this book and make helpful and insightful suggestions for their improvements and revisions. I am indebted to Tim Peyton, my editor, who has always been supportive of my projects. Tim's assistant, Alicia Kelly, provided valuable assistance and direction at critical points throughout the book's development. I also wish to extend a thanks to Jessica Sykes, the Project Manager, whose valuable efforts were quite instrumental in making sure different book features were closely monitored and completed. The entire editorial and production staff at Prentice Hall should be acknowledged. Their extensive work helped to shape and improve the present edition.

About the Author

Dean John Champion is Professor of Criminal Justice, Texas A & M International University, Laredo, Texas. Dr. Champion has taught at the University of Tennessee-Knoxville, California State University-Long Beach, and Minot State University. He earned his Ph.D. from Purdue University and B.S. and M.A. degrees from Brigham Young University. He also completed several years of law school at the Nashville School of Law.

Dr. Champion has written over 40 texts and/or edited works and maintains memberships in 11 professional organizations. He is a lifetime member of the American Society of Criminology, Academy of Criminal Justice Sciences, and the American Sociological Association. He is a former editor of the Academy of Criminal Justice Sciences/Anderson Publishing Company Series on *Issues in Crime and Justice* and the *Journal of Crime and Justice*. He is a contributing author for the *Encarta Encyclopedia 2000* for Microsoft. He has been a visiting scholar for the National Center for Juvenile Justice and is a former president of the Midwestern Criminal Justice Association. He has also designed and/or offered numerous online courses for Texas A & M International University, the University of Phoenix, ITT Tech, Excelsior College, and the University of Alaska-Fairbanks.

His published books for Prentice Hall include *The Juvenile Justice System: Delinquency, Processing and the Law,* Sixth Edition (2010); *Leading U.S. Supreme Court Cases in Criminal Justice: Briefs and Key Terms* (2009); *Administration of Criminal Justice: Structure, Function, and Process* (2003); *Statistics for Criminal Justice and the Statistics for Criminal Justice and Criminology,* Third Edition (2010); *Research Methods for Criminal Justice and Criminology,* Third Edition (2006); *Corrections in the United States: A Contemporary Perspective,* Fourth Edition (2005); *Probation, Parole, and Community Corrections,* Fifth Edition (2008); and *Policing in the Community* (w/George Rush) (1996). Works from other publishers include *The Sociology of Organizations* (McGraw-Hill, 1975); *Research Methods in Social Relations* (John Wiley & Sons, 1976); *Sociology* (Holt, Rinehart, and Winston, 1984); *The U.S. Sentencing Guidelines* (Praeger Publishers, 1989); *Juvenile Transfer Hearings* (w/G. Larry Mays) (Praeger Publishers, 1991); *Measuring Offender Risk* (Greenwood Press, 1994); *The Roxbury Dictionary of Criminal Justice: Key Terms and Leading Supreme Court Cases,* Third Edition (Roxbury Press, 2005); and *Criminal Justice in the United States,* Second Edition (Wadsworth, 1998). Dr. Champion's specialty interests include juvenile justice, criminal justice administration, corrections, and statistics/methods.

chapter 1

An Overview of Juvenile Justice in the United States

chapter objectives

As the result of reading this chapter, you will accomplish the following objectives:

1. Understand the basic components of the juvenile justice system.
2. Learn about the doctrine of *parens patriae* and how juveniles continue to be affected by this doctrine.
3. Understand the difference between juvenile delinquents and status offenders.
4. Determine what is meant by juvenile delinquency.
5. Distinguish between juvenile delinquents and the broad class of status offenders, including runaways, truants, and curfew violators.
6. Understand the meaning of the deinstitutionalization of status offenders.
7. Differentiate between and understand the primary characteristics of juvenile and criminal courts.
8. Understand the intake process for screening juveniles.
9. Learn about different prosecutorial options for pursuing cases against juveniles.
10. Acquire an understanding of the different types of juvenile court dispositions, including nominal, conditional, and custodial sanctions that may be applied.

 ## Case Study

A 16-year-old boy in Milledgeville, Georgia, was arrested for armed robbery. Police alleged that the youth assaulted and robbed a 34-year-old resident. The adult was struck in the head numerous times with a gun wielded by the youth who stole the man's wallet following the assault and fled in the victim's car. Police arrested the youth a short time later. The prosecutor said the youth would be charged as an adult and tried in criminal court. [Source: Adapted from the Associated Press, "Juvenile Arrested on Robbery Charge," October 25, 2007.]

In Clackamas County, Oregon, a 17-year-old, Jose Pablo Hernandez, armed with a knife and gun, entered and robbed a food market. Police arrested Hernandez a short time later near the store, where Hernandez was hiding in some bushes. [Source: Adapted from the Associated Press, "Clackamas County Juvenile Accused of Armed Robbery," October 29, 2007.]

 ## Case Study

At Mercer Middle School in Seattle, Washington, Tam Chau, 15, hated school. He cut classes repeatedly, preferring to hang out with his friends at a mall in an arcade room. Eventually a truancy court ordered Chau to attend school. Violating this court order three times subsequently led to Chau's arrest and confinement in a juvenile detention facility, with juvenile robbers, murderers, and thieves. Chau's arrest and detention is the result of Becca's Bill, an initiative signed into law by the Washington governor. The bill is named after Rebecca Hedman, a 13-year-old, who in 1993 had been abused by her biological mother and placed in foster care. She ran away from the foster home, becoming a drug addict and prostitute. She was found beaten to death that same year. The bill gave rise to truancy courts and empowered judges to jail runaway, at-risk, or incorrigible youths like Tam Chau. [Source: Adapted from the Associated Press, "Should Kids Serve Time for Skipping School?," May 9, 2007.]

In Fort Pierce, Florida, kids roaming the streets after 10:00 P.M. are subject to arrest and overnight detention. The procurfew argument and action taken by Fort Pierce authorities is simple: if kids don't have the opportunity to commit crime, they won't. Just ask Shelwand Riley, 15. She was punched and pepper sprayed by police officers when she resisted arrest for violating curfew and possibly possessing stolen property. [Source: Adapted from the Associated Press, "Broken Curfew=Broken Arm," October 10, 2007.]

And in Charlotte County, Florida, 17-year-old Brian Crist, a runaway teen, was arrested by police officers after he was located and found in possession of nearly three pounds of marijuana. "I just found it," Crist claimed. Crist was charged with felony—possession of marijuana with intent to distribute. [Source: Adapted from the Associated Press, "Runaway Found, Then Arrested," November 16, 2007.]

Introduction

Each of these cases is different. But there are similarities. One boy beats and robs a man and steals his car. Another youth holds up a food store at gunpoint. Another youth shuns school, is arrested by police, and is placed in detention. Another youth is arrested as a curfew violator and for possessing stolen merchandise. Another youth is a runaway with nearly three pounds of marijuana in his possession. All of these arrested youths are juveniles. Each of them has committed one or more offenses that have brought them into the juvenile justice system.

This book is about the juvenile justice system and describes its principal components. The organization of this chapter is as follows. First, the juvenile justice system is described. Sometimes the expression "juvenile justice process" is preferred, since there is much fragmentation and differentiation within organizations that process juveniles. Several of the similarities and differences among these systems will be described in greater detail in later chapters.

Juvenile delinquents are defined and described, as well as the types of offenses they commit. Different definitions of juveniles and juvenile delinquency are presented. Every jurisdiction has its own criteria for determining who juveniles are and whether they are encompassed within the jurisdiction of the juvenile court. A majority of states classify juveniles as ranging in age from 7 to 17, and juvenile courts in these states have jurisdiction over these juveniles. Some states have no minimum-age provisions and consider each case on its own merit, regardless of the youthfulness of the juvenile.

Because juveniles are not considered adults and fully responsible for some of their actions, special laws have been established that pertain only to them. Thus, violations of the laws pertaining only to juveniles are called status offenses. Juveniles who commit such infractions are called status offenders. Juveniles who commit crimes are considered juvenile delinquents, and their actions are labeled juvenile delinquency. Different types of status offenses are discussed. These offenses are not considered crimes if adults commit them. Examples of status offenses include runaway behavior, truancy, and curfew violation. These will be defined and explained. The characteristics of youths involved in such behaviors will also be described.

In 1974, the U.S. Congress passed the Juvenile Justice and Delinquency Prevention Act (JJDPA). This act, although not binding on the states, encouraged all states to remove their status offenders from secure institutions—juvenile prisons or custodial facilities—where they were being held for more or less lengthy periods. Many states subsequently removed their status offenders from these institutions and placed these youths in community, social service, or welfare agencies. This process is called the deinstitutionalization of status offenses (DSO) and will be described in some detail. Several meanings of DSO will be presented. Both anticipated and unanticipated consequences of DSO have occurred. These consequences will be listed and discussed.

Next, a general overview of the juvenile justice system will be presented. While later chapters will focus upon each of these components in greater detail, the juvenile justice system consists of all of the processes involved whenever juveniles come into contact with law enforcement. There are several parallels between the criminal and juvenile justice systems. These will be described. For those juveniles who advance further into the system, prosecutors make decisions about which cases to pursue. These decisions are often preceded by petitions from different parties requesting a formal juvenile court proceeding. When juveniles appear before a juvenile court judge, they face an adjudicatory proceeding and have their cases adjudicated. Juvenile court judges have a more limited range of punishment options compared with criminal court judges. Juvenile court judges may impose nominal, conditional, or custodial dispositions. These different kinds of dispositions will be described.

The Juvenile Justice System

The **juvenile justice system**, similar to **criminal justice**, consists of a more or less integrated network of agencies, institutions, organizations, and personnel that process juvenile offenders. This network is made up of **law enforcement agencies**; **prosecution and the courts**; corrections, probation, and parole services; and public and private community-based treatment programs that provide youths with diverse services. This definition is qualified by the phrase "more or less integrated" because the concept of juvenile justice has different meanings for individual states and for the federal government. Also, in some jurisdictions, the diverse components of the juvenile justice system are closely coordinated, while in other jurisdictions, these components are, at best, loosely coordinated. There is no single nationwide juvenile court system. Instead, there are 51 state systems, including the District of Columbia, and most of them are divided into local systems delivered through either juvenile or family courts at the county level, local probation offices, state correctional agencies, and private service providers. These systems do, however, have a common set of core principles that distinguish them from criminal courts for adult offenders, including: (1) limited jurisdiction (up to age 17 in most states); (2) informal proceedings; (3) focus on offenders, not their crimes; (4) indeterminate sentences; and (5) confidentiality (Feld, 2007).

A Process or System?

Many **criminologists** and **criminal justice professionals** prefer "process" rather than "system" when referring to juvenile justice. This is because "system" connotes a condition of homeostasis, equilibrium, or internal balance among system components. In contrast, process focuses on the different actions and contributions of each of these components in dealing with juvenile offenders at various stages of the processing through the juvenile justice system. Furthermore, system implies coordination among elements in an efficient production process; but in reality, communication and coordination among juvenile agencies, organizations, and personnel in the juvenile justice system are often inadequate or nonexistent (Congressional Research Service, 2007).

Further blurring the concept of juvenile justice is that different criteria are used to define juveniles among local, state, and federal jurisdictions. Within each of these jurisdictions, certain mechanisms exist for redefining particular juveniles as adults so that they may be legally processed by the adult counterpart to juvenile justice, the criminal justice system. Despite these definitional ambiguities and systemic interfaces among jurisdictions, most scholars who investigate juveniles understand what is meant by juvenile justice. As with pornography, these scholars and investigators recognize the juvenile justice process whenever they see its components, even if they may not always be able to define it precisely.

Who Are Juvenile Offenders?

Juvenile Offenders Defined

Juvenile offenders are classified and defined according to several different criteria. According to the 1899 Illinois Act that created juvenile courts, the **jurisdiction** of such courts would extend to all juveniles under the age of 16 who were found in violation of any state or local law or ordinance (Ferzan, 2008). About a fifth of all states place the upper age limit for juveniles at either 15 or 16. In most other states, the upper age limit for juveniles is 17, except for Wyoming, where the upper age limit is 18. Ordinarily, the jurisdiction of juvenile courts includes all juveniles between the ages of 7 and 18. Federal law defines juveniles as any persons who have not attained their eighteenth birthday (18 U.S.C., Sec. 5031, 2009).

> **juvenile offenders**
> Any infant or child who has violated juvenile laws.
>
> **jurisdiction**
> Power of a court to hear and determine a particular type of case; also, territory within which a court may exercise authority such as a city, county, or state.

The Age Jurisdiction of Juvenile Courts

The age jurisdiction of juvenile courts over juveniles depends upon established legislative definitions among the states. The federal government has no juvenile court. Although upper and lower age limits are prescribed, these age limits are not uniform among jurisdictions. Common law has been applied in many jurisdictions where the minimum age of accountability for juveniles is seven. Youths under the age of seven are presumed to be incapable of formulating criminal intent and are thus not responsible under the law. While this presumption may be rebutted, in most cases, it isn't. Thus, if a six-year-old child kills someone, deliberately or accidentally, he/she will likely be treated rather than punished. In some states, no lower age limits exist to restrict juvenile court jurisdiction. Table 1.1 shows upper age limits for most U.S. jurisdictions.

Those states with the lowest maximum age for juvenile court jurisdiction include Connecticut, New York, and North Carolina. In these states, the lowest maximum age for juvenile court jurisdiction is 15. The states having the lowest maximum age of 16 for juvenile court jurisdiction are Georgia, Illinois, Louisiana, Massachusetts, Michigan, Missouri, South Carolina, and Texas. All other states and the federal government

Table 1.1

Age at Which Criminal Courts Gain Jurisdiction over Youthful Offenders, 2008

Age (years)	States
16	Connecticut, New York, North Carolina
17	Georgia, Illinois, Louisiana, Massachusetts, Missouri, South Carolina, Texas
18	Alabama, Alaska, Arizona, Arkansas, California, Colorado, Delaware, District of Columbia, Florida, Hawaii, Idaho, Indiana, Iowa, Kansas, Kentucky, Maine, Maryland, Michigan, Minnesota, Mississippi, Montana, Nebraska, Nevada, New Hampshire, New Jersey, New Mexico, North Dakota, Ohio, Oklahoma, Oregon, Pennsylvania, Rhode Island, South Dakota, Tennessee, Utah, Vermont, Virginia, Washington, West Virginia, Wisconsin, Federal districts
19	Wyoming

Source: Jeffrey A. Butts et al. (1996). *Juvenile Court Statistics 1993: Statistics Report.* Washington, DC: Office of Juvenile Justice and Delinquency Prevention. Updated 2008 by author.

use age 18 as the minimum age for criminal court jurisdiction. Under the JJDPA, juveniles are persons who have not attained their eighteenth birthday (18 U.S.C., Sec. 5031, 2009).

Juvenile offenders who are especially young (under age seven in most jurisdictions) are often placed within the control of community agencies such as departments of human services or social welfare. These children frequently have little or no responsible parental supervision or control. In many cases, the parents themselves may have psychological problems or suffer from alcohol or drug dependencies. Youths from such families may be abused and/or neglected, and in need of supervision and other forms of care or treatment. Instead of punishing those under the age of seven, various kinds of treatment, including social therapy and psychological counseling, are most frequently required. Some states have further age-accountability provisions. Tennessee presumes, for instance, that juveniles between the ages of 7 and 12 are accountable for their delinquent acts, although this presumption may be overcome by their attorneys through effective oral arguments and clear and convincing evidence.

Some states have no minimum age limit for juveniles. Technically, these states have the power to decide matters involving children of any age. This control often involves placement of children or infants in foster homes or under the supervision of community service or human welfare agencies. Neglected, unmanageable, abused, or other children in need of supervision are placed in the custody of these various agencies, at the discretion of juvenile judges. Thus, juvenile courts generally have broad discretionary powers over most persons under the age of 18. Under certain circumstances that will be discussed in a later chapter, some juveniles, particularly young ones such as 11-year-olds and 12-year-olds, may be treated as adults for the purpose of prosecuting them in criminal court for alleged serious crimes.

Parens Patriae

parens patriae
Literally "parent of the country" and refers to doctrine where the state oversees the welfare of youth; originally established by the king of England and administered through chancellors.

Parens patriae is a concept that originated with the King of England during the twelfth century. It means literally the father of the country. Applied to juvenile matters, *parens patriae* means that the king is in charge of, makes decisions about, and has the responsibility for all matters involving juveniles. Within the scope of early English common law, parental authority was primary in the early upbringing of children. However, as children advanced beyond the age of seven, they acquired some measure of responsibility for their own actions. Accountability to parents was shifted gradually to accountability to the state, whenever youths seven years of age or older violated the law. In the name of the king, chancellors in various districts adjudicated matters involving juveniles and the offenses they committed. Juveniles had no legal rights or standing in any court. They were the sole responsibility of the king or his agents. Their future often depended largely upon chancellor decisions. In effect, children were wards of the court, and the court was vested with the responsibility of safeguarding their welfare (McGhee and Waterhouse, 2007).

Chancery courts of twelfth- and thirteenth-century England, and later years, performed many tasks, including the management of children and their affairs, as well as the management of the affairs of the mentally ill and incompetent. Therefore, an early division of labor was created, involving a three-way relationship among the child, the parent, and the state. The underlying thesis of *parens patriae* was that the parents are merely the agents of society in the area of childrearing, and that the state has the primary and legitimate interest in the upbringing of its children. Thus, *parens patriae* established a type of fiduciary or trust-like parent–child relation, with the state able to exercise the right of intervention to delimit parental rights (Friday and Ren, 2006).

Since children could become wards of the court and subject to their control, a key concern for many chancellors was for the future welfare of these children. The welfare interests of chancellors and their actions led to numerous rehabilitative and/or treatment measures. Some of these measures included placement of children in foster homes or their assignment to various work tasks for local merchants (Rockhill, Green, and Furrer, 2007). Parental influence in these child placement decisions was minimal. In the context of *parens patriae,* it is fairly easy to trace this early philosophy of child management and its influence on subsequent events in the United States, such as the child saver movement, houses of refuge, and reform schools. These latter developments were both private and public attempts to rescue children from their hostile environments and meet some or all of their needs through various forms of institutionalization.

Modern Interpretations of *Parens Patriae*

Parens patriae in the present is very much alive throughout all juvenile court jurisdictions in the United States, although some erosion of this doctrine has occurred during the past three or four decades. The persistence of this doctrine is evidenced by the wide range of dispositional options available to juvenile court judges and others involved in the early stages of offender processing in the juvenile justice system. Most of these dispositional options are either nominal or conditional, meaning that the confinement of any juvenile for most offenses is regarded as a last resort. Nominal or conditional options involve relatively mild sanctions (e.g., verbal warnings or reprimands, diversion, probation, making financial restitution to victims, performance of community service, participation in individual or group therapy, or involvement in educational programs), and these sanctions are intended to reflect the rehabilitative ideal that has been a major philosophical underpinning of *parens patriae.*

The Get-Tough Movement

However, the strong treatment or rehabilitative orientation reflected by the *parens patriae* concept is in conflict with the contemporary juvenile justice themes of accountability, justice, and due process. Contemporary juvenile court jurisprudence stresses individual accountability for one's actions. Increasingly there is a trend toward just deserts and justice in the juvenile justice system. This **get-tough movement** is geared toward providing law violators with swifter, harsher, and more certain justice and punishment than the previously dominant rehabilitative philosophy of American courts (Mears et al., 2007).

> **get-tough movement**
> View toward criminals and delinquents favoring maximum penalties and punishments for crimes or delinquent act.

For juveniles, this means greater use of nonsecure and secure custody and incarcerative sanctions in state group homes, industrial schools, or reform schools. For those juveniles charged with violent offenses, this means transferring larger numbers of them to the jurisdiction of criminal courts for adults, where more severe sanctions such as life imprisonment or the death penalty may be imposed. Not everyone agrees that this is a sound trend, however. It has been suggested that while many people favor a juvenile justice system separate from the criminal justice system, they exhibit a strong preference for a system that disposes most juveniles to specialized treatment or counseling programs in lieu of incarceration, even for repeat offenders.

Influencing the *parens patriae* doctrine are the changing rights of juveniles. Since the mid-1960s, juveniles have acquired greater constitutional rights commensurate with those enjoyed by adults in criminal courts. As juveniles are vested with greater numbers of constitutional rights, a gradual transformation of the juvenile court is occurring toward one of greater criminalization. Interestingly, as juveniles obtain a greater range of constitutional rights, they become less susceptible to the influence of *parens patriae.*

Another factor is the gradual transformation of the role of prosecutors in juvenile courts. As prosecutors become more involved in pursuing cases against juvenile

1.1   Career Snapshot

George B. Mumma, Jr.

Senior Investigator, Jefferson County,
District Attorney's Office, Littleton, CO

Statistics:
B.A. (criminal justice), Columbia College;
Certified Juvenile Court Administrator, University of Nevada,
Reno; Colorado P.O.S.T. Certified

Background

I am a Senior Investigator for the Jefferson County District Attorney's Office assigned to the Juvenile Crime Unit. I currently supervise the Special Operations Group and office firearms program. I have been in law enforcement for the past 29 years. I started out joining the Boy Scouts, earning the Eagle Scout award. Later, I was a member of the Arapahoe Rescue Patrol (ARP) for five years. The ARP is a youth search and rescue group in Littleton, Colorado. I have always enjoyed service work, and subsequently I worked as a paramedic. Eventually, I was exposed to police work. After being a paramedic for three years, I began working at the Littleton Police Department (LPD).

My life in the LPD started as a patrol officer writing tickets and taking reports, and since those early days, I have worked in a variety of assignments. I was a member of the SWAT Team, where my first assignment was as sniper/observer on a team, then breacher on an entry team, then team leader of an entry team, and now a special operations supervisor of seven operators.

I left the LPD to work for a larger department in Lakewood, Colorado, in 1983. After 10 years with that department, I left patrol work and began pursuing an investigations career where I worked briefly in Internal Affairs before taking a detective assignment in the Crimes Against Children Unit. Ultimately, I joined the Juvenile Crime Unit. It was during this time that I found my passion, though my time in Crimes Against Children took its toll. I became somewhat depressed dealing with victimized children. Many of these children had been so severely abused that I knew they would have permanent emotional and physical scars. Many of them had been sexually assaulted by teachers, babysitters, and pedophiles, and had also been forced into incestuous relationships within their own homes.

Late in 1994, I was asked by the District Attorney's Office to act as the County Law Enforcement Liaison to the Jefferson County Juvenile Assessment Center. The Juvenile Assessment Center is a collaborative operation involving partners from the school district, human services, mental health, and law enforcement, all acting in the best interests of county children. I accepted the position and was told there was no real plan, just a concept, and so I would have to create a workable plan and implement it. The Jefferson County Juvenile Assessment became a model for assessment centers across the country, and I currently work with other collaborative players to ensure that all children in our jurisdiction receive prompt and positive outreach, whether it involves juvenile justice, truancy, human service, or mental health components of the system.

In my role as the law enforcement liaison, I assist the county truancy officer, the Division of Youth Corrections, in managing the number of detainees in the detention center; teach juvenile justice to 174 area school students and parents; teach at two area colleges in the counseling program; write arrest warrants and make arrests in juvenile delinquency cases; assist with the district attorney's intake process; and review area law enforcement warrantless arrest affidavits.

At least one case stands out in my mind as motivating me to enter and stick with juvenile work. One family had some children with problems, especially their daughters. I was contacted by the school district's truancy officer who wanted me to go to an elementary school with her and talk with two secretaries who had reported two little girls with lice. While I believed this should be a human services issue, I went along anyway. When I arrived at the school and spoke to the secretaries, they advised that they had reported the problem to human services but were told that human services didn't deal with that "type of a situation." Shortly thereafter, the girls returned to school after a 52-day absence and they still had lice. The secretary worried that the man who brought the girls to school looked like "Eddie Munster" and that she was unsure of his relationship with the children. I went to the house that same day and found the two little girls, a kindergartener and a first grader, living in a trailer. The front of the trailer was missing and that turned out to be their bedroom! I knocked on the door and the little kindergartener answered. I asked where her mother was and she said she hadn't seen her for four days. I asked who was babysitting and she yelled for the babysitter who came to the door. He resembled "Eddie Munster," just as the secretaries had described. I asked him where the mother was, and he said she was with her boyfriend in another city. I told "Eddie" I would need to come in, and when I entered, I saw a large hole in the trailer roof. The home was a complete wreck, filthy and very unsafe for occupancy.

At this point, I met the first grader. I asked her if she had eaten breakfast, and she said "I wouldn't eat anything in this house." She took me to the kitchen where I found bugs crawling out of cereal boxes. The refrigerator was filthy, also filled with crawling pests. Case workers from human services were summoned to the scene and immediately took custody of the two girls. Subsequently, the mother returned and made a scene about the house becoming so dirty in just four days. This was a complete fabrication, as the house had been filthy for quite some time.

The fire department condemned the home later, and the case workers advised that the girls had been tortured and sexually molested. I arrested the mother and babysitter, charging them both with child endangerment and other offenses. The girls were placed in foster care. After two years, the girls were returned to their mother

who had become rehabilitated. This case was just one of many where children were put at risk and were saved by a public servant. When I speak to school personnel, I tell them that that they are the people who must look out for their children, and I continue to do what I can to protect youth from those who might prey on them.

I spent four months investigating the Columbine tragedy, an event that continues to haunt my community. It's been 10 years since the shootings, and the magnitude of the event is always on my mind. I am deliberate about my work and will do everything in my power to see that this type of tragedy will not happen again on my watch.

Advice to Students

- If you aren't enthusiastic about police work, you are in the wrong field.

- Police work is demanding. You may not get off when your shift ends; you must always complete your tasks thoroughly before you end your shift.

- Your report reflects your work and will be used in court. Make sure it is accurate, thorough, and complete.

- Interview everyone, don't leave out the obvious.

- Treat everyone with respect, even the suspects. You have the authority given to you and you don't have to prove that to anyone.

- Police work is 99 percent boredom, and 1 percent sheer terror.

- Train hard and practice. You must be in shape, skilled with your weapon, and prepared for anything.

- Police work is not just a job, it is a lifestyle. You are always on duty and must represent yourself and the profession in a positive way. You are viewed as a hero, act like one. There aren't many heroes anymore and you can be one.

defendants, the entire juvenile justice process may weaken the delinquency prevention role of juvenile courts (Sungi, 2008). Thus, more aggressive prosecution of juvenile cases is perceived as moving away from delinquency prevention for the purpose of deterring youths from future adult criminality. The intentions of prosecutors in most cases are to ensure that youths are entitled to due process, but the social costs may be to label these youths in ways that will propel them toward adult criminality rather than away from it (Mears et al., 2007).

Juvenile Delinquents and Delinquency

Juvenile Delinquents

infants

Legal term applicable to juveniles who have not attained the age of majority (in most states it is 18).

juvenile delinquent

Anyone who, under the age of his/her majority, has committed one or more acts that would be crimes if adults committed them.

juvenile delinquents, delinquent child

Infant of not more than a specified age who has violated criminal laws or engages in disobedient, indecent, or immoral conduct, and is in need of treatment, rehabilitation, or supervision.

juvenile delinquency

Violation of the law by any person prior to his/her eighteenth birthday; punishable by juvenile courts; violation of any law or ordinance by anyone who has not achieved the age of their majority.

In law, juveniles are referred to as **infants**. Legally, therefore, a **juvenile delinquent** is any infant of not more than a specified age who has violated criminal laws or engages in disobedient, indecent, or immoral conduct, and is in need of treatment, rehabilitation, or supervision. These youths are **juvenile delinquents**. A juvenile delinquent is a **delinquent child** (Champion, 2009). These definitions are somewhat ambiguous. What is "indecent" or "immoral conduct?" Who needs treatment, rehabilitation, or supervision? And what sort of treatment, rehabilitation, or supervision is needed? What is a "specified age?" These ambiguities have never been fully resolved.

Juvenile Delinquency

Federal law says that **juvenile delinquency** is the violation of any law of the United States by a person prior to his eighteenth birthday, which would have been a crime if committed by an adult (18 U.S.C., Sec. 5031, 2009). A broader, legally applicable, definition of juvenile delinquency is a violation of any state or local law or ordinance by anyone who has not yet achieved the age of majority. Although not especially perfect, these definitions are qualitatively more precise than the former ones.

Juvenile courts most often define juveniles and juvenile delinquency according to their own standards. For many jurisdictions, a delinquent act is whatever a court says it is. To illustrate the implications of such a definition for any juvenile, consider the following scenarios.

Scenario #1: It is 10:15 P.M. on a Thursday night in Detroit. There is a curfew in effect for youths under age 18 prohibiting them from being on city streets after 10:00 P.M. A police officer in a cruiser notices four youths standing at a street corner, holding gym bags and conversing. One youth walks toward a nearby jewelry store, looks in the window, and returns to the group. Shortly thereafter, another boy walks up to the same jewelry store window and looks in it. The officer pulls up beside the boys, exits the vehicle, and asks them for IDs. Each of the boys has a high school identity card. The boys are 16 and 17 years of age. When asked about the jewelry store interest, one boy says that he plans to get his girlfriend a necklace like one in the store window, and he wanted his friends to see it. The boys explain that they are waiting for a ride, since they are members of a team and have just finished a basketball game at a local gymnasium. One boy says, "I don't see why you're hassling us. We're not doing anything wrong." "You just did," says the officer. He makes a call on his radio for assistance from other officers, and makes all of the youths sit on the curb with their hands behind their heads. Two other cruisers arrive shortly and the youths are transported to the police station where they are searched. The search turns up two small pocket knives and a bottle opener. The youths are charged with "carrying concealed weapons" and "conspiracy to commit burglary." Juvenile authorities are notified.

Scenario #2: A highway patrol officer spots two young girls with backpacks attempting to hitch a ride on a major highway in Florida. He stops his vehicle and asks the girls for IDs. They don't have any, but claim they are over 18 and are trying to get to Georgia to visit some friends. The officer takes both girls into custody and to a local jail where a subsequent identification discloses that they are respectively 13- and 14-year-old runaways from a Miami suburb. Their parents are looking for them. They are detained at the jail until their parents can retrieve them. In the meantime, a nearby convenience store reports that two young girls from off the street came in an hour earlier and shoplifted several items. Jail deputies search the backpacks of the girls and find the shoplifted items. They are charged with "theft." Juvenile authorities are notified.

Scenario #3: A 15-year-old boy who has been suspended from a local Atlanta school for pushing another student is being held in the juvenile psychiatric wing of a mental hospital while undergoing some juvenile court-ordered tests to determine his mental condition. During the night, he sneaks away from the facility but is caught by police the next day. He is charged with "escape." Juvenile authorities are notified.

These and a thousand other scenarios could be presented. Are these scenarios the same? No. As the facts are presented, some of these scenarios are not especially serious. Can each of these scenarios result in a finding of delinquency by a juvenile court judge? Yes. Whether juveniles are "hanging out" on a street corner late at night, whether they have shoplifted, or whether they have run away from a psychiatric institution, it is possible in *some* juvenile court *somewhere* that all of them could be defined collectively as delinquent or delinquency cases. Some juvenile offending is more serious than other types of juvenile offending. Breaking windows or violating the town curfew would certainly be less serious than armed robbery, rape, or murder. The wide range of offense seriousness has caused many jurisdictions to channel less serious cases away from juvenile courts and toward various community agencies where the juveniles involved can receive assistance rather than punishment. Should one's age, socioeconomic status, ethnicity or race, attitude, and other situational circumstances influence police response one way or another? The fact is that regardless of the offenses alleged, all juveniles are confronted by subjective appraisals and judgments from the police, prosecutors, and juvenile court judges on the basis of both legal and extralegal factors. Because of their status as juveniles, youths may also be charged with various noncriminal acts. Such acts are broadly described as status offenses.

status offenses
Any act committed by a minor that would not be a crime if an adult committed it (e.g., truancy, runaway behavior).

runaways
Juveniles who leave their home for long-term periods without parental consent or supervision; unruly youths who cannot be controlled or managed by parents or guardians.

Status Offenders

Status offenders are of interest to both the juvenile justice system and the criminal justice system. **Status offenses** are any acts committed by juveniles that would (1) bring the juveniles to the attention of juvenile courts and (2) not be crimes if committed by adults. Typical status offenses are running away from home, truancy, and curfew violations. Adults wouldn't be arrested for running away from home, truancy, or walking the streets after some curfew time for juveniles. However, if juveniles do these sorts of things in particular cities, they may be grouped within the broad delinquency category, together with more serious juvenile offenders who are charged with armed robbery, forcible rape, murder, aggravated assault, burglary, larceny, vehicular theft, or illicit drug sales.

Runaways

In 2007, it was estimated there were over 300,000 **runaways** in the United States reported to police (Office of Juvenile Justice and Delinquency Prevention, 2007). This represents less than 1 percent of all offenses charged that year. Over half of those runaways were 15 to 17 years of age. Runaways are those youths who leave their homes, without permission or their parents' knowledge, and who remain away from home for prolonged periods ranging from several days to several years. Many runaways are eventually picked up by police in different

One type of status offense is underage drinking.

jurisdictions and returned to their homes. Others return of their own free will and choice. Some runaways remain permanently missing, although they are likely a part of a growing number of homeless youths roaming faraway city streets throughout the United States (Slesnick et al., 2007). Information about runaways and other types of status offenders is compiled annually through various statewide clearinghouses and the federal funded National Incidence Studies of Missing, Abducted, Runaway, and Throw-naway Children (NISMART).

Runaway behavior is complex and difficult to explain, although researchers tend to agree that many runaways generally have serious mental health needs (Chen et al., 2007). Many of these youths seek out others like them for dependency and emotional support (Kempf-Leonard and Johansson, 2007). Some runaways regard others like them as role models and peers, and often, delinquency among them occurs and increases through such peer modeling. Studies of runaways indicate that many boys and girls have psychological and/or familial adjustment problems and have been physically and sexually abused by their parents or close relatives. Evidence suggests that many runaways engage in theft or prostitution to finance their independence away from home and are exploited (Armour and Haynie, 2007).

Although all runaways are not alike, there have been attempts to profile them. Depending upon how authorities and parents react to children who have been apprehended after running away, there may be either positive or negative consequences. Empathy for runaways and their problems is important for instilling positive feelings within them. Various runaway shelters have been established to offer runaways a non-threatening residence and social support system in various jurisdictions. These shelters often locate particular services for runaways that will help meet their needs. Many children accommodated by these shelters report that they have been physically and sexually abused by family members. Thus, there is some coordination of these homes with various law enforcement agencies to investigate these allegations and assist parents in making their homes safer for their children.

Truants and Curfew Violators

Truants. Other types of status offenders are truants and curfew and liquor law violators. **Truants** are those who absent themselves from school without either school or parental permission. Very little is known about the numbers or characteristics of truants in the United States. This is due to several reasons: each school district defines truancy different from other districts; sociodemographic characteristics of truants are not normally maintained, even by individual schools; and no consistent, central reporting mechanisms exist for data compilations about truants. For instance, in Wisconsin, a truant may be a youth who absents himself/herself from school without excuse for five or more consecutive school days. In other states, a truant may be defined as someone who misses one day of school without a valid excuse.

There are probably 200,000 or more truants in the United States on any given day. This figure is most likely an underestimate of the actual number of truants. On a city-by-city basis, where records of truants are maintained, we can glean much about the true magnitude of truancy. For instance, in Pittsburgh, Pennsylvania, on any given day, there are 3,500 students absent from school, with about 70 percent of these absences unexcused. In Philadelphia, there are 2,500 students truant each day. One disturbing dimension of truancy is that about two-thirds of all juvenile males arrested while truant have tested positive for drug use (Chiang et al., 2007).

Truancy is not a crime. It is a status offense. Youths can be charged with truancy and brought into juvenile court for a status offense adjudication. Truancy is taken quite seriously in many jurisdictions, since evidence suggests that daytime crime and truancy are highly correlated.

truants
Juveniles who are habitually absent from school without excuse.

Rhode Island Truancy Court. Several states, such as Rhode Island, have established formal mechanisms to deal with the problem of truancy. The Family Court system of Rhode Island has established **truancy courts** for the purpose of heightening status offender accountability relating to truancy issues. Chronic truants are referred to the Truancy Court where their cases are formalized. This formal process dealing with truancy involves truants, their parents/guardians, a truant officer, and a Truancy Court magistrate. Participants must sign a "Waiver of Rights Form," illustrated in Figure 1.1. This form outlines the rights of truants, including the right to challenge any truancy accusation against them. Several important due process rights are included on the form. The purpose of the Truancy Court is to avoid formal juvenile court action by obeying the behavioral requirements outlined. These include (1) attending school every day; (2) being on time; (3) behaving; and (4) doing classroom work and homework. Failure to comply with one or more of these requirements may result in a referral to Family Court or placement in the Department of Children, Youth, and Families and removal from the home. This means possible institutionalization if one's truancy persists following the Truancy Court hearing.

The Truancy Court also requires parents to sign a form that permits the release of confidential information about the truant. This information is necessary in devising any type of treatment program and providing any counseling or services the truant may require. Thus, the Family Court is vested with the power to evaluate, assess, and plan activities for the truant that are designed to prevent further truancy. Various interventions are attempted in an effort to heighten the youth's awareness of the seriousness of truancy and the importance of staying in school. This form is illustrated in Figure 1.2.

Two other documents are required by the Truancy Court: a Treatment Reference Sheet (Figure 1.3) and an Official Family Court Order (Figure 1.4).

The Treatment Reference Sheet shown in Figure 1.3 is an informational document designed to provide the Truancy Court magistrate with valuable information about the student's progress prior to the Truancy Court hearing. Some of this information pertains to the parents and whether they have any criminal history, the status of their mental health, and their own educational attainment. It is believed that the parents' background is a significant consideration in any treatment recommendation made for the truant. For instance, information is acquired relating to whether the youth has any disabilities or mental health problems, which could account for his/her truant conduct. The youth's grades in different subjects are also recorded for the magistrate's inspection. Figure 1.4 is a formal court order outlining any sanctions the magistrate believes will heighten the truant's accountability. These include possible home confinement and any special conditions the court chooses to impose. Rhode Island Family Court officers are pleased with the results of the Truancy Court process thus far.

Curfew Violators. Curfew violators are those youths who remain on city streets after specified evening hours when they are prohibited from loitering or not being in the company of a parent or guardian. In 2007, there were over 282,000 youths charged with violating curfew and loitering laws in the United States (Office of Juvenile Justice and Delinquency Prevention, 2007).

Curfew violators tend to differ from runaways in that they are more serious offenders. However, truants and

Shoplifting is a common status offense.

> **truancy courts**
> Special bodies that convene to determine punishments for youths who absent themselves from school.

Figure 1.1   Rhode Island Truancy Court Waiver of Rights Form

Rhode Island Truancy Court
Waiver of Rights Form

Juvenile Name: _____
School: _____
Juvenile ID: _____
Petition Number: _____

I understand that I have the right to a trial on the truancy offense filed against me and recognize that I have the following rights should I decide to go to trial:

1. My right to a trial by a Judge and my right to appeal to the Supreme Court from any decision or finding of delinquency or waywardness.
2. The right to have the City/Town prove each and every element of the offense(s) against me by evidence and by proof beyond a reasonable doubt.
3. My right to the presumption of innocence.
4. My privilege against self-incrimination.
5. My right to confront and cross-examine the City/Town witnesses against me.
6. My right to present evidence and witnesses on my behalf and to testify in my own defense if I choose to do so.
7. My right to appeal to the Rhode Island Supreme Court from any sentence imposed by the Court after the entry of my ADMISSION OF SUFFECIENT FACTS or ADMISSION.

I understand that the Court has jurisdiction over me until my 21st birthday. I also understand that if I go to trial and am found wayward on the Truancy charge, I could be sent to the Rhode Island Training School if I refuse to obey a valid court order to attend school after I have been sentenced by a Family Court Judge.

I understand that I will have the right to an attorney if it appears that I could receive a sentence to the Rhode Island Training School.

I understand that by staying in the Truancy Court I will not go to trial and will have to abide by the Truancy Court requirements of:

1. Attending School Every Day.
2. Being on Time.
3. Behaving.
4. Doing My Classroom Work and Homework.

I agree that I will present a doctor's note or nurse's note if I am absent from school due to illness.

I understand that if I do not obey the Truancy Court requirements my case may be referred to the Family Court for trial or that I can be placed in the custody of the Department of Children, Youth, and Families and be removed from my home.

I understand that I may request a trial or hearing before a Justice of the Family Court at any time during my Truancy Court participation.

I/we have discussed the content of this document with the Truancy Court Magistrate who has explained this to me.

_____   _____
Participant's Signature   Date   Responsible Adult   Date

_____
Responsible Adult   Date

_____   _____
Truancy Court Magistrate   Date   Truant Officer   Date

TCW-1 (4/03)

Source: Reprinted by permission of the Rhode Island Family and Truancy Court.

Figure 1.2   Rhode Island Release of Confidential Information Form

RHODE ISLAND FAMILY COURT
TRUANCY COURT
CHIEF JUDGE JEREMIAH S. JEREMIAH, JR.

RELEASE OF CONFIDENTIAL INFORMATION

CLIENT'S NAME_____ DATE OF BIRTH_____

PARENT' S NAME _____

CLIENT'S ADDRESS _____

I hereby authorize all school, educational and treatment providers to release to The Rhode Island

Family Court or its representative any records concerning me and/or my children relating to

educational and school records, mental health, psychological and medical/physician records,

counseling, any treatment records, or other related documents and/or evaluations that relate to

said individuals.

This authorization is needed for the purpose of evaluation, assessment and planning by the

Rhode Island Family Court.

I understand that these records are protected by law and cannot be released without written

consent. This information may not be relayed to any other agency/facility/individual not

specified above. I understand that I may revoke this consent at any time.

_____   _____
 SIGNATURE of CLIENT/ PARENT   WITNESS

_____
DATE

Source: Reprinted by permission of the Rhode Island Family and Truancy Court.

Figure 1.3   Rhode Island Truancy Court Treatment Reference Sheet

RI Family Court / Truancy Court
TREATMENT REFERENCE SHEET

JUVENILE NAME_____ D.O.B._____

DATA: 1. Advised Child / Parent of right to trial and consequences of Truancy Court
   □ YES   □ NO

2. Number of days absent before Arraignment: _____ out of _____ days

3. Grades at Time of Arraignment:
   a. English_____   d. Math_____
   b. Reading_____   e. History_____
   c. Science_____   f. Others_____

4. Single Parent Family   □   Two Parent Family   □

5. Sibling Information (age, educational status)_____
_____

6.   Parent(s) graduated from high school: □ YES   □ NO

7.   Parent(s) has/have criminal history: □ YES   □ NO

8.   Parent(s) has/have mental health history: □ YES   □ NO

9.   Child disabilities (mental health)_____

10.   Medication_____

11.   Child's Educational Status: □ Regular Education   □ 504   □ IE
                                       □ Alternative placement

12.   Does child want to graduate from high school: □ YES   □ NO

Source: Reprinted by permission of the Rhode Island Family and Truancy Court.

Figure 1.4   Rhode Island Official Family Court Order

RHODE ISLAND FAMILY COURT
FAMILY AND JUVENILE DRUG COURT
<u>OFFICIAL FAMILY COURT ORDER</u>

Please be advised that:

PARENT'S NAME: _____

CHILD'S NAME: _____   **DATE OF BIRTH:** _____

ADDRESS: _____

_____

Has been ordered on this _____ day of _____, in the year 2005, the following:

☐ **HOME CONFINEMENT**

From _____   Until _____

☐ **SPECIAL CONDITIONS:** _____

_____

_____

_____

BY ORDER OF THE COURT:

_____   _____
DATE   **Associate Justice Kathleen A. Voccola**

Source: Reprinted by permission of the Rhode Island Family and Truancy Court.

chronic offenders

Habitual offenders; repeat offenders; persistent offenders; youths who commit frequent delinquent acts.

liquor law violators are more inclined to become **chronic offenders** and to engage in more serious, possibly criminal, behaviors. This is because truancy and curfew violations are viewed as undisciplined offenses (Chen et al., 2007).

In an effort to decrease the incidence of juvenile crime, many cities throughout the United States have enacted curfew laws specifically applicable to youths. The theory is that if juveniles are obliged to observe curfews in their communities, then they will have fewer opportunities to commit delinquent acts or status offenses (Urban, 2005). For example, in New Orleans, Louisiana, in June 1994, the most restrictive curfew law went into effect. Under this law, juveniles under age 17 were prohibited from being in public places, including the premises of business establishments, unless accompanied by a legal guardian or authorized adults. The curfew began at 8:00 P.M. on weeknights and at 11:00 P.M. on weekends. Several exceptions were made for youths who might be traveling to and from work or who were attending school, religious, or civil events. A study of the impact of this strict curfew law was conducted, and it revealed that juvenile offending shifted to non-curfew hours. Furthermore, the enforcement of this curfew law by New Orleans police was difficult, since curfew violations often occurred outside of a police presence. If anything, the curfew law tended to induce rebelliousness among those youths affected by the law. Curfew laws have not been an especially effective deterrent to status offending or delinquency generally (Urban, 2005).

Juvenile and Criminal Court Interest in Status Offenders

stigmas, stigmatize, stigmatization

Social process whereby offenders acquire undesirable characteristics as the result of imprisonment or court appearances; undesirable criminal or delinquent labels are assigned those who are processed through the criminal and juvenile justice systems.

Among status offenders, juvenile courts are most interested in chronic or persistent offenders, such as those who habitually appear before juvenile court judges (Hill et al., 2007). Repeated juvenile court exposure by status offenders may eventually be followed by adult criminality, although there is little support for this view in the research literature. The chronicity of juvenile offending seems to be influenced by the amount of contact youths have with juvenile courts. Greater contact with juvenile courts is believed by some persons to **stigmatize** youths and cause them to acquire labels or **stigmas** as delinquents or deviants (Feiring, Miller-Johnson, and Cleland, 2007). Therefore, diversion of certain types of juvenile offenders from the juvenile justice system has been advocated and recommended to minimize **stigmatization**.

One increasingly popular strategy is to remove certain types of offenses from the jurisdiction of juvenile court judges (Trulson, Marquart, and Mullings, 2005). Because status offenses are less serious than juvenile delinquency, many state legislatures have pushed for the removal of status offenses from juvenile court jurisdiction. The removal of status offenders from the discretionary power of juvenile courts is a part of what is generally known as the DSO.

JJDPA (Juvenile Justice and Delinquency Prevention Act) of 1974

Legislation recommending various alternatives to incarcerating youths, including deinstitutionalization of status offending, removal of youths from secure confinement, and other rehabilitative treatments.

The Deinstitutionalization of Status Offenses (DSO)

The JJDPA of 1974

The U.S. Congress passed the **JJDPA of 1974** in response to a national concern about growing juvenile delinquency and youth crime (Bjerk, 2007). This Act authorized the establishment of the **Office of Juvenile Justice and Delinquency Prevention (OJJDP)**, which has been extremely helpful and influential in matters of disseminating information about juvenile offending and prevention and as a general data source.

Office of Juvenile Justice and Delinquency Prevention (OJJDP)

Agency established by Congress under the JJDPA of 1974; designed to remove status offenders from jurisdiction of juvenile courts and dispose of their cases less formally.

Changes and Modifications in the JJDPA

In 1977, Congress modified the Act by declaring that the juveniles be separated by both sight and sound from adult offenders in detention and correctional facilities.

This mandate become known as the **deinstitutionalization of status offenses** or DSO. Nonoffenders, such as dependent and neglected children, were also included. Congress relaxed certain JJDPA rules and gave states additional latitude regarding their placement options for status offenders.

In 1980, Congress recommended that states should refrain from detaining juveniles in jails or lockups. Explicit compliance with this recommendation by any state is complicated by several factors. First, many juveniles appear to be adults when arrested for various offenses. Second, the relatively easy access to false identification cards and driver's licenses makes a precise determination of one's age difficult. Sometimes it may take days or weeks for police to determine the identity and age of any particular youth being held in a jail or lockup. Congress also directed that states should examine their secure confinement policies relating to minority juveniles and to determine reasons and justification for the disproportionately high rate of minority confinement. Congress also established an exception to the DSO by declaring that juveniles who violate a valid court order can be placed in secure confinement for a period of time.

By 1992, Congress directed that any participating state would have up to 25 percent of its formula grant money withheld to the extent that the state wasn't in compliance with each of the JJDPA mandates. Thus, it is clear that state compliance with these provisions of the JJDPA was encouraged and obtained by providing grants-in-aid to various jurisdictions wanting to improve their juvenile justice systems and facilities. There has been almost universal compliance with the JJDPA mandate throughout the various state juvenile justice systems, and it has served as a significant catalyst for major reform initiatives.

DSO Defined

The most popular meaning of DSO is the removal of status offenders from juvenile secure institutions. However, the JJDPA has extended the meaning of DSO to include alternative ways of ensuring that status offenders are separated from delinquent offenders. Presently, DSO occurs in three major ways: (1) decarceration; (2) diverting dependent and neglected children to social services; and (3) divestiture of jurisdiction.

Decarceration.
Decarceration means to remove status offenders from secure juvenile institutions, such as state industrial schools. Prior to the JJDPA of 1974, it was common practice in most states to incarcerate both status and delinquent offenders together in reform schools or industrial schools (Champion, 2008a). But more than a few people, scholars and the general public alike, questioned this practice. Why should truants, curfew violators, runaways, and difficult-to-control children be placed in prison-like facilities together with adjudicated juvenile murderers, rapists, burglars, thieves, robbers, arsonists, and other violent and property felony offenders? Qualitatively, there are substantial differences between status offenders and delinquent offenders. Do status offenders deserve to be treated the same as delinquent offenders for such drastically different offending behaviors? No.

Prevalent opinion suggests that causing status offenders to live and interact with delinquents in secure confinement, especially for prolonged periods of time, is definitely detrimental to status offenders. The mere exposure of status offenders to the criminogenic influence of, and close association with, hard-core delinquents adversely affects the social and psychological well-being of status offenders. The damage to a status offender's self-concept and esteem is incalculable (Champion, 2008a). This particular problem has been acknowledged outside of the United States as well. Countries such as China have implemented similar reforms in their juvenile justice systems in recent years, in order to separate less-serious juvenile offenders from more serious ones (Champion, 2008a). The many potential problems associated with combining status offenders with delinquent offenders in secure institutions no doubt was a compelling factor leading to the passage of the JJDPA.

deinstitutionalization of status offenses (DSO)
Eliminating status offenses from the broad category of delinquent acts and removing juveniles from or precluding their confinement in juvenile correctional facilities; the process of removing status offenses from jurisdiction of juvenile court so that status offenders cannot be subject to secure confinement.

decarceration
Type of deinstitutionalization where juveniles are removed from secure and nonsecure custodial facilities and put on probation, required to attend treatment or service programs, and subjected to other behavioral restraints.

Subsequently, most states have implemented decarceration policies for status offenders. For instance, Pennsylvania does not place status offenders in secure facilities. However, in some predominantly rural states, such as Montana and North Dakota, some status offenders have continued to be disposed to secure institutions by juvenile court judges. One reason is that juvenile court judges view incarcerating these youths as an appropriate punishment and a potential cure for their status offending. Another reason is that these state legislatures have not devised alternative strategies for treating status offenders through other state agencies or services. A third reason is that often, facilities simply don't exist in rural areas to meet status offender needs and provide the social services they require. Thus, the only alternative for their treatment and punishment is to be locked up in secure juvenile facilities together with delinquent offenders.

In order to expedite the decarceration of status offenders from secure juvenile facilities, the federal government has made available substantial sums of money to the states for the purpose of establishing alternative social services. Usually, states who agree to accept federal money in exchange for implementing the DSO are given several years over which to implement these reforms in how status offenders are processed. Thus, a period of time is allocated in which to phase out the incarceration of status offenders and phase in the creation of alternative social service agencies designed to accommodate them and meet their needs.

Under certain conditions, however, states may incarcerate status offenders who are under some form of probationary supervision. For instance, a Texas juvenile, E.D., was on probation for a status offense (*In re E.D.*, 2004). During the term of E.D.'s probation, one or more probation conditions were violated. The juvenile court elected to confine E.D. to an institution for a period of time as a punishment for the probation violation. The juvenile appealed, contending that as a status offender, he should not be placed in a secure facility. The appellate court disagreed and held that the juvenile court judge had broad discretionary powers to determine E.D.'s disposition, even including placement in a secure facility. The appellate court noted that secure placement of a status offender is warranted whenever the juvenile probation department (1) reviewed the behavior of the youth and the circumstances under which the juvenile was brought before the court; (2) determined the reasons for the behavior that caused the youth to be brought before the court; and (3) determined that all dispositions, including treatment, other than placement in a secure detention facility or secure correctional facility, have been exhausted or are clearly inappropriate.

The juvenile court judge set forth an order that (1) it is in the child's best interests to be placed outside of his home; (2) reasonable efforts were made to prevent or eliminate the need for the child's removal from his home; and (3) the child, in his home, can't be provided the quality of care and support that he needs to meet the conditions of probation. There was no suggestion in the record that the judge failed to comply with these three major requirements. Thus, even status offenders may suffer incarceration if they fail to obey court orders while on probation despite the deinstitutionalization initiative.

Diverting Dependent and Neglected Children to Social Services.

A second type of DSO deals with **dependent and neglected children**. While the juvenile court continues to exercise jurisdiction over dependent and neglected youths, diversion programs have been established to receive these children directly from law enforcement officers, schools, parents, or even self-referrals. These diversion programs provide crisis intervention services for youths, and their aim is to eventually return juveniles to their homes. However, more serious offenders may need more elaborate services provided by shelter homes, group homes, or even foster homes (Sullivan et al., 2007).

Divestiture of Jurisdiction.

The third type of deinstitutionalization is called **divestiture** of jurisdiction. Under divestiture, juvenile courts can't detain, petition, adjudicate, or place youths on probation or in institutions for any status offense. However, several studies of DSO implementation policies reveal that there are gaps in

dependent and neglected children
Youths considered by social services or the juvenile court to be in need of some type of adult supervision.

divestiture
Deinstitutionalizing status offenders through the act of juvenile court judges giving up their jurisdiction over status offenses.

coordinating interjurisdictional practices involving juveniles. Often, particular agencies continue to operate in their own philosophical contexts in contrast with, and sometimes in opposition to, legislative mandates for juvenile processing changes (Feld, 2007).

Potential Outcomes of DSO

Five potential outcomes of the DSO are the following:

1. DSO reduces the number of status offenders in secure confinement, especially in local facilities. Greater numbers of jurisdictions are adopting deinstitutionalization policies and the actual number of institutionalized status offenders is decreasing.

2. **Net-widening**, or pulling youths into the juvenile justice system who wouldn't have been involved previously in the system, has increased as one result of DSO. Many state jurisdictions have drawn large numbers of status offenders into the net of the juvenile justice system following DSO. In past years, many status offenders would have been ignored by police or handled informally. But when specific community programs were established for status offenders, the net widened and many status offenders were placed in these programs regardless of whether they needed specific social services.

3. **Relabeling**, or defining youths as delinquent or as emotionally disturbed who, in the past, would have been defined and processed as status offenders, has occurred in certain jurisdictions following the DSO. For instance, police officers can easily relabel juvenile curfew violators or loiterers as larceny or burglary suspects and detain these youths. In many instances, juvenile court judges have resisted DSO reforms for similar reasons (e.g., loss of discretionary control and power over status offenders).

4. DSO has had little, if any, impact on recidivism rates among status offenders.

5. DSO has created several service delivery problems, including inadequate services, nonexistent services or facilities, or the general inability to provide services within a voluntary system. This is because there is so much variation among status offenders that it is difficult to establish standardized programming and services that will be effective for all of them.

Regardless of the relative merits of DSO and the ambiguity of research results concerning its short- and long-term effects, there is no doubt that DSO is widespread nationally and has become the prevailing juvenile justice policy. The DSO has set in motion numerous programs in all jurisdictions to better serve the needs of a growing constituency of status offenders. This necessarily obligates growing numbers of agencies and organizations to contemplate new and innovative strategies, rehabilitative, therapeutic, and/or educational, to cope with these youths with diverse needs. Greater cooperation between the public, youth services, and community-based treatment programs is required to facilitate developing the best program policies and practices.

> **net-widening**
> Pulling juveniles into the juvenile justice system who wouldn't otherwise be involved in delinquent activity; applies to many status offenders (also known as "widening the net").
>
> **relabeling**
> Action, usually taken by police officers, of redefining juvenile acts as delinquent when in fact such acts are harmless or status offenses; result is harsher treatment by police of arrested juveniles.

Some Important Distinctions between Juvenile and Criminal Courts

Some of the major differences between juvenile and criminal courts are indicated below. These generalizations are more or less valid in most jurisdictions in the United States.

1. Juvenile courts are civil proceedings exclusively designed for juveniles, whereas criminal courts are proceedings designed to try adults charged with crimes. In criminal

courts, adults are targeted for criminal court actions, although some juveniles may be tried as adults in these same courts. The civil-criminal distinction is important because a civil adjudication of a juvenile court case does not result in a criminal record for the juvenile offender. In criminal courts, either a judge or jury finds a defendant guilty or not guilty. In the case of guilty verdicts, offenders are convicted and acquire criminal records. These **convictions** follow adult offenders for the rest of their lives. However, when juveniles are tried in juvenile courts, their juvenile court adjudications are sealed or expunged and generally forgotten, with exceptions, once they reach adulthood or the age of their majority.

convictions

Judgments of a court, based on a jury or judicial verdict, or on the guilty pleas of defendants, that the defendants are guilty of the offenses alleged.

2. Juvenile proceedings are more informal, whereas criminal proceedings are more formal. Attempts are made in many juvenile courts to avoid the formal trappings that characterize criminal proceedings. Juvenile court judges frequently address juveniles directly and casually. Formal rules of criminal procedure are not followed relating to the admissibility of evidence and testimony, and hearsay from various witnesses is considered together with hard factual information and evidence. Despite attempts by juvenile courts to minimize the formality of their proceedings, however, juvenile court procedures in recent years have become increasingly formalized. In some jurisdictions at least, it is difficult to distinguish criminal courts from juvenile courts in terms of their formality.

3. In 39 states, juveniles are not entitled to a trial by jury, unless the juvenile court judge approves. In all criminal proceedings, defendants are entitled to a trial by jury if they want one, and if the crime or crimes they are accused of committing carry incarcerative penalties of more than six months. Judicial approval is required for a jury trial for juveniles in most jurisdictions. This is one of the remaining legacies of the *parens patriae* doctrine in contemporary juvenile courts. Eleven states have legislative mandated jury trials for juveniles in juvenile courts if they are charged with certain types of offenses, if they are of certain ages, and if they make a timely request for a jury trial.

adversarial proceedings

Opponent-driven court litigation, where one side opposes the other; prosecution seeks to convict or find defendants guilty, while defense counsel seeks to defend their clients and seek their acquittal.

4. Juvenile court and criminal court are **adversarial proceedings**. Juveniles may or may not wish to retain or be represented by counsel (*In re Gault*, 1967). In almost every juvenile court case, prosecutors allege various infractions or law violations against juveniles, and these charges may be rebutted by juveniles or others. If juveniles are represented by counsel, these defense attorneys are permitted to offer a defense to the allegations. Criminal courts are obligated to provide counsel for anyone charged with a crime, if defendants can't afford to retain their own counsel (*Argersinger v. Hamlin*, 1972). Every state has provisions for providing defense attorneys to indigent juveniles who are adjudicated in juvenile court.

court of record

Any court where a written record is kept of court proceedings.

court reporters

Court officials who keep a written word-for-word and/or tape-recorded record of court proceedings.

5. Criminal courts are **courts of record**, whereas transcripts of most juvenile proceedings are made only if the judge decides. **Court reporters** record all testimony presented in most criminal courts. All state criminal trial courts are courts of record, where either a tape-recorded transcript of proceedings is maintained, or a written record is kept. Thus, if trial court verdicts are appealed later by either the prosecution or defense, transcripts of these proceedings can be presented by either side as evidence of errors committed by the judge or other violations of one's due process rights. Original convictions may be reversed or they may be allowed to stand, depending upon whatever the records disclose about the propriety of the proceedings. Juvenile courts are not courts of record. Thus, it is unlikely that in any given juvenile proceeding, a court reporter will keep a verbatim record of the proceedings. One factor that inhibits juvenile courts from being courts of record is the sheer expense of hiring court reporters for this work. Courts of record are expensive to maintain. Certainly in some of the more affluent jurisdictions, some juvenile court judges may enjoy the luxury of a court reporter to transcribe or record all court matters. But this is the exception rather than the rule. Furthermore, the U.S. Supreme Court has declared that juvenile courts are not obligated to be courts of record (*In re Gault*, 1967).

6. The **standard of proof** used for determining one's guilt in criminal proceedings is **beyond a reasonable doubt.** The less rigorous civil standard of **preponderance of the evidence** is used in most juvenile court matters. However, the U.S. Supreme Court has held that if any juvenile is in jeopardy of losing his/her liberty as the result of an adjudication by a juvenile court judge, then the evidentiary standard must be the criminal court standard of beyond a reasonable doubt (*In re Winship*, 1970). Losing liberty means to be locked up for any period of time, whether it is for one day, one month, or one or more years. Thus, juveniles who face charges in juvenile court where the possible punishment is confinement in a secure juvenile facility for any period of time are entitled to the beyond a reasonable doubt criminal standard in determining their guilt. Therefore, it is expected of juvenile court judges that they will always apply this standard when adjudicating a juvenile's case and where one's loss of liberty is a possibility.

7. The range of penalties juvenile court judges may impose is limited, whereas in most criminal courts, the range of penalties may include life-without-parole sentences or the death penalty. The jurisdiction of juvenile court judges over youthful offenders typically ends when these juveniles reach adulthood. Some exceptions are that juvenile courts may retain jurisdiction over mentally ill youthful offenders indefinitely after they reach adulthood. In California, for instance, the Department of the Youth Authority supervises youthful offenders ranging in age from 11 to 25.

The purpose of this comparison is to show that criminal court actions are more serious and have harsher long-term consequences for offenders compared with juvenile court proceedings. Juvenile courts continue to be guided by a strong rehabilitative orientation in most jurisdictions, where the most frequently used punishments are either verbal reprimands or probationary dispositions. Secure confinement is viewed by most juvenile court judges as a last resort, and such a punishment is reserved for only the most serious youthful offenders, with exceptions (LaMade, 2008). Probably less than 10 percent of all adjudicated delinquent offenders are incarcerated in secure juvenile facilities. However, in criminal courts, convicted offenders are more frequently jailed or imprisoned. Criminal courts also use probation as a punishment in about 60 percent of all criminal cases, especially for first-offenders or those who have committed less serious crimes. Although increasing numbers of juvenile courts are adopting more punitive sanctions similar to those of criminal courts, many youths continue to receive treatment-oriented punishments rather than incarceration in secure juvenile facilities.

An Overview of the Juvenile Justice System

The Ambiguity of Adolescence and Adulthood

Police have broad discretionary powers in their encounters with the public and dealing with street crime. Although some evidence suggests that police have shifted their policing priorities away from juveniles toward more serious adult offenders for various reasons (e.g., cases against juveniles are often dismissed or judges issue nothing more than verbal warnings to them and return them to the custody of their parents), police arrests and detentions of juveniles in local jails remains the major conduit of a juvenile's entry into the juvenile justice system.

Many juveniles are clearly juveniles. It is difficult to find youths under 13 who physically appear 18 or older. Yet, nearly 10 percent of all juveniles held for brief periods in adult jails annually are 13 years old or younger (Office of Juvenile Justice and Delinquency Prevention, 2007). For juveniles in the 14–17 age range, visual determination of one's juvenile or nonjuvenile status is increasingly difficult. Thus, at least some justification exists for why police officers take many youthful offenders to jails initially for identification and questioning.

standard of proof
The type of evidence required to sustain a petition of delinquency against a juvenile, depending on the seriousness of the offense; how guilt is measured or determined.

beyond a reasonable doubt
Evidentiary standard used in criminal courts to establish guilt or innocence of criminal defendant.

preponderance of the evidence
Standard used in civil courts to determine defendant or plaintiff liability and where the result does not involve incarceration.

Other ways that juveniles can enter the juvenile justice system include referrals from or complaints by parents, neighbors, victims, and others (social work staff, probation officers) unrelated to law enforcement. Dependent or neglected children may be reported to police initially. Following up on these complaints, police officers may take youths into custody until arrangements for their care can be made. Or police officers may arrest youths for alleged crimes.

Being Taken into Custody and Being Arrested

taken into custody

A protective action, usually taken by police officers, which is designed to offer temporary shelter for juvenile runaways or truants; not the same as an arrest.

Being **taken into custody** and being arrested are different procedures. For law enforcement officers, whenever youths are taken into custody, they are not necessarily arrested, and they may not necessarily be arrested later. Being taken into custody means precisely what it says. Officers take certain youths into custody as a protective measure so that they can determine what is best for the juvenile. Some youths who are taken into custody might be those suffering from child sexual abuse or physical abuse inflicted by parents or others, runaways, or missing children (Armour and Haynie, 2007). Youths wandering the streets may also be taken into custody by police if they are suspected of being truant from school.

When youths are arrested, this is more serious police action. An arrest means that the juvenile is suspected of committing a crime. Charges may be filed against arrested youths once it is determined who should have jurisdiction over them. Police authorities may determine that the juvenile court has jurisdiction, depending on the age or youthfulness of the offender. Or authorities may decide that the criminal court has jurisdiction and the youthful-appearing offender should be charged as an adult.

Juveniles in Jails

In 2007, there were 11,000 juveniles under the age of 18 being held in jails (Office of Juvenile Justice and Delinquency Prevention, 2007). About 89 percent of these juveniles were being held as adults. This represents about 1 percent of all jail inmates held in jails for 2007. This figure is misleading, however. It does not reflect the total number of juveniles who are brought to jails annually after they have been arrested or taken into custody by police. Many youths are jailed for short time periods, merely on suspicion, even though they haven't committed any obvious offenses. Short time periods are often two or three hours. Some states, such as Illinois, have passed laws preventing police officers from detaining juveniles in adult jails for more than six hours. Such laws reflect the **jail removal initiative**, whereby states are encouraged not to house juveniles in adult jails, even for short periods.

jail removal initiative

Action sponsored by the OJJDP and the JJDPA to deinstitutionalize juveniles from secure facilities, such as jails.

jails

City or county operated and financed facilities designed to house misdemeanants serving sentences of less than one year, pretrial detainees, witnesses, juveniles, vagrants, and others.

The Illinois policy preventing the police from detaining juveniles in jails except for limited periods is consistent with a major provision of the JJDPA of 1974. Although the JJDPA is not binding on any state, it does encourage law enforcement officials to treat juveniles differently from adult offenders if juveniles are taken to jails for brief periods. For instance, the JJDPA recommends that status offenders should be separated in jails by sight and sound from adult offenders. Furthermore, they should be held in nonsecure areas of jails for periods not exceeding six hours. They should not be restrained in any way with handcuffs or other restraint devices while detained. Their detention should only be as long as is necessary to identify them and reunite them with their parents, guardians, or a responsible adult from a public youth agency or family services.

Even more serious delinquent offenders brought to jails for processing should be subject to similar treatment by jail officials, according to JJDPA recommendations. Sight and sound separation and segregation from adult offenders is encouraged, although juveniles alleged to have committed delinquent offenses are subject to more restrictive detention provisions. The general intent of this aspect of the JJDPA is to minimize the adverse effects of labeling that might occur if juveniles were processed like adult offenders. Another factor is the recognition that most of these offenders will eventually be processed by the juvenile justice system, which is a civil entity. Any attributions of criminality arising from how juveniles are treated while they are in adult jails are considered incompatible with the rehabilitative ideals of the juvenile justice system and the civil outcomes or consequences ultimately experienced by most juvenile offenders. Thus, some of the JJDPA goals are to prevent juveniles from being influenced psychologically or physically by adults through jail contacts with them and to insulate juveniles from defining themselves as criminals which might occur through criminal-like processing.

A small proportion of juveniles engage in violent acts such as drive-by shootings.

Despite new laws designed to minimize or eliminate holding juveniles in adult **jails** or **lockups**, even for short periods, juveniles continue to be held in jails for short time periods. In more than a few instances, these detentions are unavoidable. Many juveniles appear older to police officers than they really are. They carry fake IDs or no IDs, give false names when questioned, or refuse to give police any information about their true identities. It takes time to determine who they are and what responsible adult or guardian should be contacted. Many runaways are from different states, and it takes time for their parents or guardians to reunite with them. Some of these juveniles are very aggressive, assaultive, and obviously dangerous. They must be locked up or restrained, if only to protect others. Some are suicidal and need temporary protection from themselves.

The U.S. Supreme Court has authorized the **preventive detention** of juveniles in jails for brief periods without violating their constitutional rights, especially for those offenders who pose a danger to themselves or others (*Schall v. Martin,* 1984). In this particular case, a juvenile was detained by police on serious charges. He refused to give his name or other identification, and was deemed by those in charge to be dangerous, either to himself or to others. His preventive detention was upheld by the U.S. Supreme Court as not violating his constitutional right to due process. Prior to this Supreme Court ruling, however, many states had similar laws that permitted pretrial and preventive detention of both juvenile and adult suspects. Although **pretrial detention** presupposes a forthcoming trial of those detained and preventive detention does not, both terms are often used interchangeably or even combined, as in preventive pretrial detention (Brookbanks, 2002). If 1 percent of the 13 million admissions and releases to jails annually are juveniles, a reasonable estimate would be that at least 130,000 or more juveniles spend at least some time in jails annually, if only to determine their identity and release them into the custody of their parents or guardians after a few hours.

Referrals

Figure 1.5 is a diagram of the juvenile justice system. Although each jurisdiction in the United States has its own methods for processing juvenile offenders, Figure 1.5 is sufficiently general to encompass most of these processing methods. Focusing on the diagram in Figure 1.5, a majority of juvenile encounters with the juvenile justice system are through **referrals** from police officers. Referrals are notifications made to juvenile court authorities that a juvenile requires the court's attention. Referrals can be made by anyone, such as concerned parents, school principals, teachers, neighbors, and others. However, over 90 percent of all referrals to juvenile courts are made by law enforcement officers. These referrals may be made for runaways; truants; curfew violators; unmanageable, unsupervised, or incorrigible children; children with drug or alcohol problems; or for any youth suspected of committing a crime (Kuntsche et al., 2007).

lockups
Small rooms or buildings designed for confining arrested adults and/or juveniles for short periods, such as 24 hours or less.

preventive detention
Constitutional right of police to detain suspects prior to trial without bail, where suspects are likely to flee from the jurisdiction or pose serious risks to others.

pretrial detention
Holding delinquent or criminal suspects in incarcerative facilities pending their forthcoming adjudicatory hearing or trial.

referrals
Any citation of a juvenile to juvenile court by a law enforcement officer, interested citizen, family member, or school official; usually based upon law violations, delinquency, or unruly conduct.

Figure 1.5   Diagram of the Juvenile Justice System

THE JUVENILE JUSTICE SYSTEM

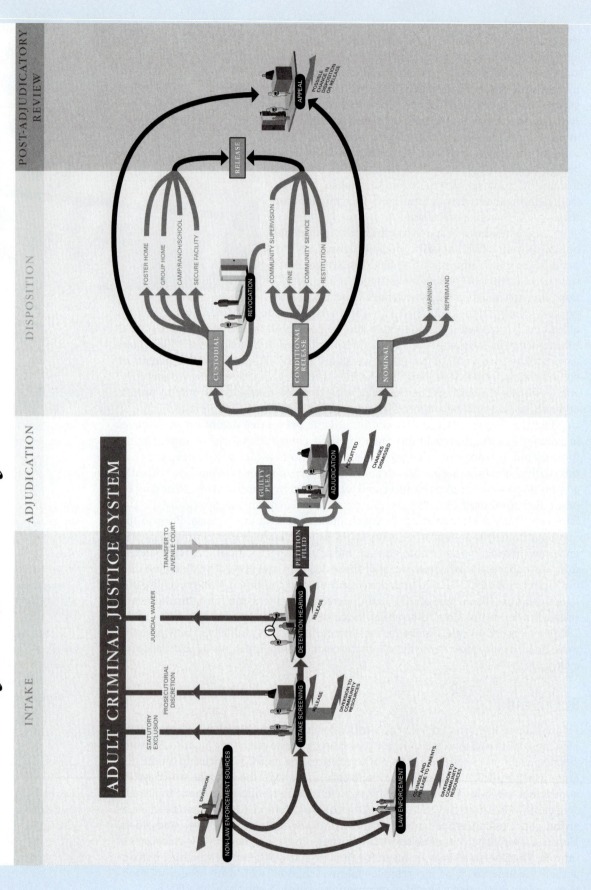

Each jurisdiction throughout the United States has its own policies relating to how referrals are handled. In Figure 1.5, following an investigation by a police officer, juveniles are either counseled and released to parents; referred to community resources; cited and referred to juvenile intake, followed by a subsequent release to parents; or transported to juvenile hall or shelter for further detention. Each of these actions is the result of police discretion. The nature of the discretionary action of police officers who take youths into custody for any reason is governed by what these officers have observed. If a youth has been loitering, especially in cities with curfew laws for juveniles, then the discretion of police officers might be to counsel the youth and turn him/her over to his/her parents without further action. In more than a few cases, youth are taken into custody and parents or guardians for these youths can't be found. In these cases, police officers turn the youths over to community resources for further action. If particular youths have violated liquor laws or committed some minor infraction, they may be cited by police and referred to a juvenile probation officer for further action. Subsequently, most of these youths are returned to the custody of their parents or guardians. However, some youths are apprehended while committing serious crimes. Police officers will likely transport these youths to a juvenile hall or shelter to await further action by juvenile justice system personnel. A law enforcement juvenile court referral form is illustrated in Figure 1.6.

In New Mexico, for example, whenever a juvenile is referred to the juvenile justice system for any offense, the referral is first screened by the Juvenile Probation/Parole Office. Juvenile probation/parole officers (JPPOs) are assigned to initially screen a police report and file. This screening is performed, in part, to determine the accuracy of the report and if the information is correct. If the information is correct, then an intake process will commence, where the youth undergoes further screening by a JJPO assigned to the case by a supervisor (New Mexico Juvenile Justice Division, 2002). Figure 1.7 is a decision tree for the New Mexico Juvenile Justice Division and provides us with an overview of how their processing of juvenile offenders works.

Figure 1.7 shows that once a referral has been made to the Juvenile Probation/Parole Office, a decision is made whether to file **petitions** or to handle the case informally. About 50 percent of all juvenile cases are handled informally. Petitions are official documents filed in juvenile courts on the juvenile's behalf, specifying reasons for the youth's court appearance. These documents assert that juveniles fall within the categories of dependent or neglected, status offender, or delinquent, and the reasons for such assertions are usually provided. Filing a petition formally places the juvenile before the juvenile court judge in many jurisdictions. But juveniles may come before juvenile court judges in less formal ways. About 45 percent of the cases brought before the juvenile court each year are nonpetitioned cases. Less than 1 percent of these cases result in out-of-home placements, 30 percent receive probation, 50 percent are dismissed, and the remainder are diverted, downgraded, or result in verbal warnings (Champion, 2008a).

When individual cases are handled informally, JPPOs in New Mexico jurisdictions have several options. Whenever youths are determined to require special care, are needy or dependent, or are otherwise unsupervised by adults or guardians, JPPOs may refer them to a Juvenile Early Intervention Program (JEIP). The JEIP is a highly structured program for at-risk, nonadjudicated youths. Figure 1.8 shows a referral form used by New Mexico JPPOs to refer youths into this early intervention program.

Juveniles referred to the program will have been assessed to need services and/or supervision due to the nature of their current offense or situation, as well as their propensity for future misconduct as determined from a preliminary inquiry by the JPPO. The target group for the JEIP ranges in age from 10 to 12 at the time of the allegation against them. Status offenders, including truants, runaways, or curfew violators, may be referred to the JEIP. Both the juvenile and his/her family must agree to participate in the JEIP and to follow through with recommendations for additional services. The JEIP consists of eight weekly sessions, including an overall presentation of the

petition
A document whereby an official or private individual can bring charges against a juvenile and ask the juvenile court to hear the case.

Figure 1.6   Juvenile Court Referral Form

Fourth Juvenile Court, Division 1, 1234 Main Street, Laredo, TX 78041
Date:_____

Juvenile Court Referral

Intake Case #   _____

Intake Officer: _____

Badge #:   _____

District: _____

_____

Name of Juvenile

_____

Address

_____

City, State

_____   _____

Name(s) of Parent(s)/Guardian(s)   **Marital Status**

_____

Address of Parent(s)/Guardian(s)

_____

Telephone Number of Parent/Guardian

Name and Relation to Juvenile of Referring Person: _____

Delinquency/Status Offense Allegation(s) _____

_____

Prior Record of Juvenile, if any: _____
_____
_____

Signed by:

_____   _____

Child/juvenile   **Date**

_____   _____

Parent/guardian   **Date**

_____   _____

Parent/guardian   **Date**
Approved by:

_____   _____

Court attorney   **Date**

_____   _____

Judge   **Date**

Source: Prepared by author.

Figure 1.7   Decision Tree for the New Mexico Juvenile Justice Division

New Mexico Juvenile Justice Division
Classification System for Juveniles
Referral Intake Process

```
                    ┌─────────────────┐
                    │   Referral to   │
                    │   JPPO Office   │
                    └────────┬────────┘
                             │
                             ▼
┌──────────────┐   No    ╱──────────────╲
│    Handle    │◄────────  Petition Filed?  
│  Informally  │         ╲──────────────╱
└──────────────┘                │
                               Yes
                                │
                                ▼
┌──────────────┐   No    ╱──────────────╲
│    Nolle/    │◄────────   Finding of
│  Dismissed   │         ╲ Delinquency?  ╱
└──────────────┘                │
                               Yes
                                │
                                ▼
                    ┌─────────────────┐         ┌──────────────────────────────────┐
                    │    Prepare      │         │ JPPO Completes:                    │
                    │ Recommendation  │────────►│                                    │
                    │  to the Court   │         │  1. Offense Severity Scale         │
                    └────────┬────────┘         │  2. Risk Assessment                │
                             │                  │  3. Needs Assessment               │
                             ▼                  │  4. Dispositional Recommendation   │
                        ╱──────────╲            │     Matrix                         │
                        │Disposition?│──────────►│  5. Risk Assessment Supplemental   │
                        ╲──────────╱            │     Information                    │
                                                │  6. Chrono                         │
                                                └──────────────────────────────────┘
```

Youthful offenders may receive any disposition but are considered convicted rather than adjudicated.

```
        ┌──────────────┐          ┌──────────────────┐
        │  Commitment  │          │    Community     │
        │    1 year    │          │   Supervision    │
        │    2 year    │          │ (Consent Decree  │
        │ until age 21 │          │   or Judgment)   │
        └──────────────┘          │ Fines, Detention │
                                  └──────────────────┘
```

Source: Reprinted by permission of the New Mexico Juvenile Justice Services.

program and expectations, choices, self-esteem including a parent's group, peer pressure, gangs, drug and alcohol issues with parents included, feelings, and a final session that includes a review and graduation ceremony. Following completion of the program, a 30-day follow-up is conducted by JPPOs.

Depending upon the jurisdiction, however, the majority of alleged juvenile delinquents will be advanced further into the juvenile justice system. Some status offenders,

REFERRAL FORM

Date: _____ File #: _____ Cause # (if appl.): _____

Client's Name: _____ DOB: _____ Age: _____

Address: _____ Zip: _____ Phone #: _____

Ethnicity: _____ Gender: _____ SS#: _____

Referral Source: _____ Primary Language Spoken: _____

Guardian's Name: _____ Relationship: _____

Guardian's Legal Status: _____

Current Offense: _____

School: _____ Grade: _____ Reg. Ed. _____ Special Ed. _____

Client's Mental Health Issues (meds, if any): _____

_____

_____

_____

Guardian's Mental Health Issues (meds, if any): _____

_____

_____

_____

Directions to client's residence:

Source: Reprinted by permission of the New Mexico Juvenile Justice Services.

intake officer
Juvenile probation officer who conducts screenings and preliminary interviews with alleged juvenile delinquents or status offenders and their families.

intake
Critical phase where a determination is made by a juvenile probation officer or other official whether to release juveniles to their parent's custody or recommend their detention for further juvenile court action.

screening
Procedure used by prosecutor to determine which cases have prosecutive merit and which ones don't.

intake hearings, intake screenings
Proceedings where juvenile official, such as juvenile probation officer, conducts an interview with a youth charged with a delinquent or status offense.

especially recidivists, will also move further into the system. Some youths may be maintained in juvenile detention facilities temporarily to await further action. Other youths may be released to their parent's custody, but these youths may be required to reappear later to face further action. Most of these youths will subsequently be interviewed by an **intake officer** in a proceeding known as **intake**.

Intake

Intake varies in formality among jurisdictions. Intake is a **screening** procedure usually conducted by a juvenile probation officer, where one or several courses of action are recommended. Some jurisdictions conduct **intake hearings** or **intake screenings**, where comments and opinions are solicited from significant others such as the police, parents, neighbors, or victims. In other jurisdictions, intake proceedings are quite informal, usually consisting of a dialogue between the juvenile and the intake officer. These are important proceedings, regardless of their degree of formality. Intake is a major screening stage in the juvenile justice process, where further action against juve- niles may be contemplated or required. Intake officers hear complaints against juveniles and informally resolve the least serious cases, or they are more often juvenile probation offi- cers who perform intake as a special assignment. Also, juve- nile probation officers may perform diverse functions, including intake, enforcement of truancy statutes, and juvenile placements (Champion, 2008a).

Intake officers also consider youths' attitudes, demeanor, age, offense seriousness, and a host of other factors. Has the juvenile had frequent prior contact with the juvenile justice system? If the offenses alleged are seri- ous, what evidence exists against the offender? Should the offender be referred to certain community social service agencies, receive psychological counseling, receive voca- tional counseling and guidance, acquire educational or technical training and skills, be issued a verbal repri- mand, be placed on some type of diversionary status, or be returned to parental custody? Interviews with parents

Police officers explain drugs and their effects to classes of students in schools.

and neighbors may be conducted as a part of an intake officer's information-gathering. Although intake is supposed to be an informal proceeding, it is nevertheless an impor- tant stage in juvenile processing. The intake officer often acts in an advisory capacity, since he/she is the first contact children and their parents will have following an arrest or being taken into custody. Figure 1.9 is a form used by intake officers in some juris- dictions that provides both parents and children with an outline of their legal options in the case. Youths and their parents have a right to know the charge(s) against their children. Also, it is indicated that the intake hearing is a preliminary inquiry and not a fact-finding session to determine one's guilt. Also, the intake officer advises that state- ments made by the child and/or parents may be used against them later in court if such action is warranted.

In most jurisdictions, depending upon the discretion of intake officers, intake results in one of five actions: (1) dismiss the case, with or without a verbal or written reprimand; (2) remand youths to the custody of their parents; (3) remand youths to the custody of their parents, with provisions for or referrals to counseling or special serv- ices; (4) divert youths to an alternative dispute resolution program, if one exists in the jurisdiction; (5) refer youths to the juvenile prosecutor for further action and possible filing of a delinquency petition (Champion and Mays, 1991).

Returning to an examination of Figure 1.9, following an intake screening, some of the options available to intake officers noted above are indicated. Theoretically, at least, only the most serious juveniles will be referred to detention to await a subsequent juve- nile court appearance. In order for a youth to be detained while awaiting a juvenile court appearance, a detention hearing is usually conducted. Most of the time, youths considered for such detention are either a danger to themselves or to others, or they are likely to flee the jurisdiction to avoid prosecution in juvenile court. Others may be released to the custody of their parents or they may be referred to one or more commu- nity resources. Usually, these community resources are intended to meet the specific needs of particular juvenile offenders. Or the intake officer may release the juvenile to his/her parents prior to a subsequent juvenile court appearance. For serious cases, a petition is filed with the juvenile court. The juvenile court prosecutor further screens these petitions and decides which ones merit an appearance before the juvenile court judge. In Alaska, for example, a petition for adjudication of delinquency is used to bring delinquency cases before the juvenile court. An illustration of such a petition is shown in Figure 1.10.

Notice in Figure 1.10 that allegations are made concerning the delinquent acts committed by the juvenile. Furthermore, supporting information accompanies the

Figure 1.9   Intake Officer's Advice to Child and Parent, Guardian, or Custodian

IN THE MATTER OF: IN THE VIGO COURT
A CHILD ALLEGED TO BE A DELINQUENT CHILD

CAUSE NUMBER: JUVENILE DIVISION

INTAKE OFFICER'S ADVICE TO CHILD AND PARENT, GUARDIAN OR CUSTODIAN
(Indiana Code 31-6-4-7)

TO SAID CHILD AND HIS OR HER PARENT, GUARDIAN OR CUSTODIAN:
You are hereby advised that:

1.   You have the right to know the allegations against said child;

2.   The undersigned intake officer is conducting a preliminary inquiry to assist in determining whether a petition should be filed alleging that said child a delinquent child;

3   The undersigned intake officer will recommend whether to file a petition, informally adjust the case, refer the child to another agency, or dismiss the case;

4.   Said child has a right to remain silent; anything said child says may be used against said child in subsequent proceedings; said child has a right to consult with an attorney before he or she talks with the Intake Officer, and said child has a right to stop at any time and consult with an attorney, and to stop talking with the intake officer at any time; said child has a right to talk with his or her parents, guardian or custodian in private before he talks with the Intake Officer;

5.   If said child cannot afford an attorney, the Court will appoint one for him or her.

DATED THIS THE_____DAY OF_____,2003

_____
PROBATION OFFICER

By signing this paper you agree only that you have received this advice

_____
SIGNATURE OF CHILD

_____
SIGNATURE OF PARENT OR GUARDIAN

_____
SIGNATURE OF PARENT OR GUARDIAN

Source: Reprinted by permission of the Vigo County juvenile court.

Figure 1.10   Delinquency Petition (Alaska)

IN THE SUPERIOR COURT FOR THE STATE OF ALASKA

_____ JUDICIAL DISTRICT AT _____

In the matter of:)
)
)   CASE NO. _____CP
)
A minor under 18 years of age   )
Date of Birth:_____)

PETITION FOR ADJUDICATION OF DELINQUENCY

The petitioner requests that the above-named juvenile be adjudicated as a delinquent under A.S 47.12.020 and that an appropriate disposition be entered.

The petitioner alleges that:

Probable cause supporting the above allegation(s) is that:

The juvenile's address is _____.

The juvenile's father is: _____, whose address is

_____.

The juvenile's mother is: _____, whose address is

_____.

The juvenile's guardian/custodian/grandmother is _____, whose address is

_____.

06-9541 (Rev. 10/97) YC   PETITION FOR ADJUDICATION OF DELINQUENCY

Figure 1.10   Delinquency Petition (Alaska) (Cont.)

In the Matter of: _____ Case No. _____

Petitioner swears or affirms upon information and belief to the above statements.

_____   _____
        Date   PETITIONER (signature)

                                _____
                                PRINT NAME AND OCCUPATION/RELATIONSHIP

                                _____
                                ADDRESS AND PHONE NUMBER

SUBSCRIBED AND SWORN TO before me on _____.
                                              Date

(SEAL)   _____
                                CLERK/NOTARY PUBLIC

                                My Commission Expires: _____

CERTIFICATE OF SERVICE
I certify that on July 21, _____
a copy of this document was sent
to: _____

By: _____ Notary

06-9541   (Rev. 10/97) YC   PETITION FOR ADJUDICATION OF DELINQUENCY
                                              2.b.2

Source: Reprinted by permission of the State of Alaska.

petition, which presumably establishes probable cause and supports the facts alleged. The petitioner signs the petition under oath and avers that the statements made are true. Their occupation and relationship with the juvenile are also included, as well as their telephone number and address. It is up to the prosecutor to determine whether action should be taken on petitions filed. Figure 1.10 alleges delinquency, or one or more crimes committed by the named juvenile. Other petitions may allege status offending, such as truancy, runaway behavior, curfew violation, or violation of drug or liquor laws (McNamara, 2008). These petitions are similar in form to Figure 1.10. Not all petitions result in formal action by a juvenile court prosecutor. Like prosecutors in criminal court, juvenile court prosecutors prioritize cases they will prosecute. Such case prioritizing depends upon the volume of petitions filed, the time estimated for the juvenile court judge to hear and act on these petitions, the sufficiency of evidence supporting these petitions, as well as an array of other factors.

Police encounters with juveniles on city streets sometimes lead to arrests and juvenile processing.

Alternative Prosecutorial Actions

Cases referred to juvenile prosecutors for further action are usually, though not always, more serious cases. Exceptions might include those youths who are chronic recidivists or technical program violators and nonviolent property offenders (e.g., status offenders, vandalism, petty theft, public order offenders).

Juvenile court prosecutors have broad discretionary powers. They may cease prosecutions against alleged offenders or downgrade the offenses alleged from felonies to misdemeanors or from misdemeanors to status offenses. Much depends upon the docket load or case activity of their own juvenile courts. In some instances, prosecutors may divert some of the more serious juvenile cases for processing by criminal courts. The least serious cases are disposed of informally. Prosecutors either file petitions or act on petitions filed by others, such as intake officers, the police, school officials, or interested family and citizens (LaMade, 2008).

Adjudicatory Proceedings

Jurisdictions vary considerably concerning their juvenile court proceedings. Increasingly, juvenile courts are emulating criminal courts in many respects. Most of the physical trappings of criminal courts are present, including the judge's bench, tables for the prosecution and defense, and a witness stand. Further, there appears to be widespread interest in holding juveniles more accountable for their actions than was the case in past years (LaMade, 2008).

Besides the more formal atmosphere of juvenile courts, the procedure is becoming increasingly adversarial, where prosecutors and defense attorneys do battle against and on behalf of juveniles charged with various offenses. However, less than 50 percent of the juvenile offenders in most jurisdictions have the assistance of counsel, although they are entitled to counsel (LaMade, 2008). Both alleged status offenders and those charged with crimes are entitled to be represented by counsel in their court cases. In most jurisdictions, juvenile court judges have almost absolute discretion in how their courts are conducted. Juvenile defendants alleged to have committed various crimes

Figure 1.11   Adjudication Form (Alaska)

IN THE SUPERIOR COURT FOR THE STATE OF ALASKA

AT _____

In the Matter of:)
)
)
)
)   CASE NO. _____CP
A minor under 18 years of age.   )
)   ADJUDICATION UPON ADMISSION
Date of birth:)
                    _____

A petition was filed on _____, 20 _____, alleging that the above-named juvenile is:

☐   a delinquent juvenile.

☐   a delinquent juvenile who has violated the conditions of his (probation) / (deferred institutional order) / (conduct agreement).

An adjudication hearing was held on the above petition on _____.
20 _____ Present were:

The court has considered the allegation in the petition and evidence presented and makes the following FINDINGS AND CONCLUSIONS:

1.   The court has jurisdiction over the parties and the subject matter of the proceedings.

2.   The child has knowingly and voluntarily admitted pursuant to Delinquency Rule 14(b)(4) that :

☐   all allegations in the petition are true.

☐   the following allegations in the petition are true:

THEREFORE, IT IS ADJUDGED that the above-named juvenile is:

☐   a delinquent juvenile.

☐   a delinquent juvenile who has violated the conditions of his (probation) / (deferred institutional order) / (conduct agreement).

Recommended on _____   Effective Date: _____

_____   _____   _____
        Superior Court Master   Superior Court Judge   Date

                                         _____
                                                Type or Print Name
I certify that on _____
a copy of this adjudication was sent to:
        DHSS, Juvenile/Attorney, Parent/Guardian, Other: _____

Clerk: _____

CP-230 (5/88) (st.5)   Del.R. 14(b) (4)
ADJUDICATION UPON ADMISSION   AS 47.10.010

may or may not be granted a trial by jury if they request one. In 2007, only 11 states provided jury trials for juveniles in juvenile courts, and these jury trials were restricted to a narrow list of serious offenses.

After hearing the evidence presented by both sides in any juvenile proceeding, the judge decides or adjudicates the matter in an **adjudication hearing**, sometimes called an **adjudicatory hearing**. An **adjudication** is a judgment or action on the petition filed with the court by others. If the petition alleges delinquency on the part of certain juveniles, the judge determines whether the juveniles are delinquent or not delinquent. If the petition alleges that the juveniles involved are dependent, neglected, or otherwise in need of care by agencies or others, the judge decides the matter. If the adjudicatory hearing fails to yield supporting facts for the petition filed, then the case is dismissed and the youth exits the juvenile justice system. If the adjudicatory hearing supports the allegations in the petition, then the judge must **dispose** the juvenile according to a range of punishments (Champion and Mays, 1991). An example of an adjudication or dispositional order form where action is taken by the juvenile court judge on facts alleged in a delinquency petition is illustrated in Figure 1.11.

In Figure 1.11, the adjudication form shows that a petition was filed with the court on a particular date, an adjudicatory hearing was conducted, and particular findings and conclusions are indicated. Notice in Figure 1.11 that juveniles may be adjudicated delinquent by the court, or they may be found in violation of one or more conditions of their probation, if they were originally disposed to probation by the juvenile court judge. This is because, like adult proceedings in criminal court, juvenile court judges retain jurisdiction over juveniles whenever they are placed on probation.

adjudication hearing, adjudicatory hearing
Formal proceeding involving a prosecuting attorney and a defense attorney where evidence is presented and the juvenile's guilt or innocence is determined by the juvenile judge.

adjudication
Judgment or action on a petition filed with the juvenile court by others.

dispose
To decide the punishment to be imposed on a juvenile following an adjudication hearing.

Juvenile Dispositions

Disposing juveniles is the equivalent of sentencing adult offenders. When adult offenders are convicted of crimes, they are sentenced. When juveniles are adjudicated delinquent, they are disposed. At least 12 different **dispositions** or punishments are available to juvenile court judges, if the facts alleged in petitions are upheld (Jarjoura et al., 2008). These dispositions are: (1) nominal, (2) conditional, or (3) custodial options.

Nominal Dispositions

Nominal dispositions are either verbal warnings or stern reprimands and are the least punitive dispositional options. The nature of such verbal warnings or reprimands is a matter of judicial discretion. Release to the custody of parents or legal guardians completes the juvenile court action against the youth (Foley, 2008). Usually nominal dispositions are most often applied to low-risk, first offenders who are the least likely to recidivate and commit new offenses (Abbott-Chapman, Denholm, and Wyld, 2007). The emphasis of nominal dispositions is upon rehabilitation and fostering a continuing, positive, reintegrative relationship between the juvenile and his/her community (Ross, 2008).

Conditional Dispositions

All **conditional dispositions** are probationary options. The most frequently imposed disposition is probation. Youths are placed on probation and required to comply with certain conditions during a probationary period lasting from several months to several years. Conditional dispositions usually require offenders to do something as a condition of probation. The nature of the conditions to be fulfilled depends on the needs of the offender and the nature of the offense committed. If youths have alcohol or drug

dispositions
Punishments resulting from a delinquency adjudication; may be nominal, conditional, or custodial.

nominal dispositions
Adjudicatory disposition resulting in lenient penalties such as warnings and/or probation.

conditional dispositions
Result of a delinquency adjudication obligating youths to comply with one or more conditions of a probation or similar program.

dependencies, they may be required to undergo individual or group counseling and some type of therapy to cope with substance abuse (McMorris et al., 2007). Juvenile murderers are often subjected to psychological counseling and clinical evaluation (Marriott, 2007). In more than a few cases, polygraph tests may be administered contemporaneous with these evaluations, counseling, and assessments.

Property offenders may be required to make restitution to victims or to compensate the court in some way for the damage they have caused (Jarjoura et al., 2008). In a growing number of jurisdictions, **restorative justice** is practiced, where offenders and their victims are brought together for the purpose of mediation. Youths learn to accept responsibility for what they have done, and their accountability is heightened (Swanson, 2005). Many jurisdictions have gravitated toward a more balanced approach in sanctioning youths, where the emphasis is upon restorative and victim-centered justice. The aim of this legislation is to (1) promote public safety and the protection of the community; (2) heighten accountability of youths toward victims and the community for offenses committed; and (3) increase competency and improve character development to assist youths in becoming responsible and productive members of society (Champion and Mays, 1991).

Offenders with behavioral disorders may require more intensive supervision while on probation (Abatiello, 2005). Those considered high risks for recidivism may be required to undergo electronic monitoring and house arrest as part of their supervision by juvenile probation officers. These and other similar control strategies are a part of the growing area of community corrections and intermediate punishments, where greater emphasis is upon community reintegration and rehabilitation (Rivers, 2005). During the 1990s there has been a gradual intensification of punishments for juveniles, including probation dispositions (Wilkerson, 2005). This emphasis on punishment is a reflection of state legislatures' tougher stance toward juveniles. Figure 1.12 is an acknowledgment of dispositional conditions and sanctions imposed by the court. Juveniles must sign this form to indicate that they have read and understood the disposition(s) imposed on them. They agree to comply with any imposed conditions.

The terms and conditions of the disposition are outlined in Figure 1.12. Obeying the law, attending school, maintaining employment, reporting to the probation officer, attending vocational training or education courses, appearing at subsequent court hearings, refraining from using drugs and alcohol, and refraining from possessing dangerous weapons are standard probation conditions. Furthermore, the judge may add other conditions, such as mandatory counseling or therapy, depending upon the particular needs exhibited by the offender and which are brought to the attention of the court.

Custodial Dispositions

Custodial dispositions are classified according to **nonsecure custody** or **nonsecure confinement** and **secure custody** or **secure confinement**. Nonsecure custody consists of placing certain juveniles into foster homes, group homes, camps, ranches, or schools. These are temporary measures often designed to lead to more permanent placement arrangements for juveniles later. Juveniles have freedom of movement, and they can generally participate in school and other youthful activities. If they are living in group homes or are on camp ranches, there are curfews to be observed. It is assumed that if they are in the care of others in foster homes or shelters, such curfews will be implicitly (if not explicitly) enforced (McNamara, 2008).

The secure custodial option is considered by most juvenile court judges as the last resort for serious juvenile offenders. Some of the reasons for this include overcrowding in secure juvenile facilities, a general reluctance among judges to incarcerate youths because of adverse labeling effects, and the potential effectiveness of certain intermediate punishments through community-service agencies. Fewer than 10 percent of all juveniles processed by juvenile courts annually are subsequently placed in either nonsecure or secure facilities (LaMade, 2008).

restorative justice
Mediation between victims and offenders whereby a suitable punishment is imposed and agreed to by offender and victim; usually involves victim compensation and some offender service.

custodial dispositions
Either nonsecure or secure options resulting from a delinquency adjudication involving out-of-home placement, ranch placement, or a juvenile custodial facility placement.

nonsecure custody, nonsecure confinement
Custodial disposition where a juvenile is placed in a group home, foster care, or other arrangement where he/she is permitted to leave with permission of parents, guardians, or supervisors.

secure custody, secure confinement
Incarceration of juvenile offender in facility which restricts movement in community; similar to adult penal facility involving total incarceration.

Figure 1.12   Conduct Agreement (State of Alaska)

IN THE SUPERIOR COURT FOR THE STATE OF ALASKA

_____ JUDICIAL DISTRICT AT _____

In the Matter of:)
)
)   CASE NO. _____CP
)
A minor under 18 years of age   )   ☐ **CONDUCT AGREEMENT**
Date of Birth: _____)   ☐ **CONDITIONS OF PROBATION**
                                                        OR DEFERRED INSTITUTIONAL
                                                        PLACEMENT

1.   I will obey all municipal, state and federal laws.

2.   I will remain in the placement designated by my Probation/Intake Officer and obey the curfew hours set by my parents, guardian, custodian or Probation/Intake Officer.

3.   I will notify my Probation/Intake Officer prior to changing my residence, employment or school.

4.   I will obey the rules and instructions set forth by my parents, guardian, custodian, and Probation/Intake Officer.

5.   I will attend school or vocational training when in session and conduct myself in accordance with school policy; otherwise, I will maintain steady employment.

6.   I will report as directed to my Probation/Intake Officer.

7.   I will appear at all scheduled court hearings.

8.   I will not ingest illegal drugs or alcohol, and will submit to random urinalysis as requested.

9.   I will not possess, have in my custody, handle, purchase or transport any firearm, knife, club or other type of weapon, ammunition or explosives. I will not carry any weapon on my person including pocket knives.

10. I will obey the following additional conditions: _____

_____

_____

_____

_____

_____

_____

Page 1 of 2
06-9555 (10/97) YC
CONDUCT AGREEMENT/CONDITIONS OF PROBATION

Del.R. 12(c), 23 & 24
AS 47.12.120

3.q.1

Figure 1.12   Conduct Agreement (State of Alaska) (Cont.)

In the Matter of: _____   Case No. _____ CP

I (have read)(have had read to me) and understand these conditions. I agree to obey them and understand that any violation may result in my being detained or having my probation revoked.

_____   _____   _____   _____
Probation/Intake Officer   Date   Juvenile   Date

We have read and understand these conditions. We agree to require the juvenile to obey them and to report any violations. We understand that if we fail to report a violation which is known to us, action may be taken against us in court. We further understand that any violation by the juvenile may result in his/her detention. We agree to bring the juvenile before the court when directed.

                                        _____   _____
                                        Parent/Guardian/Custodian   Date

ORDER

The above juvenile is hereby released under the terms and conditions agreed to in this document.

Recommended on_____   Effective Date: _____
                        Date

_____   _____   _____
Superior Court Master   Superior Court Judge   Date

                                      _____
                                      Type or Print Name

I certify that on_____
a copy of this document was sent to:

       DHSS
       Juvenile/Attorney
       Parent/Guardian
       Placement Facility
       Other:_____

Clerk: _____

Page 2 of 2   Del.R. 12(c), 23 & 24
06-9555 (10/97) YC   AS 47.12.120
CONDUCT AGREEMENT/CONDITIONS OF PROBATION   3.q.2

Juvenile Corrections

In 2006, there were over 70,000 juveniles in residential and nonresidential correctional programs other than probation (American Correctional Association, 2007). The range of juvenile corrections is almost as broad as programs for convicted adult offenders. In fact, since 1992 changes in juvenile court dispositions have been in the direction of increased incarceration of juveniles adjudicated delinquent for violent or other serious offenses without comparable attention to probation, community corrections, or other types of **aftercare** (Wilkerson, 2005).

Juvenile Probation

Juveniles adjudicated delinquent may be placed on probation or in secure confinement, depending upon juvenile court judge opinions and evaluations. Depending upon juvenile probation officer caseloads in various jurisdictions, probation may be more or less intense, commensurate with intensive supervised probation for adults. Placement in different types of probationary programs is dependent upon how the youth is originally classified. Interestingly, juvenile court judges have not consistently applied legal variables in their decision making about juvenile secure placements. More rational legal criteria for secure confinement decision making have been recommended (Sullivan et al., 2007).

Whether it is intensive, probation may be conditional and involve restitution to victims and/or community services. In 2006, there were over 650,000 juveniles on probation in various state jurisdictions (American Correctional Association, 2007). Juveniles may be placed in community-based residential programs or exposed to various therapies and treatments or training (Champion and Mays, 2001).

Confinement in state industrial schools is the juvenile equivalent of incarceration in a state prison for adults. This type of confinement is considered **hard time** for many juveniles. The California Youth Authority operates various facilities to house growing numbers of juvenile offenders in secure confinement. Lengths of commitment vary for offenders, depending upon the seriousness of their adjudication offenses (Office of Juvenile Justice and Delinquency Prevention, 2007).

Juvenile Parole

When juveniles have served a portion of their incarcerative terms, they are paroled by a juvenile paroling authority to the supervision of an appropriate state or community agency. Such supervision may be in the form of intensive aftercare (Champion, 2008a). In 2006, there were 95,000 juveniles on parole in various state jurisdictions (American Correctional Association, 2007). In Utah, for instance, a nine-member board, the Utah Youth Parole Authority, makes early-release decisions over large numbers of incarcerated youths monthly. Operated by the Utah Division of Youth Corrections, this board conducted over 385 parole hearings in 2006 (American Correctional Association, 2007). Although the board appears to be guided by certain eligibility criteria, one's institutional behavior while confined is considered quite important as an indicator of one's future community reintegration.

Summary

The juvenile justice system is an integrated network of agencies, institutions, and organizations that process juvenile offenders. Its essential components are law enforcement, prosecution and the courts, community and institutional corrections, aftercare, and parole. There is considerable diversity among jurisdictions about the

aftercare
A wide variety of programs and services for juveniles, including halfway houses, counseling services, employment assistance, and medical treatment.

hard time
Also known as flat time, actual amount of secure confinement juveniles must serve as the result of a custodial disposition from a juvenile court judge.

structure and operations of the juvenile justice system. Juveniles or infants are defined according to various ages. The maximum age limits for youths used by juvenile courts define juveniles among jurisdictions. The most common maximum age for juvenile court jurisdiction is 17, although maximum age limits of 18, 16, and 15 are found in some states. Lower age limits over juveniles used by juvenile courts also vary, with some courts having no lower age limits. Infants under age seven are generally considered incapable of formulating criminal intent and are treated by one or more community agencies rather than processed by juvenile courts.

Delinquency is any act committed by a juvenile that would be a crime if an adult committed it. Any criminal act committed by someone who has not reached the age of majority would also define delinquency. A status offense is any act committed by a juvenile that wouldn't be a crime if an adult committed it. Common status offenses include runaway behavior, curfew violation, incorrigibility, and truancy. Several policies have been established to differentiate between status and delinquent offenders. The JJDPA of 1974 was designed to remove status offenders from secure institutions where more hard-core delinquent offenders might be housed. This was called the DSO. The general meaning of DSO is broadly interpreted as decarceration of status offenders from institutions; diverting dependent and neglected children to social services; and divestiture of jurisdiction of juvenile courts over status offenders.

The traditional orientation of juvenile courts has been perpetuated by the *parens patriae* doctrine. This doctrine vests juvenile courts with individualized sanctioning powers intended to treat youths rather than punish them. Over time, juvenile courts have become increasingly adversarial, resembling criminal courts. Presently, juvenile courts are due process bodies, influenced significantly by the get-tough movement that espouses more punishment-centered options for juveniles. Despite this get-tough stance, juvenile court judges exhibit mixed philosophical principles that guide their decision making about youths. Many of these judges attempt to balance the aims of due process and justice with individualized treatments and therapies intended to rehabilitate and reintegrate youthful offenders.

The juvenile justice system and the criminal justice system parallel one another in several respects. Juveniles suspected of committing delinquent acts are taken into custody or arrested. Referrals to juvenile court by police, school authorities, neighbors, or even one's parents are common ways. These referrals are made whenever it is suspected that juveniles have violated one or more laws. About half of all juvenile cases are petitioned. A petition is a formal document seeking a hearing for the juvenile in a juvenile court. An adjudicatory hearing is a formal court proceeding much like a criminal trial. Judges usually impose dispositions on guilty juveniles, similar to criminal sentences. These include nominal dispositions or verbal warnings, conditional dispositions or probation, and custodial dispositions, which may involve incarceration.

A wide range of punishments is available to juvenile court judges that parallel the punishments available to criminal offenders, including probation and parole. Community-based punishments include probation, intensive supervised probation, home confinement, electronic monitoring, community service, restitution, fines, day reporting programs, halfway house placement, or other conditions. Other dispositons may include placement in a secure facility. Once juveniles have served a portion of their disposition in these facilities, they may be paroled. Juvenile parole is much like adult parole in that it is community-based and conditional.

Key Terms

adjudication, 37
adjudication hearing, 37
adjudicatory hearing, 37

adversarial proceedings, 22
aftercare, 41
beyond a reasonable doubt, 23

Questions for Review

1. What are the principal components of the juvenile justice system? Why do some persons view juvenile justice as a process rather than a system?

2. Why is there a general lack of uniformity among juvenile courts in the United States?

3. What is the age range for juvenile courts in the United States? What factors make it difficult to provide a consistent definition of this age range among states? Explain.

4. What is the doctrine of *parens patriae*? What are its origins? Does *parens patriae* continue to influence juvenile courts today? Why or why not?

5. What is the Juvenile Justice and Delinquency Prevention Act of 1974? What are its implications for juveniles?

6. What is meant by DSO? What are some of its outcomes for juvenile offenders?

7. What is the difference between being taken into custody and being arrested?

8. What are some major differences between juvenile courts and criminal courts?

9. What are dispositions? How do they resemble sentences for adult criminals? What are three types of dispositions? Define each and give an example.

10. Distinguish between juvenile probation and parole. What is the difference between secure and nonsecure confinement?

11. Are juvenile courts primarily treatment centered or punishment centered? What is the get-tough movement and what are some reasons for its existence?

Internet Connections

ABA Juvenile Justice Committee
http://www.abanet.org/dch/committee.cfm?com=CR200000

Center on Juvenile and Criminal Justice
http://www.cjcj.org/programs/Sentencing_Service.php

Children's Advocacy
http://www.childprotect.org/

Children's Defense Fund
http://www.childrensdefense.org/

Empowerment Resources
http://www.empowermentresources.com/

Chapter outline

The History of Juvenile Justice and Origins of the Juvenile Court

chapter objectives

As the result of reading this chapter, you will accomplish the following objectives:

1. Know about the early origins of juvenile courts in the United States.
2. Understand significant historical events in the evolution of the juvenile justice system.
3. Understand several important legal cases that have influenced juvenile offender processing in various ways.
4. Learn important differences between the *Uniform Crime Reports* and *National Crime Victimization Survey* as key indicators of delinquent behavior.
5. Learn about other important sources of information about juvenile offending, including the *National Juvenile Court Data Archive*, self-report information, and the *Sourcebook of Criminal Justice Statistics*.
6. Learn about violent and nonviolent delinquent conduct, and whether there is any career escalation among juvenile offenders.
7. Learn about several contemporary issues such as school violence, at-risk youths, career escalation, and juvenile murderers.
8. Determine some of the major differences between male and female juveniles and their offending patterns.

 ## Case Study

It happened in Kippax Fair in May 2007. A 15-year-old boy and a 12-year-old boy confronted another 12-year-old boy at gunpoint and made the victim hand over a sum of cash and a cell phone. The two robbers escaped, but their crime was reported shortly thereafter, when the 12-year-old victim contacted police and gave them the robbers' descriptions. The two youths were charged with aggravated robbery and faced juvenile court at a later date. [Source: Adapted from the Associated Press, "Juvenile in Court for Aggravated Robbery," May 7, 2007.]

In another incident on December 21, 2006, Rashawn Fernando Harris, 17, two juvenile females, and an adult male, entered and robbed the Village Inn Restaurant in Virginia Beach, Virginia. They wore masks and brandished handguns. The youths and the adult were apprehended a short time later. Harris, who had a lengthy juvenile record and was on probation at the time for robbery, was sentenced in August 2007 to 78 years in prison. All but 16 years of the sentence was suspended, and Harris was ordered on probation thereafter for 65 years, conditioned on good behavior. [Source: Adapted from the City of Virginia Beach, "*Commonwealth v. Harris*: Juvenile Restaurant Robber Sentenced to Serve 16 Years," November 2, 2007.]

 ## Case Study

In 2001, in South Carolina, Christopher Pittman, 12, shotgunned his two grandparents, Joe and Joy Pittman, as they lay sleeping in their beds. He then set fire to the house and fled, only to have his car stuck in the mud while attempting to elude police. At his trial later, he claimed that he had been taking the antidepressant Zoloft, a drug, he claimed, that clouded his judgment, leading to the murders. A jury didn't buy the theory and convicted Pittman at age 15 in 2005. A judge sentenced Pittman to 30 years. In December 2007, an appeal was launched by public defenders to seek a reduction in

Pittman's sentence, claiming that the 30-year sentence amounted to cruel and unusual punishment for a 12-year-old. [Source: Adapted from Schulyer Kropf and the *Post and Courier*, "Appeal Sought for S.C. Teen," December 19, 2007.]

In Mount Vernon, Washington, on July 21, 2007, a 23-year-old, a 16-year-old, and a 15-year-old robbed a Tacos Guadalajara, demanding a cashbox from employees at gunpoint. Shots were fired, although no one was injured. The suspects were subsequently apprehended, the escape vehicle was seized and impounded, and the cashbox was retrieved as evidence. The two juveniles were booked for armed robbery by detectives of the Skagit County Juvenile Detention Division. [Source: Adapted from the City of Mount Vernon, "July 2007 Robbery," November 2, 2007.]

Introduction

All of these cases involve crimes committed by juveniles. They differ significantly in their seriousness, and the ages of the youthful perpetrators range from 12 to 17. All of the crimes described are common for adult offenders. Did the early pioneers of the juvenile justice system ever consider that juvenile courts would have to decide cases involving such violence?

This chapter is about the history of the juvenile justice system in the United States. In 1999, the first centennial of the juvenile court in the United States was celebrated. The formality of juvenile courts today did not begin to emerge until the 1960s and 1970s. The historical antecedents of the juvenile justice system are rooted in England during the sixteenth century, when youthful offenders were under the jurisdiction of the king. Justice for youths was dispensed through political appointees known as chancellors. These persons made decisions about juveniles according to what they believed to be in the child's best interests. When the American colonies were established, English influence over how youths were treated continued. Between the early 1600s and late 1800s, a gradual transformation occurred that influenced how youthful offenders were treated. Many of the events that shaped the contemporary system of juvenile justice and offender processing are presented and described.

Two key cases, *Ex parte Crouse* (1839) and *People ex rel. O'Connell v. Turner* (1870), are presented and examined. These cases were influential in shaping policies about child welfare, guardianship, and punishments for various types of juvenile behaviors. During the 40-year interval following the Civil War, several philanthropists, religious groups, and political entities contributed to promoting several important youth reforms. The child-saving movement was created, and houses of refuge were constructed and operated. Crucial legislation in different states was enacted, establishing both truancy laws and juvenile courts. Gradually, children gained greater recognition and were given special treatment, moving them well beyond their early conceptualization as chattel, and their unfair and unilateral treatment in primitive children's tribunals. These and other critical events are described. Early juvenile courts were noted particularly for their paternalistic views toward youths through the doctrine of *parens patriae* and individualized decision making based on a youth's best interests as determined by the courts.

How much delinquency and status offending is there in the United States? While no one knows for sure, several official and unofficial measures exist that purportedly depict their frequency. Several measures used in tracking juvenile offending are described. These include the *Uniform Crime Reports* (*UCR*), the *National Crime Victimization Survey* (*NCVS*), *The National Juvenile Court Data Archive*, and the *Sourcebook of Criminal Justice Statistics*. These sources will be described and discussed. Other less-official sources include the The *National Youth Survey* and the *Monitoring the Future Survey*. These national surveys will also be defined and described. An important source of unreported delinquency and status offense information is self-reports, or disclosures by juveniles to private researchers about the nature and extent of their offending. Some of the strengths and weaknesses of these different information sources, including self-reports, will be discussed.

Classifying juvenile offending differentiates between violent offenses and property offenses. Violent offenses include murder, rape, aggravated assault, and robbery. In recent years, several incidents of school violence have been reported by the media. Thus, school violence, patterns, and trends will be depicted. This section also describes youths who are considered at risk of becoming delinquent. Several risk factors, such as family instability, poor school adjustment, lower socioeconomic status, low self-control and self-esteem, and antisocial behaviors, will be described. Some violent offending is gang related (George and Thomas, 2008). Juvenile gangs often form along racial or ethnic lines. Such gang activities will be examined. Some juveniles are murderers, although their numbers are few. These juveniles will be described.

One concern of criminologists is whether less-serious offenders, such as status offenders, progress to more serious offenses. This phenomenon is known as career escalation. It is believed by some authorities that less-serious juvenile offending, if not detected and corrected, will eventually lead to more serious offending. It is uncertain whether career escalation occurs for most juveniles who commit less-serious offenses. Career escalation and juvenile violence trends will be examined.

The chapter concludes with an examination of female juveniles and how they have emerged in recent years as a proportionately greater minority among serious juvenile offenders. Female juvenile offenders are profiled and several trends among these females are described. Female juveniles have increasingly become involved in gang activities, and juvenile female gang formation will be examined. Because more female juvenile offenders have come to the attention of police, several myths and misconceptions about female juveniles have been started and perpetuated. These myths and misconceptions will be described.

The History of Juvenile Courts

Juvenile courts are a relatively recent American creation. However, modern American juvenile courts have various less-formal European antecedents. In biblical times, Roman law vested parents with the almost exclusive responsibility for disciplining their offspring. One's age was the crucial determinant of whether youths were subject to parental discipline or to the more severe penalties invoked for adult law violators. While the origin of this cutting point is unknown, the age of seven was used in Roman times to separate infants from those older children who were accountable to the law for their actions (Congressional Research Service, 2007). During the Middle Ages, English **common law** established under the monarchy adhered to the same standard. In the United States, several state jurisdictions currently apply this distinction and consider all children below the age of seven to be not accountable for any criminal acts they may commit.

Under the laws of England during the 1500s, **shires** (counties) and other political subdivisions were organized to carry out the will of the king. Each shire had a **reeve**, or chief law enforcement officer. In later years, the term "shire" was combined with the term "reeve" (shire-reeve) to create the word, sheriff, a term that is now applied to the chief law enforcement officer of most U.S. counties. While reeves enforced both criminal and civil laws and arrested law violators, other functionaries, called **chancellors**, acted on the king's behalf and dispensed justice according to his wishes. These chancellors held court and settled disputes that included simple property trespass, property boundary disagreements, and assorted personal and property offenses, including public drunkenness, thievery, and vagrancy. The courts conducted by chancellors were known as **chancery courts** or **courts of equity**. Today, some jurisdictions in the United

common law
Authority based on court decrees and judgments that recognize, affirm, and enforce certain usages and customs of the people; laws determined by judges in accordance with their rulings.

shires
Early English counties.

reeve
Chief law enforcement officer of English counties, known as shires.

chancellors
Civil servants who acted on behalf of the King of England during the Middle Ages; chancellors held court and settled property disputes, trespass cases, and minor property offenses; thievery, vagrancy, and public drunkenness.

chancery courts
Courts of equity rooted in early English Common Law where civil disputes and matters involving children may be resolved.

States such as Tennessee have chancery courts where property boundary disputes and contested wills may be adjudicated by chancellors. These courts have other jurisdiction as well, although they deal primarily with equity cases (e.g., breaches of contract, specific performance actions, and child custody cases).

No distinctions were made regarding age or gender when punishments were administered in England during the 1700s. Youthful offenders aged seven or older experienced the same harsh punishments imposed on adults. Stocks and pillories, whipping posts, branding, ducking stools, and other forms of corporal punishment were administered to juveniles as well as to adult offenders for many different types of crimes. In some instances, **banishment** was used as a way of punishing more serious offenders. Some offenders were transported to Pacific islands, which were owned by the British and converted into penal colonies. This was known as **transportation**. Many prisoners died in these colonies. The death penalty was invoked frequently, often for petty crimes. Incarceration of offenders was particularly sordid, as women, men, and youths were confined together in jails for lengthy periods. No attempts were made to classify these offenders by gender or age, and all prisoners slept on hay loosely thrown on wooden floors.

Workhouses and Poor Laws

Eighteenth-century jails were patterned largely after **workhouses** that were still common nearly two centuries earlier. In 1557, for example, **Bridewell Workhouse** was established in London. Although the manifest aim of such places was to punish offenders, Bridewell and other similar facilities were created primarily for the purpose of providing cheap labor to satisfy mercantile interests and demands. Interestingly, jailers and sheriffs profited greatly from leasing their inmates to various merchants in order to perform semiskilled and skilled labor. These same jailers claimed that the work performed by inmates for mercantile interests was largely therapeutic and rehabilitative, although in reality the primary incentive for operating such houses was profit and personal gain. Exploitation of inmates for profit in these and other workhouses was perpetuated by jailers and sheriffs for many decades, and the general practice was accepted by an influential constituency of merchants and entrepreneurs.

At the time of the Bridewell Workhouse, English legislators had already established several statutes known as the **Poor Laws**. These laws targeted debtors who owed creditors, and sanctions for those unable to pay their debts were imposed. Debtors' prisons were places where debtors were incarcerated until they could pay their debts. Since debtors needed to work to earn the money required to pay off their debts, and since opportunities for earning money for prison labor were almost nonexistent, imprisonment for debts was tantamount to a life sentence. Many offenders were incarcerated indefinitely, or until someone, perhaps a relative or influential friend, could pay off their debts for them.

The Poor Laws were directed at the poor or socioeconomically disadvantaged. In 1601, additional statutes were established that provided constructive work for youths deemed by the courts to be vagrant, incorrigible, truant, or neglected. In general, education was not an option for these youths—it was an expensive commodity available almost exclusively to children from the upper social strata, and it provided a major means of achieving higher status over time. For the masses of poor, education was usually beyond their reach; they spent most of their time earning money to pay for life's basic necessities. They had little or no time to consider education as a realistic option (Champion, 2008a).

Indentured Servants

Many youths during this time became apprentices, usually to master craftsmen, in a system of involuntary servitude. This servitude was patterned in part after the

banishment
Sanction used to punish offenders by barring them for a specified number of miles from settlements or towns; often a capital punishment, since those banished could not obtain food or water to survive the isolation.

transportation
Early British practice of sending undesirables, misfits, and convicted offenders to remote territories and islands controlled by England.

workhouses
Early penal facilities designed to use prison labor for profit by private interests; operated in shires in mid-sixteenth century and later.

Bridewell Workhouse
Sixteenth-century London jail (sometimes gaol) established in 1557; known for providing cheap labor to business and mercantile interests; jailers and sheriffs profited from prisoner exploitation.

Poor Laws
Regulations in English Middle Ages designed to punish debtors by imprisoning them until they could pay their debts; imprisonment was for life, or until someone could pay the debtor's debts for them.

indentured servant system. Indentured servants entered voluntarily into contractual agreements with various merchants and businessmen to work for them for extended periods of up to seven years. This seven-year work agreement was considered by all parties to be a mutually beneficial way of paying for the indentured servant's passage from England to the colonies. In the case of youthful apprentices, however, their servitude, for the most part, was compulsory. Furthermore, it usually lasted until they reached adulthood, or age 21.

During the Colonial period, English influence on penal practices was apparent in most New England jurisdictions. Colonists relied on familiar traditions for administering laws and sanctioning offenders. It is no coincidence, therefore, that much criminal procedure in American courts today traces its origins to legal customs and precedents inherent in British jurisprudence during the 1600s and 1700s. However, relatively little attention was devoted to the legal status of juveniles during this period and to how to manage them. In fact, more than a few juveniles were summarily executed for relatively petty offenses (Champion, 2008a).

Hospital of Saint Michael

In other parts of the world during the same era, certain religious interests were gradually devising institutions that catered primarily to youthful offenders. For example, in Italy, a corrective facility was established in 1704 to provide for unruly youths and other young people who violated criminal laws. This facility was the **Hospital of Saint Michael,** constructed in Rome at the request of the Pope. The institution was misleadingly named, however, since the youths it housed were not ill. Rather, they were assigned various tasks and trained to perform semiskilled and skilled labor—useful tools that would enable them to find employment more easily after their release from Saint Michael. During rest periods and evening hours, youths were housed in individual cells.

The Quakers and Walnut Street Jail

Reforms relating to the treatment and/or punishment of juvenile offenders occurred slowly. Shortly after the Revolutionary War, religious interests in the United States moved forward with various proposals designed to improve the plight of the oppressed, particularly those who were incarcerated in prisons and jails. In 1787, the Quakers in Pennsylvania established the **Philadelphia Society for Alleviating the Miseries of Public Prisons**. This largely philanthropic society was comprised of prominent citizens, religious leaders, and philanthropists who were appalled by existing prison and jail conditions. Adult male, female, and juvenile offenders continued to be housed in common quarters and treated like animals. The High Street Jail in Philadelphia was one eyesore that particularly attracted the Society's attention. Because members of the Quaker faith visited this and other jail facilities regularly to bring food, clothing, and religious instruction to inmates, they were in strategic positions to observe the totality of circumstances in which those confined found themselves.

In 1790, an older Philadelphia jail facility, originally constructed in 1776, was overhauled and refurbished. It was renamed the **Walnut Street Jail**. This facility has considerable historical significance for corrections, since it was the first real attempt by jail authorities to classify and segregate offenders according to their age, gender, and crime seriousness. The Walnut Street Jail was innovative in at least three respects. First, it pioneered what is now known as **solitary confinement**. Sixteen large solitary cells were constructed to house prisoners on an individual basis during evening hours. Second, prisoners were segregated from other prisoners according to offense seriousness. More violent criminals were placed with others like them. First-offenders or petty offenders were similarly grouped together and segregated from more violent convicts. Third, women and children were maintained in separate rooms during evening hours, away from male prisoners.

The Walnut Street Jail promoted rehabilitation. It attempted to train its inmates for different types of labor, such as sewing, shoemaking, or carpentry. Unskilled laborers were assigned tasks such as beating hemp for ship caulking. Most prisoners received modest wages for their skilled or unskilled labor, although much of this pay was used to pay for their room and board. Finally, religious instruction was provided to inmates by Quaker teachers. This provision is indicative of the dramatic influence of religion in shaping prison policies and practices relating to inmate treatment and benefits (Campbell and Gonzalez, 2007).

The Child Savers and Houses of Refuge

As more families gravitated toward large cities such as New York, Philadelphia, Boston, and Chicago during the early 1800s to find work, increasing numbers of children roamed the streets, most often unsupervised by working parents who could not afford child care services. Lacking familial controls, many of these youths committed acts of vandalism and theft. Others were simply idle, without visible means of support, and were designated as vagrants. Again, religious organizations intervened in order to protect unsupervised youths from the perils of life in the streets. Believing that these youths would subsequently turn to lives of crime as adults, many reformers and philanthropists sought to save them from their plight.

Thus, in different cities throughout the United States, various groups were formed to find and control these youths by offering them constructive work programs, healthful living conditions, and above all, adult supervision. Collectively, these efforts became widely known as the **child-saving movement**. **Child savers** came largely from the middle and upper classes, and their assistance to youths took many forms. Food and shelter were provided to children who were in trouble with the law or who were simply idle. Private homes were converted into settlements where social, educational, and other important activities could be provided for needy youths. The child savers were not limited to the United States. In Scotland and England during the 1850s, child-saving institutions were abundant, with similar philosophies and interests as U.S. child-saving organizations. In England particularly, middle-class values were imposed on the children of the working class through institutional education, training, and discipline. Eventually, several juvenile reformatories were established for the purpose of institutional control (Blevins, 2005).

In the United States, more than a few child-saver organizations sought to impose their class, ethnic, and racial biases on the poor, immigrants, and minority women. A middle-class gender ideology of maternal care was imposed upon working- and lower-class mothers. Many of these mothers were declared unfit and in need of state control, since they did not conform to the cultural ideal espoused by middle- and upper-class child savers. Thus, there was the general charge that child savers sought to control and resocialize the children of the dangerous classes for the benefit of the capitalist entrepreneurs. But not everyone agrees that child savers exploited children. In certain cities, such as Wilmington, Delaware, the child-saving movement emphasized education rather than work. Furthermore, the ultimate aims of this movement in Delaware and several other states were largely altruistic and humanitarian. Even in contemporary youth corrections, the child-saver orientation influences the care and treatment strategies of contemporary personnel (Blevins, 2005).

The **New York House of Refuge** was established in New York City in 1825 by the **Society for the Prevention of Pauperism** (Campbell and Gonzalez, 2007). Subsequently imitated in other communities, **houses of refuge** were institutions largely devoted to managing status offenders, such as runaways or incorrigible children. Compulsory education and other forms of training and assistance were provided to these children. However, the strict, prison-like regimen of this organization was not entirely

child savers, child-saving movement Organized effort during early 1800s to provide assistance to wayward youths; including food and shelter.

New York House of Refuge Established in New York City in 1825 by the Society for the Prevention of Pauperism; managed largely status offenders with compulsory education provided.

Society for the Prevention of Pauperism Philanthropic society that established first public reformatory in New York in 1825, the New York House of Refuge.

houses of refuge Workhouses, the first of which was established in 1824 as a means of separating juveniles from the adult correctional process.

therapeutic for its clientele. Many of the youthful offenders who were sent to such institutions, including the House of Reformation in Boston, were offspring of immigrants. Often, they rebelled when exposed to the discipline of these organizations, and many of these youths eventually pursued criminal careers as a consequence. It would appear that at least some of these humanitarian and philanthropic efforts by child savers and others had adverse consequences for many affected juveniles.

Another facility with a notorious reputation for how it treated juveniles was the Western House of Refuge (WHR) in Rochester, New York, which operated during the 1880s. Juvenile inmates of this facility were considered deviant and criminal. In reality, the youths institutionalized at the WHR were primarily orphaned, abused, or neglected. Their treatment consisted of hard labor and rigid discipline. Not all houses of refuge were like the Western House of Refuge, however. In California, for instance, several houses of refuge were operated in ways that stressed vocational training, educational instruction, and some amount of aftercare when youths were ultimately released (Champion, 2008a).

Up until the late 1830s, there was little or no pattern to the division of labor between parental, religious, and state authority. As private interests continued to include larger numbers of juveniles within the scope of their supervision, various jurisdictions sought to regulate and institutionalize these assorted juvenile assistance, treatment, and/or intervention programs. In many communities, city councils sanctioned the establishment of facilities to accommodate youths who were delinquent, dependent, or neglected.

Ex Parte Crouse

In 1839, a decision in a state case gave juvenile authorities considerable power over parents in the management and control of their own children. *Ex parte Crouse* (1839) was a case involving a father who attempted to secure the release of his daughter, Mary Ann Crouse, from the Philadelphia House of Refuge. The girl had been committed to the Philadelphia facility by the court because she was considered unmanageable. She was not given a trial by jury. Rather, her commitment was made arbitrarily by a presiding judge. A higher court rejected the father's claim that parental control of children is exclusive, natural, and proper, and it upheld the power of the state to exercise necessary reforms and restraints to protect children from themselves and their environments. While this decision was only applicable to Pennsylvania citizens and their children, other states took note of it and sought to invoke similar controls over errant children in their jurisdictions. Essentially, children in Pennsylvania were temporarily deprived of any legal standing to challenge decisions made by the state in their behalf.

Reform Schools and *People ex rel. O'Connell v. Turner* (1870)

Throughout the remainder of the nineteenth century, different types of institutions were established to supervise unruly juveniles. At roughly mid-century, **reform schools** in several jurisdictions were created. One of the first state-operated reform schools was opened in Westboro, Massachusetts, in 1848. By the end of the century, all states had reform schools of one sort or another. All of these institutions were characterized by strict discipline, absolute control over juvenile behavior, and compulsory work at various trades. Another common feature was that they were controversial (Coalition for Juvenile Justice, 2007).

The primary question raised by reform school critics was, "Do reform schools reform?" Since many juveniles continued to commit delinquent acts after being released

reform schools
Different types of vocational institutions designed to both punish and rehabilitate youthful offenders; operated much like prisons as total institutions.

from these schools and eventually became adult criminals, the rehabilitative value of reform schools was seriously challenged. The Civil War exacerbated the problem of unruly youths, since many families were broken up. Orphans of dead soldiers were commonplace in the post–Civil War period. Such children were often committed to reform schools, regardless of whether they had committed criminal offenses. Many status offenders were sent to reform schools, simply because they were vagrants. Many of these children did not need to be reformed. Rather, they needed homes and noninstitutional care.

One state, Illinois, was particularly aggressive when it came to confining juveniles in reform schools. Many of these incarcerated juveniles were children of immigrant workers in and around Chicago, and they were often rounded up and imprisoned for simple loitering or playing in the city streets. The Chicago Reform School was especially notorious as a site where such youths were sent and confined. In 1870, however, the Illinois Supreme Court heard and decided a case which ultimately prohibited such juvenile arrests by police and incarcerations. This was the case of *People ex rel. O'Connell v. Turner* (1870). Few legal challenges of state authority were made by complaining parents, because of the awesome power of the state and its control over juvenile matters. However, an Illinois case paved the way for special courts for juveniles and an early recognition of their rights. A youth, Daniel O'Connell, was declared vagrant and in need of supervision and committed to the Chicago Reform School for an unspecified period. O'Connell's parents challenged this court action, claiming that his confinement for vagrancy was unjust and untenable. Existing Illinois law vested state authorities with the power to commit any juvenile to a state reform school as long as a "reasonable justification" could be provided. In this instance, vagrancy was a reasonable justification. The Illinois Supreme Court distinguished between misfortune (vagrancy) and criminal acts in arriving at its decision to reverse Daniel O'Connell's commitment. In effect, the court nullified the law by declaring that reform school commitments of youths could not be made by the state if the "offense" was simple misfortune. They reasoned that the state's interests would be better served if commitments of juveniles to reform schools were limited to those committing more serious criminal offenses rather than those who were victims of misfortune. The Illinois Supreme Court further held that it was unconstitutional to confine youths who had not been convicted of criminal conduct or afforded legal due process to be confined in the Chicago Reform School. One result of this decision was the eventual closure of the Chicago Reform School two years later. As one alternative to incarceration, Chicago and other Illinois youths without adult supervision were placed under the care of social service agencies and benevolent societies. Both individuals and groups established settlements for displaced or wayward youths (Champion, 2008a).

Community-Based Private Agencies

In 1889, **Jane Addams** established and operated Hull House in Chicago, Illinois. Hull House was a settlement home used largely by children from immigrant families in the Chicago area. In those days, adults worked long hours, and many youths were otherwise unsupervised and wandered about their neighborhoods looking for something to do. Using money from various charities and philanthropists, Addams supplied many children with creative activities to alleviate their boredom and monotony. Addams integrated these activities with moral, ethical, and religious teachings. In her own way, she was hoping to deter these youths from lives of crime with her constructive activities and teaching. Thus, her approach was consistent with the philosophy of **Cesare Beccaria**, the father of classical **criminology**. Beccaria wrote in 1764 that the purpose of punishment was deterrence, and that punishment should be measured according to the seriousness of the criminal acts committed.

Jane Addams
Established Hull House in Chicago in 1889; assisted wayward and homeless youths.

Cesare Beccaria
Italian criminologist known for his origination of classical criminology, emphasizing the deterrent effects of punishment.

criminology
Scientific study of the etiology of criminal behavior.

School-age youths may be truants and attract police interest.

Truancy Statutes

Truants were created as a class of juvenile offenders in Massachusetts in 1852, where the first compulsory school attendance statute was passed. Many other states adopted similar statutes, until all jurisdictions had compulsory school attendance provisions by 1918. Some historians have erroneously credited Colorado as having drafted the first juvenile court provisions. In fact, the Colorado legislature passed the Compulsory School Act of 1899, the same year that the first juvenile court was established in Illinois (Reddington, 2005). The Colorado action was aimed at preventing truancy. Colorado legislators labeled such youths "juvenile disorderly persons," but this action did not lead to the creation of a Colorado juvenile court.

The Illinois Juvenile Court Act. The Illinois legislature established the first juvenile court on July 1, 1899, by passing the **Act to Regulate the Treatment and Control of Dependent, Neglected, and Delinquent Children**, or the **Illinois Juvenile Court Act**. This act provided for limited courts of record, where notes might be taken by judges or their assistants, to reflect judicial actions against juveniles. The jurisdiction of these courts, subsequently designated as **juvenile courts**, would include all juveniles under the age of 16 who were found in violation of any state or local law or ordinance. Also, provision was made for the care of dependent and/or neglected children who had been abandoned or who otherwise lacked proper parental care, support, or guardianship. No minimum age was specified that would limit the jurisdiction of juvenile court judges. However, the act provided that judges could impose secure confinement on juveniles 10 years of age or over by placing them in state-regulated juvenile facilities such as the state reformatory or the State Home for Juvenile Female Offenders. Judges were expressly prohibited from confining any juvenile under 12 years of age in a jail or police station. Extremely young juveniles would be assigned probation officers who would look after their needs and placement on a temporary basis.

Illinois's Juvenile Court Act says much about the times and how the legal status of juveniles was interpreted and applied. The full title of the Act is revealing. According to the Act, it was applicable only to

Act to Regulate the Treatment and Control of Dependent, Neglected, and Delinquent Children
Delinquency Act passed by Illinois legislature in 1899; established first juvenile court among states.

Illinois Juvenile Court Act
Legislation passed by Illinois legislature in 1899 providing for the first juvenile court and treatment programs for various types of juvenile offenders.

juvenile courts
Formal proceeding with jurisdiction over juveniles, juvenile delinquents, status offenders, dependent or neglected children, children in need of supervision, or infants.

". . . children under the age of sixteen (16) years not now or hereafter inmates of a State institution, or any training school for boys or industrial school for girls or some institution incorporated under the laws of this State, except as provided [in other sections] . . ." For purposes of this act the words dependent child and neglected child shall mean any child who for any reason is destitute or homeless or abandoned; or dependent upon the public for support; or has not proper parental care or guardianship; or who habitually begs or receives alms, or who is found living in any house of ill fame or with any vicious or disreputable person; or whose home, by reason of neglect, cruelty or depravity on the part of its parents, guardian or other person in whose care it may be, is an unfit place for such a child; and any child under the age of eight (8) years who is found peddling or selling any article or singing or playing any musical instrument upon the streets or giving any public entertainment. The words delinquent child shall include any child under the age of 16 years who violates any law of this State or any city or village ordinance. The word child or children may mean one or more children, and the word parent or parents may be held to mean one or both parents, when consistent with the intent of this act. The word association shall include any corporation which includes in its purposes the care or disposition of children coming within the meaning of this act.

Even more insightful is what happens when such children are found. What are the limits of court sanctions? Illinois law authorized juvenile court judges to take the following actions in their dealings with dependent and neglected children:

> When any child under the age of sixteen (16) years shall be found to be dependent or neglected within the meaning of this act, the court may make an order committing the child to the care of some suitable State institution, or to the care of some reputable citizen of good moral character, or to the care of some training school or an industrial school, as provided by law, or to the care of some association willing to receive it embracing in its objects the purpose of caring or obtaining homes for dependent or neglected children, which association shall have been accredited as hereinafter provided.

For juvenile delinquents, similar provisions were made. Judges were authorized to continue the hearing for any specific delinquent child from time to time and may commit the child to the care and guardianship of a probation officer. The child might be permitted to remain in *its* own home, subject to the visitation of the probation officer. Judges were also authorized to commit children to state training or industrial schools until such time as they reach the age of their majority or adulthood (Champion, 2008a).

Juveniles as Chattel

The choice of the word, *it,* used here in reference to children, shows how youths were viewed in those days. In early English times, children were considered chattel, lumped together with the cows, pigs, horses, and other farm property one might lawfully possess. The act itself was sufficiently ambiguous so as to allow judges and others considerable latitude or discretion about how to interpret juvenile behaviors. For example, what is meant by proper parental care or guardianship? What is habitual begging? Is occasional begging acceptable? Would children be subject to arrest and juvenile court sanctions for walking city streets playing a flute or other musical devices? Who decides what homes and establishments are unfit? Where are the criteria that describe a home's fitness? It has almost always been presumed that juvenile court judges know the answers to these questions, and their judgments, regardless of their foundation, rationality, or consistency with due process, are seldom questioned.

These statements reflect the traditionalism that juvenile court judges have manifested over the years (Campbell and Gonzalez, 2007). Taking dependent and neglected or abandoned children and placing them in training or industrial schools is the functional equivalent of adult incarceration in a prison or jail. By a stroke of the pen, the Illinois legislature gave juvenile court judges absolute control over the lives of all children under age 16 in the State of Illinois. During the next 10 years, 20 states passed similar acts to establish juvenile courts. By the end of World War II, all states had created juvenile court systems. However, considerable variation existed among these court systems, depending on the jurisdiction. Not all of these courts were vested with a consistent set of responsibilities and powers.

Children's Tribunals

Earlier versions of juvenile courts were created in Massachusetts in 1874. For instance, there were **children's tribunals**, sometimes referred to as **civil tribunals**. These informal mechanisms were used to adjudicate and punish children charged with crimes. They were entirely independent from the system of criminal courts for adults. Usually, judges would confer with the equivalent of a social worker and then decide how best to deal with a wayward youth. Under the tribunal system, youths were not entitled to representation by counsel, and the proceedings occurred in secret, away from public view.

children's tribunals
Informal court mechanisms originating in Massachusetts to deal with children charged with crimes apart from the system of criminal courts for adults.

Furthermore, there were no formal presentations of evidence against the accused youth, no transcripts, no cross-examination of witnesses, and no right to appeal a judicial decision.

Some years later, Colorado implemented an education law in 1899 known as the **Compulsory School Act**. Although this act was primarily targeted at truants, it also encompassed juveniles who wandered the streets during school hours, without any obvious business or occupation. These youths were termed "juvenile disorderly persons," and they were legislatively placed within the purview of truant officers and law enforcement officers who could detain them and hold them for further action by other community agencies. While both Massachusetts and Colorado created these different mechanisms specifically for dealing with juvenile offenders, they were not juvenile courts in the same sense as those established by Illinois in 1899. Furthermore, these truancy-oriented courts are not an exclusively American creation. In England, for example, precourt tribunals have been established to decide whether families should be taken to court because of a child's nonattendance at school. The intent of such tribunals is to normalize families and destroy deviant identities juveniles might acquire because of their school absences. Both parents and children must reassure the judge that regular school attendance will be forthcoming.

Compulsory School Act
1899 Colorado law targeting truant youths; erroneously regarded as first juvenile court act, which was actually passed in Illinois in 1899, and dealt with delinquent conduct.

Informal Welfare Agencies and Emerging Juvenile Courts

The juvenile court has evolved from an informal welfare agency into a scaled-down, second-class criminal court as the result of a series of reforms that have diverted less-serious offenders from juvenile court and moved more-serious offenders to criminal courts for processing (Feld, 2007). Several policy responses have been recommended as options. These include: (1) restructuring the juvenile courts to fit their original therapeutic purposes; (2) accepting punishment as the purpose of delinquency proceedings, coupled with criminal procedural safeguards; and/or (3) abolishing juvenile courts altogether and trying young offenders in criminal courts, with certain substantive and procedural modifications.

The Lack of Juvenile Court Uniformity

Little uniformity exists among jurisdictions regarding juvenile court organization and operation. Even within state jurisdictions, great variations exist among counties and cities relating to how juvenile offenders are processed. Historically, family or domestic courts have retained jurisdiction over most, if not all, juvenile matters. Not all jurisdictions have juvenile courts, per se. Rather, some jurisdictions have courts that adjudicate juvenile offenders as well as decide child custody. Thus, while it is true that all jurisdictions presently have juvenile courts, these courts are not always called juvenile courts (Congressional Research Service, 2007).

From *Gemeinschaft* to *Gesellschaft* and Reconceptualizing Juveniles

gemeinschaft
Term created by Ferdinand Tonnies, a social theorist, to describe small, traditional communities where informal punishments were used to punish those who violated community laws.

Before the establishment of juvenile courts, how were juvenile offenders processed and punished? How were dependent and neglected children treated? Social scientists would probably describe village and community life in the 1700s and 1800s by citing the dominant social and cultural values that existed then. The term, *gemeinschaft*, might be used here to describe the lifestyle one might find in such settings. It is a term used to characterize social relations as being highly dependent upon verbal agreements and understandings and informality. Ferdinand Tonnies, a social theorist, used *gemeinschaft* to convey the richness of tradition that would typify small communities where everyone was known to all others. In these settings, formal punishments, such as incarceration in prisons or jails, was seldom used. More effective than incarceration were punishments that heightened public humiliation through stocks and pillars and other corporal measures. There was sufficient social pressure exerted so that most complied with the law. Thus, in *gemeinschaft* communities, people would probably fear social stigma, ostracism, and scorn more than their loss of freedom through incarceration (Kidd, 2007).

In these communities, children would remain children through adolescence, eventually becoming adults as they commenced to perform trades or crafts and earned independent livings apart from their families. Children performed apprenticeships over lengthy periods under the tutorship of master craftsmen and others. Many of the terms we currently use to describe delinquent acts and status offenses were nonexistent then. As the nation grew, urbanization and the increasing population density of large cities changed social relationships gradually but extensively. Tonnies described the nature of this gradual shift in social relationships from a *gemeinschaft*-type of social network to a *gesellschaft*-type of society. In **gesellschaft** societies, social relationships are more formal, contractual, and impersonal. There is greater reliance on codified compilations of appropriate and lawful conduct as a means of regulating social relations.

As urbanization gradually occurred, children were reconceptualized. During the period of Reconstruction following the Civil War, there were no child labor laws, and children were exploited increasingly by industry and businesses. Children were put to work in factories in their early years, where they were paid low wages in **sweat shops**, usually manufacturing companies where long hours were required and persons worked at repetitive jobs on assembly lines. By the end of the nineteenth century, in part because of these widespread nonunionized and unregulated sweat shop operations and compulsory school attendance for youths in their early years, loitering youths became increasingly visible and attracted the attention of the general public and law enforcement.

Specialized Juvenile Courts

Special courts were subsequently established to adjudicate juvenile matters. The technical language describing inappropriate youthful conduct or misbehaviors was greatly expanded and refined. These new courts were also vested with the authority to appoint probation officers and other persons considered suitable to manage juvenile offenders and enforce new juvenile codes that most cities created. Today, most larger police departments have specialized juvenile sections or divisions, where only juvenile law violations or suspicious activities are investigated. In retrospect, the original aggregate of child savers had much to do with inventing delinquency and its numerous, specialized subcategories as we now know them. At least they contributed to the formality of the present juvenile justice system by defining a range of impermissible juvenile behaviors that would require an operational legal apparatus to address. Once a juvenile justice system was established and properly armed with the right conceptual tools, it was a relatively easy step to enforce a fairly rigid set of juvenile behavioral standards and regulate most aspects of their conduct. This seems to be a part of a continuing pattern designed to criminalize the juvenile courts and hold juveniles accountable to the same standards as adult offenders (Blevins, 2005).

As juvenile court systems became more widespread, it was apparent that these proceedings were quite different from criminal courts in several respects. Largely one-sided affairs, these proceedings typically involved the juvenile charged with some offense, a petitioner claiming the juvenile should be declared delinquent, a status offender, dependent, or neglected; and a judge who would weigh the evidence and decide the matter. Juveniles themselves were not provided with opportunities to solicit witnesses or even give testimony in their own behalf. Defense attorneys were largely unknown in juvenile courtrooms, since there were no significant issues to defend.

Juvenile court proceedings were closed to the general public, primarily to protect the identities of the youth accused. While these proceedings were conducted behind

gesellschaft
Term created by Ferdinand Tonnies, a social theorist, to describe more formalized, larger communities and cities that relied on written documents and laws to regulate social conduct.

sweat shops
Exploitative businesses and industries that employed child labor and demanded long work hours for low pay.

closed doors for this manifest purpose, a latent function of such secrecy was to obscure from public view the high-handed and discriminatory decision making that characterized many juvenile court judges. In short, they didn't want the general public to know about the subjectivity and arbitrary nature of their decisions. On the basis of allegations alone, together with uncorroborated statements and pronouncements from probation officers and others, juvenile court judges were free to declare any particular juvenile either delinquent or nondelinquent. The penalties that could be imposed were wide ranging, from verbal reprimands and warnings to full-fledged incarceration in a secure juvenile facility. Virtually everything depended upon the opinions and views of presiding juvenile court judges. And their decisions were not appealable to higher courts.

Throughout much of the twentieth century, juveniles had no legal standing in American courts. Their constitutional rights were not at issue, because they did not have any constitutional protections in the courtroom. No rules of evidence existed to govern the quality of evidence admitted or to challenge the reliability or integrity of testifying witnesses. In most jurisdictions, juveniles were not entitled to jury trials, unless the juvenile court judge approved. And most juvenile court judges opted for bench trials rather than granting jury trials to juvenile defendants. Because these proceedings were exclusively civil in nature, the rules of criminal procedure governing criminal courts did not apply. Juveniles did not acquire criminal records. Rather, they acquired civil adjudications of delinquency. Yet, the incarceration dimension of the juvenile justice system has almost always paralleled that of the criminal justice system. Industrial or training schools, reform schools, and other types of secure confinement for juveniles have generally been nothing more than juvenile prisons. Thus, for many adjudicated juvenile offenders sentenced to one of these industrial schools, these sentences were the equivalent of imprisonment.

Kangaroo Courts in Action

Such unchecked discretion among juvenile court judges continued well into the 1960s. One explanation is mass complacency or apathy among the general public about juvenile affairs. Juvenile matters were relatively unimportant and trivial. Another explanation is the prevalent belief that juvenile court judges knew what is best for adjudicated offenders and usually prescribed appropriate punishments. Juvenile court judges and others often view juveniles as victims of their environment and peer associations. It might be easier to justify why new environments are required, including incarceration for the purpose of training, education, and rehabilitation, if the adverse effects of former environments can be illustrated. However, in 1967, the U.S. Supreme Court decided the case of *In re Gault*. This was perhaps the first major Supreme Court case which applied more stringent standards to juvenile court judge decision making, thus making them more accountable to the general public.

Briefly, Gerald Gault was a 15-year-old Arizona youth who allegedly made an obscene telephone call to an adult female neighbor. The woman called police, suggested that the youth, Gault, was the guilty party, and Gault was summarily taken into custody and detained for nearly two days. The woman was never brought to court as a witness, and the only evidence she provided was her initial verbal accusation made to police on the day of Gault's arrest. Gault himself allegedly admitted that he dialed the woman's number, but he claimed that a boyfriend of his actually spoke to the woman and made the remarks she found offensive. Partly because Gault had been involved in an earlier petty offense and had a "record," the judge, together with the probation officer, decided that Gault was dangerous enough to commit to the Arizona State Industrial School, Arizona's main juvenile penitentiary, until he reached 21 years of age or until juvenile corrections authorities decided he was rehabilitated and could be safely released. According to Arizona law, the sentence was unappealable. Any adult convicted of the same offense may have been fined $50 and/or sentenced to a 30-day jail term. But in Gault's case, he received six years in a juvenile prison, complete with correctional officers with firearms, high walls, locked gates, and barbed wire.

Appropriately, the U.S. Supreme Court referred to the court of the judge who originally sentenced Gault as a kangaroo court. Gault's sentence was reversed and several important constitutional rights were conferred upon all juveniles as a result. Specifically, all of Gault's due process rights had been denied. He had been denied counsel, had not been protected against self-incrimination, had not been permitted to cross-examine his accuser, and had not been provided with specific notice of the charges against him. Now, all juveniles enjoy these rights in every U.S. juvenile court. It is important to note that Arizona was not alone in its harsh and one-sided treatment of juvenile offenders. What occurred in the Gault case was occurring in juvenile courts in most other jurisdictions at the time. The Gault case served to underscore the lack of legal standing of juveniles everywhere, and substantial juvenile justice reforms were occurring (D'Angelo and Brown, 2005).

The Increasing Bureaucratization and Criminalization of Juvenile Justice

After the *Gault* case and several other important Supreme Court decisions affecting juveniles, the nature of juvenile courts began to change. But this transformation was anything but smooth. Even the U.S. Supreme Court continued to view juvenile courts as basically rehabilitative and treatment-centered apparatuses, thus reinforcing the traditional doctrine within the context of various constitutional restraints. Nevertheless, episodic changes in juvenile court procedures and the juvenile justice system generally suggested that it was becoming increasingly similar to criminal courts. Furthermore, many juvenile courts have moved away from traditional methods of conducting adjudicatory hearings for juveniles. Instead of individualized decision making and a rehabilitative orientation, many judges are increasingly interested in mechanisms that streamline the processing of juvenile cases and offenders. In fact, some juvenile courts have used mathematical models to establish profiles of juvenile offenders to expedite the adjudicatory process. This has been termed **actuarial justice** by some authorities, and it means that the traditional orientation of juvenile justice and punishment has been supplanted by the goal of efficient offender processing (LaMade, 2008). In Minnesota and other jurisdictions, the development of new Rules of Procedure for Juvenile Court and the current administrative assumptions and operations of these courts, with limited exceptions, often render them indistinguishable from criminal courts and the procedures those courts follow.

Measuring Juvenile Delinquency: The *Uniform Crime Reports* (UCR) and *National Crime Victimization Survey* (NCVS)

Two official sources of information about both adult and juvenile offenders are the *UCR* and the *NCVS*.

Uniform Crime Reports (UCR)

The **UCR** is published annually by the Federal Bureau of Investigation (FBI) in Washington, DC. The *UCR* is a compilation of arrests for different offenses according to several time intervals. Periodic reports of arrests are issued quarterly to interested

actuarial justice
The traditional orientation of juvenile justice, rehabilitation and individualized treatment, has been supplanted by the goal of efficient offender processing.

UCR
Official source of crime information published by Federal Bureau of Investigation annually; accepts information from reporting law enforcement agencies about criminal arrests; classifies crimes according to various index criteria; tabulates information about offender age, gender, race, and other attributes.

Table 2.1

Crime Report, Part I: Crimes and their Definition

Crime	Definition
Murder and nonnegligent manslaughter	Willful (nonnegligent) killing of one human being by another
Forcible rape	Carnal knowledge of a female, forcibly and against her will; assaults or attempts to commit rape by force or threat of force are included
Robbery	Taking or attempting to take anything of value from the care, custody, or control of a person or persons by force or threat of force or violence and/or by putting the victim in fear
Aggravated assault	Unlawful attack by one person upon another for the purpose of inflicting severe or aggravated bodily injury
Burglary	Unlawful entry into a structure to commit a felony or theft
Larceny-theft	Unlawful taking, carrying, leading, or riding away of property from the possession or constructive possession of another, including shoplifting, pocket picking, purse snatching, and thefts of motor vehicle parts or accessories
Motor vehicle theft	Theft or attempted theft of a motor vehicle, including automobiles, trucks, buses, motor scooters, and snowmobiles
Arson	Any willful or malicious burning or attempt to burn, with or without intent to defraud, a dwelling house, public building, motor vehicle, or aircraft, and the personal property of another

Source: U.S. Department of Justice, Federal Bureau of Investigation (1999). *Crime in the United States.* Washington, DC: U.S. Government Printing Office. Updated 2008 by author.

index offenses

Specific felonies used by the FBI in the *UCR* to chart crime trends; there are eight index offenses listed prior to 1988 (includes aggravated assault, larceny, burglary, vehicular theft, arson, robbery, forcible rape, murder).

felonies

Crimes punishable by imprisonment in prison for a term of one or more years; major crimes; any index offense.

index crimes

Any violations of the law listed by the *UCR* under index offenses (e.g., homicide, rape, aggravated assault, robbery, burglary, larceny, arson).

law enforcement agencies. All rural and urban law enforcement agencies are requested on a voluntary basis to submit statistical information about 29 different offenses. Most of these agencies submit arrest information, and thus, the *UCR* represents over 15,000 law enforcement agencies throughout the United States.

Crime in the *UCR* is classified into two major categories, Part I and Part II offenses. Part I offenses are considered the most serious, and eight serious felonies are listed. These include murder and nonnegligent manslaughter, forcible rape, robbery, aggravated assault, burglary, larceny-theft, motor vehicle theft, and arson. Table 2.1 shows a listing of the eight major **index offenses** (Part I offenses) and their definition.

Table 2.1 shows index crimes for 2008. These eight offenses are major offenses classified as felonies. **Felonies** are violations of criminal laws that are punishable by terms of imprisonment of one year or longer in state or federal prisons or penitentiaries. These offenses are known as index offenses because they provide readers with a sample of key or **index crimes** that can be charted quarterly or annually, according to different jurisdictions and demographic and socioeconomic dimensions (e.g., city size, age, race, gender, urban–rural). Thus, the crime categories listed are not intended to be an exhaustive compilation. However, it is possible to scan these representative crime categories to obtain a general picture of crime trends across years or other desired time segments.

The *UCR* also lists a second group of offenses known as Part II offenses. These include misdemeanors and status offenses. Offenses include embezzlement, stolen property, vandalism, carrying weapons, drug abuse violations, sex offenses, driving under the influence, liquor law violations, vagrancy, suspicion, curfew and loitering violations, runaways, and disorderly conduct (Henry and Kobus, 2007). A

misdemeanor is a violation of criminal laws that is punishable by an incarcerative term of less than one year in city or county jails. Status offenses listed, including runaway behavior, truancy, and violation of curfew, are not considered crimes, although they are reported together with criminal offenses to give a more complete picture of arrest activity throughout the United States. The offenses listed are not an exhaustive compilation. Rather, a sample listing of crimes based on arrests is provided.

NCVS

Compared with the *UCR*, the **NCVS** is conducted annually by the United States Bureau of the Census. It is a random survey of approximately 60,000 dwellings, about 127,000 youths aged 12 and over, and approximately 50,000 businesses. Subsamples of persons are questioned by interviewers who compile information about crime victims. Those interviewed are asked whether they have had different types of crime committed against them during the past six months to one year. Through statistical analysis, the amount of crime throughout the general population can be estimated (Champion, 2008a).

The *NCVS* provides information about criminal victimizations and incidents. A **victimization** is the basic measure of the occurrence of a crime and is a specific criminal act that affects a single victim. An **incident** is a specific criminal act that may involve one or more victims. Because the *NCVS* reflects an amount of crime allegedly perpetrated against a large sample of victims, it is believed to be more accurate as a national crime estimate than the *UCR*. Thus, whenever comparisons of crime from the *UCR* are made against the *NCVS*, the *NCVS* reports from two to four times the amount of crime as indicated by law enforcement agency arrest figures in the *UCR*.

Strengths of These Measures

One strength of these indicators of crime in the United States is the sheer numbers of offenses reported. Few alternative sources of information about crime in the United States exhibit such voluminous reporting. Also, regional and seasonal reports of criminal activity are provided. The *UCR* also reports the proportion of different types of crime that are cleared by arrest. **Cleared by arrest** means that someone has been arrested and charged with a particular crime. Another favorable feature of both the *UCR* and *NCVS* is that numbers of arrests and reported crimes can be compared across years. Therefore, the *UCR* reports percentage increases or decreases in the amount of different types of crime for many different jurisdictions and over various time periods. And although the *NCVS* does not purport to survey all crime victims, the randomness inherent in the selection of the target respondents is such that generalizations about the U.S. population are considered reasonably valid.

A primary advantage of the *NCVS* over the *UCR* is that victims offer interviewers information about crimes committed against them. In many instances, these respondents disclose that they do not report these crimes to police. The reasons for not reporting crimes to police vary, although these victims often believe that the police cannot do much about their victimization anyway. Sometimes, rape victims are too embarrassed to report these incidents, or they may feel that they were partially to blame. Furthermore, in some of these cases, family members or close friends may be the perpetrators, and victims may be reluctant to press criminal charges.

Weaknesses of These Measures

Certain limitations of the *UCR* and *NCVS* are well-documented. Focusing upon the *UCR* first, we may cite some of the more important weaknesses of these statistics. For instance, *UCR* figures do not provide an annual per capita measure of crime frequency.

misdemeanor
Crime punishable by confinement in city or county jail for a period of less than one year; a lesser offense.

NCVS
Published in cooperation with the United States Bureau of the Census, a random survey of 60,000 households, including 127,000 persons 12 years of age or older; includes 50,000 businesses; measures crime committed against specific victims interviewed and not necessarily reported to law enforcement officers.

victimization
Basic measure of the occurrence of a crime. A specific criminal act affecting a specific victim.

incident
Specific criminal act involving one crime and one or more victims.

cleared by arrest
Term used by the FBI in the *UCR* to indicate that someone has been arrested for a reported crime; does not necessarily mean that the crime has been solved or that the actual criminals who committed the crime have been apprehended or convicted.

Not all law enforcement agencies report crime to the FBI, and those that do may fail to report crime uniformly. Because law enforcement agencies are not compelled to submit annual information to the FBI, some agencies fail to report their arrest activity. Also, crimes of the same name vary in definition among jurisdictions. In North Dakota, for instance, "rape" is not listed as a crime. Rather, it's called "gross sexual imposition." This conceptual variation in how identical offenses are labeled among the states frustrate efforts by the FBI and others to track different types of crimes accurately.

The *UCR* only reports arrests, not the actual amount of crime. When arrests are reported in the *UCR*, only the most serious offenses are often reported. Thus, if a robbery suspect is apprehended, he/she may possess burglary tools, a concealed weapon, and stolen property. He/she may have caused physical injuries to victims. All of these events are crimes, but only the robbery, the most serious offense, will be reported to the FBI. Therefore, there is much basis for the belief that these official reports of crime are at best underestimates. Arrest activity in the *UCR* may be attributable to fluctuations in police activity rather than actual fluctuations in criminal activity. Finally, although they only make up a fraction of national criminal activity, federal crimes are not reported in the *UCR*.

Both the *NCVS* and *UCR* overemphasize street crimes and underemphasize corporate crimes. Self-reported information contained in the *NCVS* is often unreliable. Sometimes victims interviewed may not be able to identify certain actions against them as crimes. For instance, date-rapes may be reported as assaults. Also, persons may not be able to remember clearly certain criminal events. Fear of reprisals from criminals may compel some victims not to disclose their victimizations to interviewers. Some victimization data reported in the *NCVS* may be either exaggerated or more liberally reported. For various reasons, interviewees may lie to interviewers in disclosing details of crimes committed against them.

Despite these criticisms, the *UCR* and *NCVS* provide valuable data for interested professionals. The fact that virtually all law enforcement agencies rely to some extent on these annual figures as valid indicators of criminal activity in the United States suggests that their utility in this regard is invaluable. Supplementing this information are other, more detailed, reports of selected offense activity. The U.S. Department of Justice's Bureau of Justice Statistics publishes an incredible amount of information annually about different dimensions of crime and offender characteristics and behavior. This supplemental information, together with the data provided by the *UCR* and *NCVS*, may be combined to furnish us with a more complete picture of crime in the United States. Several alternative data sources are discussed in the following section.

Other Sources

National Juvenile Court Data Archive
Compendium of national statistical information and databases about juvenile delinquency.

One of the best compendiums of data specifically about juveniles and juvenile court adjudications is the ***National Juvenile Court Data Archive***. While the federal government has collected data pertaining to juveniles since 1926, the data were dependent upon the voluntary completion of statistical forms by juvenile courts in a limited number of U.S. jurisdictions. *The National Juvenile Court Data Archive* contains over 800,000 annual automated case records of juveniles in various states. Numerous data sets are currently available to researchers and may be accessed for investigative purposes. These data sets are nonuniform, although they ordinarily contain information such as age at referral, gender, race, county of residence, offense(s) charged, date of referral, processing characteristics of the case (e.g., incarceration and manner of handling), and the case disposition (Champion, 2009).

However, in 1975 the Office of Juvenile Justice and Delinquency Prevention (OJJDP) assumed responsibility for acquiring court dispositional records and publishing periodic reports of juvenile offenses and adjudicatory outcomes. Today the OJJDP publishes periodic compilations of current juvenile offender data in a statistical brief-ing book, summarizing important delinquency statistics and trends. Also, every few years the OJJDP publishes a comprehensive summary of juvenile justice information in a national report on *Juvenile Offenders and Victims* (Office of Juvenile Justice and Delinquency Prevention, 2007).

Another compendium of offender characteristics of all ages is *The Sourcebook of Criminal Justice Statistics* published annually by the Hindelang Criminal Justice Research Center and supported by grants from the U.S. Department of Justice. This is perhaps the most comprehensive source that we have discussed, since it accesses numerous governmental documents and reports annually to keep readers abreast of the latest crime figures. Among other things, it describes justice system employment and spending, jail and prison management and prisoner issues, judicial misconduct and complaints, correctional officer characteristics, crime victim characteristics and victimization patterns, delinquent behavior patterns and trends, and considerable sur-vey information. Literally hundreds of tables are presented that summarize much of the information reported by various private and governmental agencies. Useful anno-tated information is provided to supplement the tabular material.

Statistics pertaining to juvenile offenders include juvenile admissions and dis-charges from public and private incarcerative facilities, average length of stay of juve-niles in these facilities, a profile of the juvenile custody facilities, demographic information about juveniles detained for lengthy terms, criminal history or prior records of juveniles, illegal drug and alcohol use among juveniles, waiver information, and offense patterns according to socioeconomic and demographic factors. Each annual sourcebook is somewhat different from those published in previous years, although much of the material in subsequent editions has been updated from previous years.

Self-Report Information

While these official sources of crime and delinquency are quite useful, a common criti-cism is that they tend to underestimate the amount of offense behaviors that actually occur in the United States. For many years, those interested in studying juvenile offense behaviors have frequently relied upon data derived from **self-reports**. The self-report is a data collection method involving an unofficial survey of youths or adults where the intent is to obtain information about specific types of behavior not ordinarily disclosed through traditional data collection methods, including questionnaires, interviews, polls, official agency reports, or socio-demographic summaries. This information is called **self-report information**. The exact origin of the use of self-reports is unknown. However, in 1943, Austin L. Porterfield investigated hidden delinquency, or delin-quency neither detected by, nor reported to, police. He surveyed several hundred col-lege students, asking them to disclose whether they had ever engaged in delinquent acts. While all of the students reported that they had previously engaged in delinquent acts, most also reported that they had not been caught by police or brought to the attention of the juvenile court (Porterfield, 1943).

In 1958, James Short and Ivan Nye became the first investigators to conduct the first self-report study of a delinquent population. They obtained self-report informa-tion from hundreds of delinquents in several Washington State training schools. They compared this information with self-report data from hundreds of students in three Washington State communities and three Midwestern towns. Their findings revealed that delinquency was widespread and not specific to any social class. Further, both the seriousness and frequency of juvenile offending were key determinants of juvenile court treatment of youthful offenders and public policy relating to delinquents (Short and Nye, 1958).

Self-report surveys are believed to be more accurate and informative com-pared with official sources of crime and delinquency information. Before self-report surveys of such information are presented, it is helpful to become familiar with some of

The Sourcebook of Criminal Justice Statistics
Compendium of statistical information about juvenile and adult offenders; court facts, statistics, and trends; probation and parole figures; and considerable additional information; published annually by the Hindelang Criminal Justice Research Center at the University of Albany, SUNY; funded by grant from the U. S. Department of Justice, Bureau of Justice Statistics.

self-reports, self-report information
Surveys of youths (or adults) based upon disclosures these persons might make about the types of offenses they have committed and how frequently they have committed them; considered more accurate than official estimates.

the more popular crime and delinquency information sources and their strengths and weaknesses.

The research applications of self-reports are both extensive and diverse. An inspection of research articles compiled by the *Criminal Justice Abstracts* between the years 1968 and 2005 by this author revealed that 284 articles utilized self-reports for different purposes. Two-thirds of the articles involved studies of juveniles, while article subject matter was dominated by the themes of drug/alcohol use, sex offenses, spousal abuse, status offending and delinquency, and early childhood sexual, psychological, or physical abuse.

Generally, self-report studies accomplish two important research objectives: (1) describing and understanding behavior and (2) predicting behavior. Self-report information provides considerable enriching details about persons under a variety of circumstances. Self-reports furnish important descriptive information about what people think and do. Such descriptions include how persons were treated as children, and the events that were most significant to them as they grew to adulthood. The more that is learned about the significant occurrences in one's life, the better the predictive schemes to explain present and forecast future behaviors. Self-reports, therefore, are an important source of information for descriptive and theoretical purposes. From a theoretical standpoint, self-reports represent one important means of theory verification.

Some of the popular self-report surveys conducted annually are ***The National Youth Survey*** and the ***Monitoring the Future Survey***. These are large-scale surveys of high-school students that focus upon particular behaviors. In addition, the Institute for Social Research at the University of Michigan annually solicits information from a national sample of 3,000 high-school students. These informative reports are frequently cited in the research literature, which attests to the integrity, reliability, and validity of this information among noted juvenile justice professionals.

These national surveys involve administering confidential questionnaires and checklists to high-school students. Students are asked to indicate which behaviors they have engaged in during the past six months or the previous year. Assuming that their responses are truthful, researchers believe that the results are a more accurate reflection of delinquent behaviors than are official sources, such as the *UCR*. Ordinarily, simple checklists are given to students and they are asked to identify those behaviors they have done, and not necessarily those for which they have been apprehended. Considered unofficial sources of information about delinquency and delinquency patterns, these self-disclosures are considered by many professionals to be more accurate than official sources. An example of such a checklist is shown in Figure 2.1.

Self-reports enable researchers to determine whether there are changing offending patterns among juveniles over time. Substantial information exists that characterizes violent juvenile offenders and catalogs the many potential causal factors that are associated with violence, such as gang involvement (Daigle, Cullen, and Wright, 2007). Self-reported data about juvenile offenses suggest that a sizeable gap exists between official reports of delinquent conduct and information disclosed through self-reports.

Self-reports reveal much more delinquency than is reported by either the *UCR* or *NCVS*. However, since *NCVS* information is also a form of self-disclosure, some investigators have found greater compatibility between delinquency self-reporting and the *NCVS* than between delinquency self-reporting and the *UCR*, which reports only arrest information. In any case, self-reports of delinquency or status offense conduct have caused researchers to refer to these undetected offending behaviors as **hidden delinquency**.

Some investigators question whether self-report information is reliable. Do youths tell the truth about their conduct, whatever the reported behavior? Some reported information is more easily refuted or confirmed by independent means. In the cases of illicit alcohol, tobacco, or drug use, independent tests may be conducted to determine the veracity of self-report information. In one school district, for instance, over 50 percent

National Youth Survey
Study of large numbers of youths annually or at other intervals to assess hidden delinquency among high school students.

Monitoring the Future Survey
Study of 3,000 high-school students annually by Institute for Social Research at University of Michigan; attempts to discover hidden delinquency not ordinarily disclosed by published public reports.

hidden delinquency
Infractions reported by surveys of high-school youths; considered "hidden" because it most often is undetected by police officers; disclosed delinquency through self-report surveys.

Figure 2.1   A Hypothetical Checklist for Self-Report Disclosures of Delinquent or Criminal Conduct among High-School Students

"How often during the past six months have you committed the following offenses?" Check whichever best applies to you.

Offense	Frequency				
	0 times	1 time	2 times	3 times	4 or more times
Smoked marijuana	____	____	____	____	____
Stole something worth $50 or less	____	____	____	____	____
Got drunk on beer or wine	____	____	____	____	____
Got drunk on hard liquor	____	____	____	____	____
Used crack or cocaine	____	____	____	____	____

of all high-school students interviewed disclosed through self-reports that they smoked. Subsequently, analyses of saliva specimens from the same students revealed that less than 10 percent of them tested positive for tobacco use. For several reasons unknown to the researchers, about half of these high schoolers reported that they used tobacco when most of them didn't use tobacco. Were they bragging? Was this peer pressure in action? In view of the evidence, this is the strong implication.

The relation between one's early childhood and the onset of status offending or delinquency has been heavily investigated (Bowman, Prelow, and Weaver, 2007). Typically, parent–child association and attachment are linked with delinquent conduct (Beaver, Wright, and Delisi, 2007). Samples of delinquents and nondelinquents are asked to provide self-reports of their early upbringing, including their perceived closeness with parents and the disciplinary methods used to sanction misconduct. Different themes are researched. For instance, the etiology of delinquency as related to different family processes according to race/ethnicity has been studied. Does a sample of inner-city, high-risk youths reflect important differences in family processes according to race/ethnicity?

Information about runaways is almost exclusively gleaned from self-report studies. For example, it has been found that runaways compared with other types of status offenders have greater levels of family violence, rejection, and sexual abuse. Not unexpectedly, based upon self-report experiences, runaways were from families where there was less parental monitoring of juvenile behavior, warmth, and supportiveness (Chen et al., 2007).

In a more general analysis of early childhood experiences involving adolescent maltreatment and its link with delinquency, self-reports have disclosed that some youths who are violent as adults have histories of maltreatment from family members (Mersky and Reynolds, 2007).

School violence is an increasingly important topic of discussion among parents, school officials, and juvenile justice professionals (Choi, 2007). Although the media

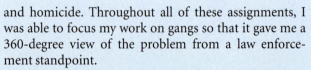

2.1   Career Snapshot

Tony Moreno

Detective Supervisor (retired),
Los Angeles Police Department, author

Statistics:
East Los Angeles Community College;
FBI Instructor Development Course;
Community College Teaching Certificate, State of California

Background

I grew up in a gang area in East Los Angeles. Although my social environment wasn't the greatest, I began to achieve personal successes at a very young age and that helped to develop the person I was to become. As I grew up, I was somewhat successful in school. I was an athlete and that kept me out of trouble. My father was also very supportive in that facet of my life. During my teenage years, with temptation and opportunities to get in trouble all around me, I stayed out of trouble for basically two reasons: (1) I never wanted to disappoint my father and (2) I never wanted to hurt my mother. Later, I attended community college for two years. When I graduated from high school, I had no idea what I wanted to do with my life. I was actually standing in line to register for my classes and saw a recruitment poster for Police Science classes. I became intrigued with that idea and enrolled in some of those classes. Since then, my life's mission has become clear. I eventually entered the Los Angeles Police Academy.

Work Experience

I didn't realize how much general gang knowledge I had absorbed over the years while growing up until I entered police work. When officers had trouble communicating and dealing with gang members, I seemed to have a natural knack for it. It was almost as if I had learned a second language by being immersed in the gang culture while growing up. I also learned very quickly that by giving people some dignity as you dealt with them, it made your job easier. This also included gang members. Through my 31+-year career in the LAPD, I worked a variety of assignments including patrol, school car, juvenile, gang detail, narcotics, organized crime, CRASH,

and homicide. Throughout all of these assignments, I was able to focus my work on gangs so that it gave me a 360-degree view of the problem from a law enforcement standpoint.

Although the great majority of gang members are adults, the gang issue is really a juvenile delinquency problem, because when the decision is actually made to join a gang, the individual is usually between the ages of 12 and 16. For that reason, I was always very cognizant of kids, teenagers, and young adults watching me as I conducted my business. When talking to younger gang members, I never really tried to change their minds about gang membership because they would usually be resistant to that. What I did do was try and have them question their own behavior and some of the customs of the gang life itself. I wholeheartedly believe that a real gang cop should not only be able to hunt down and apprehend a violent and dangerous gang member but should also be able to intervene when a 12-year-old potential gang member and his mother come to him for help and guidance. One should be a multidimensional person capable of operating within the three facets of the solution to the gang problem: prevention, intervention, and suppression.

On a personal level, I worked very hard to become the best that I could be. Law enforcement is an extremely competitive field. To be a good cop, you must have a certain amount of "ego" because you are sometimes called upon to make crucial decisions in a split-second during high-pressure situations. To put your uniform on and go back out to the street everyday knowing that means you have to maintain a healthy amount of self-confidence. You exist in a world of self-confident individuals who are constantly in competition with each other for assignments, promotions, and recognition. Even the task of acquiring a law enforcement job in the first place requires that you survive and rise from a pool of other competitors. In this environment, I focused on making myself a better, more effective "gang cop" by constantly developing information and knowledge. While other officers "leveled out" in the expertise or gang knowledge, I kept trying to make myself better and better. I eventually began to provide formal training on gangs to other law enforcement professionals and members of the community and have been doing so for over 26 years.

My oldest son decided that he wanted to become a law enforcement officer and was successful in joining the LAPD. When this happened, it caused me to look at my training methods and made me reevaluate and modify how I provided training as well as my training content. I asked myself, "If your child were going to do your job, what does he/she need to know?" This change in my perspective on gang training made me a better trainer and educator. It also was a motivating factor in writing a book, *Lessons from a Gang Cop.* The book doesn't focus on the gangs or the gang culture itself. Instead, it presents key principles that I believe are essential for the mental, emotional, and spiritual well-being of frontline professionals who are called upon to deal with the gang problem. I wrote this book to act as an inspiring and motivational piece. After over 31 years in the trenches and still maintaining a healthy appetite for gang work despite many challenges and pitfalls, I believe that I had done some things correctly and that the book was my legacy for those who become involved in gang work after me. I don't say these things in an arrogant manner. I say these things because I have worked very hard to make myself one of law enforcement's foremost gang experts and I am still able to laugh, enjoy life, and remember what is important to me and my loved ones. My head is still on straight and my heart remains in the right place.

Advice to Students

Remember that when choosing a career in criminal justice, you are entering an extremely competitive way of life that only becomes more competitive when you are successfully selected to begin your career. As a true competitor would do, you must constantly do the things that prepare and make yourself ready for the challenges you will be facing. A 20- to 30-year career will be quite a roller coaster experience for you.

You can't change people. Rather, you make them think. This tactic works especially with kids and young adults involved with or dabbling in gang activities. My primary mission was to make them think about what they were doing. If you tried to change those who were involved in criminal or anti-social behavior, you'd encounter much resistance. If you'd just point out the contradictions and fallacies in their lives, sometimes they can arrive at alternatives and solutions themselves. Remember that you will be affecting and influencing some people in a positive manner, and you may never know about it. You must maintain the faith in yourself and in your work.

Your knowledge and expertise on any given subject are personal to you. Your knowledge may be minimal, and there are no shortcuts to gaining knowledge. However, your passion does affect the rate at which you become more knowledgeable. Your goal is to become a true and practical expert. Not only will you have some knowledge, you will also know how to apply it to your best advantage. Always remember, the more knowledge you have, the safer you are. Treat people right and offer everyone some dignity. Their response to you will determine how you deal with them. In the long run, it will make your job easier.

Do things outside of your work. I coached youth soccer for over 17 years. It gave me a break from my challenging and stressful work and acted as a "breath of fresh air." It also reminds you that life occurs outside of your important work and it caused me to devote personal time to my kids. Develop and maintain your personal support system. Ideally, we all would like to be able to stand on our own two feet and handle whatever comes our way. But even in doing so, you must have your collection of friends, colleagues, and loved ones who will provide support, input, and loyalty to you when needed. My personal support system is an array of individuals who are key and significant to me. Some of them are in law enforcement and some are not. It is good to have some people who are not involved in your type of work as part of your system. They can provide an objective view of some of the things that we tend to immerse ourselves in. Your support system is for your life, not just your professional career issues. Take care of yourself. If you're no good to yourself, you're no good to anyone else.

suggests that school violence is pervasive, the sensationalism attached to school shootings does not necessarily mean that school violence is increasing (Slater, Hayes, and Ford, 2007).

Self-reports from different samples of adolescent drug users suggest that a significant association exists between drug use and involvement in delinquent behavior (Pires and Jenkins, 2007). Self-reports of crime and delinquency are a valuable source of information to researchers. Research projects with exploratory, descriptive, and/or experimental study objectives benefit from the use of self-report data. Descriptions of different types of delinquents and the development of useful intervention strategies for delinquency prevention have been assisted greatly by the use of self-reports. The broad application of self-reports in virtually every facet of criminology and criminal justice suggests the long-term application of this data collection method.

Violence and Nonviolence: Career Escalation?

How much violent crime is committed by juveniles? Are juveniles likely to escalate to more serious offenses during their youthful years as they become more deeply involved in delinquent conduct? Are there certain kinds of juvenile offenders who are more or less susceptible to intervention programs and treatments as means of reducing or eliminating their propensity to engage in delinquent conduct? Are schools new battlezones for gang warfare and other forms of violence? Certainly the media have helped to heighten our awareness of the presence and violence of youth gangs in various cities (Crooks et al., 2007). Startling information about extensive drug and alcohol use among juveniles is frequently broadcasted or reported (West, 2005). Is there currently an unstoppable juvenile crime wave prevalent throughout the United States?

School Violence

Violence among schoolchildren has received increased attention in recent years and is a serious problem in other countries as well as the United States. The media suggest that school violence is pervasive (Slater, Hayes, and Ford, 2007). In Miami, Florida, for example, high-school students have reported both serious and frequent victimization. In many of these victimizations, dangerous weapons such as firearms were used to effect the victimization (Schexnayder, 2008). There are many explanations for school violence, ranging from psychological explanations (attention deficit disorder) to sociological (peer group association, need for group recognition), to biological (glandular malfunction) (Bratina, 2008; Hinduja, Patchin, and Lippman, 2008).

Fortunately most school violence is seldom fatal. In 2007, students ranging in age from 12 to 18 were victims of about 235,000 incidents of nonfatal, serious, violent crimes in their schools. There were 720,000 similar incidents involving this age group outside of school. During the period 2003–2007, 56 percent of all public schools reported either a serious violent crime, such as murder or rape, or less serious violent crimes (e.g., assault) to the police (Office of Juvenile Justice and Delinquency Prevention, 2007). In many instances, bullying behavior has been reported as school violence, although psychological rather than physical harm is inflicted more often through bullying behavior compared with assaultive behavior that might result in student injuries (Brewer, 2008; Dussich and Maekoya, 2007; Estell, Farmer, and Cairns, 2007).

A general response to school violence throughout the United States has led to the development of several aggressive policy changes. School systems are training their teachers and students how to react in ways that will rapidly contain potentially serious school violence. Special response police forces are being trained to be more effective in providing ancillary support for school administrators and staff. Intensive prevention training for all involved parties, after-school academic enrichment programs, enforcement of and punishment for firearms possession and drug use/sales on campus, and developing a standardized system of early detection and assessment of at-risk students are being implemented on a national basis (Pires and Jenkins, 2007). Evidence

It happened on January 19, 2007. John Odgren, 16, a student at Lincoln-Sudbury Regional High School in Cambridge, Massachusetts, followed a fellow student, James Alenson, 15, into the school bathroom. Odgren was a special needs student who did not know Alenson, had never been teased by Alenson, had never been shunned by Alenson, and didn't even know his name. When inside the bathroom with Alenson, Odgren attacked Alenson with a sharp knife, slashing his throat and stabbing him through the heart and abdomen. Alenson stumbled into the hallway and collapsed. A third student in one of the bathroom stalls heard everything. He heard Alenson say, "What are you doing? You are hurting me." The student followed Odgren into the hallway where he saw Odgren stoop over Alenson and check his pulse. Odgren turned and saw the other student, and then exclaimed, "I did it. I just snapped. I don't know why." Following his arrest by police, Odgren appeared in a Middlesex Superior Court and pleaded not guilty to first-degree murder. Odgren was ordered to a state hospital for a 20-day evaluation. In the meantime, it was learned that Odgren was prone to explosive episodes, was verbally abusive, and at times became physically aggressive against his parents, teachers, and specialists.

He had been formerly placed in an alternative school, Caldwell Alternative School, in Fitchburg in 2002. At age 12, Odgren was diagnosed as a highly intelligent but troubled preadolescent with poor social skills. He had a hyperactivity disorder and Asperger's disorder, a mild form of autism. Several specialists familiar with Asperger's disorder claim that those with such a condition are no more prone toward violence than others. While at the alternative school, Odgren was suspended three times for undisclosed explosive episodes including physical aggression. Officials refused to elaborate, citing student confidentiality. In the meantime, Odgren's parents told the media that their son needed training in social skills but never received such training. Prosecutors sought to try Odgren on first-degree murder charges as an adult. Should the juvenile court have jurisdiction over this case? Who is to blame for Alenson's death? Are Massachusetts authorities at fault for placing a disturbed youth such as Odgren in a normal high school environment where he could pose a threat to others? [Source: Adapted from the Associated Press and Jesse Harlan Alderman, "Massachusetts Stabbing Victim Chosen Randomly," March 6, 2007:1–2.]

of the successfulness of these initiatives is the dramatic reduction in school violence subsequent to 1996 and through 2007. One of the contributing factors to this decline in school violence has been the establishment of a zero-tolerance policy in many school systems, which imposes more stringent penalties on youthful offenders who bring dangerous weapons to their schools (Schexnayder, 2008).

At-Risk Youths and the Pittsburgh Youth Study

Who are **at-risk youths**? At-risk youths are often those who suffer from one or more disadvantages, such as lower socioeconomic status, dysfunctional family conditions, poor school performance, learning or language disabilities, negative peer influences, and/or low self-esteem (Owens-Sabir, 2007; Abbott-Chapman, Denholm, and Wyld, 2007). It is difficult to forecast which youths will become delinquent and which ones won't. For many decades, researchers have attempted to profile so-called at-risk youths by assigning to them various characteristics that seem to be associated with hard-core delinquents (Busseri, Willoughby, and Chalmers, 2007). In 1986, and for

at-risk youths
Any juveniles considered more susceptible to the influence of gangs and delinquent peers; characterized as having less-developed reading skills, greater immaturity, lower socioeconomic status, parental dysfunction, and who are otherwise disadvantaged by their socioeconomic and environmental circumstances.

the next decade, investigators conducted a longitudinal study of 1,517 inner-city boys from Pittsburgh, Pennsylvania. The Pittsburgh Youth Study (PYS) followed three samples of boys for over a decade to determine how and why boys became involved in delinquent and other problem behaviors (Browning and Loeber, 1999:1). Initially, boys were randomly selected from the first, fourth, and seventh grades and tracked over time.

Eventually, three developmental pathways were defined that display progressively more serious problem behaviors. The first pathway, authority-conflict, involves youths who exhibit stubbornness prior to age 12, and then they move on to defiance and avoidance of authority. The second pathway, covert, includes minor covert acts, such as lying, followed by property damage and moderately serious delinquency, and then serious delinquency. The third pathway, overt, starts with minor aggression followed by fighting and violence. Risk factors identified and associated with delinquency among the Pittsburgh youth include impulsivity; IQ; personality; forces in an individual's environment, including parents, siblings, and peers; and factors related to family, school, and neighborhood (Bowman, Prelow, and Weaver, 2007).

At-risk youth in the PYS tended to have greater impulsivity; lower IQ; a lower threshold for experiencing negative emotions, such as fear, anxiety, and anger, and were more inclined to be involved in thrill-seeking and acting without caution. Family risk factors included poor supervision by parents, family receipt of public assistance (welfare), and lower socioeconomic status. The greatest demographic variable associated with delinquency was having a broken family. Living in a bad neighborhood doubled the risk for delinquency.

These aggregate data are interesting, but they fail to enable researchers to forecast with accuracy which youths will become delinquent and which ones won't. Maybe this is too much to ask without more definitive criteria for identifying potential juvenile offenders. Nevertheless, a profile of at-risk youths has slowly been generated to the extent that various intervention programs can be attempted in certain jurisdictions. The theory is that if at-risk youth can be identified according to proven prior characteristics from delinquency research, then perhaps one or more interventions can be attempted with some or all of those youths who are at risk. Many interventions attempted are flawed in different ways, however. Thus, much more is needed to establish truly effective interventions that make a difference in affecting a youth's future behavior (Case, 2007).

Juvenile courts have attempted various types of interventions involving at-risk youths (Barnes, 2005). Since the mid-1970s, the National Council of Juvenile and Family Court Judges has sought to focus national attention on abused and neglected children. Youths placed in foster care and/or suffering from various forms of sexual or physical abuse in their families are considered at-risk and in need of special treatment from various social services. It has been found, for instance, that a strategy for assisting at-risk youths is to educate family and juvenile court judges in ways to improve their court practices (Adoption and Foster Care Analysis and Reporting System, 2008). The Permanency Planning for Children Department has been established: 17 Model Courts in at least 16 states. These Model Courts have implemented a number of programs to deal with at-risk youths and their families. Such programs can easily be replicated in other jurisdictions. For instance, court calendars are generated to ensure that judicial decision makers are assigned to specific dependency cases and will remain on those cases until the children involved achieve permanence, either by being safely reunited with their rehabilitative families or by being placed in permanent adoptive homes. Family group conferencing and mediation programs are also incorporated into several of these Model Court jurisdictions. Proper handling of cases involving these types of at-risk youths tends to decrease the likelihood that placed youths will become delinquent in their future years. Family group conferencing has been extended to many states, including Indiana (McGarrell and Kroovand-Hipple, 2007).

Gang Violence

Juvenile justice professionals are interested in the increased incidence of gang formation and membership behavior. The gang phenomenon seems widespread throughout
the United States rather than being localized in major city centers. **Gangs** are found in
most jurisdictions and seem to organize along racial or ethnic lines, often for mutual
protection against other gangs. The gang problem in the United States is increasing
(Taylor et al., 2008). There has been a rapid proliferation of youth gangs in the United
States since 1980, despite our best intervention and prevention efforts. In 1980, for
instance, there were 2,000 gangs in 286 jurisdictions, with over 100,000 gang members.
By 2007, there were more than 34,500 gangs in 5,380 jurisdictions, with over 1.5 million
gang members (Office of Juvenile Justice and Delinquency Prevention, 2007). About
11 percent of all gang members are female. While definitive national trend data are
unavailable concerning female gang members and the types of offenses they commit,
independent investigations of selected jurisdictions suggest that the number of female
gangs in the United States is increasing (Graves, 2007).

gangs
Groups who form an allegiance
for a common purpose and
engage in unlawful or criminal
activity; any group gathered
together on a continuing basis
to engage in or commit
antisocial behavior.

Kids Who Kill

Juveniles who commit homicide are relatively rare (Haynie, Steffensmeier, and Bell,
2007). Of the 17,000 homicide offenders reported by the *UCR* in 2007, 1,200 (7 percent)
of these involved juveniles under age 18 (Office of Juvenile Justice and Delinquency
Prevention, 2007). Some juveniles begin their careers of gang violence, including murder and attempted murder, as early as age six. An increasing amount of youth violence,
including homicide, is linked to gang membership (Marriott, 2007). There were 1,123
gang-related juvenile murders in 2007. Actually, gang-related murders declined from
2000 (922 murders) to 2004 (580 murders), but the number of murders increased
again in 2004 and thereafter.

Apart from gang-related murders, many youths kill one or more of their family
members, such as their mothers or fathers. Studies of youths who kill their parents
show that they are often severely physically or sexually abused, and that they are particularly sensitive to stressors in the home environment. Many juvenile murderers have
chemical dependencies for which they require treatment. Juvenile murderers also
exhibit greater psychotic and conduct disorder symptoms compared with other types
of juvenile offenders (Titterington and Grundies, 2007).

Some juvenile murders are sexually motivated and occur when victims threaten to
tell others. But even something as specific as sexually motivated juvenile murder is
poorly misunderstood by the public (Hensley et al., 2005). A wide variety of explanations is provided for explaining or rationalizing adolescent murders, although any
excuse is rarely accepted as mitigating. One frequently cited reason for gang violence
was that it was an expected part of gang initiation rites. Most often cited as mitigating
factors in juvenile homicides are troubled family histories and social backgrounds;
psychological disturbances; mental retardation; indigence; and substance abuse. Treatments often include psychotherapy, psychiatric hospitalization, institutional placement, and psychopharmacological agents (Johnson, 2005; Marriott, 2007).

Juvenile Violence Trends

Violence committed by juveniles has increased during the last few decades. Between
2000 and 2007, the juvenile violent crime index soared. Subsequently, there has been a
mild decline in juvenile violence (Belshaw and Lanham, 2008). This decline in juvenile
violence has not been substantial: less than 15 percent. However, this slight decline may
be one indication that various youth crime intervention programs are working (Matrix

Research and Consultancy, 2007). One initiative is Project Safe Neighborhoods, a collaborative effort between probation, parole, and other community-based agencies and law enforcement to provide training and technical assistance relating to supervising juvenile offenders and preventing them from acquiring and using firearms (Bynum, 2005; Decker, 2005). One concomitant of youth violence is access to firearms. Gun-related violence is both a criminal justice and a public health problem. In 2000, there were 8 murders per 100,000 U.S. residents. But in 2007, the murder rate had dropped to 4.6 per 100,000.

The impact of gun violence is especially strong for juveniles and young adults (Lewis et al., 2007). There were 1,500 murder victims under the age of 18 in 2004. This is nearly 50 percent lower than the peak year of 1993, when there were 2,900 juvenile deaths. About half of these deaths were from firearms. Various policies and laws have been implemented to intervene in gun-related violence (McDevitt, 2005). Sources of illegal guns are increasingly interrupted; penalties have been increased for illegal possession and carrying of guns; and persons who supply at-risk youths with firearms for violence (e.g., probationers, gang members, and drug traffickers) are being prosecuted more aggressively. Simultaneously, programs are in place to treat and deal with those youthful offenders who have mental disorders and/or substance abuse problems (Bowman, 2005). In some studies, animal cruelty observed among certain youths has been associated with subsequent violent offending (Lea, 2007).

Career Escalation

Do status offenders progress to more serious offending, such as juvenile delinquency? Do juvenile delinquents become adult offenders? This phenomenon is known as **career escalation**. Presently, no one knows for sure whether status offenders or delinquents progress toward more serious offending as they get older. This generalization applies to both male and female offenders. One problem is that different **pathways**, or developmental sequences over the term of one's adolescence, are associated with serious, chronic, and violent offenders (Kuntsche et al., 2007). Thus, a single trajectory or pathway cannot be used as a general forecast of career escalation, whenever it occurs. Furthermore, career escalation among delinquent youths may suggest that situational factors, such as whether youths come from abusive families and where drug and/or alcohol dependencies are evident, are more significant predictors of future, more serious offending rather than the sheer onset of status of delinquent offending.

With little more information than whether youths commit particular status or delinquent acts at particular ages, long-term predictions of future career escalation among these juveniles are simply unwarranted. Arrest rates for juvenile offenders change drastically within short-term cycles of three years, rather than long-term cycles of more than three years. Also, there are different varieties of juvenile violence (McGarrell, 2005). About half of all juvenile violence is gang-related. This type of violence is quite different from the violence exhibited by youths who kill their parents or other youths out of anger or frustration. In fact, researchers have been aware of these different types of violence and their origins for several decades (Lansford et al., 2007).

Interest in career escalation among juveniles heightened during the 1970s and 1980s, when delinquency and crime increased appreciably. Statistical correlations between rising crime and delinquency rates and the amount of status and delinquent offending led to the tentative conclusion that career escalation was occurring. In retrospect, and after a closer examination of adult recidivists, a clear pattern of career escalation among juvenile offenders has not been revealed. More than any other factor, domestic violence and an abusive family environment seem to be critical determinants of whether certain youths from such families will become chronic and persistent offenders.

career escalation
Moving as a juvenile offender to progressively more serious offenses as new offenses are committed; committing new violent offenses after adjudications for property offenses would be career escalation; committing progressively more serious offenses.

pathways
Developmental sequences over the course of one's adolescence which are associated with serious, chronic, and violent offenders.

Female Versus Male Delinquency: Cataloging the Differences

In 2007, 30 percent of all juvenile arrests involved females. However, of the total number of juveniles held in either public or private juvenile secure facilities in 2007, approximately 15 percent of these detainees were female (American Correctional Association, 2007). Also, about 15 percent of all youths in juvenile community correctional programs were female (American Correctional Association, 2007). These figures indicate that female juvenile arrestees are committed to secure facilities at a lower rate than male juveniles, and that females are also returned to their communities more frequently after serving shorter secure confinement terms (Office of Juvenile Justice and Delinquency Prevention, 2007).

Profiling Female Juveniles

Are there significant differences between male and female juvenile offenders? Yes. They tend to be involved to a greater degree in less-serious types of offending, including runaway behavior, curfew violations, unruly behavior, larceny-theft, and drug abuse. In fact, the juvenile female offender of the 1990s and 2000s appears to be similar in demographic characteristics compared with female juvenile offenders of the 1980s. Survey data show that many female juveniles have prior histories of being sexually or physically abused; they come from a single-parent home; and they lack appropriate social and work-related skills (Mellins et al., 2007).

Evidence indicates that growing numbers of female juveniles are entering the juvenile justice system annually, at younger ages, and for more violent offending (Morris and Gibson, 2008). Over 60 percent of all female juveniles charged with juvenile delinquency in 2007 were under age 16. Additionally, increasing numbers of female juveniles are being transferred to criminal courts for prosecution as adult offenders. Approximately 40 percent of all transferred female juvenile cases involved a violent offense as the most serious charge. Several important risk factors have been identified and associated with greater amounts of female offending. These include the following:

1. alcohol and/or drug abuse
2. various antisocial behaviors
3. African-American background
4. depression, history of depression
5. history of parental violence
6. lower socioeconomic status
7. coming from a single parent home
8. inability to engage in problem-solving
9. poor interpersonal relations with others (Graves, 2007).

Trends in Female Juvenile Offending

However, in recent years, the pattern of female delinquent offending compared with male delinquent offending has been changing. Between 2000 and 2007, there has been a substantial increase in the number of female juvenile arrestees compared with their male counterparts.

Female delinquency seems to be increasing, although experts disagree.

In 2000, for instance, only about 15 percent of all juvenile arrestees were female. But by 2007, this figure had risen to over 30 percent. Furthermore, arrests of female juveniles for violent offenses increased during the 2000–2007 period. About 25 percent of all female arrestees in 2007 were involved in violent crimes as compared with only 15 percent of all juvenile violent crime arrestees for 2000. One reason for this increase is the increased involvement of female juveniles in gangs (Schaffner, 2006).

Like their male counterparts, female youth gangs most often form along racial and/or ethnic lines (Valdez, 2007). The most common reason for female juveniles to join gangs is for protection, often from abusive sexual or physical encounters with their fathers at home. Another important reason is simple rebellion against parents. For many female juvenile gang members, their membership gives them status among their peers and enables them to profit in illicit drug activities. It is difficult to estimate the numbers of females who are gang members. Conservatively, about 10 percent of all juvenile gang members in the United States today, or about 150,000, are female, although estimates have ranged between 9 and 22 percent, depending upon the survey conducted. Although female gangs commit fewer violent crimes compared with male gangs, 38 percent of female youth gang-offending involves violent crimes, while 37 percent of their offending involves drug offenses. Therefore, female youth gangs should be taken seriously (Graves, 2007). Studies of youth gangs in various jurisdictions, such as Alabama, suggest similar findings (Martin et al., 2008).

Is there a new breed of violent juvenile female offender emerging? No. Is female delinquency skyrocketing out of control? No. We don't know whether female juveniles are becoming more violent, although some evidence suggests that they are. We *do* know that juvenile courts are processing larger numbers of female juveniles, and that greater numbers of delinquency adjudications involve females. We suspect that in the past years, many juvenile court judges acted in a paternalistic manner toward female juveniles, and that often, their offenses were downgraded or downplayed in seriousness. These actions have not been directed at delinquency prevention among females (Burke, 2008). However, in more recent years, there has been more equitable treatment of female juveniles by the juvenile courts (Graves, 2007).

Myths and Misconceptions: Changing Views of Juvenile Females

Several important variables differentiate males and females in the juvenile justice system. First, males are more likely than females to offend at some point during their adolescence, although self-reports from female juveniles in a nationwide survey revealed that in 2007, 94 percent of them disclosed that they had committed at least one delinquent act (Office of Juvenile Justice and Delinquency Prevention, 2007). Females who offend during adolescence are often considered abnormal in some way. Second, much male offending is property-related, while it is assumed that female delinquency is predominantly sexual. Third, female delinquents seem to come from broken homes at a higher rate than their male counterparts. Therefore, their delinquency is often attributed to deficient family relationships. Fourth, female delinquents are characterized as having greater mental instability and nonrational behavior, whereas male juvenile offenders are characterized as rational and adventurous, simply testing the bounds of their adolescence.

Two major events triggered the change from a liberal to a conservative approach to juvenile justice throughout the United States. First, states passed legislation in response to public perceptions of increased violent crime among juveniles. Second, status offenses were removed from the jurisdiction of juvenile courts in many jurisdictions. Greater priority was given to getting tough with juvenile offenders. Regarding female juveniles, Schaffner (2006) has identified three major political–legal periods: (1) the paternalistic period (1960–1967), during which female delinquents were dealt with more severely than males by the juvenile courts "for their own good;" (2) a due process period (1968–1976), which reflected the impact of various legal decisions such as *In re Gault* (1967); and (3) a law-and-order phase (1977–1980), during which the court adjusted to the new conservatism of the late 1970s. Therefore, presumed changing rates in female juvenile offending were more attributable to changing policies in the treatment of female juveniles rather than actual increases in the rate of female criminality. However, as we have seen, the nature of female juvenile offending is definitely changing and increasing (Schaffner, 2006). While policy changes and juvenile court views toward female offenders have probably occurred during the early 2000s, increased female juvenile offending has been observed. At the very least, female delinquency is becoming increasingly similar to male delinquency in a number of respects, and court treatment of male and female juveniles is becoming more equalized (Schaffner, 2006).

Summary

The first juvenile court was established in 1899 in Illinois. Preceding juvenile courts were child savers. These were persons who provided food, shelter, and other services to children who wandered the streets unsupervised. Houses of refuge were established, such as the Western House of Refuge in Rochester, New York. The power of the state in regulating juvenile affairs was established by court decisions such as *Ex parte Crouse* in 1839, which usurped parental control over unmanageable children.

In Illinois and other states, reform schools were established following the Civil War, when many children were orphaned by parent deaths. Simple vagrancy, begging, or wandering the streets aimlessly were sufficient grounds to commit youths to such facilities, which were notorious for their harsh conditions, strict discipline, and compulsory labor. In 1870, the case of *People v. ex rel. O'Connell v. Turner* was decided. This case resulted in the successful removal of a juvenile from an Illinois reform school whose only offense was that he was vagrant and in need of supervision. Growing numbers of social welfare agencies were established such as Hull House, a settlement home operated by Jane Addams in Chicago in the 1880s. During the 1890s, compulsory education was the rule rather than the exception for youths, and Colorado passed the first truancy statute in 1899, thus providing for the compulsory education of juveniles. Other states quickly followed suit and passed similar laws. One function of these laws was to keep children occupied during daytime hours and under the close supervision of school authorities.

The first juvenile court was established in Illinois in 1899. This new type of court was vested with a great deal of power over juvenile affairs, and for many decades, this and similar courts in other jurisdictions functioned like social welfare agencies. Decisions were almost always made on behalf of juveniles and in their best interests, a traditional philosophy rooted in early English jurisprudence called *parens patriae*. These courts established an assortment of punishments and imposed such punishments most often in closed proceedings. Children had no legal standing, and therefore juvenile rights were never considered as an important issue.

Over the next 60 years, the similarities between juvenile and criminal courts increased. Juvenile courts evolved into due process courts emulating criminal courts in many ways, and the traditional philosophy of juvenile courts waned. Status offenders and delinquent offenders, as well as children in need of supervision, were within the purview of juvenile courts. But in time, the formality of juvenile courts intensified such that these courts became increasingly criminalized. Less-serious juveniles were gradually shifted to social welfare agencies for processing.

Several official and unofficial sources for measuring the nature and extent of delinquency and status offending include *UCR* and the *NCVS*. Both the *UCR* and *NCVS* are flawed in different respects. Other sources of crime and delinquency include the

National Juvenile Court Data Archive, the *Sourcebook of Criminal Justice Statistics,* the *National Youth Survey,* and the *Monitoring the Future Survey.* Some information about delinquency and crime is available through self-reports. Self-reports are considered less reliable by authorities, although some experts contend that they disclose hidden delinquency, thus suggesting that there is more delinquency committed annually than is officially reported. Several types of delinquency have been tracked by authorities. Delinquency trends have been charted. Presently, surveys of youth violence are mixed, and it is uncertain whether career escalation is occurring. School violence, which has captured public attention to a greater degree in recent years, continues, although recent evidence from official reports suggests that it is declining.

More than a few attempts have been made to identify children at risk. At-risk youths are the most likely juveniles to engage in delinquent behavior. Several interventions have targeted at-risk youths for participation. At-risk youths are those of lower socioeconomic statuses, lower IQs, lower school achievement, possessing more learning disabilities, having attention deficit disorders, and exhibiting more antisocial behavior. Less fully developed cognitive abilities and poor social adjustment are also associated with at-risk youths. Studies of different pathways or developmental sequences leading to different types of offending have achieved some degree of success in recent years.

Gangs and gang violence have also been studied. Although significant gang interventions have been attempted in recent years, no program seems to stem the growth of gangs and the violence such gangs exhibit. There were approximately 34,500 gangs in the United States in 2007 with approximately 1.5 million members. A growing portion of gangs consist of female juveniles, and arrests of female juveniles have increased from 10 percent to 25 percent during the period 2000–2007. Gangs offer protection, recognition and esteem, and ways of gaining status that are often unavailable to youths through their schools and other conventional organizations. Female gangs are rapidly approaching parity with their male counterparts by becoming increasingly violent and aggressive, and professional concern about female youth gangs has heightened. Although it is uncertain whether there is a new female crime wave, official figures suggest that greater attention should focus upon female juvenile gang activities and more effective deterrence interventions.

Key Terms

Act to Regulate the Treatment and Control of Dependent, Neglected, and Delinquent Children, 54
actuarial justice, 59
at-risk youths, 69
banishment, 49
Bridewell Workhouse, 49
career escalation, 72
Cesare Beccaria, 53
chancellors, 48
chancery courts, 48
child savers, 51
children's tribunals, 55
child-saving movement, 51
civil tribunals, 55
cleared by arrest, 61
common law, 48

Compulsory School Act, 56
courts of equity, 48
criminology, 53
felonies, 60
gangs, 71
gemeinschaft, 56
gesellschaft, 57
hidden delinquency, 64
Hospital of Saint Michael, 50
houses of refuge, 51
incident, 61
indentured servant system, 50
indentured servants, 50
index crimes, 60
index offenses, 60
Illinois Juvenile Court Act, 54
Jane Addams, 53

Questions for Review

1. What were workhouses and their functions? How did the poor laws influence those confined to workhouses?

2. What were houses of refuge and reform schools? Were they successful in accomplishing their objectives? Why or why not?

3. Who were child savers, and how did the child-saving philosophy influence the subsequent development of juvenile courts?

4. What were the cases of *Ex parte Crouse* and *People ex rel. O'Connell v. Turner*? What was their significance for juvenile justice?

5. What was the Illinois Juvenile Court Act and what was its significance for juvenile courts?

6. What are some important differences between the *UCR* and the *NCVS*? What are some strengths and weaknesses of the *UCR* and *NCVS*? What are some other sources of information about delinquency and crime? How reliable are these sources?

7. What is self-report information? Is it more or less accurate compared with data reported by the *UCR* or *NCVS*? What are several problems that accompany self-report information?

8. Who are at-risk youths and why do they interest criminal justice professionals? Why are such youths targeted for interventions? What are pathways and why are they significant in relation to career escalation?

9. Why is there growing interest in female juvenile gangs? What are some general trends in female juvenile delinquency, and are these trends of interest to authorities?

10. What are some myths and misconceptions about female juveniles? How have these myths and misconceptions influenced social policies relevant to female delinquents? What are some general characteristics of female delinquents?

Internet Connections

Children Now
http://www.childrennow.org/

Drug War Chronicle
http://www.stopthedrugwar.org/index.shtml

Justice Policy Institute
http://www.justicepolicy.org/

Justice Project
http://www.thejusticeproject.org/

National Council of Juvenile and Family Court Judges
http://www.ncjfcj.org/

National Council on Crime and Delinquency
http://www.nccd-crc.org/

Office for the Victims of Crime
http://www.ovc.gov/

chapter 3

Theories of Delinquency and Intervention Programs

chapter objectives

As the result of reading this chapter, you will accomplish the following objectives:

1. Understand alternative theories of juvenile conduct.
2. Differentiate between classical or biological theories and psychological theories of delinquency.
3. Understand several important sociological theories of juvenile delinquency.
4. Learn about several key psychological theories of juvenile delinquency.
5. Understand how to appreciate the importance of different theoretical explanations in terms of their successful use in forecasting delinquent behavior and creating intervention programs.

 ## Case Study

It happened in Abiline, Texas. A 15-year-old boy and another teen came upon a homeless man, Eric R. McMahon, 48. Suddenly they assaulted him, stomping, kicking, and beating him to the ground. After the man fell to the ground, the 15-year-old hit the man in the head with a large cinder block, killing him. Two witnesses saw the youths assault McMahon and called the police. The assault occurred behind the Love and Care Ministries at about 12:15 A.M. An investigation of the incident followed. According to juvenile authorities, the 15-year-old had no prior record of violent crime, had been taken into custody previously for possessing marijuana, and had made three prior runaway attempts. The 15-year-old had been under probation supervision at the time, with a curfew. He sneaked out of the house where he lived late that night after his guardian fell asleep. No link was established between the 15-year-old and the victim. When asked why he did it, the 15-year-old said, "I don't know." Authorities said that the crime was simply "random violence." [Source: Adapted from the Associated Press, "Slaying Apparently Senseless," November 1, 2007.]

 ## Case Study

It happened in Oxnard, California. Police officers on patrol spotted two juveniles spraying graffiti on a wall at 9:00 P.M. one evening, a bothersome prank that most officers prefer to ignore. The police took the boys into custody after a brief chase. After several hours of interrogation and investigation, the two juveniles were linked with an armed robbery that had occurred earlier that evening. The youths were taken to a juvenile hall where they were booked and charged with armed robbery and vandalism. The boys gave incriminating statements about their role in the robbery but no explanation for why the robbery occurred. Neither boy had a prior record of violent behavior. [Source: Adapted from the Associated Press, "2 Juveniles Arrested After Armed Robbery," October 25, 2007.]

Introduction

Why were these acts committed? Why would youths kill a homeless person unknown to them for apparently no reason? Why would juveniles commit armed robbery and then later spray graffiti on a building in plain view of a major thoroughfare? These and other apparently senseless acts of violence only scratch the surface of what some observers perceive as a growing epidemic of youth crime.

For many centuries, criminologists and others have sought to develop plausible and useful explanations for why people engage in deviant behavior and crime. Why do juveniles commit crimes? What are the different forces that cause them to rob, steal, assault, rape, and kill? This chapter describes several theories that have evolved over time to explain juvenile delinquency in various forms. Theories are tools that are useful in the development of explanations of relationships between variables such as drugs and crime, peer pressure and gang violence, and family instability and antisocial behavior. Theories attempt to explain and predict how two or more variables are interrelated. There are many types of delinquent behavior to explain, and no single theory has yet been developed to account for this behavior adequately. Instead, numerous delinquency theories have been proposed, elaborated, and tested.

This chapter is divided into four parts. The first part presents a variety of theories grouped according to biological, psychological, and sociological themes. The biological theme explores delinquency as the result of internal or biological factors. Biological determinism is discussed, which posits that much of what juveniles do is rooted in genetics and predispositions to behave in given ways (Beaver, DeLisi, and Vaughn, 2008). Heredity is examined as a possible reason for why youths might acquire delinquent propensities. Biological theories include sociobiology, the *XYY* theory, low IQ, and physical characteristics believed to be linked to delinquency.

Psychological and sociological explanations of delinquency are also presented. The importance of one's early childhood experiences on adult behavior is explored through psychoanalytic theory developed by Sigmund Freud and others. Social learning theory is also discussed, positing that there are different maturational stages influencing a youth's subsequent development and demeanor. Sociological theories are discussed, include the concentric zone hypothesis. This hypothesis attempts to link rapid urban changes, familial disruptions, and social instability with delinquency. The anomie theory of delinquency suggests that delinquents are innovators, discontent with conformity. The labeling theory is also discussed, where it is believed that associations with other delinquents and treatment as a delinquent have adverse impacts on how youths define themselves. Bonding and strain theories are also discussed. Several other theories with sociological roots include containment theory, neutralization or drift theory, differential association, and cultural transmission. Each of these views is described.

The second part of the chapter examines the general question of which theory seems best at explaining delinquency. Different criteria are examined as bases for evaluating these theories and their usefulness for explaining various types of delinquent behavior. Various factors that identify children at risk are listed and described.

The third part of this chapter evaluates several important models for dealing with juvenile offenders, such as the rehabilitation model, the treatment or medical model, the noninterventionist model, the due process model, the just-deserts or justice model, and the crime control model. These models typify how different actors in the juvenile justice system orient themselves toward delinquents and delinquency and help to explain their helping behaviors.

The chapter concludes with an examination of different interventions that have been and are continuing to be used in preventing or minimizing delinquency, and the factors or social and psychological conditions that are associated with its occurrence. Most interventions reflect one or more theories of delinquency and can easily be associated with different prevention programs. Thus, theories do not just attempt to explain behavior. They are often used to structure experiences and situations that can be applied in useful ways that might deter youths from becoming delinquents. No intervention program is foolproof. Recidivism rates vary among programs, and some intervention programs work with certain types of juvenile offenders but not with others. A positive outlook persists among criminal justice professionals, and new and different interventions and strategies for combatting delinquency are continually being explored.

Classical and Biological Theories

In this section, several classical and biological theories of criminality and delinquency will be examined. These include: (1) classical theory, (2) positivist theory or biological determinism, (3) sociobiology, and (4) the *XYY* theory.

Classical Theory

classical theory

A criminological perspective emphasizing that people have free will to choose criminal or conventional behavior as a means of achieving their personal goals.

Classical theory is a criminological perspective indicating that people have free will to choose either criminal or conventional behavior. People choose to commit crime for reasons of greed or personal need. Crime can be controlled by criminal sanctions, which should be proportionate to the guilt of the perpetrator.

Philosophers have speculated about the causes of crime for centuries, and they have elaborated diverse explanations for criminal conduct. In the 1700s, criminologists devised several explanations for criminal behavior which have persisted to the present day. Deeply rooted in the general principles of Christianity, the classical school of criminology originated with the work of Cesare Beccaria (1738–1794), *On Crimes and Punishments* (1764). Subsequent scholars who adopted perspectives about crime different from those of Beccaria labeled his views as classical, since they included an inherent conflict between good and evil and provided a standard against which other views of crime could be contrasted.

classical school

Line of thought that assumes that people are rational beings who choose between good and evil.

determinism

Concept holding that persons do not have free will but rather are subject to the influence of various forces over which they have little or no control.

The **classical school** assumes that people are rational beings who exercise free will in choosing between good actions and evil ones. At the other end of the continuum is **determinism**, the view that a specific factor, variable, or event is a determinant of one's actions or behaviors. Determinism rejects the notion of free will and choice, relying instead on properties that cause human beings to behave one way or another. Within the classical context, however, societal progress and perpetuation are paramount, and individuals must each sacrifice a degree of their freedoms in order that all persons can pursue happiness and attain their respective goals. Evil actions operate adversely for societal progress and merit punishment. Because evil acts vary in their seriousness, the severity of punishments for those actions should be adjusted accordingly. Beccaria believed that punishments should be swift, certain, and just, where the penalties are appropriately adjusted to fit particular offenses. The primary purposes of punishment are deterrence and just deserts. In an ideal world, people will refrain from wrongdoing in order to avoid the pain of punishment. Furthermore, whatever punishment is imposed is equivalent or proportional in severity with the amount of social and physical damage caused by those found guilty of crimes. Fines and/or imprisonment were common penalties for those found guilty of property crimes and violent offenses (Rhoades and Zambrano, 2005).

The origins of different sentencing schemes in the United States today can be traced to Beccaria's classical theory. Most states have mandatory sentences for specific offenses, including using a firearm during the commission of a felony. Also, most state statutes carry sentences of determinate lengths and/or fines that are roughly commensurate with the crime's severity.

Less than two decades after Beccaria outlined his philosophy of crime and punishment, Jeremy Bentham (1748–1832), an English philosopher, advanced a similar scheme in his book, *An Introduction to the Principles of Morals and Legislation* (1790). Bentham was known for his belief that **hedonism**, the pursuit of pleasure, was a primary motivator underlying much social and personal action. Simply, humans seek to acquire pleasure and avoid pain. Thus, in this pleasure–pain framework, Bentham formulated his views about the worth and intent of punishment. Like Beccaria, Bentham believed that the objectives of punishments were to deter crime and to impose sanctions sufficient to outweigh any pleasures criminals might derive from the crimes they commit. Therefore, many would-be offenders might desist from crime because the

hedonism

Jeremy Bentham's term indicating that people avoid pain and pursue pleasure.

threat of punishment would more than offset the projected pleasure derived from criminal actions. Those more persistent offenders would be subject to painful punishments adjusted according to the severity of their offenses.

Under the prevailing common law of that period, those under the age of seven were not held accountable for their actions or subject to the same kinds of punishments prescribed for adults. However, older youths eventually were vested with responsibilities for their own actions and were subject to similar adult punishments. One contemporary view of juvenile delinquents is that juveniles must accept responsibility for their actions. If they choose to ignore societal values and persist in violating the law, they must be held accountable for these offenses and punished accordingly.

In reality, the classical school of criminology is not so much an explanation of why crime or delinquency exists, but rather, it is a statement about how various offenses should be punished in order to frustrate criminal conduct. However, some elements of explanation are contained in classical thought. Bentham, for instance, would probably speculate that persistent criminal offenders are gamblers, in a sense, since they regard the calculated risk of being caught and punished for crimes as secondary to the pleasurable benefits derived from committing crimes. The pleasure of crime outweighs the pain of punishment. Beccaria might argue that criminals are comprised of those who have failed to inculcate societal values or respect for the common good.

This perspective has received attention from contemporary theorists such as Kohlberg (1981) who constructed a theory of moral development to account for both deviant and conforming behaviors. This theory is properly classified in a social learning context, and it will be discussed briefly in the section on psychological theories presented following. Although Kohlberg's theory of moral development has been both supported and rejected by adherents and critics, some experts believe that his views may have intuitive value for furnishing insight into more aberrant modes of criminality. Further, the theory may improve our understanding of a wide range of delinquent acts if integrated into a perspective that is sensitive to how varying social contexts shape individual inclinations.

Biological Theories

Determinism is strongly evident in biological theories of criminal and delinquent behavior. Generally, theories of determinism seek to associate criminal, delinquent, and deviant conduct with biological, biochemical, or genetic bases in a direct, causal relation. According to this view, juvenile delinquency is a selective phenomenon, in that it does not occur spontaneously. Delinquents are destined to become delinquent because of factors beyond their own control and/or because of the presence of certain internal factors, while nondelinquents are destined to be nondelinquent because of the presence of different internal factors. The idea that there are known, predisposing factors that cause delinquent behaviors conveniently shifts the responsibility for delinquent conduct from youths themselves to some internal or external source.

Although the attribution of criminality and delinquency to biological causes dates to prebiblical times, such determinism, **biological determinism**, was given a degree of academic dignity in the work of an Italian physician and criminologist, **Cesare Lombroso** (1835–1909), during the 1860s. Considered by many professionals to be the father of criminology, Lombroso was influenced by the work of Charles Darwin (1809–1882). Darwin's major writing, *The Origin of the Species,* was both revolutionary and evolutionary, arguing in part that human beings evolved from lower animal forms over thousands of years. Natural selection and survival of the fittest were key principles of Darwin's evolutionary theory. Lombroso was intrigued by these principles and applied them in his explanation of criminal conduct.

According to Lombroso, criminals were products of heredity. Successive generations of human beings inherited not only physical features genetically from their ancestors, but they also inherited behavioral predispositions such as propensities toward

biological determinism
View in criminology holding that criminal behavior has physiological basis; genes, foods and food additives, hormones, and inheritance are all believed to play a role in determining individual behavior; one's genetic makeup causes certain behaviors to become manifest, such as criminality.

Cesare Lombroso (1835–1909)
His school of thought linked criminal behavior with abnormal, unusual physical characteristics.

atavism
Positivist school of thought arguing that a biological condition renders a person incapable of living within the social constraints of a society; the idea that physical characteristics can distinguish criminals from the general population and are evolutionary throwbacks to animals or primitive people.

positivism
Branch of social science that uses the scientific method of the natural sciences and that suggests that human behavior is a product of social, biological, psychological, or economic factors.

positive school of criminology
School of criminological thought emphasizing analysis of criminal behaviors through empirical indicators such as physical features compared with biochemical explanations. Postulates that human behavior is a product of social, biological, psychological, or economic forces. Also known as the "Italian School."

mesomorphs
Body type described by Sheldon; persons are strong, muscular, aggressive, tough.

ectomorphs
Body type described by Sheldon; persons are thin, sensitive, delicate.

endomorphs
Body type described by Sheldon; persons are fat, soft, plump, jolly.

criminal conduct or antisocial proclivities. Since heredity is more or less binding on future generations, it made sense to Lombroso and many of his disciples that certain physical characteristics would also be inexorably related to criminal behavior. Therefore, physical appearance would be a telling factor whether certain persons would be predisposed to criminality or other types of deviant behavior. This led Lombroso to conjecture extensively about criminal types and born criminals. Height, weight, hair and eye color; physiognomic features such as jaw sizes and angles, earlobe shapes, finger lengths, and hand sizes; and assorted other anatomical characteristics were painstakingly measured and charted by Lombroso. Samples of both willing and unwilling volunteers were obtained for his analyses, including populations of Italian prisoners and soldiers. Eventually, Lombroso concluded that many of the physiological characteristics shared by criminals were indicative of stunted evolutionary growth. Indeed, Lombroso considered criminals to be throwbacks typical of earlier evolutionary stages. This view of criminals is **atavism**, strongly suggestive of subhuman qualities.

Lombroso's views become known popularly as **positivism**, and the **positive school of criminology** originated. This view rejected the free will and choice doctrines espoused by Beccaria and other classical theorists. Rather, it said that criminal conduct more likely emanated from biochemical and genetic factors peculiar to criminal types. Lombroso made further refinements by concluding that certain physical features (e.g., sloping foreheads, compressed jaws, large earlobes, long, slender fingers, excessive facial and body hair) would tend to indicate the type of criminal behavior expected from those observed.

Although Lombroso limited his theoretical and empirical work primarily to adult criminals, his strong focus upon the heredity factor was easily generalizable to juveniles. Thus, he simultaneously provided explanations for both criminal and delinquent conduct that relied almost exclusively on genetic factors. In later years, however, Lombroso changed his opinion about the key role played by genetics in promoting criminal behavior. His beliefs were changed, in part, as the result of extensive scientific studies of both juveniles and adults that disclosed little relation between physiological features and criminal behaviors. Also, the growth of other social sciences such as sociology and psychology led him to assign a more prominent role to one's social milieu as a prerequisite to criminal or delinquent conduct.

Despite the fact that specific biological features or characteristics could not be positively connected with specific types of criminal conduct, certain professionals in the early 1900s continued to regard biological determinism as a plausible explanation for criminality and delinquency. During the 1930s, Hooton (1939) and Kretschmer (1936) established physical typologies of criminals that were given some credence by the academic community. In the 1940s, William H. Sheldon (1949) provided what later became both a popular and an elaborate description of genetic types that seemingly manifested certain kinds of criminal characteristics. Sheldon defined three major categories of body types, including **mesomorphs**, strong, athletic individuals; **ectomorphs**, or thin, submissive beings; and **endomorphs**, or fat persons. He assigned point valuations to each person observed and attempted to describe behaviors most typical of them. Mesomorphs were believed to typify those who manifested criminal or delinquent behaviors. Unfortunately, little consistency existed in his descriptions of those sharing these bodily characteristics. Particularly disturbing was the fact that many nondelinquents and noncriminals were classified as mesomorphs. His work was soundly criticized by other professionals who concluded that no relation between body type and criminality could be established positively (Sutherland, 1951).

Although Sheldon's work was widely criticized and subsequently discounted, some researchers continue to investigate the relation between biology and criminal propensities and regard such a connection as plausible. For instance, research conducted by Sheldon and Eleanor Glueck in 1950 targeted 1,000 white male youths, 500 of whom were delinquent and 500 of whom were nondelinquent (Glueck and Glueck, 1950). Mesomorphic characteristics similar to those described by Sheldon were found among

60 percent of the delinquents studied, while only 30 percent of the nondelinquents shared these characteristics. While the Gluecks interpreted their findings conservatively and never said that delinquency is caused by mesomorphic characteristics, they nevertheless described delinquents generally as more agitated and aggressive compared with nondelinquents. Over five decades later, we can look back at the Gluecks' study and argue, particularly in view of the rise in the incidence of juvenile gangs in many of the United States' larger cities, that more-muscular youths are probably more likely to be gang members than less-muscular youths. Further, the fact that the Gluecks confined their analysis to white male juveniles means that they excluded from consideration several races and ethnic groups that have become increasingly conspicuous in American society and associated with certain forms of delinquency.

Sociobiology.   In recent decades, several criminologists have reaffirmed the significance of the biological contribution to criminality and delinquency (Turner, Hartman, and Bishop, 2007). Genetic researchers and biologists have evolved **sociobiology**, or the study of the biological basis for social action (Wilson, 1975:16). While this new field is not necessarily biological determinism or positivism revisited, it nevertheless stimulates interest in and directs our attention toward the role of genetics in human behavior. Presently, it is believed that a connection exists, but we are unable to elaborate this connection (Wilson, 1975).

sociobiology
Scientific study of causal relation between genetic structure and social behavior.

The *XYY* Theory.   Closely associated in principle with the sociobiological explanation of criminality and delinquency is the ***XYY* theory**. This theory asserts that certain chromosomatic abnormalities may precipitate violence and/or criminal conduct. *X* chromosomes designate female characteristics and are regarded as passive, while *Y* chromosomes designate male characteristics and are regarded as aggressive. Normally, an *XX* chromosomatic combination produces a female, while the *XY* chromosomatic combination yields a male. Sometimes, an extra *Y* chromosome insinuates itself into the *XY* formula to produce an *XYY* type. The input from this additional aggressive chromosome is believed responsible, at least in some instances, for criminal behaviors among those observed to possess it. Unfortunately, this chromosomatic combination exists in less than 5 percent of the population, and thus it lacks sufficient predictive utility when considered on its own merits.

XYY theory
Explanation of criminal behavior suggesting that some criminals are born with an extra *Y* chromosome, characterized as the "aggressive" chromosome compared with the passive *X* chromosome; an extra *Y* chromosome produces greater agitation, greater aggressiveness, and criminal propensities.

Besides designating specific body types, physical features, and heredity as crucial manifestations or causes of delinquency and criminal behavior, other biological or physical causes have been advanced in previous years. Feeblemindedness, mental illness, low intelligence, physical deformity including assorted stigmas, and glandular malfunction or imbalance have been variously described as concomitants of delinquency and criminality (Xiaoying, 2005).

Other Biologically Related Explanations.   Much research exists regarding the relation of criminal and delinquent behavior to physical deformities and glandular malfunctions. While these ideas that glandular malfunctions and physical defects are somehow causally related to various forms of deviant behavior are interesting, no consistent groundwork has been provided that empirically supports any of these notions. Regarding stigmata, for instance, Irving Goffman (1961) has observed that often, unusual behaviors are elicited from those possessing stigmata by defining audiences of others who regard such stigmata with repulsion. Thus, those with stigmas of one type or another, such as facial disfigurement, react to the reactions of others toward them, sometimes behaving as they believe others expect them to behave. It is not the stigma that causes deviant behavior, but rather the reactions of stigmatized persons who respond to the reactions of others. No scientific continuity has been conclusively established between stigmata and criminality. Some relatively recent investigations have attempted to correlate antisocial and delinquent behavior with early exposure to lead and other toxicants. These investigations have also included examinations of delinquent youth exposed to marijuana use by one or both parents and determined by prenatal and postnatal exposures to the drug. Interestingly, a positive correlation has been drawn between prenatal exposure to certain drugs and toxicants from mothers and subsequent behavioral problems of children from their infant years through adolescence (Apel et al., 2007).

A key feature of many community-based juvenile correctional programs is counseling, which is designed to assist juveniles acquire more positive self-concepts and self-assurance. Sometimes, disfigurements or physical inadequacies might cause some of these youths to feel rejected by others or left out of group activities. Wilderness experiences and outdoor-survival courses are designed, in part, to bolster one's confidence in the ability to set goals and accomplish them. If youths can cope with living in the wilderness, by learning camping, cooking, and other pioneer crafts, then they might assume that other problems can be overcome as well.

It is also the case that the ingestion of certain substances or drugs can and do interact with one's biological system to elicit different types of behaviors, some of which are deviant and delinquent (Estell et al., 2007; Tubman, Gil, and Wagner, 2004). While it is impossible to tell for sure whether biological explanations of delinquent conduct have contributed to the establishment of such programs, it is clear that many individual and group activities involving youthful offenders are geared toward developing coping skills. And often, coping with one's own physical and/or psychological inadequacies is an essential part of growing out of the delinquent mode of conduct (Lee and Hoaken, 2007).

Psychological Theories

psychological theories
Explanations linking criminal behavior with mental states or conditions, antisocial personality traits, and early psychological and moral development.

Theories that attribute criminal and delinquent behaviors to personality maladjustment or to some unusual cognitive condition are categorically known as **psychological theories**. These theories focus upon the learning process, the process whereby humans acquire language, self-definitions, definitions of others, and assorted behavioral proprieties (Chapple, 2005). Because the precise mechanisms involved in the learning process are elusive and cannot be inspected or investigated directly, each psychological theory is inherently subjective and may be debated endlessly regarding its relative merits and explanatory effectiveness. In this section, two psychological explanations for delinquent conduct will be examined: (1) psychoanalytic theory and (2) social learning theory.

Psychoanalytic Theory

psychoanalytic theory
Sigmund Freud's theory of personality formation through the id, ego, and superego at various stages of childhood. Maintains that early life experiences influence adult behavior.

Early pioneers of psychological theories were Sigmund Freud, Karen Horney, and Carl Jung. Studies concentrated on personality systems, how they are formed, and how personality and behavior are intertwined. The most popular psychologist of the period was Sigmund Freud (1856–1939). Freud was one of the first theorists to present a systematic explanatory scheme for personality emergence and development. Freud's investigations and writings eventually became widely known as **psychoanalytic theory**.

According to Freud, at the core of psychoanalytic theory are three major personality components known as the id, ego, and superego. The id is the uncontrolled "I want" component prevalent among all newborn infants. The desire of the id is for immediate gratification. Thus, infants typically exhibit little or no concern for others as they seek to acquire things they like or admire. As infants mature to young children, the id is suppressed to a degree by the ego, another personality component. The ego is a recognition of others and a respect of their rights and interests. Eventually, higher-level moral development occurs through the superego or conscience. When children begin to feel guilty when they have deprived others of something wrongfully, this is a manifestation of the superego in action, according to Freud. Eventually, a libido emerges which is a basic drive for sexual stimulation and gratification. The onset of puberty is a common event signaling the importance of the libido. Again, the ego and superego function to keep the libido in check.

Deviant behavior generally, and criminal behavior and delinquency specifically, may be explained as the result of insufficient ego and superego development (Maruna, Matravers, and King, 2004). The id dominates and seeks activities that will fulfill the urges or needs it stimulates. Parent–child relations are often cited as primary in the normal development of the ego and the superego. Therefore, if some children lack control over their impulses and desires, the blame is often placed at the parents' feet for their failure to inculcate these important inhibitors into the youth's personality system (Lord, Jiang, and Hurley, 2005).

Psychoanalytic theory stresses one's early childhood experiences as crucial for normal adult functioning to occur. Traumatic experiences may prevent proper ego or superego development. Adults may develop neuroses or psychoses that may be traceable to bizarre childhood events or other traumatic experiences. Investigations of juvenile rapists, for instance, have indicated that compared with nonrapists, rapists tended to exhibit higher rates of social isolation, physical problems, and problems with sexual identification. In fact, it may be useful to view juvenile rape as a violent, impulsive act committed by youths with a low level of ego integration.

Social Learning Theory

Social learning theory is somewhat different from psychoanalytic theory. Traumatic early childhood experiences may be important determinants of subsequent adult personality characteristics, but the primary factors influencing whether one conforms to or deviates from societal rules are those experiences youths have while learning from others such as their parents (Moseley, 2005). Adults in any institutional context (e.g., schools, churches, homes) provide role models for children to follow. Homes that are beset with violence and conflict between spouses are poor training grounds for children. Children often learn to cope with their problems in ways that are labeled antisocial or hostile (Apel et al., 2007). Even the punishments parents impose on children for disobeying them are translated into acceptable behaviors that children can direct toward their own peers (Bowman, Prelow, and Weaver, 2007).

In its most simplified form, social learning theory implies that children learn to do what they see significant others do, such as their parents. Poor parental role models have been emphasized as a probable cause of poor adolescent adjustment and delinquent behavior. The importance of the family in the early social development of children has been cited as influential in contributing to youth delinquency. Children who use violence to resolve disputes with other children likely have learned such behaviors in homes where violence is exhibited regularly by parents (Ingram et al., 2005). If delinquency is fostered through social learning, then, it seems, certain social learning intervention models might be useful for assisting youths to learn different, more acceptable behaviors. In fact, provided that certain youths, who exhibit learning or developmental disabilities in school, can be identified accurately, teachers may modify their classroom curricula in ways that increase opportunities, skills, and rewards for these children (Wallace, Minor, and Wells, 2005).

Several researchers have examined the relation between delinquency and whether children are learning-disabled (Lee and Hoaken, 2007). Learning-disabled children suffer a double disadvantage, in a sense, since their learning disabilities have likely contributed to poor school performance and social adjustments. Such learning disabilities may impair their judgment regarding peer associations, and it is possible that they might have encounters with the law more frequently than other children. When they are evaluated at intake or later in juvenile court, their school records are "evidence"

social learning theory
Applied to criminal behavior, theory stressing importance of learning through modeling others who are criminal; criminal behavior is a function of copying or learning criminal conduct from others.

Youth violence may be learned from several sources, including television, movies, and the media.

against them. Some persons may erroneously conclude that learning disabilities produce delinquent conduct, when, in fact, other factors are at work. Teachers themselves may become impatient with learning-disabled children, particularly if their conditions are unknown in advance. A lack of rewards from teachers may have deep emotional impacts for some learning-disabled children, thus creating a vicious cycle of failure for them.

These psychological theories stress one's early moral and cognitive development as influential in relation to one's later behaviors (Lee and Hoaken, 2007). Many delinquency prevention programs have been designed as interventions in one's early years. Therefore, it is not unusual to see attempts by public agencies and professionals to intervene through early training or educational programs in schools.

Sociological Theories

It is worth noting that the theories advanced thus far have related deviant, criminal, and/or delinquent behaviors to factors almost exclusively within individuals (i.e., either their minds or bodies or both). These theories have been described elsewhere as inside notions (e.g., the positivist view, glandular malfunction, *XYY* theory, sociobiology, low IQ), primarily because they identify internal factors as causally important for explaining deviation of any kind. While these inside notions have persisted over the years to provide plausible explanations for why criminals and delinquents commit their various offenses, other rival explanations have been advanced that shift certain causes of deviant conduct to factors outside of or external to individuals. Sociologists have encouraged a strong consideration of social factors as major variables that can account for the emergence and persistence of delinquent conduct (Swain, Henry, and Baez, 2004).

It is perhaps most realistic to regard these different perspectives as mutually overlapping rather than as mutually exclusive. Thus, we might view social learning theory as predominantly a psychological theory with certain sociological elements. The biological factor may figure significantly into the delinquency equation, particularly when considering the matter of developmental disabilities of a physical nature in the social learning process. A pragmatic view will be adopted here, and we will regard any explanation as useful, provided that it is accompanied by some predictive utility.

Several sociological theories of juvenile delinquency will be presented in this section. They include: (1) the concentric zone hypothesis; (2) the subculture theory of delinquency; (3) the anomie theory of delinquency; (4) labeling theory; (5) bonding theory; and (6) Agnew's general strain theory.

The Concentric Zone Hypothesis and Delinquency

interstitial area
In concentric zone hypothesis, area nearest the center of a city undergoing change, such as urban renewal; characterized by high rates of crime.

zone of transition
An area nearest center of city center undergoing rapid social change; believed to contain high rates of crime and delinquency.

During the early 1900s, large cities such as Chicago, Illinois, were undergoing rapid expansion as one result of the great influx of laborers from farms and rural regions to city centers to find work. Urbanization emanated from the center of the city outward, and such expansion caused some of the older neighborhoods in the inner city to undergo a dramatic transition. Sociologists at the University of Chicago and elsewhere studied the urban development of Chicago. Social scientists Ernest W. Burgess and Robert E. Park defined a series of concentric zones around Chicago, commencing with the core or "loop" in downtown Chicago, and progressing outward away from the city center in a series of concentric rings. The outward ring or zone immediately adjacent to the central core was labeled by Burgess and Park as an **interstitial area** or **zone of transition**. This was the immediate periphery of downtown Chicago and was characterized by slums and urban renewal projects. This area was also typified by high delinquency and crime. These researchers believed that other cities might exhibit similar growth patterns and concentric zones similar to those identified in the Chicago area. Thus, the **concentric zone hypothesis** of urban growth originated, accompanied by descriptions of different social and demographic characteristics of those inhabiting each zone. Interest in such neighborhoods affecting a youth's behavior continues (Schaefer-McDaniel, 2007).

Concurrent with Burgess and Park's efforts was an investigation of delinquency patterns in Chicago conducted by Clifford Shaw and Henry McKay (1972). These researchers studied the characteristics of delinquent youths in the zone of transition and compared the backgrounds of these youths with other youths inhabiting more stabilized neighborhoods in the zones further removed from the inner core of downtown Chicago. They based their subsequent findings and probable causes of delinquency on the records of nearly 25,000 delinquent youths in Cook County, Illinois, between 1900 and the early 1930s. Essentially, Shaw and McKay found that over the 30-year period, delinquency within the interstitial zone was widespread and tended to grow in a concomitant fashion with the growth of slums and deteriorating neighborhoods. For many of these youths, both of their parents worked in factories for long hours. Large numbers of juveniles roamed these Chicago streets with little or no adult supervision. Family stability was lacking, and many youths turned toward gang activities with other youths as a means of surviving, gaining recognition and status, and achieving certain material goals.

Compared with other zones, zones in transition were typically overcrowded, replete with families of lower socioeconomic statuses (SESs). No zones were completely free of delinquency, however. But in other zones, families were more affluent and stable, and accordingly, less delinquency was observed compared with delinquency within interstitial areas. Shaw and McKay explained delinquency in these transitional areas as likely attributable to a breakdown in family unity and pervasive social disorganization. Interstitial areas lacked recreational facilities and schools and churches were run-down. As a result, youths literally played in the streets, with little or nothing to do to occupy their time other than to form gangs and commit delinquent acts. Because many of the same gangs formed at the turn of the century were still in existence in the early 1930s, Shaw and McKay believed that gang members perpetuated gang traditions and gang culture over time through cultural transmission.

One immediate effect of Shaw and McKay's work was to divert explanations of delinquency away from biological explanations such as genetics and physical abnormalities to more sociological explanations (Ingram et al., 2005). The long-range influence of the pioneering work of Shaw and McKay is evident in contemporary studies seeking to link neighborhood characteristics with delinquent conduct (Khalili, 2008; Liberman, Raudenbush, and Sampson, 2005). Generally, these studies have been supportive of Shaw and McKay's work, although other factors closely associated with those residing in slum areas have also been causally linked with delinquency. One of these factors is SES (Dahlgren, 2005).

Studies investigating the relation between SES and delinquency have generally found more frequent and more violent types of juvenile conduct among youths of lower SES (Wolfgang and Ferracuti, 1967), while less-frequent and less-violent conduct has been exhibited by youths from families of upper SES (Liberman, Raudenbush, and Sampson, 2005). Some of this research also suggests that juveniles who are identified with lower SESs seem more likely to do less well in school than other juveniles from higher SESs.

It may be that students from families of lower SES may reflect different values and achievement orientations compared with youths from higher SES. This factor may figure significantly in the rate of juveniles' school successes or failures. School dropouts

concentric zone hypothesis
Series of rings originating from a city center, such as Chicago, and emanating outward, forming various zones characterized by different socioeconomic conditions; believed to contain areas of high delinquency and crime.

Youth gang growth in the United States and other countries has increased antisocial behavior.

or underachievers may, in fact, turn toward other underachievers or dropouts for companionship, recognition, and prestige. Thus, a complex and vicious cycle is put into motion, with certain conditions and characteristics of lower SES leading to poor academic performance, growing antisocial behavior, and subsequent delinquent conduct. However, describing the concomitants of delinquents or their prominent characteristics does not necessarily pinpoint the true causal factors associated with their conduct in any predictive sense. After all, many lower SES youths adjust well to their academic work and refrain from delinquent activities. Also, many seemingly well-adjusted and academically successful youths from higher SESs may engage in certain forms of delinquent conduct (Apel et al., 2007).

Some research has associated having money or possessing monetary resources as being positively related to delinquent conduct. Thus, especially among higher SES youth, having money becomes a risk factor to criminal conduct in that it reduces family attachments, leads to increased dating, and increases illicit drug use (Ingram et al., 2005). It may be that efforts to facilitate adolescents' entrance into the adult world of earning, spending, credit, and financial obligation may produce unintended consequences, namely increased use of drugs and greater misbehavior. The attraction of purchasing wanted luxury items, such as clothes, CDs, cellular phones, and expensive cars, may be overwhelming when compared with the mere promise that delayed gratification somehow will improve one's life at some distant, uncertain point in the future. The proceeds from adolescents' employment and parental allowance may facilitate values and behaviors that divorce youths from the responsibility accompanying entrance into the adult world of economic relationships. In a sense, then, parents and employers may be the economic agents responsible for subsidizing adolescents' delinquent involvement and drug use (Pires and Jenkins, 2007).

The Subculture Theory of Delinquency

During the 1950s, sociologist Albert Cohen (1955) focused upon and described a delinquent subculture or a **subculture of delinquency**. Delinquent subcultures exist, according to Cohen, within the greater societal culture. But these subcultures contain value systems and modes of achievement, and gaining status and recognition, apart from the mainstream culture. Thus, if we are to understand why many juveniles behave as they do, we must pay attention to the patterns of their particular subculture (Copes and Williams, 2007).

The notion of a delinquent subculture is fairly easy to understand, especially in view of the earlier work of Shaw and McKay. While middle- and upper-class children learn and aspire to achieve lofty ambitions and educational goals and receive support for these aspirations from their parents as well as predominantly middle-class teachers, lower-class youths are at a distinct disadvantage at the outset. They are born into families where these aspirations and attainments may be alien and rejected. Their primary familial role models have not attained these high aims themselves. At school, these youths are often isolated socially from upper- and middle-class youths, and therefore, social attachments are formed with others similar to themselves. Perhaps these youths dress differently from other students, wear their hair in a certain style, or use coded language when talking to peers in front of other students. They acquire a culture unto themselves and one that is largely unknown to other students. In a sense, much of this cultural isolation is self-imposed. But it functions to give them a sense of fulfillment, of reward, of self-esteem and recognition apart from other reward systems. If these students cannot achieve one or more of the various standards set by middle-class society, then they create their own standards and prescribe the means to achieve those standards.

Cohen is quick to point out that delinquency is not a product of lower SES per se. Rather, children from lower SESs are at greater risk than others of being susceptible to the rewards and opportunities a subculture of delinquency might offer in contrast with

subculture of delinquency

A culture within a culture where the use of violence in certain social situations is commonplace and normative; Marvin Wolfgang and Franco Ferracuti devised this concept to depict a set of norms apart from mainstream conventional society, in which the theme of violence is pervasive and dominant. Learned through socialization with others as an alternative lifestyle.

the system's middle-class reward structure. Several experiments have subsequently been implemented with delinquents, where these subcultures have been targeted and described, and where the norms of these subcultures have been used as intervening mechanisms to modify delinquent behaviors toward nondelinquent modes of action. The Provo Experiment was influenced, to a degree, by the work of Cohen (Empey and Rabow, 1961). Samples of delinquent youths in Provo, Utah, were identified in the late 1950s and given an opportunity to participate in group therapy sessions at Pine Hills, a large home in Provo that had been converted into an experimental laboratory.

In cooperation with juvenile court judges and other authorities, Pine Hills investigators commenced their intervention strategies assuming that juvenile participants (1) had limited access to success goals, (2) performed many of their delinquent activities in groups rather than alone, and (3) committed their delinquent acts for nonutilitarian objectives rather than for money (Empey and Rabow, 1961). These investigators believed that since the delinquents had acquired their delinquent values and conduct through their subculture of delinquency, they could unlearn these values and learn new values by the same means. Thus, groups of delinquents participated extensively in therapy directed at changing their behaviors through group processes. The investigators believed that their intervention efforts were largely successful and that the subcultural approach to delinquency prevention and behavioral change was fruitful.

The subcultural theme was devised by Wolfgang and Ferracuti (1967). It will be recalled that Wolfgang and other associates investigated large numbers of boys from Philadelphia, Pennsylvania, in a study of birth cohorts (Miller, 2007). In that study, he found that approximately 6 percent of all boys accounted for over 50 percent of all delinquent conduct from the entire cohort of over 9,000 boys (Wolfgang, Figlio, and Sellin, 1972). These were chronic recidivists who were also violent offenders. Wolfgang has theorized that, in many communities, there are subcultural norms of violence that attract youthful males. They regard violence as a normal part of their environment, they use violence, and respect the use of violence by others. On the basis of evidence amassed by Wolfgang and Ferracuti, it appeared that predominantly lower-class and less-educated males formed a disproportionately large part of this subculture of delinquency. Where violence is accepted and respected, its use is considered normal and normative for the users. Remorse is an alien emotion to those using violence and who live with it constantly. Thus, it is socially ingrained as a subcultural value. This theme would suggest that violence and aggression are learned through socialization with others, even one's siblings (Lee and Hoaken, 2007).

The Anomie Theory of Delinquency

Anomie theory was used by the early French social scientist, Emile Durkheim. Durkheim investigated many social and psychological phenomena including suicide and its causes (Springer and Frei, 2008). One precipitating factor leading to certain suicides, according to Durkheim, was anomie or normlessness. What Durkheim intended by the term was to portray a condition where people's lives, their values, and various social rules were disrupted and they found it difficult to cope with their changed life conditions. Thus, they would experience **anomie**, a type of helplessness, perhaps hopelessness. Most persons usually adapt to drastic changes in their lifestyles or patterns, but a few may opt for suicide since they lack the social and psychological means to cope with the strain of change (Konty, 2005).

Merton (1957) was intrigued by Durkheim's notion of anomie and how persons adapt to the strain of changing conditions. He devised a goals/means scheme as a way of describing different social actions that persons might use for making behavioral choices. Merton contended that society generally prescribes approved cultural goals for its members to seek (e.g., new homes, jobs, automobiles). Furthermore, appropriate, legitimate, or institutionalized means are prescribed for the purpose of attaining these

anomie theory
Robert Merton's theory, influenced by Emile Durkheim, alleging that persons acquire desires for culturally approved goals to strive to achieve, but they adopt innovative, sometimes deviant, means to achieve these goals (e.g., someone may desire a nice home but lack or reject the institutionalized means to achieve this goal) instead using bank robbery, an innovative mean, to obtain money to realize the culturally approved goal. Implies normlessness.

anomie
Condition of feelings of helplessness and normlessness.

3.1   F o c u s   o n   D e l i n q u e n c y

It happened in Georgia. T.J.S., 15, opened fire at his high school, wounding six classmates with a .22 pistol. Subsequently, he was subdued by school teachers and other students when he ran out of ammunition. T.J.S. has been maintained in juvenile detention awaiting a subsequent disposition. The authorities decided to charge T.J.S. as an adult and try him in criminal court. If convicted, T.J.S. could receive life imprisonment.

From the start, T.J.S.'s attorneys have never denied that T.J.S. was the shooter. He has acknowledged that he opened fire on other students with the rifle and that he wounded several of them during the shooting spree. One of his attorneys said, "We have never disputed that the shots were fired by T.J.S. The depths of his illness, the circumstances surrounding the case—these are the things that will be examined at the trial." T.J.S. eventually entered a plea of not guilty by reason of insanity to all of the shooting charges. If he is found not guilty by reason of insanity, he could be institutionalized in a mental hospital or freed. Should the insanity plea be accepted in cases such as this? How frequently is the insanity defense used in criminal cases? Does it excuse criminal conduct? Should T.J.S. be allowed to go free merely by alleging that he was insane at the time he shot other students? What do you think?

Source: Adapted from the Associated Press, "Georgia School Shooting Suspect Enters Insanity Plea," April 1, 2008.

---

mode of adaptation

A way that persons who occupy a particular social position adjust to cultural goals and the institutionalized means to reach those goals.

conformity

Robert K. Merton's mode of adaptation characterized by persons who accept institutionalized means to achieve culturally approved goals.

innovation

Robert K. Merton's mode of adaptation where persons reject institutionalized means to achieve culturally approved goals; instead, they engage in illegal acts, considered innovative, to achieve their goals.

goals. But not everyone is equally endowed with the desire to achieve societal goals nor are they necessarily committed to using the prescribed means to achieve these goals.

Merton described five different **modes of adaptation** that people might exhibit (Choi and Lo, 2002). These modes included **conformity** (persons accept the goals of society and work toward their attainment using societally approved means), **innovation** (persons accept the goals of society but use means to achieve goals other than those approved by society), **ritualism** (persons reject goals but work toward less lofty goals by institutionally approved means), **retreatism** (persons reject goals and reject the means to achieve goals—e.g., hermits, street people, or "bag ladies" typify those who retreat or escape from mainstream society and establish their own goals and means to achieve them), and **rebellion** (persons seek to replace culturally approved goals and institutionalized means with new goals and means for others to follow).

Of these, the innovation mode characterizes juvenile delinquents, according to Merton. Juvenile delinquency is innovative in that youths accept culturally desirable goals, but they reject the legitimate means to achieve these goals. Instead, they adopt illegitimate means such as theft, burglary, or violence. Many youths may crave new clothes, automobiles, and other expensive material items. Since they may lack the money to pay for these items, one alternative is to steal them. This is regarded by Merton as one innovative response arising from a condition of anomie and the strain it emits.

Many intermediate punishment programs today are designed to assist youths in devising new strategies to cope with everyday life rather than to use crime or delinquent conduct to achieve their goals. VisionQuest, Homeward Bound, and various types of wilderness experiences incorporate adaptive experiences as integral features of these programs. Those youths with substantial energy are sometimes placed in camps or on ranches where they can act out some of their feelings and frustrations. These programs deliberately cater to youths who are innovative, but who lack a clear sense of direction.

Labeling Theory

One of the more social sociological approaches to delinquent conduct is **labeling theory**. Labeling theory's primary proponent is Edwin Lemert (1951, 1967a, 1967b). Other social scientists have also been credited with originating this concept (Becker, 1963; Kitsuse, 1962). **Labeling** stresses the definitions people have of delinquent acts rather than delinquency itself. Applied to delinquent conduct, Lemert was concerned with two primary questions. These were: (1) What is the process whereby youths become labeled as delinquent? and (2) What is the influence of such labeling upon these youths' future behavior? Lemert assumed that no act is inherently delinquent, that all persons at different points in time conform to or deviate from the law, that persons become delinquent through social labeling or definition, that being apprehended by police begins the labeling process, that youths defined as delinquent will acquire self-definitions as delinquents, and finally, that those defining themselves as delinquent will seek to establish associations with others also defined as delinquent (Hart, 2005).

Not every youth who violates the law, regardless of the seriousness of the offense, will become a hard-core delinquent. Some infractions are relatively minor offenses. For example, experimenting with alcohol and getting drunk or trying certain drugs, joyriding, and petty theft may be one-time events never to be repeated (Kuntsche et al., 2007). However, "getting caught" enhances the likelihood that any particular youth will be brought into the juvenile justice system for processing and labeling. Youths who have adopted delinquent subcultures are often those who have attracted the attention of others, including the police, by engaging in wrongful acts or causing trouble. Wearing the symbols of gang membership such as jackets emblazoned with gang names helps to solidify one's self-definition of being delinquent (Taylor et al., 2008).

Lemert suggested that juvenile deviation may be **primary deviation** or **secondary deviation**. Primary deviation occurs when youths spontaneously violate the law by engaging in occasional pranks. Law enforcement authorities may conclude that these pranks are not particularly serious. However, if juveniles persist in repeating their deviant and delinquent conduct, they may exhibit secondary deviation. Secondary

"Getting caught" begins the cycle of delinquency for many youths.

ritualism
Mode of adaptation suggested by Robert K. Merton where persons reject culturally approved goals but work toward lesser goals through institutionalized means.

retreatism
Mode of adaptation suggested by Robert K. Merton where persons reject culturally approved goals and institutionalized means and do little or nothing to achieve; homeless persons, "bag ladies," vagrants, and others sometimes fit the retreatist profile.

rebellion
Mode of adaptation suggested by Robert K. Merton where persons reject institutional means to achieve culturally approved goals and create their own goals and means to use and seek.

labeling theory
Explanation of deviant conduct attributed to Edwin Lemert whereby persons acquire self-definitions that are deviant or criminal; persons perceive themselves as deviant or criminal through labels applied to them by others; the more people are involved in the criminal justice system, the more they acquire self-definitions consistent with the criminal label.

labeling
Process whereby persons acquire self-definitions that are deviant or criminal; process occurs through labels applied to them by others.

3.2   Career Snapshot

Christina-Louise Logue

Director—RCMP National Intervention and Diversion—National Crime Prevention Service—National Headquarters Coordinator: Ottawa Police Service-Youth Intervention and Diversion

Statistics:
C.E.G.E.P., Heritage Campus, Hull; University of Toronto School for Addiction Studies; Ohio State University Program in Functional Family Therapy, Ottawa, Ontario

Background

I graduated as a registered nurse in 1977. I grew up in a small town and was reared by a French Catholic "stay at home" mom and an Irish-Indian father. As a family, we were a very close bunch. Together we suffered through the devastations of tornados and floods in our small village. Having witnessed my father and my mother's civic-minded approach toward helping everyone through these hardships, I learned quickly that my chosen profession would have to be one that reflected the many life lessons I had learned from them.

In 1974, I started a registered nursing program. In my second year of the program, my father passed away. I never forget his caring and calming voice, encouraging me to succeed. I returned to the city to complete my nursing studies and eventually became the nurse my dad had wanted. Subsequently, I accepted the position of a psychiatric nurse, not yet knowing the interpersonal and emotional problems that accompanied such a position.

In my different shifts, I dealt with all sorts of patients. One was 42-year-old Mary, who was diagnosed with manic depression. She was kept calm through the administration of antipsychotic medications. I learned about her religious delusions, and how she believed that God was trying to date her and that He wanted sexual relations with her. She hallucinated frequently, and at one point escaped from the facility in a delusional state and committed suicide by jumping into a nearby river. No matter how hard I tried working with some of these patients, I was unable to reach some of them.

Later, I became the Head Nurse of an Adolescent Psychiatric Unit in another psychiatric facility. One particular experience there would have a very profound effect on my future life as a nurse. A young, 14-year-old female patient, Julie, was hospitalized against her will for erratic and psychotic behaviors. Her psychotic behaviors included both visual and auditory hallucinations. Julie was a drug user, primarily LSD, a powerful hallucinogenic. She also used marijuana. One evening, she pulled out a large part of her hair, believing that each strand was a snake. She was placed in a padded room and isolated. A powerful medication was prescribed for her, but I believed it was the wrong treatment. Subsequently, I was reprimanded and asked why I had refused to administer the prescribed medication. I told my superiors that administering such a powerful antipsychotic medication to someone known to hallucinate from excessive drug use was unnecessary. The doctor said he was in charge and that in the future, I should obey his orders and administer whatever he directed to his patients.

The same day I contacted the RCMP Drug Awareness Unit and asked if they had any information about the interaction effects between street drugs and powerful psychiatric medication. While my question was believed interesting, they had no answers for me. Next, I registered for a class in behavioral pharmacology, an addictions class. I learned about the dangers of the interactive effects of street drugs and psychiatric medications. Julie's problems had convinced me to learn more about addictions and about street drugs. I became totally absorbed in monitoring and correcting ways in which substance-abusing teens were being treated in psychiatric settings.

I left the nursing profession in 1989, after the incident with Julie and her psychiatrist. I have always maintained my nursing license by teaching part-time in the same nursing program where I had graduated earlier. Eventually, I took the position of Community Support Team Counselor, working with high-risk youthful offenders. I became known as the "street nurse" who worked with the highest-risk young offenders in the system. I counseled them, supported them and their families, and was often called to testify in court on their behalf.

One of my early encounters was with Trevor, a 15-year-old serving time for assault, burglary, and theft. I was assigned to counsel him while he was serving time in a youth jail. He was a large teen, nearly 6'6", and weighed over 300 pounds. He was all anger, a walking definition of aggression. The first thing he told me was, "You're wasting your time here, 'cause I have nothing to say to you and whatever you have to say to me means nothing, so get lost." I said, "Well, Trevor, that is quite the unique greeting, but if it is all the same to you, I am staying, because I am your counselor and I believe that I can help you." Trevor said nothing more to me for the next hour. At the end of a silent hour, I left and said, "Trevor, it was great meeting you. I'll be coming by each day for an hour, and so I will see you tomorrow." For the next 21 appointments, we sat facing each other in silence in the jail conference room. On the twenty-second day, he entered the room and started to laugh. I laughed along with him, finding the silence of our appointments amusing. Trevor then said, "I guess you are not going to go away, are you?" I said, "No, I guess I won't, and since you can't leave, we might as well talk to each other." Trevor agreed but insisted on me talking with him first. After that, I asked him to ask me anything he wanted, but that I would answer him based on my level of comfort with his questions. He asked me simple things, like where was I from, where did I study, why did I want to help him, and why would I just not write him off? Essentially I told him I wanted to help him, and that I was very sincere in that objective. He told me about all the people who had hurt him. He told how his mother had abandoned him, and that he had grown up with an alcoholic, abusive father. He said that teachers called him a "retard," and that he frequently got into fights with students. After several months of counseling, I asked Trevor what he wanted to be when he "grew up". Trevor said he wanted to be a machinist. In time, I learned that Trevor completed a machinist course. Ten years later, I received a call from Trevor, who was so excited to tell me that he was doing great, that he had married, was a father, and was a very successful machinist. He reminded me of our frequent conversations and my encouragement. In Trevor's case, I believed that I had made a true difference in his life.

Over the years, I have developed numerous community-based programs with special emphasis on developing social skills through training with youth and their guardians. I have always sought out to encourage single moms who reached out looking for guidance and wisdom. I have also studied functional family therapy and cognitive behavioral restructuring treatment. My studies in the field of behavioral pharmacology have resulted in my becoming qualified as a drug expert in the Supreme Courts of Ontario and Quebec since 1991. My experience as a drug addiction counselor has brought me in touch with many needful children, including Jessica. Jessica started using drugs at age 11, and by 13, she was using alcohol, marijuana, cocaine, PCP, LSD, and other drugs. She became pregnant and had an abortion. By 15, she was a chronic runaway and was supporting her drug abuse through prostitution. Her mother, Heather, looked for her frequently on the streets, showing her picture to passersby. Eventually she found her daughter and got her into drug rehabilitation. Jessica recovered, and soon, Jessica, her mother, and I embarked on a public-speaking tour to help raise awareness about teen drug use and prostitution. Jessica remains clean and sober today. She wants to be a police officer someday and I am encouraging her as much as possible to follow that dream. After five years working with high-risk young offenders, I was recruited by the Ottawa police service to work as a victim crisis counselor. However, after only two weeks in that job, I advised the Chief of Police I was quitting. When asked why, I told him I really missed working with young offenders, and that while I respected the needs of all victims, old and young, my true calling was to assist young offenders and their families. The Chief asked me to reconsider and reassigned me to work with the Ottawa Police Youth Services Section. I met several others who shared my interest in disturbed youth, and we eventually developed an early identification and early intervention program. Not everyone was enthusiastic with our interventions with youths. Some police officers worked with youths in aggressive and violent ways. Despite this opposition from the police subculture, our early intervention program with at-risk youth is now successful. In 2007, I was seconded from my role as the Ottawa Police Service Youth Intervention and Diversion Coordinator to the Director of the Royal Canadian Mounted Police National Crime Prevention Services—Intervention and Diversion Unit. In all of my duties, I advocate for youth and families in need of timely, meaningful, and appropriate services. I remain actively involved in local, national, and international level project developments and have been recognized for my efforts. I would hope that some of my experiences might motivate students to follow in my footsteps so that they, too, can feel the successes I have enjoyed over the years.

primary deviation
Part of labeling process whenever youths engage in occasional pranks and not especially serious violations of the law.

secondary deviation
Part of labeling theory which suggests that violations of the law become a part of one's normal behavior rather than just occasional pranks.

Learning about acceptable professions and occupations of adults in one's early years is a delinquency deterrent.

deviation occurs whenever the deviant conduct becomes a part of one's behavior pattern or lifestyle. Thus, delinquency is viewed as a social label applied by others to those youths who have relatively frequent contact with the juvenile justice system (Hart, 2005). The strength of such social labeling is such that juveniles themselves adopt these social labels and regard themselves as delinquent. This, too, is a vicious cycle of sorts, in that one phenomenon (social labeling by others of some youths as delinquent) reinforces the other (labeled youths acquiring self-definitions as delinquent and engaging in further delinquent conduct consistent with the delinquent label).

Lemert's labeling perspective has probably been the most influential theory relative to policy decisions by juvenile courts to divert youths away from the formal trappings of court proceedings (Hart, 2005). The sentiment is that if we can keep youths away from the juvenile justice system, they are less inclined to identify with it. Accordingly, they are less likely to define themselves as delinquent and engage in delinquent conduct. This theory is also more broadly applicable to adult first-offenders. Criminal courts often use diversion as a means of keeping first-offenders out of the system (Sullivan et al., 2007). This is done, in part, to give them another chance to conform to the law and not acquire a criminal record. Diversion doesn't always work for either adults or juveniles, but at least we can better appreciate why different justice systems employ it to deal with at least some adult and juvenile offenders in the early stages of their processing by the system (Murrell, 2005).

Bonding Theory

bonding theory
Emile Durkheim's notion that deviant behavior is controlled to the degree that group members feel morally bound to one another, are committed to common goals, and share a collective conscience.

social control theory
Explanation of criminal behavior which focuses upon control mechanisms, techniques and strategies for regulating human behavior, leading to conformity or obedience to society's rules, and which posits that deviance results when social controls are weakened or break down, so that individuals are not motivated to conform to them.

Bonding theory or **social control theory** derives primarily from the work of Travis Hirschi (1969). This theory stresses processual aspects of youths becoming bonded or socially integrated into the norms of society (Mack et al., 2007). The greater the integration or bonding, particularly with parents and school teachers, the less is the likelihood that youths will engage in delinquent activity. Different dimensions of bonding include attachment (emotional linkages with those we respect and admire), commitment (enthusiasm or energy expended in a specific relationship), belief (moral definition of the rightness or wrongness of certain conduct), and involvement (intensity of attachment with those who engage in conventional conduct or espouse conventional values) (Baron, 2007; Baron and Forde, 2007).

Hirschi investigated large numbers of high-school students in order to test his bonding theory. More academically successful students seemed to be bonded to conventional values and significant others such as teachers and school authorities compared with less-successful students. Those students who apparently lack strong commitment to school and to education generally are more prone to become delinquent than those students with opposite dispositions (McCartan and Gunnison, 2007). However, since Hirschi limited his research to students in high-school settings, he has been criticized subsequently for not applying his bonding theory to juvenile samples in other, nonschool settings. Furthermore, Hirschi has failed to explain clearly the processual aspects of bonding. Also, since rejecting or accepting conventional values and significant others is a matter of degree, and because youths may have many attachments with both delinquent and nondelinquent juveniles, bonding theory has failed to predict accurately which youths will eventually become delinquent. This is regarded as a serious limitation (Beaver, Wright, and DeLisi, 2007).

Agnew's General Strain Theory

Strain theory was developed from the anomie theory described by Emile Durkheim and Robert Merton (Baron, 2007). Anomie theory stresses the breakdown of societal restraints on individual conduct. Merton elaborated on this breakdown by describing the emerging cultural imbalance between the goals and norms of individuals in society. The strain component is apparent since, although many lower-SES youths have adopted middle-class goals and aspirations, they may be unable to attain these goals because of their individual economic and cultural circumstances (Ellwanger, 2007). This is a frustrating experience for many of these youths, and such frustration is manifested by the strain to achieve difficult goals or objectives. While middle-class youths also experience strain in their attempts to achieve middle-class goals, it is particularly aggravating for many lower-class youths, since they sometimes do not receive the necessary support from their families (Song and Royo, 2008).

Robert Agnew views strain theory as cutting across all social classes (Walls, Chapple, and Johnson, 2007). Strain theory is differentiated from control theory in that control theory is based on the premise that the breakdown of society frees individuals to commit delinquent acts. Control theory also suggests that the absence of significant relationships with nondeviant others means less social control from others over delinquent behavior. Strain theory is also differentiated from social learning theory, which stresses forces in groups that lead persons to view crime in positive ways. Social learning theory suggests that youths eventually find themselves in relationships with others who are deviant and delinquent, and these relationships are viewed as positive and rewarding. In contrast, strain theory focuses on the pressures that are placed on youths to commit delinquency. These pressures occur in the form of maltreatment by others, causing youths to become upset and turn to crime as a negative reaction (Lee and Hoaken, 2007; Mack et al., 2007).

Agnew believes that strain can be measured in different ways. One way is subjective, where investigators determine from delinquents whether they believe they dislike the way they have been treated by others. The objective method focuses upon identifying particular experiences in groups that delinquents say they would dislike if they were subjected to such experiences. Thus, different components of potential strain for juveniles can be predetermined and identified. What are the major negative determinants of strain? One of these is the failure of youths to achieve positively valued stimuli. Youths want to have money; status, especially masculine status; and respect. When youths are barred from attaining these things, strain is created. Autonomy is also highly valued. Autonomy is the power over oneself. In an effort to assert one's autonomy, some persons may be thwarted from achieving this desired state and turn to delinquency and crime to relieve strain and frustration. Thus, there are certain disjunctions in life,

strain theory
A criminological theory positing that a gap between culturally approved goals and legitimate means of achieving them causes frustration which leads to criminal behavior.

especially between aspirations and expectations. When someone achieves less than is expected, strain is experienced. This frustration to achieve whatever is desired may be judged to be the result of unfairness. When a youth expects to achieve a desired result and does not achieve it, the failure experience is an unjust one.

Another way of measuring strain is to examine potential losses of positively valued stimuli in one's life. The loss of significant others, broken relationships with friends or romantic partners, or the theft of a valued possession may create strain. Some youths react to these losses by turning to delinquency to retrieve what was lost, to prevent further loss, or to seek revenge against those perceived as causing the loss.

Yet another measure of strain consists of several negative stimuli in one's life, such as child abuse, neglect, adverse relations with parents or teachers, negative school experiences, adverse relationships with peers, neighborhood problems, and homelessness (Bowman, Prelow, and Weaver, 2007). Even parental unemployment, family deaths, and illnesses can contribute to increasing delinquent behavior in adolescents. Also, the external environment itself can create many negative feelings among youths, such as despair, defeatism, fear, and anger. Anger is especially significant as youths blame their negative circumstances and relationships on others. Those youths who experience repetitive incidents of stressful and frustrating experiences are more likely to engage in delinquent behaviors and hostile and aggressive actions (LaTorre, 2008).

Coping with strain is complex, according to Agnew. Cognitive, emotional, and behavioral coping strategies might include rationalizing, placing less importance on goals originally sought, and/or accepting the responsibility for one's failure to achieve goals. Positive stimuli rather than negative stimuli may be sought to counter the strain of one's experiences. Coping mechanisms may be either criminal or noncriminal, therefore. General strain theory includes constraints to nondelinquent behavior, as well as factors that may affect an individual's disposition to delinquent behavior. In this way, it is possible to predict the adaptations, delinquent or nondelinquent, that will be chosen.

One issue related to strain theory that Agnew addresses is that male and female delinquents adapt differently to strain. While this differential reaction has not been explained fully, it has been suggested that female juveniles may lack the confidence and self-esteem that may be conducive to committing delinquency. Females may in fact devise strategies that include avoidance and escape in an effort to reduce or eliminate strain. Furthermore, females may have stronger relational ties compared with males, and thus their strain-reduction efforts may be more successful. However, rising rates of female juvenile offending suggest that females may face strain in forms different from males. For instance, females often face sexual, emotional, and physical abuse to a greater degree than their male counterparts (Owens-Sabir, 2007). These are negative stimuli. Thus, female juvenile response to such negative stimuli may include acting out in delinquent ways. More research is needed in the study of male–female juvenile differences relative to strain theory and its gender-specific applications (Murrell, 2005).

Extraneous Factors

containment theory
Explanation elaborated by Walter Reckless and others that positive self-image enables persons otherwise disposed toward criminal behavior to avoid criminal conduct and conform to societal values. Every person is a part of an external structure and has a protective internal structure providing defense, protection, and/or insulation against one's peers, such as delinquents.

Obviously, many other explanations for delinquent conduct have been advanced by various theorists. Those selected for more in-depth coverage here are not necessarily the best theories to account for delinquency. Their inclusion is intended to describe some of the thinking about why juveniles might engage in delinquent conduct. Some of the other approaches that have been advocated include containment theory, neutralization or drift theory, differential association theory, and differential reinforcement theory.

Containment theory is associated with the work of sociologist Walter Reckless (1967). Reckless outlined a theoretical model consisting of pushes and pulls in relation to delinquency. By pushes he referred to internal personal factors, including hostility, anxiety, and discontent. By pulls he meant external social forces, including delinquent subcultures and significant others. The containment dimension of his theoretical scheme consisted of both outer and inner containments. Outer containments, according to Reckless, are social norms, folkways, mores, laws, and institutional arrangements that induce societal conformity. By inner containments, Reckless referred to individual or personal coping strategies to deal with stressful situations and conflict. These strategies might have a high tolerance for conflict or frustration and considerable ego strength. Thus, Reckless combined both psychological and social elements in referring to weak attachments of some youths to cultural norms, high anxiety levels, and low tolerance for personal stress. These persons are most inclined to delinquent conduct. A key factor in whether juveniles adopt delinquent behaviors is their level of self-esteem (Taylor et al., 2008). Those with high levels of self-esteem seem most resistant to delinquent behaviors if they are exposed to such conduct while around their friends (Mueller and Hutchison-Wallace, 2005).

Neutralization theory or drift theory was originally outlined by David Matza (1964). Matza said that most juveniles spend their early years on a behavioral continuum ranging between unlimited freedom and total control or restraint. These persons drift toward one end of the continuum or the other, depending upon their social and psychological circumstances. If youths have strong attachments with those who are delinquent, then they drift toward the unlimited freedom end of the continuum and perhaps engage in delinquent activities. However, Matza indicates that the behavioral issue is not clear-cut. Juveniles most likely have associations with normative culture, such as their parents or religious leaders, as well as the delinquent subculture, such as various delinquent youths. They may engage in delinquent conduct and regard their behavior as acceptable at the time they engage in it. Elaborate rationales for delinquent behavior may be invented by youths (e.g., society is unfair, victims deserve to be victims, nobody is hurt by our particular acts), and thus, they effectively neutralize the normative constraints of society that impinge upon them. Therefore, at least some delinquency results from rationalizations created by youths that render delinquent acts acceptable under the circumstances (Wallace and Fisher, 2007). Appropriate preventative therapy for such delinquents might be to undermine their rationales for delinquent behaviors through empathic means. Also, activities that are geared toward strengthening family bonds are important, since greater attachments with one's parents tend to overwhelm the influence of one's associations with delinquent peers (Zimmermann and McGarrell, 2005).

Differential association theory was first advanced by Edwin Sutherland (1939). In some respects, it is an outgrowth of the cultural transmission theory described by Shaw and McKay in their investigations of juvenile offenders in Chicago. Sutherland described a socialization process (learning through contact with others) whereby juveniles would acquire delinquent behaviors manifested by others among their close associates. It would certainly be an oversimplification of Sutherland's views to claim that associating with other delinquents would cause certain juveniles to adopt similar delinquent behaviors. Sutherland's scheme was more complex and multifaceted than that (Champion, 2008a). He suggested that several interpersonal dimensions characterize relations between law violators and others who behave similarly. Sutherland said that differential association consists of the following elements: frequency, priority, duration, and intensity. Thus, engaging in frequent associations and long-lasting interactions with others who are delinquent, giving them priority as significant others, and cultivating strong emotional attachments with them will contribute in a significant way to a youth's propensity to commit delinquent acts.

Explicit in Sutherland's scheme is the phenomenon of attachments with others who are delinquent. Thus, this is at least one similarity differential association theory shares with containment theory and bonding. Sutherland sought to characterize relationships some juveniles have with delinquents as multidimensional relationships, and

neutralization theory
Holds that delinquents experience guilt when involved in delinquent activities and that they respect leaders of the legitimate social order; their delinquency is episodic rather than chronic, and they adhere to conventional values while "drifting" into periods of illegal behavior. In order to drift, the delinquent must first neutralize legal and moral values.

drift theory
David Matza's term denoting a state of limbo in which youths move in and out of delinquency and in which their lifestyles embrace both conventional and deviant values.

differential association theory
Edwin Sutherland's theory of deviance and criminality through associations with others who are deviant or criminal; theory includes dimensions of frequency, duration, priority, and intensity; persons become criminal or delinquent because of a preponderance of learned definitions that are favorable to violating the law over learned definitions unfavorable to it.

cultural transmission theory
Explanation emphasizing transmission of criminal behavior through socialization. Views delinquency as socially learned behavior transmitted from one generation to the next in disorganized urban areas.

the association aspect was only one of several of these dimensions. Although Sutherland's work has been influential and has been widely quoted and utilized by criminologists, some experts have been critical of his theory on various grounds. He never fully articulated the true meaning of intensity, for instance. How intense should a relation be between a delinquent and a nondelinquent before making a difference, and causing the nondelinquent to adopt delinquent patterns of behavior? How frequently should nondelinquents be in the company of delinquents before such contact becomes crucial and changes nondelinquent behavior? These and other similar questions were never fully addressed by Sutherland. Nevertheless, differential association has influenced certain correctional policies and treatment programs for both juveniles and adults (Champion, 2008a).

Much like labeling theory, differential association theory has encouraged minimizing contact between hard-core criminal offenders and first-offenders. The use of prison is often the last resort in certain cases, since it is believed that more prolonged contact with other criminals will only serve to intensify any criminal propensities first-offenders might exhibit. If they were diverted to some nonincarcerative option, they might not become recidivists and commit new crimes. The same principle applies to delinquent first-offenders and accounts for widespread use of noncustodial sanctions that seek to minimize a juvenile's contact with the juvenile justice system.

In 1966, Robert Burgess and Ronald Akers attempted to revise Sutherland's differential association theory and derived what they termed **differential reinforcement theory**. Differential reinforcement theory actually combines elements from labeling theory and a psychological phenomenon known as conditioning. Conditioning functions in the social learning process as persons are rewarded for engaging in certain desirable behaviors and refraining from certain undesirable behaviors. Juveniles perceive how others respond to their behaviors (negative reactions) and may be disposed to behave in ways that will maximize their rewards from others (Burgess and Akers, 1966).

Also, in some respects, Burgess and Akers have incorporated certain aspects of the **looking-glass self** concept originally devised by the theorist Charles Horton Cooley. Cooley theorized that people learned ways of conforming by paying attention to the reactions of others in response to their own behavior. Therefore, Cooley would argue that we imagine how others see us. We look for other's reactions to our behavior and make interpretations of these reactions as either good or bad reactions. If we define others' reactions as good, we will feel a degree of pride and likely persist in the behaviors. But, as Cooley indicated, if we interpret their reactions to our behaviors as bad, we might experience mortification. Given this latter reaction, or at least our interpretation of it, we might change our behaviors to conform to what others might want and thereby elicit approval from them. While these ideas continue to interest us, they are difficult to conceptualize and investigate empirically. Akers and others have acknowledged such difficulties, although their work is insightful and underscores the reality of a multidimensional view of delinquent conduct.

differential reinforcement theory

Explanation that combines elements of labeling theory and a psychological phenomenon known as conditioning; persons are rewarded for engaging in desirable behavior and punished for deviant conduct.

looking-glass self

Concept originated by Charles Horton Cooley where persons learn appropriate ways of behaving by paying attention to how others view and react to them.

An Evaluation of Explanations of Delinquent Conduct

Assessing the importance or significance of theories of delinquency is difficult. First, almost all causes of delinquent conduct outlined by theorists continue to interest contemporary investigators. The most frequently discounted and consistently criticized views are biological ones, although as we have seen, sociobiology and genetic concomitants of delinquent conduct continue to raise questions about the role of heredity as a significant factor in explaining delinquency. Some evidence suggests that television and movie violence triggers aggressive and violent behavior among different youths, although blaming media violence for the actions of some youths fails to explain the absence of violence among those youths also exposed to it (Slater, Hayes, and Ford, 2007; Wallenius, Punamaki, and Rimpela, 2007). Other explanations rely on attention deficit hyperactive disorder (or ADHD) to explain why some youths become delinquent or behave in abnormal ways (Cary, 2005).

Psychological explanations seem more plausible than biological ones, although the precise relation between the psyche and biological factors remains unknown. If we focus upon psychological explanations of delinquency as important in fostering delinquent conduct, almost invariably we involve certain elements of one's social world in such explanations. Thus, one's mental processes are influenced in various ways by one's social experiences. Self-definitions, important to psychologists and learning theorists, are conceived largely in social contexts, in the presence of and through contact with others. It is not surprising, therefore, that the most fruitful explanations for delinquency are those that seek to blend the best parts of different theories that assess different dimensions of youths, their physique and intellectual abilities, personalities, and social experiences. Intellectual isolationism or complete reliance on either biological factors exclusively or psychological factors exclusively or sociological factors exclusively may simplify theory construction, but in the final analysis, such isolationism is unproductive. Certainly, each field has importance and makes a contribution toward explaining why some youths exhibit delinquent conduct and why others do not.

From a purely pragmatic approach in assessing the predictive and/or explanatory utility of each of these theories, we may examine contemporary interventionist efforts that seek to curb delinquency or prevent its recurrence. One way of determining which theories are most popular and/or influence policy and administrative decision-making relative to juveniles is to identify the ways youthful offenders are treated by the juvenile justice system when they have been apprehended and adjudicated (Wallace, Minor, and Wells, 2005).

A preliminary screening of juvenile offenders may result in some being diverted from the juvenile justice system. One manifest purpose of such diversionary action is to reduce the potentially adverse influence of labeling on these youths. A long-term objective of diversion is to minimize recidivism among divertees. While the intended effects of diversion are to reduce social stigma, such as a reduction in the degree of social stigmatization toward status offenders, the actual outcomes of diversion are presently unclear, inconsistent, and insufficiently documented (Kidd, 2007).

A promising idea is that minimizing formal involvement with the juvenile justice system is favorable for reducing participants' self-definitions as delinquent and avoiding the delinquent label. Thus, labeling theory seems to have been prominent in the promotion of diversionary programs. Furthermore, many divertees have been exposed to experiences that enhance or improve their self-reliance and independence. Many youths have learned to think out their problems rather than act them out unproductively or antisocially. When we examine the contents of these programs closely, it is fairly easy to detect aspects of bonding theory, containment theory, and differential reinforcement theory at work in the delinquency prevention process (Ousey and Wilcox, 2007).

Besides using diversion per se with or without various programs, there are elements or overtones of other theoretical schemes that may be present in the particular treatments or experiences juveniles receive as they continue to be processed throughout the juvenile justice system. At the time of adjudication, for example, juvenile court judges may or may not impose special conditions to accompany a sentence of probation. Special conditions may refer to obligating juveniles to make restitution to victims, to perform public services, to participate in group or individual therapy, or to undergo medical treatment in cases of drug addiction or alcohol abuse.

Learning to accept responsibility for one's actions, acquiring new coping skills to face crises and personal tragedy, improving one's educational attainment, and improving one's ego strength to resist the influence of one's delinquent peers are individually or collectively integral parts of various delinquency treatment programs, particularly where the psychological approach is strong (Bowman, Prelow, and Weaver, 2007).

Program successes are often used as gauges of the successfulness of their underlying theoretical schemes. Since no program is 100 percent effective at preventing delinquency, it follows that no theoretical scheme devised thus far is fully effective. Yet, the wide variety of programs that are applied today to deal with different kinds of juvenile offenders indicates that most psychological and sociological approaches have some merit and contribute differentially to delinquency reduction. Policy decisions are made throughout the juvenile justice system and are often contingent upon the theoretical views adopted by politicians, law enforcement personnel, prosecutors and judges, and correctional officials at every stage of the justice process. We may appreciate most theoretical views because of their varying intuitive value and selectively apply particular approaches to accommodate different types of juvenile offenders.

Regarding theories of delinquency generally, their impact has been felt most strongly in the area of policy-making rather than in behavioral change or modification. Virtually every theory is connected in some respect to various types of experimental programs in different jurisdictions. The intent of most programs has been to change behaviors of participants. However, high rates of recidivism characterize all delinquency prevention innovations, regardless of their intensity or ingenuity. Policy decisions implemented at earlier points have long-range implications for present policies in correctional work. Probationers and parolees as well as inmates and divertees, adults and juveniles alike, are recipients or inheritors of previous policies laid in place by theorists who have attempted to convert their theories into practical experiences and action (Sungi, 2008).

Current policy in juvenile justice favors the get-tough orientation, and programs are increasingly sponsored that heavily incorporate accountability and individual responsibility elements. At an earlier point in time, projects emphasizing rehabilitation and reintegration were rewarded more heavily through private grants and various types of government funding. No particular prevention or intervention or supervision program works best. Numerous contrasting perspectives about how policy should be shaped continue to vie for recognition among professionals and politicians. The theories that have been described here are indicative of the many factors that have shaped our present policies and practices. The influence of these diverse theories is reflected in a variety of models that have been and continue to be used by juvenile justice practitioners. Several of these models are presented in the following section.

Models for Dealing with Juvenile Offenders

Several models for dealing with juvenile offenders are presented and described here. Each of these models is driven by a particular view of juvenile delinquency and what might cause it. The causes of delinquency are many and diverse, and thus not everyone agrees with any particular explanation. Therefore, not every expert dealing with juvenile offenders agrees that one particular model is most fruitful as a basis for delinquency intervention. Rather, these models serve as a guide to the different types of decisions that are made on behalf of or against specific juvenile offenders. Because each model includes aims or objectives that are related to a degree with the aims or objectives of other models, there is sometimes confusion about model identities. For example, professionals may use a particular model label to refer to orientations that are more properly included in the context of other models. Some professionals say that they do not use any particular model, but rather, they rely on their own intuition for exercising a particular juvenile intervention.

Additionally, some recently developed interventionist activities have combined the favorable features of one model with those of others. These hybrid models are difficult to categorize, although they are believed to be helpful in diverting youths to more productive activities. One way of overcoming this confusion is to highlight those features of models that most directly reflect the hybrid models' aims. The models discussed include: (1) the rehabilitation model; (2) the treatment or medical model; (3) the non-interventionist model; (4) the due process model; (5) the "just-deserts"/justice model; and (6) the crime control model.

The Rehabilitation Model

Perhaps the most influential model that has benefited first-offender juveniles is the **rehabilitation model**. This model assumes that delinquency or delinquent conduct is the result of poor friendship or peer choices, poor social adjustments, the wrong educational priorities, and/or a general failure to envision realistic life goals and inculcate appropriate moral values (Haynie et al., 2005). In corrections, the rehabilitation model is associated with programs that change offender attitudes, personalities, or character (Salinas, 2008). These programs may be therapeutic, educational, or vocational. At the intake stage, however, there is little, if any, reliance on existing community-based programs or services that cater to certain juvenile needs. Intake officers who use the rehabilitation model in their decision-making activities will often attempt to impart different values and personal goals to juveniles through a type of informal teaching.

> **rehabilitation model**
> Concept of youth management similar to medical model, where juvenile delinquents are believed to be suffering from social and psychological handicaps; provides experiences to build self-concept; experiences stress educational and social remedies.

If a youth is being processed at the intake stage for theft, for example, the intake officer may emphasize the harmful effects of the theft for the owner from whom the merchandise was taken. Intake officers who meet with nonviolent first-offenders usually do not want to see these juveniles move further into the juvenile justice system. Therefore, these officers may attempt to get juvenile offenders to empathize with their victims and to understand the harm they have caused by their actions. While theft is a serious offense, it is less serious than aggravated assault, rape, armed robbery, or murder. Intake officers rely heavily upon their personal experience and judgment in determining the best course of action to follow. When a juvenile is very young and has committed this single theft offense, this is an ideal situation where intake officers can exercise strategic discretion and temper their decisions with some leniency. But in the context of *parens patriae,* and the rehabilitative framework guiding some of these officers, leniency does not mean outright tokenism or ineffective wrist-slapping. Doing nothing may send the wrong message to youths who have violated the law. The same may be said of police officers who encounter youths on streets and engage in police cautioning or stationhouse adjustments as alternative means of warning juveniles to refrain from future misconduct. Thus, it is believed that the informal intake hearing itself is sufficiently traumatic for most youths so that they will not be eager to reoffend. Advice, cautioning, and warnings given under such circumstances are likely to be remembered. It is also important to involve one's family members in these intake conferences. If a youth who has committed a delinquent act can see that his/her behavior has affected his/her family members, then the chances of recidivism may decline (Duran, 2005).

The Treatment or Medical Model

The **treatment model** or **medical model** assumes that delinquent conduct is like a disease, the causes of which can be isolated and attacked. Cures may be effected by administering appropriate remedies. The treatment model is very similar to the rehabilitation model. Indeed, some persons consider the treatment or medical model to be a subcategory of the rehabilitation model (Boyd and Myers, 2005). The aim of the treatment model is to provide conditional punishments for juveniles that are closely related to treatment. Intake officers have the authority to refer certain youths to select

> **treatment model, medical model**
> This model considers criminal behavior as an illness to be treated; delinquency is also a disease subject to treatment.

community-based agencies and services where they may receive the proper treatment. This treatment approach assumes that these intake officers have correctly diagnosed the illness and know best how to cure it (Davidson-Methot, 2004). Compliance with program requirements that are nonobligatory for juveniles is enhanced merely by the possibility that the intake officer may later file a delinquency petition with the juvenile court against uncooperative youths.

In growing numbers of jurisdictions, social services are being utilized increasingly by juvenile courts and juvenile justice staff in order to treat various disorders exhibited by youthful offenders. Alcohol and drug dependencies characterize large numbers of arrested youths (Kuntsche et al., 2007). Therefore, treatment programs are provided for these youths in order that they can learn about and deal with their alcohol or drug dependencies. Some youths need psychological counseling. Others require anger management training and courses to improve their interpersonal skills. In Idaho, for instance, the juvenile justice system was overhauled by the legislature in 1995. Added services included two detention centers staffed by juvenile probation officers; an alternative school; psychological assessments of juveniles; treatment provisions by private agencies for juvenile sex offenders and drug/alcohol abusers; and mentoring provided by volunteers who also served on diversion boards and youth court programs (Spencer, 2007). Juvenile mentoring in both secure and nonsecure settings is receiving greater recognition (Bouhours and Daly, 2007). The 1992 reauthorization of the Juvenile Justice and Delinquency Prevention Act of 1974 has recognized mentoring as significant for addressing problems of school attendance and delinquent activity, and a **Juvenile Mentoring Program (JUMP)** has been established in various jurisdictions.

One drawback to the treatment model generally is that great variations exist among community agencies regarding the availability of certain services as remedies for particular kinds of juvenile problems. Also, the intake officer may incorrectly diagnose one's illness and prescribe inappropriate therapy. Certain types of deep-seated personality maladjustments cannot be detected through superficial informal intake proceedings (Boyd and Myers, 2005). Simply participating in some community-based service or treatment program may be insufficient to relieve particular juveniles of the original or core causes of their delinquent behaviors. Some juveniles may have incarcerated parents, and the effects of such circumstances have been unevenly studied (Champion and Mays, 1991). Nevertheless, intake screenings may lead to community-based agency referrals that eventually may or may not be productive. In most jurisdictions, these are conditional sanctions that may be administered by intake officers without judicial approval or intervention.

Juvenile Mentoring Program (JUMP)
Federally funded program administered by the OJJDP; promotes bonding between an adult and a juvenile relating on a one-to-one basis over time; designed to improve school performance and decrease gang participation and delinquency.

The Noninterventionist Model

As the name implies, the **noninterventionist model** means the absence of any direct intervention with certain juveniles who have been taken into custody. The noninterventionist model is best understood when considered in the context of labeling theory (Lemert, 1967a). Labeling theory stresses that direct and frequent contact with the juvenile justice system will cause those having contact with it to eventually define themselves as delinquent. This definition will prompt self-definers to commit additional delinquent acts, since such behaviors are expected of those defined or stigmatized as such by others. Labeling theory advocates the removal of nonserious juveniles and status offenders from the juvenile justice system, or at least from the criminalizing influence and trappings of the juvenile courtroom.

Youth workers may testify in court about delinquency and its causes, or why some youths act in some ways.

The noninterventionist model is strategically applied only to those juveniles who the intake officer believes are unlikely to reoffend if given a second chance, or who are clearly status offenders without qualification (e.g., drug- or alcohol-dependent, chronic or persistent offenders) (Boyd and Myers, 2005). Intake officers who elect to act in a noninterventionist fashion with certain types of offenders may simply function as a possible resource person for juveniles and their parents. In cases involving runaways, truants, or curfew violators, it becomes a judgment call whether to refer youths and/or their parents to certain community services or counseling. The noninterventionist model would encourage no action by intake officers in nonserious or status offender cases, except under the most compelling circumstances. Since not all runaways are alike, certain runaways may be more in need of intervention than others, for instance. Again, the aim of nonintervention is to assist youths in avoiding stigma and unfavorable labeling that might arise if they were to be involved more deeply within the juvenile justice system. Even minor referrals by intake officers might prompt adverse reactions from offenders so that future offending behavior would be regarded as a way of getting even with the system.

The noninterventionist model is popular today, particularly because it fits well with the deinstitutionalization of status offenses (DSO) movement that has occurred in most jurisdictions. DSO was designed to divest juvenile courts of their jurisdiction over status offenders and remove status offenders from secure custodial institutions. Therefore, the primary intent of DSO was to minimize the potentially adverse influence of labeling that might occur through incarceration or if juveniles appear before juvenile court judges in a courtroom atmosphere. Also, an intended function of DSO was to reduce the docket load for many juvenile court judges by transferring their jurisdiction over status offenders to community agencies and services. The noninterventionist strategy is significant here because it advocates doing nothing about certain juvenile dispositions. The works of Lemert (1967a) and Schur (1973) are relevant for the noninterventionist perspective. These have described **judicious nonintervention** and **radical nonintervention** as terms that might be applied to noninterventionist do-nothing policy.

Radical nonintervention counters traditional thinking about delinquency, which is to assume that the juvenile justice system merely needs to be improved. Radical nonintervention argues that many of the current approaches to delinquency are not only fundamentally unsound, but they are also harmful to youth whenever they are applied. Radical nonintervention assumes the following:

1. The delinquent is not basically different from the nondelinquent.
2. Most types of youthful misconduct are found within all socioeconomic strata.
3. The primary target for delinquency policy should be neither the individual nor the local community setting, but rather the delinquency-defining processes themselves.

Radical nonintervention implies that policies that accommodate society to the widest possible diversity of behaviors and attitudes rather than forcing as many individuals as possible to adjust to supposedly common societal standards are the best policies. Subsidiary policies would favor collective action programs instead of those that single out specific individuals, and voluntary programs instead of compulsory ones. However, some critics of nonintervention suggest that such nonintervention is defeatist. Thus, rather than adopt a do-no-harm stance, juvenile justice system officials should be more concerned with doing good with their various approaches and programs.

The Due Process Model

The notion of due process is an integral feature of the criminal justice system. Due process is the basic constitutional right to a fair trial, to have an opportunity to be heard, to be aware of matters that are pending, to a presumption of innocence until

noninterventionist model Philosophy of juvenile delinquent treatment meaning the absence of any direct intervention with certain juveniles who have been taken into custody.

judicious nonintervention Use of minimal intervention in a youth's behavior and environment to effect changes in behavior.

radical nonintervention Similar to a "do-nothing" policy of delinquency nonintervention.

guilt is established beyond a reasonable doubt, to make an informed choice whether to acquiesce or contest, and to provide the reasons for such a choice before a judicial official. An important aspect of due process is that police officers must have probable cause to justify their arrests of suspected criminals. Therefore, one's constitutional rights are given considerable weight in comparison with any incriminating evidence obtained by police or others (Abatiello, 2005).

Intake officers who rely heavily upon the **due process model** in their dealings with juveniles are concerned that the juveniles' rights are fully protected at every stage of juvenile justice processing. Therefore, these officers would pay particular attention to how evidence was gathered by police against certain juveniles, and whether the juvenile's constitutional rights were protected and police officers advised the juvenile of the right to counsel at the time of the arrest and/or subsequent interrogation. The higher priority given to due process in recent years is a significant juvenile justice reform. An intake officer's emphasis of due process requirements in juvenile offender processing stems, in part, from several important U.S. Supreme Court decisions during the 1960s and 1970s, although professional associations and other interests have strongly advocated a concern for greater protection of juvenile rights.

Because of the interest certain intake officers might take in one's right to due process, some intake hearings may be more formally conducted than others. Legal variables, such as present offense, number of charges, and prior petitions, would be given greater weight in the context of due process. Many offender dispositions seem to be affected by nonlegal variables as well, including the youth's attitude, grades in school, race/ethnicity, and school status. While mildly related to dispositions, gender, race, and social class are only moderately related to offender dispositions.

Extralegal variables include race, ethnicity, gender, family solidarity, and SES. Studies of juvenile court dispositions in different jurisdictions reveal that minority offenders are dealt with more severely than white offenders. Minority youths may be more likely than white youths to be placed in custodial institutions or disposed to longer periods of probation. Besides being treated differently compared with white offenders, black juveniles have been subjected to greater detrimental labeling by the juvenile justice system over time. Differential treatment according to one's gender has also occurred in more than a few jurisdictions (Lemmon, Austin, and Feldberg, 2005). Ideally, juvenile justice decision-making should be free of the influence of these and other extralegal variables, according to the due process model.

The Just-Deserts/Justice Model

There is a strong rehabilitative orientation prevalent throughout the juvenile justice system, where the emphasis is upon serving the best interests of offending youths and the delivery of individualized services to them on the basis of their needs. *Parens patriae* explains much of the origin of this emphasis in the United States. However, the changing nature of juvenile offending during the last several decades and a gradual transformation of public sentiment toward more punitive measures have prompted certain juvenile justice reforms that are aimed at holding youths increasingly accountable for their actions and punishing them accordingly.

The **just-deserts/justice model** is punishment-centered and seemingly revenge-oriented, where the state's interest is to ensure that juveniles are punished in relation to the seriousness of the offenses they have committed. Further, those who commit identical offenses should be punished identically. This introduces the element of fairness into the punishment prescribed. The usefulness of this get-tough approach in disposing of various juvenile cases is controversial and has both proponents and opponents (Mears et al., 2007). It is significant that such an approach represents a major shift of emphasis away from juvenile offenders and their individualized needs and more toward the nature and seriousness of their actions. Just deserts as an orientation has frequently been

---

due process model

Treatment model based upon one's constitutional right to a fair trial, to have an opportunity to be heard, to be aware of matters that are pending, to a presumption of innocence until guilt has been established beyond a reasonable doubt, to make an informed choice whether to acquiesce or contest, and to provide the reasons for such a choice before a judicial officer.

---

just-deserts/ justice model

Stresses offender accountability as a means to punish youthful offenders; uses victim compensation plans, restitution, and community services as ways of making offenders pay for their offenses; philosophy which emphasizes punishment as a primary objective of sentencing, fixed sentences, abolition of parole, and an abandonment of the rehabilitative ideal; rehabilitation is functional to the extent that offenders join rehabilitative programs voluntarily.

combined with the justice model or orientation. The justice orientation is the idea that punishments should be gauged to fit the seriousness of offenses committed. Therefore, juveniles who commit more serious acts should receive harsher punishments, treatments, or sentences than those juveniles who commit less serious acts. Besides promoting punishment in proportion to offending behavior, the justice model includes certain victim considerations, such as provisions for restitution or victim compensation by offending juveniles.

The Crime Control Model

The **crime control model** theorizes that one of the best ways of controlling juvenile delinquency is to incapacitate juvenile offenders, either through some secure incarceration or through an intensive supervision program operated by a community-based agency or organization. Perhaps **consent decrees** may include provisions for the electronic monitoring of certain juvenile offenders in selected jurisdictions. Consent decrees are only for in-home placements and avoid the stigma of juvenile court appearances. They also contain conditions that must be fulfilled by the juvenile within a given time frame. These juveniles might be required to wear plastic bracelets or anklets that are devised to emit electronic signals and notify juvenile probation officers of an offender's whereabouts. Or juvenile offenders may be incarcerated in secure facilities for short- or long-term periods, depending upon the seriousness of their offenses. Figure 3.1 is a consent decree used by juvenile courts in various states Consent decrees must be signed by the juvenile, the juvenile's parents, the juvenile court prosecutor, the juvenile's attorney, if one has been retained, and a social worker. A juvenile court judge signs the consent decree. If consent decree provisions are violated, the consent decree is revoked and the case is reinstated. This reinstatement may require an appearance of the juvenile befire the juvenile court.

> **crime control model**
> Criminal justice program that emphasizes containment of dangerous offenders and societal protection; a way of controlling delinquency by incapacitating juvenile offenders through some secure detention or through intensive supervision programs operated by community-based agencies.

> **consent decrees**
> Formal agreements that involve children, their parents, and the juvenile court, where youths are placed under the court's supervision without an official finding of delinquency, with judicial approval.

The crime control perspective causes intake officers to move certain chronic, persistent, and/or dangerous juvenile offenders further into the juvenile justice system. If they believe certain juveniles pose serious risks to others or are considered dangerous, these intake officers might decide that juveniles should be held in secure confinement pending a subsequent detention hearing. If juveniles who are chronic or persistent offenders are incapacitated, they cannot reoffend. Treatment and rehabilitation are subordinate to simple control and incapacitation. Intake officers who favor the crime control view have few illusions that the system can change certain juvenile offenders. Rather, the best course of action for them is secure incarceration for lengthy periods, considering the availability of space in existing juvenile secure confinement facilities. In this way, they are directly prevented from reoffending, since they are totally incapacitated. The cost-effectiveness of such incarceration of the most chronic and persistent juvenile offenders in relation to the monies lost resulting from thefts, burglaries, robberies, and other property crimes is difficult to calculate. Incarceration is costly, and immense overcrowding in existing juvenile secure confinement facilities already plagues most jurisdictions.

An alternative to incarceration for juveniles is to focus on those most susceptible to being influenced by the potential for incarceration if they continue to reoffend. More than a few intervention programs have emphasized the adverse implications for juveniles, such as incarceration, if they continue their delinquent behavior. Stressed is the unpleasantness of prison settings. Programs, such as Scared Straight, are intended to scare some juveniles into becoming more law-abiding. For instance, selected juvenile delinquents are brought to a prison where they are confronted by several inmates. The inmates talk about what it is like to be locked up and subjected to abuse from other inmates. The intent of programs such as this is to frighten juveniles so much with what it might be like to be incarcerated that they will not be inclined to reoffend in the future.

Figure 3.1   A Consent Decree

Consent Decree

IN THE INTEREST OF: _____

Name

_____

Address

_____

City, State

The parties stipulate and agree that the court may impose a consent decree, thereby placing said child under court supervision, consistent with the following conditions:

1. Court shall locate juvenile in out-of-home placement from _____ to _____
2. Placement shall be either in child/juvenile's home or out-of-home placement
3. Child/juvenile shall not commit any offense resulting in referrals to intake or other law violations, including local, state, or federal laws.
4. Child/juvenile shall pay restitution (where required) of $_____ payable to:
   _____
5. Child/juvenile shall perform community service at court discretion for _____ hours, under supervision by designated court officers.
6. Child/juvenile shall undergo counseling at court direction to appropriate facilities at the court's discretion.
7. Other_____
   _____

Signed by:

_____
Child/juvenile   Date

_____
Parent/guardian   Date

_____
Parent/guardian   Date

Approved by:

_____
Court attorney   Date

_____
Judge   Date

Source: Author

Delinquency Prevention Programs and Community Interventions

Since the 1980s, much has been done to establish delinquency prevention programs in various communities and to involve both citizens and the police in joint efforts to combat juvenile crime (Schaffner, 2005). Because of the great diversity of offending among juveniles, it has been necessary to devise specific types of programs to target certain juvenile offender populations. For instance, a significant amount of youth violence occurs in school settings. As a result, considerable resources have been allocated to address the problem of school violence and reduce its incidence (Schexnayder, 2008). At the same time that school violence is targeted for reduction, certain programs seek to heighten the accountability of offenders who are most prominently involved in school violence. Programs that implement accountability principles often include school-based probation that provides skills training for high-risk youths (Schexnayder, 2008).

Some programs are aimed at youthful sex offenders (van Wijk et al., 2007). Sex offender services and counseling are provided in various communities to assist those youths with these specific problems (Bouhours and Daly, 2007). Youths may be targeted who engage in hate crimes. Such programs attempt to educate youths about the risks of gang membership as well as some of the personal and social reasons youths seek out gangs initially (Taylor et al., 2008). Even youths who are presently incarcerated in secure facilities are considered potential subjects for intervention programs. Therefore, various forms of assistance and services are made available to youthful inmates in juvenile industrial schools for their rehabilitation and reintegration.

Effective intervention programs designed to prevent delinquent conduct should be started early in a youth's life, probably through school programs (Crawley et al., 2005). School systems are logical conduits through which intervention programs can be channeled. A wide range of ages is targeted by various intervention programs. Some of these programs are described following. In each case, various models for dealing with delinquent offenders are associated with these programs and activities, and a brief reference to them will be given to establish meaningful links.

The Support Our Students Program

The **Support Our Students (SOS) program** is based loosely on the crime control model and targets school-age children for after-school programs designed to provide them with extra learning opportunities. The SOS program is established to operate during the afternoon hours, when most of the juvenile delinquency in the community occurs. SOS is important for at least three reasons: (1) too many children have little or no adult supervision after school; (2) unsupervised children are more likely to become involved in criminal activities and other related behaviors; and (3) after-school programs have been shown to prevent many of the consequences of leaving children unsupervised.

> **Support Our Students (SOS) program** After-school intervention providing learning opportunities to children in high-crime areas.

SOS has six important goals. These are to: (1) reduce the number of students who are unsupervised after school, otherwise known as latch-key children; (2) improve the academic performance of students participating in the program; (3) meet the physical, intellectual, emotional, and social needs of students participating in the program and improve their attitudes and behavior; (4) improve coordination of existing resources and enhance collaboration so as to provide services to school-age children effectively and efficiently; (5) reduce juvenile crime in local communities served by the program; and (6) recruit community volunteers to provide positive adult role models for school-age children and to help supervise their after-school activities (North Carolina Department of Juvenile Justice and Delinquency Prevention, 2008).

CASASTART Programs

CASASTART programs target high-risk youths, aged 11–13, who are exposed to drugs and criminal activity. They are neighborhood-based, school-centered programs that work with youth, their families, and their communities. Runaways and curfew violators may be referred to CASASTART by intake officers who believe this type of intervention will interrupt the cycle of social stigmatization that occurs if youths interact closely with their delinquency peers at school and elsewhere. To some extent, at least, CASA-START is driven by the noninterventionist model.

Since their inception, CASASTART programs have been established in numerous communities throughout the United States. In McKeesport, Pennsylvania, for instance, a CASASTART program has been operating for several years. Its goals are to prevent and reduce drug and alcohol use; promote good school attendance and academic performance, while lowering the incidence of disruptive behavior at school; reduce drug-related crime and violence; and reduce delinquent behavior. The McKeesport program achieves these goals on three levels: (1) building resiliency in children; (2) strengthening families; and (3) making neighborhoods safer for children and their families (McKeesport CASASTART, 2008). By reaching children at the early ages of 11–13, it is believed that many youths can be diverted away from the negative influence of their delinquent peers.

Eight core components of CASASTART include: (1) community-enhanced policing/enhanced enforcement; (2) case management (13–18 families); (3) criminal/juvenile justice intervention; (4) family services, including parent programs, counseling, and organized parent–child activities; (5) after-school and summer activities for personal and social development, improving self-esteem, and studying one's cultural heritage; (6) education services, offering tutoring as well as work preparation opportunities; (7) mentoring through one-on-one relationships; and (8) incentives, both monetary and nonmonetary. CASASTART has reported lower rates of drug use among participants as well as more prosocial behavior (McKeesport CASASTART, 2008).

Project Safe Neighborhoods and Operation TIDE

Project Safe Neighborhoods is a national initiative implemented to reduce violence attributable to firearms. It is also aimed at reducing gun violence among juveniles by deterring juveniles from gaining access to or possessing firearms. Under this initiative, persons banned from possessing firearms include: (1) convicted felons; (2) fugitives from justice; (3) illegal immigrants in the U.S.; (4) mental defectives or persons committed at any time to a mental institution; (5) persons who have given up their U.S. citizenship; (6) persons dishonorably discharged from the armed forces; (7) anyone under court order to refrain from stalking, harassing, or threatening an intimate partner or other person; and (8) anyone convicted of a misdemeanor crime involving violence or a threat with a deadly weapon (Crawford, 2007).

Partnerships are established among various agencies of the federal government and local law enforcement agencies, schools, and other organizations. Intelligence gathering includes crime mapping, identifying hot spots which are high-crime areas of communities, tracing, and ballistics technology. Local and regional training occurs relating to the proper use of firearms for interested persons. A deterrence message is delivered by different means, in order to deter local youths from possessing firearms. This initiative is aimed at gangs, who most frequently use firearms in their illegal activities. Results thus far suggest that this initiative is having an impact on reducing the rate of firearm use among teens and particularly gangs. The rehabilitation model and its principal components have been used as inputs for driving safe neighborhood initiatives (Khalili, 2008).

Flint, Michigan, is a part of the "Three Cities Initiative" sponsored by the U.S. Department of Justice's Project Safe Neighborhoods. The other two cities in Michigan targeted for this program are Saginaw and Jackson. One integral component of Project Safe Neighborhoods is a program called **Operation TIDE**. "TIDE" is an acronym for Tactical Intelligence Driven Enforcement. It is a task force comprised of federal, state, and local law enforcement agencies and officers devoted to reducing and/or eliminating gun and gang violence. Operation TIDE is effective because it prosecutes youthful offenders in accordance with stiff federal gun laws and sentences (Free Press, 2007).

Such interventions are only a few of many similar types of programs operating throughout the United States involving police and interested citizens in proactive and positive roles, where they are taking an active interest in preventing delinquent conduct through interacting closely with youths. These programs will not make juvenile offenders desist from delinquency, but many of them will heighten juvenile awareness of positive influences in their lives. Another positive effect of such programs is to assist police officers in understanding juveniles and their motives (Free Press, 2007).

> **Operation TIDE**
> A composite of federal, state, and local law enforcement officers dedicated to reducing violence attributable to guns and gangs.

Summary

Theories about crime and delinquency have been classified into several broad areas. These include classical and biological theories, psychological theories, and sociological theories. Classical theories assume that persons have free will to choose between good and evil, and that they weigh the advantages and disadvantages of committing crime to achieve their various goals. Biological theories are rooted in the belief that a primary cause of delinquency and crime is one's biological make-up and genetic structure. Determinism is often used as an explanation for why delinquency and criminal acts are committed. Determinism rejects free will and rational choice in explaining whether one conforms to or deviates from society's rules.

Biological theories include biological determinism, *XYY* theory, and sociobiology. Psychological theories stress the importance of cognitive development in acquiring criminal and delinquent characteristics. Psychoanalytic theory stresses one's early childhood experiences as crucial to determining one's adult behaviors. Another psychological theory is social learning theory. This is the idea that different levels of learning occur at different stages in one's maturational development. Sociological theories stress social environmental factors as they impact on one's behavior to produce criminal or delinquent conduct.

The subculture theory of delinquency has been examined. This theory suggests that a delinquent subculture exists within the larger culture, complete with its own norms and status structure. Several offshoots of this theory are strain theory, anomie theory, and labeling theory. Labeling theory is one of the more influential sociological theories to account for delinquent conduct. Labeling stresses the definitions people have of delinquent acts and how they come to define themselves as delinquent. Bonding or social control theory is also popular. It suggests that youths who bond successfully with school authorities and teachers, religious leaders, and family members will be less likely to engage in delinquent activities. Several other sociological theories have been posited, including containment theory, neutralization theory, differential association theory, and cultural transmission theory. Each of these theories focus upon social forces that impact one's decision-making and individual choices and social interactions at critical points in one's development.

Evaluating theories of delinquency is often based on the predictive utility of particular theoretical schemes and the frequency with which any particular theory is used in prevention programs or delinquency intervention activities. However, each explanation of delinquency has variable importance according to how much recidivism is reduced resulting from a theory's application. Many youths simply mature or grow out of their delinquency behavior. Thus, evaluations of theories are difficult to make.

Several models for dealing with juvenile offenders have been identified. These models include rehabilitation, the treatment or medical model, the noninterventionist model, the due process model, the just-deserts or justice model, and the crime control model. Each of these models reflects one's professional orientation toward delinquents as well as the particular strategies one adopts for helping them. The due process and just-deserts/justice models emphasize one's legal rights and equal protection under the law. There is a strong legal emphasis underlying such approaches. The crime control model stresses close supervision of those offenders most likely to reoffend, or incarceration in a secure facility. This is not an especially popular strategy, since alternatives to incarceration are believed to be more conducive to one's rehabilitation and eventual societal reintegration.

Several delinquency prevention programs were described. These are often community interventions intended to bring about changes in one's life. Targeted for interventions are at-risk youths, or those who require more personalized guidance and supervision. Each year new interventions are proposed and some of the older intervention programs are abandoned or used less frequently. Usually, a particular theory or combination of theories of delinquency underlie these intervention programs to one degree or another.

Key Terms

anomie, 91
anomie theory, 91
atavism, 84
biological determinism, 83
bonding theory, 96
CASASTART programs, 110
Cesare Lombroso, 83
classical school, 82
classical theory, 82
concentric zone hypothesis, 89
conformity, 92
consent decrees, 107
containment theory, 98
crime control model, 107
cultural transmission theory, 99
determinism, 82
differential association theory, 99
differential reinforcement theory, 100
drift theory, 99
due process model, 106
ectomorphs, 84
endomorphs, 84
hedonism, 82
innovation, 92
interstitial area, 88
judicious nonintervention, 105
just-deserts/justice model, 106
Juvenile Mentoring Program (JUMP), 104
labeling, 93

labeling theory, 93
looking-glass self, 100
medical model, 103
mesomorphs, 84
mode of adaptation, 92
neutralization theory, 99
noninterventionist model, 105
Operation TIDE, 111
positive school of criminology, 84
positivism, 84
primary deviation, 96
Project Safe Neighborhoods, 110
psychoanalytic theory, 86
psychological theories, 86
radical nonintervention, 105
rebellion, 93
rehabilitation model, 103
retreatism, 93
ritualism, 93
secondary deviation, 96
social control theory, 96
social learning theory, 87
sociobiology, 85
strain theory, 97
subculture of delinquency, 90
Support Our Students (SOS) program, 109
treatment model, 103
XYY theory, 85
zone of transition, 88

Questions for Review

1. What is theory? What are some important components of theory? What are theories designed to do? Explain and discuss.

2. What is meant by biological determinism? How does biological determinism conflict with the classical school of criminology? Which theories are associated with determinism?

3. What are the major components of psychoanalytic theory? Describe the importance of one's formative years to psychoanalytic theory. In what respect is one's childhood regarded as one's "formative years?"

4. How does social learning theory differ from psychoanalytic theory?

5. How is cultural transmission theory related to the concentric zone hypothesis?

6. What is the role of SES in juvenile delinquency? Who are at-risk youths? What are their characteristics?

7. What is meant by a delinquent subculture? How can we use information about a delinquent subculture to change delinquent behaviors in various communities?

8. What are some similarities and differences between Merton's theory of anomie and strain theory? In the theory of anomie, what mode of adaptation is most likely to be invoked by juvenile delinquents? What other modes of adaptation have been identified?

9. How are different theories of delinquent conduct evaluated? Which types of evaluation seem most useful?

10. What are the four delinquency intervention programs? What is their relative successfulness in reducing delinquency?

Internet Connections

National Center for Missing and Exploited Children
http://www.missingkids.com

National Center for Youth Law
http://www.youthlaw.org/

National Center on Education, Disability, and Juvenile Justice
http://www.edjj.org/

National Clearinghouse on Child Abuse
http://www.happinessonline.org/LoveAndHelpChildren/p7.htm

Open Society Institute
http://www.soros.org/crime/

Youth Gangs in the Schools
http://ncjrs.org/html/ojjdp/jjbul2000_8_2/contents.html

chapter 4

The Legal Rights of Juveniles

Chapter outline

chapter objectives

As the result of reading this chapter, you will accomplish the following objectives:

1. Understand the historical context within which juvenile rights were gradually acquired.
2. Learn about the hands-off doctrine as it once applied to juvenile cases.
3. Understand critical events in the emergence of juvenile rights.
4. Learn about key landmark cases advancing constitutional rights for juveniles charged with crimes.
5. Distinguish between criminal courts and juvenile courts in terms of the rights of offenders processed by each.
6. Understand the debate over whether the death penalty shall be applied to selected juvenile offenders who commit capital murder, including the pros and cons of this process.
7. Learn about several important death penalty cases involving juveniles.
8. Learn about court unification and some of the reasons for its implementation.

 ## Case Study

It was another gang fight at a fast-food restaurant in San Jose, California. A Jack-in-the-Box restaurant was the scene of two teen deaths in January 2004. The victims were Diego Gutierrez and Miguel Romero, both 17 and gang members. A third youth was wounded in the gunfire. The assailants, James Ortega, 14, Malik Alayube, 18, and a 14-year-old boy burst into the restaurant and flashed a gang hand sign at the rival gang members, and Ortega shot all three youths in the back several times. Ortega was charged as an adult under California law that mandates prosecution of those 14 or older as adult offenders. On February 23, 2007, Ortega was sentenced to 36 years to life in prison for the murders. He will be eligible for parole when he is 50. Alayube pleaded guilty to his role in the murders and received a sentence of 20 years to life. [Source: Adapted from the *San Francisco Chronicle* and John Cote, "Murderer at 14 Sentenced to 36 Years to Life," February 23, 2007.]

 ## Case Study

It happened in St. Louis, Missouri, on July 5, 2007. Alexus Purtty, 13, was in front of her home as a boy walked by at 10:30 P.M. Purtty was frightened of the boy, who was suspected of burglarizing her home on a previous evening. Some shouting occurred, according to neighbors, and then a scuffle between the boy and Purtty occurred. The boy grabbed a knife and stabbed Purtty in the chest. The girl died at the hospital shortly thereafter. The boy was arrested and charged with second-degree murder. On September 18, 2007, the boy, just having turned 13, was found guilty and committed to the Missouri Division of Youth Services until he turned 18. According to officials, the boy had been living with his elderly father after being placed in foster care for 3 years. Allegedly, the boy's mother had abused and neglected him for several years. He had no prior criminal history. [Source: Adapted from Heather Ratcliffe and the *St. Louis Dispatch*, "Judge Finds Boy, 13, Guilty of Second-Degree Murder," September 19, 2007.]

Introduction

One of the most controversial issues in the United States today is how to confront and deal with juvenile crime, especially violent crime. Increasingly, the juvenile justice system must decide how to deal with murderers such as James Ortega in San Jose and the 13-year-old killer in St. Louis. Decisions about youth violence such as these incidents depict are not easy to make. No easy answers can be given for why such violence occurs or how it can be prevented. But the juvenile justice system must deal with these and other violent crimes on a daily basis.

How should we judge the perpetrators in these two scenarios? How should youths, ranging in age from 14 to 17, be processed and treated when they have committed murder, rape, aggravated assault, and other serious offenses? Can they be rehabilitated and should states attempt to rehabilitate them? Do they have a right to be rehabilitated? When juveniles kill, especially in a deliberate, cold, calculating fashion, what sort of punishments should the states impose?

This chapter explores the legal rights of juveniles. The chapter opens with a brief examination of a historical account of the emerging rights of juveniles in the United States. Since Colonial times and up until the mid-1960s, juveniles had no universally applicable legal entitlements. Subsequently, different states adopted a variety of policies for juveniles and how they ought to be treated. Illinois established the first juvenile court in 1899. For the next 67 years, most juvenile courts functioned much like social welfare agencies rather than legal apparatuses. Juveniles enjoyed few if any legal rights commensurate with those of adults.

The next section examines several landmark juvenile cases decided by the U.S. Supreme Court. The first three cases, *Kent v. United States* (1966), *In re Gault* (1967), and *In re Winship* (1970), are considered the "big three" legal cases that opened the floodgates of juvenile litigation before the U.S. Supreme Court. Once the *Kent* case had been decided in 1966, it became much easier for the U.S. Supreme Court to impose its vast precedent-setting powers on juvenile courts in all jurisdictions. Other important cases soon followed, including *McKeiver v. Pennsylvania* (1971), *Breed v. Jones* (1975), and *Schall v. Martin* (1984), which granted various constitutional rights to juveniles. These cases will be presented and discussed.

Explored next are the various implications of granting juveniles greater constitutional rights. Juvenile courts in all jurisdictions have moved away from traditional approaches to juvenile offending and punishments and toward due process commensurate with adult offenders. Today the presence of attorneys in juvenile courts is more the rule rather than the exception. Although the U.S. Supreme Court refrained from granting jury trials to juveniles as a matter of right, several states presently grant jury trials to juvenile offenders. These and other issues will be examined as the juvenile justice process has become increasingly legalistic and bureaucratized.

The death penalty for juveniles is also examined. The death penalty is inherently controversial. The history of the death penalty applied to juveniles is briefly explored. Several important cases decided by the U.S. Supreme Court are described, together with their implications, for whether juveniles are executed for capital offenses. In 2005, the U.S. Supreme Court ruled that the application of the death penalty was unconstitutional for any youth who committed a capital offense under the age of 18. This and other important cases will be described. A listing of key arguments both for and against the death penalty will be featured.

The chapter concludes with an examination of court unification. Juvenile court organization and operations have changed significantly such that some experts believe the two court systems should be merged. This is court unification and there is presently mixed support for it. The implications of court unification for the future of juvenile courts and the juvenile justice system will be explored.

Original Juvenile Court Jurisdiction: *Parens Patriae*

Until the mid-1960s, juvenile courts had considerable latitude in regulating the affairs of minors. This freedom to act in a child's behalf was rooted in the largely unchallenged doctrine of *parens patriae*. Whenever juveniles were apprehended by police officers for alleged crimes, they were eventually turned over to juvenile authorities or taken to a juvenile hall for further processing. They were not advised of their right to an attorney, to have an attorney present during any interrogation, or to remain silent. They could be questioned by police at length, without parental notification or legal contact. In short, they had little, if any, protection against adult constitutional rights violations on the part of law enforcement officers and others. They had no access to due process because of their status or standing as juveniles (Rehling, 2005).

When juveniles appeared before juvenile court judges in the early years of juvenile courts, youths almost never had the opportunity to rebut evidence presented against them or to test the reliability of witnesses through cross-examination. This was rationalized at the time by asserting that juveniles did not understand the law and had to have it interpreted for them by others, principally juvenile court judges. Subsequent investigations of the knowledge youths have of their rights seems to confirm this assertion. These early adjudicatory proceedings were very informal. They were also conducted without defense counsel being present to advise their youthful clients. In one-sided affairs, facts were alleged by various accusers, often persons such as probation officers or police officers, and youthful defendants were not permitted to give testimony in their own behalf or cross-examine those giving testimony.

Prosecutors were seldom present in juvenile proceedings since they were largely nonadversarial, and juvenile court judges handled most cases informally, independently, and subjectively, depending upon the youth's needs and the seriousness of the offense. If judges decided that secure confinement would best serve the interests of justice and the welfare of the juvenile, then the youth would be placed in a secure confinement facility (juvenile prison) for an indeterminate period. These decisions were seldom questioned or challenged. If they were challenged, higher courts would dismiss these challenges as frivolous or without merit.

The "Hands-Off" Doctrine

A major reason for the silent acceptance of juvenile court judges' decisions was that the U.S. Supreme Court had repeatedly demonstrated its reluctance to intervene in juvenile matters or question decisions made by juvenile court judges. In the case of *In re Gault* (1967), Justice Stewart typified the traditional orientation of former Supreme Courts by declaring:

hands-off doctrine
Policy practiced by the federal courts, where official court policy was not to intervene in matters relating to adult corrections; belief that correctional superintendents and wardens and departments of corrections are in best position to make decisions about welfare of inmates; applied to juvenile corrections and juvenile courts similarly.

> The Court today uses an obscure Arizona case as a vehicle to impose upon thousands of juvenile courts throughout the Nation restrictions that the Constitution made applicable to adversary criminal trials. I believe the Court's decision is *wholly unsound* [emphasis mine] as a matter of constitutional law, and sadly unwise as a matter of judicial policy . . . The inflexible restrictions that the Constitution so wisely made applicable to adversary criminal trials have no inevitable place in the proceedings of those public social agencies known as juvenile or family courts (387 U.S. at 78–79).

The **hands-off doctrine** of the U.S. Supreme Court toward juvenile court matters was similar to their hands-off policy toward corrections (Gomez and Ganuza, 2002). In the case of *Ruffin v. Commonwealth* (1871), a Virginia judge declared that "prisoners have no more rights than slaves." Thus, during the next 70 years, prisoners were used as guinea pigs in various biological and chemical experiments, particularly in the testing of gases used on the front lines in Europe during World War I. Such tests of chemical agents on prisoners were conducted at the Michigan State Prison at Jackson. Some prisons mandated inmate sterilization, because it was believed that criminal behavior was hereditary. No committees for the protection of human subjects existed to protest these inmate treatments. Inmates had absolutely no rights, including mail privacy, visitation, or other privileges, other than those rights dispensed or withheld by prison authorities (Myers, 1973).

The U.S. Supreme Court commenced to change this state of affairs toward corrections in 1941 in the case of *Ex parte Hull* (1941). This case involved attempts by prisoners to petition the courts to hear various grievances or complaints. Prison superintendents and staff would routinely trash these petitions, contending that they were improperly prepared and hence, legally unacceptable. In the *Hull* decision, the court held that no state or its officers could abridge inmates of their right to access the federal or state courts through their petitions. Once the *Hull* decision had been made, there was a proliferation of inmate rights cases in subsequent years, known as a **litigation explosion**. Two decades later, a similar litigation explosion would occur. This time the subject matter would be juvenile rights (Anderson and Dyson, 2001).

In many respects, juveniles were treated like adult inmates in prisons. Youths had no legal standing and virtually no rights other than those extended by the courts. The right to a trial by jury, a basic right provided any defendant who might be incarcerated for six months or more by a criminal court conviction, did not exist for juveniles unless juvenile court judges permitted such trials. Most juvenile court judges abhor jury trials for their juveniles and refuse to permit them. Even today, juveniles do not have an absolute right to a trial by jury, with few exceptions through state statutes. Thus, juveniles may be deprived of their freedom for many years on the basis of a personal judicial decision.

Because of the informality of juvenile proceedings in most jurisdictions, there were frequent and obvious abuses of judicial discretion. These abuses occurred because of the absence of consistent guidelines whereby cases could be adjudicated. Juvenile probation officers might casually recommend to judges that particular juveniles "ought to do a few months" in an industrial school or other secure confinement facility, and the judge might be persuaded to adjudicate these cases accordingly.

However, several forces were at work simultaneously during the 1950s and 1960s that would eventually have the conjoint consequence of making juvenile courts more accountable for specific adjudications of youthful offenders. One of these forces was increased parental and general public recognition of and concern for the liberal license taken by juvenile courts in administering the affairs of juveniles. The abuse of judicial discretion was becoming increasingly apparent. Additionally, there was a growing disenchantment with and apathy for the rehabilitation ideal, although this disenchantment was not directed solely at juvenile courts (LaMade, 2008; Sungi, 2008).

The juvenile court as originally envisioned by Progressives was procedurally informal, characterized by individualized, offender-oriented dispositional practices. However, the contemporary juvenile court departs markedly from this Progressive ideal. Today, juvenile courts are increasingly like criminal courts, featuring an adversarial system and greater procedural formality. This formality effectively inhibits any individualized treatment these courts might contemplate, and it has increased the perfunctory nature of sentencing juveniles adjudicated as delinquent.

The transformation of juvenile courts into more formal proceedings as part of the national trend toward bureaucratization, and as an institutional compromise between law and social welfare, has occurred. Bureaucracy stresses a fixed hierarchy of authority, task specialization, individualized spheres of competence, impersonal social relationships between organizational actors, and impartial enforcement of abstract rules. Thus, in the context of bureaucracy, decision making is routinized rather than arbitrary. Personalities and social characteristics are irrelevant.

litigation explosion
Rapid escalation of case filings before appellate courts, often based upon a landmark case extending rights to particular segments of the population, such as jail or prison inmates or juveniles.

Applied to juvenile court proceedings, juvenile court decision making would most likely be a function of the nature and seriousness of offenses committed and the factual delinquent history of juvenile defendants. Emotional considerations in bureaucratic structures are nonexistent. The bureaucratic approach would be that juveniles should be held to a high standard of accountability for their actions. Furthermore, an individualized, treatment-oriented sanctioning system would be inconsistent with bureaucracy and would violate its general principles of impartiality. This type of system for juvenile justice seems consistent with the sentiments of a large portion of U.S. citizens and their belief that juvenile courts should get tough with juvenile offenders. Despite this due process and bureaucratic emphasis, juvenile courts have continued to retain many of their seemingly haphazard characteristics. Sound policies have been established, but their implementation has remained inconsistent and problematic for many juvenile courts (Whitehead, 2008).

A major change from the *parens patriae* state-based interests to a due process juvenile justice model means that decision making about youthful offenders is increasingly rationalized, and the principle of just-deserts is fundamental. This means that less discretionary authority will be manifested by juvenile court judges, as they decide each case more on the basis of offense seriousness rather than according to individual factors or circumstances, and prescribe punishments (LaMade, 2008). Table 4.1 provides a general chronology of events relating to juvenile rights during the last 200 years.

During the mid-1960s and through the 1980s, significant achievements were made in the area of juvenile rights. Although the *parens patriae* philosophy continues to influence juvenile proceedings, the U.S. Supreme Court has vested youths with certain constitutional rights. These rights do not encompass all of the rights extended to adults who are charged with crimes. But those rights conveyed to juveniles thus far have had far-reaching implications for how juveniles are processed. The general result of these U.S. Supreme Court decisions has been to bring the juvenile court system under constitutional control. Several landmark cases involving juvenile rights will be described in the following section.

Landmark Cases in Juvenile Justice

Several significant changes have been made in the juvenile justice system and how youths are processed in recent decades. In this section, we will examine several important rights bestowed upon juveniles by the U.S. Supreme Court during the period 1960–1990. Describing these rights will make clear those rights juveniles did not have until the landmark cases associated with them were decided. Then, a comparison will be made of juvenile rights and those rights enjoyed by adults charged with crimes in criminal courts. Despite sweeping juvenile reforms and major legal gains, there are still several important differences between the rights of juveniles and adults when both are charged with crimes (Wilkerson, 2005).

Currently, juvenile courts are largely punishment-centered, with the justice/just-deserts model influencing court decision making. Interests of youths are secondary, while community interests are seemingly served by juvenile court actions. Juveniles are being given greater responsibility for their actions, and they are increasingly expected to be held accountable for their wrongdoing (Feld, 2007). At the same time, some evidence suggests that youths have a poor understanding of their legal rights and are thus disadvantaged by a more legalistic juvenile justice system (Billings et al., 2007).

Each of the cases presented following represents attempts by juveniles to secure rights ordinarily extended to adults. Given these cases, juveniles have fared well with the U.S. Supreme Court in past years. While juveniles still do not enjoy the full range of rights extended to adult offenders who are tried in criminal courts, juveniles have acquired due process privileges that were not available to them prior to the 1960s. The first three cases presented, *Kent v. United States, In re Gault,* and *In re Winship,* comprise

Table 4.1

Chronological Summary of Major Events in Juvenile Justice

Year	Event
1791	Bill of Rights passed by U.S. Congress
1825	New York House of Refuge established
1828	Boston House of Refuge founded
1839	*Ex parte Crouse*, established right of juvenile court intervention in parent-child matters
1841	John Augustus initiates probation in Boston
1847	State institutions for juveniles opened in Boston and New York
1851	First adoption act in U.S. passed in Massachusetts
1853	New York Children's Aid Society established
1853	New York Juvenile Asylum created by Children's Aid Society
1855	Death penalty imposed on 10-year-old, James Arcene, in Arkansas for robbery and murder; earliest juvenile execution was Thomas Graunger, 16-year-old, for sodomizing a cow in 1642
1866	Massachusetts statute passed giving juvenile court power to intervene and take custody of juveniles under age 16 whose parents are unfit
1868	Fourteenth Amendment passed by U.S. Congress, establishing right to due process and equal protection under the law
1870	*People ex rel. O'Connell v. Turner* case holding that reform school commitments of youths could not be made on the basis of simple misfortune or vagrancy; limited institutionalization of youths to those who committed crimes; denied confinement of youths who were not afforded legal due process
1874–1875	Massachusetts established first Children's Tribunal to deal with youthful offenders
1881	Michigan commences child protection with the Michigan Public Acts of 1881
1884	*Reynolds v. Howe* case gives state authority to place neglected children in institutions
1886	First child neglect case is heard in Massachusetts
1889	Indiana established children's guardians to have jurisdiction over neglected and dependent children
1890	Children's Aid Society of Pennsylvania, foster home for juvenile delinquents used as an alternative to reform schools, is established
1891	Minnesota Supreme Court establishes doctrine of parental immunity
1897	*Ex parte Becknell* case reverses disposition of juvenile who has not been given a fair trial
1899	Hull House established in Chicago by Jane Addams to assist unsupervised children of immigrant parents
1899	Compulsory School Act, Colorado; statutory regulation of truants
1899	Illinois Act to Regulate the Treatment and Control of Dependent, Neglected, and Delinquent Children; first juvenile court established in United States
1900	Case law begins to deal with children's protective statutes
1901	Juvenile court established in Denver, Colorado
1906	Massachusetts passes act providing for treatment of children not as criminals but as children in need of guidance and aid
1907	Separate juvenile court with original jurisdiction in juvenile matters established in Denver, Colorado
1908	*Ex parte Sharpe* defines more clearly power of juvenile court to include *parens patriae*
1910	Compulsory school acts passed in different state jurisdictions
1912	Creation of U.S. Children's Bureau, charged with compiling statistical information about juvenile offenders; existed from 1912 to 1940
1918	Chicago slums studied by Shaw and McKay; delinquency related to urban environment and transitional neighborhoods
1924	Federal Probation Act passed
1930	Children's Charter
1938	Federal Juvenile Court Act passed
1954	*Brown v. Board of Education* school desegregation decision
1959	Standard Family Court Act of National Council on Crime and Delinquency establishes that juvenile hearings are to be informally conducted

Table 4.1   (Cont.)

Chronological Summary of Major Events in Juvenile Justice

Year	Event
1966	*Kent v. United States* case established juvenile's right to a hearing before transfer to criminal court, right to assistance of counsel during police interrogations, right to reports and records relating to transfer decision, and right to reasons given by the judge for the transfer
1967	*In re Gault* case established juvenile's right to an attorney, right to notice of charges, right to confront and cross-examine witnesses, and right against self-incrimination
1968	*Ginsberg v. New York* establishes that it is unlawful to sell pornography to a minor
1969	*Tinker v. Des Moines Independent Community School District* establishes that the First Amendment applies to juveniles and protects their constitutional right to free speech
1970	*In re Winship* case established juvenile's right to criminal court standard of "beyond a reasonable doubt" where loss of freedom is a possible penalty
1971	*McKeiver v. Pennsylvania* case established that juvenile's right to a trial by jury is not absolute
1971	Twenty-sixth Amendment to Constitution is passed granting the right to vote to 18-year-olds
1972	*Wisconsin v. Yoder* case gives parents the right to impose their religion on their children
1972	Marvin Wolfgang publishes *Delinquency in a Birth Cohort*
1973	*In re Snyder* gives minors the right to bring legal proceedings against their parents
1973	*San Antonio Independent School District v. Rodriguez* establishes that differences in education based on wealth are not necessarily discriminatory
1974	Juvenile Justice and Delinquency Prevention Act, intended to deinstitutionalize status offenders, separate delinquents from status offenders generally, and divest juvenile court judges of their jurisdiction over status offenders
1974	Office of Juvenile Justice and Delinquency Prevention, instrumental in promoting deinstitutionalization of status offenders
1974	Federal Child Abuse Prevention Act
1974	Buckley Amendment to Education Act of 1974, the Family Education Rights and Privacy Act; students have right to see their own files with parental consent
1975	*Goss v. Lopez* case establishes that a student facing school suspension has right to due process, prior notice, and an open hearing
1975	*Breed v. Jones* case established that double jeopardy exists if juvenile is adjudicated as delinquent in juvenile court on a given charge and tried for same offense later in criminal court; prohibits double jeopardy
1977	Report of the Committee on the Judiciary, especially concerning the rights of the unborn and the right of 18-year-olds to vote
1977	Juvenile Justice Amendment of 1977
1977	*Ingraham v. Wright* case establishes that corporal punishment is permissible in public schools and is not a violation of the Eighth Amendment
1977	American Bar Association, Standards on Juvenile Justice
1977	Washington State amends its sentencing policies
1979	*Fare v. Michael C.* case established "totality of circumstances" standard for evaluating propriety of custodial interrogations of juveniles by police without parents or attorneys present; defines *Miranda* rights of minors
1980	National concern over child abuse and neglect
1982	*Eddings v. Oklahoma* case established that death penalty applied to juveniles is not cruel and unusual punishment per se
1982	Efforts to decarcerate status offenders escalate
1984	*Schall v. Martin* case established the constitutionality of the preventive detention of juveniles
1985	*New Jersey v. T.L.O.* case established lesser standard of search and seizure on school property; searches and seizures permissible without probable cause or warrant
1985	Wilson and Herrnstein publish *Crime and Human Nature*, focusing attention on the biological causes of delinquency
1985	United Nations General Assembly adopts "Standard Minimum Rules for the Administration of Juvenile Justice"
1986	*Woods v. Clusen* case established right of juveniles against aggressive police interrogation tactics by failing to observe juvenile's constitutional rights and provide for fundamental fairness

Table 4.1   (Cont.)

Chronological Summary of Major Events in Juvenile Justice

Year	Event
1986	Juvenile offenders waived to criminal court are executed, focusing attention on the death penalty administered to children
1987	Conservative trends result in 10,000 juvenile waivers to criminal courts
1988	Re-emergence of nationwide gang problem
1988	*Thompson v. Oklahoma* case established that death penalty applied to juveniles convicted of murder who were under age 16 at time of murder is cruel and unusual punishment
1989	*Stanford v. Kentucky* and *Wilkins v. Missouri* cases established that the death penalty is not cruel and unusual punishment applied to juveniles convicted of murder who were ages 16 or 17 at the time the murder was committed
1990	*Maryland v. Craig* allows child abuse victims to testify on closed-circuit television in courts
1991	Juvenile violence rate hits all-time high of 430 acts per 100,000 adolescents
1995	Reported child abuse cases exceed three million
1996	Michigan parents criminally convicted for failing to supervise delinquent son
1997	Juvenile crime rates begin to remain stable in U.S
1998	School shooting in Jonesboro, Arkansas leaves five killed, raises questions about children and access to firearms
1999	School shoootings on rise; Littleton, Colorado high school scene of mass murders of 15 persons by two students who commit suicide; public policies implemented about safeguarding school systems from similar incidents in future
2000	*Santa Fe Independent School District v. Jane Doe* case bans student-led prayer at sporting events, further defining separation of church and state in school settings
2002	U.S. Supreme Court strikes down federal law banning computer-generated images of minors engaging in sex, thereby allowing virtual kiddie porn to be sold freely over the Internet
2004	40-year follow-up of Perry Preschool Project; fewer lifetime arrests and other social benefits accrue to participants
2005	*Roper v. Simmons* case determines that execution of persons who are under age 18 at time they commit capital crimes is prohibited by Eighth and Fourteenth Amendments; overturned *Stanford v. Kentucky* and *Wilkins v. Missouri* decided in 1989

Source: Compiled by author, 2008.

the "big three" of juvenile cases involving their legal rights. The remaining cases address specific rights issues, such as the right against double jeopardy, jury trials as a matter of right in juvenile courts, preventive detention, and the standards that should govern searches of students and seizures of contraband on school property.

Kent v. United States (1966)

Regarded as the first major juvenile rights case to preface further juvenile court reforms, *Kent v. United States* (1966) established the universal precedents of requiring waiver hearings before juveniles could be transferred to the jurisdiction of a criminal court (excepting legislative automatic waivers as discussed in this and other chapters, although reverse waiver hearings must be conducted at the juvenile's request) and juveniles being entitled to consult with counsel prior to and during such hearings (Grisso, 1998).

The facts of the case are that in 1959, Morris A. Kent, Jr., a 14-year-old in the District of Columbia, was apprehended as the result of several housebreakings and attempted purse snatchings. He was placed on probation in the custody of his mother. In 1961, an intruder entered the apartment of a woman, took her wallet, and raped her. Fingerprints at the crime scene were later identified as those of Morris Kent, who was fingerprinted when apprehended for housebreaking in 1959. On September 5, 1961,

A vacant building in Baltimore, Maryland, was the scene of a fatal shooting that led to the death of a 14-year-old boy. Police were summoned to the vacant building by passersby who noticed a hole in a large fence and what appeared to be a fire in one of the upper floors of the building. When police arrived at the scene, they saw smoke coming out of a second-story window of the building and investigated. As they climbed the stairs of the building, they suddenly heard movement and yelling coming from above them. They entered the second story and came face-to-face with five persons who were wearing hooded sweatshirts. One person reached in his pocket and pulled out a shiny object that police believed to be a weapon. They drew their own pistols and fired several shots, wounding three of the persons. A third threw his hands over his head and lay on the floor. One suspect appeared to be bleeding profusely. As police approached, they observed that the bleeding person had been shot in the head and was dead. The other suspects were wounded in their chests and upper arms. Emergency vehicles were summoned and the wounded persons were treated at a nearby hospital. The persons turned out to be five juveniles, aged 15–17. They were using the vacant building to do drugs. What was believed to be a firearm turned out to be a crack pipe. The surviving youths were charged with criminal trespass and possession of controlled substances, including crack cocaine and a firearm, which was in the pocket of the youth who surrendered and lay on the floor. The firearm was an unloaded .22 pistol. The youths were being held in juvenile detention pending a hearing. A background check of the youths revealed gang affilia-tions and lengthy juvenile records. [Source: Adapted from the Associated Press, "Four Youths Arrested for Drugs, One Killed," June 24, 2008.]

A trio of murders: (1) 18-year-old Justice Blackshere was found guilty of first-degree murder on August 22, 2007, for stabbing two former co-workers at a downtown restaurant in Detroit, Michigan. He murdered Chelios Chili Bar manager Megan Soroka, 49, and chef Mark Barnard, 52. Blackshere had been fired in November 2006 from his busboy position and wanted to get his job back. Seven witnesses saw him kill the two victims. Mandatory life imprisonment was prescribed. (2) 16-year-old Jacob Brighton shot and killed his parents, 47-year-old Richard Brighton and 46-year-old Penny Brighton in Fort Pierce, Florida. In August 2007, Jacob was indicted by a grand jury on first-degree murder charges. Deputies who went to the Brighton home following reports of gunshots found Jacob, who flagged them down. "I've shot my parents. There's no point in rescue. They're dead," he said. No motive for the shootings was given. (3) 17-year-old Freddy Tellez, of Hailey, Idaho, was arrested by police following the murder of his 16-year-old girlfriend, Margarita Guardado. Guardado was struck in the head with a blunt object and then her body was set on fire. Tellez faces life in prison if convicted. No motive was given for the murder. [Adapted from the Associated Press, "First-Degree Murder: Detroit Teen Found Guilty in Cheli's Restaurant Killings," August 22, 2007; adapted from the Associated Press, "Teen, 16, Formally Indicted for Killing Parents," August 23, 2007; adapted from "Former Boyfriend Charged with Hailey Teen's Murder," *Idaho News Now,* August 21, 2007].

Kent, 16, was taken into custody, interrogated for seven hours by police, and admitted the offense as well as volunteering information about other housebreakings, robberies, and rapes. Although the records are unclear about when Kent's mother became aware of Kent's arrest, she did obtain counsel for Kent shortly after 2:00 P.M. the following day. She and her attorney conferred with the Social Service Director of the Juvenile Court and learned there was a possibility Kent would be waived to criminal court. Kent's attorney advised the Director of his intention to oppose the waiver.

Kent was detained in a Receiving Home for one week. During that period, there was no arraignment and no determination by a judicial officer of the probable cause for Kent's arrest. His attorney filed a motion with the juvenile court opposing the waiver as well as a request to inspect records relating to Kent's previous offenses. Also, a psychiatric examination of Kent was arranged by Kent's attorney. Kent's attorney argued that because his client was "a victim of severe psychopathology," it would be in Kent's best interests to remain within juvenile court jurisdiction where he could receive adequate treatment in a hospital and would be a suitable subject for rehabilitation.

Typical of juvenile court judges at the time, the juvenile court judge failed to rule on any of Kent's attorney's motions. He also failed to confer with Kent's attorney and/or parents. In a somewhat arrogant manner, the juvenile court judge declared that "after full investigation, I do hereby waive" jurisdiction of Kent and directed that he be "held for trial for [the alleged] offenses under the regular procedure of the U.S. District Court for the District of Columbia." He offered no findings, nor did he recite any reason for the waiver or make mention of Kent's attorney's motions. Kent was later found guilty of six counts of housebreaking by a federal jury, although the jury found him "not guilty by reason of insanity" on the rape charge. Because of District of Columbia law, it was mandatory that Kent be transferred to a mental institution until such time as his sanity is restored. On each of the housebreaking counts, Kent's sentence was 5 to 15 years, or a total of 30 to 90 years in prison. His mental institution commitment would be counted as time served against the 30- to 90-year sentence.

Arrested youths have legal rights similar to adults.

Kent's conviction was reversed by a vote of 5–4. This is significant, because it signified a subtle shift in Supreme Court sentiment relating to juvenile rights. The majority held that Kent's rights to due process and to the effective assistance of counsel were violated when he was denied a formal hearing on the waiver and his attorney's motions were ignored. It is also significant that the Supreme Court stressed the phrase "critically important" when referring to the absence of counsel and waiver hearing, respectively. In adult cases, critical stages are those that relate to the defendant's potential loss of freedoms (i.e., incarceration). Because of the Kent decision, waiver hearings are now critical stages. Regarding the effective assistance of counsel, this was also regarded by the court as a "critically important" decision. They observed that

the right to representation by counsel is not a formality. It is not a grudging gesture to a ritualistic requirement. It is of the essence of justice . . . . Appointment of counsel without affording an opportunity for a hearing on a 'critically important' decision is tantamount to a denial of counsel (383 U.S. at 561).

In re Gault (1967)

In re Gault (1967) is perhaps the most noteworthy of all landmark juvenile rights cases. Certainly, it is considered the most ambitious. In a 7–2 vote, the U.S. Supreme Court articulated the following rights for all juveniles: (1) the right to a notice of charges; (2) the right to counsel; (3) the right to confront and cross-examine witnesses; and (4) the right to invoke the privilege against self-incrimination. The petitioner, Gault, requested the court to rule favorably on two additional rights sought: (1) the right to a transcript of the proceedings and (2) the right to appellate review. The court elected not to rule on either of these rights.

The facts of the case are that Gerald Francis Gault, a 15-year-old, and a friend, Ronald Lewis, were taken into custody by the Sheriff of Gila County, Arizona, on the morning of June 8, 1964. At the time, Gault was on probation as the result of "being in the company of another who had stolen a wallet from a lady's purse," a judgment entered February 25, 1964. A verbal complaint had been filed by a neighbor of Gault, Mrs. Cook, alleging that Gault had called her and made lewd and indecent remarks. [With some levity, the Supreme Court said that "It will suffice for purposes of this opinion to say that the remarks or questions put to her were of the irritatingly offensive, adolescent, sex variety" (387 U.S. at 4)]. When Gault was picked up, his mother and father were at work. Indeed, they did not learn where their son was until much later that evening. Gault was being held at the Children's Detention Home.

Gault's parents proceeded to the Home. Officer Flagg, the deputy probation officer and superintendent of the Children's Detention Home where Gault was being detained, advised Gault's parents that a hearing would be held in juvenile court at 3:00 P.M. the following day. Flagg filed a petition with the court on the hearing day, June 9. This petition was entirely formal, stating only that "said minor is under the age of 18 years, and is in need of the protection of this Honorable Court; [and that] said minor is a delinquent minor." It prayed for a hearing and an order regarding the "care and custody of said minor." No factual basis was provided for the petition, and Gault's parents were not provided with a copy of it in advance of the hearing.

On June 9, the hearing was held, with only Gault, his mother and older brother, probation officers Flagg and Henderson, and the juvenile court judge present. The original complainant, Mrs. Cook, was not there. No one was sworn at the hearing, no transcript was made of it, and no memorandum of the substance of the proceedings was prepared. The testimony consisted largely of allegations by Officer Flagg about Gault's behavior and prior juvenile record. A subsequent hearing was scheduled for June 15. On June 15, another hearing was held, with all above present, along with Ronald Lewis and his father, and Gault's father. What actually transpired is unknown, although there are conflicting recollections from all parties who were there. Mrs. Gault asked why Mrs. Cook was not present. Judge McGhee said "she didn't have to be present at that hearing." Furthermore, the judge did not speak to Mrs. Cook or communicate with her at any time. Flagg spoke with her once by telephone on June 9. Officially, the charge against Gault was "Lewd Telephone Calls." When the hearing was concluded, the judge committed Gault as a juvenile delinquent to the Arizona State Industrial School "for a period of his minority" [until age 21]. [Parenthetically, if an adult had made an obscene telephone call, he would have received a $50 fine and no more than 60 days in jail. In Gerald Gault's case, he was facing nearly six years in a juvenile prison for the same offense.]

habeas corpus

Writ meaning "produce the body;" used by prisoners to challenge the nature and length of their confinement.

A *habeas corpus* hearing was held on August 17, and Judge McGhee was cross-examined regarding his actions. After "hemming and hawing," the judge declared that Gault had "disturbed the peace" and was "habitually involved in immoral matters." Regarding the judge's reference to Gault's alleged "habitual immorality," the judge made vague references to an incident two years earlier when Gault had been accused of stealing someone's baseball glove and had lied to police by denying that he had taken it. The judge also recalled, again vaguely, that Gault had testified some months earlier about making "silly calls, or funny calls, or something like that."

After exhausting their appeals in Arizona state courts, the Gaults appealed to the U.S. Supreme Court. Needless to say, the court was appalled that Gault's case had been handled in such a cavalier and unconstitutional manner. The Supreme Court reversed the Arizona court's decision, holding that Gault did, indeed, have the right to an attorney, the right to confront his accuser (Mrs. Cook) and to cross-examine her, the right against self-incrimination, and the right to have notice of the charges filed against him. Perhaps Justice Black summed up the current juvenile court situation in the United States when he said, "This holding strikes a well-nigh fatal blow to much that is *unique* [emphasis mine] about the juvenile courts in this Nation." The right to an attorney, as well as other rights conveyed to Gault, are now a pervasive feature of juvenile offender processing. Figure 4.1 shows an acknowledgment of one's rights when a juvenile is initially apprehended and his/her processing begins.

Career Snapshot   4.2

William Hitchcock

Juvenile Court Judge, Alaska Court System,
Anchorage, Alaska

Statistics:
B.A. (political science), Whitman College (1967);
J.D., University of Oregon School of Law (1975)

Background

When I was growing up in the 50s and 60s, young people were expected to decide fairly early whether they were going to select college and a professional career path, or something else such as a career in the military. I knew from junior high that I wanted to pursue a college education and professional career. I thought I would go into a scientific field because of the obsession with science that was created by Sputnik and the dawn of the space race. I pursued physics and math until in high school, it became apparent that I had no aptitude for anything that complicated. I was better at acting in plays and being in debates, so I was on my way to becoming a liberal arts major. The field of law soon became my ambition, so I majored in Political Science and began law school immediately after getting my undergraduate degree.

I lost my draft deferment just as my second year of law school began, meaning I would have to enter the military. This was in 1969, when the Vietnam War was underway. I enlisted in the U.S. Air Force, where I became a personnel specialist at Elmendorf Air Force Base in Anchorage, Alaska. I landed a unique opportunity there to run an ombudsman program that aimed at improving the quality of life for airmen and their families.

After concluding my four-year tour of duty in the Air Force, I returned to the University of Oregon's School of Law to resume my second year. After graduation, I returned to Anchorage and snagged a job as a law clerk for the Alaska Court System. Soon, I was elevated to the position of court master, a judicial position hearing divorce and other uncontested routine civil matters, eventually growing into handling delinquency and child protection matters as well. In other states, this kind of position may be called a "referee," "court commissioner," or "magistrate." These terms are basically meant to describe a judicial position with limited powers.

In the mid-1980s, the Alaska Court System divested itself of the function of juvenile intake for delinquency cases, and the administrative function of case management became my responsibility. This period of time also saw the beginning of tremendous growth in the number of child protection cases coming to the court. By the early 1990s, juvenile crime waves were sweeping more delinquency cases into court as well. I became much more involved in the administration and management of children's court at this time.

The 1980s also marked the beginning of my involvement with the National Council of Juvenile and Family Court Judges, which had a significant impact on my career. I became aware of the importance of becoming educated in understanding the behavioral and societal issues underpinning our children's caseload. I also began to see that judges handling these matters needed to be involved in system improvement efforts and that they could do so without violating the boundaries of judicial ethics. My first real endeavor in that area was to lead the implementation of a new process called citizen foster care review, whereby citizens from the community would become trained and tasked with reviewing abuse/neglect cases and holding systems accountable for performance. That led to my being appointed to the Board of Directors of the National Association of Foster Care Reviewers and a nearly 10-year stint in a volunteer capacity with citizen review nationally.

Over the past 10 years, I have undertaken a number of other initiatives designed to improve the handling of children's cases. I developed an interagency network of juvenile justice agencies and providers in Anchorage, which meets regularly to exchange information and promote collaborative projects and processes. I was also involved in the design and implementation of a domestic violence coordinating council that remains active. In 2001, I facilitated the planning of a proposal that led to a multi-year grant called Reclaiming Futures, which aimed to create an effective community care system for substance-abusing juveniles.

Like everyone else who deals with juveniles, I have had my share of interesting cases. The saddest are the cases of young children who come from abusive homes and who cannot bond with normal caretakers. Many of these kids also suffer the further victimization of having their foster or adoptive home placements fail as well. I have seen delinquency cases in which kids acting out their rage have done wanton and malicious destruction of property, even killing pets in the course of burglarizing or vandalizing a home. However, I still believe that the majority of the kids who commit crimes have a core of positive assets that can be tapped into and developed so that they may redirected into productive lifestyles.

Among the more difficult cases are those presented by kids who have been fetally affected by alcohol. I think Alaska sees more of these kids than those in other states because of the high rates of alcoholism here. I remember a kid who became involved in the juvenile justice system from a very young age. He could not internalize or learn anything because of his fetal alcoholism, and always seemed to be stuck in a continuing cycle of failure. He was an example of the difficulties of applying the traditional justice system to kids who can't learn anything from generic behavioral modification programs. It's the same for kids with mental health needs. It's kids like that who are driving the interest in problem-solving courts, such as drug courts, or mental health courts. This trend is changing the way traditional courts operate and forcing us to address what causes kids to get involved in crime in the first place.

What do I like about my work? The power of a judge to influence the way the case may move is appealing. But only part of that power is exerted in the courtroom. I'm a big believer in being engaged in the community—in being involved in local activities and initiatives, and taking a leadership role in efforts to make our justice system more responsive to the community. I believe the time spent on these efforts is as important as the time I spend wearing the robe and working in the courtroom. I believe in leading from in front of the bench as well as behind the bench.

Advice to Students

A lot of people who go into law do so because they think they can make a lot of money. But others go into the field because they want to change society for the better. There's not as much money if you go in the direction of public service, and a lot of people don't stay in those kinds of jobs because they can make more money elsewhere. But I believe public service work is just as rewarding because you can make a difference.

To anyone who goes into this work, I would say two things. First, if you want a long-term career in helping people, you need to stay current in understanding what the literature and research tells us about human behavior. The traditional view of our judicial work is that one simply needs to know the law and how it applies in particular cases. Judges and helping professionals alike need to understand the dynamics and implications of child abuse, of bonding and attachment, and the impact of domestic violence, to name a few.

Second, don't ever forget that you need to take something away for yourself. Working with child abuse and delinquency can be very stressful, so you need to recognize your achievements, celebrate your victories. Don't get caught up in crises and gloss over your achievements. Every individual who touches these cases can make a difference in the lives of children and their families.

In re Winship (1970)

In re Winship was a less-complex case compared with Gault. But it established an important precedent in juvenile courts relating to the standard of proof used in establishing defendant guilt. The U.S. Supreme Court held that "beyond a reasonable doubt," a standard ordinarily used in adult criminal courts, was henceforth to be used by juvenile court judges and others in establishing a youth's delinquency. Formerly, the standard used was the civil application of "preponderance of the evidence."

The facts in the *Winship* case are that Samuel Winship was a 12-year-old charged with larceny in New York City. He purportedly entered a locker and stole $112 from a woman's pocketbook. Under Section 712 of the New York Family Court Act, a juvenile delinquent was defined as "a person over seven and less than 16 years of age who does any act, which, if done by an adult, would constitute a crime." Interestingly, the

Figure 4.1 Acknowledgment of Rights (Glynn County, GA)

In the Juvenile Court for Glynn County State of Georgia

IN THE MATTER OF:	§	**CASE NO.**
	§	**SEX:**
	§	**DOB:**
A CHILD.	§	**AGE:**

ACKNOWLEDGMENT OF RIGHTS

The above-named child, along with the undersigned parent/guardian and/or attorney, state(s) as follows:

I understand that I have been charged with   and that I am here today to answer to that charge(s). I have had explained and further understand the following:

1. I do not have to admit to the charge(s) against me or even say anything at all, and that if I choose not to say anything it will not be used against me.
2. I have the right to have the charge(s) against me served upon me in writing within a reasonable time.
3. I have the right to have a lawyer represent me, and if I cannot afford to hire a lawyer, the Court will provide one for me.
4. I understand that a lawyer is trained to understand court procedure and proceedings, knows how to conduct trials and how to properly introduce evidence and exclude improper evidence, knows how the law applies to the circumstances of my case, and knows how my rights and liberties may be affected by the court proceedings and how to protect my rights and liberties, and how to present my case and all matters favorable to me to the court, all of which I may not know.
5. I have had my right to be represented by a lawyer explained to me and I understand the danger of proceeding without a lawyer.
6. I have been told of the possible dispositions which the court can order if I admit to the charge(s) or if I am found to have committed a delinquent or unruly act(s) and those dispositions may include but are not limited to dismissal, informal adjustment, probation, commitment to the Department of Human Resources, Commitment to the Department of Juvenile Justice not to exceed six months, placement in the custody of the Division of Family and Children Services, community service, suspension of driving privileges, requiring school attendance, and restitution.
7. I have talked with my parents/guardian and/or lawyer about this case and have had all of the above explained to me and had the opportunity to ask questions and have had all my questions answered.
8. I have the right to have a trial before the judge. I can have witnesses there to testify for me, and I can question anyone who might testify against me. I have the right to an appeal from the trial if I disagree with the decision, and I have a right to receive a record and/or transcript of the proceedings in the event of an appeal.

After having been advised of the above, I do hereby:

( ) Elect to have a lawyer   ( ) Elect not to have a lawyer

This _____ day of _____, 20 _____.

_____   _____
Signature of Child   Signature of Parent

_____   _____
Signature of Person Advising Rights   Signature of Attorney/GAL

juvenile court judge in the case acknowledged that the proof to be presented by the prosecution might be insufficient to establish the guilt of Winship beyond a reasonable doubt, although he did indicate that the New York Family Court Act provided that "any determination at the conclusion of [an adjudicatory hearing] that a [juvenile] did an act or acts must be based on a preponderance of the evidence" standard (397 U.S. at 360). Winship was adjudicated as a delinquent and ordered to a training school for 18 months, subject to annual extensions of his commitment until his eighteenth birthday. Appeals to New York courts were unsuccessful.

The U.S. Supreme Court heard Winship's case and, in a 6–3 vote, reversed the New York Family Court ruling. A statement by Justice Brennan succinctly states the case for the beyond-a-reasonable-doubt standard:

> In sum, the constitutional safeguard of proof beyond a reasonable doubt is as much required during the adjudicatory stage of a delinquency proceeding as are those constitutional safeguards applied in *Gault*—notice of charges, right to counsel, the rights of confrontation and examination, and the privilege of self-incrimination. We therefore hold, in agreement with Chief Justice Fuld in dissent in the Court of Appeals, that where a 12-year-old child is charged with an act of stealing which renders him liable to confinement for as long as six years, then, as a matter of due process, the case against him must be proved beyond a reasonable doubt (397 U.S. at 368).

McKeiver v. Pennsylvania (1971)

The McKeiver case was important because the U.S. Supreme Court held that juveniles are not entitled to a jury trial as a matter of right. [It should be noted that as of 1990, 12 states legislatively mandated jury trials for juveniles in juvenile courts if they so requested such trials, depending upon the seriousness of the offense(s) alleged.] The facts are that in May 1968, Joseph McKeiver, 16, was charged with robbery, larceny, and receiving stolen goods. Although he was represented by counsel at his adjudicatory hearing and requested a trial by jury to ascertain his guilt or innocence, Judge Theodore S. Gutowicz of the Court of Common Pleas, Family Division, Juvenile Branch, of Philadelphia, Pennsylvania, denied the request. McKeiver was subsequently adjudicated delinquent. On subsequent appeal to the U.S. Supreme Court, McKeiver's adjudication was upheld. Again, of interest to criminal justice analysts, the remarks of a U.S. Supreme Court Justice are insightful. Justice Blackmun indicated:

> If the formalities of the criminal adjudicative process are to be superimposed upon the juvenile court system, there is little need for its separate existence. Perhaps that ultimate disillusionment will come one day, but for the moment, we are disinclined to give impetus to it (403 U.S. at 551).

Throughout the opinion delivered in the *McKeiver* case, it is apparent that the Supreme Court was sensitive to the problems associated with juvenile court procedure. Since criminal courts were already bogged down with formalities and lengthy protocol that frequently led to excessive court delays, it was not unreasonable for the court to rule against perpetuating such formalities in juvenile courts. But we must recognize that in this instance, the court merely ruled that it is not the constitutional right of juveniles to have the right to a jury trial upon their request. This proclamation had no effect on individual states that wished to enact or preserve such a method of adjudicating juveniles as delinquent or not delinquent. Therefore, about a fourth of the states today have legislative provisions for jury trials in juvenile courts.

Breed v. Jones (1975)

The *Breed v. Jones* case raised the significant constitutional issue of **double jeopardy**. Double jeopardy means being tried for the same crime twice. The Fifth Amendment provides protection against double jeopardy. Thus, if someone is charged with a crime and acquitted, they cannot be tried again for that same offense. This would violate their Fifth Amendment right against double jeopardy. In *Breed v. Jones,* the U.S. Supreme Court concluded that after a juvenile has been adjudicated delinquent for a particular offense, the youth cannot be tried again as an adult in criminal court for that same offense.

The facts of the case are that on February 8, 1971, in Los Angeles, California, Gary Steven Jones, 17, was armed with a deadly weapon and allegedly committed robbery. Jones was subsequently apprehended and an adjudicatory hearing was held on March 1. A petition was filed against Jones. After testimony was taken from Jones and witnesses, the juvenile court found that the allegations in the petition were true and sustained the petition. A dispositional hearing date was set for March 15. At that time, Jones was declared "not . . . amenable to the care, treatment and training program available through the facilities of the juvenile court" under a California statute. Jones was then transferred by judicial waiver to a California criminal court where he could be tried as an adult. In a later criminal trial, Jones was convicted of robbery and committed for an indeterminate period to the California Youth Authority. The California Supreme Court upheld the conviction.

When Jones appealed the decision in 1971, the U.S. Supreme Court reversed the robbery conviction. Chief Justice Warren Burger delivered the court opinion:

> We hold that the prosecution of [Jones] in Superior Court, after an adjudicatory proceeding in Juvenile Court, violated the Double Jeopardy Clause of the Fifth Amendment, as applied to the States through the Fourteenth Amendment.

The court ordered Jones' release outright or a remand to juvenile court for disposition. In a lengthy opinion, Justice Burger targeted double jeopardy as (1) being adjudicated as delinquent on specific charges in a juvenile court and (2) subsequently being tried and convicted on those same charges in criminal court. Within the context of fundamental fairness, such action could not be tolerated.

Schall v. Martin (1984)

In the *Schall* case, the U.S. Supreme Court issued juveniles a minor setback regarding the state's right to hold them in preventive detention pending a subsequent adjudication. The court said that the preventive detention of juveniles by states is constitutional, if judges perceive these youths to pose a danger to the community or an otherwise serious risk if released short of an adjudicatory hearing. The *Schall v. Martin* decision was significant, in part, because many persons advocated the separation of juveniles and adults in jails, those facilities most often used for preventive detention. Also, the preventive detention of adults was not ordinarily practiced at that time. [Since then, the preventive detention of adults who are deemed to pose societal risks has been upheld by the U.S. Supreme Court (*United States v. Salerno,* 1987).]

The facts are that 14-year-old Gregory Martin was arrested at 11:30 P.M. on December 13, 1977, in New York City. He was charged with first-degree robbery, second-degree assault, and criminal possession of a weapon. Martin lied to police at the time, giving a false name and address. Between the time of his arrest and December 29 when a fact-finding hearing was held, Martin was detained (a total of 15 days). His confinement was based largely on the false information he had supplied to police and the seriousness of the charges pending against him. Subsequently, he was adjudicated a delinquent

double jeopardy
Subjecting persons to prosecution more than once in the same jurisdiction for the same offense, usually without new or vital evidence. Prohibited by the Fifth Amendment.

and placed on two years' probation. Later, his attorney filed an appeal, contesting his preventive detention as violative of the Due Process Clause of the Fourteenth Amendment. The U.S. Supreme Court eventually heard the case and upheld the detention as constitutional. Table 4.2 summarizes some of the major rights available to juveniles and compares these rights with selected rights enjoyed by adults in criminal proceedings.

Table 4.2

Comparison of Juvenile and Adult Rights Relating to Delinquency and Crime

Right	Adults	Juveniles
1. "Beyond-a-reasonable-doubt" standard used in court	Yes	Yes
2. Right against double jeopardy	Yes	Yes
3. Right to assistance of counsel	Yes	Yes
4. Right to notice of charges	Yes	Yes
5. Right to a transcript of court proceedings	Yes	No
6. Right against self-incrimination	Yes	Yes
7. Right to trial by jury	Yes	No in most states
8. Right to defense counsel in court proceedings	Yes	No
9. Right to due process	Yes	No[a]
10. Right to bail	Yes	No, with exceptions
11. Right to cross-examine witnesses	Yes	Yes
12. Right of confrontation	Yes	Yes
13. Standards relating to searches and seizures:		
a. "Probable cause" and warrants required for searches and seizures	Yes, with exceptions	No
b. "Reasonable suspicion" required for searches and seizures without warrant	No	Yes
14. Right to hearing prior to transfer to criminal court or to a reverse waiver hearing in states with automatic transfer provisions	N/A	Yes
15. Right to a speedy trial	Yes	No
16. Right to *habeas corpus* relief in correctional settings	Yes	No
17. Right to rehabilitation	No	No
18. Criminal evidentiary standards	Yes	Yes
19. Right to hearing for parole or probation revocation	Yes	No
20. Bifurcated trial, death penalty cases	Yes	Yes
21. Right to discovery	Yes	Limited
22. Fingerprinting, photographing at booking	Yes	No, with exceptions
23. Right to appeal	Yes	Limited
24. Waivers of rights:		
a. Adults	Knowingly, intelligently	
b. Juveniles	Totality of circumstances	
25. Right to hearing for parole or probation revocation	Yes	No, with exceptions
26. "Equal protection" clause of Fourteenth Amendment applicable	Yes	No, with exceptions
27. Right to court-appointed attorney if indigent	Yes	No, with exceptions
28. Transcript required of criminal/delinquency trial proceedings	Yes	No, with exceptions
29. Pretrial detention permitted	Yes	Yes
30. Plea bargaining	Yes, with exceptions	No, with exception
31. Burden of proof borne by prosecution[b]	Yes	No, with exceptions
32. Public access to trials	Yes	Limited
33. Conviction/adjudication results in criminal record	Yes	No

[a]Minimal, not full, due-process safeguards assured.

[b]Burden of proof is borne by prosecutor in 23 state juvenile courts; the remainder make no provision or mention of who bears the burden of proof.

Source: Compiled by author, 2008.

Implications of More Constitutional Rights for Juveniles

Some of the major implications of more constitutional rights for juveniles include: (1) more equitable treatment through less disparity in dispositions among juvenile judges; (2) greater certainty of punishment through the new justice orientation; (3) less informality in dispositions and less individualized rehabilitative treatments; (4) greater likelihood of acquiring a juvenile offender record, since procedures from intake through adjudication are increasingly codified; and (5) greater likelihood of being transferred to criminal courts through waivers, since the most serious cases will move forward more frequently to juvenile courts.

Almost all juvenile courts in the United States are civil courts. When juveniles are adjudicated delinquent by these courts, they don't acquire criminal records. Once youths reach the age of majority or adulthood, their juvenile records are expunged, forgotten, or sealed. They begin a fresh life as adults without a prior record of delinquency or criminal activity. This works to their advantage. However, the jurisdiction of juvenile courts in various states is changing. As we will see in subsequent chapters, the powers of juvenile court judges are being extended. Increasingly, it is possible for these judges to impose both juvenile and adult penalties on youths adjudicated delinquent. These dual sanctions are both innovative and controversial (Bilchik, 1996). Furthermore, many states are lowering the age at which a juvenile may be tried as an adult in criminal court.

For the majority of jurisdictions as of 2005, while most juveniles remain within juvenile court jurisdiction, they are subject to harsher penalties as juveniles than might otherwise be the case if they were treated as adults. For instance, the case of *Gault* reported earlier in this chapter saw a boy disposed to nearly six years in a state industrial school for allegedly making an obscene telephone call, a low-level misdemeanor. For offenses such as this, adults would not be incarcerated. Rather, they would be fined a nominal amount. Currently, juvenile court judges have considerable power to influence a juvenile's liberty to the limits of one's infant status. Even now in most jurisdictions, if juvenile court judges wish, they may dispose youths to long-term secure confinement far beyond incarcerative terms for sentenced adults who have been convicted of similar offenses. This unfairness is a carry-over from the *parens patriae* years of juvenile courts.

The Juvenile's Right to Waive Rights

With all of the legal rights extended to juveniles since 1966, there are more than a few occasions when juveniles may waive various rights, such as the right to counsel at one or more critical stages of their juvenile justice system processing. For instance, a 1968 case decided following the *In re Gault* decision was *West v. United States* (1968). In the *West* case, a juvenile had waived his right to counsel, as well as several other important rights that had been extended to juveniles through the *Gault* case. A nine-point standard for analysis was established by the Fifth Circuit Court of Appeals when the *West* disposition was imposed and an appeal followed. The nine-point standard was devised in order for judges to determine whether *any* juvenile is capable of understanding and waiving one or more of their constitutional rights. These nine points are:

1. Age
2. Education
3. Knowledge of the substance of the charge, and the nature of the right to remain silent and the right to an attorney
4. Whether the accused is allowed contact with parents, guardian, attorney, or other interested adult
5. Whether the interrogation occurred before or after indictment

6. Methods used in interrogation
7. Length of interrogation
8. Whether the accused refused to voluntarily give statements on prior occasions
9. Whether the accused had repudiated an extra-judicial statement at a later date

While these nine points are interesting and relevant, the fact that they were articulated by the Fifth Circuit Court of Appeals meant that they were not binding on federal district courts in other circuits. For that matter, since these were rights conveyed through a federal circuit, they were not binding on any particular state jurisdiction, even a state within the territory of the Fifth Circuit Court of Appeals.

Subsequently, a totality of circumstances test was established in the case of *Fare v. Michael C.* (1979), involving a juvenile who was interrogated by police without parental consent or attorney presence. Michael C. was a youth on probation and charged with murder. Michael C. asked to see his probation officer during a later police interrogation, but the investigating detectives denied his request. They said that probation officers are not attorneys and thus are not permitted to participate in interrogations of suspects. Michael C. subsequently waived his right to an attorney, answered police questions, and gave incriminating evidence that led to his conviction for murder. He later appealed, contending that his right to counsel was violated when police officers refused to allow him to see his probation officer. However, the U.S. Supreme Court found that Michael C. had made an intelligent, understanding, and voluntary waiver of his rights when questioned by police. The court used the totality of circumstances standard which was adopted from an earlier case involving an adult offender. This U.S. Supreme Court case has resulted in several mixed decisions among appellate courts concerning interrogations of youthful suspects. For instance, in *Woods v. Clusen* (1986), the Seventh Circuit Court of Appeals ruled that a 16.5-year-old's confession was inadmissible because the juvenile had been taken from his home at 7:30 A.M., handcuffed, stripped, forced to wear institutional clothing but no shoes or socks, was shown pictures of the crime scene, and intimidated and interrogated for many hours. These police tactics were criticized by the court and the investigators were reprimanded for their failure to uphold and respect the offender's constitutional rights and provide fundamental fairness.

Research by Grisso (1998), for instance, shows that juveniles have little grasp of their constitutional rights. Grisso studied a large sample of juveniles and found that only 10 percent of them chose not to waive their rights where serious charges were alleged. Grisso found that they (1) demonstrated less comprehension than adults of their *Miranda* rights; (2) had less understanding of the wording of the **Miranda warning**; (3) misunderstood their right to counsel; and (4) did not understand their right to remain silent, believing that they could later be punished if they failed to tell about their criminal activities (*Miranda v. Arizona,* 1966).

States are unevenly distributed when it comes to providing counsel for juveniles. Different circumstances on a state-by-state basis show significant variation. Table 4.3 shows a distribution of the states according to this and other legal rights of juveniles regarding defense counsel appointments and waivers of the right to counsel as of 2008. Only about half of all states have vested juvenile court judges with the discretion to appoint counsel for juveniles, while even fewer states provide strict rights waiver requirements and mandatory defense counsel appointments.

Miranda warning
Sanction given to suspects by police officers advising suspects of their legal rights to counsel, to refuse to answer questions, to avoid self-incrimination, and other privileges.

The Continued Leniency of Juvenile Court Adjudications and Dispositions

Juvenile court actions continue to be fairly lenient. The sanction of choice among juvenile court judges is probation. Even those offenders who appear multiple times before

Table 4.3

Right to Counsel for Juveniles by State, 2008

Conditions Under Which the Right to Counsel Is Invoked[a]

State	Specific Juvenile Statute	Discretionary Appointment	Strict Waiver Requirements	Mandatory Appointment
Alabama	x	x		
Alaska	x			
Arizona	x	x		
Arkansas	x	x	x	
California	x	x		x
Colorado	x	x	x	
Connecticut	x	x	x	
Delaware				
Florida	x			
Georgia	x	x		
Hawaii				
Idaho	x	x		
Illinois	x	x		x
Indiana	x	x		
Iowa	x	x	x	
Kansas	x	x		x
Kentucky	x			
Louisiana	x		x	x
Maine	x			
Maryland	x	x	x	
Massachusetts		x	x	x
Michigan				
Minnesota	x			
Mississippi				
Missouri				
Montana	x	x	x	
Nebraska	x			
Nevada	x			
New Hampshire				
New Jersey	x		x	
New Mexico	x	x	x	x
New York	x			
North Carolina		x		x
North Dakota		x		
Ohio	x	x	x	
Oklahoma	x	x	x	
Oregon	x	x		
Pennsylvania	x	x	x	
Rhode Island		x		
South Carolina		x		
South Dakota		x	x	
Tennessee	x	x		
Texas	x	x	x	x
Utah	x	x		
Vermont	x	x		

Table 4.3   (Cont.)

Right to Counsel for Juveniles by State, 2008

Conditions Under Which the Right to Counsel Is Invoked[a]

State	Specific Juvenile Statute	Discretionary Appointment	Strict Waiver Requirements	Mandatory Appointment
Virginia	X	X	X	
Washington	X			
West Virginia		X		
Wisconsin	X	X		
Wyoming	X			

[a]Five states—Delaware, Hawaii, Michigan, Missouri, and New Hampshire—do not have statutory references to a juvenile's right to legal counsel in their state legal codes.

Source: Caeti, Hemmens, and Burton, 1996:622–623. Reprinted with permission of the *American Journal of Criminal Law* and the authors. Updated 2008 by author.

the same judge are likely to continue to receive probation for their persistent offending. However, the many juvenile justice reforms that have occurred during the 1980s and 1990s have caused some persons to see little difference between how adults are processed by criminal courts and how juveniles are processed by juvenile courts (Feld, 2007). However, despite the increased similarities with criminal courts, there are significant differences that serve to differentiate criminal courts and criminal processing from how youths are treated or processed by the juvenile justice system.

Perhaps the most important implication for juveniles is that in most cases, juvenile court adjudications do not result in criminal records. These courts continue to exercise civil authority. Once juveniles reach adulthood, their juvenile records are routinely expunged and forgotten, with some exceptions. But having one's case adjudicated by a juvenile court operates to a youth's disadvantage in some respects. For instance, the rules governing the admissibility of evidence or testimony are relaxed considerably compared with the rules governing similar admissions in criminal courts. Thus, it is easier in juvenile courts to admit inculpatory evidence and testimony than in criminal courtrooms.

Further, cases against juveniles don't need to be as convincing as cases against criminal defendants. Lower standards of proof are operative relative to search and seizure and the degree of probable cause required. Schoolchildren are particularly vulnerable in this regard, in view of *New Jersey v. T.L.O.* (1985). In this case, a 14-year-old girl was caught smoking a cigarette in the school bathroom, violating school rules. When confronted by the principal, she denied that she had been smoking. The principal examined her purse and discovered a pack of cigarettes, some rolling papers, money, marijuana, and other drug materials. This information was turned over to police, who charged the girl with delinquency. She was convicted. The girl's attorney sought to exclude the seized evidence because it was believed to be in violation of her Fourth Amendment right against unreasonable searches and seizures. The U.S. Supreme Court heard the case and ruled in favor of school officials, declaring that they only need reasonable suspicion, not probable cause, in order to search students and their possessions while on school property. When students enter their schools, they are subject to a lower standard than that applied to adult suspects when suspected of wrongdoing or carrying illegal contraband in violation of school rules.

Adversely, juveniles don't always receive jury trials if they request them. Less than a fourth of all states permit jury trials for juveniles by statute. In the remaining states, jury trials are available to juveniles only if judges permit them. In most cases, therefore, the judgment of the juvenile court is final, for all practical purposes. Appeals of decisions by juvenile court judges are relatively rare. Long-term dispositions of incarceration may be imposed by juvenile court judges at will, without serious challenge. Current profiles of long-term detainees in secure juvenile facilities suggests that judges impose dispositions of secure confinement frequently. Further, a majority of these long-term detainees are less-serious property offenders who show some chronicity in their rate of re-offending.

An Update on Jury Trials for Juvenile Delinquents

The National Center for Juvenile Justice has investigated various state jurisdictions to determine their present status concerning jury trials and other formal procedures for juveniles. The categories created by this investigation included the following: (1) states providing no right to a jury trial for juvenile delinquents under any circumstances; (2) states providing a right to a jury trial for juvenile delinquents under any circumstances; (3) states not providing a jury trial for juvenile delinquents except under specified circumstances; (4) states providing the right to a jury trial for juvenile delinquents under specified circumstances; and (5) states with statutes allowing juvenile delinquents with a right to jury trial to waive that right.

1. States not providing jury trials for juvenile delinquents under any circumstances: Alabama; Arizona; Arkansas; California; District of Columbia; Georgia; Hawaii; Indiana; Kentucky; Louisiana; Maryland; Mississippi; Nevada; New Jersey; North Dakota; Ohio; Oregon; Pennsylvania; South Carolina; Tennessee; Utah; Vermont; and Washington.

2. States providing jury trials for juvenile delinquents under any circumstances: Alaska; Massachusetts; Michigan; and West Virginia.

3. States not providing jury trials for juvenile delinquents, except under specified circumstances:

Defense counsels represent youths charged with crimes.

Colorado: All hearings, including adjudicatory hearings, shall be heard without a jury; juvenile not entitled to a trial by jury when petition alleges a delinquent act which is a class 2 or class 3 misdemeanor, a petty offense, a violation of a municipal or county ordinance, or a violation of a court order if, prior to the trial and with the approval of the court, the district attorney has waived in writing the right to seek a commitment to the department of human services or a sentence to the county jail.

District of Columbia: Probation revocation hearing heard without a jury.

Florida: Adjudicatory hearing heard without a jury.

Louisiana: Adjudication hearing heard without a jury.

Maine: Adjudicatory hearing heard without a jury.

Montana: Hearing on whether juvenile should be transferred to adult criminal court heard without a jury; probation revocation proceeding heard without a jury.

Nebraska: Adjudicatory hearing heard without a jury.

New Mexico: Probation revocation proceedings heard without a jury.

North Carolina: Adjudicatory hearing heard without a jury.

Texas: Detention hearing heard without a jury; hearing to consider transfer of child for criminal proceedings and hearing to consider waiver of jurisdiction held without a jury; disposition hearing heard without a jury, unless child in jeopardy of a determinate sentence; hearing to modify a disposition heard without a jury, unless child in jeopardy of a sentence for a determinate term.

Wisconsin: No right to a jury trial in a waiver hearing.

Wyoming: Probation revocation hearing heard without a jury; transfer hearing heard without a jury.

4. States where juvenile delinquent has a right to a jury trial under specified circumstances:

Arkansas: If amount of restitution ordered by the court exceeds $10,000, juvenile has right to jury trial on all issues of liability and damages.

Colorado: No right to a jury trial unless otherwise provided by this title; juvenile may demand a jury trial, unless the petition alleges a delinquent act which is a class 2 or class 3 misdemeanor, a petty offense, a violation of a municipal or county ordinance, or a violation of a court order if, prior to the trial and with the approval of the court, the district attorney has waived in writing the right to seek a commitment to the department of human services or a sentence to the county jail; any juvenile alleged to be an aggravated juvenile offender (defined in statute) has the right to a jury trial.

Idaho: Any juvenile aged 14–18 alleged to have committed a violent offense (defined in statute) or a controlled substance offense has the right to a jury trial.

Illinois: Any habitual juvenile offender (defined in statute) has the right to a jury trial.

Kansas: Any juvenile alleged to have committed an act that would be a felony if committed by an adult has the right to a jury trial.

Minnesota: Child who is prosecuted as an extended jurisdiction juvenile has the right to a jury trial on the issue of guilt.

Montana: Any juvenile who contests the offenses alleged in the petition has the right to a jury trial.

New Mexico: Jury trial on issues of alleged delinquent acts may be demanded when the offenses alleged would be tried by a jury if committed by an adult.

Oklahoma: Child has right to a jury trial in adjudicatory hearing.

Rhode Island: Child has right to jury when court finds child is subject to certification to adult court.

Texas: Child has right to jury trial at adjudicatory hearing; child has right to a jury trial at disposition hearing only if child is in jeopardy of a determinate sentence; child has right to a jury trial at a hearing to modify the disposition only if the child is in jeopardy of a determinate sentence on the issues of the violation of the court's orders and the sentence.

Virginia: If juvenile indicted, juvenile has the right to a jury trial; if found guilty of capital murder, court fixes sentence with intervention of a jury; where appeal is taken by child on a finding that he or she is delinquent and the alleged delinquent act would be a felony if done by an adult, the child is entitled to a jury.

Wyoming: Juvenile has a right to jury trial at adjudicatory hearing.

5. States providing right to a jury trial for juvenile delinquents where juvenile delinquents can waive their right to a jury trial:

Colorado: Unless a jury is demanded, it shall be deemed waived.

Illinois: Minor can demand in open court and with advice of counsel, a trial by the court without a jury.

Massachusetts: Child can file written waiver and consent to be tried by the court without a jury; this waiver cannot be received unless the child is represented by counsel or has filed, through his parent or guardian, a written waiver of counsel.

Montana: In the absence of a demand, a jury trial is waived.

Oklahoma: Child has right to waive jury trial.

Texas: Trial shall be by jury unless jury is waived.

Wyoming: Failure of party to demand a jury no later than 10 days after the party is advised of his rights is a waiver of this right.

Source: Compiled by author, 2008.

Gelber (1990) has speculated what the juvenile court might be like during the first several decades of the twenty-first century. He envisions a court, conceivably renamed the Juvenile Services Consortium, with two tiers. The first tier will be devoted to adjudicating offenders under age 14. These offenders will always receive rehabilitative sanctions, such as probation or placement in conditional, community-based correctional programs. The second tier consists of those aged 14 to 18. For these juveniles, jury trials will be available and these offenders will be subject to the same incarcerative sanctions that can be imposed by criminal courts.

Gelber's two-tiered juvenile court projection for the twenty-first century may not be far off the mark in relation to societal expectations for such courts in future years. The public mood seems to be in favor of deserts-based sentencing and toward due process for juvenile offenders. The two-tiered nature of Gelber's projected court organization would seemingly achieve this get-tough result, although provisions would remain for treatment-centered rehabilitative sanctions for younger offenders. In a sense, this two-tiered court projection seems to be nothing more than lowering the age jurisdiction of criminal courts from 18 to 14. However, Gelber's intent is to preserve the jurisdictional integrity of the juvenile justice system in relation to the criminal justice system. In any case, this would be an effective compromise between those favoring the traditional rehabilitative posture of juvenile courts and those favoring a shift to more punitive court policies and practices.

The Death Penalty for Juveniles

At the beginning of 2008, there were 3,263 prisoners on death row. Less than 2 percent of all death row inmates are age 20 or under. In 2005, the youngest inmate on death row was Devin Thompson (DOB May 15, 1985) from Alabama, and in October 2005, he was 20 years 5 months old (Death Penalty Information Center, 2008). In March 2005, it was decided in the case of *Roper v. Simmons* (to be discussed later in this section) that the minimum age at which a juvenile could be executed was 18. Prior to the *Roper* decision, the minimum age of execution was 16. Presently very few persons under age 20 are on death row throughout the United States.

The first documented execution of a juvenile occurred in 1642. Thomas Graunger, a 16-year-old, was convicted of bestiality. He was caught sodomizing a horse and a cow. Graunger was tried, convicted, and executed. The youngest age where the death penalty was imposed was 10. A poorly documented case of a 10 year old convicted murderer in Louisiana occurred in 1855. A more celebrated case, that of 10-year-old James Arcene, occurred in Arkansas in 1885. Arcene was 10 years old when he robbed and murdered his victim. He was eventually arrested at age 23 before being executed (Streib, 1987:57).

Arguments for or against the death penalty for adults pertain to juveniles as well. The media have assisted in sensationalizing capital crimes by juveniles, and to some extent, this has caused a substantial number of persons to approve the death penalty for certain juveniles. Those favoring the death penalty say it is "just" punishment and a societal revenge for the life taken or harm inflicted by the offender. It is an economical way of dealing with those who will never be released from confinement. It may be administered humanely, through lethal injection. It functions as a deterrent to others to refrain from committing capital crimes. Opponents say it is cruel and unusual punishment. They claim the death penalty does not deter those who intend to take another's life. It is barbaric and uncivilized (Buckler et al., 2008). Other countries do not impose it for any type of offense, regardless of its seriousness. It makes no sense to kill as a means of sending messages to others not to kill (Dario and Holleran, 2008).

For juveniles, the argument is supplemented by the fact that age functions as a mitigating factor. In any capital conviction, the convicted offender is entitled to a bifurcated trial where guilt is established first, and then the punishment is imposed in view of any prevailing mitigating or aggravating circumstances. Was the crime especially brutal? Did the victim suffer? Was the murderer senile or mentally ill? Or was the murderer a juvenile? Since age acts as a mitigating factor in cases where the death penalty is considered for adults, there are those who say the death penalty should not be applied to juveniles under any condition. Early English precedents and common law assumed that those under age seven were incapable of formulating criminal intent, and thus, they were absolved from any wrongdoing. Between age 7 and age 12, a presumption exists that the child is capable of formulating criminal intent, and in every jurisdiction, the burden is borne by the prosecution for establishing beyond a reasonable doubt that the youth was capable of formulating criminal intent.

While each case is judged on its own merits, there are always at least two sides in an issue involving the murder of one by another. The survivors of the victim demand justice, and the justice they usually seek is the death of the one who brought about the death of their own. This is a manifestation of the eye-for-an-eye philosophy. In many respects, it is an accurate portrayal of why the death penalty is imposed for both juveniles and adults. It is supposed to be a penalty that fits the crime committed. But attorneys and family members of those convicted of capital crimes cannot help but feel compassion for their doomed relatives. Someone they love is about to lose his or her life. But hadn't they taken someone's life in the process? But does taking another life bring back the dead victim? But does taking the life of the murderer fulfill some higher societal purpose? The arguments about this issue are endless.

In 1977, in Fort Jackson, South Carolina, a 17-year-old mentally retarded youth and a 16-year-old companion were living with a 22-year-old soldier in a rented, run-down house. [The following account has been adapted from Streib, 1987:125–127.] Alcohol, THC, PCP, marijuana, and other drugs were readily available. On a warm Saturday, October 29, after heavy drinking and consuming drugs, the three decided to look for a girl to rape. They drove to a baseball park in nearby Columbia. They parked next to a young couple, a 17-year-old boy and his 14-year-old girlfriend. On orders from the soldier, they shot the boy three times with a high-powered rifle, killing him instantly. Then they drove off with the girl to a secluded area where each raped her repeatedly. Finally, they finished her off by shooting her and mutilating her body.

The three were soon arrested by police. The youngest youth agreed to testify against the soldier and the 17-year-old in exchange for a lighter punishment. Both the soldier and the 17-year-old eventually entered guilty pleas and were sentenced to death. After lengthy appeals, the soldier was executed by South Carolina authorities on January 11, 1985. Finally, on January 10, 1986, James Terry Roach, the 17-year-old who killed the boy and girl and mutilated the girl's body, was executed in the South Carolina electric chair. Justice was served. Or was it? A crowd cheered outside the prison walls as the execution of Roach occurred. Roach wrote his last letter, and as he was strapped into the electric chair, he read it with shaky hands: "To the families of the victims, my heart is still with you in your sorrow. May you forgive me just as I know that my Lord has done." Two one-minute surges of electricity hit him and he was pronounced dead at 5:16 A.M. (Streib, 1987:125–127). The minimum offender age for the death penalty in those states that have the death penalty for capital crimes is 18. As the result of *Roper v. Simmons* (2005), the minimum age is now 18 for all states that use the death penalty as the maximum punishment for the most serious offenses. Some of these states may have higher minimum ages for executing youthful offenders.

Before the *Roper v. Simmons* case, the U.S. Supreme Court consistently refused to become embroiled in the capital-punishment-for-juveniles issue, although it heard several juvenile death penalty appeals in past years. One frequently cited case in these appeals is *Eddings v. Oklahoma* (1982). This case raised the question of whether the death penalty as applied to juveniles is cruel and unusual punishment under the Eighth Amendment. The U.S. Supreme Court avoided the issue. The justices did not say it was cruel and unusual punishment, but they also did not say that it wasn't. What they said was that the youthfulness of the offender is a mitigating factor of great weight that may be considered. Therefore, all jurisdictions where death penalties are imposed were left to draw their own conclusions and interpretations of U.S. Supreme Court remarks about death penalty cases.

Reasons for Supporting the Death Penalty

The primary reasons for supporting the death penalty in certain capital cases are three-fold: (1) retribution; (2) deterrence; and (3) just deserts.

1. The death penalty is retribution. Retribution is defended largely on the basis of the philosophical just-deserts rationale. Offenders should be executed because they did not respect the lives of others. Death is the just desert for someone who inflicted death on someone else. Retribution is often regarded as the primary purpose of the death penalty.

2. The death penalty deters others from committing murder. The deterrence function of the death penalty is frequently questioned as well. An examination of homicide rates in Illinois during a 48-year period (1933–1980) was conducted. It revealed that average homicide rates for three different periods did not fluctuate noticeably. These periods included (1) times when the death penalty was allowed; (2) years when the death penalty was allowed but no executions were performed; and (3) years when the death penalty was abolished (Bonczar and Snell, 2004:3). Another view is that no criminal act ever justifies capital punishment (Death Penalty Information Center, 2008).

3. The death penalty is a just desert for commission of a capital offense. The "just-deserts" philosophy is that the death penalty is just punishment for someone who has committed murder. The U.S. Supreme Court has indirectly validated this reasoning by refusing to declare the death penalty cruel and unusual punishment (Ingram, 2008).

Reasons for Opposing the Death Penalty

Some of the reasons persons use to oppose the death penalty are that (1) it is barbaric; (2) it may be applied in error to someone who is not actually guilty of a capital offense; (3) it is nothing more than sheer revenge; (4) it is more costly than life imprisonment; (5) it is applied arbitrarily; (6) it does not deter others from committing murder; and (7) most persons in the United States are opposed to the death penalty.

1. The death penalty is barbaric. Some persons say that the death penalty is barbaric and violates international law. There are other avenues whereby convicted capital offenders can be punished. The United States is one of the few civilized countries of the modern world that still uses the death penalty. Portraits of persons condemned to death include accounts of their past lives by close friends and family members who oppose capital punishment in their cases. Even statements from various family members of victims express opposition to the death penalty because of its alleged barbarism (Ingram, 2008).

2. The death penalty is unfair and may be applied erroneously. Some convicted offenders are wrongly convicted. Evidence subsequently discovered has led to freeing

several persons who were formerly on death row awaiting execution. The American Civil Liberties Union and Amnesty International are strong death penalty opponents. This possibility of an erroneous conviction is one of their strongest arguments against its application. Thus, this view proposes an outright ban on the death penalty because of the mere possibility that some persons sentenced to death are actually innocent and should not be executed.

3. The death penalty is nothing more than revenge. Some observers argue that by condoning the death penalty, the U.S. Supreme Court has sanctioned vengeance, which is an unacceptable justification for imposing capital punishment. For persons who are retarded or intellectually disabled, it is likely that they cannot reach the level of culpability necessary to trigger the need for the death penalty. They cannot engage in cold calculus to weigh committing the crime against the potential death penalty used to punish it.

4. The death penalty is more costly than life-without-parole sentences. Executing prisoners under death sentences may be more costly over time than imprisoning them for life. However, a key reason for the high cost of executing prisoners is that they have been entitled to file endless appeals and delay the imposition of their death sentences. In 1996, Congress acted to limit the number of appeals inmates on death rows could file. Thus, it is expected in future years that the length of time between conviction and imposition of the death penalty will be greatly abbreviated. This shorter period of time will decrease the expense of death penalty appeals and undermine this particular argument (Death Penalty Information Center, 2008).

5. The death penalty is still applied arbitrarily despite efforts by legislatures and Congress to make its application more equitable. Although bifurcated trials have decreased the racial bias in death penalty applications, disproportionality in death sentences according to race and ethnicity have not been completely eliminated. While some persons argue that some races and ethnic categories have higher rates of capital murder and thus are disproportionately represented on death row, other persons say that the death penalty continues to be applied in a discriminatory manner in many jurisdictions (Ingram, 2008).

6. The death penalty does not deter others from committing murder. The literature strongly supports the idea that the death penalty apparently has no discernable deterrent effect. Persons will commit murder anyway, even knowing that there is a chance they may be caught eventually and executed for the crime. An examination of crime statistics and comparisons of those jurisdictions where the death penalty is applied and jurisdictions where it isn't applied show few, if any, differences in capital murder cases. Thus, the argument is that if capital punishment fails to deter capital murder, then it should be abolished (Dario and Holleran, 2008).

7. Most persons in the United States are against the death penalty. One view is that there is growing lack of public support for the death penalty in the United States. However, several national surveys show that over 75 percent of those interviewed support the death penalty and its application. Certainly, knowledge about the death penalty and its deterrent and retributive effects makes a difference in whether persons support or oppose its use. Growing violent street crimes, especially violent street crimes resulting in the deaths of innocent victims, do nothing but trigger pro–capital-punishment reactions from an increasingly frightened public (Death Penalty Information Center, 2008).

All of the arguments that function as either pros or cons relative to the death penalty also apply directly to the issue of juvenile executions. However, the nature of juvenile justice reforms is such that a strong belief persists that substantial efforts must be made by juvenile courts and correctional facilities to rehabilitate juveniles rather than incarcerate or execute them. In those states where executions are conducted, where should the line be drawn concerning the minimum age at which someone becomes liable, accountable, and subject to the death penalty?

U.S. Supreme Court Death Penalty Cases

Several U.S. Supreme Court cases have been decided in recent years involving questions of executions of juveniles. These cases have been especially significant in providing a legal foundation for such executions. These include *Eddings v. Oklahoma* (1982), *Thompson v. Oklahoma* (1988), *Stanford v. Kentucky* (1989), *Wilkins v. Missouri* (1989), and *Roper v. Simmons* (2005). As a prelude to discussing these cases, it should be noted that until 1988, 16 states had minimum-age provisions for juvenile executions (under age 18), where the range in minimum age was from 10 (Indiana) to 17 (Georgia, New Hampshire, and Texas). When the *Thompson v. Oklahoma* case was decided in 1988, the minimum age for juvenile executions in all states was raised to 16. The following year, the U.S. Supreme Court upheld death sentences of a 16-year-old and a 17-year-old as well.

Eddings v. Oklahoma (1982)

On April 4, 1977, Monty Lee Eddings and several other companions ran away from their Missouri homes. In a car owned by Eddings's older brother, they drove without direction or purpose, eventually reaching the Oklahoma Turnpike. Eddings had several firearms in the car, including several rifles that he had stolen from his father. At one point, Eddings lost control of the car and was stopped by an Oklahoma State Highway Patrol officer. When the officer approached the car, Eddings stuck a shotgun out of the window and killed the officer outright. When Eddings was subsequently apprehended, he was waived to criminal court on a prosecutorial motion. Efforts by Eddings and his attorney to oppose the waiver failed.

In a subsequent bifurcated trial, several aggravating circumstances were introduced and alleged, while several mitigating circumstances, including Eddings's youthfulness, mental state, and potential for treatment, were considered by the trial judge. However, the judge did not consider Eddings's "unhappy upbringing and emotional disturbance" as significant mitigating factors to offset the aggravating ones. Eddings's attorney filed an appeal that eventually reached the U.S. Supreme Court. Although the Oklahoma Court of Criminal Appeals reversed the trial judge's ruling, the U.S. Supreme Court reversed the Oklahoma Court of Criminal Appeals. The reversal pivoted on whether the trial judge erred by refusing to consider the "unhappy upbringing and emotionally disturbed state" of Eddings. The trial judge had previously acknowledged the youthfulness of Eddings as a mitigating factor. The *fact* of Eddings's age, 16, was significant, precisely because the majority of justices didn't consider it as significant. Rather, they focused upon the issue of introduction of mitigating circumstances specifically outlined in Eddings's appeal. Oklahoma was now in the position of lawfully imposing the death penalty on a juvenile who was 16 years old at the time he committed murder.

Thompson v. Oklahoma (1988)

In the case of William Wayne Thompson, he was convicted of murdering his former brother-in-law, Charles Keene. Keene had been suspected of abusing Thompson's sister. In the evening hours of January 22/23, 1983, Thompson and three older companions left his mother's house, saying "We're going to kill Charles." Facts disclose that early the next morning Charles Keene was beaten to death by Thompson and his associates with fists and hand-held weapons, including a length of pipe. Thompson later told others, "We killed him. I shot him in the head and cut his throat in the river." Thompson's accomplices told police shortly after their arrest that Thompson had shot Keene twice in the head, and then cut his body in several places (e.g., throat, chest, and abdomen), so that, according to Thompson, "the fish could eat his body." When Keene's body was recovered on February 18, 1983, the medical examiner indicated that Keene had been shot twice in the head, had been beaten, and that his throat, chest, and abdomen had been cut.

Since Thompson was 15 years old at the time of the murder, juvenile officials transferred his case to criminal court. This transfer was supported, in part, by an Oklahoma statutory provision indicating that there was "prosecutive merit" in pursuing the case against Thompson. Again, the subject of the defendant's youthfulness was introduced as a mitigating factor (among other factors), together with aggravating factors such as the "especially heinous, atrocious, and cruel" manner in which Keene had been murdered. Thompson was convicted of first-degree murder and sentenced to death.

Thompson filed an appeal which eventually reached the U.S. Supreme Court. The court examined Thompson's case at length, and in a vigorously debated opinion, it overturned Thompson's death sentence and indicated in its conclusory dicta that

> petitioner's counsel and various *amici curiae* have asked us to "draw the line" that would prohibit the execution of any person who was under the age of 18 at the time of the offense. Our task, today, however, is to decide the case before us; we do so by concluding that the Eighth and Fourteenth Amendments prohibit the execution of a person who was under 16 years of age at the time of his or her offense (108 S.Ct. at 2700).

Accordingly, Thompson's death penalty was reversed. Officially, this Supreme Court action effectively drew a temporary line of 16 years of age as a minimum for exacting the death penalty in capital cases. This "line" awaited subsequent challenges, however.

Stanford v. Kentucky (1989)

Kevin Stanford was 17 when, on January 17, 1981, he and an accomplice repeatedly raped and sodomized and eventually shot to death 20-year-old Baerbel Poore in Jefferson County, Kentucky. This occurred during a robbery of a gas station where Poore worked as an attendant. Stanford later told police, "I had to shoot her [since] she lived next door to me and she would recognize me . . . I guess we could have tied her up or something or beat [her up] . . . and tell her if she tells, we would kill her."

A corrections officer who interviewed Stanford said that after Stanford made that disclosure, "he (Stanford) started laughing." The jury in Stanford's case found him guilty of first-degree murder and the judge sentenced him to death. The U.S. Supreme Court eventually heard his appeal, and in an opinion that addressed the "minimum age for the death penalty" issue, decided both this case and the case of Heath Wilkins in the paragraphs to follow. Subsequently, in December 2003, the governor of Kentucky commuted Stanford's death sentence to life imprisonment without parole, with the proclamation that "we ought not to be executing people who, legally, were children" (*Lexington Herald Leader,* December 9, 2003:B3).

Wilkins v. Missouri (1989)

Heath Wilkins, a 16-year-old at the time of the crime, stabbed to death Nancy Allen Moore, a 26-year-old mother of two who was working behind the counter of a convenience store in Avondale, Missouri. On July 27, 1985, Wilkins and his accomplice,

Patrick Stevens, entered the convenience store to rob it, agreeing with Wilkins's plan that they would kill "whoever was behind the counter" because "a dead person can't talk." When they entered the store, they stabbed Moore, who fell to the floor. When Stevens had difficulty opening the cash register, Moore, mortally wounded, offered to help him. Wilkins stabbed her three more times in the chest, two of the knife wounds penetrating Moore's heart. Moore began to beg for her life, whereupon Wilkins stabbed her four more times in the neck, opening up her carotid artery. She died shortly thereafter. Stevens and Wilkins netted $450 in cash and checks, some liquor, cigarettes, and rolling papers from the robbery/murder site. Wilkins was convicted of first-degree murder and the judge sentenced him to death.

The U.S. Supreme Court heard both cases simultaneously, since the singular issue was whether the death penalty was considered cruel and inhumane as it pertained to 16- and 17-year-olds. At that time, not all states had achieved consensus about applying the death penalty to persons under the age of 18 as a punishment for capital crimes. Although several justices dissented from the majority view, the U.S. Supreme Court upheld the death sentences of Stanford and Wilkins, concluding that:

> we discern neither a historical nor a modern societal consensus forbidding the imposition of capital punishment on any person who murders at 16 or 17 years of age. Accordingly, we conclude that such punishment does not offend the Eighth Amendment's prohibition against cruel and unusual punishment (109 S.Ct. at 2980).

Thus, this crucial opinion underscored age 16 as the minimum age at which the death penalty may be administered. But this age standard would be changed 16 years later in the case of *Roper v. Simmons* (2005).

Roper v. Simmons (2005)

In March 2005, the U.S. Supreme Court revisited the issue of administering the death penalty to juveniles under the age of 18. Despite their decisions in the cases of *Wilkins v. Missouri* (1989) and *Stanford v. Kentucky* (1989), evolving community standards between 1989 and 2005, public opinion surveys concerning the application of the death penalty to juveniles, as well as United Nations sentiment and pressure, created a sociopolitical climate that placed the United States almost alone in its stance toward the application of the death penalty to persons under the age of 18. The case heard and decided was *Roper v. Simmons* (2005).

The facts of the case are as follows. In 1993, in Fenton, Missouri, Christopher Simmons, 17, told two other youths, Charles Benjamin, 15, and John Tessmer, 16, that he wanted to murder someone. Simmons said that he wanted to commit burglary by breaking and entering and then commit murder, tying up a victim, and then throwing the victim from a bridge. Simmons assured Benjamin and Tessmer that they could "get away with it because they were minors." At 2:00 A.M. one morning, Simmons, Benjamin, and Tessmer met to carry out a burglary and murder, but Tessmer left before they started out to do their deeds. Simmons and Benjamin went to the home of Shirley Crook, a woman who had previously been involved in an auto accident with Simmons. They entered her home through an open window and she awakened. She recognized Simmons, who bound her with duct tape, including placing duct tape over her eyes and mouth. They took her to a railroad trestle spanning the Meramec River, tied her hands and feet with wire, and then covered her entire face with duct tape. Next, they threw her from the trestle into the river where she drowned. Simmons later bragged to others that he had killed a woman because "the bitch had seen my face." Fishermen in the river found Crook's body and investigating detectives linked her death with Simmons, who was taken into custody for questioning. Simmons gave a videotaped confession, describing his heinous actions to police. He was subsequently convicted of first-degree murder and sentenced to death. Aggravating factors included the especially heinous nature of the murder; committing the murder for money; and attempting to conceal the crime by disposing of Crook's body into the river. His acts were described as wantonly vile, horrible, and inhuman. Mitigation included that Simmons had no prior juvenile record.

He appealed his conviction to the Missouri Supreme Court, alleging incompetence of counsel, since he had a difficult home environment, had poor school attendance and performance, abused alcohol and drugs, and exhibited dramatic changes in behavior, suggesting an altered mental state. The Missouri Supreme Court affirmed his conviction and death sentence. A second appeal was subsequently filed, alleging that it was a violation of his Eighth and Fourteenth Amendment rights for the state to execute him, since he was under 18 and a juvenile at the time he committed the crime. The Missouri Supreme Court set aside his death sentence and resentenced him to life imprisonment without the possibility of parole or release except by act of the governor. Prosecutors appealed and the U.S. Supreme Court heard the case.

In a precedent-setting action, the U.S. Supreme Court in a 5–4 decision affirmed the Missouri Supreme Court, effectively overturning their earlier decisions in the cases of *Stanford v. Kentucky* (1989) and *Wilkins v. Missouri* (1989), where the ages of 16 and 17, respectively, were approved for lawful executions. The U.S. Supreme Court declared that it is unconstitutional to execute juveniles under the age of 18 at the time they committed a capital offense. In its lengthy opinion, the court noted United Nations provisions against executing persons under the age of 18; the fact that the United States was among a very limited number of countries that continued to execute juveniles under age 18; and evolving community standards that increasingly opposed executing juveniles. The court alluded to a "national consensus" against the death penalty for juveniles, although evidence presented to support such a view of national sentiment was sketchy.

It is quite likely that this U.S. Supreme Court decision was influenced to some extent by international sentiment and an emerging socio-political climate that opposed executing juveniles under the age of 18 for any reason. The decision brought the United States into line with most other world nations. The court supported its decision with alternative rationales other than political ones, however. The court observed that juveniles are not fully formed adults; that they have an underdeveloped sense of responsibility; that they lack maturity; that they are more vulnerable or susceptible to negative influences and outside pressures, including peer pressure; and that they have less control over their own environment. Further, the court said that the character of juveniles is not as well formed as that of adults, and that their personality traits are more transitory and less fixed. Thus, the court recognized the diminished culpability of juveniles in capital cases. The court also observed that retribution and deterrence fail to justify imposing the death penalty on juvenile offenders. Table 4.4 shows the minimum age allowable or authorized by statute for juveniles in those states with death penalties in 2008.

Recognizing that some persons may take issue with their decision to raise the legal age at which youthful offenders may be executed, the U.S. Supreme Court noted that drawing the line at 18 years of age is subject to the objections always raised against categorical rules. The qualities that distinguish juveniles from adults do not disappear when an individual turns 18. By the same token, some under 18 already have attained a level of maturity some adults will never reach. But for the reasons the court has noted, a line must be drawn. The age of 18 is the point where society draws the line for many purposes between childhood and adulthood. The court therefore concludes that 18 is the age at which the line for death eligibility ought to rest.

Because of this U.S. Supreme Court decision, it is likely that all juveniles who were convicted for capital crimes and sentenced to death when they were under 18 at the time their crimes were committed will have their death sentences set aside. Much U.S. Supreme Court decision making is not retroactively applicable to previous decisions by

Table 4.4

Minimum Age Authorized for Capital Punishment of Juveniles, 2008

Age 18	None Specified
Alabama	Arizona
Arkansas	Idaho
California	Louisiana
Colorado	Montana
Connecticut	Pennsylvania
Delaware	South Carolina
Federal System	South Dakota
Florida	
Georgia	
Illinois	
Indiana	
Kansas	
Kentucky	
Maryland	
Mississippi	
Nebraska	
Nevada	
New Hampshire	
New Jersey	
New Mexico	
New York	
North Carolina	
Ohio	
Oklahoma	
Oregon	
Tennessee	
Texas	
Utah	
Virginia	
Washington	
Wyoming	

Source: Compiled by author, 2008.

other courts. But this decision will profoundly affect the status of all persons on death row in the United States who were under age 18 when they committed their crimes. Also affected are those youths under age 18 who are presently undergoing capital murder trials where the death penalty is sought. This decision effectively eliminates the death penalty for these juveniles as a prosecutorial option. No doubt most, if not all, states with capital murder statutes for juveniles under the age of 18 will commute these sentences either to life imprisonment or to life without the possibility of parole. In almost every state, the governor exercises the power to grant clemency, pardons, and other more lenient actions relative to juveniles convicted of capital crimes.

Because of the declining frequency with which juveniles have been executed in recent years, the death penalty issue as it applies to juveniles does not seem as strong as it once was. There will always be many persons in society who will oppose the death penalty for any reason (Dario and Holleran, 2008). But with the 2005 U.S. Supreme Court decision of *Roper v. Simmons,* it is doubtful that future major changes will be made concerning death penalty policy toward youthful offenders aged 18 or over, since the United States is now aligned with United Nations policy. While public sentiment is not always easy to measure, there seems to be a strong sentiment for harsher penalties to be meted out to juveniles. This doesn't necessarily mean the death penalty or life imprisonment, but it does mean tighter laws and enforcement of those laws where juveniles are concerned.

Public Sentiment about the Death Penalty for Juveniles

Views of criminologists are not that different from the views held by the general public about juvenile delinquency and what should be done to prevent or punish it. Victor Streib (1987:189) has summarized succinctly a commonly expressed solution that

> our society must be willing to devote enormous resources to a search for the causes and cures of violent juvenile crime, just as we have done in the search for the causes and cures of such killer diseases as cancer. And we must not demand a complete cure in a short time, since no one knows how long it will take.

Obviously, we have not cured cancer. We are even further away from discovering the etiology of delinquent behavior in all of its diverse forms and finding one or more satisfactory cures for it.

Early identification of at-risk youths who have suffered some type of child abuse from their parents is valuable in that it has enabled youth authorities to link many of these at-risk youths with subsequent youth violence. Family dysfunction has been linked with assault behavior manifested by youths who have witnessed it compared with those who have not witnessed it (Salzinger, Rosario, and Feldman, 2007; Sullivan et al., 2007). Explanations for youth violence are varied and complex. So far, we don't have a good grasp of the specific factors that produce violent behavior among adolescents. We can say, for instance, that in certain instances, childhood victimization has increased the overall risk of violent offending among affected juveniles. But we are not yet in a position to say which juveniles will commit specific violent types of offenses in their future years (Olivero, 2005).

Unification of Criminal and Juvenile Courts

Presently, there are several different types of courts in every U.S. jurisdiction. Usually, these courts have general, original, and concurrent jurisdiction, meaning that some courts share adjudicatory responsibilities involving the same subject matter. In Arkansas, for example, chancery courts have jurisdiction over juvenile delinquency cases, although separate county courts may also hear cases involving juveniles. In Colorado, district courts have general jurisdiction over criminal and civil matters, probate matters, and juvenile cases. However, there are specific juvenile courts in Colorado that hear juvenile cases as well. Tennessee county courts, circuit courts, and juvenile courts have concurrent jurisdiction over delinquency and other types of juvenile cases (e.g., children in need of supervision, child custody cases).

Court unification is a general proposal that seeks to centralize and integrate the diverse functions of all courts of general, concurrent, and exclusive jurisdiction into a more simplified and uncomplicated scheme. One way of viewing court unification is that it is ultimately intended to abolish concurrent jurisdiction wherever it is currently shared among various courts in a common jurisdiction, although no presently advocated court unification model has been shown to be superior to others proposed. Thus, there are different ways of achieving unification, although not everyone agrees about which method is best. One example of court unification is Pennsylvania.

Prior to 1969, Pennsylvania had two appellate courts and numerous local courts that functioned independently of one another (Yeager, Herb, and Lemmon, 1989). Even the Pennsylvania Supreme Court lacked full and explicit administrative and supervisory authority over the entire judicial system. As the result of the Pennsylvania Constitutional Convention of 1967–1968, a new judiciary article, Article V of the Pennsylvania Constitution, was framed. Vast changes were made in court organization and operations. A family division was established to deal exclusively with all juvenile matters. A 10-year follow-up evaluation of Pennsylvania's court unification concluded that the present court organization is vastly superior to the pre-1969 court organization. Efficiency and economy were two objectives sought by these court changes. Both aims were achieved.

Earlier studies of jurisdictions representing various degrees of unification have been conducted to assess whether there is necessarily greater economy, coordination, and speed associated with maintaining records and processing cases (Hill et al., 2007). Georgia, Iowa, Colorado, New Jersey, and Connecticut were examined. Data were collected from records maintained by state administrative officials and local trial courts, and interviews were conducted with key court personnel. A total of 103 courts were selected for analysis, including 20 courts of general jurisdiction, 69 courts of limited jurisdiction, and 15 juvenile courts. More centralized organizational schemes only partially fulfilled the expectations of these researchers. Henderson et al. (1984) report that under centralization, poorer areas were likely to do better financially, although courts in well-off areas faced tighter budget restrictions. Greater uniformity of operations was observed in most jurisdictions. Further, centralization of court organization tended to highlight problems in previously neglected areas, including family and juvenile services. Their findings relating to differences in the effectiveness and efficiency of case processing in trial courts in both decentralized and centralized systems were inconclusive, however.

> **court unification**
> Proposal that seeks to centralize and integrate the diverse functions of all courts of general, concurrent, and exclusive jurisdiction into a more simplified and uncomplicated scheme.

Implications of Court Unification for Juveniles

For juveniles, court unification poses potentially threatening consequences. For example, in those jurisdictions where considerable fragmentation exists in the processing of juvenile cases or where concurrent jurisdiction distributes juvenile matters among several different courts, juveniles, especially habitual offenders, may be able to benefit because of a general lack of centralization in record keeping. Thus, juveniles may be adjudicated delinquent in one juvenile court jurisdiction, but this record of adjudication may not be communicated to other courts in adjacent jurisdictions. In time, it is likely that a national record-keeping network will exist, where all juvenile courts may access information from other jurisdictions. Currently, however, the confidentiality of record keeping is a structural constraint that inhibits the development of such extensive record sharing. However, as has been reported in earlier chapters, one major change in juvenile justice record keeping has been the creation of various state repositories of juvenile information that can be shared among interested agencies. This is considered a part of the get-tough movement and is intended to hold juveniles more accountable for their offending by giving authorities in different jurisdictions greater access to their prior offense records (Mears et al., 2007).

A separate and distinct juvenile justice system apart from the criminal justice system has the primary goal of individualized treatment, with therapy and rehabilitation as dominant factors. But a separate juvenile justice system is also designed to hold juveniles strictly accountable for their actions. Thus, less use may be made of secure confinement, and greater use be made of probation and parole, with the primary objectives of offering restitution to victims, compensating communities and courts for the time taken to process cases, and performing community services to learn valuable lessons.

Getting Tough and Court Unification

There is no question that the get-tough movement is still in force and is pervasive throughout the juvenile justice system. One indication of this is the increased use of waivers or transfers, as more juveniles are shifted to the jurisdiction of criminal courts. We have seen certain implications of juveniles as they enter criminal courts for processing, although some of these implications are not entirely unfavorable. Increasing numbers of juvenile court judges are soliciting the involvement of members of the community to voluntarily assist in monitoring adjudicated youths. Greater responsibilities are shifting toward parents in many jurisdictions, particularly when their children commit crimes against property.

Public policy currently favors protecting juveniles as much as possible from the stigmatization of courts and criminal labeling, including the large-scale removal of youths from jails and prisons. Accordingly, recommendations from the public include greater use of nonsecure facilities and programs as opposed to confinement in secure facilities. Especially manifest is the concern for very young offenders. More children under age 12 are entering the juvenile justice system annually. Clearly, effective programs and procedures for processing such youths need to be in place and operative. Encouragement for greater use of community-based services and treatment programs, special education services, and school-based, early intervention programs is apparent (Whitehead, 2008).

There is an increasing bureaucratization of juvenile courts, indicated in part by greater formality of juvenile case processing. Juvenile proceedings are increasingly adversarial, similar to criminal courts. Almost all of the criminal court trappings are found in juvenile courts (Feld, 2007). Most juvenile courts are not courts of record, and much informality exists regarding calling witnesses and offering testimony. Federal and state rules of evidence are relaxed considerably and do not attach directly to juvenile civil proceedings.

Juvenile courts are sometimes classified according to a **traditional model** or **family model** and due process distinction. Traditional courts perpetuate the doctrine of *parens patriae,* and juvenile court judges retain a good deal of discretion in adjudicating offenders. They rely more heavily on confinement as a punishment. The due process juvenile courtroom relies more heavily on preadjudicatory interactions between defense counsels and prosecutors, and nonjudicial handling of cases is more the rule rather than the exception. More frequently used in such courts are nonsecure facilities, community-based programs, probation, and diversion with conditions (Sullivan et al., 2007).

Politicizing Juvenile Punishments

The political approach to punishing juveniles is to rely heavily on the sentiments expressed by voting constituencies. State legislators are at the helm of juvenile justice reforms currently, and several organizations are in strategic positions to offer their guidance and assistance in formulating new juvenile policies. The American Bar Association,

traditional model
Juvenile court proceedings characterized by less formal adjudications, greater use of detention.

family model
Established under the Juvenile Law of 1948, exists in all Japanese jurisdictions and hears any matters pertaining to juvenile delinquency, child abuse and neglect, and child custody matters; both status offenders and delinquents appear before Family Court judges; similar to juvenile court judges in U. S. jurisdictions, Family Court judges have considerable discretionary authority; decide cases within the *parens patriae* context.

the American Legislative Exchange Council, and the Institute of Judicial Administration have provided legislators with model penal codes and proposed juvenile court revisions to introduce consistency throughout an inconsistent juvenile justice system. Two model juvenile justice acts have evolved—the Model Delinquency Act and the Model Disobedient Children's Act. Among other things, these acts, respectively, distinguish between delinquent and status offenders and make provisions for their alternative care, treatment, and punishment. Both acts are designed to hold juveniles responsible for their acts and to hold the system accountable for its treatment of these youths as well.

It is doubtful whether these codes are functional and in the best interests of those youths. Some persons say that these codes will weaken the current protection extended to dependent children or children in need of supervision. Furthermore, a serious erosion of judicial discretion may occur, accompanied by increased use of pretrial detention for juveniles where serious crimes are alleged. Also, status offenders may be jailed for violating court orders. It is difficult to devise a code of accountability founded on the principle of just deserts that nevertheless performs certain traditional treatment functions in the old context of *parens patriae*. Additionally, codes of any kind promote a degree of blind conformity or compliance with rules for the sake of compliance. With greater codification of juvenile procedures, less latitude exists for judges and others to make concessions and impose individualized dispositions where appropriate. The very idea of individualized dispositions, while appealing to just-deserts interests, invites abuse through discriminatory treatment on racial, ethnic, gender, and socioeconomic grounds.

Summary

For over 150 years since the United States was formed, juveniles had little or no legal standing. Matters were decided on their behalf according to their best interests by judges in accordance with the *parens patriae* doctrine. Although this doctrine is inherently discriminatory in its individualization of decision making relative to juveniles, it persists today among juvenile courts.

The U.S. Supreme Court was reluctant to become involved in juvenile matters for many decades because it believed that a youth's interests were the province of juvenile courts. However, discriminatory treatment of juveniles became too substantial for the high court to ignore. In 1966, a precedent-setting case, *Kent v. United States,* was decided. It was declared that juveniles have a right to a hearing prior to being transferred to criminal court for prosecution as an adult. Two cases immediately followed. These were *In re Gault* (1967) and *In re Winship* (1970). These cases gave youths the right to a notice of charges against them, to confront and cross-examine their accusers, the right against self-incrimination and to give testimony in their own behalf, and the right to an attorney. Additionally, the civil standard of proof necessary to confine youths in secure facilities, the preponderance of the evidence, was changed to the criminal standard of beyond a reasonable doubt. A pattern of gradually accruing rights for juveniles was established. Today juveniles enjoy almost the full range of rights as adults.

Several implications of greater rights for juveniles include more equitable treatment for juveniles through less juvenile court disparity; greater certainty of punishment through greater emphasis upon due process and justice; greater likelihood of juveniles acquiring juvenile records; and a greater likelihood of having one's case moved from the jurisdiction of juvenile courts to criminal courts.

A controversial issue relating to juveniles is the age at which they can be executed for committing capital crimes. Until 2005, juveniles aged 16 or over could be executed for capital offenses in most of the jurisdictions with death penalties. The landmark death penalty cases as the bases for this decision were *Wilkins v. Missouri* and *Stanford v.*

Kentucky. However, in March 2005, the U.S. Supreme Court decided the case of *Roper v. Simmons*. The high court declared that executions of juveniles under the age of 18 were unconstitutional. All juveniles on death row at the time of this decision had their sentences commuted to life, either with or without the possibility of parole. This newer standard comports with most other United Nations members where juveniles are defined as those under age 18 and executions of such persons are prohibited. Both proponents and opponents of the death penalty have advanced arguments favoring their respective positions. These arguments were discussed.

Because juveniles have acquired greater rights commensurate with those of adult criminal offenders, court unification has been proposed. Arguments for and against court unification were examined. Presently, public policy favors maintaining separate court systems for adults and juveniles. This situation is unlikely to change in the near future.

Key Terms

court unification, 149
double jeopardy, 131
family model, 150
habeas corpus, 126

hands-off doctrine, 118
litigation explosion, 119
Miranda warning, 134
traditional model, 150

Questions for Review

1. How has the get-tough movement influenced juvenile rights?

2. What is the hands-off doctrine? What corrections case seemed to establish this doctrine in corrections? What case undermined this doctrine? What is the significance of the hands-off doctrine for juvenile cases appealed to the U.S. Supreme Court? What juvenile case set a precedent by eliminating the hands-off doctrine?

3. What was the significance of (a) *Kent v. United States* and (b) *In re Gault*?

4. What is the standard of proof currently used in juvenile courts, where a juvenile's liberty is in jeopardy? What case was significant in evolving this standard of proof?

5. What is the case of *Breed v. Jones* and its significance for juvenile rights?

6. What is the minimum age for seeking the death penalty against a juvenile who has allegedly committed capital murder? What are some distinctions between the cases of *Wilkins v. Missouri* and *Stanford v. Kentucky* on the one hand and *Roper v. Simmons* on the other?

7. What are three arguments for and three arguments against the death penalty?

8. What was the significance of the case of *Thompson v. Oklahoma* and whether juveniles could be executed for committing capital crimes?

9. What is meant by court unification? What are some implications of court unification for juvenile offenders?

10. What are some problems with establishing court unification in the United States?

Internet Connections

Building Blocks for Youth
http://www.buildingblocksforyouth.org/issues/jjdpa/factsheet.html

Children and Family Justice Center
http://www.law.northwestern.edu/cfjc/

Criminal Justice Policy Foundation
http://www.cjpf.org/

Equal Rights for All
http://www.equalrights4all.org/

Juvenile Justice Center
http://www.abanet.org/crimjust/juvjus/

Juvenile Justice Information Center
http://www.cjcj.org/jjic/index.php

chapter 5

Juveniles and the Police

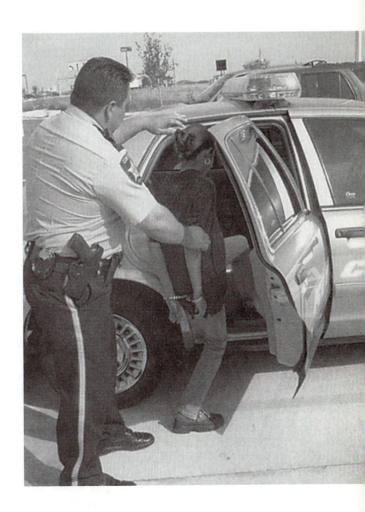

chapter objectives

As the result of reading this chapter, you will accomplish the following objectives:

1. Learn about police discretion relative to juvenile offenders.
2. Assess the importance of youth squads in police departments that interdict delinquent conduct.
3. Understand the differential response of youths to contacts with police.
4. Understand the ambiguity associated with juvenile arrests.
5. Understand how police officers distinguish between and process status and delinquent offenders.
6. Learn about several important delinquency intervention programs within communities and their effectiveness.

 ## Case Study

For at least two weeks, Oregon City, Oregon, was plagued with acts of vandalism: items stolen out of cars; food stolen out of garages; screens taken off windows; homes egged. Police suspected juveniles of perpetrating such acts. On the night of December 20, 2007, the police received a report from an anonymous caller that some kids were walking down the road and appeared to be drunk. A police car was dispatched and the youths fled when police approached. Three youths were apprehended and eventually confessed, implicating others in their vandalism. The youths were housed at the Clackamas County Juvenile Department, where they were charged with criminal mischief and theft. Monetary losses from the vandalism were estimated to be in excess of $5,000. In an unrelated incident in Midland, Texas, police arrested four males aged 14–16 on graffiti charges. They were accused of spray painting fences, sheds, vehicles, and walls. Graffiti damage was estimated at $5,000. [Sources: Adapted from the *Oregon City News,* "Police Arrest Juveniles Suspected in Crime Spree," December 20, 2007; adapted from the *Midland Reporter-Telegram,* "Police Arrest Four Juveniles for August Graffiti Incidents," September 19, 2007.]

 ## Case Study

In Alameda, California, police arrested six juveniles between the ages of 13 and 16 in early November 2007 in connection with the shooting death of Ichinkhorloo Bayarsaikhan on Halloween night a week earlier. Bayarsaikhan, 15, was shot at about 10:30 P.M. at Washington Park while she and a group of 10 friends were being robbed. The victim's family was thankful that the six suspects were arrested. In an unrelated incident in Pemberton Township, New Jersey, police observed a suspiciously young driver behind the wheel of a dark vehicle at 5:15 A.M. A brief investigation of the car and its occupants showed that six teens were in the car; the driver had no license; liquor bottles were discovered; and an automatic handgun was recovered from the floor of the rear seat. One round appeared to be jammed in the gun barrel. The youths were charged with possession of a handgun, possession of alcoholic beverages, and curfew violations. [Sources: Adapted from the *Alameda Examiner,* "Alameda Police Arrest 6 Juveniles in Teen Killing," November 9, 2007; adapted from *The Times of Trenton,* "Police Arrest Six Juveniles," September 24, 2007.]

Introduction

Police officers encounter youths on city streets every day and night. They never know how serious the youths are or the potential dangers they pose. In two incidents described above, petty offenders were involved in acts of vandalism, theft, and defacing property with graffiti. In other incidents described, cold-blooded murderers were apprehended and innocent-appearing youths were prevented from using a dangerous weapon to harm officers or others. Every police officer has at least one story to tell about his/her encounters with different types of youths. These encounters can range from harmless to lethal. One certainty is that the outcomes of these continuous encounters are completely unpredictable.

This chapter describes various interactions between the police and juveniles. An examination of police discretionary powers and how the exercise of this discretion is both used and abused is presented. Police departments are increasingly sensitive to the issue of how juveniles should be treated. Many larger police agencies today have established juvenile units whose exclusive function is to investigate juvenile offending whenever it occurs. These units have evolved policies that will be described and examined.

Juvenile gangs, and their formation and growth, are examined next, as well as the efforts of police to respond to gangs and gang problems. Contemporaneous with juvenile gang formation and growth have evolved numerous myths and misconceptions about who gang members are and what they do. These myths and misconceptions are listed and described. Over the years different authorities have classified and categorized various types of gangs according to their structure, organization, and operation. Some of these classification schemes will be described and discussed. Female juveniles have also formed gangs, and these gangs seem to be increasing in greater proportion to their male juvenile counterparts. Female gang formation and growth will also be described.

Next, a description of several types of responses by juveniles to their contacts with the police is presented. Several important factors are considered as dimensions affecting the nature of this contact. Socioeconomic status (SES), race/ethnicity, and gender all play important roles in how different juvenile–police encounters occur as well as the resulting outcomes of these encounters. These factors will be discussed in some detail.

The nature of decision making relative to juvenile arrests is described next. Arresting juveniles is complicated by the fact that it is not always easy for police officers to know the ages of youths they encounter and how these youths ought to be processed. Many juveniles possess false identification information or no information whatsoever, thus making it impossible for police officers to know with certainty who they have arrested and how such persons should be processed. Many juveniles are booked, photographed, fingerprinted, and otherwise subjected to many of the procedures associated with adult offender processing. These procedures are described.

In a majority of U.S. jurisdictions, juvenile courts have divested themselves of jurisdiction over status offenders. Despite divestiture, some police officers have continued to interact with status offenders as though they were delinquents. Status offending may be relabeled by police as delinquency, and police officers act accordingly. The influence of race, ethnicity, SES, and gender on such police behaviors toward juvenile status offenders has not gone unnoticed. The implications of divestiture of jurisdiction over status offenders will be discussed in some detail. Despite divestiture, both status and delinquent offenders are held in police stations for more or less lengthy periods. This detention process will be discussed.

Police Discretion: Use and Abuse

Police officers make up the front line or first line of defense in the prevention and/or control of street crime committed by juveniles, although the effectiveness of this line in

discretionary powers
Relating to the police role, police discretion is the distribution of nonnegotiable coercive force employed in accordance with the dictates of an intuitive grasp of situational exigencies; police have authority to use force to enforce the law, if, in the officer's opinion, the situation demands it.

situationally based discretion
Confronting crime in the streets on the basis of immediate situational factors, time of night, presence of weapons, numbers of offenders; requires extensive personal judgments by police officers.

community policing
Activities conducted by law enforcement officers to enhance public relations between police and the community; foot patrols and other "back-to-the-people" patrol strategies are considered integral elements of community policing.

crime control continues to be questioned (Myers, 2004). Police officers are vested with considerable **discretionary powers**, depending upon the circumstances, ranging from verbal warnings in confrontations with the public to the application of deadly force (*Tennessee v. Garner,* 1985). Police discretion is the range of behavioral choices police officers have within the limits of their power. Beyond the formal training police officers receive from law enforcement agency training academies, police discretion is influenced by many other factors, including the situation, as well as the race, ethnicity, gender, SES, and age of those confronted. Many of those stopped by police who are questioned, and subsequently arrested and detained in jails or other lockup facilities, even for short periods, are juveniles (Eitle, Stolzenberg, and D'Alessio, 2005).

The Diffuseness of Police Officer Roles

The public tends to define the police role diffusely, where police are expected to address a wide variety of human problems. The nature of this intervention is that they will intervene in various situations and ensure that matters do not get worse. Thus, police training in various jurisdictions is geared to reflect this broad public expectation of the police role (Shafer, Carter, and Katz-Bannister, 2004). Training manuals for police officers include numerous examples of field situations, including how to deal with domestic disturbances, traffic violations, narcotics, civil disorders, vice, drunkenness, federal offenses, and juveniles (Myers, 2004).

Much of this **situationally based discretion** in confronting crime in the streets and the public is covert. Most of what transpires in the interaction between police officers and suspects is known only to these actors. Thus, it is often difficult to enforce consistently high standards of accountability for police to observe in their diverse public encounters. In short, police officers make on-the-spot decisions about whether to move beyond simple verbal warnings or reprimands to more formal actions against those stopped and questioned on suspicion. Considering the circumstances or situation, law enforcement officers may be more or less aggressive.

Contributing to the diffuseness of police officer roles in communities is a relatively recent phenomenon known as **community policing**. Community policing is a major policing reform that broadens the police mission from a narrow focus on crime to a mandate that encourages the police to explore creative solutions for a host of community concerns, including crime, fear of crime, disorder, and neighborhood decay. It rests on the belief that only by working together will people and the police be able to improve the quality of life in the community, with the police not only as enforcers, but also as advisors, facilitators, and supporters of new community-based, police-supervised initiatives.

One immediate effect of community policing in many neighborhoods is to place greater discretionary power in the hands of police officers, whether they are on foot or in cruisers. An implicit effect of community policing is to create better relations between the police department and the community, in order for community residents to place greater trust in the police rather than to fear them (Myers, 2004). In communities where such discretion power shifts occur through planning, police officers may be expected by higher-ups to take a greater interest in youths, even where petty infractions are involved. Police officers may be punished for failing to take seriously minor infractions and for not intervening when necessary. Thus, they are in a dilemma about whether to get involved in the activities of minor offenders. In more sensitive settings, where ethnicity may play

Police discretion is exercised when groups of teens are hanging out in front of stores or gas stations.

an important role, law enforcement officers may be criticized unfairly by citizens for simply doing their jobs.

For many police officers, stopping and detaining juveniles is not a particularly popular activity. One reason is that juvenile court judges are inclined to be quite lenient with juvenile first-offenders or minor offenders. Many juvenile courts consider youths chronic offenders only after they have been adjudicated as delinquents five or six times. Thus, the considerable time police officers spend by taking youths into custody and filling out extensive paperwork seems like so much wasted time when these youths are released later with only verbal warnings from judges. There are also additional regulations governing how juveniles should be processed and detained when brought to jails following their encounters with police officers. These increasingly complex procedures for juvenile-offender processing discourage police–juvenile interactions except under the most serious circumstances and where serious crimes have been committed.

Nevertheless, police officers in every jurisdiction encounter large numbers of juveniles annually during their patrols or **beats**. Because of the informal nature of many of these police–juvenile encounters, the *Uniform Crime Reports* (*UCR*) and other official sources for arrest information fail to disclose the true incidence of all juvenile contacts with the law. In 2007, there were approximately 2.2 million juvenile arrests, about half of which were petitioned to juvenile courts for further action. Furthermore, self-reports from juveniles in elementary schools and high schools suggest considerably greater delinquent activity as well as contacts with police that don't necessarily result in arrests or being taken into custody for brief periods (Office of Juvenile Justice and Delinquency Prevention, 2007).

beats
Patrol areas assigned to police officers in neighborhoods.

Juvenile Gang Units in Police Departments

In the early years of police–juvenile encounters, police departments operated under a type of siege mentality. In Los Angeles, for example, the Zoot Suit Riots of 1943 involved a 10-day attack by civilians on alleged Mexican-American youth gang members. Extraordinarily repressive police policies were implemented at that time, and police–juvenile relations were strained for many decades (Mauro, 2005). Subsequently, police departments throughout the nation, particularly larger municipal police departments with 200 or more officers, established specialized juvenile units as a part of their organizational structure to deal with different types of offenders. Even relatively small departments in remote geographical areas have at least one juvenile officer who deals exclusively with juvenile affairs. Despite this specialization, however, every police officer who encounters juveniles while policing becomes a juvenile officer temporarily. Not all of the police activities in these juvenile units have been directed at gang violence or violent offenses committed by juveniles, however. Those targeted for active police intervention and assistance have included truants; runaways and missing children; property offenders and those who commit vehicular theft; curfew violators; and school-related offenses (Thurman and Zhao, 2004).

Police interest in gangs is most often focused upon prevention rather than retaliation (Mauro, 2005). Prevention measures by police include profiling gang members; methods used by gangs to recruit new members; neighborhood roots that spawn and perpetuate gang activity; the influence and presence of gang members in prison settings; providing materials and strategies for parents and school authorities to use for coping with gang activities; and examining gang structure (Katz, Webb, and Decker, 2005).

By 1997, all 51 jurisdictions in the United States had made extensive changes in their laws concerning juveniles who commit violent or serious crimes (Torbet and Szymanski, 1998). In turn, these legislative changes have caused numerous police departments to implement programs that will achieve certain delinquency prevention objectives contemplated by these changes (West, 2005). Many of these programs involve the establishment of gang units.

5.1   Focus on Delinquency

It happened in Jacksonville, Florida. Fourteen-year-old Latosha Marks was charged with first-degree murder in the stabbing death of her 15-year-old foster brother, DeShawn Hutchinson. Subsequently convicted of murder, Marks was sentenced to seven years in prison and 10 years of probation. Hutchinson's biological mother said, "I still can't sleep and it's bothering me badly. That was my child. She's a child still, but just like they give adults time, they should give her time. Murder's a murder." Marks was also ordered to undergo psychiatric counseling. [Source: Adapted from the Associated Press, "Teenage Girl Gets 7 Year Sentence for Slaying Foster Brother," March 2, 2006.]

It happened in Honolulu, Hawaii. A 15-year-old boy was arrested on May 25, 2007, on charges that he raped and murdered 51-year-old Karen Ertell in Honolulu, Hawaii. The unnamed boy was also charged with additional counts of murder and rape of another woman. Other charges against the boy included burglary, possession of confidential personal information, theft of credit cards, and fraudulent use of credit cards. Authorities are seeking to try the youth as an adult. [Source: Adapted from the Associated Press, "Rape Added to Juvenile Murder Suspect's Offenses," *Honolulu Advertiser*, July 30, 2007.]

youth squads

Teams of police officers in police departments whose responsibility is to focus upon particular delinquency problems and resolve them.

reactive units

Police youth squad units that respond to calls for service whenever gangs are terrorizing neighborhoods.

proactive units

Police youth squad units assigned special duties of aggressively patrolling high-delinquency areas in an effort to deter gangs from operating.

restorative policing

Police-based family group conferencing uses police, victims, youths, and their families to discuss the harm caused by the youth and creates an agreement to repair the harm; similar to restorative justice.

Actually, the activities of juvenile units or **youth squads** are largely directed toward delinquency prevention (Santana, 2005). These units tend to be **reactive units**, in that they respond to public requests for intervention and assistance whenever offenses committed by juveniles are reported. That is, these officers react to calls from others about crimes that have already been committed or are in progress. Gang fights or break-ins involving youths would activate these juvenile units. In contrast, police officers who patrol city streets are most often **proactive units** involved in contacts with juveniles who may or may not be offenders and/or law violators. These officers are almost constantly on the lookout for suspicious activities. They monitor the streets and investigate potentially troublesome situations.

Proactive Restorative Policing

In Bethlehem, Pennsylvania, a Police Family Group Conference Project (FGC) was established in the mid-1990s and coordinated by the Bethlehem Police Department (McCold and Wachtel, 1998). First-time, moderately serious juvenile offenders were randomly assigned either to formal adjudication in juvenile court or to a diversionary **restorative policing** process involving family group conference. Police-based family group conferencing uses trained police officers to facilitate meetings, which are attended by juvenile offenders, their victims, and their families and/or friends to discuss the harm caused by the offender's action and to create an agreement to repair the harm. Data were obtained and analyzed for 80 FGC participants, 180 victims, and 169 parents. These data were compared with control groups with similar characteristics. The FGC participation rate was 42 percent; 100 percent of the conferences produced an agreement on restorative actions; and 94 percent of all offenders were in full compliance with the agreements. The FGC seemed to produce lower rearrest rates among participants, and perceptions of fairness were as high as 96 percent for all participants.

Researchers concluded that the Bethlehem Police Department was able to reduce recidivism substantially among FGC participants while avoiding net-widening. It was also demonstrated that police officers were able to conduct FGCs successfully and without special training. Thus, the potential for applying FGCs in other jurisdictions was demonstrated.

Youth Gangs, Minority Status, and Gender

Types and Numbers of Gangs. The increased visibility of delinquent gangs organized along ethnic and racial lines in many cities and the violence such gangs manifest have caused police departments to establish task forces of special police officers who do nothing but monitor and investigate gang activities (Santana, 2005). Gangs have been classified as **scavenger gangs**, **territorial gangs**, and **corporate gangs**. Scavenger gangs form primarily as a means of socializing and for mutual protection. Territorial gangs are organized for the purpose of preserving a fixed amount of territory, such as several city blocks (Crawford, 2007). They maintain control over these geographical areas and repel efforts by other gangs to invade their territory or turf. The most violent gangs are corporate gangs. These types of gangs emulate organized crime syndicates. While all types of gangs pose dangers to the public, corporate gangs are more profit motivated and rely on illicit activities such as drug trafficking to further their profit interests (Katz, Webb, and Decker, 2005). Thus, corporate gangs are more dangerous than scavenger or territorial gangs. Corporate gangs use excessive violence including murder to carry out their goals. Often, innocent bystanders are gunned down as victims of gang retaliation against rival gangs and gang members (Martin et al., 2008).

Less-conventional gangs, such as the Skinheads, have been targeted by some youth gang bureaus and other police agencies within departments. For example, the Skinheads claimed at least 100,000 members worldwide in 2004. They have a cumulative record of gang violence involving weapons. And it is not always cities with large populations where police gang units are deployed. In Alabama, for instance, law enforcement agencies in 46 cities with populations of 10,000 or more have reported substantial gang activities in their jurisdictions (Martin et al., 2008). Alabama officials report that their gang visibility is comparable to that reported by larger cities, especially concerning the amount of female involvement or participation in gangs, the trappings of gang culture, and other critical gang elements. Officials in other jurisdictions have reported similar gang presence and activity (Grant, 2008).

In 1995, the National Youth Gang Center (NYGC) conducted an extensive survey, which became known as the **National Youth Gang Survey (NYGS)** (Wilson, 2001). Subsequently, the NYGS has been conducted annually to track gang activities and describe critical gang components and characteristics. At least nine types of gangs were identified in the original survey: (1) juvenile gangs; (2) street gangs; (3) taggers; (4) drug gangs; (5) satanic groups; (6) posses; (7) crews; (8) stoners; and (9) terrorist groups. Traditionally, gangs were formed by racial, ethnic, or religious groups. Gangs of today are based on needs to identify with a group (Martin et al., 2008). However, not all gangs today are limited to youths. Increasing numbers of youth gangs have adults as members. One estimate is that in 2007, there were over 34,500 gangs with a membership in excess of 1.5 million (Office of Juvenile Justice and Delinquency Prevention, 2007).

Myths and Truths about Gangs

Joan Moore (1993:28–29) has described several stereotypes of gangs that are not true. These include

1. Gangs are exclusively males who are violent, addicted to drugs and alcohol, sexually hyperactive, unpredictable, and confrontational.
2. They are either all African-American or all Hispanic.

---

scavenger gangs
Groups formed primarily as a means of socializing and for mutual protection.

territorial gangs
Groups of youths organized to defend a fixed amount of territory, such as several city blocks.

corporate gangs
Juvenile gangs emulating organized crime; profit-motivated gangs that rely on illicit activities, such as drug trafficking, to further their profits.

National Youth Gang Survey (NYGS)
Conducted annually since 1995; purpose of survey is to identify and describe critical gang components and characteristics.

5.2   Career Snapshot

Alana Malloy

Police Officer, Fairbanks, AK Police Department

Statistics:
B.A., M.A. (Justice), University of Alaska-Fairbanks

Background and Interests

I am a police officer for the Fairbanks Police Department. The department has 47 sworn officers. I have the best job in the world, although I wasn't one of those kids who had it figured out when I was five years old. In fact, I thought my career would be trying out all types of careers in an effort to find something that fit. Well, this is it. I work with an amazing group of sworn officers and civilian staff who make this job an adventure filled with challenge, growth, and new experiences every day. I graduated from the University of Alaska-Fairbanks with my B.A. in Justice, worked at an internship in rural Alaska as a juvenile probation officer, and then headed off to law school in California. I returned to Alaska and worked as an Assistant Teaching Parent at a residential treatment program for juvenile offenders and youth who were unable to remain in foster care placements. During this time, I also completed my M.A. in Administration of Justice.

Fairbanks is a unique community in many ways. I have lived in Alaska for about 14 years, of which I spent three as a police officer. Through personal experience and professional exposure, I have learned that Alaska is a culture of extreme living. We live hard and we play hard. Alaska has a high level of alcohol abuse and domestic violence. Add this to extreme cold temperatures, rural isolation, and a struggling culture trying to reclaim traditional values, and you begin to understand life in the far north.

During my initial interview to become a police officer, the investigator asked why I wanted to be a cop. I thought it was simple, I wanted to help people. I explained about my desire to help people, to restore societal chaos, and beamed with positive idealism. When I was done, he sat there for a minute, and finally asked what if I couldn't help these people; what if there weren't

happy endings? First lesson; just when you think you have something figured out, you usually don't. Now, with three years on the job, I understand what he was asking me. Very rarely do police officers get to see a positive end result to the contacts they make. There is the occasional parade, public event, or career day at a school, but people don't call 911 because something is going right. We usually respond to calls and in five minutes, try to restore order to situations that take a lifetime to create. Police work, by its very nature, is reactive. To help put this in perspective, consider this: the Fairbanks Police Department responded to 26,521 calls for service in 2007, an average of 73 calls for service per day. There are four to five officers on duty during a 10-hour shift, three shifts a day, 24 hours a day, 365 days a year, serving a city of 30,000 people. You do the math; we keep busy. Proactive policing is an effective tool in crime prevention, and it makes sense that if you spend the time utilizing proactive strategies, police calls for service may decrease and crime may be reduced. But, when is there time for proactive policing when calls for service are nonstop and increasing manpower is not an immediate option? The short answer is when you team up with the federal government.

Experiences

I am currently assigned to Project Weed and Seed. The Weed and Seed program is a community-based strategy sponsored by the U.S. Department of Justice. This strategy involves a two-pronged approach: law enforcement agencies and prosecutors cooperate to *weed out* violent criminals and drug abusers, and public service agencies and community-based private organizations collaborate to *seed in* much-needed social services including prevention, intervention, treatment, and neighborhood restoration programs. The community-oriented policing component bridges the weeding and seeding elements. This program is better understood as a strategy, rather than just as a program. When a new program starts up, it is alive and thriving as long as the money is there to support it, but when the money runs out, the program usually fades away. The Weed and Seed strategy sets a five-year timeline with the operational mission to organize and empower a community to build a partnership that sustains itself when federal support ends. This can be renewed annually for up to five years, with continued financial support from the community and demonstrated partnership growth.

The first year of any new program implementation strategy is full of challenges and endless variables. Even operating under a community-oriented policing philosophy, police departments struggle to utilize proactive strategies. The Weed and Seed program recognizes this dilemma. My current assignment allows me to do the extensive community outreach and partnership building with residents, businesses, and schools that every busy police department wants to do, but are usually unable to focus on due to limited resources and manpower. The program supports a dedicated law enforcement officer and a civilian program site coordinator, and is awarded to a recognized site area, referred to as the *footprint*.

The footprint in Fairbanks is made up of about 3,000 residents, five public schools, and many businesses. The area was chosen due to several demographic factors, including increased calls for police service concentrated in a set area, higher instances of juvenile crime, numerous low-income rental housing complexes with absentee landlords, and lower youth education scores. During the first year of the program, I attended several trainings identified in the program mission tailored specifically to the needs of the Fairbanks community. These trainings have included advanced courses in crime prevention and instruction, gang awareness and education, sexual-assault-response team training, and interviewing and interrogation skills.

I am the link between this *footprint community* and the police department. I respond to calls for service in the footprint. By only responding to this designated area, I build a relationship with the residents and employees. This programs brings back the traditional idea of the "beat cop"; a police officer who knows the area and the people in it, and they know that police officer. As the program continues to identify needs, my duties evolve. In addition to responding to calls for service, I conduct security checks on businesses and schools to deter crime. During summer months, I am out on foot patrol in the parks and public-gathering areas. I give public presentations on crime prevention strategies and provide trainings to businesses and their staff on shoplifting and robbery prevention. I help establish Neighborhood Watch programs in the footprint, empowering the residents to take back their neighborhood. I am currently working on forming a graffiti abatement program that will work towards neighborhood restoration and resistance to gang influences. I identify chronic nuisance businesses and properties based on repeated police calls for service and work with owners to resolve these issues. If these attempts are unsuccessful, I enforce city ordinances to fine or close down those nuisance properties. I work with the Juvenile Probation Department on a joint gang task force that facilitates a multiagency response toward an increasing gang concern in our community through awareness and education.

I perform extensive outreach in the schools, from elementary through high school. The five schools in the footprint now meet monthly with parents and kids at a Community Family Night to educate and celebrate their partnership through games and skill building. This partnership with the schools has fostered positive role modeling for youth. I stop by the schools and join the kids during recess and school functions. I walk the halls with principals and teachers during passing periods, go to football and basketball games, and attend proms (two last year).

Advice to Students

The best advice I can give to students is the same advice I was given. Try it all. Find out what challenges you, and then find someone to teach it to you. Find those internships and job-shadowing opportunities that expose you to fields you're interested in. Paid internships always seem preferable, but don't discount volunteer internships. Prospective employers may see a dedication and desire when you are there because you want to be, rather than just for the benefit of a paycheck.

If you're on the fence and not sure if you want to be a police officer, go on ride-along's with officers, volunteer with community nonprofits, such as Volunteers in Policing, and participate in various law enforcement internships. This process doesn't stop once you get the job. Law enforcement is a unique field because it encompasses so many facets of the law and public service. There are endless specialties, and countless avenues for growth and development.

3. They thrive in inner-city neighborhoods where they dominate, intimidate, and prey upon innocent citizens.
4. They all deal heavily in drugs, especially crack cocaine.
5. All gangs are alike.
6. There is no good in gangs; it is all bad.
7. Gangs are basically criminal enterprises and youths start gangs in order to collectively commit crimes.

Findings that challenge these erroneous and stereotypical gang characteristics are

1. Gangs, drugs, and violence appear to apply more to adult drug and criminal gangs than to youth gangs.
2. The connection between gangs, drugs, and violence is not as strong as it has been believed.
3. More young adult males than juveniles are involved in most criminal youth gangs, and they appear to be disproportionately involved in serious and violent crimes.
4. It is not as difficult for adolescents to resist gang pressures as was commonly believed. Youths can refuse to join gangs without reprisals.
5. Gang members can usually leave their gangs without serious consequences.
6. Modern gangs make less use of gang symbols and rites than gangs of the past.
7. Modern youth gangs are based less on territory than in the past.
8. More adolescents are gang members than in past years.
9. More gangs are in suburban areas, small towns, and rural areas than in the past.
10. There is more gang presence in the schools than in the 1980s and 1990s.
11. White gang members are more prevalent in adolescent gangs than in the past.
12. Females are more prevalent in adolescent gangs than previously reported.
13. Gangs in rural and sparsely populated areas are quite different from city gangs (Wilson, 2001:49–50).

The fact of racial and ethnic disproportionality in the juvenile justice system is underscored by a study undertaken by Darlene Conley in 1994. The juvenile justice system of a western state was investigated. Juvenile courts in six counties were selected as the target for her research. A representative sample of 1,777 juvenile cases was drawn, together with 170 in-depth interviews with court personnel, community leaders, defense attorneys, prosecutors, law enforcement officers, parents, youths, and others. The study also included 65 hours of participant observation covering court proceedings and plea bargaining involving adjudicated juveniles. Focus group interviews with juveniles were also conducted. It was found that blacks were 2 times more likely than whites to be arrested; 5 times more likely to be referred to juvenile court; 5 times more likely to be detained; 3 times more likely to be charged; 2.5 times more likely to be adjudicated delinquent; and 11 times more likely to be placed in secure confinement for a lengthy period. Hispanics were also overrepresented in the same counties, although they were not processed as extensively as blacks.

Suspected gang members may be searched and/or taken into custody by police on suspicion.

Similar findings relative to dissimilar treatment of minority juveniles have been reported elsewhere (Proctor and Mullings, 2008; Taylor et al., 2008).

Female Gangs

How prevalent are female gangs in the United States? Do female gangs commit similar types of offenses compared with male gangs? In 2007, it was estimated that there were over 150,000 female gang members in the United States, accounting for about 10 percent of all gang membership (Office of Juvenile Justice and Delinquency Prevention, 2007). Contemporary descriptions of female gang members suggest that they typically lack a formal education; have violent experiences at their schools; have seriously dysfunctional family lives; and have social problems including poverty, substance abuse, and gang violence. Interviews with a sample of female gang members from Texas indicated that they often join gangs to achieve power and protection, engendering respect from others based upon fear; and they often resort to more-serious criminal conduct. Often, membership in female gangs is contingent upon one's ethnic or racial status. Family disintegration and community deterioration often lead female gang members to create their own subculture where recognition can more easily be attained. Another factor is the lack of appropriate intervention, diversion, and treatment alternatives available to female juveniles compared with their male counterparts. With the presence of such gender inequities, young female involvement in delinquent behavior is more easily explained (Valdez, 2007).

Profiling of female gang members has been limited, in part because of their inaccessibility by researchers. It is too early to make sweeping generalizations about female delinquents and whether they are becoming more violent (Kelly, 2005). More attention needs to be directed toward understanding their interpersonal behaviors as well as certain institutionalized patterns of a patriarchal society.

Rising proportional female gang membership has been associated with rising female juvenile violence.

Juvenile Response to Police Officer Contacts

Police officers who observe juveniles in pairs or larger groupings, particularly in areas known to be gang dominated, may assume that these youths are gang members, and this observation may heighten police officer interest in and activity against them. The nature of this heightened interest and activity may be more frequent stopping and questioning of juveniles on the basis of their appearance and geographical location and whether they are minority youths. The precise impact of police–gang interactions is unclear, although in some jurisdictions, proactive policing against gang members has created sufficient conflict necessary to unify and perpetuate some gangs.

While it is unknown whether police officers discriminate against certain youths or single them out for stopping and questioning on the basis of racial or ethnic factors, there may be patterns of police behavior that appear discriminatory on racial or ethnic grounds. In some jurisdictions, minority youth stops, arrest rates, and detentions are at least three times as high as those for white youths.

Female youth gangs make up over 10 percent of all juvenile gangs in the United States.

However, much police officer activity is centered in high-crime areas that tend to be inhabited by large numbers of persons of lower SESs. And those areas with large numbers of persons of lower SESs are also those that contain larger concentrations of minorities (Greenleaf, 2005). Thus, some selectivity regulates where police officers will concentrate their patrol efforts as well as which youths they target for questioning and who they choose to ignore. Some observers believe that this opens the door to allegations of police officer harassment against certain classes of juvenile offenders on the basis of subjectively determined stereotypical features such as a youth's appearance (Crawford, 2007).

Interestingly, how youths behave toward police officers whenever they are stopped and questioned seems to make an important difference about what the officers will eventually do. The appearance and demeanor of those youths stopped by police officers and their subsequent actions seems to indicate that youths who are poorly dressed and/or behave defiantly and belligerently toward police are more likely to be harassed, possibly arrested. Related research is consistent with these early findings and suggests that cooperative, neatly dressed youths stand a better chance of avoiding being stopped, questioned, or arrested by police (Crawford, 2007).

In fact, some police officers insist that a youth's demeanor when responding to police questioning on the street is crucial to whether the youth will be taken into custody, even if temporarily. Therefore, if youths don't display the proper amount of deference toward police officers whenever they are stopped and questioned, the youths stand a good chance of being taken to the police station for further questioning (Grant, 2008). Interestingly, youths also may be too polite and arouse the suspicions of police officers. Thus, there is an elusive range of politeness that minimizes a youth's chances of being taken into custody. It is possible to be too polite or not polite enough so that police officers are sufficiently aggravated or motivated to act. Despite statutory safeguards about detaining youths in adult jails for long periods and the division of labor relating to youthful offender processing in any jurisdiction, police officers are free to do pretty much whatever they want relative to juveniles they question who are either acting suspiciously or belligerently. If any pretext exists for assuming that certain youths have been or are engaging in delinquent acts, they are subject to temporary detention by police officers. In many instances, these detention decisions by police are purely arbitrary.

The following is a listing of discretionary actions that may be taken by police officers when encountering youths on the street:

1. Police officers may ignore the behaviors of youths they observe in the absence of citizen complaints. The most frequent types of encounters police officers have with juveniles do not stem from complaints filed by others. Rather, police officers observe youths under a wide variety of circumstances. The situation and circumstances are important, since youths walking down a street in pairs during daylight hours would not attract the same kind of attention as pairs of youths walking the streets late at night. It depends upon what the officers regard as serious behaviors: If youths are on skateboards on the sidewalks of the main street of a local community, they may or may not be posing risks to other pedestrians; if youths are playing ball on a vacant lot near other homes in a neighborhood, they may or may not be disturbing others. Police action in each case is probably unwarranted.

2. Police officers may act passively on someone's complaint about juvenile behaviors. If a store owner complains that youths are jeopardizing the safety of store customers by riding their skateboards down crowded city streets, police officers may respond by directing youths to other streets for their skateboarding. If neighbors complain that youths are making too much noise playing in a nearby vacant lot, police officers may appear and advise youths to play elsewhere. The intent of police officers in these situations is two-fold. First, they want citizens to know they are there doing something. Second, they want citizens to know action has been taken and the problem no longer

exists. Police officers continue to view the behaviors they observe as not especially serious. In these instances, police warnings are ordinarily sufficient to satisfy complainants. Since complaints were made, dispositions of those complaints are usually logged officially. Police officers may or may not choose to name those youths warned. Rather, they may file a generalized report briefly describing their action taken. A sample complaint form is shown in Figure 5.1.

3. Police officers may take youths into custody and release them to parents or guardians without incident. Those youths who may be acting suspiciously or who are in places where their presence might indicate an intent to do something unlawful (e.g., youths crashing in an

Police interest in youths on city streets may be aroused by loitering, acting too polite, or acting too impolite.

uninhabited house after their party) are likely to be taken into custody for more extensive questioning. In many instances, these **stationhouse adjustments** may result in their release to parents with warnings from police about refraining from suspicious conduct in the future. While these actions are official in the sense that police officers actually took youths into custody for a brief period and made records of these temporary detentions, they do not result in official action or intervention by intake officers or juvenile courts.

4. Police officers may take youths into custody and refer them officially to community service agencies for assistance or treatment. Sometimes, youths appear to police to be under the influence of drugs or alcohol when they are stopped and questioned. Other youths may not have parents or guardians responsible for their conduct. They may be classified by police officers as runaways. In these cases, police officers arrange for various community services to take custody of these juveniles for treatment or assistance. These youths will be under agency care until arrangements can be made for their placement with relatives or in foster homes. Those youths with chemical dependencies may undergo medical treatment and therapy. In either case, juvenile courts are avoided. In many jurisdictions, drug courts are being established to deal with juveniles who are dependent on alcohol or chemicals (Armstrong, 2008; Miller, Miller, and Barnes, 2007).

5. Police officers may take youths into custody, file specific charges against them, and refer them to juvenile intake where they may or may not be detained. Only a small percentage of all juveniles detained by police will subsequently be charged with offenses. Conservatively, probably less than 10 percent of all juveniles who have contact with police officers annually engage in serious violent or property offenses. Therefore, many youths are taken into custody for minor infractions, and their referrals to juvenile intake may or may not result in short- or long-term confinement. The discretion shifts from police officers to intake officers—whether to process certain juveniles further into the juvenile justice system. Those juveniles who are deemed dangerous, violent, or persistent-nonviolent are most likely to be subject to detention until adjudication by a juvenile court. Police officers may respond to citizen complaints or actually observe juveniles engaging in illegal conduct. The likelihood of taking these youths into custody for such wrongdoings alleged or observed is increased accordingly.

6. Police officers may take youths into custody, file criminal charges against them, and statutorily place them in jails pending their initial appearance, a preliminary hearing, and a subsequent trial. Some juveniles may be classified as adults for the purpose of

stationhouse adjustments
Decisions made by police officers about certain juveniles taken into custody and brought to police stations for processing and investigation; adjustments often result in verbal reprimands and release to custody of parents.

Figure 5.1   Complaint against Juvenile (Dougherty County, GA)

COMPLAINT
IN THE JUVENILE COURT OF
DOUGHERTY COUNTY, GEORGIA

State F.F. #   Case #   File #

Name: (last, F, M)	Age:
AKA:	DOB:

Race: Lives	Res.: _____
Sex: With:	Bus.: _____

Child's   (Name)   (Phone)
Address:
(Street)   (Apt.#)   (City)   (County)   (State)   (Zip)

Mother's   Res.: _____
Name: Phone: Bus.: _____

Mother's   (Include Mother's Maiden Name in Parenthesis)
Address:
(Street)   (Apt.#)   (City)   (County)   (State)   (Zip)

Father's   Res.: _____
Name: Phone: Bus.: _____

Father's
Address:
(Street)   (Apt.#)   (City)   (County)   (State)   (Zip)

Legal   Res.: _____
Custodian: Phone: Bus.: _____

Custodian's
Address
(Street)   (Apt.#)   (City)   (County)   (State)   (Zip)

Complaint:
(Code Section)   (Misd./Fel.)   (Date of Offense)

Complaint:
(Code Section)   (Misd./Fel.)   (Date of Offense)

Complaint:
(Code Section)   (Misd./Fel.)   (Date of Offense)

Taken Into Custody: Yes ( ) No ( )
By Whom:

Placement of (Name) (Agency)	Date: _____
Deprived Child	Time: _____

Person Notified	Date: _____
By: Via	Time: _____

Detained: Yes ( ) No ( ) Place	Date: _____
Authorized By: Detained	Time: _____

Released To:	Date: _____
Relation:	Time: _____

Co-Perpetrators:
(Names and Ages)

Co-Perpetrators:
(Names and Ages)

Victim's Name:	Phone #: _____
Victim's Address:	
Victim's Name:	Phone #: _____
Victim's Address:	

JUVENILE COURT # 41 (A&M)

Source: Reprinted by permission of Dougherty County, Georgia Juvenile Court.

transferring them to criminal courts where they might receive harsher punishments. Jurisdictions such as Illinois; Washington, DC; New York; and California are a few of many places where **automatic transfer laws** exist and where some juveniles are automatically placed within the power of criminal courts rather than juvenile courts. Therefore, police officers *must* act in accordance with certain statutory provisions when handling certain juvenile offenders, whenever they effect arrests of suspects. Often, they have no choice in the matter. Changing get-tough policies toward violent or serious juvenile offenders are making it more difficult for police to be lenient when confronting juveniles on city streets.

Therefore, police discretion is exercised the most during the normal course of police patrols. Those youths who stand the best chance of being targeted for special police attention include minorities who are acting suspiciously and live in high-crime neighborhoods known as gang territories (Khalili, 2008). Also, increasing the likelihood of being taken into custody is the demeanor or behaviors exhibited by youths, whether they are polite or impolite to police officers. Apart from any illicit conduct actually observed by or reported to police officers, a youth's appearance and behaviors are key considerations in whether they will be harassed and/or detained temporarily by police. However, comparatively few youths are actually arrested in relation to the actual number of police–juvenile encounters on city streets.

> **automatic transfer laws**
> Jurisdictional laws that provide for automatic waivers of juveniles to criminal court for processing; legislatively prescribed directive to transfer juveniles of specified ages who have committed especially serious offenses to jurisdiction of criminal courts.

Arrests of Juveniles

Police officers need little, if any, provocation to bring juveniles into custody. Arrests of juveniles are, by degree, more serious than acts of bringing them into custody. Since any juvenile may be taken into custody for suspicious behavior or on any other pretext, all types of juveniles may be detained at police headquarters or at a sheriff's station, department, or jail temporarily. Suspected runaways, truants, or curfew violators may be taken into custody for their own welfare or protection, not necessarily for the purpose of facing subsequent offenses. It is standard policy in most jurisdictions, considering the sophistication of available social services, for police officers and jailers to turn over juveniles to the appropriate agencies as soon as possible after these youths have been apprehended or taken into custody (Burek et al., 2008).

Before police officers turn juveniles over to intake officials or juvenile probation officers for further processing, they ordinarily complete an arrest report, noting the youth's name; address; parent's or guardian's name and address; offenses alleged; circumstances; whether other juveniles were involved and apprehended; the juvenile's prior record, if any; height; weight; age; and other classificatory information. If immediate action against the juvenile is warranted, the police officer may complete and file an application for filing of a juvenile court petition.

Except in unusual circumstances and where youths are especially violent and pose a danger to others or themselves, they will be released to the custody of their parents or guardians following a brief detention and booking. In some instances, juveniles fail to appear later at their scheduled appointments with either the juvenile court or intake officers. When such persons fail to appear for scheduled proceedings against them, juvenile court judges issue orders for their immediate apprehension and detention. Figure 5.2 shows an apprehend and detain order for Glynn County, Georgia. Parents may become involved as well, since it is their responsibility to ensure that their children appear at any scheduled proceedings against them by the juvenile court.

Juvenile–Adult Distinctions

According to the Juvenile Justice and Delinquency Prevention Act of 1974 (JJDPA) and its subsequent amendments, juveniles must be separated from adults, both by sight and

Figure 5.2   Apprehend and Detain Order (Glynn County, GA)

In the Juvenile Court for
Glynn County State of Georgia

IN THE MATTER OF:

A Child.

§ <u>DESCRIPTION</u>
§
§ SEX:
§ DOB:
§ AGE:
§ FURTHER DESCRIPTION:

<u>ORDER TO APPREHEND</u>

To any Sheriff, Deputy Sheriff, or ay Peace Officer of said State or subdivision thereof–GREETINGS:

A complaint being made before me this the _____ day of ____, 20____, _____

_____

you are therefore commanded to take into custody the above-named juvenile and _____ pending a hearing before me to be dealt with as the law directs.

Witness my hand and official signature as Judge, this the _____ day of ____, 20____.

_____

Richard Douglas, Judge
JUVENILE COURT OF GLYNN COUNTY

Source: Reprinted by permission of Glynn County, Georgia Juvenile Court.

sound, and treated as juveniles as soon as possible following their apprehension. If juveniles are brought into custody and charged with offenses that might be either felonies or misdemeanors if committed by adults, they may be clearly distinguishable as juveniles. It would be difficult to conclude that an 8-, 9-, or 10-year-old could pass for 18 or older. But many juveniles who are taken into custody may or may not be under 18. Their appearance is deceptive, and if they deliberately wish to conceal information about their identity or age from officers, it is relatively easy for them to do so. This is a common occurrence, since many juveniles are afraid that police will notify their parents. Fear of parental reaction may sometimes be more compelling than the fear of police officers and possible confinement in a jail.

Because juveniles generally have less understanding of the law compared with adults, especially those who make careers out of crime, they may believe that they will fare better if officers believe that they are adults and not juvenile offenders. Perhaps there is a chance they might be released after spending a few hours or even a day or two confined in a jail cell. However, if they are identified positively as juveniles, then parents will invariably be notified of their arrest. But these youths often underestimate the resources police have at their disposal to verify information received from those booked after arrests. With proper identification, adults are ordinarily entitled to make bail and obtain early temporary release from jail. If fake IDs are used by these juveniles, however, this phony information is easily detected and arouses suspicions and interest in these youths. They will likely be detained as long as it takes to establish their true identities and ages. Furnishing police officers with false information is a rapid way to be placed in preventive detention for an indefinite period. And police officers are entitled to use preventive detention lawfully in such cases (*Schall v. Martin*, 1984).

The Ambiguity of Juvenile Arrests

Little uniformity exists among jurisdictions about how an arrest is defined. There is even greater ambiguity about what constitutes a juvenile arrest (Burek et al., 2008). An arrest is the legal detainment of a person to answer for criminal charges or (infrequently at present) civil demands. It is suggested that increasing numbers of police departments are proactively changing their police–juvenile policies so that decision making regarding juvenile processing will be more rational and effective.

Early research by Klein, Rosenzweig, and Bates (1975) focused upon juvenile arrest procedures followed by 49 suburban and urban police departments in a large metropolitan county. Over 250 police chiefs and juvenile officers and their supervisors were surveyed, some of whom participated in follow-up, in-depth interviews about juvenile arrests and processing. Among police chiefs, for example, fewer than 50 percent were in agreement that booking juvenile suspects was the equivalent of arresting them. Further, respondents variously believed that arrests involved simple police contact with juveniles and cautioning behavior. Others believed that taking youths into custody and releasing them to parents constituted an arrest. Less than half of those surveyed appeared thoroughly familiar with juvenile rights under the law and the different restrictions applicable to their processing by police officers. Record keeping and other activities related to juvenile processing by police have not changed much in subsequent years (Bureau of Justice Statistics, 2008).

Booking, Fingerprinting, and Photographing Juvenile Suspects

Under the JJDPA of 1974, its subsequent revisions, and recommendations from the National Advisory Committee on Criminal Justice Standards and Goals in 1976, significant restrictions were placed on law enforcement agencies concerning how juveniles should be processed and the nature and types of records that may be maintained relating to such processing. Under the 1974 act, for instance, status offenders were separated from delinquent offenders through deinstitutionalization of status offenders (DSO). According to the act, status offenders should not be taken to jails for temporary detention. Rather, they should be taken to social service agencies for less-formal dispositions. One intent of the act was to minimize the adverse impact and labeling influence associated with jails (Decker, 2005). While DSO is fairly common in most jurisdictions, police discretion causes a significant proportion of status offenders to be processed as delinquent anyway. Thus, some status offenders fall through the cracks and continue to be placed in U.S. jails annually, even though such housing is only for a few hours.

Since most juveniles are under the jurisdiction of juvenile courts, extensions of civil authority, procedural safeguards for juveniles are in place to prescribe conduct for both police and jail officers in their dealings with juveniles. For example, it is common practice for jail officers to photograph and fingerprint adult offenders. This is basic booking procedure. However, juveniles are often processed differently at the point of booking. Most jurisdictions have restricted photographing and fingerprinting juveniles for purposes related solely to their identification and eventual placement with parents or guardians. Fingerprinting is also useful if property crimes have been committed and fingerprints have been left at crime scenes.

Interrogations of Juvenile Suspects

Until 1966, custodial interrogations of criminal suspects by police were largely unregulated. Many of these custodial interrogations involved police brutality against particular suspects who were believed guilty of certain crimes. Suspects were denied access to defense counsel, and they were interrogated for many hours at a time, often without food, water, or rest. More than a few suspects confessed to crimes they didn't commit simply to end these brutal interrogations. However, in 1966 the U.S. Supreme Court heard the case of *Miranda v. Arizona*. Miranda was arrested on suspicion of rape and kidnapping. He was not permitted to talk to an attorney, nor was he advised of his right to one. He was interrogated by police for several hours, eventually confessing and signing a written confession. He was convicted. Miranda appealed, contending that his right to due process had been violated because he had not first been advised of his right to remain silent and to have an attorney present during a custodial interrogation. The U.S. Supreme Court agreed and set forth what later became known as the Miranda warning. This monumental decision provided that confessions made by suspects who were not notified of their due process rights cannot be admitted as evidence. Suspects must be advised of certain rights before they are questioned by police; these rights include the right to remain silent, the right to counsel, the right to free counsel if suspects cannot afford one, and the right to terminate questioning at any time.

When the Miranda warning became official policy for police officers when arresting criminal suspects, the warning and accompanying constitutional safeguards were not believed by them to be applicable to juveniles. Thus, law enforcement officers continued to question youths about crimes during several post-Miranda years. Since it is generally accepted that a juvenile's understanding of the law is poor, it might be further assumed that juveniles might be more easily manipulated by law enforcement authorities (Rehling, 2005).

A decision to protect juveniles from themselves by making incriminating Fifth Amendment–type statements was made by the U.S. Supreme Court in 1979. In that year, the U.S. Supreme Court decided the case of *Fare v. Michael C.* Michael C. was a juvenile charged with murder. During a preliminary interrogation, Michael C. was alone with police officers and detectives. Neither his parents nor an attorney were present. Michael C. asked to see his probation officer, but the interrogating detectives denied this request, since a probation officer is not an attorney and cannot be permitted to function as a defense counsel under these circumstances. Subsequently, Michael C. waived his right to counsel and answered police questions. He was convicted of murder and appealed, alleging that his right to counsel had been violated when he asked to see his probation officer and his request had been denied by the investigating officers. The court considered Michael C.'s case and determined that Michael C. had, indeed, made an intelligent, understanding, and voluntary waiver of his rights. The standard devised by the U.S. Supreme Court was the **totality of circumstances** test, which was essentially a standard they had adopted earlier in a criminal case involving an adult offender. Thus, the U.S. Supreme Court said that juvenile rights waivers should not be based on one sole characteristic or procedure, but rather, on all of the relevant circumstances of the case.

totality of circumstances

Sometimes used as the standard whereby offender guilt is determined or where search and seizure warrants may be obtained; officers consider entire set of circumstances surrounding apparently illegal event and act accordingly.

Michael C.'s case involved a juvenile who waived his constitutional right to be questioned by police about his involvement in a crime. The court ruled that the totality of circumstances test should govern whether juveniles intelligently and knowingly waived their rights to be questioned by police about crimes, and whether it is necessary first to obtain parental consent. Undoubtedly, this decision had led many states to enact statutes that specifically render inadmissible any admissions juveniles might make to police in the absence of parental guidance or consent.

Expungement and Sealing Policies

Historically, once photographs and fingerprints had been taken, they were destroyed as soon as possible following their use by police (Torbet et al., 1996:14). If such records exist in police department files after juveniles have reached the age of their majority, they may have their records expunged or sealed through **expungement orders**. Expungement orders are usually issued from judges to police departments and juvenile agencies to destroy any file material relating to one's juvenile offense history. Policies relating to records expungements vary among jurisdictions. Expunging one's juvenile record, sometimes known as **sealing records of juveniles**, is a means of preserving and ensuring confidentiality of information that might otherwise prove harmful to adults if disclosed to others such as employers.

> **expungement orders, sealing records of juveniles**
> Deletion of one's arrest record from official sources; in most jurisdictions, juvenile delinquency records are expunged when one reaches the age of majority or adulthood.

Theoretically, sealing of records is intended as a rehabilitative device, although not all juvenile justice professionals believe that sealing one's records and enforcing the confidentiality about one's juvenile past through expungement is always beneficial to the general public. State policies about police fingerprinting of juvenile suspects are diverse and inconsistent among jurisdictions. Further, there continues to be considerable disagreement about how such fingerprint and related information should be used by either juvenile or criminal courts in their subsequent processing of youthful offenders. In 2007, 47 states permitted fingerprinting of juveniles, while 46 states allowed photographing of them for law enforcement purposes (Office of Juvenile Justice and Delinquency Prevention, 2007).

By 2008, many jurisdictions extended the time interval for sealing or expunging one's juvenile record. Most states have increased the number of years that must pass before one's juvenile record can be expunged. Thus, one's juvenile record may not be expunged for several years after the person has become an adult. In fact, by 2008, 25 states specified that if any juvenile has committed a violent or other serious felony, his/her juvenile record cannot be sealed or expunged. Indications are that more states will adopt similar policies in the immediate future. Figure 5.3 shows an order to seal a juvenile's records used by the juvenile court in Glynn County, Georgia.

By 2007, 34 states had mandated open proceedings and the release of juvenile records to the public, particularly where serious offenses are involved. Furthermore, many states now expose juvenile court records to school officials or require that schools be notified whenever a juvenile is taken into custody for a violent crime or when a deadly weapon is used. Another widely adopted policy change is that 44 states have lowered the age at which juvenile court records may be made available to the public. Also, these states have established statewide repositories of information about violent and serious juveniles (Office of Juvenile Justice and Delinquency Prevention, 2007).

Status Offenders and Juvenile Delinquents

One of the more controversial issues in juvenile justice is how status offenders should be classified and managed. The fact that status offenders are labeled as status offenders contributes significantly to this controversy (Ross, 2008). Such a label implies that all status offenders are somehow alike and should be treated similarly in all jurisdictions. But this implication is about as valid as assuming that all juvenile delinquents are alike

Figure 5.3   Order Sealing Records (Glynn County, GA)

IN THE JUVENILE COURT OF GLYNN COUNTY
STATE OF GEORGIA

IN THE INTEREST OF:

—
—
—
—
—
—

ORDER SEALING RECORDS

     The above-named Petitioner having come before this Court with his/her application to seal his/her records, and it having been shown to the satisfaction of the Court that the Petitioner has been rehabilitated and that he/she has not been charged with any crime during the period of time between his/her termination of probation and the filing of this application and it being further found that the **District Attorney's Office, Glynn County Police Department, Glynn County Sheriff's Office and the Brunswick City Police Department** were apprised of the Application for Sealing Records and they agree to a waiver of Hearing on the same as evidenced by Exhibit "A".

     It is **ORDERED** that the records of   are sealed and all index references to the Petitioner shall be deleted. The Court, the Petitioner, law enforcement officers and all departments shall reply that no record exists with respect to the Petitioner upon inquiry in any matter.

     IT IS FURTHER ORDERED that a copy of this **ORDER** shall be transmitted forthwith to the **District Attorney's Office, Glynn County Police Department, Glynn County Sheriff's Office and the Brunswick City Police Department**.

     Inspection of the Petitioner's sealed files and records may hereafter be permitted only upon **Order of this Court**.

     This the

_____

Source: Reprinted by permission of Glynn County, Georgia Juvenile Court.

and should be treated similarly. If we think about the etiology of runaway behavior compared with the respective etiologies of curfew violation, truancy, incorrigibility, liquor law violation, and sex offenses, it is likely that different sets of explanatory factors account for each type of deviant conduct. Thus, different treatments, remedies, or solutions would be required for dealing with each effectively.

In 1974, the JJDPA acknowledged some major differences between status offenders and delinquents by mandating that status offenders should not be institutionalized as though they had committed crimes. Rather, they should be diverted away from the trappings of juvenile courts that seemingly criminalize their behaviors. By managing status offenders less formally and dealing with their behaviors largely through counseling and assistance provided through community-based services, it was reasoned that they would be less likely to define themselves as delinquent and that others would be less likely to define them as delinquent as well. The long-range implication of such differential treatment is that status offenders will not be inclined to progress or escalate to more serious types of offenses compared with those more-serious delinquent offenders who are exposed to the **criminogenic environment** of the juvenile courtroom (Austin, 2003).

Between the time the JJDPA was implemented and individual states adopted policies to DSO, there was a 95 percent reduction in the number of status offenders who are placed in some type of secure confinement (Office of Juvenile Justice and Delinquency Prevention, 2007). However, a portion of those detained consisted of status offenders who violated court orders or one or more conditions imposed by juvenile court judges at the time of their adjudications. Status offenders tend to exhibit less recidivism compared with those referred to juvenile court for delinquent acts. Further, the earlier juveniles are referred to juvenile court, for whatever reason, the more likely they will be to reoffend and reappear in juvenile courts. Therefore, diversionary procedures employed by police officers at their discretion when confronting extremely youthful offenders or those who are not doing anything particularly unlawful would seem to be justified on the basis of existing research evidence (Champion, 2008a).

But DSO is seen by some persons as tantamount to relinquishing juvenile court control over them, and not all persons favor this particular maneuver. A strong undercurrent of *parens patriae* persists, especially pertaining to those status offenders who need supervision and guidance from caring adults. Retaining control over status offenders is one means whereby the juvenile court can compel them to receive needed assistance and/or appropriate treatment. But disagreement exists about the most effective forms of intervention to be provided status offenders. One problem experienced by more than a few juvenile justice systems is inadequate resources for status offenders, and others require less-drastic interventions as alternatives to incarceration.

criminogenic environment
Setting where juveniles may feel like criminals or may acquire the characteristics or labels of criminals; settings include courtrooms and prisons.

Divestiture and Its Implications: Net-Widening

Divestiture means that juvenile courts relinquish their jurisdiction or authority over certain types of offenders, such as status offenders. Thus, if a juvenile court in Kansas or Colorado were to divest itself of authority over status offenders or children in need of supervision (CHINS), then those processing status offenders, such as police officers, would probably take such offenders to social service agencies or other community organizations designed to deal with these youths. Under divestiture provisions, status offenses are simply removed from the jurisdiction of juvenile courts. Various community agencies and social service organizations take over the responsibility for ensuring that status offenders will receive proper assistance and treatment. Referrals to juvenile court, incarceration, and the imposition of formal sanctions are no longer justified on the basis that one is a status offender and should suffer this processing and these punishments.

Relabeling Status Offenses as Delinquent Offenses

Because of police discretion, curfew violation, runaway behavior, and truancy can easily be reinterpreted or relabeled as attempted burglary or attempted larceny. Hanging out or common loitering may be defined by police as behaviors associated with casing homes, businesses, and automobiles as future targets for burglary and theft. And these acts are sufficiently serious and provocative to bring more juveniles into the juvenile justice system, thereby widening the net. Widening the net occurs whenever juveniles are brought into the juvenile justice system who would ordinarily have been dealt with by police differently prior to divestiture (Norris, Twill, and Kim, 2008). Prior to divestiture, many status offenders would have received wrist-slaps and verbal warnings by police instead of being taken into custody. However, when police officers resort to relabeling status offenses as conceivably criminal actions, greater rather than fewer numbers of juveniles will be netted into the juvenile justice system in the postdivestiture period than was the case in the predivestiture period. Sometimes, such relabeling occurs because of police attitudes toward youths or personal idiosyncrasies that cannot be legislated away or controlled by police departments. Police discretion is very individualized.

In the cities of Yakima and Seattle in Washington, police officers in the late 1970s were not particularly receptive to the idea that their discretion in certain juvenile matters was abolished by a legislative mandate. In effect, the police officers in these cities literally created a fictitious juvenile delinquency wave in the postdivestiture period, where the rate of delinquency appeared to double overnight. Such an artificial wave was easily accomplished, since these front-line officers merely defined juvenile behaviors differently according to their unchecked discretion.

Protecting Status Offenders from Themselves

Many runaways and truants may have certain mental health or educational needs that can only be met through mandatory participation in a mental health therapy program or educational intervention (Salinas, 2008). Court intervention may be necessary to ensure that juveniles take advantage of these services. Informal dispositions of status offense cases may not have the legal coercion of a juvenile court order. Thus, one's participation in various assistance programs is either voluntary or strongly recommended. However, agency response in accommodating youths with various problems seems selective and discriminatory. Often, those youths most in need of certain agency services are turned away as unqualified. Thus, status offender referrals to certain agencies may be unproductive, particularly if the status offenders are psychotic, violent, or drug/alcohol dependent (Kuntsche et al., 2007).

Parens Patriae Versus Due Process

The *parens patriae* philosophy is in increasing conflict with the due process orientation that typifies most juvenile court procedures today. Status offenders represent a juvenile offender class clearly in the middle of this conflict. Reducing admissions of status offenders to various detention centers and treatment facilities may result in a reversal of the hardening effect of custodial confinement on these youths.

Gender Stereotyping and DSO

A continuing problem of DSO in any jurisdiction is how male and female status offenders are differentially treated by juvenile court judges. To some extent the differential treatment of females by juvenile courts has become routinized and institutionalized. DSO has failed to change how juvenile court judges dispose of female status offense cases compared with how cases were disposed prior to DSO. It has been suggested that judicial stereotyping of female status offenders is such that many judges act to protect females from the system and society by placing them in restrictive circumstances such as secure confinement, even if their offenses do not warrant such placement. Thus, a double standard continues to be applied, despite the best intentions of DSO.

Race and Ethnicity

Do police officers and juvenile court judges stereotype status offenders on other factors besides gender? Some jurisdictions report that disproportionately high numbers of black youths are represented in their juvenile justice system. In Georgia, for instance, a youth's race has had a direct impact upon disposition decision making, as well as at the law enforcement, intake, and adjudication decision points (Owens-Sabir, 2007). Closely related to the race variable was SES. Thus, race and SES operated in this instance to predict correctly more-adverse consequences for youths who were black compared with youths who had committed similar offenses, had similar delinquency histories, but were white.

Presently, juvenile justice policy statements have been made declaring differential treatment on the basis of race/ethnicity, gender, and SES to be illegal, immoral, and inadvisable (Robbers, 2008). Such extralegal factors should have no place in determining one's chances in the juvenile justice system, whether one is a delinquent or a status offender (Zhang, 2008).

Redefining Delinquency

Police officers might consider taking a more proactive role as interventionists in the lives of juvenile offenders encountered on the street. For instance, Trojanowicz and Bucqueroux (1990:238) say that

> young people do not launch long-term criminal careers with a daring bank robbery, an elaborate kidnapping scheme, or a million-dollar dope deal. Yet the traditional police delivery system does not want officers "wasting" much time tracking down the kid who may have thrown rocks through a few windows at school. Narcotics officers on their way to bust Mr. Big at the dope house cruise right by those fleet-footed 10-year-old lookouts. And a call about a botched attempt by a youngster to hotwire a car would not be much of a priority, especially where far more serious crimes occur every day.

These criminologists indicate that officers should be encouraged to intervene and to take these petty offenses and juvenile infractions seriously. It is possible for police officers to identify those at-risk youngsters in particular neighborhoods and perhaps do something to assist them to refrain from future lives of crime (Khalili, 2008).

But the nature of systems is such that the actions of particular parts of the system may not function properly or be permitted to function properly in relation to other systemic parts. This was especially the case when divestiture of jurisdiction was implemented in Yakima and Seattle, Washington, during the 1980s and status offenders were removed from the jurisdiction of the juvenile courts. Whether or not Yakima or Seattle police officers were justified in doing so, they intervened in the lives of numerous status offenders after divestiture was enacted and relabeled status offenses as delinquent offenses. This intervention was contrary to the spirit of intervention explicitly outlined by Trojanowicz and Bucqueroux in their description of police actions under community policing policies. More status offenders and petty offenders on the streets of Yakima and Seattle were taken to jails and juvenile halls following divestiture than in previous years. This is quite different from officers acting as interventionists in positive ways and doing things for youths rather than against them.

There are obvious gaps between different contact points in the juvenile justice system. It is one thing to legislate change and remove status offenders from the jurisdiction of juvenile court judges and police officers. It is quite another thing to expect that juvenile court judges and police officers will automatically relinquish their powers over status offenders. While many juvenile court judges and police officers won't admit it to others, they do not like having their discretionary powers limited or undermined by legislatures.

Some observers have recommended that police departments should have separate units to interface with juveniles and manage them. This has already been accomplished in many of the larger city police departments throughout the United States. However, many smaller police departments and sheriff's offices simply lack the staff or facilities to accommodate such special units. These luxuries are usually enjoyed only by larger departments. Smaller departments must be content with individual officers who assume responsibilities for managing juvenile offenders and perform related tasks. Most initial contact with juveniles who roam the streets in various cities are usually made by patrolling uniformed police officers (Greenleaf, 2005).

Police officers will continue to exhibit interest in those juveniles who violate criminal laws. Offense seriousness and the totality of circumstances will usually dictate their reactions in street encounters with these youths (Duran, 2005). But most juveniles who are the subjects of police-initiated contacts have committed no crimes. These may be status offenders or those reported to police as **CHINS** (Lee, 2008). The wise use of discretion by police officers is especially crucial in dealing with status offenders. Fine lines may be drawn by academicians and others to distinguish between offender arrests and temporary detentions resulting from being taken into custody, but the bottom line is usually a record of the contact being entered in a juvenile file. One buffer between police actions against status offenders and less-serious delinquents is to divert certain juveniles to alternative and informal mechanisms where their cases can be disposed of with minimal visibility.

CHINS

Any children determined by the juvenile court and other agencies to be in need of community care or supervision.

Summary

The relationship between the police and juveniles is considered diffuse, since police officers are able to exercise much situationally-based discretion. Police officers have generally regarded contact with juveniles on the streets unfavorably, since the juvenile justice system deals with a majority of juvenile cases with great leniency. Most juvenile offending involves minor delinquent conduct, and therefore many police officers regard crime fighting and real police work as catching criminals rather than processing juveniles.

Most large police departments in the United States have gang units, which are largely reactive. These youth squads are oriented toward delinquency prevention and respond to reports of delinquent activity whenever it occurs, especially if it appears to be gang related. Studies of youth gangs are abundant, and several types of youth gangs have been identified. There are several myths and misconceptions about gangs. Several of these myths were described. Greater numbers of gang members are females, and the rate of female gang membership is growing annually. Gang members are younger each year, and rural- and urban-based gangs differ considerably.

Responses by juveniles to police officer contacts are sketchy. Police officers need relatively little if any justification to interfere in juvenile activities, regardless of their innocence or seriousness. Police officers have absolute discretionary powers over juveniles they confront. They can ignore youths; they may act passively on citizen complaints about juveniles; officers may take some youths into custody for a few hours and release them later through station house adjustments; they may take youths into custody and refer them to some social service agency or to juvenile court authorities; or they may arrest youths and charge them with various offenses.

Whenever juveniles are arrested, these arrests may or may not be clear-cut. Many arrested juveniles have false identifications or no identification. Arrested youths who are believed to have committed more serious offenses are usually photographed, fingerprinted, and booked like criminal offenders. Status offenders are qualitatively different from juvenile delinquents. A significant effort is made in most jurisdictions to separate status offenders from delinquent offenders. Relabeling and net-widening may occur and are unfortunate results of police discretionary powers. Several important factors have been linked with how juveniles are treated by the police and the juvenile justice system generally. Gender, SES, race, and ethnicity continue to be extralegal factors that are used by different actors throughout the juvenile justice system to make decisions and impose sanctions. Presently, there are mixed opinions about whether the juvenile justice system discriminates in significant ways against juveniles of different ethnicities, races, genders, or SES.

Key Terms

automatic transfer laws, 169
beats, 159
CHINS, 178
community policing, 158
corporate gangs, 161
criminogenic environment, 175
discretionary powers, 158
expungement orders, 173
National Youth Gang Survey
   (NYGS), 161

proactive units, 160
reactive units, 160
restorative policing, 160
scavenger gangs, 161
sealing records of juveniles, 173
situationally based discretion, 158
stationhouse adjustments, 167
territorial gangs, 161
totality of circumstances, 172
youth squads, 160

Questions for Review

1. What is situationally based police discretion? How is such discretion used and abused?

2. How are police officer roles considered diffuse regarding interactions with juveniles?

3. What are youth squads and gang units? What are their functions?

4. What is proactive, restorative policing? What are some of its characteristics?

5. What are several myths and truths about juvenile gangs and their membership?

6. What proportion of gangs in the United States are female gangs? What are some general characteristics of female gang members?

7. What are the four different discretionary actions police officers may take in relation to juveniles they encounter?

8. Why are the arrests of juveniles sometimes considered ambiguous?

9. Under what circumstances can police officers book, fingerprint, and photograph juvenile suspects?

10. What is meant by expungement or sealing juvenile records? How does divestiture of jurisdiction lead to net-widening?

Internet Connections

Federal Gang Violence Act
http://feinstein.senate.gov/03Releases/r-gangs1022.htm

Fight Crime, Invest in Kids
http://www.fightcrime.org/

Juvenile Justice Reform Initiatives
http://www.ojjdp.ncjrs.org/pubs/reform/ch2_k.html

Juvenile Law Center
http://www.juvenilelawcenter.com/pages/1/index.htm

Justice Policy Institute
http://www.justicepolicy.org/

National Youth Gang Center
http://www.iir.com/NYGC/

National Youth Violence Prevention Resource Center
http://www.safeyouth.org/scripts/index.asp

PreventViolence.org: Strategies to Keep Youth Safe
http://www.preventviolence.org/

chapter **6**

Intake and Preadjudicatory Processing

chapter objectives

As the result of reading this chapter, you will accomplish the following objectives:

1. Understand the intake process.
2. Learn about the roles of juvenile intake officers and the screening decisions they make.
3. Understand different models for dealing with juvenile offenders.
4. Distinguish between and learn about several important legal and extralegal factors that affect how juveniles are processed and treated within the juvenile justice system.
5. Describe several preliminary options available for juvenile offenders in lieu of formal juvenile court processing.

 ### Case Study

In Boulder, Colorado, intake officers are confronted regularly with juveniles of all ages and backgrounds. They must decide what action should be taken for many of these youths, including those charged with serious crimes. The Colorado Children's Code provides guidelines for these professionals to follow. The Boulder District Attorney's Juvenile Prosecution Unit, staffed with four attorneys, two paralegals, and a victim/witness advocate, seeks timely interventions and consequences with delinquent children. Not all kids who get into trouble need the same consequences. For instance, first-time felony offenders or misdemeanants may be offered juvenile diversion. Kids with more serious histories of delinquency may obtain firmer consequences. The most serious youths may be considered for placement in the Department of Institutions for up to two years. No case is clear-cut, and no decision about a juvenile's eventual outcome is perfect. [Source: Adapted from Colorado District Attorney's Office, Boulder County, Colorado, "Juvenile Prosecution Unit," January 15, 2008.]

 ### Case Study

In Montgomery County, Maryland, a juvenile intake officer faced two juveniles, brothers aged 13 and 16, who had recently been arrested for brandishing toy guns at a motorist. The guns appeared to be real, and the motorist advised police of the incident. The youths were arrested and charged with first-degree assault, which carries a maximum penalty of 25 years imprisonment. [Source: Adapted from the Department of Police, Montgomery County, Maryland, "Police Arrest Juveniles for First-Degree Assault with Toy Weapons," August 1, 2006.]

Introduction

Intake officers, usually juvenile probation officers assigned to juvenile courts for the purpose of screening juveniles, face all types of juveniles in their work. In many cases, they make decisions about which cases should be moved forward to the desks of juvenile prosecutors. In other cases, they may recommend diversion to juvenile court judges. Each jurisdiction differs in handling juveniles who commit similar offenses. Should juveniles who wave toy guns at passing motorists be treated in ways similar to those youths who commit armed robbery or attempted rape? What criteria should intake officers use in influencing a youth's life chances?

Approximately 2.2 million juveniles a year come into contact with police, school authorities, and others to have their cases heard in juvenile courts. Almost all of these juveniles are screened before moving further into the juvenile justice system. About half are diverted from the juvenile justice system through intake. This chapter describes the intake process. Intake is usually considered the first screening of youths where important decisions are made them. The intake process is examined, as well as a description provided of persons known as intake officers who perform these screening chores.

Because juveniles have acquired many of the same constitutional rights enjoyed by adult offenders charged with crimes, the intake process itself has been affected in various ways. Due process has become an increasingly important theme governing juvenile offender processing, and the intake process is affected accordingly. The formalization of the intake process is described. A portion of juvenile cases is plea bargained. While it is unknown precisely how much plea bargaining occurs in the juvenile justice system, it seems to be extensive. The discretionary powers of intake officers are examined, and the parallels between the intake process and plea bargaining are described.

Next described is an assortment of legal and extralegal factors that influence how juvenile offenders are treated. These factors include offense seriousness, the type of crime committed, the nature of evidence, the prior record of the juvenile, age, gender, race/ethnicity, and socioeconomic status (SES). The importance of these factors in juvenile offender processing is examined.

Subjective judgments about which juveniles are arrested and which ones are released with verbal warnings or reprimands are made by the police, and this subjectivity continues throughout the juvenile justice system at different points. Intake officers make decisions based on one's appearance, the type of attorney representing a juvenile, and the demeanor of the parents or the youths themselves. Both legal and extralegal factors are explored in some detail, and research is presented to indicate the presence of such factors in judicial decision making as well as at other points in juvenile offender processing and treatment. The nature of one's offending is a determining factor as well. Different dimensions of the decision-making process about juvenile offenders are examined.

What Is Intake?

Processing serious youthful offenders begins with an arrest and detention.

Intake or an intake screening is the second major step in the juvenile justice process. Intake is a more or less informally conducted screening procedure whereby intake probation officers or other juvenile court functionaries decide whether detained juveniles should be (1) unconditionally released from the juvenile justice system, (2) released to parents or guardians subject to a subsequent juvenile court appearance, (3) released or referred to one or more community-based services or resources, (4) placed in secure confinement subject to a subsequent juvenile court appearance, or (5) waived or transferred to the jurisdiction of criminal courts (Toth, 2005). The first step of the intake process is gathering information about the juvenile. A social history report is prepared by the intake officer. Such a report is illustrated in Figure 6.1.

Intake usually occurs in the office of a juvenile probation officer away from the formal juvenile court area. The juvenile probation officer, or intake officer, schedules an appointment with the juvenile and the juvenile's parents to consider the allegations made against the juvenile. The meeting is informal. The attorney representing the juvenile's interests may attend, although the primary purpose of the intake hearing is to

Figure 6.1   Social History Report

Social History Report

Routing Information   Case Identification

TO: _____   CASE   NAME: _____

FROM: _____ DATE: _____   SERIAL: _____ STATUS: _____

AREA: _____ OFFICE: _____   BIRTH DATE: _____ SEX: ___ RACE: _____

REPORT REQUESTED BY: _____   JPC ASSIGNED CASE: _____

1. IDENTIFYING DATA
    a. Youth's birthplace:
    b. Youth's birth status:
    c. Other names used:
    d. Youth's address at time of commitment:
    e. With whom living at time of commitment:
    f. Family's relationship to youth:
    g. Legal guardian:
    h. Social security number: Youth: Father: Mother:

2. PERSONS AND AGENCIES INTERVIEWED

3. AGENCIES THAT HAVE WORKED WITH YOUTH AND FAMILY

4. DELINQUENCY HISTORY (USE ONLY AS SUPPLEMENTAL TO COURT REPORT. IDENTIFY ANY PARTICULAR
    CHRONIC AND/OR PECULIAR PROBLEMS.)

5. DEVELOPMENTAL HISTORY
    a. Early history (Use only when obvious value in detailing youth's problems.)
    b. Medical history (Detail only if pertinent.)
    c. Description of youth (How parents perceive youth, attitudes, and behavior patterns.)

6. FAMILY HISTORY—REVISED
    a. Marital history and youth's previous living situations
    b. Father
    c. Mother
    d. Siblings
    e. Family income
    f. Parents' perception of problem
    g. Impression of family functioning
        (1) How parents relate to youth
        (2) Parents' concept of discipline
        (3) Evaluation of parent role (how they should/do perform as parents)
        (4) JPC's impression of performance and evaluation (identify strengths and weaknesses)
        (5) Family's financial resources, including benefits, veterans, Social Security, welfare, etc., medical/hospital insurance
             (Note: Income is reported elsewhere—preadmission history.)

7. COMMUNITY INFORMATION
    a. Placement possibilities, including own home. (Note attitudes, family structural compatibility, and other placement con-
        siderations.)
    b. Community attitudes toward placement
        (1) Neighbors
        (2) School officials

8. SCHOOL AND VOCATIONAL HISTORY
    a. School performance
        (1) Last school attended and grade completed
        (2) Level of scholastic performance
    b. Vocational history
        (1) Part-time or full-time jobs held
        (2) Performance evaluation

9. IMPRESSIONS AND RECOMMENDATIONS
    a. Overall evaluation by JPC
    b. Family's willingness to become involved and cooperate
    c. Problem list (JPC's perception of specific problems)
    d. Strengths and assets of family and youth which can be used in dealing with problems.

Source: Author.

screen juveniles and determine who deserve further attention from the juvenile justice system. Juvenile probation officers are vested with limited powers, and they do not have full adjudicatory authority possessed by juvenile court judges. For especially petty offending, intake officers can divert a case to social services, recommend a full-fledged juvenile prosecution, or request deferred prosecution in the least serious cases. A deferred prosecution agreement from a Wisconsin court is illustrated in Figure 6.2. The juvenile court prosecutor must consent to deferring prosecution of the juvenile. The intake officer oversees any special conditions or orders set forth in the deferred prosecution order. The juvenile, the juvenile's parents, and the intake officer sign the form, which has a beginning and an ending date. The agreement may be terminated for a variety of reasons, such as the juvenile or the juvenile's parent(s) failing to observe one or more conditions of the agreement. The favorable outcome of such an agreement is that the juvenile need not appear in a juvenile court. Even though the form is "formal," the process is quite informal compared with conventional juvenile court proceedings. Figure 6.3 is a notice to victims and a summary of the action taken as the result of the deferred prosecution of the juvenile. This notification is a courtesy to victims, and they cannot prevent the deferred prosecution. Wisconsin and other jurisdictions make every effort to keep victims notified as to the status of the juvenile and his/her progress during the period of deferred prosecution. When the period of deferred prosecution ends, the victims are notified of that event as well.

The Discretionary Powers of Intake Officers

The pivotal role played by intake probation officers cannot be underestimated. While police officers are often guided by rules and regulations that require specific actions such as taking juveniles into custody when certain events are observed or reported, the guidelines governing intake actions and decision making are less clear-cut. In most jurisdictions, intake proceedings are not open to the public, involve few participants, and do not presume the existence of the full range of a juvenile's constitutional rights. This is not meant to imply that juveniles may not exercise one or more of their constitutional rights during an intake hearing or proceeding, but rather the informal nature of many intake proceedings is such that one's constitutional rights are not usually the primary issue. The primary formality of these proceedings consists of information compiled by intake officers during their interviews with juvenile arrestees. The long-range effects of intake decision making are often serious and have profound implications for juvenile offenders once they reach adulthood (Toth, 2005).

Intake officers must often rely on their own powers of observation, feelings, and past experiences rather than a list of specific decision-making criteria to determine what they believe is best for each juvenile. Each juvenile's case is different from others, despite the fact that several types of offenses occur with great frequency (e.g., shoplifting and theft, burglary, and other property crimes). Some juveniles have lengthy records of delinquent conduct, whereas others are first-offenders. As we have seen, many jurisdictions have standard forms completed by probation officers during intake interviews.

Sometimes intake officers will have access to several alternative indicators of a juvenile's behavior, both past and future, through the administration of paper–pencil instruments that purportedly measure one's risk or likelihood of reoffending. Armed with this information, intake officers attempt to make important decisions about what should be done with and for juveniles who appear before them.

Various studies of intake officers have been conducted in an effort to determine the successfulness of their actions in influencing the lives of those they screen. For instance, during the period 1986–1987, 81 juvenile male offenders were court-referred to Lakeside Center, a residential treatment center in St. Louis, Missouri. Previously these juveniles had been rated and evaluated by intake officers. The officers reviewed social

Figure 6.2   Deferred Prosecution Agreement

State of Michigan, Circuit Court
_____ County

IN THE INTEREST OF: Deferred Prosecution Agreement

_____

Name

_____

Date of Birth   Case # _____

The prosecutor for the County of _____ comes before the court and requests deferred prosecution for the above titled juvenile. Neither the interests of the state nor the juvenile will be served at this time by formal adjudicatory proceedings, and it is the intake officer's belief that a delinquency petition not be filed presently. Rather, the juvenile, parents/guardians, and/or counselors appointed by the county will carry out the following conditions and terms, between the dates of _____ and _____. Upon the termination of this time period, a re-evaluation will be conducted by the court and prosecutor to determine the nature of future action against the juvenile. Satisfactory fulfillment of all terms and conditions contained in this agreement may lead to an expungement recommendation and such an order shall be entered by the court. If it is deemed that one or more court-ordered obligations have not been fulfilled as outlined below, the court at it's discretion will reinstitute proceedings against the juvenile and move forward with an adjudicatory hearing.

Court-Ordered Obligations:

❑ Restitution in the amount of $_____
❑ Obedience of all local, state, and federal ordinances
❑ Attendance at school and satisfactory academic performance
❑ Submission to recommended psychological testing and assessment
❑ Obedience to lawful legal guardians and/or parents or *guardians ad litem*
❑ Participation in teen court program or other suitable rehabilitative intervention
❑ Parental participation in parenting skills courses as designated by the court
❑ Avoidance of association with others involved in delinquent acts or who are truant
❑ Other: _____

It is so ordered on this date: _____

❑ **The deferred prosecution is granted**
❑ **The deferred prosecution is denied**

_____

Signature of Judge

_____

Signature(s) of parents, guardians, *guardians ad litem*

_____

Source: Author.

Figure 6.3 Notice to Victims

State of Michigan
Circuit Court _____
Juvenile Court Intake

Date: _____

Notice to Victims

Under Paragraph §3406.9221 of the Michigan Juvenile Code, the following information is being provided on your behalf because you were a victim of a crime committed by the following juvenile:

_____
Name of Juvenile

❑ The juvenile's case was adjudicated on: _____
❑ The disposition for the juvenile was: _____
❑ The juvenile's case was closed in _____ County and referred to _____ County where the juvenile resides.
❑ The juvenile was placed under a deferred prosecution agreement with court-ordered obligations.
❑ Restitution in the amount of $ _____ has been ordered paid to you as victims by _____
_____

❑ Repairs or services to victims are required and must be performed by _____
_____

❑ The juvenile has been placed in   ❑ secure   ❑ nonsecure confinement at _____
_____

and will be released from confinement on or about: _____

An agreement was reached between the juvenile court and juvenile/juvenile's attorney to restitution orders and/or repairs or services to restore any victim damages and the fair value of losses.

If the obligations of this agreement are not fulfilled in their entirety, then the juvenile's program may be revoked. At such time, a hearing will be conducted to determine further disposition of the juvenile. You will be notified in writing and by mail of the time and place of such a hearing, if one is needed and scheduled. You are permitted to present information, verbal and/or written, unfavorable or favorable to the juvenile involved at any future hearing.

Any questions relating to the above actions we have taken may be directed to the _____County Court, 1224 S. 4th Place, Grand Rapids, MI, 55667. You may also telephone this court at 555-236-4298 to determine the status of the juvenile's disposition at any time.

Please refer to Case # _____ as required by law under §3406.2668 of the Michigan Juvenile Code for any future inquiries.

All decisions by this court are reviewed by the juvenile court prosecutor and judge.

_____   _____   _____
Signature of Victim   Date   Telephone Number

Source: Author.

Arrested youths often appear before juvenile court judges for a preliminary review of their cases.

and referral history information, and they conducted an admission interview with each youth. The intake officers rated these juveniles as "good," "fair," or "poor" in terms of their prognosis for whether each juvenile would reoffend. Later, after the juveniles had attended the Lakeside Center for a period of time, a majority successfully completed the program, while 27 percent failed to complete it. Those who completed the program were far less likely to reoffend later when follow-ups were conducted. However, specific juveniles who were rated earlier by intake officers as having a "fair" or "poor" prognosis reoffended at a much higher rate compared with those rated by these officers as "good." Researchers concluded that intake officer assessments of the future conduct of juveniles they screened were highly reliable, especially when accompanied by an independent risk assessment device to measure their propensity to reoffend (Sawicki, Schaeffer, and Thies, 1999).

The process of intake is far from uniform throughout all U.S. jurisdictions. Often, intake officers do not believe that a comprehensive assessment of all juveniles is necessary at the point of intake (Toth, 2005). Juvenile probation office policies may not be clearly articulated, thus causing some confusion among intake officers about how intake screenings should be conducted and which variables should be considered most crucial in intake decision making. A wide variety of early interventions suggests a lack of consistency among jurisdictions and how effectively intake officers perform their jobs.

Florida Assessment Centers

assessment centers
Organizations selecting entry-level officers for correctional work; assessment centers hire correctional officers and probation or parole officers.

due process
Basic constitutional right to a fair trial, presumption of innocence until guilt is proven beyond a reasonable doubt, the opportunity to be heard, to be aware of a matter that is pending.

In Florida, juvenile **assessment centers** have been established as processing points for juveniles who have been taken into custody or arrested (Dembo and Schmeidler, 2003). These centers provide comprehensive screenings and assessments of youths to match various available services to client needs, to promote interagency coordination, and to generate data relevant to resource investment and treatment outcomes. Florida intake officers conduct clinical screenings, recommend confinement, make provisions for youth custody and supervision, arrange transportation, and track juveniles as they move throughout the juvenile justice system.

The U.S. Supreme Court has rejected attempts by various interests to extend the full range of **due process** guarantees for juveniles to intake proceedings, largely because of the informal nature of them. Thus, there are numerous interjurisdictional variations concerning the intake process and the extent to which one's constitutional rights are safeguarded or protected. Generally, these proceedings are conducted informally, without court reporters and other personnel who are normally equated with formal court decorum. A casually dressed, folksy juvenile probation officer sits at a desk with the juvenile accused of some infraction or crime, or who is alleged to be in need of some special supervision or care. One or both parents may be present at this informal hearing, although it is not unusual for parents or guardians to be absent from such proceedings. Victims may or may not attend, again depending upon the jurisdiction.

The Increasing Formalization of Intake

Intake is such an important stage of a juvenile's processing that it must be scrupulously monitored so that fairness and equitable treatment of juveniles by intake officers is preserved. Both legal and extralegal factors have been found to influence intake decision making in various jurisdictions. For instance, a study of the intake process in Iowa provides information about intake proceedings suggesting that extralegal factors are often at work to influence intake officer decision making. Leiber (1995) investigated a random sample of referrals to juvenile courts in Iowa during the period 1980–1991. Included in his study were 3,437 white juveniles, 2,784 black juveniles, and 350 Hispanic juveniles. Agency records provided detailed information about how the cases were disposed and processed at different stages, commencing with intake. Leiber found that the ultimate case outcome was influenced mostly by legal factors, such as offense seriousness, prior record of offending, and one's age. However, he found compelling evidence of discrimination in offender processing at the intake stage. Black juveniles tended to receive a larger proportion of recommendations from intake officers for further proceedings in the juvenile justice system. Black juveniles were also far less likely than whites and Hispanics to receive diversion or other lenient outcomes from the intake proceeding.

Often, these disparities in processing juveniles at the intake stage are attributable to the subjective impressions of intake officers. While most of these officers are perhaps well-intentioned in their individualization of juvenile treatment, there is some general bias inherent in such individualization. This bias occurs most likely as the result of gender, race/ethnic, and socioeconomic factors (Baron, 2007).

Regardless of whether any particular jurisdiction exhibits differential, preferential, or discriminatory treatment toward juvenile offenders at *any* stage of their processing, there are those who believe that increased defense attorney involvement for at least the most serious juveniles is a necessity (Burke, 2008). The primary reason for the presence of defense attorney involvement in the early stages of a juvenile's processing is to ensure that the juvenile's due process rights are observed. If there are extralegal factors at work that somehow influence an intake officer's view of a particular juvenile's case, then the impact of these extralegal factors can be diffused or at least minimized by the presence of someone who knows the law—a defense attorney. During the 1980s where data were available from reporting states, the amount of attorney use in juvenile proceedings increased substantially (Champion, 2008a). Specific states involved in a 10-year examination of juvenile attorney use trends were California, Montana, Nebraska, North Dakota, and Pennsylvania. Attorney use increased systematically during this decade.

The increased presence of counsel in juvenile proceedings at virtually any stage may have both positive and negative effects (Feld, 2007). An attorney's presence can preserve due process. Intake officers and other juvenile court actors, including judges, are inclined to apply juvenile law more precisely than under circumstances where defense counsel are not present to represent youthful offenders. Where defense counsel are not present, however, the law might be relaxed to the point where some juveniles' rights are ignored or trivialized. But an attorney's presence in juvenile proceedings criminalizes these proceedings to a degree. The fact of needing an attorney for one's defense in juvenile court is suggestive of criminal proceedings and ensuring a criminal defendant's right to due process. In circumstances where defense counsel and prosecutors argue the facts of particular cases, juveniles cannot help but be influenced by this adversarial event.

This experience is sometimes so traumatic that juveniles come to identify with criminals who go through essentially the same process. Many persons believe that youths who identify with criminals will eventually label themselves as criminal or delinquent, and thus they will be harmed from the experience. This is consistent with labeling theory, where self-definitions of particular types of persons are acquired by others, such as juveniles identifying with criminals on the basis of how they, the juveniles themselves, are treated and defined by others. To the

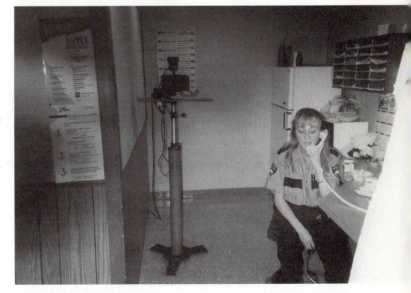

Youths taken into custody may be booked, including being photographed and fingerprinted.

extent that labeling theory adversely influences youths who either are first-offenders or have only committed minor infractions including status offenses, then some thought ought to be given to maintaining a degree of informality in intake proceedings. Nevertheless, it is important to emphasize a youth's accountability at all stages of juvenile justice processing (Ross, 2008).

The Need for Greater Accountability

More than a few persons seek greater accountability from those who work with juvenile offenders from intake through adjudication and disposition (Feld, 2007). Presently there is much variation among juvenile justice systems throughout the United States. Different types of family courts attempt to apply juvenile law in resolving a wide assortment of familial disputes and juvenile matters. Juvenile courts are increasingly seeking new methods and techniques, such as expanded intake functions and nonadversarial resolution of disputes, not only to create smoother case processing for juvenile courts, but also to provide more efficient, just, and enforceable social solutions to diverse juvenile problems. Accountability for judicial power requires that the court act comprehensively in providing social services either directly or by way of referral. This accountability involves not only the enforcement of dispositional orders requiring the parties and families to respond, but also the agencies and service providers to function effectively and the court to hold itself responsible for its case processing and management systems. This is a significant shift from the traditional treatment of juveniles by courts under the doctrine of *parens patriae*.

Intake Proceedings: Where Do We Go from Here?

Intake Compared with Plea Bargaining

A parallel has been drawn between what goes on in juvenile intake hearings and criminal plea bargaining (Champion, 2008a). In plea bargaining, prosecutors and defense attorneys will negotiate a guilty plea and a punishment that are acceptable to both parties. Ordinarily, plea bargaining occurs before any formal disposition or trial. Thus, the accused waives certain constitutional rights, including the right to a trial by jury, the right to confront and cross-examine witnesses, and the right against self-incrimination. A plea bargain is an admission of guilt to one or more criminal charges, and it is anticipated by those entering guilty pleas that leniency will be extended to them in exchange for their guilty pleas. The theory is that the accused will save the state considerable time and expense otherwise allocated to trials as well as the important prosecutorial burden of proving the defendant's guilt beyond a reasonable doubt. Although some jurisdictions prohibit plea bargaining (e.g., Alaska and selected counties throughout the United States), the U.S. Supreme Court has ruled that plea bargaining is constitutional in any jurisdiction that wishes to use it (*Brady v. United States*, 1970).

For many cases, this exchange is a reasonable one. In adult cases, crime for crime, other factors being reasonably equal, convicted offenders who plea bargain receive more lenient treatment compared with those who subject the state to the time and expense of jury trials (Champion, 2008a). Plea bargaining is favored by those who believe that it accelerates the criminal justice process.

During intake hearings, intake probation officers have almost unlimited discretion regarding specific outcomes for youths, especially those where minor offending is alleged. Apart from certain state-mandated hearings that must precede formal adjudicatory proceedings by juvenile court judges, no constitutional provisions require states to conduct such hearings. Intake officers seldom hear legal arguments or evaluate the sufficiency of evidence on behalf of or against youths sitting before them. These proceedings, which most often are informally conducted, usually result in adjustments, where intake officers adjust disputes or allegations informally. Thus, it may not be in the child's best interests for parents to hire attorneys to represent their children at this early and critical screening stage.

Intake officers are in the business of behavioral prediction. They must make important predictions about what they believe will be the future conduct of each juvenile, depending upon their decision. Sometimes personality tests are administered to certain youths to determine their degree of social or psychological adjustment or aptitude. Those considered dangerous, either to themselves or to others, are detained at youth centers or other juvenile custodial facilities, until a detention hearing is conducted. Florida Juvenile Assessment Centers administer a battery of tests to juveniles during intake, including clinical screenings by psychiatric professionals (Dembo et al., 2000b). For sex offenders in some jurisdictions, other psychological assessments are made and inventories administered, such as the Tennessee Self-Concept Scale, Beck Depression Inventory, the Rape-Myth Acceptance Scale, the Adversarial Sexual Attitudes Scale, the Assessing Environments Scale, the Buss-Durkee Hostility Inventory, and the Youth Self-Report (Worling, 1995). On the basis of these and other criteria, decisions are made by intake officers about whether additional steps are necessary in juvenile offender processing.

Increasing numbers of juvenile cases are plea bargained.

Intake officers may decide to refer juveniles to community-based services or agencies where they can receive needed treatment in cases such as alcohol or drug dependency. They may decide that certain juveniles should be detained in secure facilities to await a subsequent adjudication of their cases by juvenile court judges. Therefore, any action they take, other than outright dismissal of charges, that requires juveniles to fulfill certain conditions (e.g., attend special classes or receive therapy from some community agency or mental health facility) is based upon their presumption that the juvenile is guilty of the acts alleged by complainants.

If parents or guardians or the juveniles themselves insist that the intervention of an attorney is necessary during such informal proceedings, this effectively eliminates the informality and places certain constraints on intake officers. The coercive nature of their position is such that they may compel youths to receive therapy, make restitution, or comply with any number of other conditions to avoid further involvement in the juvenile justice process. It is relatively easy to file petitions against juveniles and compel them to face juvenile court judges.

Parens Patriae Perpetuated

Some evidence indicates that intake probation officers in many jurisdictions are perpetuating the *parens patriae* philosophy. For example, a study of intake probation officers in a southwestern U.S. metropolitan jurisdiction revealed that probation officers believed that they were the primary source of their juvenile clients' understanding of their legal rights, although these same probation officers did not themselves appear to have a sound grasp or understanding of these same juvenile rights (Lawrence, 1984). In this same jurisdiction, juveniles believed that they clearly understood their legal rights. However, interview data from them suggested that in general, they tended to have a very poor understanding of their rights. Emerging from this study was a general recommendation that probation officers who perform intake functions should receive more training and preparation for these important roles.

Juvenile court judges have been criticized for ineffective decision making about the conditions of one's probation and the social and community services they should receive. In more than a few instances, judges are limited primarily because there are limited social services available in their communities. Thus, even if judges wanted to maximize their effectiveness in placing youths in treatment programs that could help them, their actions would be frustrated by an absence of such programs.

Studies of intake dispositions in several jurisdictions have found that most intake dispositions tend to be influenced by extralegal factors, such as family, school, and employment. The preoccupation of intake probation officers in this jurisdiction with social adjustment factors rather than legalistic ones reflected a strong paternalistic orientation in dispositional decision making. Many intake officers dispose of cases according to what they perceived to be in the best interests of the children involved, rather than according to legalistic criteria, such as witness credibility, tangible evidence, and one's prior offending record (Holsinger and Latessa, 1999).

Intake probation officers are not inundated exclusively with cases that require fine judgment calls and discretionary hairsplitting. Many youths appearing before intake officers are hard-core offenders and recidivists who have previously been there. Also, evidentiary information presented by arresting officers is overwhelming in many cases, and a large portion of these cases tends to be rather serious. Therefore, intake officers will send many of these juveniles to juvenile court and/or arrange for a detention hearing so that they may be confined for their own safety as well as for the safety of others. Increasingly, serious juvenile offenders will be referred to juvenile prosecutors with recommendations that these juveniles should be transferred to the jurisdiction of criminal courts. The theory for this measure is that juveniles who are transferred to criminal courts will be amenable to more severe punishments normally meted out to adult offenders. However, it is questionable at present whether those who are transferred to criminal courts actually receive punishments that are more severe than they would otherwise receive if their cases were adjudicated in juvenile courts (Champion, 2008a).

Thus, intake is a screening mechanism designed to separate the more serious cases from the less serious ones as juveniles are processed by the system. Intake officers perform classificatory functions, where they attempt to classify informally large numbers of juveniles according to abstract criteria. Clearly, intake is not an infallible process. Much depends upon the particular experience and training of individual intake probation officers, juvenile court caseloads, and the nature of cases subject to intake decision making.

The discretionary powers of intake probation officers are in some ways equivalent to prosecutors in criminal courts. Intake officers may direct cases further into the system, they may defer certain cases pending some fulfillment of conditions, or they may abandon cases altogether and dismiss them from further processing. This powerful discretion can be used in both positive and negative ways, however. In response to a growing demand for juvenile justice reforms, numerous juvenile court judges have urged that more objective criteria be used for evaluating youthful offenders in the early stages of their processing, particularly at intake.

legal factors

Variables influencing the intake decision relating to the factual information about delinquent acts: crime seriousness, type of crime committed, prior record of delinquency adjudications, and evidence of inculpatory or exculpatory nature.

extralegal factors

Characteristics influencing intake decisions, such as juvenile offender attitudes, school grades and standing, gender, race, ethnicity, SES, and age.

Legal Factors: Crime Seriousness, Type of Crime Committed, Evidence, and Prior Record

A distinction is made between **legal factors** and **extralegal factors** that relate to intake decision making, as well as at other stages of the juvenile justice process. Legal factors relate to purely factual information about the offenses alleged, such as crime seriousness, the type of crime committed, any inculpatory (incriminating) or exculpatory (exonerating) evidence against offending juveniles, and the existence or absence of prior juvenile records or delinquency adjudications. Extralegal factors include, but are not limited to, juvenile offender attitudes, school grades and standing, gender, race or ethnicity, SES, and age. Age also functions as a legal factor for certain types of offenses. Specific legal variables examined here include: (1) offense seriousness, (2) type of crime committed, (3) inculpatory or exculpatory evidence, and (4) prior record.

Offense Seriousness

Offense or crime seriousness pertains to whether bodily harm was inflicted or death resulted from the youth's act. Those offenses considered as serious include forcible rape, aggravated assault, robbery, and homicide. These are crimes against persons or violent crimes. By degree, they are more serious than the conglomerate of property offenses, including vehicular theft, larceny, and burglary. In recent years, drug use has escalated among youths and adults in the United States and is considered as one of the most serious of the nation's crime problems (Pires and Jenkins, 2007). One general deterrent in every jurisdiction has been the imposition of stiff sentences and fines on those who sell drugs to others, and lesser punishments were imposed on those who possess drugs for personal use. All large cities in the United States today have numerous youth gangs, many of which are involved rather heavily in drug trafficking (Frisher et al., 2007). One result of such widespread drug trafficking among youths is the provision, in most juvenile courts, for more stringent penalties to be imposed on drug sales and possession. Thus, crimes don't always have to be violent to be considered serious.

Type of Crime Committed

Another key factor in screening cases for possible subsequent processing by the juvenile justice system is the type of crime or offense committed (Holsinger and Latessa, 1999). Is the offense property-related or violent? Was the act either a felony or a misdemeanor? Were there victims with apparent injuries? Did the youths act alone or in concert with others, and what was the nature of their role in the offense? Were they initiators or leaders, and did they encourage or incite others to offend? Intake officers are more likely to refer cases to juvenile prosecutors where juveniles are older (i.e., 16 years of age and over), and where the offenses alleged are especially serious, compared with referring younger, petty, first-offenders to prosecutors for additional processing.

Regarding juvenile justice policy, greater leniency with many offenders, particularly first-offenders, is often accompanied by less recidivism. Shay Bilchik says that greater intrusion into the juvenile justice system characterizes more serious offenders, probably meaning more chronic, persistent, dangerous, or habitual offenders—precisely the category of youthful offenders who are more likely to reoffend anyway (Bilchik, 1996). Perhaps the term **strategic leniency** is appropriate. The implication is that at least some punishment, properly administered, appears to have therapeutic value for many juvenile offenders compared with no punishment. For more violent or chronic, persistent offenders, however, leniency may be unwarranted.

> **strategic leniency**
> Less harsh dispositions meted out to certain offenders believed to be nonviolent and least likely to reoffend.

Inculpatory or Exculpatory Evidence

Offense seriousness and type of crime are considered quite influential at intake hearings, but some attention is also given by intake officers to the evidence police officers and others have acquired to show the offender's guilt. Direct evidence such as eyewitness accounts of the youth's behavior, tangible objects such as weapons, and the totality of circumstances give the intake officer a reasonably good idea of where the case would end eventually if it reached the adjudicatory stage in a juvenile court.

Also, intake officers can consider exculpatory evidence or materials and testimony from others informally that provide alibis for juveniles or mitigate the seriousness of their offenses. Evidentiary factors are important in establishing one's guilt or innocence, but referrals of juveniles by police officers to intake are usually indicative of the fact that the officers were persuaded to act in accordance with the situation they confronted. It is extraordinary for officers to pursue juvenile cases to the intake stage purely on the basis of whim, although some officers do so as a means of punishing certain juvenile offenders with poor attitudes. Most intake officers screen the least serious cases quickly at intake or provide dispositions for juveniles other than formal ones.

Prior Record

Intake officers use prior records of delinquency adjudications and factor these data into their decisions. In other jurisdictions, even jurisdictions in other countries such as Canada, prior records strongly suggest that prior treatments and/or punishments were apparently ineffective at curbing offender recidivism (Peterson, Ruck, and Koegl, 2001). It would be logical to suspect that intake officers would deal more harshly with those having prior records of delinquency adjudications. One's prior record of juvenile offenses would suggest persistence and chronicity, perhaps a rejection of and resistance to prior attempts at intervention and treatment. And in some of these cases, harsher punishments and dispositions have been observed. However, this is not a blanket generalization designed to cover all offense categories. Some offense categories have greater priority over others for many intake officers.

Also, the previous disposition of a particular juvenile's case seems to be a good predictor of subsequent case dispositions for that same offender. For instance, dispositions for prior offenses seem very similar to new dispositions for these very same offenses, regardless of the type or seriousness of the offense. Thus, if a juvenile has formerly been adjudicated delinquent on a burglary charge and probation for six months was imposed as the punishment, a new burglary charge against that same juvenile will likely result in the same probationary punishment for six months.

Extralegal Factors: Age, Gender, Race/Ethnicity, and SES of Juvenile Offenders

Most intake officers have vested interests in the decisions they make during screening hearings. They want to be fair to all juveniles, but at the same time, they are interested in individualizing their decision making according to each juvenile case. This means that they must balance their interests and objectives to achieve multiple goals, some of which may be in conflict. Furthermore, in recent years, greater pressure has been exerted on all juvenile justice components to implement those policies and procedures that will increase offender accountability at all stages of processing. Thus, a balanced approach may be recommended. Three major goals of the balanced approach for probation officers serving in various capacities in relation to their clients include: (1) protecting the community, (2) imposing accountability for offenses, and (3) equipping juvenile offenders with competencies to live productively and responsibly in the community.

In the context of attempting to achieve these three objectives and balance them, several extralegal characteristics of juvenile offenders have emerged to influence adversely the equality of treatment these youths may receive from probation officers at intake: (1) age, (2) gender, (3) race/ethnicity, and (4) SES.

Age

Age is both a legal and an extralegal factor in the juvenile justice system. Age is legally relevant in decisions about waivers to criminal court jurisdiction. Waivers of juveniles

Career Snapshot   6.1

Jeremiah S. Jeremiah, Jr.

Chief Judge, Rhode Island Family Court

Statistics:
B.A., J.D., Boston University

Background

I was appointed as the Chief Judge of the Rhode Island Family Court in 1987 after having served as an Associate Justice of the Court since 1986. As Chief Judge, I oversee 11 associate justices, 1 general magistrate, 6 magistrates, and 180 employees. For 25 years prior to my appointment to the bench, I was an attorney in private practice. My service to the public began in 1963 when I was appointed as an Assistant City Solicitor in Cranston, Rhode Island; I was promoted to County Solicitor in 1978 and served in that position until 1984.

In 1984 and until 1986, I served as Executive Counsel to the Governor of Rhode Island, the lead attorney position in the executive branch. I have been active in civic and professional affairs for over 40 years. I have been a member of numerous boards and committees dedicated to the improvement of justice for Rhode Island's children and families. In December 2000, I received the U.S. Department of Justice, Office of Justice Programs, Certificate of Appreciation for outstanding service and dedication to the young people and their families of Rhode Island. The recipient of many honors and awards, including the Giannini Award for Outstanding Contributions to Law-Related Education in Rhode Island and the Jack and Ruth Eckerd Achievement for Youth Award, I was recently recognized by the Urban League of Rhode Island for my dedication with their Community Service Award. In May 2001, the City of Woonsocket bestowed upon me its Award for Innovation for my creation of the city's first Truancy Court. I have created various innovative and user-friendly programs in the Family Court to better serve the public.

The highly successful Rhode Island Juvenile Drug Court was instituted in December 1999 under my leadership, as well as the state's first school-located Truancy Courts in 2000. I have since implemented other Specialty Court programs entitled the Family Treatment Drug Court, Juvenile Re-Entry Court, and the Domestic

Violence Court. I have also initiated court-mandated case management systems for the domestic relations and child protection dockets. I have also developed court-based mediation alternatives for the miscellaneous complaint and termination of parental rights calendars along with voluntary mediation and video education for divorcing couples. Other noteworthy projects include juvenile victim/offender mediation, supervised child/parent visitation, the adoption registry, and juvenile hearing boards.

Experiences

I have devoted my entire adult life to public service. The greater part of that service has been working to improve the lives of children. I have a very positive philosophy that I truly believe in. That is that the right motivation and circumstances can turn the lives of children around and set them on the path toward a successful and rewarding future. As the Chief Judge of the Rhode Island Family Court, not a day goes by that as I do not see or hear about youngsters who, unfortunately, have chosen the wrong path to go down. I cannot emphasize to children enough the importance of building and strengthening their leadership skills now so, as they continue to grow and mature, they will have the necessary tools to effectively respond and react in the most beneficial and productive ways when they are faced with difficult situations.

Unfortunately some children like those who enter my Juvenile Drug Court or Truancy Court programs are dealt a difficult hand. Whether it is making a bad decision, succumbing to peer pressure, having an unsupportive or unloving family, physical and/or developmental disabilities, economic disadvantages, or a combination of a host of other obstacles to overcome, these children are in desperate need of our support. We need to provide the resources to afford them an opportunity to become successful and productive citizens. Blame is not a solution! We need to educate and embrace the less fortunate and take responsibility for doing the best we can with everyone.

I have found nothing that is more rewarding than when I hear a success story about a child who has overcome hardship and prevailed! It is even more meaningful when I know that it is the direct result of the interaction of the Family Court. Five years ago, I began implementing a number of Specialty Court programs that were designed to deal with specific problems in a therapeutic, nonpunitive manner. The Specialty Courts (e.g., Juvenile Drug Court, Truancy Court, Family Treatment Drug Court, Re-Entry Court, and the Domestic Violence Court) are examples of the creative solutions that the Family Court has instituted to improve access to and appropriately address the complexity of issues that are presented so frequently to our court. These programs have become critical components and are essential to successfully treating the juveniles and the families that we encounter. They strive to encourage juveniles and their families to progress and succeed and not punish through the traditional adversarial process.

The Truancy Program is a prime example of the success we have seen since the implementation of our Special Court programs. The mission of the Family Truancy Court is to reduce the statewide truancy rate and to maximize juveniles' opportunities and likelihood of success. The Truancy Court program's growth and expansion is a testimony to the expertise, enthusiasm, and determination of all those involved and committed to ensuring the success of not only the Truancy Court, but also the success of each student it encounters. I started this program in one high school in 2000. Currently there are Truancy Court programs in 59 schools (a combination of high schools, middle school/junior high schools, and elementary schools) in 21 different cities and towns. In 2004, we serviced over 1,500 juveniles and their families in this one program alone. Over the past three years, an average of 66 percent of the children involved in the program have increased their school attendance and an average of 63 percent of these children have shown an increase in their academic performance. The pre-arraignment rate among middle-school children was 49 percent, while the post-arraignment rate after the

Truancy Court intervention was 89 percent. These facts are motivation for us to continue to improve, enhance, and expand our current Truancy Court program. However, the real driving force remains to be ensuring that every child is afforded the opportunity to the best education possible.

The keys to the success of the Rhode Island Family Court Truancy Court program are the following:

1. Court is held directly in the school rather than the court house, allowing for the child to lose less time in class.
2. Students are arraigned quickly, and the presiding magistrate assigns each juvenile in the system to a social worker to work with to see what is at the root of the absenteeism.
3. Truancy Court participants are frequently seen, with a parent or guardian initially, and then, as they progress, their time between court dates may be extended.

The majority of the students sent to the Truancy Court are between the ages of 13 and 14.

Advice to Students

Stay in school and learn all you can to improve your future. Make a commitment to improve your life and the lives of others. Be a role model for less fortunate or misdirected children who are in compromising situations, some by no choice of their own. Be a leader, in your school, in community, and in the future. Grasp any and all opportunities to create and mold a better and promising future. Be a part of a future that is more willing to embrace others, is more sensitive and understanding of the wrong choices and misfortunes that others endure, and is more compassionate and willing to lend a helping hand to those in need.

I remain steadfast in my commitment to ensuring that appropriate services are available and accessible to everyone who the Family Court serves. I am proud of the Rhode Island Family Court and the vast amount of recognition we have received from across the country that has acknowledged our success with the Specialty Court programs and want to emulate them in their respective communities, cities, and states.

under the age of 16 to criminal courts are relatively rare. Also, age has extralegal relevance. Older youths perhaps are assumed to be more responsible for their actions compared with younger youths, and they are often treated accordingly. Also, arrest data show that the peak ages of criminality lie between the sixteenth and twentieth birthdays

(Office of Juvenile Justice and Delinquency Prevention, 2007). Perhaps some intake officers believe that more aggressiveness in their decision making should be directed against older juveniles than against the younger ones.

However, the earlier the onset of a juvenile's contact with the juvenile justice system and police, the more serious the problem (Passetti and Merlo, 2008). Thus, younger offenders rather than older offenders are often treated with greater interest and attention. This is supported by the array of risk assessment instruments used by both juvenile and adult corrections departments throughout the United States today. Almost all these instruments use age as an important component in arriving at one's degree of risk or dangerousness. The younger the offender, the greater the weight assigned. This means that if youths become involved with delinquent acts at earlier ages, then greater weight is given and one's dangerousness score increases (Champion, 1994). This evidences the seriousness with which age is regarded as a predictor of chronic and persistent recidivism, whether property or violent offending is involved.

For many intake officers, the age factor appears to function in much the same fashion in influencing their intake decision making as it does when prosecutors assess the seriousness of identical offenses committed by both youths and adult offenders. For an assortment of nonrational reasons, armed robbery is not as serious for some prosecutors when committed by a 12-year-old as it is when it is committed by a 21-year-old. Applied to intake decision making, probation officers may regard certain serious offenses as less serious when committed by those aged 13 and under, while 14-year-olds and older youths may have those same offenses judged as more serious. There are no precise age divisions that separate younger from older youthful offenders when one's age is functioning as an extralegal factor (Toth, 2005).

Gender

Generally, traditional patterns of female delinquency have persisted over the years. Because there are so few female juvenile offenders compared with their male counterparts, the influence of gender on intake decision making and at other stages of the juvenile justice process has not been investigated extensively. Juvenile females make up approximately 14 percent of the juvenile incarcerative population in the United States annually (American Correctional Association, 2007). Females are only slightly more represented proportionately among those on probation or involved in assorted public and private aftercare services. Explanations for gender differences in their comparative rate of offending have ranged from different socialization experiences to impulsivity, self-control differentials, or low constraint/negative emotionality compared with male delinquents (Chapple and Johnson, 2007).

Differential treatment of males and females in both the juvenile and the criminal justice systems is well documented. However, some of the traditional reasons given for such differential treatment, especially about female juveniles and their delinquency patterns, appear to be misconceived or have no basis in fact (Beaver, DeLisi, and Vaughn, 2008). Selected assessments of the impact of gender on intake decision making show that it is only moderately related to dispositions, consistent with intake guidelines in selected jurisdictions such as Arizona and Florida.

Within the just deserts, justice, or crime control frameworks, the attention of those interested in the juvenile justice system is focused upon the act more than upon the juveniles committing the act or their physical or social characteristics. Thus, gender differences leading to differential treatment of offenders who behave similarly would not be acceptable. However, the differential treatment of male and female juveniles in the United States and other countries persists (Chapple and Johnson, 2007).

A strong contributing factor is the paternalistic view of juvenile court judges and others in the juvenile justice system that has persisted over time in the aftermath and influence of *parens patriae*. Differences between the arrest rates of female and male

6.2   Focus on Delinquency

It happened in Minnesota. A newborn baby was found dead on the back porch of a house in freezing cold. The site of the death is a farming community. Residents in the community named the dead baby A.Z., and gave it a proper burial. No one knew whose baby it was or who had left it to die on the back porch of the house. The secret of A.Z. was eventually revealed when it was determined that a 15-year-old admitted she had been pregnant. K.L., the female teen, wore baggy clothes to hide her pregnancy. She gave birth to a 7-pound baby girl in her bedroom while her parents were asleep. K.L. then bathed the baby, dressed her in pajamas, wrapped her in a towel, and left her on the back steps of the house next door with part of her umbilical cord still attached. A few days later, K.L. attended the baby's funeral with her parents at a church a few blocks from her house, showing no emotion.

Subsequently during a domestic disturbance between K.L., 20, and the dead baby's father, R.M., with whom she was living now, she blurted out what she had done with the newborn baby. At that point, R.M. struck at her head and face. K.L. threatened to call the police, but R.M. said that if she did, he would tell them about her baby and what she had done. She kept quiet about it, but later, under questioning from her parents about bruises on her face, the truth was eventually told. R.M. was arrested for domestic battery and K.L. was arrested and charged with first-degree murder. If convicted, she could receive life imprisonment. A defense attorney for K.L. advised that she would plead not guilty to the charge. What should the penalty be for the murder of a baby, when the murderer is a 15-year-old unmarried girl? Do you think K.L. is guilty of first-degree murder? If convicted of the baby's murder, what do you think should be K.L.'s punishment? How should the judge decide? [Source: Adapted from the Associated Press, "Girl Confesses to Baby's Death," July 7, 2008.]

juveniles and the proportion of females to males who are subsequently adjudicated as delinquent suggest that the case attrition rate for females is significantly higher at intake than it is for male juveniles. However, gender may have only an indirect impact on such decision making by intake officers.

Race and Ethnicity

More important as predictors of decision making at virtually every stage of the juvenile justice process are race and ethnicity. Race and ethnicity appear to be significant predictor variables in arrest and detention discretion as well as referrals. Minority overrepresentation throughout the juvenile justice process has been reported in various jurisdictions (Burek et al., 2008).

SES

Closely related to racial and ethnic factors as extralegal considerations in intake decision making is the **SES** of juvenile offenders. It has been found that, generally, the poor as well as racial and ethnic minorities are disenfranchised by the juvenile justice system at various stages. This is true not only of juvenile courts in the United States but also in those of other countries. One explanation for this alleged disenfranchisement is more limited access to economic resources among the poor and minorities. More restricted economic resources reduce the quality of legal defenses that may be accessed by the socioeconomically disadvantaged. Greater reliance on public defenders is observed among the poor compared with those who are financially advantaged.

A greater proportion of the socioeconomically disadvantaged tends to acquiesce and quietly accept systemic sanctions that accompany charges of wrongdoing rather than acquire counsel and contest the charges formally in court. But not all investigators believe that the relation between SES and delinquency is necessarily strong or negative.

Preliminary Decision Making: Diversion and Other Options

Diverting Certain Juveniles from the System

A long-range interest of most, if not all, intake officers is minimizing recidivism among those diverted from the system at the time of an intake hearing. **Recidivism** is also a commonly used measure of program effectiveness in both adult and juvenile offender treatment and sanctioning schemes. Because of the fragmented nature of the juvenile justice systems throughout the United States, it is extremely difficult to compile reliable, accurate information about the extent of juvenile delinquent recidivism. However, criminal justice practitioners estimate that the rate of recidivism among juveniles is similar to that for adult criminal offenders (Office of Juvenile Justice and Delinquency Prevention, 2007).

> **recidivism**
> Repeat offending, convictions or adjudications for new offenses after prior convictions or adjudications, or any type of new offense following prior offense history.

Intake officer interest in the type of offense committed is triggered not only by the seriousness of the act itself and what should be done about it, but by evidence from various jurisdictions which suggests that recidivism rates vary substantially for different types of juvenile offenders. For example, studies of violent and nonviolent and chronic and nonchronic juvenile recidivists suggest that greater proportions of chronic offenders repeat violent offenses than nonchronic offenders (Belshaw and Lanham, 2008). However, chronic offenders also commit subsequent nonviolent acts as well as violent ones. Despite increasing juvenile violence, it remains the case that only a small proportion of youths accounts for a majority of the violent crimes committed (Lansford et al., 2007).

How Should We Deal with Chronic Violent Offenders?

Closely associated with recidivism among chronic violent offenders in certain jurisdictions are predictor variables such as whether the delinquent has delinquent siblings and/or significant others as associates, whether the delinquent has school problems, and whether the acts committed were misdemeanors or felonies. In growing numbers of jurisdictions, chronic violent or serious offenders and other aggressive youths have been targeted for priority processing at intake and other stages. Harsher measures, including rapid identification of youths, expedited hearings, close monitoring of their cases, and their segregation from other, less serious offenders, have been employed by different Hawaiian juvenile justice units as a means of crime control. Continuous counseling, placement in long-term secure confinement facilities, extended court jurisdiction, and the revelation of these youths' identities to the public seem effective at curbing recidivism among these hard-core offenders. Several constitutional issues that must be resolved concern identities of juvenile offenders and the publication of information about them made available to others.

The Inadequacy of Treatment and Community Services

Also, many jurisdictions are hard-pressed to provide adequate treatment facilities and interventions that contain the ingredients for effectiveness. Some programs might have security without a jail-like atmosphere, close coordination and cooperation between the community and the criminal justice system, paraprofessional staffs, and provisions for remedial education and job training for these youths. But existing limited budgets and other priorities in many jurisdictions prevent the development of such sophisticated interventions. Yet another view is that interventions should be aimed at modifying one's social and psychological environment that fostered such violence and chronicity originally (Supancic, 2005).

Getting Tough with Persistent Offenders

For persistent offenders and otherwise hard-core violent recidivists, even for some violent first-offenders, the strategy employed at intake may be a waiver of jurisdiction to criminal courts (Champion, 2008a). Some jurisdictions, such as New York, Washington, and Illinois, have automatic transfer laws that compel juvenile authorities to send certain types of juvenile offenders in a particular age range (normally age 16 or 17) directly to criminal court to be processed as adults. The manifest intent of such waivers to criminal court is for harsher punishments to be imposed on these youthful offenders beyond those that can ordinarily be administered within the power of juvenile court judges (Kuanliang, 2008).

The get-tough movement clearly has incarceration in mind for those youths who have been adjudicated delinquent for violent offenses (Vivian, Grimes, and Vasquez, 2007). Anything less than secure confinement for such youths adjudicated for aggravated assault, rape, robbery, or homicide is considered as too lenient. However, some juvenile justice observers argue that there is presently too much incarceration, that incarceration is overdone, and that many youths can remain in their communities under close supervision, participating in productive self-improvement and rehabilitative programs (Mears et al., 2007).

Is There Too Much Juvenile Incarceration?

Several alternatives to confinement have been investigated (Trulson and Haerle, 2008). In 1987, the Delaware Plan was established, whereby certain community programs were established as alternatives to incarcerating certain types of delinquent offenders. Brandau found that, over time, a sample of 363 youths adjudicated for various serious delinquency offenses was assigned randomly to reform school, placed on probation, or sent to the Delaware Bay Marine Institute (DBMI). The DBMI was a community-based program designed to equip certain youths with coping skills and other useful experiences. Legal, social, and demographic variables were controlled, and all youths were evaluated according to whether they were more likely to be assigned to the reform school following their delinquency adjudications. Subsequently, recidivism information was compiled for all youths to determine the influence of the different experiences on them. Youths in the DBMI program had recidivism rates similar to those placed on straight probation and those placed in reform schools. This finding is significant because it shows in this instance, at least, that the DBMI program was about as effective as incarceration or probation for decreasing one's likelihood of recidivating. Since incarcerating juveniles is more expensive than placing them on probation or in the DBMI program, it is suggested that nonincarcerative community-based alternatives should be used more frequently, even for serious offenders.

Some criminologists argue that secure confinement is overused in many instances where juveniles have been adjudicated (Champion, 2008a). Surveys of incarcerated youth suggest that many do not need to be incarcerated. Over a third of all youths in state training schools probably belong in less secure settings. In more than a few jurisdictions, juvenile court judges may be exercising a rather heavy hand when meting out punishments and disposing of cases through secure custody rather than imposing alternative community-based punishments (Xiaoying, 2005). Increasingly emphasized, particularly as a cost-cutting measure, is focusing attention on methods or interventions that will reduce the recidivism rates of previously committed youth (Champion, 2008a).

Assessment of Guardianship

While most cases that are furthered to the intake stage of the juvenile justice process involve some type of juvenile offending, criminal or otherwise, intake officers are often confronted with cases that require assessments of a youth's parents or guardians and the general sociocultural environment (Souhami, 2007). Ordinarily, children in need of supervision (CHINS), including unruly or incorrigible youths, dependent and/or neglected youths, and abused children are channeled by police officers to certain community agencies for special services and placement. Departments of Health and Human Services, social welfare agencies, and family crisis or intervention centers are frequently contacted and receive youths for further processing. However, if some youths in need of supervision are eventually subject to intake screenings, probation officers must evaluate the nature of one's needs and the seriousness of the situation before a disposition of the case is made. Beyond the broad classification of CHINS, many youths may have chemical dependencies that precipitated their delinquent conduct and require medical attention rather than punishment.

Examples of such youths include youthful male and female prostitutes who originally may have been runaways and/or incorrigible, alcohol- or drug-dependent youths who have turned to burglary and petty theft to support their dependencies, psychologically disturbed or mentally retarded juveniles, and sexually exploited children (Kuntsche et al., 2007). If the facts disclosed at intake enable probation officers to make the strong presumption that certain youths should be diverted to human services shelters or community welfare agencies for treatment or temporary management, then this conditional disposition can be made of the case. This decision is often predicated upon the belief that a strong connection exists between the child's delinquency and physical, psychological, or sexual abuse received from adults or significant others. Thus, it is imperative that early interventions be attempted with those considered to be at the greatest risk of chronic offending (Feiring, Miller-Johnson, and Cleland, 2007).

Summary

Intake is a preliminary screening stage for deciding which juveniles should be moved further into the juvenile justice system. It is performed by persons hired for this purpose, usually by juvenile probation officers who work closely with juvenile courts. Intake officers have broad discretionary powers, and their decisions about juveniles are based on both legal and extralegal factors.

Little uniformity exists among jurisdictions relating to the intake process. Defense counsels have increased involvement in juvenile matters. One consequence is that there has been greater formalization of the intake process. With the greater involvement of defense counsels, intake officers have been increasingly concerned about a youth's right to due process. This emphasis has been examined. Increasingly, informal negotiations transpire between defense counsels and intake officers that resemble plea bargaining. This phenomenon and its pervasiveness was examined.

Both legal and extralegal factors are considered in determining outcomes for youths appearing at different stages of offender processing. Several legal variables are seriousness, type of crime committed, the presence or absence of inculpatory or exculpatory factors, prior record, and age. Extralegal factors include age, gender, race/ethnicity, and SES. How these factors are involved in offender processing was examined.

Preliminary decision making about youthful offenders may involve diversion, where a juvenile's case is temporarily removed from the juvenile justice system. Some juveniles are persistent offenders who may be either serious or nonserious. How should less serious offenders who chronically offend be treated? There are no easy answers to this question. More serious offenders may be incarcerated in secure facilities, although more than a few authorities believe that there is already too much juvenile incarceration. The tension between rehabilitation and lenient treatment on the one hand and the get-tough movement on the other persists.

Key Terms

assessment centers, 188
due process, 188
extralegal factors, 192

legal factors, 192
recidivism, 199
strategic leniency, 193

Questions for Review

1. What is the intake process? Who performs the intake officer role? What are the duties of intake officers?

2. How much discretion does an intake officer have? In what respects is intake compared with plea bargaining?

3. What is an assessment center? What are some general features of the Florida Assessment Center? What are some of its functions?

4. How has intake become increasingly formalized? How does the growing presence of defense counsels in juvenile matters increase intake formality?

5. How has the doctrine of *parens patriae* influenced the intake process?

6. What are several legal factors and how do they influence intake decision making?

7. What are several extralegal factors that influence decision making about juvenile offenders? Should extralegal factors be considered in any particular juvenile's case? Why or why not?

8. What types of juvenile offenders should be diverted from the juvenile justice system? Why?

9. Who are chronic and violent juvenile offenders? How should they be treated by the juvenile justice system?

10. Do we use incarceration too much for punishing juvenile offenders? Under what circumstances should incarceration be used? Which factors should determine whether a particular juvenile should be confined to an industrial school?

Internet Connections

Aspen Youth Services
http://www.aspenyouth.com

Believing in Girls
http://www.pacecenter.org

Human Rights and the Drug War
http://www.hr95.org/

Safe and Responsive Schools Project
http://www.indiana.edu/~safeschl/

Schools, Not Jails
http://www.schoolsnotjails.com/

Urban Institute
http://www.urban.org/

Vera Institute of Justice
http://www.vera.org/

Youth Law Center
http://www.ylc.com/

chapter

7

Prosecutorial Decision Making in Juvenile Justice

chapter objectives

As the result of reading this chapter, you will accomplish the following objectives:

1. Understand the importance of defense counsels for juveniles charged with crimes.
2. Learn about the changing prosecutorial role relative to juvenile offenders.
3. Learn about important procedural safeguards to protect the privacy of juveniles, including rules governing photographing and fingerprinting juveniles, and making juvenile records accessible to the public.
4. Learn about the time restrictions governing juvenile offender processing.
5. Understand the speedy trial rights for juvenile offenders.
6. Understand the growing formality of juvenile offender processing and the greater adversarial nature of juvenile court proceedings.
7. Understand the importance of plea bargaining in juvenile cases.

 ## Case Study

It happened in Milledgeville, Georgia. A 34-year-old man was called to the home of another individual one evening, and a 16-year-old entered the residence with a bandana over his face and a gun. He approached the victim and struck him with the gun. After striking the victim on the head several times, the youth took the victim's wallet and fled. The youth was later identified and arrested. Although he was only 16, the prosecutor decided to charge him as an adult for the aggravated armed robbery offense. [Source: Adapted from the *Union-Recorder* and Hannah Marney, "Juvenile Arrested on Robbery Charge," October 25, 2007.]

 ## Case Study

It happened in Cincinnati, Ohio. Zach Hassell, 15, and a friend, Germaine Taylor, 17, confronted another man, Michael Aufrance, 37, who they believed had been stealing drugs from them. Hassell got into a fight with Aufrance and ordered his friend, Taylor, to kill Aufrance. Before Aufrance could be killed, police were called and intervened. Hassell was charged as a juvenile for ordering the death of Aufrance, while his co-defendant, Taylor, was charged as an adult for complicity to commit murder. Had prosecutors decided to charge Hassell as an adult, which was their right, he could have faced life imprisonment. As a juvenile, if Hassell is found guilty, he can be placed in the state juvenile prison until age 21. [Source: Adapted from Sharon Coolidge and *The Enquirer*, "Death-Order Case Kept in Youth Court," January 15, 2008.]

Introduction

Should prosecutorial charging decisions be influenced by a juvenile's age? What criteria should be used to determine whether youths can be charged as adults? Should a 16-year-old youth who pistol whips and robs another be tried as an adult or a juvenile? Should a 15-year-old who orders the death of another be tried as an adult or a juvenile? These are tough calls to make for any prosecutor. Prosecutorial discretion varies among jurisdictions. The same behaviors committed by youths in one jurisdiction may lead to criminal trials, whereas in other jurisdictions, youths will have their cases and fates determined by juvenile court judges.

This chapter examines the role of juvenile court prosecutors. Juvenile court prosecutors enjoy considerable discretionary powers in deciding whether to pursue particular charges against juvenile suspects. The chapter begins with an examination of the transformation of the prosecutorial role, especially the changes in this role resulting from the greater rights extended to juveniles by the U.S. Supreme Court. The criminal standard of "beyond a reasonable doubt" has raised the bar concerning what prosecutors must prove in juvenile courts to make their cases against juveniles charged with serious offenses.

Next, this chapter examines the general advocacy role of public defenders and defense counsels who represent youthful clients in juvenile courts. While juveniles are not entitled to speedy trials like adults, the time lines associated with scheduling juvenile court adjudicatory proceedings and other stages of juvenile defendant processing are accelerated and in fact are more immediate. There are several reasons for accelerating the juvenile justice process, and these reasons will be examined and explained.

Defense counsels are available to any juvenile defendant as a matter of right. Defense counsels are advocates for juveniles and seek outcomes most favorable to their clients. The nature and influence of the defense counsel role in plea bargaining will be described. Working closely with some defense counsels are *guardians ad litem,* or special guardians appointed by the juvenile court to assist in ensuring that a juvenile's rights are observed. Parents are also involved to varying degrees in seeing to the legal needs of their children. The roles of *guardians ad litem* and parents respective to youthful defendants will be examined.

The Changing Prosecutorial Role in Juvenile Matters

Juvenile court prosecutors have had to make several adjustments in their orientation toward and treatment of juvenile defendants during the last several decades. As juveniles acquire more legal rights, prosecutors must be increasingly sensitive to these rights and constitutional safeguards and ensure that they are not violated. Constitutional rights violations can and will be challenged in the event of unfavorable juvenile court adjudications and/or sentences (White, 2008).

For example, the standard of proof in juvenile proceedings, as well as the introduction of evidence against youths, are currently different compared with pre-*Gault* years. Defense counsel may now aggressively challenge the quality of evidence against youths and how it was obtained, the accuracy of confessions or other incriminating utterances made by youths while in custody and under interrogation, the veracity of witnesses, and whether juveniles understand the rights they are asked to waive by law enforcement officers and others. Competency hearings may be required before certain juveniles are subjected to an adjudicatory hearing (LaSean, 2008).

Modifying Prosecutorial Roles by Changing the Standard of Proof in Juvenile Proceedings

Regarding the standard of proof in juvenile courts prior to 1970, it was customary to use the "preponderance of the evidence" standard in determining whether a juvenile was delinquent. This was a far less stringent standard compared with criminal court proceedings, where the standard of proof used to determine a defendant's guilt is "beyond a reasonable doubt." On the basis of using the preponderance of the evidence standard, juvenile court judges could find juveniles delinquent and incarcerate them in industrial schools or detention facilities for long periods. Thus, the loss of a juvenile's liberty rested on a finding by the juvenile court judge based upon a relatively weak civil evidentiary standard. However, the case of *In re Winship* (1970) resulted in the U.S. Supreme Court decision to require the beyond-a-reasonable-doubt standard in all juvenile court cases where the juvenile was in danger of losing his/her liberty. Although every juvenile court jurisdiction continues to use the preponderance of the evidence standard for certain juvenile proceedings, these jurisdictions are required to use the criminal standard of "beyond a reasonable doubt" whenever an adjudication of delinquency can result in confinement or a loss of liberty.

Juveniles have benefited in at least one respect as the result of these new rights and standards of proof. These changed conditions have forced law enforcement officers, prosecutors, and judges to be more careful and discriminating when charging juveniles with certain offenses. However, changing the technical ground rules for proceeding against juveniles has not necessarily resulted in substantial changes in police officer discretion, prosecutorial discretion, or judicial discretion. Juveniles remain second-class citizens, in a sense, since they continue to be subject to street-level justice by police officers. Nevertheless, juveniles are entitled to almost all constitutional protections. This includes determining their competency to be adjudicated if this issue arises (Sungi, 2008).

Despite the increased bureaucratization of juvenile courts, they continue to exhibit some of the traditionalism of the pre-*Gault* years. This means that relatively little change has occurred in the nature of juvenile adjudications. Juvenile court judges, with the exception of those few jurisdictions that provide jury trials for serious juvenile cases, continue to make adjudicatory decisions as they did prior to *In re Winship* (1970). Regardless of new evidentiary standards and proof-of-guilt requirements, these judges continue to exercise their individual discretion and decide whether a juvenile's guilt or delinquency has been established beyond a reasonable doubt. The fact is that nearly 80 percent of all states do not provide jury trials for juveniles in juvenile courts. Therefore, bench trials are used where the judge decides each case. We don't know how many judges are, or are not, complying with the beyond-a-reasonable-doubt standard, since these judges are exclusively fact-finders. In one respect at least, the *In re Winship* case was a somewhat hollow victory for juveniles in jeopardy of losing their liberty. The beyond-a-reasonable-doubt standard was established, but its use is dependent upon the subjective judgments of juvenile court judges.

For juvenile court prosecutors, changing the standard of proof to beyond a reasonable doubt made their cases harder to prove, even under bench trial conditions compared with jury trial conditions. Thus, the stage was set for greater use of plea bargaining in juvenile cases, especially when the evidence was weak and not particularly compelling. One important reason for weak evidence in juvenile cases is that in many jurisdictions, police officers don't regard juvenile offending to be as serious as adult offending. Therefore, evidence-gathering procedures relating to delinquent acts may not be as aggressive when compared with serious adult crimes. Lackluster evidence gathering by police in juvenile delinquency cases may be explained by the fact that juvenile courts have exhibited extraordinary leniency toward juveniles, even where serious crimes were alleged and the evidence was strong. It is discouraging for police officers to see their best evidence-gathering efforts wasted when a juvenile court judge disposes an adjudicated juvenile delinquent to probation or some other lenient punishment.

For the most part, however, juvenile court prosecutors have adapted well to their changing roles as the juvenile court has gradually transformed. The due process emphasis has prompted many prosecutors to prioritize their prosecutorial discretion according to a juvenile's offense history and crime seriousness. Nevertheless, this priority shift has not caused prosecutors to ignore potentially mitigating factors in individual juvenile cases, such as undue exposure to violence and domestic abuse.

Eliminating the Confidentiality of Juvenile Court Proceedings and Record Keeping

Enhancing the accountability of juvenile courts is greater public access to them under the provisions of the First Amendment. This also applies to interjurisdictional requests for juvenile information among the states. During the 1990s, considerable changes occurred regarding the confidentiality of juvenile court matters as well as juvenile records. Table 7.1 shows a summary of confidentiality provisions of the various states for 2008.

Table 7.1

Summary of Confidentiality Provisions Relating to Serious and Violent Juvenile Offenders, 2008

State	Open Hearing	Release of Name	Release of Court Record[a]	Statewide Repository[b]	Finger-printing	Photo-graphing	Offender Registration	Seal/Expunge Records Prohibited
Totals	30	42	48	44	47	46	39	25
Alabama			•	•	•	•	•	
Alaska	•	•	•	•	•	•	•	•
Arizona	•	•	•	•	•	•	•	•
Arkansas		•	•	•	•	•	•	
California	•	•	•	•	•	•	•	
Colorado		•	•	•	•	•	•	
Connecticut			•					
Delaware	•	•	•	•	•	•	•	•
District of Columbia			•		•	•		
Florida	•	•	•	•	•	•	•	•
Georgia	•	•	•	•	•	•	•	•
Hawaii	•	•	•	•	•	•	•	•
Idaho	•	•	•	•	•	•	•	
Illinois	•	•	•	•	•	•	•	
Indiana	•	•	•	•	•	•	•	
Iowa	•	•	•	•	•	•	•	•
Kansas	•	•	•	•	•	•	•	•
Kentucky		•	•	•	•	•	•	
Louisiana	•	•	•	•	•	•	•	•
Maine	•	•	•	•	•		•	
Maryland	•		•	•	•	•		
Massachusetts	•	•	•	•	•	•	•	
Michigan	•	•	•	•	•	•	•	•
Minnesota	•	•	•	•	•	•	•	
Mississippi		•	•	•	•	•	•	
Missouri	•	•	•	•	•	•	•	
Montana	•		•	•	•	•	•	
Nebraska		•		•	•			
Nevada	•	•	•	•	•	•	•	•
New Hampshire		•	•			•	•	

Table 7.1   (Cont.)

Summary of Confidentiality Provisions Relating to Serious and Violent Juvenile Offenders, 2008

State	Open Hearing	Release of Name	Release of Court Record[a]	Statewide Repository[b]	Finger-printing	Photo-graphing	Offender Registration	Seal/Expunge Records Prohibited
New Jersey		•	•	•	•	•	•	
New Mexico	•			•	•	•	•	
New York			•	•	•	•		
North Carolina			•	•	•	•		
North Dakota		•		•	•	•		
Ohio			•	•	•	•	•	
Oklahoma	•	•	•	•	•	•		•
Oregon		•	•	•	•	•	•	
Pennsylvania	•	•	•	•	•	•	•	
Rhode Island		•	•		•	•	•	
South Carolina		•	•	•	•	•	•	•
South Dakota	•	•	•	•	•	•	•	•
Tennessee		•	•	•	•	•	•	
Texas	•	•	•	•	•	•	•	
Utah	•	•	•	•	•	•	•	
Vermont					•	•		
Virginia	•	•	•	•	•	•	•	
Washington	•	•	•	•	•	•	•	•
West Virginia		•	•		•			•
Wisconsin	•	•		•			•	
Wyoming		•	•		•	•	•	•

Legend: • indicates the provision(s) allowed by each state as of the end of the 1997 legislative session.

[a]In this category, • indicates a provision for juvenile court records to be specifically released to at least one of the following parties: the public, the victims(s), the school(s), the prosecutor, law enforcement, or social agency; however, all states allow records to be released to any party who can show a legitimate interest, typically by court order.

[b]In this category, • indicates a provision for fingerprints to be part of a separate juvenile or adult criminal history repository.

Source: Patricia Torbet and Linda Szymanski. 1998. *State Legislative Responses to Violent Juvenile Crime: 1996–1997 Update*. Washington, DC: U.S. Department of Justice, p. 10. Updated 2008 by author.

In 2008, for instance, 30 states had provisions for open hearings in juvenile or family court proceedings. Only eight states did not provide for the release of the names of those juveniles charged with serious offenses. Only two states did not permit court record releases to interested parties. In fact, all states currently make available juvenile court records to any party showing a legitimate interest. In such cases, information is ordinarily obtained through a court order. Fingerprinting and photographing of juveniles is conducted routinely in most states. Half the states require registration of all juvenile offenders when they enter new jurisdictions. Also, most states presently have state repositories of juvenile records and other relevant information about juvenile offending. Seventeen states prohibited sealing or expunging juvenile court records after certain dates, such as a juvenile's age of majority or adulthood. Therefore, juveniles today are considerably more likely to have their offenses known to the public. Open-records policies are increasingly favored by the public and juvenile justice professionals.

Kansas is an example of a state that made substantial changes in its confidentiality provisions governing juvenile offenders. The juvenile crime rate rose nationwide during the 1990s, and juvenile crime in Kansas escalated accordingly during this same time period. In an effort to hold juveniles more accountable for their actions, the Kansas State Legislature demanded a more open juvenile justice system. Several measures to enhance accountability were established:

1. Parents of offenders younger than 18 may be assessed the cost of certain services, such as probation and out-of-home placement services; juvenile offenders 18 and older can be assessed the costs.
2. Courts may order families to attend counseling together.
3. Parents' health insurance policies may be accessed to pay for their child's care while in state custody. Kansas previously paid for drug treatment and medical care expenses for juvenile offenders because most insurance policies did not cover these costs while a juvenile offender was in state custody.
4. Hearings for juvenile offenders 16 and older are open to the public.
5. Official file records for juvenile offenders are open to the public (Musser, 2001:112–113).

The Kansas law now states that the official file shall be open for public inspection for any juvenile 14 or more years of age at the time any act is alleged to have been committed or for any juvenile less than 14 years of age at the time any act is alleged to have been committed, except if the judge determines that opening the official file for public inspection is not in the best interest of the juvenile who is less than 14 years of age. Not all records are open. Personal history files, including reports and information the court receives, are privileged and may only be seen by the parties' attorneys and juvenile intake and assessment staff, or by order of a district court judge. Between 1995 and 2001, the Office of Juvenile Justice and Delinquency Prevention noted that more states have made substantial changes with juvenile records, such as greater identification of juveniles, while others are considering making juvenile records available to the public (Musser, 2001:113). This means that the **confidentiality privilege** juveniles have enjoyed for many decades is rapidly disappearing.

Open Juvenile Court Proceedings

The greater formality of juvenile proceedings, as well as their accessibility to the general public, may restrict the discretion of juvenile court judges, although this limitation is not particularly an undesirable one. Juvenile court judges have been known to make decisions that only incidentally relate to a juvenile's alleged offense. For instance, the presence of a defense counsel representing a juvenile's interests and promoting due process would tend to deter judges from such conduct.

The Prosecution Decision Beyond 2000

The juvenile justice system has been notoriously slow in its case processing of juvenile offenders. In fact, delays in filing charges against juveniles and the eventual adjudicatory hearing are chronic in many jurisdictions. Juveniles arrested for various types of offenses may wait a year or longer in some jurisdictions before their cases are heard by juvenile court judges. Juvenile court prosecutors may delay filing charges against particular juveniles for a variety of reasons. Competency decisions must be made in certain cases where a youth's mental state is an issue.

The most obvious reasons for delays—court caseload backlogs, crowded court dockets, insufficient prosecutorial staff, too much paperwork—are not always valid reasons. In many instances, the actors themselves are at fault. In short, prosecutors and judges may simply be plodding along at a slow pace, because of their own personal dispositions and work habits. It has been illustrated that in many jurisdictions where

confidentiality privilege
Right between defendant and his/her attorney where certain information cannot be disclosed to prosecutors or others because of the attorney–client relation; for juveniles, records have been maintained under secure circumstances with limited access, and accessed only by those in authority with a clear law enforcement purpose.

prosecutors and judges have aggressively tackled their caseload problems and forced functionaries to work faster, juvenile caseload processing has been greatly accelerated. Thus, the time between a juvenile's arrest and disposition has been greatly shortened because of individual decision making and not because of any organizational constraints or overwork (Jarjoura et al., 2008).

Another factor contributing to juvenile court delays is the sizeable increase in juvenile court caseloads. Many of these cases involve serious and violent offenses, as well as an ever-expanding number of drug offenses. For instance, drug offense cases accounted for 11 percent of all delinquency cases in 2000, compared with only 8 percent of all cases in 1993. The proportionate female juvenile involvement in drug cases increased from 14 to 16 percent between 1993 and 2000 as well. These types of cases take more time to resolve, simply because of their greater complexity. By 2007, the number of alleged drug offenses represented nearly 20 percent of all juvenile court cases. The juvenile courts have simply failed to keep pace with the growth of juvenile crime over the last few decades (Office of Juvenile Justice and Delinquency Prevention, 2007).

In 34 states in 2007, juvenile court prosecutors were at liberty to file charges against juvenile offenders whenever they decided (Office of Juvenile Justice and Delinquency Prevention, 2007). No binding legislative provisions were applicable to these actors to force them to act promptly and bring a youth's case before the juvenile court. In the meantime, 20 states established time limits that cannot be exceeded between the time of a juvenile's court referral and the filing of charges by prosecutors. Table 7.2 shows various time limits imposed by various states for juvenile court adjudication and disposition of cases. For instance, in Minnesota, juvenile court prosecutors must file charges against juveniles within 30 days of their referral to juvenile court by police, if such juveniles are placed in secure confinement. These same prosecutors must file charges against undetained juveniles within 60 days following the juvenile's referral to juvenile court by police. In Maryland, prosecutors have 60 days to file charges against either detained or undetained juveniles following their court referrals. And in Georgia and Ohio, prosecutors must file charges within 10 days, if juveniles are being detained. A failure to file charges against juveniles in these jurisdictions within the time periods specified results in a dismissal of their cases **with prejudice**, meaning that the prosecutors cannot refile charges against the same offenders.

with prejudice
To dismiss charges, but those same charges cannot be brought again later against the same defendant.

Judges must determine offense seriousness in order to make a proper determination of a case's course.

Time Standards in Juvenile Court for Prosecutors and Other Actors

Establishing time standards for accomplishing various procedures within the juvenile justice process are not new. As early as 1971, various organizations were at work to encourage the juvenile justice system to process cases more quickly. It was believed at the time that only legislatively created time standards would cause police, intake officers, prosecutors, and judges to take faster action in processing juvenile offenders.

For instance, Butts (1996a:544–547) notes that the Joint Commission on Juvenile Justice Standards led the way in 1971 with early time standards for juvenile processing. A product of the Institute of Judicial Administration (IJA) and the American Bar Association (ABA), the project convened periodically over the next several years and issued 27 different volumes during the years 1977–1980. The standards promulgated by the project were intended as guidelines for juvenile courts and the juvenile justice system generally. The commission formed through the project was guided by the principle that juvenile court cases should always be processed without unnecessary delay.

Career Snapshot   7.1

Tamara M. Carter

Juvenile Probation Officer, Vigo County, Terre Haute, IN

Statistics:
B.S.W. (social work), Indiana State University

Background

July 7, 1985, was the day that changed my life. I became a juvenile probation officer in Vigo County, Terre Haute, Indiana. Twenty years later, I am still here and amazed. I am a 1982 graduate of Indiana State University with a Bachelor of Social Work degree. I had enrolled with the intention of majoring in dietetics, but Chemistry 104 told me to leave! Social work became my new major. The day of graduation, I went back to my home-town of Bloomington, Indiana. With a degree in hand (which came a month later in the mail), I was ready for the world. Then tragedy struck. My father died one month after I graduated. We were devastated but our faith and the prayers of others got us through. This put my job seeking on hold for a while. My family was more important.

Before I had moved back to Terre Haute, I had inter-viewed for a position of social worker at a nursing home. I had interviewed very well. Then the topic of salary came up. I told them that I wanted $10,000 a year. I did not get the job. My request was too high and more than the minimum wage. I had a college degree! What a real-ity check.

Fast forward to 1985. The first day was quite inter-esting as a probation officer. My office had a window and I was able to see some of the kids who were being brought in handcuffed. This was an eye-opener. Many looked sad and scared, but a few acted like it was no bother. I found out later that they were the "regulars" and they knew the routine. After a while, it did not bother me as much. In fact, if I saw them coming up the walk or knew they were on their way, I'd meet them at the door. They hated that!

The building we worked in had been the "Colored Orphanage." It had housed both boys and girls since the 1920s through the 1960s. I have met many people who were reared there and/or had family members there. For them, it had a lot of good and sad memories.

After it became a juvenile center, the probation department, court, kitchen, and detention were housed in the same building. Male detainees were held on one side downstairs and the females were confined on the other side. The building sat on a hill out in the county. Many kids talked about being transported there and how scary it seemed. Imagine driving up a hill hand-cuffed in a police car late at night. The moon is shining through the trees, the building is old red brick, it looks dark and cold, and you are going to be placed in a cell in the basement, and your parents are going to be called. Whew, what an eerie feeling! For a lot of the kids, it was their first and last time in this facility.

In 2001, we moved into a new building. The court and probation department are in one building and the detention center is in the other one, although we are connected by a hallway. It is a much nicer building, and it is in the city limits. Many of our families do not have transportation and/or little money. They are able to ride the city bus or walk.

In 20 years of working, I have seen a lot of changes in the kids and their families. The biggest change is respect. They have very little. In the past, 10 to 15 years ago, even if the kids were involved with our system, they still showed more respect toward their parents. For some, they would have rather stayed at the center than face their parents. Today, many show no respect for their parents, teachers, the court, or even themselves. This is so sad. I know that you cannot group all young people together, but because it does exist, it makes you stop and wonder about the future.

As a probation officer, I have had the opportunity to supervise many college students. Many were social work majors from Indiana State University and I have had a few criminology and psychology majors too. The length of internship, one semester or two, determines how soon they are able to work on their own. By the time they fin-ish, they have met with the kids and their families, made decisions for the outcome, school visits, referrals, and of course, paperwork!

Advice to Students

I try to stress that each day is different just as each situation is different. You cannot look at the offense on paper and make a good decision until you get the full report and background about the child and his/her family. There will be times that you will have to make decisions quickly. You will not have time to think about the theory, open-ended questions. If you have learned anything, it'll come to you as you are working.

Do not prejudge because of what is written down. One intern stated, "Well, there is no father and they are poor. What do you expect?" First of all, she never said that again! Then I showed her my case load, and those who had two parents in the home outnumbered the single-parent household. The father had just died and the mother was starting over. By the way, the intern graduated, earned her M.S.W., and is an outstanding social worker in her field. Students, while in your internship, be excited, willing to listen and learn. There are so many areas that a social work degree can take you and for you to do some good. Dietetics is a great field, but my social work degree has given me so much more experience and joy than I could ever imagine.

Table 7.2

Time Limits (in days) for Juvenile Court Adjudication and Disposition Hearings, in Cases Not Involving Proceedings for Transfer to Criminal Court

State	Court Referral	Start of Adjudication Deadline Filing of Charges (detained/ undetained)	Preliminary Hearing (detained/ undetained)	Detention Admission	Detention Hearing	Start of Disposition Deadline Filing of Charges (detained/ undetained)	Adjudication (detained/ undetained)
Alaska							Immediately[b]
Arizona			30/60				30/45
Arkansas					14		14/—
California	30	30[b]		15			
Delaware				30[c]			
Florida		21/90[c]					15/—
Georgia		10/60					30/—
Illinois		120[b,c]		10[c]			
Iowa		60[b,d]					ASAP[b]
Louisiana			30/90				30[b]
Maryland		60[b]		30			30[b]
Massachusetts	60						
Michigan		180[b]		63			35/—
Minnesota		30/60					15[c]/45[c]
Mississippi		90/—		21			14/—
Montana							ASAP
Nebraska		180/—				180[c]	
New Hampshire		21/30					21/30
New Jersey				30			30/60
New Mexico							20/—
New York			14/60				10/50

Table 7.2   (Cont.)

Time Limits (in days) for Juvenile Court Adjudication and Disposition Hearings, in Cases Not Involving Proceedings for Transfer to Criminal Court

State	Court Referral	Start of Adjudication Deadline Filing of Charges (detained/ undetained)	Preliminary Hearing (detained/ undetained)	Detention Admission	Detention Hearing	Start of Disposition Deadline Filing of Charges (detained/ undetained)	Adjudication (detained/ undetained)
North Dakota		30[b]		14			
Ohio		10/—					Immediately[b]
Oregon	56			28			28[c]
Pennsylvania		10/—					20/—
Rhode Island				7			
South Carolina		40[b]					
Tennessee		—/90		30			15/90
Texas		10/—					
Vermont		15/—					30[b]
Virginia		—/120		21			30/—
Washington		30[b]/60[b]					14/21
Wisconsin			20[e]/30[e]			10[e]/30[e]	10/30
Wyoming					60		

[a]Twenty states did not have time limits for adjudication as of 1993: AL, AK, CO, CT, DC, HI, ID, IN, KS, KY, ME, MO, MT, NV, NM, NC, OK, SD, UT, and WV. Twenty-six states did not have time limits for dispositions: AL, CA, CO, CT, DE, DC, HI, ID, IL, IN, KS, KY, ME, MA, MO, NV, NC, ND, OK, RI, SC, SD, TX, UT, WV, and WY.
[b]Statute did not distinguish detention status.
[c]Extensions are possible.
[d]If statutory right to speedy trial is waived.
[e]Statute-specified time from "plea hearing."
Source: Butts, Data source: Analysis by the National Center for Juvenile Justice. Reprinted by permission of the *American Journal of Criminal Law* and the authors, 1996b:557–558. Updated 2008 by author.

The IJA/ABA standards relating to processing juveniles were as follows:

Time	Action
2 hours	Between police referral and the decision to detain
24 hours	Between detention and a petition justifying further detention
15 days	Between police referral and adjudication (if youth is detained)
30 days	Between police referral and adjudication (if youth is not detained)
15 days	Between adjudication and final disposition (if youth is detained)

Note that in these time guidelines, law enforcement officers are not given much time to detain youths once they have been taken into custody. Once police officers have referred a youth to juvenile court, only two hours is recommended in order for a decision to be made about detaining the youth. If a youth is detained, then only 24 hours are allowed between the start of a youth's detention and filing a petition to justify further detention. And depending upon whether youths are detained or undetained, the time limits recommended are either 15 or 30 days, respectively, between detention and adjudication. These guidelines are rather rigorous compared with the traditional sluggishness of juvenile offender processing. Table 7.2 shows that only a handful of states thus far have adopted these or more rigorous standards for filing charges against juveniles (e.g., Georgia, Ohio, Pennsylvania, Texas, and Vermont). These figures remained unchanged until 2008.

Butts also says that similar time limits for juvenile processing were recommended contemporaneously by the National Advisory Committee for Juvenile Justice and Delinquency Prevention in 1980. These limits are shown below (Butts, 1996b:546–547):

Time	Action
24 hours	Between police referral and the report of intake decision (if youth is detained)
30 days	Between police referral and the report of intake decision (if youth is undetained)
24 hours	Between detention and detention hearing
2 days	Between intake report and the filing of a petition by the prosecutor (if detained)
5 days	Between intake report and the filing of a petition by the prosecutor (if undetained)
5 days	Between filing of the petition and the initial arraignment hearing
15 days	Between filing of the petition and adjudication (if detained)
30 days	Between filing of the petition and adjudication (if undetained)
15 days	Between adjudication and final disposition

Again, the National Advisory Committee gave little latitude to juvenile court prosecutors in dispatching juvenile cases. In this particular arrangement of scenarios, however, the intake stage was addressed, and rather strongly. Not only were prosecutors obligated to file petitions against specified juveniles more quickly following intake, but intake officers were required to make their assessments of juveniles and file reports of these assessments within a two-day period. One major difference in the National Advisory Committee recommendations and guidelines was the fact that if certain actors in the juvenile justice system did not comply with these time standards, then cases against certain juveniles could be dismissed, but **without prejudice**. This meant that juvenile court prosecutors could resurrect the original charges and refile them with the juvenile court at a later date. Thus, no particularly compelling constraints were placed on either intake officers or prosecutors to act in a timely manner, according to this second set of standards. However, we must recognize that neither the IJA/ABA time guidelines nor the National Advisory Committee guidelines are binding on any state jurisdiction. They are set forth as strongly recommended guidelines for juvenile court officials to follow.

without prejudice
To dismiss charges, but those same charges can be brought again later against the same defendant.

Why Should the Juvenile Justice Process Be Accelerated?

Several compelling arguments are made for why juvenile justice should be applied quickly. One such is that adolescence is a critical period wherein youths undergo many changes. Maturational factors seem especially accelerated, while a juvenile's personality and response to peer pressures are modified and enhanced in diverse ways. A month may seem like a year to most adolescents. Secure confinement of 24 hours is a serious deprivation of a juvenile's freedom. When some juvenile cases undergo protracted delays of up to a year or longer, it is difficult for many youths to accept their subsequent punishment for something they did long ago. More than a few juveniles grow out of delinquency by the time their cases come before the juvenile court, and they wonder why they are now being punished for something they did when they were younger.

Studies of juvenile justice system delays disclose that the size of a jurisdiction plays an important part in how fast juvenile cases are concluded. In 1985, for example, the median processing time for juvenile cases in a large sample of U.S. county jurisdictions was about 44 days. By 1994, the median processing time in these same counties was 92 days (Butts and Halemba, 1996:131). For smaller jurisdictions, with fewer and presumably less-serious cases to process, case-processing time ranged from 34 to 83 days in 1994, while larger counties took from 59 to 110 days.

These juvenile justice processing delays parallel criminal court processing of adult defendants. We might be inclined to accept these long juvenile justice delays if the cases processed were sufficiently serious to warrant more court time. However, only about 17 percent of all cases handled by both small and large county jurisdictions involved serious or person offenses in 1994 (Butts and Halemba, 1996:129).

Therefore, it has been recommended that juvenile justice case-processing time be decreased so as to move the disposition closer to the time when the offense was committed. Juveniles should be able to relate whatever happens to them in court later to the offense they committed earlier. In more than a few instances, juveniles awaiting trial on one charge have had subsequent opportunities to reoffend. When they are arrested for new offenses before being adjudicated for earlier offenses, their cognitive development may inhibit their understanding of the process and their disposition (Butts, 1996b:525).

Shine and Price (1992) provide two important reasons for why juvenile cases should be processed quickly:

1. To maximize the impact upon the juvenile that s/he has been caught in a criminal act, that s/he will be held accountable for what s/he has done, and that there will be consequences for this action, it is important that the case be resolved quickly. If the case continues too long, the impact of the message is diluted, either because the juvenile has been subsequently arrested for other offenses and loses track of just what it is that s/he is being prosecuted for or because the juvenile has not engaged in any further delinquent acts and feels that any consequences for the past offense are unfair.

2. If there are victims, then unwarranted delays in juvenile case processing are unfair and damaging to victims. Many victims suffer some type of financial loss or physical injury. Expenses are incurred. Faster resolutions of juvenile court cases can lead to more rapid compensation and victim restitution plans imposed by the court. Such compensation of victim restitution can do much to alleviate any continued suffering victims may endure.

Public Defenders for Juveniles

Greater procedural formality in the juvenile justice system has occurred with respect to the appointment of public defenders for indigent juveniles. Every juvenile court jurisdiction provides public defenders for juveniles and their families who cannot afford to appoint private counsel, especially in more-serious cases where incarceration in secure confinement facilities is a strong possibility. Formerly, defense counsels for juveniles often were the juvenile's probation officer or a social case worker with a vested interest in the case. It is not entirely clear how these officers and workers were able to separate their law enforcement and defense functions to avoid allegations of conflicts of interest. But little interest in the quality of defense of juvenile cases was exhibited by the public in previous years anyway. While some persons believe that juveniles are now insulated to some extent from the whims of juvenile court prosecutors and judges, others suspect that defense attorneys have in some instances made it more difficult for juveniles to receive fair treatment (Office of Juvenile Justice and Delinquency Prevention, 2007).

During intake, it has been found that the presence of attorneys, who represent juvenile's interests and attempt to protect them so that all their constitutional rights are observed at each stage of the juvenile justice process, actually detracts from the informal

7.2   Focus on Delinquency

Two similar rape cases in a midwestern state had two very different outcomes. The first rape case involved M.J., 16. M.J. was accused of breaking into his neighbor's apartment and raping her 13-year-old daughter, R.P. He was arrested shortly after the incident when the girl's mother called police and reported the rape and gave an accurate description of the rapist. R.P. said that she was glad the guy got caught. M.J. was transferred to adult court to stand trial for rape. M.J. decided to plead guilty in a plea bargain agreement, where he would be sentenced to 20 years, with 12 years served in the state prison and the other 8 years served on probation. In addition, M.J. will be required to register as a sexual offender with the state and serve a concurrent 10-year sentence for the burglary.

The second rape case involved a 16-year-old female, S.V. S.V. had a sexual relationship with one of her male neighbors, U.A., who was 13 years old. She believed that U.A. was in love with her and that this feeling somehow excused the sexual assault. The incidents were admittedly consensual between S.V. and U.A. But between the arrest of S.V. and her trial, U.A. changed his mind. After S.V. had been transferred to adult court for a trial, U.A. told the jury, "I just feel like I've lost a lot of years being young. I want S.V. to go to jail because I don't want her doing it to anyone else." The prosecutor asked the judge to sentence S.V. to 20–35 years with 15 years suspended. However, the defense attorney asked for a three-year sentence of probation because he said S.V. and U.A. were in love with each other. S.V. received five years of probation. The prosecutor was obviously disappointed with the sentence and said it was inappropriate.

These two cases of rape both occurred in the same state. Yet, there are very different outcomes. Should 16-year-old male rapists be treated differently from 16-year-old female rapists? What factors do you think account for the great disparity in sentencing in the two cases? [Sources: Adapted from the Associated Press, "Boy Pleads Guilty to Rape, Gets 20 Years," June 4, 2008; adapted from the Associated Press, "S.V., 16-Year-Old Female Rapist, Given Probation," June 26, 2008.]

nature of intake. Intake officers change these proceedings into formal hearings, and recommendations for subsequent dispositions might be more severe than if defense attorneys were not present. In fact, intake officers have openly discouraged juveniles and their parents from availing themselves of an attorney's services at this stage, since their presence hampers informal adjustments of cases and limits a youth's informal compliance with informal probationary conditions. In some cases, intake officers consider themselves the primary source of a youth's understanding of legal rights, although a recommendation that these officers receive more training and preparation in law and juvenile rights suggests that their own understanding of the law merits improvement.

In a growing number of instances, cases are being diverted to victim–offender mediation, where various nonprofit, private organizations receive referrals from juvenile courts. The intent of such victim–offender mediation is to reach a resolution between victims and offenders without subjecting offenders to juvenile court and its adverse labeling impact. In communities with mediation programs, there is support from community residents. Financial support in the form of grants is provided from local, state, and federal agencies. Mediators may be interested citizens, retired judges, community leaders, or even intake officers who undertake these tasks during nonworking hours (Aisenberg et al., 2007).

Despite these alternatives to juvenile court action, it is true that juvenile court proceedings have become increasingly formalized. Further, public access to these proceedings in most jurisdictions is increasing (Champion, 2008a). Thus, the presence of defense counsel, an adversarial scenario—a trial-like atmosphere where witnesses testify for and against juvenile defendants—and adherence to Rules of Procedure for Juvenile Courts are clear indicators of greater formalization, bureaucratization, and criminalization, as Feld (2007) has suggested.

Two problems have been highlighted relating to the use of public defenders in juvenile courts. These problems include the limited resources and growing caseloads of public defenders for juveniles in many jurisdictions. A study examined the access to counsel in selected states and local juvenile delinquency proceedings (U.S. General Accounting Office, 1995b). Data sources were relevant state statutes, state administrative procedures, and case law in 15 states; National Council on Juvenile Justice statistics for three states; national surveys of county prosecutors and public defenders; telephone interviews with selected state and local judges in eight states; and site visits to juvenile justice officials in four states. Statutes guaranteeing a juvenile's right to counsel were found in all 15 states examined. Overall, the rate of defense counsel representation for juveniles varied from 65 percent in Nebraska to 97 percent in California. Representation by offense category varied, as did the overall impact of representation on case outcomes. In most cases where juveniles were not represented by counsel, juveniles were less likely to receive out-of-home placements, such as a disposition to an industrial school. This shouldn't be interpreted to mean that defense counsel cause more juveniles to receive out-of-home placements. Rather, a better explanation is that defense counsel were not used in the least-serious cases, those that didn't merit placement in an institution anyway. Prosecutors and juvenile justice officials were generally pleased with the quality of counsel provided to juveniles, apart from their concerns about scarce resources and growing caseloads (U.S. General Accounting Office, 1995b).

The Speedy Trial Rights of Juveniles

Juveniles have no federal constitutional right to a speedy trial. The U.S. Supreme Court has not decided any juvenile case that would entitle a juvenile to a speedy trial commensurate with adults in criminal courts. Criminal defendants are assured a speedy trial through the Sixth Amendment and the leading 1972 case of *Barker v. Wingo*. This case led to the establishment of the **Barker balancing test**. Each state and the federal government has established speedy trial procedures that establish time standards between different events, such as between the time of arrest and initial appearance, between a juvenile's initial appearance and arraignment, and between a juvenile's arraignment and trial. The federal government uses a 100-day standard. New Mexico is perhaps the most liberal, providing a 180-day period. Many states have adopted the federal standard.

For juveniles, standards vary among jurisdictions between comparable stages of juvenile justice processing, such as between arrest and intake, between intake and prosecutorial decision making and case filing, between case filing and adjudication, and between adjudication and disposition. However, some state legislatures have provided time standards that proscribe different maximum time limits between each of these events.

It seems that the longer juveniles remain within the juvenile justice system, the more adverse the consequences for their subsequent recidivism and seriousness of offending (Hill et al., 2007). One reason juvenile case processing has been sluggish is that the doctrine of *parens patriae* has been pervasive, suggesting rehabilitation over other themes, such as punishment, crime control, or due process. According to the *parens patriae* concept, juvenile courts need a certain amount of time to provide for the needs of youths drawn into the system. If insufficient time is allocated for rehabilitation, then rehabilitation will not occur. However, the U.S. Supreme Court has characterized the doctrine of *parens patriae* as "murky" and of "dubious historical relevance" in the case of *In re Gault* (1967). The U.S. Supreme Court also declared in *Gault* that

Barker balancing test
Speedy trial standard, where delays are considered in terms of the reason, length, existence of prejudice against the defendant by the prosecutor, and the assertion of the defendant's speedy trial rights [from the case of *Barker v. Wingo*, 407 U.S. 514 (1972)].

juveniles don't need to give up their due process rights under the Fourteenth Amendment in order to derive juvenile justice system benefits because of their status as juvenile offenders, such as the greater concern for their well-being supposedly inherent in juvenile court proceedings. Instead, the U.S. Supreme Court suggested that the due process principles of fairness, impartiality, and orderliness were of paramount importance in contrast with the *parens patriae* philosophy. Essentially, the U.S. Supreme Court has acted to bring the juvenile court system under constitutional control.

Examinations of juvenile court prosecutorial opinions about the effectiveness of juvenile court processing indicate that in at least some jurisdictions, such as Illinois, prosecutors perceive juvenile courts to be relatively ineffective at rehabilitating juveniles (Ellsworth, Kinsella, and Massin, 1992). These prosecutors believe that probation services are most vital to a youth's rehabilitation, and that specific community programs and services intended to prevent delinquency are either inadequate, nonexistent, or ineffective. Specific sectors of the community were targeted as most important by these prosecutors. They believe that greater juvenile court intervention should occur in school matters. All things considered, however, these prosecutors believe that their rehabilitative impact in specific juvenile cases becomes less effective as their involvement in such cases increases. Again, this suggests moving youths through the system more quickly to minimize their exposure to the process.

The Advocacy Role of Defense Attorneys

statute of limitations
Maximum time period within which a prosecution can be brought against a defendant for a particular offense; many criminal statutes have three- or six-year statute of limitations periods; there is no statute of limitations on homicide charges.

For especially serious cases, defense attorneys are increasingly useful and necessary as a means of safeguarding juvenile rights and holding the juvenile justice system more accountable regarding its treatment of juvenile offenders. For instance, it is important for defense counsel to advise their clients about the **statute of limitations** associated with various offenses, where the government can bring charges within specified time periods following the crime's occurrence. Some crimes, like murder, have no statute of limitations, and thus, there is an indefinite period of time when the state can bring charges against a potential defendant. Widespread abuse of discretion by various actors throughout all stages of the juvenile justice process is well documented. The intrusion of defense attorneys into the juvenile justice process, under a new due process framework, is anticipated as a logical consequence of the rights juveniles have obtained from the U.S. Supreme Court.

Attorneys for Juveniles as a Matter of Right

Although juveniles are entitled to the services of attorneys at all stages of juvenile proceedings, some investigators have shown that about half of all youths processed in the juvenile justice system are not represented by counsel (Feld, 2007). Shortly after the *Gault* decision in 1967, the Minnesota legislature mandated the assistance of counsel for all juveniles in delinquency proceedings. It was believed that making provisions for defense counsel would maximize the equitable treatment of youths by Minnesota juvenile courts (Feld, 2007).

Analyzing adjudication data from an earlier period in five other jurisdictions besides Minnesota, Feld (2007) discovered similar figures. Roughly half of all juveniles adjudicated delinquent in these state juvenile courts had legal representation at the time of their adjudications. It is unclear whether the juveniles who did not have defense counsel also did not request defense counsel. It would have been inconsistent with *Gault*, as well as unconstitutional, if these juveniles had requested defense counsel and been denied it in those jurisdictions. But Feld may have provided at least two plausible explanations for this finding. He found that juveniles who were represented by attorneys in each of these jurisdictions, and who were also adjudicated as delinquent, tended to receive harsher sentences and dispositions from juvenile court judges compared with those juveniles who did not have defense counsel to represent them. Thus, it would seem that the presence of defense counsel in juvenile courts, at least in those jurisdictions examined by Feld, actually aggravated the dispositional outcome rather than mitigated it. An alternative explanation is that the more serious offenders in those jurisdictions were more likely to acquire counsel. Thus, they would logically receive harsher sentences compared with less-serious offenders, if they were ultimately adjudicated as delinquents.

Subsequent to Feld's research, the presence of defense counsel in juvenile proceedings has escalated dramatically. Although there continue to be regional variations in the proportionate representation of juveniles by defense counsel, especially rural areas contrasted with urban areas, the overall trend has been toward increased attorney representation. With the presence of defense counsel in juvenile proceedings becoming increasingly commonplace, it is also likely that the adverse impact of defense attorneys on the outcomes of these proceedings has lessened accordingly.

Defense Counsel and Ensuring Due Process Rights for Juveniles

The manifest function of defense attorneys in juvenile courts is to ensure that due process is fulfilled by all participants. Defense attorneys are the primary advocates of fairness for juveniles who are charged with crimes or other types of offenses. Minors, particularly very young youths, are more susceptible to the persuasiveness of adults. Law enforcement officers, intake officers, and prosecutors might extract incriminating evidence from juveniles in much the same way as police officers and prosecutors might extract inculpatory information from suspects in criminal cases, provided that certain constitutional safeguards were not in place. For adults, a major constitutional safeguard is the Miranda warning, which, among other things, advises those arrested for crimes of their right to an attorney, their right to terminate police interrogations whenever they wish and remain silent, their right to have their attorneys present during questioning, and the right to have an attorney appointed for them if they cannot afford one (LaSean, 2008).

Some persons believe that the U.S. Supreme Court has always supported the *parens patriae* nature of juvenile courts, and that their purportedly liberal decisions about juvenile constitutional guarantees have been intended only to provide minimal procedural protections. Nevertheless, the possibilities of incarceration in secure juvenile facilities and/or transfer to criminal court jurisdiction where harsher penalties may be administered are sufficient to warrant the intervention of defense counsel in many juvenile cases. At the very least, defense counsel may prevent some youths from being railroaded into accepting unnecessary conditional interventions from intake officers or juvenile court judges. It is not the intention of defense attorneys to aggravate matters and cause their juvenile clients to receive harsher punishments than they would normally receive from the same judges if defense counsel weren't present. But it is a curious paradox that those seeking justice and due process and who exercise their rights for these aims are often penalized for exercising these rights.

In many respects, this paradox is similar to the disparity in sentencing among those who have similar criminal histories and are convicted for the same offenses, but who receive widely disparate sentences depending upon whether their convictions are obtained through plea bargaining or a jury verdict in a criminal trial. There is no particular reason for judges to impose harsher punishments on convicted offenders who exercise their right to a jury trial compared with those who enter into plea agreements and plead guilty, but differential punishments are frequently administered. One explanation, an extralegal and nonlegal one, is that the extra punishment is the penalty for obligating the state to prove its case against the defendant in open court. Being aware of this type of sentencing disparity, many defense attorneys counsel their clients, especially where there

Family court judges determine guardianship matters as well as eventual dispositions for adjudicated youths.

is strong inculpatory evidence, to plead guilty to lesser charges and accept a lesser penalty to avoid more severe punishments that judges almost certainly will impose upon conviction through a trial. It would appear from the available evidence that juvenile court judges may be guilty of the same behavior when relating to juvenile clients who are represented by counsel and those who are not. For the present, anyway, being represented by counsel in juvenile court seems more of a liability than an asset.

Are Attorneys Being Used More Frequently by Juvenile Defendants?

Yes. One survey of five states during the 1995–2005 period (California, Montana, Nebraska, North Dakota, and Pennsylvania) found that attorney use by juvenile offenders increased systematically across these years (Champion, 2008b). Attorney use varies by jurisdiction, however. In the early 2000s, over 90 percent of all California juvenile cases involved either private or publicly appointed defense counsel. However, in states such as Nebraska and North Dakota, attorney use by juveniles occurred in about 65 percent of the cases.

It may seem that whenever youths invoke their right to an attorney, it would be under circumstances where the offenses alleged are serious or violent. While it is true that attorney use was more prevalent in these states where serious and violent offenses were alleged, it is also true that attorney use increased during the 10-year period for status offenders and those charged with public order, property, and drug offenses as well. The primary implication of this research is that juvenile courts are experiencing greater defense attorney involvement each year. If these states are representative of all U.S. jurisdictions, then the formalization of juvenile courtrooms is definitely increasing with greater involvement of defense counsel in juvenile cases.

Do Defense Counsel for Juveniles Make a Difference in Their Case Dispositions?

The use of defense counsel by juveniles results in mixed outcomes. In some instances, because of the greater formality of the proceedings because defense counsel are present, outcomes occur that may be unfavorable to juvenile defendants. For instance, if an intake officer were inclined to divert a particular case from the juvenile justice system because of his/her judgment that the youth will probably not reoffend, this decision may not be made if an attorney is present to represent the juvenile's interests. The intake officer may feel that a higher authority should decide the case. The defense counsel may be intimidating. In an attorney-free environment, the intake officer would act differently. Thus, different actions by different actors in the system may be anticipated, depending upon the presence or absence of an attorney.

In cases adjudicated before juvenile court judges, a defense counsel's presence seems to work for the juvenile's benefit. Judicial discretion is affected to the extent that stricter or less-strict adherence to juvenile laws is affected. There seems to be a tendency for juvenile court judges to be more lenient with juveniles who are represented by defense counsel compared with those juvenile defendants who are not. This leniency manifests itself in various ways. For instance, juvenile court judges may impose probation more often than incarceration where juveniles are represented by counsel. Represented juveniles who are disposed to a secure facility for a period of months may serve shorter incarcerative terms compared with those juveniles sent to the same secure facilities but who were not represented by counsel. More frequent granting of juvenile parole occurs among those youths represented by counsel compared with those youths not represented by counsel.

Defense Counsel as *Guardians Ad Litem*

In some juvenile cases, child abuse has been alleged. Thus, defense counsel perform additional responsibilities as they attempt to ensure that the best interests of their clients are served in ways that will protect children from parents who abuse them (Salzinger, Rosario, and Feldman, 2007). *Guardians ad litem* are special guardians appointed by the court in which a particular litigation is pending to represent a youth, ward, or unborn person in that particular litigation (Champion, 2009). Most juvenile court jurisdictions have *guardian ad litem* programs, where interested persons serve in this capacity. In some cases, defense counsel for youths perform the dual role of defense counsel and the youth's *guardian ad litem*. *Guardians ad litem* are supposed to work in ways that will benefit those they represent, and such guardians provide legal protection from others. Defense counsel working as *guardians ad litem* may act to further the child's best interests, despite a child's contrary requests or demands. Thus, it is a different type of nonadversarial role performed by some defense counsel.

> **guardians ad litem**
> Special authorities appointed by the court in which particular litigation is pending to represent a youth, ward, or unborn person in that particular litigation.

Juvenile Offender Plea Bargaining and the Role of Defense Counsel

Often, we think that plea bargaining occurs only within the criminal justice system. The fact is that juveniles enter into plea agreements with juvenile court prosecutors with great frequency. Plea bargaining is an invaluable tool with which to eliminate case backlogs that might occur in some of the larger juvenile courts. Defense counsel entering into plea agreements with juvenile court prosecutors usually want the least-restrictive option imposed on their juvenile clients. Most frequently sought by defense counsel are charge reductions against their clients by prosecutors. Defense counsel are interested in reducing the stigma of a serious, negative juvenile court profile of their youthful clients by seeking reduced charges from prosecutors (Kidd, 2007). Prosecutors would benefit in that plea agreements would speed up case processing and save them time from having to prove critical elements of crimes against juvenile defendants. Actors, prosecutors, and defense attorneys are interested in achieving personal goals instead of pursuing some type of *parens patriae* objective. Prosecutors are interested in concluding adjudications with sanctions, while defense counsel are interested in protecting their clients from more-serious charges that could influence their future lives.

The degree to which *parens patriae* is alive and well depends on how much a particular court has accepted and furthered the due process renovation created by *Gault*. If fairness is to be realized in the adjudicatory hearing of juveniles, judges and defense attorneys should know the rules of criminal procedure and evidence, and they must be made aware that adjudications are serious for youths. Defense lawyers should also be reminded that appellate review is both a necessary and valuable weapon, although few juvenile court decisions are ever appealed. However, one continuing and troublesome aspect of plea bargaining in the juvenile justice system is that admissions of guilt are elicited from juveniles without benefit of a trial.

Parental Intrusion in Juvenile Courts Is Often More Damaging Than Attorney Involvement

The impact of the parents of juveniles who appear in juvenile courts has been investigated (Pierce and Brodsky, 2002). The attitudes and opinions of various juvenile justice actors, such as judges, prosecutors, defense attorneys, and probation officers have been investigated. In more than a few instances, parents of processed juveniles tend to make matters for their children worse by their own actions. Some parents threaten intake officers, prosecutors, and/or judges. Many of those surveyed viewed the interventions of parents in juvenile proceedings as primarily negative. Some of their negative behaviors might be due to a basic misunderstanding of the due process rights of their children. Other parents may feel that the juvenile court is not a formally contrived proceeding with legal powers. As some parents attempt to intervene and circumvent procedural matters before the juvenile court, all actors, including defense counsel, become exasperated and tend to impose harsher sanctions than would otherwise be imposed if the parents were not there. However, parental involvement in juvenile matters is often required according to court or procedural rules.

It is clear from juvenile justice trends observed in most states thus far that defense counsel are increasingly present during all stages of juvenile processing (Bradley, 2005). This increased involvement of defense counsel is intended to ensure that a juvenile's constitutional rights are observed. Another intention of counsel is to ensure the best dispositional outcome for their youthful clients. This usually means some form of lenient treatment from the system. We have seen that attorney involvement does preserve a juvenile's rights at different processing stages; however, it is not yet clear whether a defense counsel's presence is totally beneficial to juvenile clients at all times. Too much formalization may cause various actors (e.g., intake officers, prosecutors, judges) to act differently when others are present who monitor their actions. The traditional view of juvenile courts is that whatever is done to and for the juvenile will be in the youth's best interests. Sometimes, this means making one type of decision for one offender and a different type of decision for another offender, even when the offenders share similar backgrounds and have committed similar offenses.

Extralegal factors, such as race/ethnicity, socioeconomic status, gender, age, and a youth's demeanor all contribute to decision making at different processing stages (Burke, 2008). Ideally, these criteria should not be considered when making decisions about juvenile offenders. But sometimes judges and others will respond and make decisions about some youths based upon these and other variables (Dimmick, 2005). In many cases, these decisions are favorable for the youths involved, but outsiders may perceive this differential treatment to be inherently unequal treatment. Thus, questions arise about a juvenile's equal protection rights as set forth in the Fourteenth Amendment. Therefore, judges and others may tend to deal with some offenders more severely, simply to preserve due process. And this greater harshness is sometimes the result of a defense attorney's presence.

Consider the following scenario. Two 12-year-old youths have been taken into custody for theft. One boy stole some candy from a grocery store, while the other boy stole some pencils from a convenience store. Both boys have no prior juvenile records. One boy is Hispanic, while the other is Asian. The intake officer, who is black, sees both boys and their families, with no defense counsel present. The Hispanic boy utters various obscenities at the intake officer. The Asian boy sits calmly and responds politely to questions asked. The intake officer might be inclined to recommend further juvenile justice processing for the Hispanic juvenile, while he might be inclined to divert the Asian juvenile from the system. Is this decision motivated by prejudice? Or is the decision motivated by the attitude or demeanor displayed by each youth? If, in fact, these different decisions are made, the Hispanic boy is adversely affected by the intake officer's decision. But the Asian boy benefits from the informal handling of his case by the intake officer.

Now, let's consider these same scenarios, but in each case, we will place in the room defense counsel for both youths. Whether the defense counsel are privately retained or publicly appointed, they are interested in justice for their respective clients. Because of the presence of an attorney in each of the cases, the intake officer decides to apply standard decision-making criteria. Both of these boys have committed theft, at least a misdemeanor if an adult committed these acts. Thus, the intake officer moves both boys further into the system, so that a juvenile court prosecutor can take over from there. In the Hispanic boy's case, the presence of his defense counsel merely gave credence to the intake officer's decision to move the boy further into the system. The boy's demeanor or attitude didn't help matters, but the intake officer is merely following the rules. The letter of the law is applied. In the Asian youth's situation, the intake officer moves the boy further into the system, even though he believes this decision is *not* in the boy's best interests. But the intake officer is treating both boys equally, thus ensuring their due process and equal protection rights under the Fourteenth Amendment. The presence of defense counsel explains the consistency of the intake officer's conduct in both cases.

Some get-tough observers may say, so what? The boys stole something of value and they must learn not to steal. If we excuse the Asian boy from the system without punishing him, he will learn contempt for the system because the system is lenient and tolerates theft. The due process view is that both boys need to be punished equally, because they have equal background characteristics and have committed commensurate offenses. Should they be punished equally? At the other end of the spectrum are those who wish to preserve the *parens patriae* concept of juvenile courts. Doing things that are in a youth's best interests may involve making decisions that may be inherently discriminatory. Should we punish a juvenile's demeanor or attitude, which varies greatly from youth to youth; or should we punish the same delinquent acts in the same ways? This hypothetical example shows both the good and bad stemming from greater attorney involvement in juvenile proceedings at any stage (Mears et al., 2007).

Summary

Juvenile court prosecutors have considerable discretionary powers. But as greater rights have been extended to juveniles, prosecutors have been held to a higher standard in determining whether to prosecute youths. Seeking a youth's confinement now means that prosecutors must prove beyond a reasonable doubt the criminal court standard that juveniles are guilty of the offenses alleged against them. The changing nature of the prosecutorial role was described.

The time lines governing the processing of juveniles are greatly abbreviated compared with adult offenders. The acceleration of the juvenile justice process is due in large part to the belief that juveniles will experience greater accountability and associate their illegal actions with the punishments they will eventually receive. The appointment of public defenders and defense counsels to safeguard a youth's constitutional rights is an integral part of the juvenile justice system.

The rate of attorney use by juveniles has increased steadily in the United States for the past 35 years. Every indication suggests that this trend will continue. Defense counsels have learned to plea bargain juvenile cases increasingly such that more formal and costly court actions are circumvented. Strategic leniency was described to typify recent court orientations toward punishing adjudicated juvenile offenders.

Key Terms

Barker balancing test, 219
confidentiality privilege, 211
guardians ad litem, 223

statute of limitations, 220
with prejudice, 212
without prejudice, 216

Questions for Review

1. How are juvenile courts becoming increasingly adversarial proceedings? How has the prosecutorial role in juvenile courts changed in recent years?

2. How has the standard of proof "beyond a reasonable doubt" modified the prosecutorial role?

3. Should confidentiality of juvenile records be maintained? Why or why not?

4. What are some reasons for removing confidentiality surrounding juvenile records and opening juvenile courts to the general public?

5. What kinds of time standards govern prosecutorial decision making in the juvenile justice system? Are these time standards uniform for all jurisdictions?

6. What are some reasons for accelerating juvenile case processing?

7. Under what circumstances are public defenders appointed for juveniles? Do different types of defense counsel, public or private, make a difference in juvenile proceedings? If yes, why? If no, why not?

8. Do juvenile offenders have the right to a speedy trial? In what ways do more accelerated time lines for concluding juvenile cases parallel the speedy trial provisions of criminal courts?

9. What is the significance of the *Barker v. Wingo* case? Does the *Barker* case have any influence on juvenile matters? Why or why not?

10. How do defense counsels ensure that a juvenile's due process rights are preserved? What are *guardians ad litem* and what are their functions?

Internet Connections

Action without Borders
http://www.idealist.org/

Criminal Justice Consortium
http://www.bapd.org/gcrium-1.html

Federal Youth Court Program
http://www.youthcourt.net

Fortune Society
http://www.fortunesociety.org/

National Council on Crime and Delinquency
http://www.nccd-crc.org/nccd/n_more_pass.html

NetAction
http://www.netaction.org/

Network for Good
http://www.networkforgood.org/

Office of Juvenile Justice and Delinquency Prevention
http://www.ojjdp.ncjrs.org/

chapter 8

Classification and Preliminary Treatment

Waivers and Other Alternatives

chapter objectives

As the result of reading this chapter, you will accomplish the following objectives:

1. Distinguish between different types of offenses in terms of their seriousness.
2. Understand the criminal justice and juvenile justice system responses to juvenile violence.
3. Understand the get-tough movement and the policies advocated toward violent juveniles.
4. Understand the meaning of juvenile transfers, waivers, and certifications.
5. Understand different types of waiver actions and their implications for juvenile offenders.
6. Learn about the ages at which juveniles may be transferred to criminal court for processing.
7. Understand the importance of waiver hearings for juveniles.
8. Become familiar with important case law governing juvenile transfers or waivers.
9. Understand blended sentencing statutes as emerging optional punishments for juveniles who commit serious crimes.

 ## Case Study

It happened in Ewa Beach, Hawaii. Karen Ertell, a teenager, was allegedly raped and murdered by a 15-year-old Ilima Intermediate School student in May 2007. He lived down the street from the victim and had broken into her house on several occasions prior to the rape and murder. The youth had a lengthy prior record of juvenile offending, including burglary, robbery, auto theft, and credit card fraud. Ertell was scheduled to testify against him when she was raped and murdered. The suspect was being held in the Alder Street Youth Detention Facility while a family court decided whether to try the youth as an adult or juvenile. If the suspect is adjudicated of first-degree murder in juvenile court, he could be held in the Hawaii Youth Correctional Facility until age 21. If tried as an adult, the youth would face life imprisonment without the possibility of parole. [Source: Adapted from Treena Shapiro and the *Honolulu Advertiser,* "Hawaii Bill Calls for Trials as Adults for Teens," January 15, 2008.]

 ## Case Study

Robert Jobe is 15 and a resident of Toledo, Ohio. He is accused of murdering police Vice Detective Keith Dressel. Lucas County Juvenile Court Judge James Ray gave his decision regarding Jobe's disposition a great deal of thought. Jobe had a lengthy juvenile record. He had been on electronic monitoring previously and had cut off his electronic bracelet. He had numerous run-ins with the law. He defied court orders and was cited for contempt on several occasions. In 2006, he was caught with a gun. A hearing was held to determine whether Jobe should be tried as a juvenile or an adult for the crime he allegedly committed. Ray reasoned that if Jobe were tried as a juvenile, and if he were adjudicated delinquent on the murder charge, he would be released from custody when he reached age 21. However, if he were tried and convicted as an adult for the murder, he could face life imprisonment. Had Jobe been 16 when he allegedly killed Detective

Dressel, he would have automatically been tried as an adult for the offense. However, for 15-year-olds, the call to prosecute Jobe as an adult or a juvenile is up to the juvenile court judge. In this case, considering community safety and other factors, Judge Ray ordered Jobe to criminal court to face the murder charge as an adult. [Source: Adapted from *The Toledo Blade,* "Adult Trial for Adult Crime," January 15, 2008.]

Introduction

Rape and murder are two of the most serious violent offenses anyone can commit. When juveniles commit these offenses, these acts are especially troubling for the juvenile courts who must decide whether to prosecute youths as juveniles or adults. Whichever decision is made can have radically different consequences for these youths if they are found guilty.

This chapter is about how juveniles are classified and charged with various types of offenses. Virtually all jurisdictions distinguish between status and delinquent offenders and have procedures for dealing with them. Some youths commit such serious offenses that juvenile courts are incapable of punishing them sufficiently. Juvenile court judges may or may not be given choices concerning the ultimate outcomes of these cases. The decision-making criteria used by judges in making these difficult choices will be examined.

Next described is the waiver or transfer process, which is a mechanism used to transfer or waive jurisdiction over certain juveniles from juvenile courts to criminal courts. All waiver proceedings involve hearings to determine one's suitability for transfer. Also known as certification, these mechanisms are ways that youths can be treated as adults for the purpose of criminal prosecution. The nature and use of waivers or transfers, as well as the rationales they use, are discussed. A description of transferred juveniles is provided, and several explanations are given for why many of these youths are processed by criminal courts.

Several types of waivers or transfers are distinguished. The next section examines different types of waivers, which include judicial waivers, direct file, statutory exclusion, and demand waivers. Judicial waivers, initiated by judges, may be discretionary, mandatory, or presumptive. Other types of waivers are prosecutor initiated, such as direct file actions. State legislatures have adopted statutory exclusion, where the juvenile court is barred from hearing particular kinds of cases. Also, juveniles may demand to have their cases heard and decided in criminal courts instead of juvenile courts. Several other options are described about how juveniles are treated in different jurisdictions.

The implications of waiver actions for juveniles are listed and described. Two favorable outcomes of resulting from transfers to criminal court are that transferred or waived youths are entitled to a jury trial as a matter of right, and the full range of rights enjoyed by adult offenders are also extended to transferred juveniles. Several advantages and disadvantages of transfers for juveniles will be discussed. Time standards also govern the transfer process. These time standards will be defined and explained.

The chapter concludes by examining blended sentencing statutes. In a growing number of jurisdictions, juvenile and criminal courts are devising mechanisms for processing juveniles more effectively and that circumvent the cumbersome transfer or waiver process. Blended sentencing statutes enable juvenile and criminal court judges to impose both juvenile and adult punishments on particular juvenile offenders simultaneously, depending upon the jurisdiction and the particular blended sentencing statutes that the jurisdiction has adopted. Several variations of blended sentencing statutes will be described, and several examples will be provided concerning how these proceedings may be applied.

Seriousness of the Offense and Waiver Decision Making

Seriousness of the Offense

Investigations of the nature and seriousness of violent juvenile offending have been conducted by several researchers (Spano, Rivera, and Bolland, 2006). It may be that today's juveniles don't commit more acts of violence than did juveniles in previous generations, but more juveniles are violent. Some of the major causes of juvenile violence may be poor family relations, socioeconomically disadvantaged neighborhoods, poor school adjustments, peer pressure, greater availability of firearms, and greater dependence on alcohol or drugs (Mack et al., 2007).

Separating Status Offenders from Delinquent Offenders

One of the first steps taken to separate juveniles into different offending categories was the deinstitutionalization of status offenses (DSO). Also including divestiture, this major juvenile justice system reform was designed to remove the least-serious and non-criminal offenders from the jurisdiction of juvenile courts in every jurisdiction. Presumably and ideally, after DSO has occurred, only those juveniles who are charged with felonies and/or misdemeanors, delinquents, will be brought into the juvenile justice process and formally adjudicated in juvenile courts. These courts would also retain supervisory control over children in need of supervision, abused children, or neglected children. In reality, events have not turned out as legislators had originally anticipated or intended. Many status offenders continue to filter into the juvenile justice system in most jurisdictions (Feld, 2007).

When DSO occurred on a large scale throughout the United States during the late 1970s, several jurisdictions, including West Virginia, made policy decisions about how both nonserious and serious offenders would henceforth be treated by their juvenile justice systems. In West Virginia, for instance, the Supreme Court of Appeals ruled in 1977 that an adjudicated delinquent was constitutionally entitled to receive the least-restrictive alternative treatment consistent with his or her rehabilitative needs (*State ex rel. Harris v. Calendine,* 1977). While this decision didn't eliminate institutionalizing more serious or violent juveniles, it did encourage juvenile court judges to consider seriously various alternatives to incarceration as punishments for youthful offenders. Relating to DSO, the court also prohibited the commingling of adjudicated status offenders and adjudicated delinquent offenders in secure, prison-like facilities. Again, the court didn't necessarily rule out the secure confinement, long-term or otherwise, of status offenders as a possible sanction by juvenile court judges, despite encouragement by the court for judges first to attempt to apply nonincarcerative sanctions before imposing incarcerative penalties.

These mixed messages sent by the Supreme Court of Appeals of West Virginia did little, if anything, to restrict the discretionary powers of juvenile court judges. The court's emphasis on rehabilitation and alternative treatments to be considered by juvenile court judges reinforced the traditional concept of juvenile courts as rehabilitative rather than punitive sanctioning bodies. However, the court's ruling led to a substantial overhaul of the West Virginia juvenile code as well as a substantial drop in the incarcerated juvenile offender population in state-operated correctional facilities.

Juvenile Court Adjudications for Status Offenders

In many jurisdictions, DSO has reduced the volume of juvenile court cases over the years, but it has not prevented juvenile courts from continuing to adjudicate large numbers of status offenders annually. In 1997, an estimated 158,500 status offense cases were formally processed by juvenile courts through referrals and subsequent status offender petitions. By 2006, these types of cases represented about a fifth of all status offenses that came to the attention of juvenile courts (American Correctional Association, 2007). Proportionately, status offense cases processed formally by juvenile courts comprised only 15 percent of the entire delinquency and status offense court caseload. In 2006, juvenile courts formally processed approximately 27,000 runaway cases, 48,000 truancy cases, 26,500 ungovernability cases, 44,900 status liquor law violation cases, and 38,000 other miscellaneous status offense cases. Thus, truancy and liquor law violations were most often referred to juvenile courts for some type of action. About half of these referrals were made by police officers. About 52 percent of all of these cases were adjudicated as status offenders (Office of Juvenile Justice and Delinquency Prevention, 2007). Among those status offense cases that were not adjudicated, 68 percent were dismissed, 22 percent resulted in informal sanctions other than probation or out-of-home placement (e.g., fines, community service, restitution, or referrals to other community agencies for services), 9 percent resulted in informal probation, and less than 1 percent resulted in placement. **Placement** refers to out-of-home placement, such as in a group home or foster care. Seldom does placement mean secure confinement for status offenders in a state industrial school or reform school. Thus, juveniles who are subjected to these dispositional options are considered **placed**.

Formal adjudications become an official part of a juvenile's record. For offenders who are nonadjudicated, a formal decision is not rendered; rather, an informal declaration is made by the judge to dispose of these cases with minimal intrusion into the families and lives of those affected by the court decision.

The Use of Contempt Power to Incarcerate Nondelinquent Youths

While most adjudicated status offenders are not sent to industrial schools or directed to alternative out-of-home placements, it is the case that juvenile court judges wield considerable power to make status offenders comply with routine court directives. Truants may be ordered by the judge to attend school. Incorrigible youths may be ordered to obey their parents and remain law-abiding (Lee, 2008). Runaways may be ordered to participate in group counseling. Those youths with alcohol or drug dependencies may be ordered to attend individual counseling and alcohol/drug education sessions on a regular basis. If certain status offenders fail to obey these judicial directives in any way, they are at risk of being cited for **contempt of court**. A contempt-of-court citation is a misdemeanor, and juvenile court judges can use their contempt power to incarcerate any status offenders who do not comply with their orders. This judicial contempt power is unlimited.

Some observers believe that the use of contempt power by juvenile court judges is an abuse of judicial discretion. This is because some juvenile court judges hold juveniles accountable for their actions and consider them like adults in terms of their understanding of the law. Also, contempt power allows judges to circumvent and suspend procedural protections provided under state juvenile court acts. Further, incarcerating status offenders as a punishment for contempt of court is inconsistent with legislative priorities. Thus, citing and incarcerating status offenders for contempt has created a dual system in which judges are free to uphold protective provisions of the act or ignore them in favor of punishment by invoking contempt power. Therefore, status offenders are not fully insulated from incarceration as a punishment, despite the prevalence of DSO throughout the United States.

Delinquent Offenders and Juvenile Court Dispositions

Assuming that for the majority of jurisdictions, juvenile courts have effectively weeded out the bulk of the nonserious, nondelinquent cases, the remainder should theoretically

placement
One of several optional dispositions available to juvenile court judges following formal or informal proceedings against juveniles where either delinquent or status offenses have been alleged; adjudication proceedings yield a court decision about whether facts alleged in petition are true; if so, a disposition is imposed which may be placement in a foster or group home, wilderness experience, camp, ranch, or secure institution.

placed
Judicial disposition where juvenile is disposed to a group or foster home, or other type of out-of-home care; also includes secure confinement in an industrial school or comparable facility.

contempt of court
A citation by a judge against anyone in court who disrupts the proceedings or does anything to interfere with judicial decrees or pronouncements.

consist of those charged with delinquent offenses or acts that would be criminal if adults committed them. In 2004, there were approximately 70 million youths in the United States under the age of 18. Juvenile courts in the United States processed about 2.2 million delinquency cases (about 3 percent of all youths) in 2006 (Office of Juvenile Justice and Delinquency Prevention, 2007). This number represents a 50 percent increase over the number of delinquency cases handled in 1993. About 60 percent of all cases processed in 2007 were handled formally, where a petition was filed requesting an adjudicatory hearing. Furthermore, about 60 percent of these formally processed cases resulted in delinquency adjudications. About half of all adjudicated delinquents received probation or some other conditional release. About 30 percent of those adjudicated delinquent were ordered placed in a residential facility, such as a group home or a foster home. Approximately 12 percent of all adjudicated delinquency cases resulted in placement in secure detention facilities, such as industrial schools. The juvenile courts waived jurisdiction and transferred youths to criminal courts in 1 percent of all formally handled cases (Office of Juvenile Justice and Delinquency Prevention, 2007).

Between 1972 and 2006, several interesting trends have occurred with respect to juveniles who have been arrested or taken into police custody. In 1972, for instance, 50.8 percent of all juveniles taken into police custody were referred to juvenile courts, whereas 48 percent of these cases were handled within the department and subsequently released. However, during the next 32 years, the percentage of referrals to juvenile court systematically increased so that by 2004, 65 percent of all juveniles taken into custody by police were referred to juvenile court. Only 18 percent were handled within police departments and released through stationhouse adjustments (Office of Juvenile Justice and Delinquency Prevention, 2007). The remainder of youths in police custody were referred to social service agencies for further processing. Many of these referrals were status offenders.

Less than 1 percent of all juvenile cases are transferred annually from the jurisdiction of juvenile courts to the jurisdiction of criminal courts. By year-end 2004, 48 state jurisdictions and the District of Columbia gave juvenile court judges the power to waive their jurisdiction over certain juveniles so that they could be transferred to criminal court. However, in 2007, all states had some type of mechanism in place so that specific juvenile offenders could be treated as adults for the purpose of a prosecution in criminal courts (Office of Juvenile Justice and Delinquency Prevention, 2007).

Transfers, Waivers, and Certifications

Transfers, waiver
Proceedings where juveniles are remanded to the jurisdiction of criminal courts; also known as certifications and waivers.

transfer hearings
Proceeding to determine whether juveniles should be certified as adults for purposes of being subjected to jurisdiction of adult criminal courts where more severe penalties may be imposed.

certification
Similar to waivers or transfers; in some jurisdictions, juveniles are certified or designated as adults for the purpose of pursuing a criminal prosecution against them.

What are Transfers? **Transfers** refer to changing the jurisdiction of certain juvenile offenders to another jurisdiction, usually from juvenile court jurisdiction to criminal court jurisdiction. Transfers are also known as waivers, referring to a **waiver** or change of jurisdiction from the authority of juvenile court judges to criminal court judges (Haraway, 2008). Prosecutors or juvenile court judges decide that in some cases, juveniles should be waived or transferred to the jurisdiction of criminal courts. Presumably, those cases that are waived or transferred are the most-serious cases, involving violent or serious offenses, such as homicide, aggravated assault, rape, robbery, or drug dealing. These jurisdictions conduct **transfer hearings** (Kwak and Jeong, 2008).

In some jurisdictions, such as Texas and Utah, juveniles are waived or transferred to criminal courts through a process known as **certification** (Texas Youth Commission, 2005). A certification is a formal procedure whereby the state declares the juvenile to be an adult for the purpose of a criminal prosecution in a criminal court (McSherry, 2008). The results of certifications are the same as for waivers or transfers. Thus, certifications, waivers, and transfers result in juvenile offenders being subject to the jurisdiction of criminal courts where they are prosecuted as adult offenders. A 14-year-old murderer, for instance, might be transferred to criminal court for a criminal prosecution on the murder charge. In criminal court, the juvenile, now being treated as an adult, can be convicted of murder and sentenced to a prison term for one or more years. If the juvenile is charged with capital murder, is 16 or older, and lives in a state where the death penalty is administered to those convicted of capital murder, then he/she can potentially receive the death penalty as the maximum punishment for that offense, provided there is a capital murder conviction. Or criminal court judges might impose life-without-parole sentences on these convicted 16- or 17-year-olds. Imposing life-without-parole sentences or the death penalty are *not* within the jurisdiction of juvenile court judges. Their jurisdiction ends when an offender becomes an adult. Thus, a delinquency adjudication on capital murder charges in juvenile court might result in a juvenile being placed in the state industrial school until he is 18 or 21, depending upon whichever is the age of majority or adulthood.

The actual numbers of juveniles waived to the jurisdiction of criminal courts annually has fluctuated. Waivers declined in 1997 from earlier years (5,000-6,000) to 8,400 juveniles. However, from 1997 through 2006, the use of waivers has gradually increased and fluctuated between 11,000 and 13,000 juveniles per year (Office of Juvenile Justice and Delinquency Prevention, 2007).

The Rationale for Using Transfers, Waivers, or Certifications.

The basic rationale underlying the use of waivers is that the most serious juvenile offenders will be transferred to the jurisdiction of criminal courts where the harshest punishments, including capital punishment, may be imposed as sanctions (Brown, 2005). Since juvenile courts lack the jurisdiction and decision-making power to impose anything harsher than secure confinement dispositions of limited duration in industrial or reform schools, it would seem that the waiver would be an ideal way to impose the most severe punishments on those juveniles who commit the most violent acts (Watts-Farmer, 2008). A list of reasons for using transfers, waivers, or certifications are as follows:

1. To make it possible for harsher punishments to be imposed.
2. To provide just deserts and proportionately severe punishments on those juveniles who deserve such punishments by their more violent actions.
3. To foster fairness in administering punishments according to the seriousness of one's offense.
4. To hold serious or violent offenders more accountable for what they have done.
5. To show other juveniles who contemplate committing serious offenses that the system works and harsh punishments can be expected if serious offenses are committed.
6. To provide a deterrent to decrease juvenile violence.
7. To overcome the traditional leniency of juvenile courts and provide more realistic sanctions.
8. To make youths realize the seriousness of their offending and induce remorse and **acceptance of responsibility**.

Ideal Offender Characteristics for Justifying Transfers to Criminal Courts.

Those designated for transfer or waiver by various participants in the juvenile justice process should exhibit certain consistent characteristics (McSherry, 2008). Age, offense seriousness, and prior record (including previous referrals to juvenile court, intake proceedings and dispositions, or juvenile court delinquency adjudications) are some of these characteristics.

Juvenile offenders most in need of processing by criminal courts should be chronic, persistent, and violent offenders (Haraway, 2008). Person offenses, such as rape, murder, robbery, and aggravated assault, should top the list of those who merit transfer from the jurisdiction of juvenile courts to criminal courts for criminal prosecutions. Because of the therapeutic environment generated by juvenile courts and their emphasis upon rehabilitation, treatment, and reform, less-serious property and drug offenders, a largely nonviolent class, might benefit more from juvenile court processing. Therefore, we would expect to see almost all transferred cases to criminal court typified by person or

acceptance of responsibility
Genuine admission or acknowledgment of wrongdoing; in federal presentence investigation reports, for example, convicted offenders may write an explanation and apology for the crime(s) they committed; a provision that may be considered in deciding whether leniency should be extended to offenders during the sentencing phase of their processing.

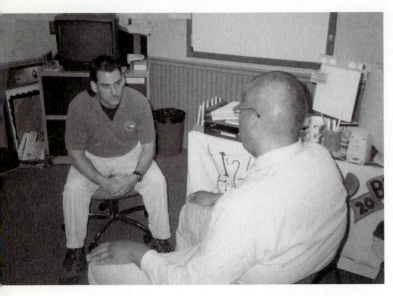

Informal conferences with youths often precede further juvenile court action.

violent offenders, clearly the most serious and dangerous juvenile offender class (Brown, 2005).

Actual Characteristics of Transferred Juveniles.

Are the most-serious juveniles actually transferred to criminal courts for processing? No. In 2006, transfers of violent juvenile offenders increased to 42 percent, and property offenders represented 39 percent of those transferred (McSherry, 2008). Drugs and public order offenses accounted for the remaining 19 percent. By 2006, however, violent offenders represented only 34 percent of all transferred youths. Those juveniles charged with various drug offenses represented 15 percent of all transferred youths. Those charged with public order offenses represented 7 percent of those transferred. Property offenders accounted for 44 percent of those transferred. Therefore, if we combine the nonviolent categories of property offending, drug offending, and public order offending, they account for 66 percent of all transferred youths in 2006. Clearly the most violent person offenders are not being targeted for transfer to criminal courts. Juvenile court judges ought to be concerned about these alarming figures (Office of Juvenile Justice and Delinquency Prevention, 2008). It should be noted that the abrupt increase in transfers of juveniles charged with various drug crimes in the early 1990s probably reflects various federal and state initiatives to prosecute drug offenders more aggressively and subject them to more severe punishments.

Despite earlier references to more extensive and violent female juvenile offending, female juveniles transferred to criminal court increased from 5 percent in 2000 to 12 percent in 2007. It is also significant to note that youths under age 16 were being transferred to a greater degree in 2006 compared with 2000. In 2000, for instance, only 11 percent of those transferred to criminal court were under age 16. In 2006, however, this figure had grown to 20 percent. This is likely reflective of the get-tough movement reaction toward more violent crimes committed by younger juveniles. The percentage of white youths transferred to criminal courts increased from 56 percent in 2000 to 64 percent in 2006, whereas the percentage of black youths declined from 41 percent to 28 percent during the same time interval (Office of Juvenile Justice and Delinquency Prevention, 2007). The disproportionate representation of blacks transferred to criminal courts is apparent.

Youngest Ages at Which Juveniles Can Be Transferred to Criminal Court.

Table 8.1 shows the youngest ages at which juveniles could be transferred or waived to criminal courts in all U.S. jurisdictions in 2006 (Office of Juvenile Justice and Delinquency Prevention, 2007).

In 2006, 14 states and all federal districts had no specified age for transferring juveniles to criminal courts for processing. Two states, Vermont and Wisconsin, specified age 10 as the minimum age at which a juvenile could be waived. Colorado, Missouri, Montana, and Oregon established age 12 as the earliest age for a juvenile waiver. Eighteen states used age 14 as the minimum transfer age, while the District of Columbia set the minimum transfer age at 15, and one state, Hawaii, used the minimum transfer age of 16. Thus, since 1987 a majority of states substantially reduced the age at which juveniles could be tried as adults in criminal courts.

Some idea of the aggressiveness of state governments and public policies directed toward getting tough toward violent juvenile offending is provided by Table 8.2. Table 8.2 shows the various states that have modified or enacted changes in their transfer provisions for juveniles during 1996–2005.

Under judicial waiver modifications, four states have lowered the age limit at which juveniles can be transferred to criminal court. One example of a significant age

Table 8.1

Minimum Age for Transferring Juveniles to Adult Court, 2008

Minimum Age	States
None	Arizona, Florida, Georgia, Indiana, Maine, Maryland, Nebraska, Nevada, New Hampshire, Oklahoma, Pennsylvania, Rhode Island, South Carolina, South Dakota, Tennessee, Washington, West Virginia
10	Vermont, Wisconsin
12	Colorado, Missouri, Montana, Oregon
13	Illinois, Mississippi, New York, North Carolina, Wyoming
14	Alabama, Arkansas, California, Connecticut, Iowa, Kansas, Kentucky, Louisiana, Massachusetts, Michigan, Minnesota, New Jersey, New Mexico, North Dakota, Ohio, Texas, Utah, Virginia
15	District of Columbia
16	Hawaii

Source: Compiled by author 2008.

modification is Missouri, where the minimum age for juvenile transfers was lowered from 14 to 12 for any felony. In Texas, the minimum transfer age was lowered from 15 to 10. Virginia lowered the transfer age from 15 to 14. Table 8.2 also shows that other modifications were made to get tough toward juvenile offenders. Ten states added crimes to the list of those qualifying youths for transfer to criminal courts. In 6 states, the age of criminal accountability was lowered, while 24 states authorized additional crimes to be included that would automatically direct that the criminal court would have jurisdiction rather than the juvenile court.

Waiver Decision Making

Organizational and political factors are at work to influence the upward trend in the use of transfers. Politicians wish to present a get-tough facade to the public by citing waiver statistics and showing their increased use is the political response to the rise in serious youth crime. Despite political rhetoric, there has been a general increase in the use of waivers, although from 1998 to 2007, at least, the number of waivers has remained fairly constant (Office of Juvenile Justice and Delinquency Prevention, 2007).

Several types of waivers are used by different jurisdictions for transferring jurisdiction over juveniles from juvenile to criminal courts (Zhang, 2008). One of these is the automatic transfer or automatic waiver which several jurisdictions currently employ. This means that if youthful offenders are within a particular age range, such as ages 16 or 17, and if they are charged with specific types of offenses (usually murder, robbery, rape, aggravated assault, and other violent crimes), they will be transferred automatically to criminal courts. These types of waivers, also known as legislative waivers because they were mandated by legislative bodies in various states and carry the weight of statutory authority, involve no discretionary action among prosecutors or judges. For other types of waivers, the decision-making process is largely discretionary (Champion, 2008a).

Because of the discretionary nature of the waiver process, large numbers of the wrong types of juveniles are transferred to criminal courts. They are wrong because

Table 8.2

States Modifying or Enacting Transfer Provisions, 2008

Type of Transfer Provision	Action Taken (Number of States)	States Making Changes	Examples
Discretionary Waiver	Added crimes (7 states)	DE, KY, LA, MT, NV, RI, WA	Kentucky: 1996 provision permits the juvenile court to transfer a juvenile to crime court if 14-years-old and charged with a felony with firearm.
	Lowered age limit (4 states)	CO, DE, HI, VA	Hawaii: 1997 provision adds language that allows to waiver a minor at any age (previous 16) if charged with first- or second-degree murder (or attempts) and there is no evidence that the person is committable to an institute for the mentally defective/mentally ill.
	Added or modified prior record provisions (4 states)	FL, HI, IN, KY	Florida: 1997 legislation requires that if the juvenile, 14 at the time of a fourth felony and certain conditions apply, the state's attorney must ask the court to transfer him or her and certify the child as an adult or must provide written reasons for not making such a request.
Presumptive Waiver	Enacted provisions (2 states)	KS, UT	Kansas: 1996 legislation shifts the burden of proof to the child to rebut the presumption that the child is an adult.
Direct File	Enacted or modified (8 states)	AR, AZ, CO, FL, GA, MA, MT, OK	Colorado: 1996 legislation adds vehicular homicide, vehicular assault, and felonious arson to direct file statute.
Statutory Exclusion	Enacted provision (2 states)	AZ, MA	Arizona: 1997 legislation establishes exclusion for 15- to 17-year-olds charged with certain violent felonies.
	Added crimes (12 states)	AL, AK, DE, GA, IL, IN, OK, OR, SC, SD, UT, WA	Georgia: 1997 legislation adds crime of battery if victim is a teacher or other school personnel to list of designated felonies.
	Lowered age limit (1 state)	DE	Delaware: 1996 legislation lowers from 16 to 15 the age for which the offense of possession of a firearm during the commission of a felony is automatically prosecuted in criminal court.
	Added lesser-included offense (1 state)	IN	Indiana: 1997 legislation lists exclusion offenses, including any offense that may be joined with the listed offenses.

Source: Patricia Torbet and Linda Szymanski. (1998). *State Legislative Responses to Violent Juvenile Crime: 1996–1997 Update*. Washington, DC: U.S. Department of Justice, p. 5. Updated 2008 by author.

they are not those originally targeted by juvenile justice professionals and reformers to be the primary candidates for transfers. The primary targets of waivers are intended to be the most-serious, violent, and dangerous juveniles who also deserve more serious sanctions criminal courts can impose. But there is a serious credibility gap between the types of juveniles who are actually transferred each year and those who should be transferred. In 1994, for instance, nearly half (45 percent) of all youths transferred to criminal court were charged with property or public order offenses. These types of offenses include theft, burglary, petty larceny, and disturbing the peace. Only 44 percent of those transferred in 1994 were charged with person offenses or violent crimes. If transfers, waivers, or certifications were applied as they should be applied, 100 percent of those transferred annually would be serious, violent offenders. Juvenile courts would handle all of the other cases (Haraway, 2008).

Why Do Property and Public Order Offenders Get Transferred to Criminal Court?

An interested public wants to know why juvenile courts would send property offenders or public order offenders to criminal courts for processing. After all, these are the least-serious offenders compared with those committing aggravated assault, attempted murder, homicide, rape, and armed robbery. Studies of juvenile court judges disclose that often, persistent nonserious offenders are transferred from juvenile courts because juvenile court judges are tired of seeing these same offenders in their courts. They believe that if such persistent offenders are sent to criminal courts, this will be a better deterrent to their future offending (McNeill and Batchelor, 2004). What these judges do not understand is that criminal court prosecutors and judges often tend to downplay the significance of these small-time offenders. At least half the nonserious property offenders will have their cases dismissed, diverted, or downgraded (Champion, 2005). Another 40 percent will enter plea bargains and receive probation from criminal court judges. Most criminal court judges do not want to put 14-year-old property offenders or public order offenders in adult prisons, where chronic overcrowding and the potential for sexual exploitation are pervasive. Thus, only about 10 percent of nonserious offenders who are transferred annually will be placed in confinement for a term of months or years. About 90 percent will return to their neighborhoods and continue to reoffend (Champion and Mays, 1991).

A list of some of the factors cited by juvenile court judges that result in the transfer of nonserious property, public order, or drug offenders to criminal court are:

1. Although property offenders aren't especially serious or violent, their persistence in offending causes juvenile court judges to tire of their frequent appearances; transfers of these offenders to criminal court will "teach them a lesson."
2. Some jurisdictions mandate transfers to criminal court of those offenders who exceed some previously determined maximum of juvenile court adjudications; these may include property or public order offenders.
3. Individual differences among juvenile court judges will dictate which juveniles are transferred, despite the seriousness of their offense; if the judge doesn't like a particular youth's attitude, the youth will be transferred.
4. Any kind of drug offense should be dealt with by criminal courts; thus, a simple "possession of a controlled substance" charge (e.g., prescription medicine) may be sufficient to qualify a juvenile for a criminal court transfer.
5. What is a serious or violent offense in one juvenile court jurisdiction may not be considered serious or violent in another jurisdiction; thus, different standards are applied to the same types of juveniles in different jurisdictions.

It is questionable whether waivers have functioned as effective deterrents to future juvenile offending (Haraway, 2008). In some jurisdictions where gang presence is strong, for instance, local task forces have targeted gangs for harsher treatment, including the greater likelihood of being transferred to criminal court. A study of 38 state jurisdictions disclosed, however, that most prosecutors had no specific plans relating to dealing with gang members when they were transferred to criminal courts. Further, specialized gang prosecution units were rare (5 percent), even though it was believed that tougher juvenile laws would help combat the gang problem (Knox, Martin, and Tromanhauser, 1995). Most jurisdictions continue to experiment with various strategies that will target the most-serious offenders for criminal prosecutions (Taylor et al., 2008).

Types of Waivers

There are four types of waiver actions. These include: (1) judicial waivers, (2) direct file, (3) statutory exclusion, and (4) demand waivers.

Judicial Waivers. The largest numbers of waivers from juvenile to criminal court annually come about as the result of direct judicial action. **Judicial waivers** give the juvenile court judge the authority to decide whether to waive jurisdiction and transfer the case to criminal court. There are three kinds of judicial waivers: (1) discretionary; (2) mandatory; and (3) presumptive.

Discretionary Waivers. **Discretionary waivers** empower the judge to waive jurisdiction over the juvenile and transfer the case to criminal court. Because of this type of waiver, judicial waivers are sometimes known as discretionary waivers (Champion, 2008a). This is because the judge may or may not decide to waive particular youths to criminal courts for processing (Congressional Research Service, 2007).

Mandatory Waivers. In the case of a **mandatory waiver**, the juvenile court judge *must* waive jurisdiction over the juvenile to criminal court if probable cause exists that the juvenile committed the alleged offense.

Presumptive Waivers. Under the **presumptive waiver** scenario, judges still decide to transfer youths to criminal courts. However, the burden of proof concerning a transfer decision is shifted from the state to the juvenile. It requires that certain juveniles shall be waived to criminal court unless they can prove that they are suited for juvenile rehabilitation. In this respect, at least, they are similar to mandatory waivers. Defense counsel who wish to keep their juvenile clients within the jurisdiction of the juvenile court have a relatively difficult time arguing that their clients deserve a juvenile court adjudicatory hearing instead of prosecution in criminal court.

Judicial waivers are often criticized because of their subjectivity. Two different youths charged with identical offenses may appear at different times before the same judge. On the basis of impressions formed about the youths, the judge may decide to transfer one youth to criminal court and adjudicate the other youth in juvenile court. Obviously, the intrusion of extralegal factors into this important action generates a degree of unfairness and inequality. A youth's appearance and attitude emerge as significant factors that will either make or break the offender in the eyes of the judge. These socioeconomic and behavioral criteria often overshadow the seriousness or pettiness of offenses alleged. In the context of this particular type of transfer, it is easy to see how some persistent, nonviolent offenders may suffer waiver to criminal court. This is an easy way for the judge to get rid of them.

Although judges have this discretionary power in most jurisdictions, youths are still entitled to a hearing where they can protest the waiver action. While it is true that the criminal court poses risks to juveniles in terms of potentially harsher penalties, it is also true that being tried as an adult entitles youths to all of the adult constitutional safeguards, including the right to a trial by jury. In a later section of this chapter, we will examine closely this and other options that may be of benefit to juveniles. Thus, juveniles may not want to fight waiver or transfer actions, largely because they may be treated more leniently by criminal courts.

Direct File

Whenever offenders are screened at intake and referred to the juvenile court for possible prosecution, prosecutors will conduct further screenings of these youths. They determine which cases merit further action and formal adjudication by judges. Not

judicial waivers
Decision by juvenile judge to waive juvenile to jurisdiction of criminal court.

discretionary waivers
Transfers of juveniles to criminal courts by judges, at their discretion or in their judgment; also known as judicial waivers.

mandatory waiver
Automatic transfer of certain juveniles to criminal court on the basis of (1) their age and (2) the seriousness of their offense; e.g., a 17-year-old in Illinois who allegedly committed homicide would be subject to mandatory transfer to criminal court for the purpose of a criminal prosecution.

presumptive waiver
Requirement that shifts the burden to the juvenile for defending against their transfer to criminal court by showing that they are capable of being rehabilitated; following automatic or legislative waiver, juveniles can challenge the waiver in a hearing where they must demonstrate to the court's satisfaction their capability of becoming reformed.

all cases sent to prosecutors by intake officers automatically result in subsequent formal juvenile court action. Prosecutors may decline to prosecute certain cases, particularly if there are problems with witnesses who are either missing or who refuse to testify, if there are evidentiary issues, or if there are overloaded juvenile court dockets. A relatively small proportion of cases may warrant waivers to criminal courts (Toth, 2005). Table 8.3 shows the states that had direct file or concurrent jurisdiction provisions in 2004.

Table 8.3

States with Concurrent Jurisdiction and Direct File Provisions, by Offense, 2008

Concurrent Jurisdiction Offense and Minimum Age Criteria, 2008

States	Minimum Age for Concurrent Jurisdiction	Any Criminal Offense	Certain Felonies	Capital Crimes	Murder	Certain Offenses			
						Person Offenses	Property Offenses	Drug Offenses	Weapon Offenses
Arizona	14		14						
Arkansas	14		14	14	14	14			14
Colorado	14		14		14	14	14		14
District of Columbia	16				16	16	16		
Florida	NS*	16[a]	16	NS[b]	14	14	14		14
Georgia	NS			NS					
Louisiana	15				15	15	15	15	
Massachusetts	14		14			14			14
Michigan	14		14		14	14	14	14	
Montana	12				12	12	16	16	16
Nebraska	NS	16[c]	NS						
Oklahoma	15				15	15	15	16	16
Vermont	16	16							
Virginia	14				14	14			
Wyoming	14	17	14						

Examples: In Arizona, prosecutors have discretion to file directly in criminal court those cases involving juveniles aged 14 or older charged with certain felonies (defined in state statutes). In Florida, prosecutors may "direct file" cases involving juveniles aged 16 or older charged with a misdemeanor (if they have a prior adjudication) or a felony offense and those aged 14 or older charged with murder or certain person, property, or weapon offenses; no minimum age is specified for cases in which a grand jury indicts a juvenile for a capital offense.

Ages in minimum age column may not apply to all offense restrictions but represent the youngest possible age at which a juvenile's case may be filed directly in criminal court.

*"NS" indicates that in at least one of the offense restrictions indicated, no minimum age is specified.

[a]Applies to misdemeanors and requires prior adjudication(s), which may be required to have been for the same or a more serious offense type.

[b]Requires grand jury indictment.

[c]Applies to misdemeanors.

Source: Adapted from H. Snyder and M. Sickmund. (1999). *Juvenile Offenders and Victims: 1999 National Report*. Washington. DC: U.S. Department of Justice. Office of Justice Programs. Office of Juvenile Justice and Delinquency Prevention. Updated 2008 by author.

direct file
Prosecutorial waiver of jurisdiction to a criminal court; an action taken against a juvenile who has committed an especially serious offense, where that juvenile's case is transferred to criminal court for the purpose of a criminal prosecution.

concurrent jurisdiction
Power to file charges against juveniles in either criminal courts or juvenile courts.

statutory exclusion
Provisions that automatically exclude certain juveniles and offenses from the jurisdiction of the juvenile courts; e.g., murder, rape, armed robbery.

legislative waiver
Provision that compels juvenile court to remand certain youths to criminal courts because of specific offenses that have been committed or alleged.

demand waiver
Requests by juveniles to have their cases transferred from juvenile courts to criminal courts.

reverse waiver
Motion to transfer juvenile's case from criminal court to juvenile court following a legislative or automatic waiver action.

Under **direct file**, the prosecutor has the sole authority to decide whether any given juvenile case will be heard in criminal court or juvenile court. Essentially, the prosecutor decides which court should have jurisdiction over the juvenile (Feld, 2007). Prosecutors with direct file power are said to have **concurrent jurisdiction**. This is another name for direct file. In Florida, for example, prosecutors have concurrent jurisdiction. They may file extremely serious charges (e.g., murder, rape, aggravated assault, robbery) against youths in criminal courts and present cases to grand juries for indictment action. Or prosecutors may decide to file the same cases in the juvenile court (D'Angelo and Brown, 2005).

Statutory Exclusion

Statutory exclusion means that certain juvenile offenders are automatically excluded from the juvenile court's original jurisdiction. Legislatures of various states declare a particular list of offenses to be excluded from the jurisdiction of juvenile courts. Added to this list of excluded offenses is a particular age range. Thus, in Illinois, if a 17-year-old juvenile is charged with murder, rape, or aggravated assault, this particular juvenile is automatically excluded from the jurisdiction of the juvenile court. Instead, the case will be heard in criminal court. In 2007, 30 states had statutory exclusion provisions and excluded certain types of offenders from juvenile court jurisdiction (Office of Juvenile Justice and Delinquency Prevention, 2007). Because state legislatures created statutory exclusion provisions, this waiver action is sometimes known as a **legislative waiver**. And because these provisions mandate the automatic waiver of juveniles to criminal court, they are also known as automatic waivers. States with statutory exclusion provisions by minimum age for 2008 are shown in Table 8.4.

Demand Waivers

Under certain conditions and in selected jurisdictions, juveniles may submit motions for **demand waiver** actions. Demand waiver actions are requests or motions filed by juveniles and their attorneys to have their cases transferred from juvenile courts to criminal courts. Why would juveniles want to have their cases transferred to criminal courts?

One reason is that most U.S. jurisdictions do not provide jury trials for juveniles in juvenile courts as a matter of right (*McKeiver v. Pennsylvania*, 1971). However, about a fifth of the states have established provisions for jury trials for juveniles at their request and depending upon the nature of the charges against them. In the remainder of the states, jury trials for juveniles are granted only at the discretion of the juvenile court judge. Most juvenile court judges are not inclined to grant jury trials to juveniles. Thus, if juveniles are (1) in a jurisdiction where they are not entitled to a jury trial even if they request one from the juvenile court judge; (2) face serious charges; and (3) believe that their cases would receive greater impartiality from a jury in a criminal courtroom, they may seek a demand waiver in order to have their cases transferred to criminal court. Florida permits demand waivers as one of several waiver options (Office of Juvenile Justice and Delinquency Prevention, 2007).

Other Types of Waivers

Reverse Waivers. A **reverse waiver** is an action by the criminal court to transfer direct file or statutory exclusion cases from criminal court back to juvenile court, usually at the recommendation of the prosecutor. Typically, juveniles who would be involved in these reverse waiver hearings would be those who were automatically sent to criminal court because of statutory exclusion. Thus, criminal court judges can send at least some of these juveniles back. Reverse waiver actions may also be instigated by defense counsels on behalf of their clients.

Table 8.4

States with Statutory Exclusion by Offense and Minimum Age, 2008

Statutory Exclusion Offense and Minimum Age Criteria, 2008

States	Minimum Age for Concurrent Jurisdiction	Any Criminal Offense	Certain Felonies	Capital Crimes	Murder	Certain Offenses: Person Offenses	Property Offenses	Drug Offenses	Weapon Offenses
Alabama	16		16	16				16	
Alaska	16					16	16		
Arizona	15		15[a]		15	15			
Delaware	15		15						
Florida	NS*	NS[a]				NS			
Georgia	13				13	13			
Idaho	14				14	14	14	14	
Illinois	13		15[b]		13	15		15	15
Indiana	16		16		16	16		16	16
Iowa	16		16					16	16
Louisiana	15				15	15			
Maryland	14			14	16	16			16
Massachusetts	14				14				
Minnesota	16				16				
Mississippi	13		13	13					
Montana	17				17	17	17	17	17
Nevada	NS	NS[a]			NS	16[a]			
New Mexico	15				15[c]				
New York	13				13	14	14		
Oklahoma	13				13				
Oregon	15				15	15			
Pennsylvania	NS				NS	15			
South Carolina	16		16						
South Dakota	16		16						
Utah	16		16[d]	16					
Vermont	14				14	14	14		
Washington	16				16	16	16		
Wisconsin	NS				10	NS[e]			

Examples: In Delaware, juveniles aged 15 or older charged with certain felonies must be tried in criminal court. In Arizona, juveniles aged 15 or older must be tried in criminal court if they are charged with murder or certain person offenses or if they have prior felony adjudications and are charged with a felony.

Ages in minimum age column may not apply to all offense restrictions but represent the youngest possible age at which a juvenile's case may be excluded from juvenile court.

* "NS" indicates that in at least one of the offense restrictions indicated, no minimum age is specified.

[a] Requires prior adjudication(s), or conviction(s), which may be required to have been for the same or a more serious offense type.

[b] Only escape or bail violation while subject to prosecution in criminal court.

[c] Requires grand jury indictment.

[d] Requires prior commitment in a secure facility.

[e] Only if charged while confined or on probation or parole.

Source: Adapted from H. Snyder and M. Sickmund. (1999). *Juvenile Offenders and Victims: 1999 National Report*. Washington. DC: U.S. Department of Justice, Office of Justice Programs, Office of Juvenile Justice and Delinquency Prevention. Updated 2008 by author.

8.1   F o c u s   o n   D e l i n q u e n c y

It happened in Leonardtown, Maryland. Corey Ryder, a 17-year-old youth accused of attempting to murder his parents, stood before a criminal court judge at a hearing. Ryder had been arrested following his attempt to hire an undercover police officer to kill his parents. The undercover officer asked Ryder how he (Ryder) wanted the killing to be done. Ryder said in the tape-recorded conversation, "Two bullets is all it takes." Given Ryder's age, and under Maryland's statutory exclusion rules for juvenile offenders, Ryder was arrested, charged as an adult, and sent to criminal court. Ryder's defense counsel, public defender John Getz, asked the criminal court judge, Karen Abrams, to allow Ryder to be tried as a juvenile in juvenile court. A hearing followed to determine whether Ryder ought to be tried in juvenile court rather than in a criminal court.

Several state witnesses were called to testify that Ryder would benefit from state treatment for juveniles which he would be denied if convicted of the crime in criminal court. Other witnesses testified about alleged abuse suffered by Ryder at the hands of his parents which led to his anger against them. Ryder had earlier moved out of his parent's home and had issues with parental authority. Another witness was Tara Klysz, Ryder's probation officer. Klysz said that Ryder had a long history of juvenile offending, including property destruction, drug abuse, and poor school behavior.

Countering the defense was Ryder's mother, who testified that her son had threatened to cut her throat and discovered a large knife hidden in his room. She told the court she feared for her life. Another contrary testi-

mony revealed that Ryder had been in several previous treatment programs, and that he had failed to make visible progress in any of them. One electronic monitoring program appeared successful when Ryder was obligated to attend school and conform to school rules. But as soon as he was free of the electronic monitoring program, his bad behavior returned.

Judge Karen Abrams considered the juvenile court option, eventually opting to send Ryder's case to juvenile court for processing. She justified her action by saying that there was something obviously wrong with Ryder, and that prison was not the answer. She said that the juvenile court had the power to order psychiatric evaluations and furnish Ryder with needed services not otherwise provided for adult offenders. She advised Ryder in open court to take advantage of the treatment opportunities from the state and to learn to deal with anger issues that caused him to commit the alleged offense in the first place. Probation Officer Klysz agreed with Judge Abrams that treatment would benefit Ryder more than imprisonment. Ryder's mother was visibly shaken by Judge Abrams' decision. She was upset over the prospect that in the juvenile justice system, Ryder would be released on his 21st birthday, only 4 short years away. She said, "How do I live? How does my family live?" The mother continued to fear for her life at the hands of her son, and she had no faith that any juvenile treatment program would improve him. Should Ryder's case have been returned to juvenile court? Or should Ryder have been tried as an adult, considering his past failure record with so many interventions? What do you think?

Source: Adapted from Guy Leonard and the Associated Press, "Teen's Attempted Murder Trial Will Move to Juvenile Court," September 21, 2007.

Once an Adult/Always an Adult. The **once an adult/always an adult provision** is perhaps the most serious and long-lasting for affected juvenile offenders. This provision means that once juveniles have been convicted in criminal court, they are henceforth considered adults for the purpose of criminal prosecutions. For instance, suppose a 12-year-old is transferred to criminal court in Vermont and subsequently convicted of a crime. Subsequently, at age 15, if the same juvenile commits another crime, such as vehicular theft, he would be subject to prosecution in criminal court. Thus, a criminal court conviction means that the juvenile permanently loses his access to the juvenile court. In 2004, two-thirds of all states had once an adult/always an adult provisions (Office of Juvenile Justice and Delinquency Prevention, 2007).

Interestingly, the once an adult/always an adult provision is not as ominous as it appears. It requires that particular jurisdictions keep track of each juvenile offender previously convicted of a crime. This record keeping is not particularly sophisticated in different jurisdictions. Some juveniles may simply move away from the jurisdiction where they were originally convicted. Fourteen-year-old juveniles who are convicted of a crime in California may move to North Dakota or Vermont, where they may be treated as first-offenders in those juvenile courts. How are North Dakota and Vermont juvenile courts supposed to know that a particular 14-year-old has a criminal conviction in California? Information sharing among juvenile courts throughout the United States is very limited or nonexistent. Thus, the intent of the once an adult/always an adult provision can often be defeated simply by relocating and moving to another jurisdiction. This is true also of juvenile court jurisdictions within the same state. In California, for instance, a state with the once an adult/always an adult provision, if a juvenile has been transferred to a criminal court for prosecution in Long Beach, California and moves to Bellflower, Carson, Paramount, or Pomona, other California cities, it is very likely that the juvenile courts in those cities will be unaware of the fact that the juvenile was treated as an adult for purposes of a criminal prosecution in Long Beach. Such is the state regarding juvenile record information sharing among California juvenile courts. The fact is that most states have a combination of various transfer or waiver provisions.

The most popular type of waiver action is the judicial waiver, where 46 states and the District of Columbia had judicial waiver provisions in 2006 (Office of Juvenile Justice and Delinquency Prevention, 2007). Over half of all states (30) had statutory exclusion provisions in 2004. Reverse waivers, which result from automatic or legislative waivers, were used in 25 states in 2008. Also, 33 states enacted the once an adult/always an adult provision. Fifteen states had concurrent jurisdiction or direct file provisions. A summary of the juvenile transfer provisions for all states for 2008 is shown in Table 8.5.

once an adult/always an adult provision Ruling that once a juvenile has been transferred to criminal court to be prosecuted as an adult, regardless of the criminal court outcome, the juvenile can never be subject to the jurisdiction of juvenile courts in the future; in short, the juvenile, once transferred, will always be treated as an adult if future crimes are committed, even though the youth is still not of adult age.

Table 8.5

Juvenile Transfer Provisions for All States, 2008

State	Judicial Waiver Discretionary	Presumptive	Mandatory	Concurrent Jurisdiction	Statutory Exclusion	Reverse Waiver	Once an Adult/ Always an Adult
Total Number of States	46	15	14	15	28	23	31
Alabama	•				•		•
Alaska	•	•			•		
Arizona	•	•		•	•	•	•
Arkansas	•			•		•	
California	•	•					•
Colorado	•	•		•		•	
Connecticut			•			•	
Delaware	•		•		•		•
District of Columbia	•	•		•			•
Florida	•			•	•		

Table 8.5   (Cont.)

Juvenile Transfer Provisions for All States, 2008

State	Judicial Waiver			Concurrent Jurisdiction	Statutory Exclusion	Reverse Waiver	Once an Adult/ Always an Adult
	Discretionary	Presumptive	Mandatory				
Georgia	•		•	•	•	•	
Hawaii	•						•
Idaho	•				•		•
Illinois	•	•	•		•		•
Indiana	•			•	•		•
Iowa	•				•	•	•
Kansas	•	•					•
Kentucky	•		•			•	
Louisiana	•		•	•	•		
Maine	•						•
Maryland	•				•	•	
Massachusetts					•		•
Michigan	•			•			•
Minnesota	•	•			•		•
Mississippi	•				•	•	•
Missouri	•						•
Montana	•			•			
Nebraska	•			•			
Nevada	•	•			•	•	•
New Hampshire	•	•					•
New Jersey	•	•					
New Mexico					•		
New York					•	•	
North Carolina	•		•				
North Dakota	•	•	•				•
Ohio	•		•				•
Oklahoma	•			•	•	•	•
Oregon	•				•	•	•
Pennsylvania	•	•			•	•	
Rhode Island	•	•			•		•
South Carolina	•		•		•	•	
South Dakota	•				•		•
Tennessee	•					•	
Texas	•						•
Utah	•	•			•		
Vermont	•			•	•	•	
Virginia	•			•	•		•
Washington	•				•		•
West Virginia	•		•				
Wisconsin	•				•	•	•
Wyoming	•			•		•	

In states with a combination of transfer mechanisms, the exclusion, mandatory waiver, or concurrent jurisdiction provisions generally target the oldest juveniles and/or those charged with the most-serious offenses, while those charged with relatively less-serious offenses and/or younger juveniles may be eligible for discretionary waiver.

Source: Adapted from H. Snyder and M. Sickmund. (1999). *Juvenile Offenders and Victims: 1999 National Report*. Washington, DC: U.S Department of Justice, Office of Justice Programs, Office of Juvenile Justice and Delinquency Prevention. Updated 2008 by author.

Waiver and Reverse Waiver Hearings

Waiver Hearings

All juveniles who are waived to criminal court for processing are entitled to a hearing on the waiver if they request one (Massachusetts Statistical Analysis Center, 2001). A **waiver hearing** is a formal proceeding designed to determine whether the waiver action taken by the judge or prosecutor is the correct action, and that the juvenile should be transferred to criminal court. Many waiver hearings are preceded by a petition for a waiver of jurisdiction. Such a petition is illustrated in Figure 8.1.

Waiver hearings are normally conducted before the juvenile court judge. Waiver hearings are initiated through a **waiver motion**, where the prosecutor usually requests the judge to send the case to criminal court. Following a petition for a waiver of jurisdiction, a notice of a hearing on such a waiver petition is issued. Figure 8.2 is notice of hearing for a waiver action which is used by various juvenile courts.

Such hearings are to some extent evidentiary, since a case must be made for why criminal courts should have jurisdiction in any specific instance. Usually, juveniles with lengthy prior records, several previous referrals, and/or one or more previous adjudications as delinquent are more susceptible to being transferred. While the offenses alleged are most often crimes, it is not always the case that the crimes are the most serious ones. Depending upon the jurisdiction, the seriousness of crimes associated with transferred cases varies. As has been shown by previous research, large numbers of cases involving property crimes are transferred to criminal courts for processing. In some instances, chronic, persistent, or habitual status offenders are potential candidates for transfer or waiver, particularly if they have violated specific court orders to attend school, participate in therapeutic programs, perform community service, make restitution, or engage in some other constructive enterprise.

If waivers are to be fully effective, then only the most-serious offenders should be targeted for transfer. Transferring less-serious and petty offenders accomplishes little in the way of enhanced punishments for these offenders. Following a transfer or waiver hearing, the juvenile court judge either grants or denies the order to waive juvenile court jurisdiction over the juvenile. An order waiving juvenile court jurisdiction is shown in Figure 8.3. Once such an order has been issued, the juvenile is transferred to the jurisdiction of criminal court. The order may be contested or appealed. But this matter must be taken up with a criminal court judge, who now has jurisdiction over the transferred or waived juvenile and makes a determination if an appeal opposing the waiver has been filed.

Criminal courts often regard transfers of such cases as nuisances, and it is not uncommon to see the widespread use of probation or diversion here. Criminal court prosecutors may **nolle prosequi** many of these cases before they reach the trial stage. These are plea agreement hearings which require judicial approval before guilty pleas are accepted.

Reverse Waiver Hearings

In those jurisdictions with direct file or statutory exclusion provisions, juveniles and their attorneys may contest these waiver actions through **reverse waiver hearings** or **reverse waiver actions**. Reverse waiver hearings are conducted before criminal court judges to determine whether to send a juvenile's case back to juvenile court. For both waiver and reverse waiver hearings, defense counsel and the prosecution attempt to make a case for their desired action. In many respects, these hearings are similar to preliminary hearings or preliminary examinations conducted within the criminal justice framework. Some evidence and testimony are permitted, and arguments for both sides are heard. Once all arguments have been presented and each side has had a chance to rebut the opponents' arguments, the judge decides the matter.

waiver hearing
Request by prosecutor to transfer juvenile charged with various offenses to a criminal or adult court for prosecution; waiver motions make it possible to sustain adult criminal penalties.

waiver motion
Formal request by prosecutor to send juvenile's case from juvenile court to criminal court.

nolle prosequi
Decision by prosecution to decline to pursue criminal case against defendant.

reverse waiver hearings, reverse waiver actions
Formal proceedings to contest automatic transfer of juveniles to jurisdiction of criminal courts; used in jurisdictions with automatic transfer laws.

Figure 8.1   Petition for Waiver of Jurisdiction

STATE OF MAINE, CIRCUIT COURT_____**COUNTY**

In the interest of:

PETITION FOR WAIVER OF JURISDICTION

_____
Name

_____   **Case #**_____
Date of Birth

1. It is requested that the court waive the juvenile to adult court.
2. I am the: ☐ prosecuting attorney   ☐ juvenile   ☐ judge
3. This petition is filed:

before the plea hearing
before adjudication, juvenile is 16 years of age or older, and denies charges

4. This request is based on the following allegation(s):

☐ Aggravated assault
☐ Felony murder
☐ Rape/forcible/statutory
☐ Armed robbery/robbery
☐ Distribution/possession of controlled substances
☐ Other: Describe_____

5. On or before the juvenile's 15th birthday, it is alleged the juvenile committed the following crime(s):

Crime   **Definition**   **Statute**

6. The facts supporting this waiver include the following:
_____
_____
_____

_____
Signature of petitioner
_____
Name (typed or printed)
_____
Date

Source: Author.

Figure 8.2   Notice of Hearing

STATE OF MICHIGAN, CIRCUIT COURT_____ COUNTY

IN THE INTEREST OF: **NOTICE OF HEARING**

_____

Name

_____

Date of Birth   Case # _____

This case is scheduled for a hearing in at the following time and place:

Date: _____

Time:_____

Place:_____

Purpose(s):

☐ Temporary custody (custodial or noncustodial)
☐ Waiver of juvenile court jurisdiction
☐ Plea
☐ Hearing on the petition
☐ Motion(s)
☐ Disposition
☐ Change of placement
☐ Other: specifiy_____

All hearings involving transfer of jurisdiction must include either private or court-appointed counsel for juvenile. A request for court-appointed counsel must be made in a timely manner, at least 5 working days prior to hearing.
Any juvenile 15 or under has the right to have an attorney present during this hearing. If a delinquency charge is alleged, the juvenile must be represented by an attorney.
The costs of court-appointed counsel, if necessary, are based on the parental ability to pay. Indigence will waive all attorney's fees. Otherwise, parents will be obliged to reimburse the state for all attorney costs associated with this hearing.

_____

Signature of juvenile   Date

_____

Signature(s) of Parents   Date

Source: Author.

Figure 8.3   Order Waiving Juvenile Court Jurisdiction

STATE OF MICHIGAN, CIRCUIT COURT_____ **COUNTY**

IN THE INTEREST OF: **Order Waiving Juvenile**
                                                                     Court Jurisdiction

_____

Name

_____

Date of Birth   Case # _____

The waiver was held on: _____which is the effective date of this order.
The court holds:
1. Petition alleging delinquency and waiver petition were filed.
2. Case has prosecutive merit.
3. Waiver petition is uncontested.
4. Juvenile was represented by an attorney, if required.
5. The court has reviewed the record of all factors indicated below in determining its action and why the
   juvenile was waived:

Prior Record and Personality Factors
☐ Was the juvenile developmentally or mentally disabled?
☐ Was the juvenile found delinquent on prior occasions?
☐ Did the juvenile inflict serious bodily injury to one or more victims?
☐ What were the juvenile's motives, attitude, and living pattern?
☐ What is the physical and mental maturity of the juvenile?
☐ What is the juvenile's prior treatment history, medical or otherwise?
☐ What were the juvenile's living conditions prior to the delinquent act?
☐ What is the juvenile's potential for responding to future treatment?
☐ Other: _____

Seriousness of offense
☐ Crime against persons/property
☐ Crime was violent in nature, aggravated, willful, premeditated

Adequacy of Juvenile System Facilities
☐ Nature of services available, including medical and psychiatric staff
☐ Suitability of placement of juvenile among others which will minimize risk
☐ Suitability of juvenile for placement in treatment/counseling program

It is so ordered:
☐ **The waiver petition is granted**
☐ **The waiver petition is denied**

_____

Signature of Judge   Date

_____

Source: Author.

Time Standards Governing Waiver Decisions

Although only less than 1 percent of all juveniles processed by the juvenile justice system annually are transferred to criminal courts for processing as adults, only nine states had time limits governing transfer provisions for juveniles as of 1993 (Butts, 1996b:559). These states included Arizona, Indiana, Iowa, Maryland, Massachusetts, Michigan, Minnesota, New Mexico, and Virginia. See Table 7.2 for the time limits that govern juvenile court handling of delinquency cases considered for transfer to criminal court.

Table 7.2 shows for Maryland, for example, a 30-day maximum time limit between one's detention and the transfer hearing. If the transfer hearing results in a denial of the transfer, then there is a 30-day maximum between the denial of the transfer and the juvenile court adjudication. In contrast, Minnesota provides only a one-day maximum between placing youths in adult jails and filing transfer motions by juvenile court prosecutors. New Mexico's provisions are similar to those of Maryland.

Implications of Waiver Hearings for Juveniles

Those juveniles who contest or fight their transfers to criminal courts or attempt to obtain a reverse waiver wish to remain within the juvenile justice system, be treated as juveniles, and be adjudicated by juvenile court judges. But not all juveniles who are the subject of transfer are eager to contest the transfer. There are several important implications for youths, depending upon the nature of their offenses, their prior records, and the potential penalties the respective courts may impose. Under the right circumstances, having one's case transferred to criminal court may offer juvenile defendants considerable advantages not normally enjoyed if their cases were to remain in the juvenile court. In the following discussion, some of the major advantages and disadvantages of being transferred will be examined.

Positive Benefits Resulting from Juvenile Court Adjudications

The positive benefits of having one's case heard in juvenile court are that:

1. Juvenile court proceedings are civil, not criminal; thus, juveniles do not acquire criminal records;
2. Juveniles are less likely to be incarcerated;
3. Compared with criminal court judges, juvenile court judges have considerably more discretion in influencing a youth's life chances prior to or at the time of adjudication;
4. Juvenile courts are traditionally more lenient than criminal courts;
5. There is considerably more public sympathy extended to those who are processed in the juvenile justice system, despite the general public advocacy for a greater get-tough policy;
6. Compared with criminal courts, juvenile courts do not have as elaborate an information-exchange apparatus to determine whether certain juveniles have been adjudicated delinquent by juvenile courts in other jurisdictions; and
7. Life imprisonment and the death penalty lie beyond the jurisdiction of juvenile judges, and they cannot impose these harsh sentences.

First, since juvenile courts are civil bodies, records of juvenile adjudications are suppressed, expunged, or otherwise deleted when these adjudicated juveniles reach adulthood. Also, juvenile court judges often act compassionately, by sentencing youthful offenders to probation, or by issuing verbal warnings or reprimands, or by imposing nonincarcerative, nonfine alternatives as sanctions.

8.2   Career Snapshot

Michael D. Downey

District Supervisor, Community Services Division, Minnesota Department of Corrections

Statistics:
B.A. (criminal justice studies); graduate work in Psychology, St. Cloud State University; past President, Minnesota Corrections Association

Background

Corrections was actually my second career looking back at the past 36 years I have been in this field. While in my early years of college, I had a serious motorcycle accident. During this time, I came into contact with many medical and human services professionals. I admired their caring and warm spirit. Those experiences caused me to rethink my career plans. Eventually, I read an ad seeking college-trained individuals who would dedicate at least one to two years to be trained and serve as volunteer juvenile probation officers for Hennepin County. I was interviewed, accepted, and underwent extensive training to prepare predispositional investigations and make sentencing recommendations to the juvenile court. This was the beginning of what I have found to be a very interesting and fulfilling career path.

Work Experience

My first position in corrections was as a Volunteer Probation Officer for Hennepin County. I was assigned to a unit of staff covering the southern region of Minneapolis. Offense severity varied greatly with the youths from possession of marijuana by a first-time offender to a 15-year-old young man awaiting sentencing for his fifth felony-level burglary who was known to every police officer in his south Minneapolis precinct. With this experience, I applied for a job as correctional counselor trainee with the Minnesota Department of Corrections at their prison in St. Cloud, Minnesota. That job was a truly interesting experience and involved very extensive training, including college classes and on-the-job training in every aspect of prison operations. While there, I worked in the prison reception unit. The prison held

male offenders ages 18–25 but also juveniles who were certified to stand trial as adults. The youngest juvenile in the unit got a .45 caliber pistol as a present from his girlfriend for his fifteenth birthday, then shot and killed a grocery clerk after robbing the store. It was while working at the prison that I changed my college major and entered criminal justice, working the midnight shift and then attending college classes during the day. Being involved in academics by day and working nights in the prison were amazing learning experiences. I was able to work briefly, out of class, as a case manager, then called a corrections agent. I met corrections agents in our field services unit who worked in the communities and cites throughout Minnesota, and I tried to get a job in that area.

My first experience was as a probation officer in a small, two-county department in central Minnesota. My caseload consisted of adult offenders and those juvenile offenders who were certified as adults. I started with a caseload of 35 in two counties. I worked in that county-managed department for 10 years, eventually leaving with a caseload of over 125 felony-level offenders. After 10 years of service, an opportunity developed, again with the Minnesota Department of Corrections.

I started as a corrections agent supervising an adult felony caseload, covering six counties, out of an office in Morris, Minnesota, in late 1986. In the summer of 1988, I took what would be my last field agent job in Alexandria, Minnesota, supervising a caseload in only one county. This experience was an excellent one in that the county criminal justice system was one of the best networks I have ever worked in. I worked closely and partnered with juvenile probation officers on a regular basis. All partners in the county criminal justice systems worked very well together in providing excellent service to the community and making everyone safer. In the fall of 1993, a District Supervisor vacancy occurred in southeast Minnesota, and I was encouraged to apply.

In December 1993, I was promoted as District Supervisor of the Albert District for the state department of corrections. The district included offices throughout the region bordering Wisconsin to the east and Iowa to the south. It currently consists of eight offices in six counties with 32 staff members under my supervision. They are comprised of adult and juvenile corrections agents, Sentencing-to-Service Crew Leaders, and professional support staff. Currently 1,760 adults and 140 juveniles are under my supervision in that region. Supervising our Sentencing-to-Service Crew Leaders is a very unique part of my job. This program is an opportunity for juvenile and adult offenders to be under close supervision while working on projects for the public good and meeting the conditions of their supervision.

Experiences

I have had the good fortune of working with some of the best professionals in the Minnesota corrections field over the past 36 years. Statewide associations have been many in the areas of planning, training, and career development. I have had the privilege of serving as the President of the Minnesota Correction Association and continue to serve on a program committee that sets the topics and training for our Annual Training Institute that has attracted over 1,000 colleagues in past years. My current affiliations enable me to utilize restorative justice practices in corrections throughout the state. I also represent our department on the Department of Human Services Problem Gambling Advisory Committee that works on the awareness and prevention of problem gambling. I continue to encourage staff members to get involved in similar projects that take them out of day-to-day probation work in the hopes these activities enhance their careers and take them into larger realms of our business.

Working in the field of corrections can be very rewarding at times and also frustrating, but it is always interesting. With each new offender/client, we have the opportunity to make their lives richer and rewarding by working with case plans that meet their individual needs. Working with juveniles and their families is especially rewarding because of the opportunities we provide. With those many opportunities come many accounts of challenging and rewarding experiences. In one of my first cases, I was directed to do a predispositional investigation on a 15-year-old boy adjudicated for his fifth burglary conviction. When I first met with him, he disclosed that he had a stomach ulcer. He was truly conflicted by the young criminal life he was living. I worked with him closely through sentencing, and then

the case was transferred to a field supervision officer. I lost track of him. While attending a wedding reception many months later, I met the boy's mother who was working as a waitress, and she remembered me. She thanked me for all of my time spent with her son, and the concern I had for him. She said he had turned his life around in many areas.

Although rewarding, our positions can be, at times, physically and emotionally challenging. I had a young adult under supervision for making threats of violence to family members, generally while intoxicated. The first months of supervision did not go well as he challenged my authority at every meeting. I had concerns that he may be still abusing alcohol. On a very cold February Sunday evening, I received a call from the local sheriff's department that the offender was again making threats of violence to neighboring family members and may be intoxicated. Assistance was requested and two deputies accompanied me to the offender's residence. After knocking on the door, we announced our presence and were coming in. The offender was just inside the door and passed out in a reclining chair. As we looked behind us, there was a shotgun hanging above the door we had just entered. I asked the one of the deputies to see if it was loaded. It was. We were three very lucky people that cold winter evening. The good ending to that story is that after his arrest, detention, and a court violation hearing, the offender entered in-patient alcohol rehabilitation and remained sober until his eventual discharge from supervision several years later.

Advice to Students

The most successful probation officers have some common qualities. They approach the job realizing their daily challenges will have them responding to job duties along a continuum of a police officer on one end and a social worker on the other. In the same day, maybe with the same offender, they will act accordingly to situations presented to them. They realize the job demands enforcement of rules and conditions that provide for the public safety but that is not their only responsibility. Along the continuum, they will also foster a relationship with the offender that provides for positive growth and change by effective counseling, case planning, and brokering of rehabilitative services. At the end of the day, they are more proud of offenders they have helped along a positive path, rather than the ones they have had to lock up. I have been fortunate to work with many student interns and have attended student job fairs representing our agency. My advice to students is generally the same:

1. Don't be too impatient in getting hired right away in your chosen job.

2. Take advantage of entry-level positions in related fields such as residential treatment centers, prisons, or county jails. Two of the last probation officers I hired had experience working with inmates in county jails. This is very transferable experience.

3. Keep up your network contacts. Keep in touch with those in the business, like supervisors of internships and local criminal justice partners.

4. If you are in an entry-level position, volunteer in an office like the one you want to eventually work in. This has the added benefit of learning and practicing the skills you will need for that job.

5. Update your resume frequently as new experiences and skill development, paid or unpaid, have been completed.

6. Learn what is expected of the position you ultimately want. The Minnesota Correction Association is guided by evidence-based practices, as is much of the national scene. Learn risk assessment tools, presentence investigation practices, cognitive skill development of offenders, and case planning techniques.

7. Don't rely on just a related degree. Take advantage of continuing education opportunities as this business keeps changing.

A fourth advantage is that juvenile courts are traditionally noted for their lenient treatment of juveniles. This seems to be more a function of the influence of priorities in dealing with juvenile offenders rather than some immovable policy that might impose standard punishments of incarceration as penalties. For example, a national conference of juvenile justice researchers in New Orleans, Louisiana, recommended that juvenile courts should emphasize three general goals in their adjudication decisions: (1) protection of the community; (2) imposing accountability; and (3) helping juveniles and equipping them to live productively and responsibly in the community (Maloney, Romig, and Armstrong, 1988). This balanced approach is largely constructive, in that it heavily emphasizes those skills that lead to the rehabilitation of youthful offenders. And in the minds of many citizens, rehabilitation is equated with leniency. Increasingly used, however, are residential placement facilities in various jurisdictions, where the rate of recidivism among juveniles is relatively low compared with those offenders with more extensive histories of delinquent conduct (Trulson and Haerle, 2008).

A fifth advantage of juvenile court processing is that sympathy for youths who commit offenses is easier to extend in sentencing. Many juveniles get into trouble because of sociocultural circumstances. Individualized treatment may be necessary, perhaps administered through appropriate community-based facilities, in order to promote greater respect for the law as well as to provide needed services. Mandatory diversion policies have received some public support in various jurisdictions, especially where less-serious youthful offenders are involved and they are charged with nonviolent, petty crimes. Many of these juveniles may not require intensive supervised probation or incarceration, but rather, they require responsible supervision to guide them toward and assist them in various services and treatments (Dembo, Turner, and Jainchill, 2007).

Juvenile courts do not ordinarily exchange information with most other juvenile courts in a massive national communication network. Local control over youthful offenders accomplishes only this limited objective—local control. Thus, juveniles might migrate to other jurisdictions and offend repeatedly, where getting caught in those alternative jurisdictions would not be treated as recidivism in the original jurisdiction. This is beneficial for juveniles, who might seek to commit numerous offenses in a broad range of contiguous jurisdictions. The probability that their acts in one jurisdiction would come to the attention of juvenile officials in their own jurisdiction is often remote.

Furthermore, juveniles in certain jurisdictions may reappear before the same juvenile court judge frequently. Multiple adjudications for serious offenses do not mean automatically that these youths will be placed in juvenile detention or transferred to criminal court (Feld, 2007). Even those who reappear before the same juvenile court judge may be adjudicated repeatedly without significant effect. Juvenile court judges may give juveniles the benefit of the doubt and impose nondetention alternatives. Nondetention alternatives as sentences are influenced significantly by the degree of overcrowding in secure juvenile facilities (King, Melvin, and Biederman, 2008). Thus, leniency displayed by juvenile court judges may really be due to necessity rather than because of some personal belief that incarceration should be avoided.

Finally, it is beyond the jurisdiction of juvenile court judges to impose life imprisonment and/or the death penalty, despite the potential for jury trials in some juvenile court jurisdictions. Thus, if offenders come before a juvenile court judge for processing and have committed especially aggravated violent or capital offenses, the juvenile court judge's options are limited. Incarceration in a juvenile facility, possibly for a prolonged period, is the most powerful sanction available to these judges. However, if waiver actions are successful, the road is paved for the possible application of such punishments in criminal courts.

Any possibility of juvenile confinement triggers the need for legal assistance, including public defenders.

Unfavorable Implications of Juvenile Court Adjudications

Juvenile court adjudications of cases may not always be favorable toward juveniles. The major drawbacks to having one's case heard by juvenile court judges are the following:

1. Juvenile court judges have the power to administer lengthy sentences of incarceration, not only for serious and dangerous offenders, but for status offenders as well;
2. In most states, juvenile courts are not required to provide juveniles with a trial by jury;
3. Because of their wide discretion in handling juveniles, judges may underpenalize a large number of those appearing before them on various charges; and
4. Juveniles do not enjoy the same range of constitutional rights as adults in criminal courts.

Adverse to juveniles, juvenile court judges may impose short- or long-term secure confinement on offenders, regardless of the nonseriousness or pettiness of their offenses. The case of *In re Gault* (1967) makes it abundantly clear that juvenile court judges can impose lengthy custodial dispositions for youths adjudicated delinquent for relative minor offending. For committing the same offense, an adult would have been fined $50 and may have served up to 30 days in a local jail. As we learned in the case of *Gault*, the disposition to an industrial school for nearly six years was excessive and there were constitutional irregularities. This unusual incarcerative sentence was subsequently overturned by the U.S. Supreme Court on several important constitutional grounds. However, juvenile court judges continue to have broad discretionary powers and may impose similar sentences, provided that the constitutional guarantees assured by the *Gault* decision are present in any subsequent case.

The case of *Gault* is not an isolated instance of disposing of youths who have committed petty offenses with long periods of secure confinement. Some juvenile court judges typically impose longer incarcerative sentences on property offenders compared with how criminal courts sentence convicted transferred juvenile property offenders. The policies governing the nature and types of dispositions imposed on adjudicated juvenile offenders vary greatly among jurisdictions presently. There is much diversity among juvenile court judges about the nature and types of dispositions they impose on juveniles adjudicated for similar offenses.

Another disadvantage of juvenile courts is that granting any juvenile a jury trial is mostly the discretion of prosecutors and juvenile court judges. If the judge approves, the juvenile may receive a jury trial in selected jurisdictions, if a jury trial is requested. This practice typifies juvenile courts in 38 states. In the remaining states, juveniles may request and receive trials under certain circumstances. In other words, the state legislatures of at least 12 states have made it possible for juveniles to receive jury trials upon request, although the circumstances for such jury trial requests parallel closely the jury trial requests of defendants in criminal courts. Again, we must consider the civil–criminal distinction that adheres, respectively, to juvenile and criminal court proceedings. Jury trials in juvenile courts retain the civil connotation, without juveniles acquiring criminal records. However, jury trials in adult criminal courts, upon the defendant's conviction, result in the offender's acquisition of a criminal record.

A third limitation of juvenile proceedings is that the wide discretion enjoyed by most juvenile court judges is often abused. This abuse is largely in the form of excessive leniency, and it doesn't occur exclusively at the adjudicatory stage of juvenile processing. Because of this leniency and wide discretionary power, many juvenile courts have drawn criticisms from both the public and juvenile justice professionals. One continuing criticism is that juvenile courts avoid the accountability issue through excessive use of probation or diversion.

One significant drawback for juveniles is that they don't enjoy the full range of constitutional rights as adults in criminal courts. In many jurisdictions, transcripts of proceedings are not made or retained for juveniles where serious charges are alleged, unless special arrangements are made beforehand. Thus, when juveniles in these jurisdictions appeal their adjudications to higher courts, they may or may not have the written record to rely upon when lodging appeals with appellate courts.

Defense and Prosecutorial Considerations Relating to Waivers

Juvenile Trial Options: Interstate Variations

Juveniles are only infrequently given a jury trial if their cases are adjudicated by juvenile courts. Table 8.6 shows the interstate variation in jury trials for juveniles in juvenile courts in 2008. In nearly 80 percent of all state juvenile courts, jury trials for juveniles are denied. There is a great deal of variation among jurisdictions relating to trying and disposing of juvenile offenders.

Implications of Criminal Court Processing

When juveniles are waived to criminal court, then the full range of constitutional guarantees for adults also attaches for them (Champion, 2008a). We have already examined the advantages of permitting or petitioning the juvenile court to retain jurisdiction in certain cases. An absence of a criminal record, limited punishments, extensive leniency, and a greater variety of discretionary options on the part of juvenile court judges make juvenile courts an attractive adjudicatory medium, if the juvenile has a choice. Of course, even if the crimes alleged are serious, leniency may assume the form of a dismissal of charges, charge reductions, warnings, and other nonadjudicatory penalties.

The primary implications for juveniles being processed through the criminal justice system are several, and they are quite important. First, depending upon the seriousness of the offenses alleged, a jury trial may be a matter of right. Second, periods of lengthy incarceration in minimum, medium, and maximum security facilities with adults becomes a real possibility (Champion, 2008a). Third, criminal courts in a majority

Table 8.6

Interstate Variation in Jury Trials for Juveniles, 2008

Provision	States
Jury trial granted upon request by juvenile	Alaska, California, Kansas, Massachusetts, Michigan, Minnesota, New Mexico, Oklahoma, Texas, West Virginia, Wisconsin, Wyoming
Juvenile denied right to trial by jury	Alabama, Florida, Georgia, Hawaii, Indiana, Iowa, Louisiana, Maine, Maryland, Mississippi, Nebraska, Nevada, New Jersey, North Carolina, North Dakota, Ohio, Oregon, Pennsylvania, South Carolina, Tennessee, Utah, Vermont, Washington
No mention	Alaska, Arizona, California, Connecticut, Colorado, Idaho, Illinois, Missouri, New Hampshire, New Mexico, New York, Virginia
By court order	South Dakota

Source: Patricia Torbet and Linda Szymanski. (1998). *State Legislative Responses to Violent Juvenile Crime: 1996–1997 Update*. Washington, DC: U.S. Department of Justice. Updated 2008 by author.

of state jurisdictions may impose the death penalty in capital cases. A sensitive subject with most citizens is whether juveniles should receive the death penalty if convicted of capital crimes. In recent years, the U.S. Supreme Court has addressed this issue specifically and ruled that in those states where the death penalty is imposed, the death penalty may be imposed as a punishment on any juvenile who was age 18 or older at the time the capital offense was committed (*Roper v. Simmons,* 2005).

Jury Trials as a Matter of Right for Serious Offenses

A primary benefit of a transfer to criminal court is the absolute right to a jury trial. This is conditional, however, and depends upon the minimum incarcerative period associated with one or more criminal charges filed against the defendants. In only 12 state jurisdictions, juveniles have a jury trial right granted through legislative action (Office of Juvenile Justice and Delinquency Prevention, 2007). However, when juveniles reach criminal courts, certain constitutional provisions apply to them as well as to adults. First, anyone charged with a crime where the possible sentence is six months' incarceration or more, with exceptions, is entitled to a jury trial if one is requested (*Baldwin v. New York,* 1970). Therefore, jury trials are not discretionary matters for judges to decide. Any defendant who may be subject to more than six months' incarceration in a jail or prison as the prescribed statutory punishment associated with the criminal offenses alleged may request and receive a jury trial from any U.S. judge, in either state or federal courts.

Juveniles who are charged with particularly serious crimes, and where several aggravating circumstances are apparent, stand a good chance of receiving favorable treatment from juries. Aggravating circumstances include a victim's death or the infliction of serious bodily injuries, committing an offense while on bail for another offense or on probation or parole, use of extreme cruelty in the commission of the crime, use of a dangerous weapon in the commission of a crime, a prior record, and leadership in the commission of offenses alleged. However, mitigating circumstances, those factors that tend to lessen the severity of sentencing, include duress or extreme provocation, mental incapacitation, motivation to provide necessities, youthfulness or old age, and no previous criminal record.

Among the several aggravating and mitigating circumstances listed preceding, having a prior record or being a first-offender becomes an important consideration. Youths who are transferred to criminal courts sometimes don't have previous criminal records. This doesn't mean that they haven't committed crimes earlier, but rather, that their records are **juvenile court records**. Juveniles may have **sustained petitions**, where the facts alleged against them have been determined to be true by the juvenile court judge. However, this adjudication hearing is a civil proceeding. As such, technically, these youths don't bring prior criminal records into the criminal courtroom. This is a favorable factor for juveniles to consider when deciding whether to challenge transfers or have their automatic waivers reversed. However, changes in state laws regarding the confidentiality of juvenile court records have been made so that greater access to such records is available to others, and for longer periods beyond one's adulthood. Increasingly, one's juvenile past may affect one's criminal court trial outcome and sentencing.

Another important factor relative to having access to a jury trial is that prosecutors often try to avoid them, opting for a simple plea bargain agreement instead. Plea bargaining or plea negotiating is a preconviction bargain between the state and the defendant where the defendant enters a guilty plea in exchange for leniency in the form of reduced charges or less-harsh treatment at the time of sentencing. It is well-known that plea bargaining in the United States accounts for approximately 90 percent of all criminal convictions. But plea bargaining also involves an admission of guilt without benefit of a trial. For this reason, plea bargaining is often criticized.

Jury trials are costly and the results of jury deliberations are unpredictable. If prosecutors can obtain guilty pleas from transferred juveniles, they assist the state and themselves, both in terms of the costs of prosecution and avoidance of jury whims in youthful offender cases. Also, plea bargaining in transferred juvenile cases often results in convictions on lesser charges, specifically charges that would not have prompted the transfer or waiver from juvenile courts initially. However, this is a bit ironic, since it suggests that the criminal justice system is inadvertently sabotaging the primary purpose of juvenile transfers through plea bargaining arrangements that are otherwise commonplace for adult criminals. Furthermore, when prosecutors decide to file charges, sufficient evidence should exist to increase the chances of a successful prosecution. Also, the charges alleged should be serious ones. But many transferred juveniles are not necessarily the most-serious youthful offenders, and the standard of evidence in juvenile courts is sometimes not as rigorous as it is in criminal courts. Thus, many transferred juvenile cases fail from the outset and are dismissed by the prosecutors themselves, often because of inadequate or poor evidence.

Closely associated with prosecutorial reluctance to prosecute many of these transferred juveniles is the fact that a majority of those transferred are charged with property crimes. While these cases may stand out from other cases coming before juvenile court judges, prosecutors and criminal court judges might regard them as insignificant. Thus, juveniles enter the adult system from juvenile courts, where their offenses set them apart from most other juvenile offenders. But alongside adults in criminal courts, they become one of many property offenders who face criminal processing. Their youthful age works in their behalf to improve the chances of having their cases dismissed or of being acquitted by juries. Most prosecutors wish to reserve jury trials for only the most-serious offenders. Therefore, their general inclination is to treat youthful property offenders with greater leniency, unless they elect to nolle prosequi outright.

The Potential for Capital Punishment

The most important implication for juveniles transferred to criminal courts is the potential imposition of the **death penalty** upon their conviction for a capital crime (Buckler et al., 2008). About two-thirds of the states use **capital punishment** for prescribed

---

juvenile court records
Formal or informal statements concerning an adjudication hearing involving sustained allegations against a juvenile; a written document of a juvenile's prior delinquency or status offending.

sustained petitions
Adjudications resulting in a finding that the facts alleged in a petition are true; a finding that the juvenile committed the offenses alleged, which resulted in an adjudication and disposition.

capital punishment, death penalty
Imposition of the death penalty for the most-serious crimes; may be administered by electrocution, lethal injection, gas, hanging, or shooting.

offenses that are especially aggravated (Ingram, 2008). For youths who are age 18 or older at the time they commit a capital offense and who live in a state that has the death penalty, they are in jeopardy of being sentenced to death (*Roper v. Simmons*, 2005).

An alternative to the death penalty applied to juveniles is the life-without-parole option. In 2007, 43 states had **life-without-parole** provisions for capital murder statutes, including aggravated homicide as well as for habitual or career offenders (Bureau of Justice Statistics, 2008). Thus, it is possible for youths to be sentenced to life without the possibility of parole if they are convicted of a capital offense in a state with or without the death penalty (Dario and Holleran, 2008). In these instances, juveniles take their chances in criminal courts, often not knowing what outcome can be expected.

life-without-parole
Penalty imposed as maximum punishment in states that do not have death penalty; provides for permanent incarceration of offenders in prisons, without parole eligibility; early release may be attained through accumulation of good time credits.

Blended Sentencing Statutes

In recent years, many states have legislatively redefined the juvenile court's purpose and role by diminishing the role of rehabilitation and heightening the importance of public safety, punishment, and accountability in the juvenile justice system (Champion, 2008a). One of the most dramatic changes in the dispositional/sentencing options available to juvenile court judges is **blended sentencing**. Blended sentencing statutes represent a dramatic change in dispositional/sentencing options available to judges. Blended sentencing refers to the imposition of juvenile and/or adult correctional sanctions on serious and violent juvenile offenders who have been adjudicated in juvenile court or convicted in criminal court. Blended sentencing options are usually based upon age or upon a combination of age and offense.

There are five blended sentencing models. Figure 8.4 shows these five models. These include: (1) juvenile-exclusive blend; (2) juvenile-inclusive blend; (3) juvenile-contiguous blend; (4) criminal-exclusive blend; and (5) criminal-inclusive blend.

blended sentencing
Any type of sentencing procedure where either a criminal or juvenile court judge can impose *both* juvenile and/or adult incarcerative penalties.

The Juvenile-Exclusive Blend

The **juvenile-exclusive blend** involves a disposition by the juvenile court judge which is either a disposition to the juvenile correctional system or to the adult correctional system, but not both. Thus, a judge might order a juvenile adjudicated delinquent for aggravated assault to serve three years in a juvenile industrial school; or the judge may order the adjudicated delinquent to serve three years in a prison for adults. The judge cannot impose *both* types of punishment under this model, however. In 2008, only one state, New Mexico, provided such a sentencing option for its juvenile court judges.

juvenile-exclusive blend
Sentencing form where a juvenile court judge can impose either adult or juvenile incarceration as a disposition and sentence but not both.

The Juvenile-Inclusive Blend

The **juvenile-inclusive blend** involves a disposition by the juvenile court judge which is both a juvenile correctional sanction and an adult correctional sanction. For example, suppose the judge had adjudicated a 15-year-old juvenile delinquent on a charge of vehicular theft, then the judge might impose a disposition of two years in a juvenile industrial school or reform school. Further, the judge might impose a sentence of three additional years in an adult penitentiary. However, the second sentence to the adult prison would typically be suspended, unless the juvenile violated one or more conditions of his/her original disposition and any conditions accompanying the disposition. Usually, this suspension period would run until the youth reaches age 18 or 21. If the offender were to commit a new offense or violate one or more program conditions, he/she would immediately be placed in the adult prison to serve the second sentence originally imposed.

juvenile-inclusive blend
Form of sentencing where a juvenile court judge can impose *both* adult and juvenile incarceration simultaneously.

Figure 8.4   Models of Blended Sentencing Statutes

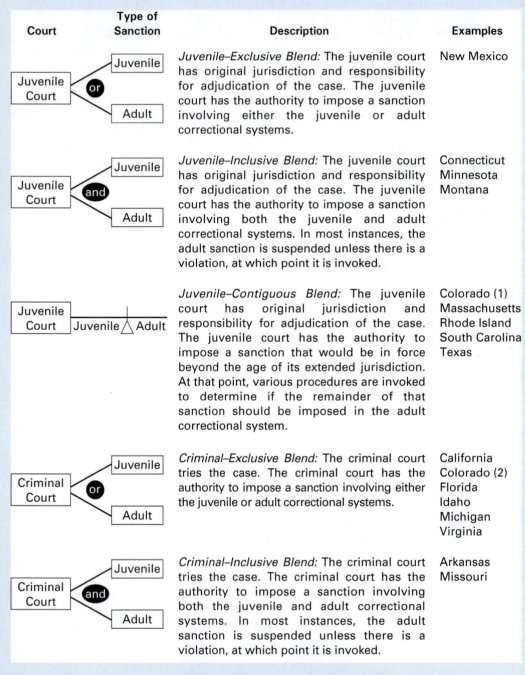

Court	Type of Sanction	Description	Examples
Juvenile Court	Juvenile **or** Adult	*Juvenile–Exclusive Blend:* The juvenile court has original jurisdiction and responsibility for adjudication of the case. The juvenile court has the authority to impose a sanction involving either the juvenile or adult correctional systems.	New Mexico
Juvenile Court	Juvenile **and** Adult	*Juvenile–Inclusive Blend:* The juvenile court has original jurisdiction and responsibility for adjudication of the case. The juvenile court has the authority to impose a sanction involving both the juvenile and adult correctional systems. In most instances, the adult sanction is suspended unless there is a violation, at which point it is invoked.	Connecticut Minnesota Montana
Juvenile Court	Juvenile △ Adult	*Juvenile–Contiguous Blend:* The juvenile court has original jurisdiction and responsibility for adjudication of the case. The juvenile court has the authority to impose a sanction that would be in force beyond the age of its extended jurisdiction. At that point, various procedures are invoked to determine if the remainder of that sanction should be imposed in the adult correctional system.	Colorado (1) Massachusetts Rhode Island South Carolina Texas
Criminal Court	Juvenile **or** Adult	*Criminal–Exclusive Blend:* The criminal court tries the case. The criminal court has the authority to impose a sanction involving either the juvenile or adult correctional systems.	California Colorado (2) Florida Idaho Michigan Virginia
Criminal Court	Juvenile **and** Adult	*Criminal–Inclusive Blend:* The criminal court tries the case. The criminal court has the authority to impose a sanction involving both the juvenile and adult correctional systems. In most instances, the adult sanction is suspended unless there is a violation, at which point it is invoked.	Arkansas Missouri

Source: Bilchik, 1996:13; Torbet et al., "State Responses to Serious and Violent Crime," OJJDP.

The Juvenile-Contiguous Blend

The **juvenile-contiguous blend** involves a disposition by a juvenile court judge that may extend beyond the jurisdictional age limit of the offender. When the age limit of the juvenile court jurisdiction is reached, various procedures may be invoked to transfer the case to the jurisdiction of adult corrections. States with this juvenile-contiguous blend include Colorado, Massachusetts, Rhode Island, South Carolina, and Texas. In 1987, the Texas legislature enacted a determinate sentencing law that is an example of the juvenile-contiguous blended sentencing model, whereby for certain offenses the juvenile court may impose a sentence that may remain in effect beyond its extended jurisdiction. In Texas, for example, a 15-year-old youth who has been adjudicated delinquent on a murder charge can be given a determinate sentence of from 1 to 30 years. At the time of the disposition in juvenile court, the youth is sent to the Texas Youth Commission and incarcerated in one of its facilities (similar to reform or industrial schools). By the time the youth reaches age 17.5, the juvenile court must conduct a hearing to determine whether the youth should be sent to the Texas Department of Corrections to serve some or all of the remaining sentence. At this hearing, the youth may present evidence in his/her favor to show why he/she has become rehabilitated and no longer should be confined. However, evidence of institutional misconduct may be presented by the prosecutor to show why the youth should be incarcerated for more years in a Texas prison. This hearing functions as an incentive for the youth to behave and try to improve his/her behavior while confined in the juvenile facility. This particular sentencing blend seems most effective at punishing serious and violent offenders while providing them with a final chance to access certain provided Texas rehabilitative programs.

> **juvenile-contiguous blend**
> Form of sentencing by a juvenile court judge where the judge can impose a disposition beyond the normal jurisdictional range for juvenile offenders; e.g., a judge may impose a 30-year term on a 14-year-old offender, but the juvenile is entitled to a hearing when he/she reaches the age of majority to determine whether the remainder of the sentence shall be served.

The Criminal-Exclusive Blend

The **criminal-exclusive blend** involves a decision by a criminal court judge to impose either a juvenile court sanction or a criminal court sanction, but not both. For example, a criminal court judge may hear the case of a 15-year-old youth who has been transferred to criminal court on a rape charge. The youth is convicted in a jury trial in criminal court. At this point, the judge has two options: the judge can sentence the offender to a prison term in an adult correctional facility, or the judge can impose an incarcerative sentence for the youth to serve in a juvenile facility. The judge may believe that the 15-year-old would be better off in a juvenile industrial school rather than an adult prison. The judge may impose a sentence of adult incarceration, but he/she may be inclined to place the youth in a facility where there are other youths in the offender's age range.

> **criminal-exclusive blend**
> Form of sentencing by a criminal court judge where either juvenile or adult sentences of incarceration can be imposed, but not both.

The Criminal-Inclusive Blend

The **criminal-inclusive blend** involves a decision by the criminal court judge to impose both a juvenile penalty and a criminal sentence simultaneously. Again, as in the juvenile court-inclusive blend model, the latter criminal sentence may be suspended depending upon the good conduct of the juvenile during the juvenile punishment phase. For example, suppose a 13-year-old boy has been convicted of attempted murder. The boy participated in a drive-by shooting and is a gang member. The criminal court judge sentences the youth to a term of five years in a juvenile facility, such as an industrial school. At the same time, the judge imposes a sentence of 20 years on the youth to be spent in an adult correctional facility, following the five-year sentence in the juvenile facility. However, the adult portion of the sentence may be suspended, depending upon whether the juvenile behaves or misbehaves during his five-year industrial school incarceration. There is an additional twist to this blend. If the juvenile violates one or more conditions of his confinement in the juvenile facility, the judge has the power to revoke that sentence and invoke the sentence of incarceration in an adult facility. Thus, a powerful incentive is provided for the youth to show evidence that rehabilitation has occurred. It is to the youth's advantage to behave well while confined, since a more ominous sentence of confinement with adult offenders may be imposed at any time.

> **criminal-inclusive blend**
> Form of sentencing by a criminal court judge where both juvenile and adult sentences can be imposed simultaneously.

Further, with good behavior, the youth can be free of the system following the period of juvenile confinement; the adult portion of the sentence is suspended if the youth deserves such leniency. One state that has the revocation power and ability to place youths in adult correctional facilities is Arkansas, although this power is rarely used by criminal court judges.

Blended sentencing statutes are intended to provide both juvenile and criminal court judges with a greater range of dispositional and/or sentencing options. In the 1980s and earlier, juvenile courts were notoriously lenient on juvenile offenders. Dispositions of juvenile court judges were mostly nominal or conditional, which usually meant verbal warnings and/or probation. While probation continues to be the sanction of choice in a majority of juvenile courts following delinquency adjudications, many states have armed their juvenile and criminal court judges with greater sanctioning powers. Thus, it is now possible in states such as Colorado, Arkansas, and Missouri for juvenile court judges to impose sanctions which extend well-beyond their original jurisdictional authority. Juvenile court judges in New Mexico, for instance, can place certain juveniles in either adult or juvenile correctional facilities. Criminal court judges in Florida, Idaho, Michigan, or Missouri can place those convicted of crimes in either juvenile or adult correctional facilities, depending upon the jurisdiction. These are broader and more powerful dispositional and sentencing options to hold youthful offenders more accountable for the serious offenses they commit.

Jury Trials as a Matter of Right in All Juvenile Court Blended Sentencing Proceedings

When juveniles are tried as adults in criminal court, they are entitled to the full range of constitutional rights extended to criminal defendants, including the right to a jury trial. This same provision exists whenever juveniles are tried in juvenile courts, and where the juvenile is subject to the application of blended sentencing statutes. All states with either the juvenile-inclusive blend, the juvenile-exclusive blend, or the juvenile-contiguous blend must grant juvenile defendants the right to a jury trial in juvenile court upon request.

If the jury verdict is "guilty," then the juvenile court judge has the right under one of these blended sentencing statutes, depending upon the state jurisdiction, to impose both a juvenile penalty and a criminal penalty, or either a juvenile penalty or a criminal penalty but not both. Thus, juvenile court judges may exercise considerable discretion relating to dispositions and sentencing. If the juvenile court judge is in a state where both juvenile and criminal penalties may be imposed, such as Michigan, he/she may impose both types of penalties on a convicted juvenile or he/she may impose the juvenile penalty but not the criminal penalty. This aspect of blended sentencing is totally discretionary with the judge.

One of the positive aspects of blended sentencing statutes is that the use of transfers or waivers and subsequent waiver hearings are rendered obsolete. By statute, juveniles in one state or another with blended sentencing statutes are either in juvenile or criminal court where the court can exercise one or both types of juvenile and adult sanctions.

Surprisingly, some judges have resisted applying blended sentencing statutes in their jurisdictions, even when they have been authorized to use them. In Michigan, for instance, one juvenile court judge chided the Michigan legislature for passing a blended sentencing statute. When sentencing a juvenile offender who had been convicted of a heinous, premeditated murder, the judge sentenced the juvenile only to the juvenile punishment and did not impose the criminal punishment. He took it upon himself to chastise the Michigan legislature for its abuse of authority in changing the sentencing laws governing youthful offenders.

The primary positive implication for juveniles sentenced under such blended sentencing statutes is that it provides them with a strong incentive to behave well and to participate in needed counseling, training, or other activities that will improve their skills and psychological and social development. If they know that poor behavior will jeopardize their chances of being released upon reaching adulthood, then they will be motivated to behave in a law-abiding and productive fashion for the period of their confinement in the juvenile facility. The juvenile court judge who fails to recognize the motivational value of these blended sentencing statutes seriously undermines a significant juvenile justice reform.

Blended sentencing options demonstrate the ambivalence of what to do about serious and violent juvenile offenders. The creation of middle ground disposition/sentencing and correctional options demonstrates a lack of resolve on two fronts: (1) coming to closure on (i.e., removing) certain juveniles for whom the juvenile justice system is inadequate, or (2) bolstering the resolve and resources of the juvenile justice system to adequately address the needs of these very difficult young offenders. Blended sentencing creates confusing options for all system actors, including offenders, judges, prosecutors, and corrections administrators. Contact with juvenile and criminal justice personnel across the country revealed that confusion exists about these statutes and the rules and regulations governing them, especially with respect to the juvenile's status during case processing and subsequent placement. This has repercussions on the definition of a juvenile with regard to compliance with the Juvenile Justice and Delinquency Prevention Act mandates. Perhaps in time, the good stemming from the application of these blended sentencing statutes by growing numbers of states will outweigh the negative perceptions of it by various system actors.

Summary

Distinguishing between different types of offenders is an integral part of juvenile offender processing. Status offenders are most frequently given lenient treatment, while delinquents are usually given harsher punishments. For the most-serious offenders, jurisdictions use waivers, transfers, or certifications for treating juveniles as adults for the purpose of criminal prosecutions. The rationale for using waivers is to provide for harsher penalties for more serious offenses; to hold offenders more accountable because of the more serious offenses they commit; to promote greater fairness and just deserts in punishments according to offense seriousness; to provide a broader range of penalties that fit these crimes in terms of proportionality of the seriousness of them; to overcome the traditional leniency of juvenile courts; to promote deterrence for other juveniles who might contemplate committing serious offenses; and to encourage youthful offenders to accept responsibility for their actions.

While only the most-serious juvenile offenders are designated for transfer to criminal courts, only about 40 percent of all transferred persons each year are violent offenders. Most other transferred juveniles are property offenders or drug users/abusers. Less-serious offenders are often repeat offenders, and many juvenile court judges will transfer these youths simply to eliminate their continued juvenile court appearances. These actions defeat the true purposes of transfers.

Types of waivers include judicial waivers, discretionary waivers, mandatory waivers, presumptive waivers, direct file, and statutory exclusion. Another type of waiver is a demand waiver, where a juvenile asks the juvenile court to waive him/her to the jurisdiction of the criminal court. Other types of actions are once an adult/always an adult provisions where juveniles who have been transferred to criminal court once are subsequently considered adults for criminal prosecutions if they continue to reoffend as juveniles and until they reach the age of their majority. Waiver hearings are conducted, and judges decide whether waivers should be granted. Stringent time standards exist governing the use of waiver actions. Hearings are proceedings where the relative merits of the transfer are discussed by the prosecutor and defense counsel. The presiding judge makes the final determination.

Both positive and negative implications of waivers for juveniles were described. Some juvenile court judges may impose secure confinement. Juvenile court adjudications seldom result in criminal records for adjudicated delinquents. Often, these records are expunged when one becomes an adult. Juvenile courts don't have the same range of punishments that exist for adults who are processed by criminal courts. The death penalty and life-without-parole dispositions are not within juvenile court jurisdiction.

During the past 20 years, significant modifications have occurred in how juveniles are processed. Blended sentencing statutes have been created, where it is possible for either juvenile or criminal courts to impose either juvenile court punishments, criminal court punishments, or both. Various blended sentencing statutes were described.

Key Terms

acceptance of responsibility, 233
blended sentencing, 257
capital punishment, 256
certification, 232
concurrent jurisdiction, 240
contempt of court, 231
criminal-exclusive blend, 259
criminal-inclusive blend, 259
death penalty, 256
demand waiver, 240
direct file, 240
discretionary waivers, 238
judicial waivers, 238
juvenile-contiguous blend, 259
juvenile court records, 256
juvenile-exclusive blend, 257
juvenile-inclusive blend, 257
legislative waiver, 240

life-without-parole, 257
mandatory waiver, 238
nolle prosequi, 245
once an adult/always an
    adult provision, 243
placed, 231
placement, 231
presumptive waiver, 238
reverse waiver, 240
reverse waiver actions, 245
reverse waiver hearings, 245
statutory exclusion, 240
sustained petitions, 256
transfer hearings, 232
transfers, 232
waiver, 232
waiver hearing, 245
waiver motion, 245

Questions for Review

1. What are the implications of offense seriousness for the use of waivers in the juvenile justice system?

2. What is the rationale for distinguishing between status offenders and delinquent offenders in juvenile justice system processing?

3. What is contempt power used by juvenile court judges? How does the use of contempt power by juvenile court judges influence status offenders?

4. What are several types of judicial waivers? What is the rationale for using transfers?

5. What are some of the ideal characteristics of youths targeted for transfers to criminal courts? What are the actual characteristics of youths who are transferred to criminal courts?

6. What is meant by the once an adult/always an adult provision? What implications does this policy have for affected youths?

7. What are some contrasts between direct file, legislative waivers, and demand waivers?

8. Under what circumstances are juveniles entitled to hearings on transfer decisions?

9. What are some favorable and unfavorable implications for juveniles if their cases are heard in juvenile courts instead of criminal courts? What are some positive and negative implications for juveniles if they have their cases heard in criminal courts?

10. What are five different types of blended sentencing statutes? What are some positive benefits of blended sentencing statutes for serious and violent juvenile offenders?

Internet Connections

Criminal Justice Policy Foundation
http://www.cjpf.org/

CURE-NY
http://www.users.bestweb.net~cureny/cure-ny.htm

National Coalition to Abolish the Death Penalty
http://www.ncadp.org/

National Criminal Justice Reference Service
http://www.ncjrs.gov/

Open Society Institute
http://www.soros.org/crime/

Sentencing Project
http://www.sentencingproject.org/

Unusual Suspects Theatre Company
http://www.theunusualsuspects.org/index.html

The Adjudicatory Process

Dispositional Alternatives

chapter objectives

As the result of reading this chapter, you will accomplish the following objectives:

1. Differentiate between first-offenders and repeat offenders.
2. Understand the differences between aggravating and mitigating circumstances.
3. Learn about juvenile dangerousness and risk, as well as how these phenomena can be assessed.
4. Learn about selective incapacitation and how it is used in juvenile cases.
5. Learn about anamnestic, actuarial, and clinical prediction and how each is used to forecast juvenile offender dangerousness.
6. Examine several risk instruments, their applications, and limitations.
7. Understand the importance of victim-impact statements in dispositional hearings for juvenile offenders.
8. Learn about predispositional reports, who prepares them, and how they are used for sanctioning juveniles.

 ## Case Study

Jose Pablo Hernandez, 17, was positively identified by convenience store personnel as the one who robbed them at gunpoint at night in late October 2007. Hernandez is accused of robbing the Clackamas Food Market in Clackamas County, Oregon, and was ordered held in a juvenile facility on $500,000 bail to await trial on the charges. Reports say that a male was hiding in the bushes near the store just prior to robbing it using a knife and a gun. The weapons were seized from Hernandez when he was arrested. Clackamas County officials believe that Hernandez is the one who robbed the same store earlier in the year. His detention pending trial is based in part on his predicted dangerousness and the seriousness of the charge of first-degree robbery. [Source: Adapted from *The Oregonian*, "Clackamas County Juvenile Accused of Armed Robbery," October 29, 2007.]

 ## Case Study

Brian Crist, 17, is a runaway teen from Charlotte, North Carolina. Initially, Crist's parents reported him missing and a search was conducted by police. Subsequently, police discovered Crist on a road heading for Englewood Beach. He was standing next to a bicycle and was carrying a large piece of luggage. An inspection of the luggage contents revealed 5 one-gallon-sized plastic bags full of marijuana, 2.5 pounds. Crist was immediately arrested and taken to a hospital for examination. Later, he was charged with possession of marijuana with intent to sell or distribute, possession of marijuana over 20 grams, and possession of drug paraphernalia. Because of his runaway behavior and the amount of drugs in his possession, Crist was ordered held indefinitely without bond pending trial. [Source: Adapted from the *Associated Press*, "Runaway Teen Found, Then Arrested," November 16, 2007.]

Introduction

How do we know if arrested youths are dangerous? Should all dangerous youths be detained pending trial? Is a runaway youth in possession of 2.5 pounds of marijuana dangerous? What critiera should be used to decide which youths should be detained and which ones shouldn't? Youths who rob stores at gunpoint and threaten the lives of others are likely dangerous. Freeing them pending a trial may put a community in jeopardy. But what about those possessing large amounts of drugs? If they are freed pending a trial, they may not hurt anyone, but they also may flee the jurisdiction to avoid prosecution. Often, these are the two primary criteria used by authorities for making detention decisions.

This chapter examines the adjudicatory process, focusing upon factors that influence youthful offender dispositions. The first part of the chapter describes the nature of offenses charged and whether youths are first-offenders or repeat offenders. Offense seriousness is a primary consideration, together with one's age, one's association with others when the offense was committed, the nature of one's participation in the offense, and a variety of other legal and extralegal factors. Juveniles are assessed and disposed by evaluating both aggravating and mitigating factors, or factors that intensify or lessen one's culpability in the offense as well as one's punishment. Several important aggravating factors are listed and described. Other factors, known as mitigating factors, are also listed and described. These factors tend to minimize the seriousness of the offenses committed.

About half of all juvenile courts during the 1980s had devised measures of risk or dangerousness as well as assessments of youthful client needs. By 2009, almost every juvenile court had devised such instrumentation. The next part of this chapter examines the concepts of dangerousness, risk, and needs assessment as these terms apply to evaluations of juveniles. While these instruments are not used exclusively to determine one's subsequent disposition in the juvenile justice system, they provide different actors in the system with a sense of the nature and extent of services required to meet individual needs as well as the degree and type of supervision required for each offender. Risk and needs assessments are conducted by both juvenile probation and parole personnel. Several important elements of risk assessment instruments will be listed and described.

Several types of risk predictions are listed and defined. These include actuarial, anamnestic, and clinical prediction. It will be evident that no prediction method is foolproof and that errors in prediction occur. Some offenders are predicted to be dangerous and turn out not to be dangerous. These are known as false positives. Other offenders are predicted not to be dangerous but turn out to be dangerous. These are known as false negatives. There will always be false positives and false negatives in the juvenile justice system, despite the fact that this instrumentation is constantly being revised and improved. Because of prediction errors, some youths are confined in secure facilities longer than other youths, and these incarceration differences are unjustified. The issue of selective incapacitation will be examined.

Next explored are several instruments devised by different states to assess one's risk and needs. Examples are provided and hypothetical calculations made to illustrate how assessments of juveniles are performed. The contents of these instruments are listed and explained. Also described are the individual weighting criteria for items included on these instruments and how they are used to measure one's potential for recidivism.

One of the most critical documents in juvenile offender processing is the predispositional report. The chapter concludes with a detailed presentation and analysis of such reports and how they are used in the juvenile justice process. Similar to presentence investigation reports (PSIs) prepared by probation officers for criminal offenders, predispositional reports furnish information about youths. Plans are often devised for one's aftercare based on the contents of these reports. Samples of actual predispositional reports are provided.

The Nature of the Offense

In 2006, it is estimated that there were 2.3 million arrests of youths under age 18 (Office of Juvenile Justice and Delinquency Prevention, 2007). About 1.8 million cases were sent to the juvenile justice system for processing. About half of these cases were processed formally. Of the 840,000 petitioned cases that were handled formally, 515,000 juveniles were adjudicated. Of these, about 125,000 were placed in secure institutions, such as industrial schools. About 12,700 cases were recommended for transfer to criminal courts (Office of Juvenile Justice and Delinquency Prevention, 2007). Of all arrests of youths under age 18 in 2006, approximately 510,000 were for violent or person offenses, such as aggravated assault, rape, and murder.

During the period 1986–1996, violent crime by juveniles increased by nearly 70 percent nationally. This dramatic increase in juvenile violence has drawn greater public attention to juveniles and to how juvenile courts deal with them. Violence by juveniles grew at uneven rates among various state jurisdictions during the 1990s. More recent figures suggest that juvenile violence is decreasing in most jurisdictions. The incidence of violence among younger juveniles leveled off during the late 1990s and through 2006, declining slightly for offense-specific categories (Office of Juvenile Justice and Delinquency Prevention, 2007).

Adjudicated juveniles are subject to a limited range of juvenile court penalties, from verbal warnings and reprimands to secure confinement in a state industrial school. Delinquent acts involving physical harm to others or the threat of physical harm are considered violent offenses, in contrast to the larger category of property offenses that encompasses vehicular theft, petty larceny, or burglary. Intake officers perform the initial screening function by sending forward only the more serious offenders or those who the intake officers believe should have their cases adjudicated by juvenile court judges.

Juvenile court prosecutors screen those cases further by deciding which cases have the most prosecutive merit. Prosecutors are influenced by numerous factors whether to prosecute juveniles formally. Age, offense seriousness, and one's previous record often convince prosecutors to move forward with selected cases, whereas they may divert less serious cases to informal arbitration through alternative dispute resolution (Dembo et al., 2006).

One important consideration is the willingness of juveniles to compensate victims for their monetary losses through a program of restitution. Juries comprised of one's peers may impose restitution as a condition of diversion, and a youth's satisfactory completion of such a diversion program will likely avoid the scars of a formal delinquency adjudication. Juvenile courts continue to view their roles as largely rehabilitative, and judges seek to assist youths in avoiding any negative consequences of secure confinement (Bowman, Prelow, and Weaver, 2007). Various interventions are believed beneficial to juveniles in lieu of formal adjudicatory actions in juvenile courts.

In many jurisdictions, secure confinement is the last resort for judges when disposing serious juvenile offenders. This reluctance to incarcerate juveniles has prompted criticisms that juvenile courts are soft on crime and that present juvenile crime control policies are insufficiently stringent. Some jurisdictions, such as New York, have established juvenile offender laws designed to transfer the most serious juvenile offenders from juvenile court to criminal court. However, such laws have proved ineffective at deterring juvenile violence (Buffington-Vollum, Edens, and Keilen, 2008).

Nevertheless, growing rates of violence among juveniles during the early 1990s, especially for offenses such as first-degree sexual assault, aggravated robbery, and homicide, and the increasing influence of the get-tough movement in juvenile courts caused juvenile court judges to impose harsher dispositions for those juveniles who committed more serious offenses. Thus, the nature of the offenses alleged, together with inculpatory evidence against youths charged, weighed heavily in favor of moving certain more serious offenders into the system toward formal adjudication. Even though juvenile violence has tapered off and even decreased in most jurisdictions, the get-tough initiatives spawned by early 1990s juvenile violence continue. The rise of youth gangs in large U.S. cities, together with greater involvement in illicit drug trafficking, has done much to place more youths at risk regarding possible incarceration in secure facilities (Taylor et al., 2008).

First-Offender or Repeat-Offender?

Is a juvenile a **first-offender** or a **repeat offender**? First-offenders have no prior record of delinquency, and it is presumed that their current offense is their first offense. Repeat offenders have prior delinquency or criminal records, either delinquency adjudications or criminal convictions or both. This is a key question raised by prosecutors when examining one's file to determine whether to prosecute the case in court. The overwhelming tendency among prosecutors is either to divert petty first-offenders to some conditional program or to dismiss these cases outright. Many diversionary programs involve restitution or victim compensation in some form. Contracts are arranged between youths and their victims, whereby youths reimburse victims, either partially or completely, for their financial losses. These programs often involve mediators who are responsible for securing agreements between juvenile offenders and their victims. Known as alternative dispute resolution, these mediation programs are believed to be fairly widespread and effective (Champion, 2008a).

Whether they are violent or property offenders, youths with prior records stand good chances of receiving some nonincarcerative sanction, if they are eventually adjudicated as delinquent. However, chronic juvenile offenders compared with first-offenders also have a greater chance of pursuing criminal careers as adults. Currently, no uniform policies exist among jurisdictions about how chronic offenders should be identified. Because of poor record keeping and the lack of interjurisdictional record sharing, many youthful offenders are continually diverted from formal juvenile court processing, despite their chronic recidivism (Trulson and Haerle, 2008). Some jurisdictions measure whether formal action against juveniles should be taken on the basis of the number of times they have been arrested. After four arrests, youths in some jurisdictions may be considered serious enough to have petitions filed against them as delinquents. During the 1990s, however, the compilation and centralization of state delinquency figures has increased, as well as the openness and availability of this information to the public sector.

Despite the relatively greater seriousness of violent offenses compared with property offenses, property offenders account for nearly two-thirds of all petitioned juveniles annually in most juvenile courts (Champion, 2005). Substantial numbers of status offenders continue to be processed by the juvenile justice system as well. Thus, it is unclear who is being targeted by get-tough policies nationwide. Ideally, only those most serious chronic and violent juveniles should be targeted for the harshest juvenile court penalties. However, an overwhelming majority of long-term detainees in public and private secure facilities are property offenders, again by a substantial margin of two to one (Office of Juvenile Justice and Delinquency Prevention, 2007). One implication of this finding is that those most likely to be targeted for juvenile court action are persistent or chronic and nonviolent property offenders. They are considered the most troublesome in several respects. They clog juvenile court dockets again and again, and they sluggishly abandon their pattern of delinquent conduct. Further, they consume valuable juvenile court time, which costs taxpayers considerable money.

The strong rehabilitative and reintegrative principles upon which the juvenile courts have operated for most of the twentieth century continue to influence how violent juvenile offenders are treated. For instance, various reintegrative programs have been described that are designed especially for violent juvenile offenders, called **Violent Juvenile Offender Programs (VJOPs)**. These programs provide several positive interventions and treatments (Fagan, 1990). Instead of long-term incarceration in secure confinement, many violent juvenile offenders are placed in community-based secure facilities, where they remain for short periods before being reintegrated into their communities. Transitional residential programs include sustained intensive supervision as youths are gradually given freedoms and responsibilities.

first-offender
Criminals who have no previous criminal records; these persons may have committed crimes, but they have only been caught for the instant offense.

repeat offender
Any juvenile or adult with a prior record of delinquency or criminality.

Violent Juvenile Offender Programs (VJOPs)
Procedures designed to provide positive interventions and treatments; reintegrative programs, including transitional residential programs for those youths who have been subject to long-term detention; provides for social networking, provision of educational opportunities for youths, social learning, and goal-oriented behavioral skills.

The VJOP is based upon a theoretical model integrating strain, control, and learning theories. Four program dimensions include:

1. **Social networking:** the strengthening of personal bonds (attitudes, commitment, and beliefs) through positive experiences with family members, schools, the workplace, or nondelinquent peers.
2. **Provision of opportunities for youths:** the strengthening of social bonds (attachment and involvement) through achievement and successful participation in school, workplace, and family activities.
3. **Social learning:** the process by which personal and social bonds are strengthened and reinforced; strategies include rewards and sanctions for the attainment of goals or for contingent behaviors.
4. **Goal-oriented behaviors:** the linking of specific behaviors to each client's needs and abilities, including problem behaviors and special intervention needs (e.g., substance-abuse treatment or psychotherapy) (Fagan, 1990:240).

Violent juvenile offenders who have participated in these programs seem less inclined to recidivate. He believes that "carefully implemented and well-managed intervention programs," those that involve "early reintegration activities preceding release from secure care and intensive supervision in the community, with emphasis on gradual reentry and development of social skills to avoid criminal behavior," do much to "avert the abrupt return to criminality after release from the program" of these youths. Those youths exposed to more conventional and longer, secure confinement and treatment appear to recidivate at greater rates and to persist in their delinquent behaviors (Fagan, 1990:258). Therefore, it is difficult to formulate specific guidelines about how violent juvenile offenders ought to be handled in their juvenile court processing. Currently, competing philosophies of rehabilitation and just deserts recommend polarities in treatments, ranging from total diversion to total secure confinement (Kubena, 2008).

Is the First-Offender/Repeat-Offender Distinction Relevant? Race, Ethnicity, and Socioeconomic Status Revisited

Juvenile courts are supposed to be objective in their adjudicatory hearings and imposition of sanctions. Legal variables, such as prior record and the seriousness of the current offense, are supposed to be defining criteria for a system of graduated sanctions. Indeed, investigations of selected juvenile courts reveal that current offense seriousness and prior record are the most important variables in determining the dispositions of repeat delinquents. But juvenile courts in virtually every jurisdiction have drawn criticism that adjudications and dispositions are more a function of race, ethnicity, and socioeconomic status than of offense seriousness and prior record (Champion, 2008a). This is because of the disproportionately high representation of minorities in juvenile arrests, adjudications, and incarcerative dispositions (Eitle, Stolzenberg, and D'Alessio, 2005).

In many jurisdictions, white juveniles stand a better chance than blacks or Hispanics of not being detained following their arraignment. White juveniles also have a better chance of avoiding incarceration compared with blacks and Hispanics if they are adjudicated delinquent (Bradley, 2005). This charge against juvenile justice systems in the United States has led to a federal mandate to document the existence and nature of minority overrepresentation and to devise strategies to reduce such overrepresentation. One strategy designed to overcome the prejudicial effects of race, ethnicity, and social class is to establish objective criteria for juvenile justice decision making (Eitle, Stolzenberg, and D'Alessio, 2005).

Several objective criteria might be applied to decision making at various points throughout the juvenile justice system. These criteria are found in most state criminal codes and describe various conditions or circumstances that are more or less influential regarding juvenile offender dispositions, regardless of their seriousness. Some of these objective criteria include aggravating and mitigating circumstances.

Aggravating and Mitigating Circumstances

Playing an important part in determining how far any particular juvenile moves into the juvenile justice system are various aggravating and mitigating circumstances accompanying their acts. In the early stages of intake and prosecutorial decision making, aggravating and mitigating circumstances are often informally considered, and much depends upon the amount of detail furnished by police officers about the delinquent events. Aggravating circumstances are usually those actions on the part of juveniles that tend to intensify the seriousness of their acts. Accordingly, where aggravating circumstances exist, one's subsequent punishment might be intensified. At the other end of the spectrum are mitigating circumstances, or those factors that might weigh in the juvenile's favor. These circumstances might lessen the seriousness of the act as well as the severity of punishment imposed by juvenile court judges. A list of aggravating and mitigating circumstances are presented as follows.

Aggravating Circumstances

Aggravating circumstances applicable to both juveniles and adults include:

1. **Death or serious bodily injury to one or more victims.** The most serious juvenile offenders are those who cause death or serious bodily injury to their victims. Homicide and aggravated assault are those offenses that most directly involve death or serious physical harm to others, although it is possible to inflict serious bodily injury or inflict deep emotional scars through armed robbery and even some property crimes, including burglary (Champion, 2008a). The harshest option available to juvenile court judges is direct commitment to secure confinement, such as an industrial school or reform school.

2. **An offense committed while the offender is awaiting other delinquency charges.** Are juveniles awaiting an intake hearing after being arrested for previous offenses? Many juveniles commit new delinquent acts between the time they are arrested for other offenses and the date of their intake hearing. These offenders are probably good candidates for temporary confinement in secure holding facilities until their cases can be heard by intake officers and delinquency petitions can be filed.

3. **An offense committed while the offender is on probation, parole, or work release.** Offenders with prior adjudications and who are currently serving their sentences may reoffend during these conditional periods. Usually, a condition of diversionary and probationary programs is that youths refrain from further delinquent activity. Thus, they may be in violation of a program condition. Probation, parole, and work-release program violations are separate offenses that are accompanied by harsher penalties. In effect, these are incidents of contempt of court, since they involve violations of direct court-ordered conditional activities. The probation, parole, or work-release conditional programs have usually been granted to certain offenders because they have been deemed trustworthy by officials. Therefore, violations of the court's trust are especially serious, and it becomes less likely that these juveniles will be extended such privileges in the future.

4. **Previous offenses for which the offender has been punished.** Having a prior record is a strong indicator of one's chronicity and potential for future offending behavior. Juvenile court judges may be less inclined to be lenient in sentencing those with prior records, especially where serious delinquent acts have been committed. For example, repeat sex offenders are often treated more harshly by juvenile court

> **aggravating circumstances**
> Factors that may enhance the severity of one's sentence; these include brutality of act, whether serious bodily injury or death occurred to a victim during crime commission, and whether offender was on probation or parole when crime was committed.

judges, because of their suspected high rate of relapse. Thus, whether or not the belief that a high rate of relapse among sex offenders is justified, the mere fact of being a sex offender becomes an unofficial aggravating factor for many juvenile court judges (Bouhours and Daly, 2007).

5. **Leadership in the commission of the delinquent involving two or more offenders.** Especially in gang-related activities, one's leadership role is an aggravating circumstance. Are certain youths gang leaders? Do they incite others to commit delinquent acts? Gang leaders are often targeted for the harshest punishments, since they are most visible to their peers and serve as examples of how the system deals with juvenile offenders. Those playing minor roles in gang-related activity might be treated more leniently by judges.

6. **A violent offense involving more than one victim.** As the number of victims increases as the result of any delinquent conduct, the potential for physical harm and death rapidly escalates. Robberies of convenience stores and other places where large numbers of customers might be are likely to involve multiple victims. The number of victims or potential victims aggravates the initial delinquent conduct.

7. **Extreme cruelty during the commission of the offense.** Maiming victims or torturing them during the commission of delinquent acts is considered extreme cruelty and worthy of enhanced punishments by juvenile court judges.

8. **Use of a dangerous weapon in the commission of the offense, with high risk to human life.** The second and third leading causes of death among juveniles under age 21 are homicides and suicides, and most of these events include the use of firearms (Metts, 2005). Using firearms to commit delinquent acts increases greatly the potential harm to victims of such acts. Many states currently have mandatory **flat time** or hard time associated with using firearms during the commission of felonies. This means that if someone uses a dangerous weapon during the commission of a crime, a mandatory sentence enhancement is included, which may be an additional two- to five-year sentence in addition to the initial punishment, which might be a 10-year sentence for armed robbery.

Mitigating Circumstances

Mitigating circumstances include:

1. **No serious bodily injury resulting from the offense.** Petty property offenders who do not endanger lives or injure others may have their sentences mitigated as a result. Interestingly, however, property offenders account for a majority of long-term juvenile detainees in industrial schools or secure juvenile facilities.

2. **No attempt to inflict serious bodily injury on anyone.** Those juveniles who commit theft or burglary usually wish to avoid confrontations with their victims. While some juveniles prepare for such contingencies and therefore pose bodily threats to others, most youthful offenders committing such acts run away from the crime scene if discovered. This is evidence of their desire to avoid inflicting serious bodily harm on their victims.

3. **Duress or extreme provocation.** A compelling defense used in criminal court cases is that offenders were under duress at the time they committed their crimes. They may have been forced to act certain ways by others. Under certain circumstances, youths may plead that they were coerced or were acting under duress when committing delinquent acts in concert with others. Gang membership and gang violence may be precipitated to a degree because of duress. Youths may join gangs for self-protection and to avoid being assaulted by other gang members.

4. **Circumstances that justify the conduct.** Any circumstance that might justify one's conduct is a mitigating factor. If youths act to protect themselves or others from

flat time
Frequently known as hard time, meaning the actual amount of time one must serve while incarcerated.

mitigating circumstances
Factors that lessen the severity of the crime and/or sentence; such factors include old age, cooperation with police in apprehending other offenders, and lack of intent to inflict injury.

physical harm, then judges may find these circumstances strong enough to justify whatever conduct was exhibited.

5. **Mental incapacitation or a physical condition that significantly reduced the offender's culpability in the offense.** This factor specifies conditions that relate to drug or alcohol dependencies or to mental retardation or mental illness. If youths are suffering from some form of mental illness or are retarded, or if they are alcohol or drug dependent, their condition may limit their capacity to understand the law and interfere with their ability to comply with it.

6. **Cooperation with authorities in apprehending other participants in the act or making restitution to the victims for losses they suffered.** Those youths who assist police in apprehending others involved in delinquent acts are credited with these positive deeds. Also, juveniles who make restitution to victims or compensate them in part or in whole for their financial losses stand a good chance of having their cases mitigated through such restitution and good works.

7. **No prior record of delinquency.** First-offender juveniles, particular those under age 16, are especially targeted for more lenient treatment compared with recidivists.

8. **One's youthfulness.** The younger the juvenile, the greater the mitigation. Under common law, for instance, persons who commit crimes and who are under the age of seven are presumed incapable of formulating criminal intent. However, those who are 8, 9, 10, 11, and 12 years of age are entitled to some mitigation as well, in the opinions of some observers. Not being a fully formed adult renders a juvenile less mature and capable of sound decision making. One line of thought is that it is simply more difficult for juveniles to understand the law and comply with it. Thus, one's youthfulness should be weighed against any aggravating circumstances that might exist.

These lists of aggravating and mitigating circumstances are not exhaustive. Other factors may affect the judicial decision. At each stage of the juvenile justice process, interested officials want to know whether certain offenders will recidivate if they receive leniency. No one knows for sure whether certain offenders will recidivate more frequently than do other offenders, although certain factors correlate highly with recidivism (Trulson and Haerle, 2008). In the following section, we will examine several ways of assessing a juvenile's dangerousness or risk to the community. Such assessments are crucial in many jurisdictions in influencing prosecutorial and judicial decision making.

Juvenile Risk Assessments and Predictions of Dangerousness

Risk assessment is an element of a classification system and traditionally means the process of determining the probability that an individual will repeat unlawful or destructive behavior (Miller and Lin, 2007). Risk **prediction** takes several forms, including the prediction of violent behavior, predictions of new offenses (recidivism), and the prediction of technical program violations associated with probation and parole. Most states have some semblance of risk assessment of juvenile offenders, but only about half of the states have formal risk assessment instruments (Case, 2007).

Dangerousness and Risk

The concepts of **dangerousness** and **risk** are often used interchangeably. Dangerousness and risk both convey propensities to cause harm to others or oneself. What is the likelihood that any particular offender will be violent toward others? Does an offender

prediction
Assessment of some expected future behavior of a person, including criminal acts, arrests, or convictions.

dangerousness
Defined differently in several jurisdictions; prior record of violent offenses; potential to commit future violent crimes if released; propensity to inflict injury; predicted risk of convicted offender or prison or jail inmate; likelihood of inflicting harm upon others.

risk
Potential likelihood for someone to engage in further delinquency or criminality.

predictors of dangerousness and risk
Assessment devices that attempt to forecast one's potential for violence or risk to others; any factors that are used in such instruments.

risk/needs assessment instruments
Predictive device intended to forecast offender propensity to commit new offenses or recidivate.

needs assessment
[TK]

selective incapacitation
Incarcerating individuals who show a high likelihood of repeating their previous offenses; based on forecasts of potential for recidivism; includes but not limited to dangerousness.

pose any risk to public safety? What is the likelihood that any particular offender will commit suicide or attempt it? Risk (or dangerousness) instruments are screening devices intended to distinguish among different types of offenders for the purposes of determining initial institutional classification, security placement and inmate management, early release eligibility, and the level of supervision required under conditions of probation or parole. These instruments contain information believed useful in forecasting future delinquent conduct or criminality (Case, 2007). This information is collectively referred to as **predictors of dangerousness and risk**. Most state jurisdictions and the federal government regard these measures that forecast future criminality or delinquency as **risk/needs assessment instruments** rather than dangerousness instruments (Case, 2007). There is considerable variability among states regarding the format and content of such measures.

Needs Assessment and Its Measurement

Needs assessment instruments are instruments that measure an offender's personal/social skills, health well-being and emotional stability, educational level and vocational strengths and weaknesses, alcohol/drug dependencies, mental ability, and other relevant life factors, and which highlight those areas for which services are available and could or should be provided (Salinas, 2008).

Attempts to forecast juvenile dangerousness/risk and needs are important, because many actors in the juvenile justice system use these predictions or forecasts as the basis for their decision making (Case, 2007). Intake officers who initially screen youthful offenders try to decide which offenders are most deserving of leniency and which should be pushed further into the system for formal processing. Prosecutors want to know which juveniles are most receptive to diversion and amenable to change. Thus, they can ensure that only the most serious and chronic offenders will be processed, while the remaining youths will have another chance to live reasonably normal lives in their communities without juvenile justice system supervision. And judges want to know which youths will likely reoffend if returned to their communities through probation or some other nonincarcerative option. Some juvenile offenders may be penalized purely on the basis of their likelihood of future offending. Others may receive leniency because they are considered good probation or parole risks and unlikely to reoffend. Thus, some juveniles are selectively incapacitated. **Selective incapacitation** is confining those who are predicted to pose a risk to others, usually on the basis of their prior record and/or risk score on some risk instrument.

Who are dangerous youths and how do judges decide?

Selective Incapacitation

False Positives and False Negatives.

There are at least two major dangers inherent in risk or dangerousness predictions. First, youths who are identified as likely recidivists may receive harsher treatment compared with those who are considered unlikely to reoffend. In fact, many of those youths considered as good risks for probation or diversion may eventually turn out to be dangerous, although predictions of their future conduct gave assurances to the contrary. Second, those youths who receive harsher punishment and longer confinement because they are believed to be dangerous may not, in fact, be dangerous. Therefore, we risk overpenalizing those who will not be dangerous in the future, although our forecasts suggest they will be dangerous. We also risk underpenalizing those believed by our forecasts not to be dangerous, although a portion will eventually turn out to be dangerous and kill or seriously injure others (Case, 2007).

These two scenarios depict **false positives** and **false negatives**. False positives are those persons predicted to be dangerous in the future but who turn out not to be dangerous. False negatives are those persons predicted not to be dangerous in the future but turn out to be dangerous anyway. False positives are those who are unduly punished because of our predictions, while false negatives are those who do not receive needed punishment or future supervision (Champion, 2008a). For adult criminals, attempts to forecast criminal behaviors have led to recommendations for selective incapacitation in many jurisdictions. Selective incapacitation involves incarcerating or detaining those persons believed to be likely recidivists on the basis of various behavioral and attitudinal criteria. The theory behind selective incapacitation is that if high-risk offenders can be targeted and controlled through long-term confinement, then their circulation will be limited as well as the potential crimes they might commit.

Basically, incapacitation is a strategy for crime control involving the physical isolation of offenders from their communities, usually through incarceration, to prevent them from committing future crimes. The major harm is penalizing certain youths for acts they haven't yet committed. Can we legitimately punish anyone in the United States for suspected future criminality or delinquency? Whatever one's personal feelings in this regard, the answer is that such punishments are imposed each time parole boards deny parole requests or probation recommendations are rejected in favor of incarceration.

Two types of incapacitation are (1) collective and (2) selective. Under collective incapacitation, crime reduction would be accomplished through traditional offense-based sentencing and incarcerative policies, such as mandatory minimum sentences. Under selective incapacitation, however, those offenders predicted to pose the greatest risk of future crimes would become prime candidates for incarceration and for longer prison sentences. A major problem throughout both the criminal justice system and the juvenile justice system is that no universally acceptable implementation policies have been adopted in most jurisdictions supporting the use of such incapacitation strategies. Further, there are serious problems with many of these instruments because they cannot distinguish adequately between risks posed by male and female juvenile offenders (Case, 2007).

The quality of risk assessment devices is such at present that we cannot depend upon them as absolutely perfect indicators of one's future conduct (Champion, 1994). One problem is that many risk assessment instruments are almost exclusively tested on adult offenders rather than juvenile offenders. Also, follow-up periods for the assessments of predictive effectiveness are often relatively short, thus preventing researchers from validating the predictive utility of these scales over time. Despite the continuing controversy surrounding the application of risk prediction measures and the criticisms by some researchers that such predictions are either impossible or inappropriate, such predictions continue to be made.

Generally, risk assessment measures are one of the three following categories: (1) anamnestic prediction; (2) actuarial prediction; and (3) clinical prediction.

false positives
Offenders predicted to be dangerous who turn out not to be dangerous.

false negatives
Offenders predicted not to be dangerous who turn out to be dangerous.

anamnestic prediction
Projection of inmate behavior according to past circumstances.

actuarial prediction
Projection of future inmate behavior based on a class of offenders similar to those considered for parole.

clinical prediction
Forecast of inmate behavior based upon professionals' expert training and working directly with offenders.

Anamnestic Prediction. **Anamnestic prediction** uses past sets of circumstances to predict future behaviors. If the current circumstances are similar to past circumstances, where previous offense behaviors were observed, then it is likely that youths will exhibit future offending.

Actuarial Prediction. **Actuarial prediction** is an aggregate predictive tool. Those youthful offenders who are being considered for diversion, probation, or parole are compared with former offenders who have similar characteristics. Performances and records of previous conduct in view of diversion, probation, or parole decisions serve as the basis for profiling the high-risk recidivist. Certain youths may exhibit characteristics similar to those of previous juveniles who became recidivists. The expectation is that current youths will likely recidivate as well.

Clinical Prediction. **Clinical prediction** involves professional assessments of diagnostic examinations and test results. The professional training of probation officers, prosecutors, and judges, as they experience working with youthful offenders directly, enables them to forecast probable behaviors of their present clients. Clinical prediction involves the administration of psychological tools and personality assessment devices. Certain background and behavioral characteristics are assessed as well. Some persons consider clinical prediction to be superior to actuarial and anamnestic prediction, although there is little support for this claim. In fact, actuarial prediction, the simplest prediction form, is either equal to or better than clinical prediction under a variety of circumstances.

Common Elements of Risk Assessment Instruments

Most risk assessment measures for juvenile offenders contain several common elements (Case, 2007). Adapting these common elements to youthful offender scenarios, the following elements seem prevalent:

1. Age at first adjudication
2. Prior delinquent behavior (a combined measure of the number and severity of priors)
3. Number of prior commitments to juvenile facilities
4. Drug/chemical abuse
5. Alcohol abuse
6. Family relationships (parental control)
7. School problems
8. Peer relationships

For each of the elements above, some evidence has been found to establish a definite association between these and a youth's recidivism potential. These associations are not always strong, but in an actuarial prediction sense, they provide a basis for assuming that each of these elements has some causal value. The earlier the age of first adjudication and/or contact with the juvenile justice system, the greater the risk of recidivism. Poor school performance, family problems and a lack of parental control, drug and/or alcohol dependencies, prior commitments to juvenile facilities, and a history of juvenile offending are individually and collectively linked with recidivism.

For example, the California Youth Authority includes the following variables and response weights as a means of assessing one's risk level:

1. Age at first police contact:
   9 = score 6 points
   10 = score 5 points
   11 = score 4 points
   12 = score 3 points
   13 = score 2 points
   14 = score 1 point
   15 = score 0 points

2. Number of prior police contacts (number):
   Score actual number

3. Aggression and/or purse snatching:
   "Yes" = score 1
   "No" = score 0

4. Petty theft:
   "Yes" = score 1
   "No" = score 0

5. Use of alcohol or glue:
   "Yes" = score 1
   "No" = score 0

6. Usually three or more others involved in delinquent act:
   "Yes" = score 1
   "No" = score 0

7. Family on welfare:
   "Yes" = score 1
   "No" = score 0

8. Father main support in family:
   "No" = score 1
   "Yes" = score 0

9. Intact family:
   "No" = score 1
   "Yes" = score 0

10. Number of siblings:
    3 = score 1 point
    4 = score 2 points
    5+ = score 3 points

11. Father has criminal record:
    "Yes" = score 1
    "No" = score 0

12. Mother has criminal record:
    "Yes" = score 1
    "No" = score 0

13. Low family supervision:
    "Yes" = score 1
    "No" = score 0

14. Mother rejects:
    "Yes" = score 1
    "No" = score 0

15. Father rejects:
    "Yes" = score 1
    "No" = score 0

16. Parents wanted youth committed:
    "No" = score 1
    "Yes" = score 0

17. Verbal IQ:
    ≤ 69 = score 4
    70–79 = score 3
    80–89 = score 2

90–99 = score 1
100+ = score 0

18. Grade level:
    at grade level = score 1
    1 year retarded = score 2
    2 years retarded = score 3
    3 years retarded = score 4
    4+ years retarded = score 5

19. Negative school attitude:
    score 0–3

20. School disciplinary problems:
    "Yes" = score 1
    "No" = score 0

On the basis of the score obtained, youths might be assigned the following risk levels:

Risk Level Score	Degree of Risk
0–22	Low
21–31	Medium
32+	High

(Adapted from the California Youth Authority, 2008.)

Youths who receive scores of 0–22 are considered low risks, while those with scores of 32 or higher are considered high risks. California Youth Authority officials believe that while these scores do not necessarily indicate that all youths with higher scores will be recidivists and all those with lower scores will be nonrecidivists, there does appear to be some indication that these categorizations are generally valid ones. Thus, these classifications might be used to segregate more serious offenders from less serious ones in secure confinement facilities. Or such scores might be useful in the forecasts of future performance in diversion or probationary programs.

When measures or indices such as these are examined critically, it is interesting to note how such important life-influencing decisions are reduced to six or seven predictive criteria. In the instrumentation devised by the California Youth Authority, decisions about youths made by this organization are supplemented with several other important **classification** criteria, such as personality assessment tools, youth interviews, and professional impressions.

classification

Means used by prisons and probation/parole agencies to separate offenders according to offense seriousness, type of offense, and other criteria; no classification system has been demonstrably successful at effective prisoner or client placements.

The Functions of Classification

1. Classification systems enable authorities to make decisions about appropriate offender program placements.
2. Classification systems help to identify one's needs and the provision of effective services in specialized treatment programs.
3. Classification assists in determining one's custody level if confined in either prisons or jails.
4. Classification helps to adjust one's custody level during confinement, considering behavioral improvement and evidence of rehabilitation.
5. While confined, inmates may be targeted for particular services and/or programs to meet their needs.
6. Classification may be used for offender management and deterrence relative to program or prison rules and requirements.
7. Classification schemes are useful for policy decision making and administrative planning relevant for jail and prison construction, the nature and number of facilities required, and the types of services to be made available within such facilities.

8. Classification systems enable parole boards to make better early-release decisions about eligible offenders.
9. Community corrections agencies can utilize classification schemes to determine those parolees who qualify for participation and those who don't qualify.
10. Classification systems enable assessments of risk and dangerousness to be made generally in anticipation of the type of supervision best suited for particular offenders.
11. Classification schemes assist in decision making relevant for community crime control, the nature of penalties to be imposed, and the determination of punishment.
12. Classification may enable authorities to determine whether selective incapacitation is desirable for particular offenders or offender groupings.

For most states, the following general applications are made of risk assessment instruments at different client-processing stages:

1. To promote better program planning through optimum budgeting and deployment of resources.
2. To target high-risk and high-need offenders for particular custody levels, programs, and services without endangering the safety of others.
3. To apply the fair and appropriate sanctions to particular classes of offenders and raise their level of accountability.
4. To provide mechanisms for evaluating services and programs as well as service and program improvements over time.
5. To maximize public safety as well as public understanding of the diverse functions of corrections by making decision making more open and comprehensible to both citizens and offender-clients.

Sound predictive models should exhibit validity and reality, be dynamic rather than fixed, serve practical purposes, reflect responsible judgment, and have both qualitative and quantitative components. Various states such as Washington have experimented with different types of rehabilitative models involved in the custody and treatment of committed youths. The goals of such models are to teach offenders accountability; provide preventative and rehabilitative programming and public protection; and reduce repetitive criminal behavior using the least restrictive setting necessary. Many rehabilitative models move youths through a continuum of care, from structured residential settings through community parole. Community placement eligibility criteria are often established, together with a variety of rehabilitative treatment programs. Core treatment programming includes substance-abuse education, work, vocational and life skills, problem-solving, constructive response to frustration, and victim empathy/restoration (Salinas, 2008). Specialized treatment programming is provided for sex offenders, mentally ill offenders, and substance abusers. Such programming has also been attempted in other countries, such as Australia (McMorris et al., 2007).

Risk Prediction from Arizona and Florida

Two different risk prediction instruments have been devised by Arizona and Florida. As a simple exercise, read the following scenarios involving several hypothetical delinquents. Next, read through the particular risk prediction instruments, paying attention to their instructions for score determinations. Then, complete each instrument and determine the total score for each juvenile. It will be apparent that this task is easier for some instruments than for others. You will need to do several things when you compute scores for each of these juvenile offenders. You will need to keep track of their ages, how many formal and informal delinquency or status offender adjudications they have acquired, and whether they have escaped or attempted escape from a secure juvenile facility. In some of the instruments, you will need to determine whether they are drug or alcohol dependent. A brief solution will be provided at the end of these two scenarios.

Scenario 1: Arizona and Ronald M. Ronald M. lives in Phoenix, Arizona. He is 14 years old. Ronald M. is a member of the Scorpions, a Phoenix juvenile gang. He has been a gang member for three years and has participated in several drive-by shootings, none of which has resulted in fatalities to intended victims. Ronald M. is known to the police. When Ronald M. was 11, he was taken into custody for assaulting another student in his school. This was the result of a referral by the school principal. An intake officer adjusted the case and returned Ronald M. to the custody of his parents. Two months later, Ronald M. was taken into custody again, this time for beating another student with a lead pipe and causing serious bodily injuries. Again, the school principal referred Ronald M. to juvenile authorities for processing, and a delinquency petition was filed. This time, the juvenile court judge heard Ronald M.'s case and adjudicated Ronald M. delinquent on the assault charge. Ronald M. was disposed to probation for one year.

While on probation, Ronald M. joined the Scorpions and was involved in at least three convenience store thefts and five crack cocaine sales. During the last crack cocaine sale, an undercover police officer posing as a crack cocaine customer arrested Ronald M. and two of his gang companions and took them to the police station for processing. Ronald M. appeared again before the same juvenile court judge after a police referral. This time, the judge adjudicated Ronald M. delinquent on the drug charge and disposed him to an 18-month probationary term. In the meantime, a routine drug screen at the local jail where Ronald M. was being detained in preventive detention revealed that he tested positive for cocaine and alcohol use. Under questioning, Ronald M. admitted to using drugs occasionally, as well as consuming alcohol at gang meetings. When Ronald M. was 12 and still on probation, he was taken into custody by police following a burglary report at a local drug store. When officers apprehended Ronald M., he was crawling out of a back window of the drug store with several bottles of Percodan, a prescription pain reliever. Officers confiscated a loaded .22-caliber pistol, which Ronald M. was carrying in his jacket pocket. Officers filed a delinquency petition with the juvenile court, alleging several law violations, including burglary, theft, and carrying a concealed firearm. Ronald M.'s probation officer also referred Ronald M. to the juvenile court and recommended that Ronald M.'s probation program be revoked, since he was in clear violation of his probation program requirements. The juvenile court judge adjudicated Ronald M. delinquent on the firearms charge as well as on the burglary and theft charges. He also revoked Ronald M.'s probation after a two-stage hearing where substantial evidence was presented of Ronald M.'s guilt. Ronald M. was disposed to six months' intensive supervised probation with electronic monitoring.

Subsequently, Ronald M. has been adjudicated delinquent three more times. Police officers filed petitions with the juvenile court on all three occasions. Two of these delinquency adjudications were for felonies (aggravated assault and selling one kilogram of cocaine). For the aggravated assault offense, the juvenile court judge disposed Ronald M. to the Arizona State Industrial School, a secure-custody facility, for a term of six months. The judge also revoked Ronald M.'s probation program. A predispositional report filed by the juvenile probation officer disclosed that Ronald M. has frequently been truant from school and has had serious behavioral problems when in school. He has had difficulty relating with other youths. Two weeks ago, Ronald M. was taken into custody and charged with arson, a felony. He and two Scorpion gang members were observed by three eyewitnesses setting fire to the occupied home of a rival gang member. Fortunately, no one was injured in the resulting fire. The juvenile court judge has just adjudicated Ronald M. delinquent on the arson charge and has committed him to the Arizona State Industrial School for two years.

Using the Arizona Department of Juvenile Corrections (ADJC) Risk Assessment form illustrated in Figure 9.1, determine Ronald M.'s total risk score. What is Ronald M.'s risk category? What is Ronald M.'s most serious commitment offense? What is Ronald M.'s most serious prior adjudicated offense?

Figure 9.1　The Arizona ADJC Risk Assessment Instrument

ADJC RISK ASSESSMENT

YOUTH NAME _____ K# _____ DATE OF ASSESSMENT _____

COMMITTING COUNTY _____ DATE OF ADMISSION _____ DOB _____

R1 Number of Referrals   (__)　　　　　　　　　　　　　　　　SCORE
　　1 to 4 ....0　　　　　____
　　5 or More ....+1

R2 Number of Adjudications   (__)
　　1 or 2 ....-1
　　3 or 4 0
　　5 or More ....+1　　　____

R3 Age at First Juvenile Referral (__)
　　12 yrs 5 mos. or Younger...................................+1
　　12 yrs 6 mos. or Older.......................................0　　　　____

R4 Petition Offense History (check applicable below and add for score)
　　A.(__) 2 or More Assaultive Offenses..................+1
　　B.(__) 2 or More Drug Offenses..........................+2
　　C.(__) 3 or More Property Offenses....................+1
　　D.(__) Weapons Offense or use in above.............+1　　____

　　　　　　　　R 4 Sub Total   ____

R5 Petitions for Felony Offenses (__)
　　0 to 2..0
　　3 or More...+1　　____

R6 Affiliation with a Delinquent Gang
　　No...0
　　Yes...+1　　____

R7 Enrolled in School with no Serious Truancy or Behavioral Problems
　　No...0
　　Yes...-1　　____

R8 Known Use of Alcohol or Drugs
　　No...-1
　　Yes...0　　____

　　　　　　　TOTAL RISK SCORE　　　　　____

RISK CATEGORY (CHECK ONE)		
[ ] LOW(1 or Less)	[ ] MEDIUM (2-4)	[ ] HIGH (5+)

_____
Signature of Staff Completing Assessment Instrument

CURRENT COMMITMENT TYPE (CHECK ONE):　　[ ] NEW COMMIT　　[ ]ADJC REVOCATION

MOST SERIOUS COMMITMENT OFFENSE:

OFFENSE DESCRIPTION　ARS CODE　F/M CLASS　SUBCLASS　DATE
_____　_____　_____　_____　_____

MOST SERIOUS PRIOR ADJUDICATED OFFENSE:

OFFENSE DESCRIPTION　ARS CODE　F/M CLASS　SUBCLASS　DATE
_____　_____　_____　_____　_____

CLASS: 1,2,3,4,5,6 OR 9 = NOT APPLICABLE
F=FELONY　　M=MISDEMEANOR　　V=VIOLATION PROB. OR PAROLE　　O=OTHER

Scenario 2: Florida and Susan R. Susan R. is 15 years old. She lives in Tampa, Florida, and is a sophomore in high school. Recently, a juvenile court judge adjudicated Susan R. delinquent for stealing a neighbor's car and joyriding. She drove the car into another state, where she wrecked it. She was accompanied by two other girls, who were subsequently identified as members of a female gang from Tampa. Susan R. has admitted that she, too, is a member of that same gang. The auto theft charge is a third-degree felony. The judge has disposed her to two years' probation, together with mandatory psychological and substance-abuse counseling, since she had been using marijuana at the time of her arrest. She is currently receiving both psychological counseling and treatment for her substance abuse. The marijuana possession was a second-degree misdemeanor, although this charge was subsequently dropped pursuant to a plea bargain with the juvenile court prosecutor. A predispositional report prepared by a juvenile probation officer for the juvenile court disclosed the following background factors for Susan R. She began her career of delinquency when she was 12 years of age. At that time, she shoplifted some cosmetics from a local department store. When she was confronted by a store security officer, Susan R. assaulted the officer by pushing her into a display counter. The glass broke and the officer sustained severe lacerations. Susan R. was charged with theft and aggravated assault. The theft was related to a gang initiation. The juvenile court judge adjudicated her delinquent on both charges and ordered her committed to the Florida Industrial School, a secure facility, for a term of six months. Susan R. and another inmate escaped from this facility one evening, although they were apprehended three days later and returned to custody. Over the next few months, Susan R. tried to escape from the facility on at least four different occasions. The juvenile court judge adjudicated her delinquent on an escape charge, and the term of her confinement in the Florida Industrial School was extended to one year. Susan R. was subsequently released from secure confinement at age 13, and she returned to school. Over the next two years, Susan R. was involved in several minor incidents involving low-level misdemeanors. In one instance, she was placed on diversion by the prosecutor, with judicial approval. A part of her diversion was performing 200 hours of community service as well as observance of a curfew. Her juvenile probation officer caught her violating curfew on at least three occasions and filed an affidavit with the juvenile court. The juvenile court judge verbally reprimanded Susan R. on this occasion, but he did not impose other sanctions.

An interview with Susan R.'s parents revealed that Susan R. is incorrigible. The parents say that they have no control over Susan R.'s actions. However, Susan R.'s siblings, a younger brother and a sister, report that their parents, who have physical altercations frequently in front of them and use drugs themselves, are seldom home to monitor them and their sister, Susan R. A counselor has concluded independently that the family has a history of domestic violence and that the home is quite unstable. Susan R.'s mother has been committed to a psychiatric institution in previous years for depression as well as schizophrenia. The mother is currently on medication for managing her depression. Susan R.'s father has a previous conviction for receiving stolen property, a second-degree misdemeanor. He has also been previously convicted of sexual battery and served six months in the county jail for this crime. In fact, at the present time, the Florida Department of Human Services is conducting an investigation of Susan R.'s family on charges of alleged child neglect.

Susan R. herself has no obvious developmental disabilities nor prior mental illnesses and appears to be in good physical health. However, because of the history of her family, it has been recommended that she have a psychological assessment to determine her present mental state. Susan R. is currently unemployed and has no marketable skills. Thus, she would be unable to obtain and/or sustain employment if she were expected to work. It has been recommended that she take several vocational/technical courses to improve her skill level. Her peer relations are poor, and she is socially immature and withdrawn. She is easily led by others, as evidenced by the ease with which she was recruited into her gang. Most of Susan R.'s close peers are other gang members. Although she is currently enrolled in school, she has poor attendance. During periods when she has attended school, she has been compliant and not disruptive. According to her teachers, Susan R. reads well and has no obvious learning disabilities. But it has been determined that Susan R. has used marijuana frequently with her gang friends. Susan R.'s home situation has been cited by the juvenile probation officer as a substantial mitigating circumstance, and she recommends a 5-point reduction in Susan R.'s risk score. The probation supervisor, who oversees risk assessment instrument preparation and administration, concurs with this recommendation and has chosen not to override it.

Figure 9.2 shows the Florida Department of Juvenile Justice Supervision Risk Classification Instrument. Notice that it consists of two parts. The first part is a risk assessment scale. The second part is a needs assessment scale.

Figure 9.2 also illustrates the Florida Department of Juvenile Justice Classification Matrix. This matrix is used to determine the level of a youth's placement in the Florida Department of Juvenile Justice based on a combination of one's needs assessment score and risk assessment score. For Susan R., and using the information in the above scenario, determine Susan R.'s risk assessment and needs assessment scores. Next, place Susan R. in the classification matrix according to the scores you have calculated.

Calculating the ADJC Risk Score for Ronald M.

Before determining Ronald M.'s score on the Arizona Risk Assessment instrument, familiarize yourself with the instrument's contents. There are eight categories: (1) number of referrals, (2) number of adjudications, (3) age at first juvenile referral, (4) petition offense history, (5) petitions for felony offenses, (6) affiliation with a delinquent gang, (7) enrolled in school with no serious truancy or behavioral problems, and (8) known use of alcohol or drugs.

First, let's count the number of times Ronald M. has been referred to juvenile court on various charges. We can count both referrals and delinquency petitions filed against Ronald M., because both actions are intended to bring juveniles before the juvenile court. Delinquency petitions are only filed in about half of all juvenile cases that reach the juvenile courts annually throughout the United States. The other types of cases are nonpetitioned cases. In Ronald M.'s case, he was referred by the school principal on two occasions, with a delinquency petition filed on the second occasion. Ronald M. was referred again to juvenile court by police officers for selling crack cocaine. Later, Ronald M. was referred to the juvenile court for burglary, theft, and carrying a concealed weapon. Ronald M.'s probation officer also referred him to the juvenile court because of a probation violation. Subsequently, Ronald M. was referred to juvenile court three more times, all resulting in delinquency adjudications. Two of these offenses were felonies: aggravated assault and selling cocaine. Finally, Ronald M. was most recently referred to the juvenile court for arson and adjudicated delinquent on that charge. Therefore, there are at least nine referrals of Ronald M. to juvenile court. Since this is "5 or more," we will give Ronald M. a + 1 for R1, as shown in Figure 9.1.

Next, we determine the number of Ronald M.'s adjudications. He was adjudicated delinquent on the school assault charge; the drug charge; the firearms, burglary, and theft charges; three additional adjudications for offenses, including aggravated assault and selling cocaine; and for arson. This adds up to seven delinquency adjudications. For R2, this is "5 or more," and therefore, we score R2 with a + 1.

Ronald M.'s age at his first juvenile court referral was 11. For R3, this is "12 years, 5 months or younger," and therefore, we score Ronald M. a + 1.

Ronald M.'s petition offense history includes "2 or more assaultive offenses." We score this portion of the risk instrument with a + 1. Ronald M. also has "2 or more drug offenses," and therefore, we assign him a + 2. Although Ronald M. has participated in several thefts, as mentioned in the scenario, we should count only what police and other authorities actually know about Ronald M. and which types of offenses resulted in petitions filed with the juvenile court. He has a burglary and a theft charge for which

Figure 9.2   Florida Department of Juvenile Justice Supervision Risk Classification Instrument

**FLORIDA DEPARTMENT OF JUVENILE JUSTICE
SUPERVISION RISK CLASSIFICATION INSTRUMENT**

Youth's Name: Sharon H Test   Court Docket #: _____

Juvenile Probation Officer: _____   Unit: _____

Date Completed: _____   DJJID: 532950   Referral ID: 1507938

RISK ASSESSMENT

A. INSTANT OFFENSE (most serious) ....

- Capital or life felony — 32 points
- 1st degree felony (violent) — 20 points
- 1st degree felony/2nd degree felony (violent) — 18 points
- 2nd degree felony/3rd degree felony (violent) — 15 points
- 3rd degree felony — 7 points
- 1st degree misdemeanor (violent) — 5 points
- 1st degree misdemeanor — 3 points
- 2nd degree misdemeanor — 1 point

B. PRIOR HISTORY (highest applicable score)

- Meets the criteria for Level 10 placement — 7 points
- Has met the definition of a SHO/IRT with this offense — 6 points
- Two or more prior non-related felonies resulting in adjudication or withheld adjudication — 3 points
- One felony or two or more non-related misdemeanors resulting in adjudication or withheld adjudication — 2 points
- One prior misdemeanor resulting in adj. or withheld adj. — 1 point

C. OTHER SCORING FACTORS (combined score) ....

- Current legal status CC/F (2 pts) - committed (4 pts)
- Previous completed CC/F (2 pts) committed (4pts)
- Previous technical violation (1 point. per affidavit)
- Youth 12 years old/under at time of 1st charge (1pt)
- Substance use/abuse involved (1 pt.)
- History of escape or absconding (1pt.)
- Current or previous JASP/community arb. (2 pts each)
- Other previous or current diversion (1 pt. each)
- Domestic violence involved (youth as perpetrator) (2 pts each)
- Gang related offense (2 pt.)

D. A+B+C = SUBTOTAL 0

Mitigating (maximum 5 pts.)..........................(-)

Justification _____

Aggravating-consider pending offenses (max 5) ......(+)

Justification _____

TOTAL: A+B+C – mitigation + aggravating = 0

TOTAL RISK SCORE 0   **TOTAL NEEDS SCORE** 0

CLASSIFICATION DECISION (see matrix on page 3):

☐ Diversion   ☐ Minimum   ☐ General   ☐ Intensive
☐ Level 2   ☐ Level 4   ☐ Level 6   ☐ Level 8/10

OVERRIDE CLASSIFICATION DECISION (if applicable):

☐ Diversion   ☐ Minimum   ☐ General   ☐ Intensive
☐ Level 2   ☐ Level 4   ☐ Level 6   ☐ Level 8/10

OVERRIDE JUSTIFICATION: _____

JPO Initials _____ Date: _____
Supervisor Initials _____ Date: _____

NEEDS ASSESSMENT

FAMILY RELATIONSHIPS (score total points)

A.   0
- Parents unable/unwilling to control youth — 3 pts.
- Parent cooperative, some control — 1 pt.
- Youth in unstable independent living situation — 2 pts.
- Family history of domestic violence — 2 pts.
- Family history of abuse/neglect — 2 pts.
- Parent or sibling with criminal history — 1 pt.
- Parent with mental illness — 2 pts.
- Parent with substance abuse — 2 pts.
- Out of home dependency placement — 2 pts.
- Current abuse/neglect investigation — 3 pts.
- Youth is a parent — 3 pts.

B. PEER RELATIONSHIPS (score total pts)   0
- Socially immature — 1 pt.
- Socially withdrawn — 1 pt.
- Easily led by others — 1 pt.
- Exploits or aggressive to others — 2 pts.
- Peers have delinquent history or gang involvement — 3 pts.

C. SIGNIFICANT ADULT RELATIONS (score highest)   0
- Authority figure relationships are inconsistent — 1 pt.
- Youth unavailable/unwilling to positively relate to adult authority figures — 2 pts

D. EDUCATIONAL (score total pts.)   0
- Poor attendance/not enrolled (under 16) — 3 pts.
- Disruptive school behavior — 2 pts.
- Literacy problems — 2 pts.
- Learning disability — 2 pts.
- Withdrawn/expelled/suspended — 3 pts.
- Enrolled and failing — 2 pts.

E. YOUTH'S EMPLOYMENT (score total pts)   0
(youth over 16, not in school or youth with monetary needs)
- Currently developing marketable skills/no school — 1 pt.
- Needs to develop marketable skills — 2 pts.
- Currently unemployed — 2 pts.

F. DEVELOPMENTAL DISABILITY (score highest)   0
- Known dev. disability/no current services — 3 pts.
- Known dev. disability/with current services — 2 pts.
- Disability suspected/no diagnosis — 2 pts.

G. PHYSICAL HEALTH & HYGIENE (score total pts.)   0
- Medical or dental referral needed — 1 pt.
- Health or hygiene education needed — 1 pt.
- Handicap or illness limits functioning — 3 pts.

H. MENTAL HEALTH (score total pts.)   0
- Assessment needed — 2 pts.
- Prior history of mental health problems — 2 pts.
- Currently in treatment — 2 pts.
- Assessment indicates treatment needs/no current services — 3 pts.

I. SUBSTANCE ABUSE (score total pts.)   0
- Assessment needed — 2 pts.
- Occasional user — 1 pt.
- Frequent user — 3 pts.
- Assessment indicates treatment needs/no services — 3 pts.
- Receiving treatment services — 2 pts.

TOTAL NEEDS SCORE   0

April, 1998   Case Management: Intake   DJJ/IS Form 4

Page 1 of 3

Source: Reprinted with permission by the Florida Department of Juvenile Justice.

Figure 9.2   Florida Department of Juvenile Justice Supervision Risk Classification Instrument (Cont.)

FLORIDA DEPARTMENT OF JUVENILE JUSTICE
CLASSIFICATION MATRIX

NEEDS	RISK			
	LOW 0 10	MODERATE 11 17	HIGH 18 24	VERY HIGH 25 32
LOW 0 : : : : 15	Diversion	Minimum Supervision General Supervision	Minimum Supervision General Intensive Supervision	Level 4 Level 6 Level 8/10
MODERATE 16 : : : : 30	Diversion	Minimum Supervision General Supervision	Intensive Level 2 	Level 4 Level 6 Level 8/10
HIGH 31 : : : : 45	Diversion Minimum Supervision	General Supervision	Intensive Level 2 Level 4	Level 6 Level 8/10
VERY HIGH 46+ : : : :	Diversion Minimum Supervision	General Supervision Intensive Supervision	Level 2 Level 4 Level 6	Level 8/10

petitions have been filed. Since this is not "3 or more property offenses," we do not assign Ronald M. a score. However, we can give Ronald M. a + 1 for "weapons offense or use in above." Thus, for the R4 Petition Offense History score, Ronald M. should receive a "4."

R5 is "Petitions for Felony Offenses," and Ronald M. has at least three or more of these. Therefore, we assign him a + 1 for R5.

R6 is easy to score. Is Ronald M. a gang member? Yes. Therefore, he receives a + 1 for R6.

R7 is also easy to score. Ronald M. has been enrolled in school in the past, but he has serious truancy problems. We must assign him a "0" for R7.

Finally, for R8, Ronald M. is known for his use of alcohol and drugs. We must assign him a "0" for R8.

Summing R1 through R8, we have $1 + 1 + 1 + 4 + 1 + 1 + 0 + 0 = 9$. Ronald M.'s total risk assessment score is 9. According to the ADJC Risk Assessment instrument, the risk category where we would place Ronald M. is "High" (5+ points).

Notice that there are other items to fill in on this form. One space is for "Most Serious Commitment Offense." We are not in a position to know how Arizona rates the seriousness of aggravated assault in relation to arson. But these are the two offenses resulting in Ronald M.'s commitment to the Arizona State Industrial School. If "arson" were the more serious offense, then we would list this in the first space for "Most Serious Commitment Offense," with an appropriate code and date. It would be a felony. For the "Most Serious Prior Adjudicated Offense," we would have to list "aggravated assault" as the offense, which is also a felony. We would also enter a code for this offense, as well as the date of the adjudication.

Without the accompanying ADJC instruction manual for this instrument, we don't know how Ronald M.'s score of "9" will be used. In all likelihood, it will relate to his placement in the secure facility and the intensity of supervision he will receive while confined. He is definitely a risk to others and must be monitored carefully. However, this score is only one of many criteria that are used in placement and level-of-custody decision making.

It should be noted that if Ronald M. is alternatively considered for admission into a community-based program by the juvenile court judge instead of placement in a secure facility, another form is used by the ADJC. This form is very similar to the form shown in Figure 9.1 and is illustrated in Figure 9.3.

Figure 9.3 is a reassessment form, and it serves to give us an impression of how much Ronald M. has improved his behavior since being admitted into the community-based program. In this form, attention is focused on one's peer relationships within a 30- to 90-day period; whether there have been problems with school or work adjustment within a similar time interval; and whether the client has had problems adjusting to supervision or compliance with program requirements within the most recent 30- to 90-day period.

In Ronald M.'s case, if he were placed in a community program instead of being incarcerated, he would be evaluated within a 30- to 90-day period following his community program placement. If he improved his behavior, there is a good possibility that his risk level (or risk category) could be reduced. This possible risk category reduction may have implications for how closely or loosely Ronald M. is supervised in his community-based program. It is also indicative of whether he is becoming rehabilitated and reintegrated.

Calculating the Florida Risk Assessment Score for Susan R. The Florida Department of Juvenile Justice Risk Classification Instrument, Figure 9.2, is divided into two parts: (1) risk assessment and (2) needs assessment. Again, when determining the score for any juvenile, we must first familiarize ourselves with the instrument's contents before computing a risk score. There are three categories (A, B, and C), which refer to (1) the instant offense, (2) prior history, and (3) other scoring factors.

Figure 9.3   ADJC Risk Reassessment for Youth in Community Programs

ADJC RISK REASSESSMENT
FOR YOUTH IN COMMUNITY PROGRAMS

YOUTH NAME _____ K# _____ DOB _____ DATE OF REASSESSMENT _____

For items 1 - 4 use initial Risk Assessment information

SCORE

RE 1. **Age At First Referral** (____)
        12 Years or Less ....+1
        13 Years or Older 0
        _____

RE 2. **Number of Prior Referrals** (____)
        4 or Less 0
        5 or More ....+1
        _____

RE 3. **Prior Petition Offense History**
        A (____) 3 or More Property ....+1
        B (____) 2 or More Assaultive Offenses ....+1
        C (____) 2 or More Drug Offenses ....+2
        D (____) Weapons Offense...+1
        _____

        RE 3 SUBTOTAL   _____

RE 4. **Prior Petitions For Felony Offenses** (____)
        2 or Less 0
        3 or More ....+1
        _____

Score All Following Items for Last 30/90 Days.

RE 5. **Referrals To Court or For Revocation Hearing (Last 30/90 days)**
        None ....-1
        One ....+1
        Two or More..+2

RE 6. **Use of Alcohol or Other Drugs (Last 30/90 Days)**
        No...0
        Yes..+1
        _____
        Check type (if any)   _____Alcohol   _____ Marijuana   _____ Other Drug

RE 7. **Peer Relationships (Last 30/90 Days)**
        No Problems 0
        Associates with Delinquent Peers ....+1
        Associates with Gang Members ....+2
        _____

RE 8. **School or Work Adjustment (Last 30/90 Days)** _____ Where
        No Problems or Minor Problems..0
        Some Attendance /Behavior Problems ....+1
        Serious Work or School Attendance/Behavior Problems...................+2
        _____

RE 9. **Adjustment to Supervision/Compliance with Plan (Last 30/90 Days)**
        No Problems ....-1
        Minor Problems...0
        Serious Compliance Problems with Plan ....+1
        _____

        TOTAL SCORE   _____

RISK CATEGORY (CIRCLE ONE)

LOW (5 or Less) = LEVEL III   MEDIUM (6 - 10) = LEVEL II   HIGH (11 or HIGHER) = LEVEL I

Assigned Supervision Level_____   Override Y/N   Reason _____
        _____
        _____
        _____

Parole Officer's Signature _____ Date _____

Supervisor's Signature _____ Date _____

Source: Reprinted with the permission of Arizona Department of Juvenile Corrections.

For category A, "Instant Offense," Susan R. has recently been adjudicated delinquent on an auto theft charge, which is a third-degree felony. According to this risk assessment scale, a third-degree felony rates a score of 7 points.

For category B, we are to assign Susan R. the "highest applicable score." This means that we are not supposed to add or sum the scores for all categories that fit Susan R. Given her delinquency history since age 12, including her escape from a secure facility, an assault on a store security officer, and gang membership, she probably meets the criteria for "Level 10 placement." According to Florida officials, the risk score derived from this instrument at the time of a youth's arrest is used to make an appropriate recommendation to the state attorney's office (Champion, 2008a). Let's assume that Susan R. qualifies for Level 10 placement, and therefore we will assign her a "7."

Category C is additive in that we are to consider a number of factors, each associated with specific points. These factors include current legal status (presently committed to a secure facility), previous completed commitment (to a secure facility), previous technical violation (in connection with a probation or parole program or diversion), age at the time of first charge, substance use/abuse involvement, history of escape or absconding, current or previous community arbitration (alternative dispute resolution), other previous or current diversion, and a gang-related offense. For each category that applies to Susan R., we should assign a score. Subsequently we will sum the individual scores to determine the combined score for "C."

Currently Susan R. is on probation. However, she has had a previous commitment to the Florida Industrial School. We assign her 4 points for this category. She has a technical violation, violating curfew while on probation, and an affidavit has been filed in connection with this violation. Therefore, Susan R. receives 1 point for this category.

Susan R. began her career of delinquency at age 12. Therefore, she receives 1 point for this category. She is a substance abuser, and therefore she receives 1 point for this category. She has a history of escape from the secure facility where she was placed, and this entitles her to 1 point. She has never participated in alternative dispute resolution, and therefore she receives no points for this category. However, she has been placed on diversion once in the past, and she receives 1 point for this category. Although there is domestic violence in Susan R.'s home, Susan R. has never been the perpetrator. Therefore, she receives no points for this category. Finally, she has had at least one gang-related offense, shoplifting. We assign her 2 points for this category. There are 10 categories as subparts of "C," and we sum the various subparts as follows: $0 + 4 + 1 + 1 + 1 + 1 + 0 + 1 + 0 + 2 = 11$ points. Susan R.'s score for category C is 11.

Summing her scores for categories A, B, and C, we have $7 + 7 + 11 = 25$ points. Notice that for "D," adjustments may be made for the presence of aggravating or mitigating circumstances. Anyone completing this risk assessment might choose to focus upon Susan R.'s violent acts, such as pushing the store security officer. They might also focus upon Susan R.'s escape from the Florida Industrial School and subsequent attempts to escape. These factors might be considered as aggravating. However, substantial evidence exists that might constitute mitigating circumstances. Susan R.'s home life is a disaster. She has a dysfunctional family where frequent physical altercations and drug use are evident. Background information about Susan R. from school officials suggests that but for her gang affiliation, Susan R. is a compliant and reasonably intelligent student. In the present scenario, the juvenile probation officer has recommended a 5-point reduction for Susan R., given her home circumstances. The probation supervisor has concurred with this recommendation. Therefore, there will probably be a 5-point reduction in Susan R.'s final score. This would be $25 - 5 = 20$ points. Thus, Susan R.'s final risk assessment score would be 20.

One final word about the Florida risk reassessment device is in order. At the very bottom of the risk reassessment instrument shown in Figure 9.3, a classification decision is illustrated. But immediately below this classification decision is an override classification decision. **Overrides** are decisions by someone in authority and with pertinent expertise to change whatever classification is yielded from the original risk score that has been computed. For instance, Susan R.'s score of 20 can be overridden for one or more reasons. The nature of the override is either to increase or to decrease the resulting score or classification decision. No risk assessment instrument captures every single facet of one's existence or circumstances. If there are circumstances of facts that are relevant to cases such as Susan R.'s, then the original classification decision may be overridden. For instance, Susan R. may have been coerced into committing burglaries

overrides
Actions by an authority in an institution or agency that overrule a score or assessment made of a client or inmate; raw scores or assessments or recommendations can be overruled; the function of override is to upgrade the seriousness of offense status or downgrade the seriousness of offense status, thus changing the level of custody at which one is maintained in secure confinement; may also affect the type and nature of community programming for particular offenders.

and thefts by her other gang members. Duress might be a mitigating circumstance that is otherwise undetected through conventional measurement methods. Or Susan R. may be emotionally immature for her age. Factors such as these may be detected through interviews with juvenile clients. Perhaps information is yielded through other means, such as reports from school or church officials. In any case, any particular score assigned to a juvenile client may be overridden. It may be raised or lowered, provided that a reasonable justification is articulated to account for the change.

Needs Assessments

Besides measuring a juvenile's potential risk or dangerousness, it is important for juvenile justice practitioners to know what types of problems afflict particular youths. Many youths who enter the juvenile justice system are drug or alcohol dependent, have psychological problems, suffer from maladjustments in their homes or schools, or are impaired physically in some respect. Therefore, to determine the needs of juveniles, practitioners must assess juveniles who are processed. Sometimes, scales are combined to obtain information about both risk and needs. These risk/needs assessment instruments enable those conducting such assessments to obtain both types of information from youths in one test administration. Not all juveniles need the same community services. There are diverse community resources available to meet a wide variety of needs exhibited by the youths who enter the juvenile justice system. Some juveniles require minimal intervention, while other youths need extensive treatments and services. Whether youths are confined in secure facilities or allowed to attend their schools and remain with their families in their communities, different provisions often must be made to individualize their needs. Needs assessment instruments are used to determine which specific services and treatments ought to be provided to each youth.

For example, with regard to the Florida Risk Classification Instrument described earlier and our hypothetical case of Susan R., Figure 9.2 contains both a "needs assessment" component and a "risk assessment" component. We calculated the risk assessment component. In the next section, we will compute Susan R.'s needs assessment score based on the scenario information provided earlier.

Computing Susan R.'s Florida Needs Assessment Score.

Again, we should familiarize ourselves with the needs assessment instrument, the second part of the Risk Classification Instrument as shown in Figure 9.2. There are nine areas covered: family relationships, peer relationships, significant adult relations, educational factors, youth's employment, developmental disability (if any), physical health and hygiene, mental health, and substance abuse. Some of these areas contain additive components, meaning that we must assign points to juveniles such as Susan R. if certain subparts of these areas pertain to her or her circumstances.

For Part A, "Family Relationships," we know from the above scenario about Susan R. that her parents cannot control her. We also know that she lives in an unstable family environment with a family history of domestic violence, abuse and/or neglect, and that one parent has a criminal history. We also know that the parents use drugs or abuse various substances. Further, there is an ongoing investigation of this allegedly abusive environment conducted by the Florida Department of Human Services. Susan R. herself is not a parent. There are 11 subparts for Part A. We would score these subparts sequentially as follows: $3 + 0 + 2 + 2 + 2 + 1 + 2 + 2 + 0 + 3 + 0 = 17$ points. The Part A calculation is determined as follows:

Parents unable/unwilling to control youth?	Yes	3 points
Parent cooperative, some control?	No	0 points
Youth in unstable independent living situation?	Yes	2 points
Family history of domestic violence?	Yes	2 points
Family history of abuse/neglect?	Yes	2 points

Parent or sibling with criminal history?	Yes	1 point
Parent with mental illness?	Yes	2 points
Parent with substance abuse?	Yes	2 points
Out-of-home dependency placement?	No	0 points
Current abuse/neglect investigation?	Yes	3 points
Youth is a parent?	No	0 points

Part B has five subparts: socially immature, socially withdrawn, easily led by others, exploits or aggressive to others, and peers have delinquent history or gang involvement. We would score these subparts as follows: $1 + 1 + 1 + 0 + 3 = 6$ points. The Part B calculation is determined as follows:

Socially immature?	Yes	1 point
Socially withdrawn?	Yes	1 point
Easily led by others?	Yes	1 point
Exploits or aggressive to others?	No	0 points
Peers have delinquent history or gang involvement?	Yes	3 points

Part C deals with significant adult relations. We can assign Susan R. 1 point for "authority figure relationships are inconsistent," although we have no data to suggest that Susan R. is unavailable/unwilling to positively relate to adult authority figures. Thus, for Part C, Susan R.'s score would be 1 point.

For Part D, "Educational," there are six components: poor attendance/not enrolled, disruptive school behavior, literacy problems, learning disability, withdrawn/expelled/suspended, and enrolled and failing. Susan R. has poor attendance at school, although she is not disruptive and has no literacy or learning disability problems. She has not withdrawn from school, nor has she been expelled or suspended. She is not failing her classes, despite her truancy. We would give her 3 points for poor attendance, but "0" points for the other subparts. Her score for Part D, therefore, would be 3 points.

For Part E, "Youth's Employment," since Susan R. is not "over 16," these subparts are not relevant for her. She receives a "0" for Part E.

For Part F, "Developmental Disability," Susan R. has no known developmental disabilities. Therefore, she will receive a "0" for this part.

For Part G, "Physical Health and Hygiene," Susan R. is in good physical health. She needs no health or hygiene education, and no obvious handicaps or illnesses limit her functioning. Therefore, she receives a "0" for Part G.

For Part H, "Mental Health," there are four subparts: assessment needed, prior history of mental health problems, currently in treatment, and assessment indicates treatment needs/no current services. Susan R. will receive 3 points because of the recommended mental health assessment. Furthermore, she is currently receiving psychological counseling for her substance-abuse problems. She receives 2 points for this subpart. Otherwise, no other points apply to Susan R. Part H, therefore, is scored as $3 + 2 = 5$ points.

Lastly for Part I, "Substance Abuse," an assessment of her substance-abuse problem is needed, and she is a frequent user of marijuana. Although a substance-abuse assessment is recommended and will likely be conducted, Susan R. is currently receiving mandatory substance-abuse counseling/treatment. We would score Part I as follows: $2 + 0 + 3 + 0 + 2 = 7$ points. This score accrues as follows:

Assessment needed?	Yes	2 points
Occasional user?	No	0 points
Frequent user?	Yes	3 points
Assessment indicates treatment needs/no services?	No (not yet, anyway)	0 points
Receiving treatment services?	Yes	2 points

If we sum the various parts, we would have the following cumulative score:

Part	Points
A	17
B	6
C	1
D	3
E	0
F	0
G	0
H	5
I	7
Total	39

Susan R.'s total needs score is 39 points.

Together with this needs assessment score of 39, we can use Susan R.'s risk score of 20 and determine where Susan R. should be placed in the Florida Department of Juvenile Justice Classification Matrix illustrated in Figure 9.2. This matrix cross-tabulates one's risk and needs scores, with one's risk score across the top and one's needs score down the left-hand side. Where these scores intersect in the body of the table defines the suggested nature of supervision Susan R. should receive by Florida juvenile corrections officials. Where a needs score of 39 (High) intersects with a risk score of 20 (High), a square is indicated with "Intensive," "Level 2," and "Level 4." Since we have no interpretive booklet from the Florida Department of Juvenile Justice, we don't know what these different levels mean, although we can glean that the levels range from 2 to 10, with 2 being the lowest level and 10 being the highest level. "Intensive" would suggest to us that Susan R. should receive intensive supervision, regardless of the program, community or institutional, where she is ultimately placed. We know from Susan R.'s scenario that the juvenile court judge disposed Susan R. to two years' probation, with mandatory psychological and substance-abuse counseling. No doubt there were other conditions, such as community service and/or restitution. This is because she stole a neighbor's car and wrecked it. Some compensation to the neighbor for the loss of the car will be provided. Susan R. will be expected to make some restitution for the car loss.

It should be emphasized that juvenile justice officials do not depend entirely on risk/needs instruments for their information about youth needs. Interviews with youths and their families are often conducted. Intake officers acquire extensive information about a youth's background. If certain youths are recidivists and have extensive juvenile records, some indication of their needs will already be on file. Thus, we will know what interventions have been applied in the past and whether these interventions have helped in any way. If not, then we might try alternative interventions and programs. Furthermore, the needs of male juvenile offenders often differ from the needs of female juvenile offenders. These gender differences are important and should be taken into consideration whenever assessment instruments are devised. Another source of information about youths and their needs comes from juvenile probation officers. These court officials compile information about a youth's background and furnish this material to juvenile court judges. Subsequently, dispositions are individualized according to the probation officer's report. This is known as a predisposition report.

Predisposition Reports

Assisting juvenile court judges in their decision making relating to sentencing juvenile offenders during adjudicatory proceedings are predisposition reports that are often filed by juvenile probation officers, especially in serious cases (Foley, 2008). Predisposition

9.1   Career Snapshot

Kristie M. Stake

Probation Officer, Elko County Juvenile Probation, Elko, Nevada

Statistics:
Bachelor's Degree in Social Work, University of Nevada;
POST Certified Instructor Training Coordinator

Background

As far back as I can remember, I envisioned a career in some form of law enforcement. When I was in college I went on a few ride-alongs with the Reno Police Department where my desire to enter into the field grew. I decided early on in my college education that I wanted to work with children and geared my curriculum toward social work in the event that a career in law enforcement did not pan out.

During the last year as an undergraduate, I had the opportunity of interning at the Carson City Juvenile Probation Department. I realized then that I had found my career preference and could not fathom finding something I would enjoy more. The department hired me as a probation officer aide, which pretty much meant I was a probation officer without the power of arrest and I had to run all my decisions by an official probation officer. I remained a probation officer aide for approximately one year when a probation officer position came open within the department. I applied for the position and was extremely thrilled when I was hired.

Work Experience

After working with the Carson City Juvenile Probation Department, my husband was offered a law enforcement position in Elko, Nevada. We relocated there and I was eventually hired as a probation officer for the Elko County Juvenile Probation Department.

When I first entered the field as an intern, I had a difficult time separating my personal feelings and the job. I believed every excuse and story I was told, and at times I went home depressed because of the home lives of families I worked with. Unfortunately, one consequence of this job is developing a jaded view of the world. Constantly I have to remind myself that not all juveniles are lying or scheming. There are those cases that pull at your heartstrings, but you have to have the ability to ask yourself if what you are doing is in their best interests or if it is because it will make you feel better.

A misconception some people have when dealing with juveniles is that they are "just kids," and at times you may let your guard down. You must keep in mind if choosing this career path that juveniles are very impulsive and rarely think before they act. Once I was in a meeting with one of my girls who was just kicked out of a counseling group. I told her she was going to jail, and as I was walking down the hall with her to the detention facility, she took off running. I was pregnant at the time and couldn't chase her. I had to call for police assistance, and they eventually apprehended her. What I should have done was called another probation officer into my office to escort her to detention.

Advice to Students

First and foremost, I would have to say that if you want to choose the field *parole* or *probation*, a degree is preferred if not mandatory in many departments. Although this does not necessarily make you better at your job, it will open doors for advancement and will also give you the "edge" when you are writing reports or testifying in court. When working on this degree, learning a second language is something I would recommend and personally wished I would have done, preferably one that is prevalent in your community.

You should involve yourself as much as you can with the occupation you are exploring. If you want to be a police officer, go on ride-alongs or volunteer in at the jail. If you want to be a probation officer, volunteer in the local detention center or any other juvenile facility. If internships are available in your field, take full advantage of these opportunities. If you are volunteering your time or you are an intern, never think that you are too good to do something. If you are diligent and do what is asked of you without complaining, the department is more likely to hire you if a position becomes available. If you are lazy and pick and choose what you want to do because you are waiting for more exciting things to happen, you may pass up your dream job. Law enforcement is not all glitz and glory. Much of the time you are dealing with people who are having the worst day of their lives and hate you. However, if you stick it out, you will likely help somebody more than you will ever know.

reports contain background information about juveniles, the facts relating to their delinquent acts, and possibly probation officer recommendations for particular dispositions. They serve the function of assisting judges in making more informed sentencing decisions. They also serve as needs assessment devices, where probation officers and other juvenile authorities can determine high-need areas for certain youths and channel them to specific community-based organizations and agencies for particular treatments and services.

The Predisposition Report and Its Preparation

Juvenile court judges in many jurisdictions order the preparation of **predisposition reports**, which are the functional equivalent of PSIs for adults. Trester (1981:89–90) has summarized four important reasons for why predisposition reports should be prepared:

1. These reports provide juvenile court judges with a more complete picture of juvenile offenders and their offenses, including the existence of any aggravating or mitigating circumstances.
2. These reports can assist the court in tailoring the disposition of the case to an offender's needs.
3. These reports may lead to the identification of positive factors that would indicate the likelihood of rehabilitation.
4. These reports provide judges with the offender's treatment history, which might indicate the effectiveness or ineffectiveness of previous dispositions and suggest the need for alternative dispositions.

predisposition reports
Documents prepared by juvenile intake officer for juvenile judge; purpose of report is to furnish the judge with background about juveniles to make a more informed sentencing decision; similar to the PSI report.

It is important to recognize that predisposition reports are not required by judges in all jurisdictions. By the same token, legislative mandates obligate officials in other jurisdictions to prepare them for all juveniles to be adjudicated. Also, there are no specific formats universally acceptable in these report preparations. An example of a predispositional report from New Mexico is shown in Box 9.2.

Several juvenile justice experts have described predisposition reports and their preparation. These reports contain much enriching information about youths and can be helpful to juvenile court judges prior to sentencing (Barfeind, 2008; Foley, 2008). Several aspects of a person's life are crucial for investigations, analysis, and treatment. These include (1) personal health, physical and emotional; (2) family and home situation; (3) recreational activities and use of leisure time; (4) peer group relationships (types of companions); (5) education; and (6) work experience. Predisposition reports are frequently recommended in all cases where the offenders are minors. However, the details required of predisposition reports, together with the limited resources of juvenile courts, limit their preparation to all but the most serious cases. There is no typical predisposition report in any U.S. jurisdiction (Foley, 2008).

Various characteristics are included in most predisposition reports. These include the following: (1) gender; (2) ethnic status; (3) age at first juvenile court appearance;

9.2   A Sample Predispositional Report from New Mexico

Children, Youth and Families Department Juvenile Justice Division

Identifying Information*

*Fictitious names used because of New Mexico confidentiality provisions

Name: Mary Gleaves
DOB: October 15, 1993
SSN: Not applicable
Address: 301 1st St.
Las Cruces, NM
Phone Number: (444)(555-1212)
P/G/C: Parents
Religious Preference: Unknown
Primary Language Spoken: English
Final Disposition: No contest plea
Final Disposition Date: Pending
AKA: Not applicable

Court Information

Completed By: Ann Jordan
Date Completed: October 10, 2007
Case Number: 123456
Cause Number: 7890
Judge: Hon. Mark VanMeter
County: McNabb
Defense Attorney: Charles Heffler
CCA: Unknown

I. Referral Information

Current Offense: On January 2, 2007 at 3:40 A.M., Mary Gleaves was taken (by her parents) to the hospital after she was bleeding profusely. Doctors there notified Mary Gleaves's parents that it was apparent that she had just given birth to a baby. The location of the baby was unknown at the time, and doctors suspected that Mary Gleaves had possibly killed the baby. Police were notified and searched her room where they found a full-term baby (deceased) in a trash can in Mary Gleaves's bedroom. Mary Gleaves allegedly told police that she did not know she was pregnant, but gave birth to the baby, by herself, on December 30, 2006. An autopsy report indicates that the baby girl, who was found with the umbilical cord still attached and wrapped around her neck, was alive at birth and died of asphyxiation. Mary Gleaves was arrested on January 11, 2007 and booked into McNabb County Jail, Juvenile Unit, at approximately 6:00 P.M.

On January 13, 2007, a petition was filed charging Mary Gleaves with: Count 1: child abuse (intentionally caused) (death); or in the alternative, child abuse (negligently caused) (death); or in the alternative, child abuse (negligently permitted) (death); and Count 2: tampering with evidence. Mary Gleaves's parents were able to post the 10 percent cash deposit of $10,000 bond, and Mary Gleaves was released home on January 14, 2007. A forensic evaluation was ordered at this time.

On September 22, 2007, Mary Gleaves entered into a plea agreement with the Children's Court Attorney. Mary Gleaves pleaded No Contest to Alternative Count 1: Child Abuse (Negligently Permitted) (Death). In exchange for the plea, the remaining counts in the petition were dismissed and the state agreed to handle the case in a juvenile setting. There was no agreement as to the disposition in the matter and a predispositional report was ordered.

Number of Co-offenders: 0
Victim Impact Mailed: ☐ Yes   ☐ No   ☐ Not applicable Response   ☐ Yes   ☐ No
Victim Requests Restoration:

Victim-Impact Summary: A victim-impact statement is not applicable in this case. It should be noted, however, that Mary Gleaves has given two names for the father of her child. Initially, Mary Gleaves told investigators that she had sexual intercourse with Walter Brooks and that the condom broke. She said she had taken a pregnancy test at Planned Parenthood with negative results. During this officer's conversation with Mary Gleaves, however, she indicated that the father is John Johnson. She said that Johnson denied that he is the father and that they do not have any contact with each other.

Chronological Report Attached: ☐ Yes   ☐ No
Currently on Probation/Parole: ☐ Yes   ☐ No Location:

Prior Supervision

Cause Number	Begin Date	Type	Length	Expiration	Release Date	Release Type
Not applicable	October 13, 2005	Informal supervision	3 months	January 12, 2006	January 12, 2006	Now supervising under conditional release

Comments: Mary Gleaves was placed on informal supervision after her first referral to the probation department in October 2005. Mary Gleaves was referred to juvenile probation for a citation she had received for criminal trespass. Mary Gleaves and her two sisters, who were cited as a group of teens, were caught loitering at Grady's, a restaurant and popular hangout for youths. Mary Gleaves came to see this officer at least one time every week, without fail. Mary Gleaves turned in weekly grade checks from school and attendance was verified.

Prior Commitment to Correctional Facility

Cause Number	Commit Date	Type	Length	Expiration	Dispatch Date	Dispatch Type
Not applicable	Not applicable	Not applicable	Not applicable	Not applicable	Not applicable	Not applicable

Comments: Mary Gleaves has had no prior commitments to correctional facilities.

Prior Youthful Offender: ☐ Yes   ☐ No
Outstanding Restitution: ☐ Yes   ☐ No   ☐ Amount: $0.00
Outstanding Community Service: ☐ Yes   ☐ No   ☐ Hours: 0

II. Social, Educational, and Substance-Abuse History

(Please include information on siblings, dependents, employment, parents' marital status, primary language spoken in home, current school status, special expectations, truancy, behavior problems, gang activity, weapons, extracurricular activities, alcohol, marijuana, and other drug use.)

A. Social

Mary Gleaves is the youngest of three daughters born to Martin and Jane Gleaves. Jean Gleaves is 19 years old, married, and living with her husband, William Smith, 21, and their infant son, Frederick. Olivia Gleaves, 18, lives in the family home along with Mary Gleaves. The family lives in a rented house in the Northeast Heights of Las Cruces and has for the past four years. The home is a three-bedroom home, which appears cluttered but clean. The front- and backyards seem moderately maintained, and the inside is well furnished. The ashes of Mary Gleaves's deceased baby sit on the fireplace mantel in an urn the shape of an angel. Baby Gleaves was cremated on January 28, 2007, after the Office of Medical Investigators released the body. For weeks after the incident, the mailbox outside the house and the cars belonging to the family and friends were decorated with tiny pink ribbons in remembrance of the baby. Mary Gleaves has moved out of the bedroom that she resided in at the time of the incident. Mary Gleaves's parents have moved into that room and report that Mary Gleaves is unable (emotionally) to go in there. As of May 1, 2007, Mary Gleaves was working at Best Industries. Mary Gleaves previously worked at McDonald's but lost her job shortly after the events of this case came to light. Mary Gleaves had to take four months off of work after the incident. She was an emotional wreck, making her "dysfunctional" and therefore unable to complete her job as expected. Taking this time off paid its toll on the family as well, and Martin Gleaves was forced to work even more at his job of 11 years. Martin Gleaves said that he had to "keep the family going" in a time when it seemed everything was falling apart. Mary Gleaves is currently working with her father at Best Industries, where she is working in the mail room. Mary Gleaves is currently considered a part-time employee, although she works 7.5 hours a day. Mary Gleaves has been there for three months and currently makes $6.50/hour. The remainder of her day is spent on her home schooling. Mary Gleaves spends much of her weekends babysitting her five-month-old nephew, Frederick.

Mary Gleaves attended Las Cruces Elementary School where her mother was the President of the PTA. Both Mrs. Gleaves and her father report that Mary Gleaves was a good student and did fine in elementary school. Once in middle school, Mary Gleaves attended Craig Middle School. She and her family lived in the south valley, and Mary Gleaves said she was one of the very few blonde-haired, blue-eyed girls there. Mary Gleaves reported that she did fine in school but had problems with peers because of her race. The family eventually moved, and Mary Gleaves began attending Burgess Middle School. Mary Gleaves reported no problems at Burgess. Once in high school, Mary Gleaves began attending informal student parties and she was very much into marijuana in her ninth grade year. Mary Gleaves became involved with a boyfriend, who proved to be a bad influence on her. After her ditching classes became a habit, Mary Gleaves was referred to a truancy officer and ordered to complete community service. Mary Gleaves reportedly got back on track after her parents placed her on more structure and restriction. By the time this incident took place, Mary Gleaves was seemingly doing much better. Mary Gleaves was in the midterm of her sophomore year when this incident occurred and did not return following her arrest in January 2007. Mary Gleaves plans to continue with her home schooling until graduation. Incidentally, Mary Gleaves has done very well in this program and is now classified as a Junior, ahead of her schedule in mainstream educational setting. Mary Gleaves's sister, Olivia, left her school after the incident as well when the publicity brought adverse reactions from her peers. Olivia, however, has since returned to the school and reportedly is not having any problems there. Jean Gleaves graduated from school before any of these circumstances arose.

As mentioned earlier, Mary Gleaves was referred to the probation department on one other occasion. In July 2005, police officers working a tac-plan in the northeast heights cited Mary Gleaves and her sisters for trespassing at a local restaurant. Officers were working in an effort to reduce the number of young people loitering in the various parking lots. Mary Gleaves and her sisters were at Grady's when the three of them were cited. Mary Gleaves came in to see this officer for her preliminary inquiry on October 13, 2005, and was placed on informal supervision. Mary Gleaves made weekly visits with this officer, called in regularly, and turned in school reports as requested. There does not appear to be any other legal history with the family; however, it has been reported that things have been tense at home.

There does not appear to be any physical evidence in the home; however, it has been reported that there is tension and that marital conflict is present. According to the forensic evaluation, dated January 20, 2006, there were frequent fights about issues relating to the three daughters, money, and dad's drinking. Martin Gleaves has been said to have a "long-standing alcohol abuse Hell." Counseling was offered initially to help cope with the surrounding offense and any issues exacerbated by it; however, Martin Gleaves advised that he does not need any more counseling. Martin Gleaves reports that he will support Mary Gleaves throughout her counseling, but that he has no intention of continuing himself. Martin Gleaves reported that he does not believe the incident should be "dwelled on" and that "you have to go on, or it will tear you up." It was unclear whether Martin Gleaves would participate in further counseling or not.

Initially, Martin Gleaves sought counseling services for his family through the Employee Assistance Program that his employer provides. This program only allowed for five visits, and the family quickly exhausted that service. Dr. Martha Jordan, a private psychologist, was recommended, and Mary Gleaves has been seeing her for some time now. Mary Gleaves sees Dr. Jordan every two weeks, but no other family member attends. Mary Gleaves's sessions are on average one hour at a time. Mary Gleaves reports that she likes Dr. Jordan and feels comfortable working with her.

Mary Gleaves has admitted to using substances in the past, such as marijuana and acid. It is this officer's understanding that Mary Gleaves used acid on an experimental basis only and that marijuana was her drug of choice while in the ninth grade. It is also this officer's understanding that Mary Gleaves has not used any marijuana since June 2006. It is a concern, however, that Mary Gleaves admits to using alcohol on New Year's Eve 2005. This apparently took place at the house with her parents present along with other friends drinking as well. It is concerning that Mary Gleaves's parents would allow minors to drink in their home. This was not typical, however, according to Mary Gleaves, but rather something of a celebration of the upcoming new year. Mary Gleaves advised her parents allow drinking on special occasions only.

B. Education/Employment

Diploma
☐ HS Diploma   ☐ GED Certificate
Graduation Date: Pending   GED Date: Not applicable

Special Education
☐ Eligible for special education   ☐ Ineligible for special education   ☐ May require special education
Qualifications for Special Education: Not applicable
Level: Not applicable   Effective Date: Not applicable

C. School History

School Name	Type	Program	Program Type	Grade/Special Education	Start Date
Harcourt Learning Direct	Home school	Mail/correspondence school	Regular education	10	March 1, 2007

Comments: As mentioned earlier, Mary Gleaves is doing well in school and is now classified as a Junior in high school. Mary Gleaves mails in her school work and completes the assignments that she is provided through the Harcourt Learning Direct Program. Mary Gleaves has goals of completing her high school education and eventually obtaining a degree in automobile mechanics.

D. Mental Health/Substance Use History

Treatment
☐ Prior treatment inpatient   ☐ Prior treatment outpatient   Date of Last Psychological
                                                                        Evaluation: April 17, 2006

Substance Use
☐ Alcohol   Frequency: Special occasions
☐ Marijuana   Frequency: Daily in the past
☐ Drugs   Frequency: Experimental
☐ Solvents   Frequency:
☐ Date Updated: November 7, 2006

Comments: Please refer to Section II above for details.

III. Juvenile Probation and Parole (JPPO) Overview Recommendation

(Include core services, P/G/C and client's view of needs, issues and strengths, treatment/residential placement, JPPO areas of concern and community-based service required if removal of client from home is recommended.)

Mary Gleaves appeared to be very nervous about the outcome of this case. Mary Gleaves acknowledged that she would like to continue working and complete her education. Mary Gleaves described herself as a very caring person who is "good minded" and prides herself in her good grades and employment history. Mary Gleaves's father was equally complimentary in his description of Mary Gleaves. Martin Gleaves described Mary Gleaves as a hard worker, energetic, focused, and good with chores at home, never having to be reminded to do them. The only negative issue that Mary Gleaves and her father could pinpoint was her need to stay on track with school. Nothing was mentioned in regard to counseling or the deep issues associated with the death of her child.

It is difficult to ascertain what Mary Gleaves's thoughts are about the incident itself. It is unfortunate that she was able to plead No Contest in that she now can keep her side of the story to herself. It has been very difficult to assess the situation given that much of the very important information will never have to be given by Mary Gleaves. It impedes treatment as well by not having to talk about the incident or specific actions in the matter as long as that is the case. Mary Gleaves's own state of mind is at risk. As Dr. Jordan described it, "Mary Gleaves has been greatly limited in her ability to work with other students, as she has not been permitted to talk about the offense." Dr. Jordan has been hampered in her ability to investigate with Mary Gleaves and her family the causes of the offense and to directly address them. When weighing the distinction between retribution, safety of the public, and the best interest of the child, it is difficult to suggest that incarceration is the most appropriate outcome. Mary Gleaves has been afforded the opportunity to show that she can comply with the structure and rules that the probation department can provide and she has done that. Incarcerating her at this point would serve no purpose other than punishment, and this could impede the treatment process even further. Dr. Jordan feels that Mary Gleaves does not lack the capacity for empathy and concern for others. Further, it is this officer's understanding that Mary Gleaves does not pose a threat to anyone. The amount of denial in this case is insurmountable and the plea agreement encourages it. It is imperative that Mary Gleaves be allowed to engage in therapy to the point that she can talk about the incident and work, with her parents, to move past this and begin the lengthy process of intensive therapy. It is equally important that Mary Gleaves's family engage in therapy. According to the forensic evaluation, a likely factor in Mary Gleaves's situation is the stress in the family characterized by parental alcohol abuse, depression, and chronic marital conflict. The results of these family problems affected the whole family. Mary Gleaves, it has been reported, is deficient in coping skills, judgment, problem solving, and decision making. Mary Gleaves, according to the forensic evaluation appears to be "overwhelmed by especially stressful circumstances, and to ill-judged behavior at such times." Mary Gleaves, it reports, "does not seem to be a girl with antisocial or prominent aggressive tendencies, or characteristic tendencies toward remorseless use of others." Given these findings, it would seem appropriate to think

that with support and supervision, and with intense therapy to recognize these contributing factors, Mary Gleaves would seem to be a low risk for repeat offenses and danger to others.

It is this officer's recommendation that Mary Gleaves be given a term of probation for an extended period of time to be determined by the court, but that addresses these crucial elements. It is highly recommended that Mary Gleaves be monitored closely to determine her progress and participation. It is also recommended that Mary Gleaves's parents be made party to the petition and monitored for their compliance in therapy as well. A referral to the Juvenile Intensive Probation Supervision (JIPS) program could also be made to address what could be a rocky transition from intense publicity of this case back to more routine circumstances. It is also recommended that Mary Gleaves continue with intense psychotherapy and address specifics of the incident. The probation department would ideally work with the therapist in maintaining compliance and progress. Incarceration at this point would serve no other purpose than to address punishment and retribution. These issues could be served in the context of probation supervision just as well, while allowing Mary Gleaves to obtain the therapy that she desperately needs. Periodic judicial reviews could be used to further monitor compliance and progress. Community service is advised and possible options with meaningful results could be explored through the context of therapy.

IV. Clinical Social Worker Comments

(Must be completed for mandatory referrals and court order.)
    Please refer to forensic evaluation dated January 20, 2007.

Respectfully Submitted,

_____

Jane Brown, JPPO

Clinical Social Worker

Approved: _____

_____

Chief JPPO/Supervisor

(4) source of first referral to juvenile court; (5) reason(s) for referral; (6) formal court disposition; (7) youth's initial placement by court; (8) miscellaneous court orders and conditions; (9) type of counsel retained; (10) initial plea; (11) number of prior offenses; (12) age and time of initial offense; (13) number of offenses after first hearing; (14) youth's total offense number; (15) number of companions, first offense; (16) number of detentions; (17) no-contact recommendations, and (18) number of out-of-home placements (Barfeind, 2008). A no-contact recommendation may be ordered by the court. It is illustrated by Figure 9.4.

Figure 9.4   No Contact/Association Defined

COMMUNICATION: Communication in any form is contact. This includes verbal communication such as talking, and/or written communication such as letters, notes, messages, etc.

DIRECT CONTACT: One-on-one contact. This includes in person visits, touching, talking on the phone, letters, written notes, E-Mail, and/or making proximity contact.

PROXIMITY CONTACT: Being in the proximity (visual or physical presence) of a person (such as in the same house, yard, store, restaurant, vehicle, room, church, movie theater, etc.) where communication could be established. This includes driving by, following and/or waiting outside the home, property, place of employment, school, church and/or daycare of the victim/prohibited party.

INDIRECT CONTACT: Making contact through another person (such as friends or family) to send messages, pictures, and deliver or receive packages, gifts, notes, money, etc.

NON-VERBAL CONTACT: This includes waving, smiling, sign language, mouthing words, facial or body language, and obscene gestures.

SUPERVISED CONTACT: When an offender is allowed to have contact with the victim/prohibited party under prearranged conditions and times. These conditions and times must be approved **in writing prior to the contact.** Contact can only be approved by the supervising P.O. Your counselor or attorney <u>cannot</u> give approval.

I understand I am **not to contact or associate** (as defined above) with the victim/prohibited party until I receive written permission by the Court/Parole Board/Supervisory Authority and/or my Parole & Probation Officer. I understand that because of the nature of my offense, I have lost my privilege to have contact with the victim/prohibited party at this time. I understand it is **MY RESPONSIBILITY** to make every attempt to avoid contact with the victim/prohibited party. I also understand that if the victim/prohibited party attempts contact with me I am not to respond to or acknowledge them.

_____   _____
Parolee/Probationer Signature   Date

_____   _____
Parole & Probation Officer Signature   Date

Not all juvenile courts require the preparation of predisposition reports. They take much time to prepare, and their diagnostic information is often limited, since juvenile justice system budgets in many jurisdictions are restricted. In many respects, these reports are comparable to **PSIs** filed by probation officers in criminal courts for various convicted adult offenders.

In recent years, various juvenile justice reforms have been implemented in many juvenile courts. Some of these reforms have been mandated by U.S. Supreme Court decisions regarding more extensive rights of juvenile offenders. Greater uniformity in

PSIs
Inquiry conducted about a convicted defendant at the request of the judge; purpose of inquiry is to determine worthiness of defendant for parole or sentencing leniency.

handling and less disparity in sentencing are desirable outcomes in the aftermath of extensive informal juvenile processing that characterized the juvenile courts of previous decades. Nevertheless, there continues to exist a great deal of individualism exhibited among juvenile court judges in different jurisdictions and how the various laws and decisions pertaining to juveniles should be interpreted.

Victim-Impact Statements in Predisposition Reports

victim-impact statement

Appendage to a predisposition report or PSI that addresses the effect of the defendant's actions against victims or anyone harmed by the crime or delinquent act; usually compiled by the victim.

Predisposition reports may or may not contain a **victim-impact statement**. PSIs that are prepared for adults who are convicted of crimes in criminal courts are the adult equivalents of predisposition reports. It is more common to see such victim-impact statements in PSI reports, although some predisposition reports contain them in certain jurisdictions. These statements are often prepared by victims themselves and appended to the report before the judge sees it. They are intended to provide judges with a sense of the physical harm and monetary damage victims have sustained, and thus, they are often aggravating factors that weigh heavily against the juvenile to be sentenced.

Since 1992, however, there has been a trend among state legislatures to increase the rights of victims of juvenile crime (Herman and Wasserman, 2001). By 1996, 22 state legislatures had enacted legislation addressing the victims of juvenile crime (Erez and Laster, 1999). This state legislation addresses the role of victims in various ways, including the following:

1. Including victims of juvenile crime in the victim's bill of rights.
2. Notifying the victim upon release of the offender from custody.
3. Increasing opportunities for victims to be heard in juvenile court proceedings.
4. Expanding victim services to victims of juvenile crime.
5. Establishing the authority for victims to be notified of significant hearings (e.g., bail disposition).
6. Providing for release of the name and address of the offender and the offender's parents to the victim upon request.
7. Enhancing sentences if the victim is elderly or handicapped (Torbet et al., 1996:48). States enacting such legislation include Alabama, Alaska, Arizona, California, Connecticut, Florida, Georgia, Idaho, Iowa, Louisiana, Minnesota, Montana, New Mexico, North Dakota, Pennsylvania, South Dakota, Texas, Utah, Virginia, and Wyoming.

A strong consideration when enacting this legislation is the matter of restitution to victims. Restitution is increasingly regarded as an essential component of fairness in meting out dispositions for juvenile offenders. Offender accountability is heightened as restitution is incorporated into the disposition, especially if there was some type of property loss, damage, physical injury, or death. In reality, however, many states continue to haggle over how reparations will be imposed on either the youths or the families or both.

Some states have incorporated into their juvenile statutes high dollar limits relating to parental liability whenever their children destroy the property of others or cause serious physical injuries. The theory is that if parents are held accountable, they will hold their own children accountable. Thus, reparations assessed against parents for the wrongdoing of their children is an indirect way of preventing delinquency, or so some state legislatures have contemplated. Another accountability measure is to include victim-impact statements to these reports. This makes judges aware of the true nature and extent of victim injuries and/or financial losses suffered because of the juvenile perpetrator. These statements are not obligatory, but they do assist judges in determining which dispositions should be imposed.

It happened in West Palm Beach, Florida. On Wednesday, May 16, 2001, a jury in West Palm Beach, Florida, convicted Nathaniel Brazill, 14, of second-degree murder in the shooting death of a teacher, 35-year-old Barry Grunow. Brazill was also convicted of aggravated assault for pointing a .25-caliber semiautomatic pistol at a math teacher as he fled.

Brazill could be sentenced up to 25 years in prison for the conviction. Brazill sat without emotion as the jury delivered its verdicts. He frowned as each verdict was read. Brazill had shot Grunow once between the eyes in the doorway of the teacher's Lake Worth Middle School classroom on May 26, 2000, after being sent home for throwing water balloons just before summer vacation. Bob Hatcher, the school principal, expressed relief over the verdict, saying that the justice system

worked. He said, "The jury found a verdict. I think it was a very fair and equitable trial." Brazill had claimed that the gun went off unintentionally. During the trial itself, he showed some emotion, crying after the prosecutor asked him what had happened to Grunow after the shooting. Brazill had left school and returned later with the weapon, which he used to kill Grunow. He said he wanted to talk to his girlfriend in Grunow's classroom. What can school officials do to prevent such violence in the future? Should all schools have metal detectors through which students must pass? Should we make all schools in America similar to airport security? What do you think? [Source: Adapted from Amanda Riddle and the *Associated Press*, "Boy Who Shot Teacher Convicted of Second-Degree Murder," May 17, 2001.]

Summary

Dispositions of juvenile offenders following the conclusion of an adjudicatory hearing consist of several options available to juvenile court judges, ranging from nominal to custodial sanctions, with or without conditions. Those receiving harsher sanctions have usually been adjudicated of more serious violent offenses. Dispositional options also appear related in some instances to extralegal factors, such as gender, race, ethnicity, and/or socioeconomic status, although the literature relating to this issue is inconsistent. Some of these inconsistencies were explored.

Juvenile court judges consider both aggravating and mitigating circumstances whenever deciding which dispositions to impose. Aggravating circumstances are any factors that make one's offense more serious. Mitigating factors are also considered. These factors decrease the seriousness of one's offense or mitigate it. Both types of factors were described.

Most states have constructed risk assessment measures. These measures attempt to forecast the risk a juvenile may pose if released or if placed in a particular therapeutic program. The greater the risk posed, the greater the supervision required. One objective of risk assessments is to determine one's type of supervision. Sometimes, selective incapacitation is used to describe detention or incarceration of those offenders deemed most dangerous to society.

Needs assessments are also made. These are also instruments that determine one's particular circumstances and needs and indicate particular interventions or social services. Almost every risk and needs instrument is flawed in one respect or another. Some juveniles may be incarcerated who should not be incarcerated. Also some juveniles may receive nonincarcerative dispositions when incarceration is what they require. Persons believed to be dangerous but are not actually dangerous are called false positives. Those who are considered nondangerous but turn out to be dangerous anyway are called false negatives.

Three general types of prediction have been identified. These are actuarial prediction, anamnestic prediction, and clinical prediction. Studies comparing the effectiveness of all prediction schemes show that they exhibit little differences in their overall effectiveness at predicting one's future behaviors successfully.

Risk instrumentation varies greatly among jurisdictions. However, most risk instruments share several common elements. Risk criteria usually include age, prior record of delinquent or status offending, number of prior commitments to juvenile facilities, escapes from those facilities, drug or chemical dependencies, alcohol abuse, family relationships and stability or instability, school adjustment problems and academic performance, and peer relationships. One major purpose of such instrumentation is classification. Classification enables authorities to place youths in programs that seem most helpful as treatments for particular youths.

Predisposition reports are also prepared, often by juvenile probation officers. These reports are similar to PSIs prepared for criminal offenders. These documents assist judges in their decision making since the juvenile probation officer often makes a dispositional recommendation based on the report's contents.

Key Terms

actuarial prediction, 276
aggravating circumstances, 271
anamnestic prediction, 276
classification, 278
clinical prediction, 276
dangerousness, 273
false negatives, 275
false positives, 275
first-offender, 269
flat time, 272
mitigating circumstances, 272
needs assessment, 274
overrides, 288

prediction, 273
predictors of dangerousness and risk, 274
predisposition reports, 293
PSIs (presentence investigation reports), 299
repeat offender, 269
risk, 273
risk/needs assessment instruments, 274
selective incapacitation, 274
victim-impact statement, 300
Violent Juvenile Offender Programs (VJOPs), 269

Questions for Review

1. How do first-offenders and repeat-offenders differ? How does being a first-offender as opposed to a repeat-offender make a difference in how one's dangerousness or risk is assessed?

2. What are aggravating circumstances? What are several types of aggravating circumstances? How might these circumstances affect judicial decision making in a juvenile's disposition?

3. What are four mitigating circumstances? How do judges use these mitigating circumstances to lessen one's punishment?

4. What are some major differences between risk instruments and needs assessments?

5. What is meant by selective incapacitation? How is it used? What are false positives and false negatives? How do such designations occur?

6. What are the three types of predictions? Which ones are most effective and why?

7. What is a predisposition report? Who prepares this report? How are such reports used for determining a juvenile's disposition?

8. What is a victim-impact statement? How is it used to modify the severity of one's disposition?

9. What are VJOPs? What are their functions?

10. What are some moral and ethical questions that have been raised about selective incapacitation? Is selective incapacitation successful? Why or why not?

Internet Connections

Bibliography on Gang Culture
http://www.streetgangs.com/bibliography/gangbib.html

Center for Community Development
http://socialwork.rutgers.edu/cscd.html

Center for the Prevention of School Violence
http://www.learnnc.org/bestweb/cpsv

Debt to Society
http://www.motherjones.com/prisons/

Helping.org
http://www.ideafinder.com/guest/madlist/amd-helping.htm

Help My Teen
http://www.helpmyteen.com/

Teenage Curfews
http://www.mapletreepublishing.com/Parenting/Teenagerse_curfews.htm

Youth Activism Project
http://www.youthactivism.com

Youth Alternatives, Inc.
http://www.volunteersolutions.org/volunteer/agency/one_177937.html

chapter 10

Nominal Sanctions

*Warnings, Diversion, and
Alternative Dispute Resolution*

As the result of reading this chapter, you will accomplish the following objectives:

1. Understand what is meant by nominal dispositions.
2. Learn about several important juvenile dispositions, including diversion and alternative dispute resolution, as well as their functions and dysfunctions.
3. Understand what is meant by teen courts and why teen courts are important in delinquent offender processing.
4. Learn about day treatment centers and how they operate in communities as important services for juveniles.

 ## Case Study

B.H. is a 13-year-old ninth grader at a Plano, Texas, high school. In June 2008, B.H. was discovered in the boys' restroom flushing several rolls of tissue down the toilet. Already he had flooded the lavatory floor with water. B.H. had been in trouble at the school before for minor infractions. He broke scoring pencils for examinations. He scratched blackboards with a paint scraper. School officials contacted the Plano Police Department about B.H. and they suggested a teen court to deal with him. Within the next few weeks, a teen court was convened at a local community center at 6:00 P.M. with B.H. and his parents in attendance. B.H. admitted guilt in the flooding incident and was ultimately ordered to perform 20 hours of community service. The community service related to cleaning debris from local city parks and recreational areas. B.H. is now free of the juvenile justice system and has no juvenile record. [Source: Adapted from The City of Plano, "Teen Court Works for High School Vandal," July 28, 2008.]

 ## Case Study

J.K. is a 14-year-old youth who does not respect the property of others. J.K. lives in Phoenix, Arizona, in an affluent neighborhood. One evening in May 2008, J.K. and some friends returned from a party at 2:30 A.M., and when his friends drove into his driveway, they drove over a flower garden belonging to a neighbor. The garden was ruined, but the youths simply dropped off J.K. and drove away. Coincidentally, a woman saw the incident from across the street from her bedroom window and reported it to the neighbors the next morning. The neighbors contacted J.K.'s parents and J.K. admitted to the incident, but he refused to name the boys who drove him home. A police investigation of the property damage followed. J.K. was sent to a community center where he participated in an alternative dispute resolution program. He agreed to pay for the replacement costs of the neighbor's flower garden in lieu of a formal court proceeding. All parties seemed satisfied with how the matter was resolved. [Source: Adapted from the Superior Court, Maricopa County, Arizona, "Justice Is an End, Not the Means," July 29, 2008.]

Introduction

A youth floods bathroom toilets with tissue paper in a high-school bathroom. Another youth destroys a neighbor's flower garden. Are either of these cases worthy of a prosecution in a juvenile court?

This chapter examines a broad range of dispositional options available to juvenile courts known as nominal sanctions, diversion, and alternative dispute resolution (ADR). These types of sanctions or dispositions are applied only for those juveniles considered to pose the least amount of risk to others or are considered low-risk first-offenders unlikely to recidivate. The first part of the chapter defines nominal dispositions. Nominal dispositions are typically verbal warnings issued by judges in lieu of any formal adjudication for either status offending or delinquency.

Many juveniles are diverted from the juvenile justice system through deferred prosecution and diversion. Diversion is defined and discussed. There are many types of diversion programs. One shared feature of these programs is that they attempt to provide constructive interventions in the lives of youths that will hold them accountable for their actions without the formality of juvenile court processing. Different types of diversion programs are described, together with their general functions and dysfunctions for juveniles. The use of teen courts, youth courts, or peer courts is increasing not only in the United States but internationally. In 2005, there were over 1,000 teen courts in the United States, and by 2008, there were nearly 2,000. Teen courts are described in detail, including their respective strengths, weaknesses, and applications. Several teen courts are illustrated to show how the youth court process functions.

The next section of this chapter describes day reporting centers. Located in one's community, day reporting centers offer an extensive array of services and assistance to youths. The goals and functions of day reporting centers are described. Several examples of day reporting centers are given, together with an estimate of their successfulness in treating and supervising less serious juveniles.

The chapter concludes with an examination of ADR and restorative justice. These types of programs are known collectively as victim–offender mediation programs. Mediation programs are intended to unite victims and their youthful victimizers for constructive purposes. These programs offer youths the opportunity to face their victims and accept responsibility for their actions. The functions, uses, and operations of victim–offender mediation programs will be examined.

Nominal Dispositions Defined

Nominal dispositions are verbal and/or written warnings issued to low-risk juvenile offenders, often first-offenders, for the purpose of alerting them to the seriousness of their acts and their potential for receiving severe conditional punishments if they ever should reoffend. These sanctions are the least punitive alternatives. Nominal dispositions may be imposed by police officers in their encounters with juveniles. These verbal warnings or reprimands are often in the form of stationhouse adjustments, where youths are taken into custody and released to their parents later, without a record being made of the incident.

Juvenile court judges are encouraged in most states to utilize the least restrictive sanctions after adjudicating juveniles as delinquents, status offenders, or children in need of supervision (CHINS). The use of incarceration as a sanction is within the judicial powers of juvenile courts, although these courts are obliged and encouraged to seek other options as sanctions. Secure confinement as a disposition may be overused, but public safety seems better served to the extent that many juveniles can remain at home within their communities, where a more therapeutic milieu exists for them to become rehabilitated. One community-based option in Delaware is the Delaware Bay Marine Institute (DBMI), a program that emphasizes sea-related activities and underwater skills. While the results of this research were inconclusive, the fact remains that there are viable alternatives to incarcerating juveniles that may work as good as or better than simply incarcerating them (Brandau, 1992). For some juveniles, even better alternatives include doing little or nothing other than issuing certain verbal warnings or reprimands.

For example, intake officers may also use nominal dispositions against certain juveniles, if it is perceived that they merit only verbal warnings instead of more punitive sanctions. If petitions against certain juveniles are filed, depending upon the circumstances, judges may find them to be delinquent as alleged in these petitions. However, these adjudications do not automatically bind judges to implement conditional or custodial sanctions. Thus, judges may simply issue warnings to adjudicated juveniles. These warnings are serious, especially after a finding that the juvenile is delinquent. Juveniles with prior records face tougher sentencing options if they reoffend in the same juvenile court jurisdiction and reappear before the same judges. Actually, various juvenile court actors engage in the process of attempting to forecast a youth's behavior if certain actions are taken or not. Some persons have created decision trees to operationalize this process. Ashford and LeCroy (1988) suggest the decision tree shown in Figure 10.1.

This juvenile aftercare decision tree begins with the question of whether the youth is violent. Depending upon the answer to this question, either "yes" or "no," the tree branches two different ways where other questions are posed. Notice that if the answers to successive questions are "yes," the degree of restrictiveness recommended to the juvenile court increases. The more "no" answers suggest less restrictiveness. This tree merely conceptualizes court thinking, particularly following an adjudication. However, actors may utilize similar decision trees much earlier in the system. For instance, intake officers and prosecutors may use **diversion** for some youths.

diversion
Official halting or suspension of legal proceedings against criminal defendants after a recorded justice system entry, and possible referral of those persons to treatment or care programs administered by a nonjustice or private agency.

Diversion

The Juvenile Justice and Delinquency Prevention Act of 1974, and its subsequent amendments, was intended, in part, to deinstitutionalize status offenders and remove them from the jurisdiction of juvenile courts. Another provision of this Act was to ensure that all other adjudicated delinquent offenders would receive the least punitive sentencing options from juvenile court judges in relation to their adjudication offenses. In fact, the National Advisory Committee for Juvenile Justice and Delinquency Prevention declared in 1980 that juvenile court judges should select the least restrictive sentencing alternatives, given the nature of the offense; the age, interests, and needs of the juvenile offender; and the circumstances of the conduct. Thus, judicial actions that appear too lenient are the result of either federal mandates or national recommendations.

Diversion is not new. It is regarded as a form of deferred prosecution where offenders, especially low-risk ones, can have a chance to prove that they are law-abiding persons. An early instance of diversion was created by Conrad Printzlien, New York's first chief probation officer. Printzlien was concerned that many youths were stigmatized by rapid prosecution and conviction, and thus he set out to find an alternative to unnecessary and unwarranted incarceration of juveniles. The result was the Brooklyn Plan, a deferred prosecution program that provided a way to distinguish situational offenders from more serious chronic and persistent juvenile delinquents. Between 1936 and 1946, 250 youths were handled as divertees. The program proved successful at decreasing recidivism among divertees and eventually was operated in other cities besides New York.

According to some persons, a primary, intended consequence of diversion is to remove large numbers of relatively minor offenders from juvenile court processing as quickly as possible. However, other professionals caution that one unintended consequence of diversion is the development of wider, stronger, and different nets. This means, in simplest terms, that those youngsters diverted from the

Diversion may involve participation in community programs where assistance from others is given.

Figure 10.1   Juvenile Aftercare Decision Tree (from Ashford and LeCroy, 1988)

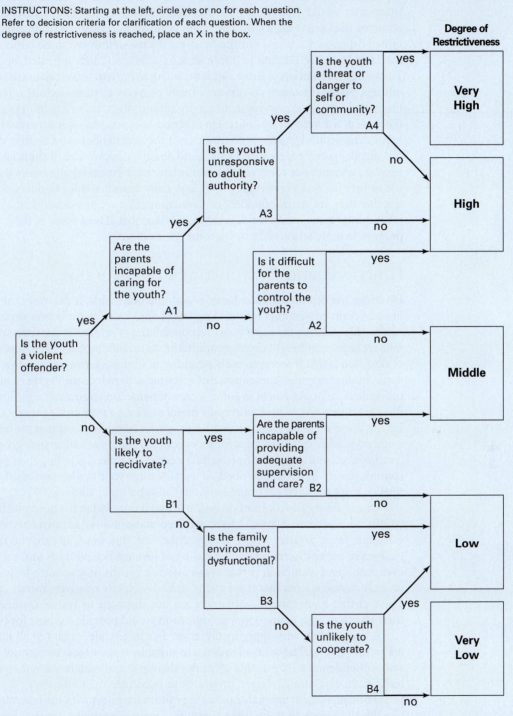

INSTRUCTIONS: Starting at the left, circle yes or no for each question. Refer to decision criteria for clarification of each question. When the degree of restrictiveness is reached, place an X in the box.

Source: From Jose B. Ashford and Craig Winston LeCroy "Decision Making for Juvenile Offenders in Aftercare," p. 49, vol 39 (1988). Reprinted with permission by Juvenile Family Court Journal and the National Council of Juvenile and Family Court Judges.

formal juvenile justice system are captured in nets formed by the community-based agencies. Thus, if we view social control in its broadest terms, this means that more, not fewer, children will fall under some form of social control through diversionary programs.

Some authorities say that diversion of offenders should be aimed at the client population that would otherwise have received formal dispositions if diversion had not occurred (Gavazzi et al., 2000). This client population consists of youths who have committed delinquent acts and not simply status offenses. However, some critics say that status offenders may escalate to more serious offenses if left untreated by the system. Therefore, intervention of some sort is necessary to prevent this escalation of offense seriousness. Status offenders do not necessarily progress to more serious offenses. Sometimes, their apparent involvement in more serious offenses is a function of relabeling of the same acts differently by police. On other occasions, status offenders may be upgraded to misdemeanants by juvenile court judges if they fail to obey valid court orders. If a status offender is ordered to attend school and doesn't, this provides the judicial grounds for issuing a contempt of court citation, a misdemeanor. Not everyone favors this particular use of juvenile court contempt power, especially against status offenders. Regardless of whether they are status offenders or have committed serious delinquent acts, divertees often exhibit some recidivism. Therefore, it is true that at least some of these divertees do progress to more serious offenses as some critics allege.

Functions and Dysfunctions of Diversion

Diversion has certain logistical benefits and functions. First, it decreases the caseload of juvenile court prosecutors by shuffling less-serious cases to probation departments. Of course, this increases the supervisory responsibilities of probation departments who must manage larger numbers of divertees in addition to juvenile probationers. Another function of diversion is that it seems to reduce recidivism in those jurisdictions where it has been used. Another intended consequence of diversion is to reduce the degree of juvenile institutionalization or placement in either secure or nonsecure incarcerative facilities. A fourth function is that diversion is potentially useful as a long-range crime prevention measure. Finally, diversion reduces certain youth risks, such as suicide attempts as the result of being confined in adult jails or lockups for short periods. The stress and anxiety generated as the result of even short-term confinement for certain juveniles, including their propensity to commit suicide, has been described. At least for some youths, diversion assists in avoiding the stresses of confinement or prosecution (Gallagher and Dobrin, 2007).

One of the dysfunctions of diversion is that it may widen the net by including some youths who otherwise would have received stationhouse adjustments by police or warnings from juvenile court judges. Much of this net-widening occurs through changes in police discretion and relabeling of juvenile behaviors as more serious, however. Another dysfunction is that some affected youths may acquire beliefs about the juvenile justice system that it is lenient and will tolerate relatively minor lawbreaking. The fact that many juvenile offenders are not disposed to secure confinement until their fourth or fifth delinquency adjudication would provide support for these beliefs.

A key problem with applying diversion on a large scale is that not all status offenders or low-level delinquent offenders are suitable as divertees. We cannot say that all status offenders are alike or that all minor delinquent offenders share the same characteristics. In order for diversion programs to maximize their effectiveness, they should target offenders most amenable to having minimal contact with the juvenile justice system. Ideally, we ought to be able to identify certain youths who are at risk of becoming more-serious delinquent offenders or dangerous adult criminals. This means that it is necessary to identify particular factors that qualify certain youths as being at risk (Bernat, 2005). Thus, diversion could be selectively applied, depending upon whether certain youths possess more risk characteristics than others (Loukas, Suizzo, and Prelow, 2007). Net-widening would be minimized and the sheer operating costs would be reduced substantially (Kennedy, 2005).

Diversion Programs for Juveniles

The Diversion Plus Program

An alternative to formal court processing for status and less-serious delinquent offenders is the **Diversion Plus Program**. This program was established in Lexington, Kentucky, in July 1991 and operated until November 1992 (Kammer, Minor, and Wells, 1997:52). Besides reducing recidivism among its clients, the goal of the program was to promote conformity to the law without stigmatization. Eligibility requirements were that youths had to be (1) between the ages of 11 and 18, (2) charged with a status or less-serious delinquent offense, and (3) free of any prior record of delinquency.

The entire program consisted of eight separate sessions during a two-month period, Monday through Friday, from 6:00 to 9:00 P.M. Group size was limited to 12 persons. The first few sessions were designed to orient clients and teach them to work as a group. A variety of exercises were used to promote interpersonal trust and cooperation. The needs of program participants were assessed initially, and one-on-one counseling and small-group interaction emphasizing active learning occurred through hands-on projects. Each session emphasized a core curriculum: building self-esteem and self-control, improvement in decision-making processes, independent-living skills, career exploration, substance-abuse prevention, recreation, and team challenges (p. 52). After learning about a particular topic (e.g., independent living), participants used the knowledge acquired to complete specific tasks (e.g., budgeting money). A points system was used to encourage compliance with the requirements. Points could be earned for participating and completing requirements, and points could be lost for noncompliance. Persons could use their points at the end of the program to purchase items in an auction during the final evening. Also, a $100 gift certificate was given to the person earning the most points.

During the Diversion Plus Program, there were 94 participants. Half were female, and the average age was 14.5 years. Subsequently, 81 clients graduated from the program. Most of the 13 nongraduates terminated the program because of noncompliance. A follow-up showed that 63 percent of the graduates were subsequently rearrested for various charges. Interestingly, the rearrests of status offenders most often involved delinquent offenses. This finding shows, at least for this sample, that some offense escalation occurred. However, the escalation was from status offending to minor delinquent offending. No strong pattern of escalation to felonious offenses was detected. Thus, it cannot be said in the present instance that high levels of program involvement and completion are sufficient to ensure low recidivism. However, the investigators conjectured that had this program not been available, more youths would have penetrated the juvenile justice system further with perhaps more serious types of offending (p. 54).

> **Diversion Plus Program**
> Established in Lexington, Kentucky, in 1991, designed to reduce recidivism and promote conformity to the law without stigmatization; includes first-offenders, low-risk delinquent offenders, and any youth without a prior juvenile record.

> **See Our Side (SOS) Program**
> Juvenile aversion program in Prince George's County, Maryland, designed to prevent delinquency.

See Our Side Program

In Prince George's County, Maryland, a program was established in 1983 called **See Our Side (SOS) Program** (Mitchell and Williams, 1986:70). SOS is referred to by its directors as a juvenile aversion program and dissociates itself from shock programs such as Scared Straight. Basically, SOS seeks to educate juveniles about the realities of life in prison through discussions and hands-on experience and attempts to show them the types of behaviors that can lead to incarceration. Clients coming to SOS are

Youth programs may involve learning skills such as home remodeling and handiwork.

referrals from various sources, including juvenile court, public and private schools, churches, professional counseling agencies, and police and fire departments. Youths served by SOS range in age from 12 to 18, and they do not have to be adjudicated as delinquent to be eligible for participation. SOS helps any youth who might benefit from such participation.

SOS consists of four, three-hour phases. These are described below:

Phase I: Staff orientation and group counseling session where staff attempt to facilitate discussion and ease tension among the youthful clients; characteristics of jails are discussed, including age and gender breakdowns, race, and types of juvenile behavior that might result in jailing for short periods.

Phase II: A tour of a prison facility.

Phase III: Three inmates discuss with youths what life is like behind bars; inmates who assist in the program are selected on the basis of their emotional maturity, communications skills, and warden recommendations.

Phase IV: Two evaluations are made: an evaluation of SOS sessions by the juveniles and a recidivism evaluation for each youth one year after they participated in SOS. Relative program successfulness can therefore be gauged.

An evaluation of the program by SOS officials in 1985 found that SOS served 327 youths during the first year of operation and that a total of 38 sessions were held. Recidivism of program participants was about 22 percent. Again, this low recidivism rate is favorable. Subsequent evaluations of the SOS program showed that the average rate of client recidivism dropped to only 16 percent. The cost of the program was negligible. During the first year, the program cost was only $280, or about 86 cents per youth served.

The Community Board Program

Reparative Probation Program
Voluntary civil mediation agenda involving minor offenders, where mediators determine fair compensation to victims through a series of meetings.

mediation
A process whereby a third party intervenes between a perpetrator and a victim to work out a noncriminal or civil resolution to a problem that might otherwise result in a delinquency adjudication or criminal conviction.

mediator
Third-party arbiter in ADR.

One innovation introduced by the Vermont juvenile courts is the **Reparative Probation Program**, which is a civil **mediation** mechanism. This program involves first- and second-time juvenile offenders who have been charged with minor offenses, often property offenses, where damage to or loss of property was sustained by one or more victims. The Community Board Program uses volunteers to meet with both offenders and their victims as an alternative to a full juvenile court adjudicatory hearing (Karp, 2001). Mediation is conducted wherein a mutually satisfactory solution is arranged by the **mediator**.

One of the positive aspects of this program is that victims can meet and confront their attackers. Victims may become involved and empowered. Their face-to-face encounters with youths who victimized them enable victims to tell them of the harm they caused. In a selective way, the mediation program was successful. That is, some types of juveniles directly benefited from their confrontation experience. This type of mediation program doesn't seem to work well with particularly youthful offenders. Older juveniles have higher maturity levels and are more responsive to mediation (Bannan, 2008).

Implications of Diversion Programs for Juveniles

One result of the Juvenile Justice and Delinquency Prevention Act of 1974 was to deinstitutionalize status offenders and remove them from the jurisdiction of juvenile courts. This has been done in some jurisdictions, but not in all of them. One result is that there is much variation among jurisdictions about how juvenile offenders are

Career Snapshot   10.1

Chanda Galloway Miller

Coordinator, City of Holland Teen Court, Holland, MI

Statistics:
B.A. (English education), Hastings College (Hastings, NE);
J.D., University of South Dakota

Background

I did not set out in life to become a lawyer. My goal was teaching English to middle-school students. I have a heart for teens. They are in a vital stage of development and discovery, full of energy, and terribly vulnerable, unknown to themselves. While I did teach in middle school, my career path has been varied since.

Twelve years after receiving my B.A., I entered law school. By then my son was in elementary school. My husband's work responsibilities required us to live quite a distance from the university, so I commuted all three years. After being in private practice in South Dakota for a few years, we moved to Michigan, where I joined another private practice. While doing so, I heard of an opportunity to teach part-time at a local college in business law and, since I had missed teaching, I got onboard and taught for a couple of years. Another move brought us to Iowa where I chaired a paralegal program at a community college. This was an excellent combination of teaching and law that I enjoyed enormously. As my husband's career evolved, we then began working internationally. Our first assignment was in Jakarta, Indonesia, where we lived for five years. There I joined an international law office where I worked with the young attorneys to improve their English and their writing and case management skills. Our next assignment was in Beijing, P.R. China, where I lived for three years and again did some teaching of business law to university students before we decided to again establish a home in the United States.

We chose to return to Michigan since our son, now married, was living here. After examining the local job opportunities, it became apparent that there wasn't a lot of call for someone who hadn't practiced law in the United States for over eight years, so I decided to change to a lifestyle of volunteering. It wasn't long until an announcement in the newspaper led me to the position of Teen Court Coordinator.

Experiences

Our Teen Court program is one of the oldest in the country, having started in 1991. It is also entirely operated by volunteers. Referrals to the program from the police and prosecutor's office come to me. Since participation in the program is voluntary, one of my first responsibilities is to meet with the teen offender and his/her parents/guardians to review the process and obtain signatures on a consent form. Since we require the offenders to plead guilty and not use lawyers, they opt to give up some important rights.

One of the most interesting parts of the interview is talking with the teen about the offense committed. I would have already seen the police report, but hearing their version of the events is always revealing. I always preface this by telling them it will be the first question they are asked in court, so they get to have a practice run by telling me what happened. There are times when the answer is quite eye-opening for the parents as well. With some regularity, information is given to me that the parents haven't heard previously. I then review the court process in detail to be certain that everyone is clear on what will happen, what the consequences may be, and stressing the confidentiality of the proceedings.

We conduct trials in a regular county courtroom after the court has closed for the day. I escort offenders and families in and out, review procedures with them, and handle all the necessary paperwork for the proceeding. Watching the demeanor of the teens as they actually enter the courtroom is fascinating. Quite often, kids who've been giving me a lot of attitude during the interview and prior to trial undergo an amazing transformation as they enter the courtroom door. This is a sobering experience.

Sitting in on the trials and listening to the questions of the jurors is one of the best parts of this work. I quickly reached the conclusion that while a teen offender may be very capable of misleading an adult or presenting dishonest answers to an adult's questions, this does not happen with other teens. The jurors seek the truth, know when they aren't hearing it, and ask the questions necessary to make it come out. They seek to get to know more about the offenders than just what they did wrong, inquiring about school, after-school activities, relationships with friends and family, and the impact their arrest has had not only on them but on their families. This is often another moment of considerable impact on the offenders as they quite often haven't really considered the effects of their action, especially on younger siblings. Jurors inquire about consequences given at home as a result of the arrest. If told the offender was grounded, they may ask what specifically that entailed, how long it was supposed to last, and whether it actually continued that length of time. Once the sentence is announced, I follow up with the offenders to provide them information on likely locations for them to perform community service hours, always a part of our sentences, as well as other details. We do not set up community service for the offenders; that is their responsibility. We are fortunate to be in a community with a large number of not-for-profit organizations making it easier for the students to locate placement.

A source of great satisfaction for me is seeing an offender seize this opportunity to clear his/her record, carry out the consequences assigned in a timely manner, and move forward with a different attitude. We have had a number of kids who found locations for their community service where they enjoyed serving and continued volunteering there. Juries may make recommendations along with their sentences. When we have an offender take those to heart and make positive changes such as becoming involved in after-school activities, it greatly increases their likelihood of success and makes all of us smile. The most difficult times are when an offender gets back into trouble immediately after going through our process. We offer a wonderful opportunity for teens to start fresh and when they fail to do so, it is disappointing to all of us who are involved.

I vividly recall one young man a few years ago who came to us on a disorderly conduct charge for some poor behavior choices. Meeting with him and his parents, I found him to be deeply troubled and showing behavior that I found indicative of a need for major counseling intervention at the very least. A week later when they appeared for his trial, they informed me that the night before he had again been arrested, this time for graffiti. He told his parents he had been spraying graffiti in an effort to handle the stress caused by the upcoming trial. Looking into his eyes that night, I already knew the future was likely to be a downward spiral, as his parents seemed oblivious to the depth of his problems despite my urging them to seek counseling for him immediately.

We recently tried a girl in her junior year of high school. She had stopped attending classes, taken up tobacco use, and was then arrested for shoplifting. During the proceedings, she demonstrated enormous disrespect for her mother, a single parent, and testified to a number of clashes between the two of them. When she left the courtroom, we all agreed it was likely she would soon be in trouble again. Within two weeks, her mother phoned to inform me she had again been arrested and this time was incarcerated in a county juvenile facility. She chose to forfeit the opportunity provided by teen court.

Advice to Students

There are no magic bullets when working with juveniles. Positive peer pressure can be significant. Youth courts throughout the country are built on that principle. Statistics are instructive but are no substitute for actually seeing a kid grow and change. Juveniles often make poor decisions but must be responsible for the consequences. After working in this field for awhile, it is easy to become jaded. Try to view each offender individually. You can make a difference. Each time you reach a young person and help change his/her behavior pattern, you also reach everyone in that teen's sphere of influence. The ripple effect is amazing. There is no stereotype for juvenile offenders. Don't think of them in clichés.

---

processed and treated. In recent years, however, an increasing number of juvenile courts have imposed dispositions according to offender needs as well as according to what is just and deserved. Better classifications of offenders need to be devised. Additional information is needed about offender characteristics, their backgrounds, and specific circumstances in order that proper punishments and treatments can be imposed by juvenile court judges. For diversion programs to be successful, they must be targeted at the most successful juvenile candidates. Most frequently, these are low-risk, first-offenders or juveniles who are quite young.

Some diversion programs, especially for youthful sex offenders, include some rather stringent conditions and may even involve participation in intervention projects designed to remedy certain manifested problems. Some participants may receive individual, group, and family counseling and other therapies. Youths may also be exposed to psychophysiological assessments and various testing procedures (Bouhours and Daly, 2007).

Juvenile courts have come under attack in recent years as the result of what the public considers excessive judicial leniency in dealing with youthful offenders. Often, juvenile cases are dismissed. This occurs not only during formal adjudicatory proceedings by juvenile court judges but also by intake officers in earlier screenings of offenders. Thus, it is unreasonable to identify any specific part of the juvenile justice process as unusually lenient in juvenile case processing. All phases of the system seem to be influenced by the rehabilitative philosophy.

In addition to charges of being too lenient with offenders and dismissing or diverting their cases, the juvenile court has been targeted for other criticisms. Critics say that the juvenile court has failed to distinguish adequately between less-serious and more-serious offenders, it has often ignored the victims of juvenile violence, it has often failed to correct or rehabilitate juveniles in a manner consistent with its manifest purposes, it has been unconcerned or complacent about juvenile offenders and how they should be punished, it has confined children at times in adult jails, it has failed often to protect juveniles' rights, its services have been too thinly spread, and it has been too resistant to self-examination and suggestions for improvement. But one criticism of these criticisms is that, collectively, they do not apply to any single juvenile court at a particular point in time. Rather, they are loosely distributed and shared by many juvenile courts. By the same token, there are many juvenile courts operating with few serious flaws.

The goals of diversion can be achieved more effectively, according to some authorities, if divertees are obligated to accept responsibility for their actions through restitution or community service. When youths must do something constructive and repay victims for damages to property, they learn valuable lessons concerning their actions and how they affect others. Sometimes diversion coupled with other program elements has been termed creative diversion and is used throughout the United States in diverse jurisdictions.

teen courts
Tribunals consisting of teenagers who judge other teenagers charged with minor offenses, much like regular juries in criminal courts, where juvenile prosecutors and defense counsel argue cases against specific juvenile offenders; juries decide punishment with judicial approval.

Teen Courts

Increasing numbers of jurisdictions are using **teen courts** as an alternative to juvenile court for determining one's guilt and punishment. Teen courts are informal jury proceedings, where jurors consist of teenagers who hear and decide minor cases. First-offender cases, where status offenses or misdemeanors have been committed, are given priority in a different type of court setting involving one's peers as judges. Judges may divert minor cases to these teen courts. Adults function only as presiding judges, and these persons are often retired judges or lawyers who perform such services voluntarily and in their spare time. The focus of teen courts is upon therapeutic jurisprudence, with a strong emphasis upon rehabilitation. One objective of such courts is to teach empathy to offenders. Victims are encouraged to take an active role in these courts. Youths become actively involved as advisory juries (Peterson, 2005).

Teen courts are also known as youth courts, peer courts, and student courts (Preston and Roots, 2004). In 1997, there were 78 active teen courts. By 2005, there were 1,019 youth-court programs operating in juvenile justice systems, schools, and community-based organizations throughout the United States, with an anticipated 2,000 youth courts being established over the next few years (Peterson, 2005).

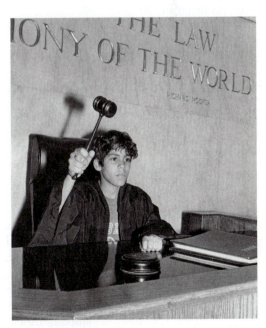

Teen courts are used increasingly to settle minor offending.

10.2   Resolution by American Probation and Parole Association in Support of Youth Courts

In 2004, the American Probation and Parole Association adopted the following resolution in support of youth courts:

Whereas, youth courts, also known as teen courts, peer courts, and student courts, are one of the fastest growing crime intervention and prevention programs in the nation.

Whereas, youth volunteers under the supervision of adult volunteers act as judges, jurors, clerks, bailiffs, and counsel for youth who are charged with minor delinquent and status offenses, problem behaviors or minor infractions of school rules, and who consent to participate in the program.

Whereas, youth courts engage the community in a partnership with the juvenile justice system, youth programs, schools, attorneys, judges, and police departments working together to form and expand diversionary programs responding to juvenile crime and problem behavior.

Whereas, youth courts increase the awareness of delinquency issues and problem behavior on a local level and mobilize community members, including youth, to take an active civil role in addressing the problem. Youth courts exemplify the practices of empowering youth through involvement in developing community solutions to problems, teaching decision making and applying leadership skills.

Whereas, youth courts design effective program services and sentencing options that hold youth accountable, repair the harm to the victim and the community, and contribute to public safety.

Whereas, youth courts promote attitudes, activities, and behaviors that create and maintain safe and vital communities where crime and delinquency cannot flourish; and youth court practices provide a foundation for crime prevention and community justice initiatives, as well as embrace the principles of restorative justice.

Therefore, be it resolved, that the American Probation and Parole Association hereby recognizes the importance of youth courts to our communities and recommends that probation, parole, and community supervision agencies support and assist in the formation and expansion of diversionary programs, known as youth courts.

Source: Reprinted with permission from "Resolution in Support of Youth Courts," *APPA Perspectives* 28:8 (2004a).

The Use of Teen Courts

Among the first cities to establish teen courts were Seattle, Washington, and Denver, Colorado (Rasmussen, 2004). Subsequently, teen courts have been established in many other jurisdictions, including Odessa, Texas. In Odessa, for instance, juveniles are referred to teen courts for Class C misdemeanors and minor traffic violations. Defendants range in age from 10 to 16. Traffic citation cases result in teen court referrals by municipal judges, who give youths the option of paying their fines or having their cases heard by the teen court. If youths select the teen court for adjudication, then they do not acquire a juvenile record. The teen court listens to all evidence and decides the matter (Peterson, 2005). Juvenile participation in teen court is usually preceded by a referral. A referral order to a teen court used by Wisconsin is shown in Figure 10.2.

Figure 10.2   Teen Court Referral

A|D|R

CENTER

Alternative Dispute Resolution Services and Training

TEEN COURT REFERRAL FORM

Teen/ Court is for first-time offenders only. Once we receive the referral, our office will verify that the student is a first-time offender. The student must also be enrolled and attending school full-time.

[Student has been cleared as a first-time offender by: _____ _____]
                                                         Last Name   Date

Referred by: _____   Referral Date: ____/____/____

Agency: _____   Phone #: _____

Student name: _____   DOB: ____/____/____ Age:_____

School: _____ Grade: _____   Race: _____ Sex: _____

Parent/Guardian: _____   Phone: (_____) _____-_____

Address: _____   Zip: _____

(Please circle type of crime)

Charge: _____   Victimless Crime—Person Crime—Property Crime

Date and time of incident: ____/____/_____   _____:_____

Explanation of charge:

_____

_____

_____

_____

_____

_____

Victim: _____ Parent: _____   Phone: _____

Address: _____   DOB: _____

Witness: _____   Phone: _____

Address: _____   DOB: _____

Please attach citation and other reports. Include any witness and/or victim statements.

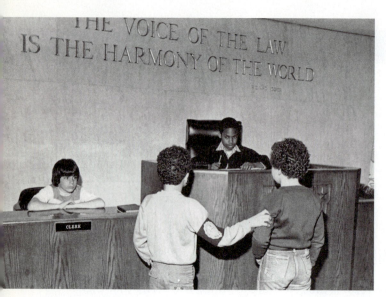

Teen court dispositions are always related closely to community service as well as jury service (Karp, 2004). Thus, juveniles who are found guilty by teen courts may, in fact, serve on such juries in the future, as one of their conditional punishments (Rasmussen, 2004). Or they may be required to perform up to 22 hours of community service, such as working at the animal shelter, library, or nursing home; picking up trash in parks or ball fields; or working with various community agencies. The teen court program in Odessa has been very successful. Prior to using teen courts, the recidivism rate for all juvenile offenders in the city was between 50 and 60 percent. However, teen court adjudications all but eliminated this recidivism figure. Interestingly, juveniles who are tried by the teen court often develop an interest in the legal system. Teen courts place a high priority on educating young people about their responsibilities of being individuals, family members, and citizens. As a part of one's diversion, conditional options such as restitution, fines, or community service may be imposed in those cases where property damage was incurred as the result of the juvenile's behavior (Chapman, 2005). Juvenile court judges must exercise considerable discretion and impose dispositions that best meet the juvenile's needs and circumstances. Two detailed examples of the workings of teen courts are the Anchorage Youth Court (AYC), Alaska, and the Holland Teen Court (HTC), Michigan.

The Anchorage Youth Court (AYC)

By 2005, there were over 1,000 teen courts established in most states (Peterson, 2005). These courts are not always known as teen courts. In Anchorage, Alaska, for instance, a teen court program was established in 1989 and exists today as the **Anchorage Youth Court (AYC)**. Subsequently 14 other youth courts have been established in various Alaska cities and modeled after the AYC (Anchorage Youth Court, 2005). Funding for youth courts in Alaska varies. AYC receives one-third of its funds from federal block grants, United Way, and program fees; one-third from fund-raising and donations; and one-third from the Anchorage Assembly. The AYC targets first-offenders and makes extensive use of volunteers from the community. The protocol of the AYC is outlined below.

Anchorage Youth Court (AYC)

Teen court established in Anchorage, Alaska, in 1999; cases include minor misdemeanor offenders; juries of one's peers decide punishments, after defendants admit guilt in advance of trial proceedings; sanctions include restitution and community service.

Intake and No-Contest Pleas. At the intake stage, a decision is made whether to recommend a youth for AYC. Not all youths are eligible. Youths with extensive juvenile records or who are charged with extremely serious felonious offenses are usually prohibited from participating in AYC. For low-risk, first-time juveniles, however, they may be offered the opportunity to enter "no-contest" pleas and attend AYC for sentencing. A no-contest plea means that the youth admits to the offense and avoids formal adjudication by a juvenile court judge. An appointment date is scheduled for the youth's subsequent appearance before the AYC for sentencing. The AYC utilizes volunteers from grades 7 to 12 who serve in different capacities. Thus, youths who volunteer may serve as prosecutors, defense counsels, judges, clerks, bailiffs, and jurors for youths who have committed misdemeanors and minor felonies. There are three AYC juvenile judges who hear each case and impose a punishment or sentence. Offenders and their parents are given a detailed list of instructions about when to appear, where, and how to behave while the AYC progresses. These instructions pertain to a courtroom dress code, courtroom decorum, courtroom attendance, and client contact. Also covered in detail is a list of consequences for not following AYC courtroom guidelines. If youths scheduled for AYC fail to appear, such nonappearances will be taken into account at a subsequent rescheduled sentencing hearing. The conduct of all participants, including judges, is also governed. An ethics committee has sanctioning power over all court officers who fail to appear for AYC duty. All AYC sessions are tape-recorded. Thus, the AYC is like a court of record in the event a dispute arises later over what was said or if any evidence presented is questioned.

The Sentencing Options. The following sentencing options are available to impose on any defendant: (1) AYC classes, including anger management class, defensive driving class, property and theft crimes class, skills for life class, "Start Smart" and "Stay Smart" classes, victim impact class, and weapons safety class; (2) apology letter to family; (3) apology letter to victim; (4) community work service (CWS); (5) diversity awareness; (6) drug/alcohol assessment; (7) essay; (8) fire prevention program; (9) jail tour; (10) juvenile anti-shoplifting program, parent–adolescent mediation, restitution, and victim–offender mediation.

No-Contest Script. A no-contest script is presented to the defendant, the prosecutor, defense counsel, and the judges. This script is shown in Figure 10.3.

The AYC no-contest script outlines the entire protocol for the AYC proceeding. The defendant is advised that one or more persons have been appointed to defend him/her. Prosecutors are named. Although AYC uses three-judge panels, sometimes two-judge panels are permitted, with defendant approval. The charging document is read, outlining all charges against the defendant as well as the defendant's admissions to all offenses alleged. The defendant is asked whether the facts outlined in the charging document are true and enters a no-contest plea.

Prosecution and Defense Sentencing Recommendations. Both the prosecution and the defense have the opportunity to examine the case, the facts, and the circumstances and make a recommendation to the AYC judges. Both prosecutors and defense counsels are provided with prep lists that outline their specific duties and options. These prep lists are quite specific, and defense counsels go over them with their clients to make sure all procedures are understood fully. Both sides also have access to the list of sentencing options noted earlier in this section. This listing is also detailed, and it describes the nature of each sentencing option. In the process of considering the case, both sides examine the AYC Sentencing Matrix, which includes a listing of both aggravating and mitigating factors. These are shown in Figure 10.4.

Figure 10.4 not only lists aggravating and mitigating factors that may be considered by both sides but also lists a sentencing matrix for calculating CWS hours. Every youth processed by AYC performs a certain number of CWSs determined by the seriousness of the offense and the presence or absence of aggravating and mitigating circumstances.

Figures 10.5 and 10.6 show the defense's and prosecution's sentencing recommendations, respectively. These recommendations take into account any and all aggravating and mitigating factors from both the defense's and the prosecution's point of view.

It is not unusual for the defense and prosecution to disagree about which aggravating or mitigating factors should be counted or how many CWS hours should be performed. Both sides can recommend that the defendant should write an essay of a specified length, make restitution, attend one or more classes as needed, and engage in other activities.

Probation Officer's Recommendation, Victim Impact Statement, and Recommendation to Judges. A juvenile probation officer may prepare the equivalent of a predispositional report for any particular juvenile and make a recommendation. A probation officer's recommendation may be given considerable weight or it may be discounted. All of this information is considered by the judges, who ultimately decide the nature and amount of punishment to impose.

Figure 10.3   Anchorage Youth Court No-Contest Script

ANCHORAGE YOUTH COURT NO-CONTEST SCRIPT

1.   "This is the case of State of Alaska versus __[defendant's name]__; case number 04- __[case #]__. Is the defendant present in the courtroom?"

2.   "Mr./Ms. __[defendant's last name]__, the record reflects your true name as _____, spelled _____. Is this information correct?
    a.   [*If YES*] "Then let the record stand."
    b.   [*If NO*] "Please spell your name for the court."... "Let the record stand correct."

3.   "You have the right to have an Anchorage Youth Court attorney and (one has/two have) been appointed to represent you."
    a.   "At this time, will defense counsel please identify themselves."
    b.   "Will the prosecutors please identify themselves."

4.   [*If there are only 2 judges present, state:*] "For the record, there are only 2 AYC judges present. You have the right to have your sentence decided by 3 AYC judges. Please confer with your attorney and decide whether you agree to proceed with 2 judges or want to reschedule for a time when 3 judges are available." [*If the defendant want to reschedule, recess the case.*]

5.   "You entered into Anchorage Youth Court by signing an agreement at Juvenile Intake."
    a.   "Please look at a copy of this agreement in your attorney's case file."
    b.   "Did you read and understand this agreement prior to signing it?"
    c.   "Did you knowingly and willingly sign this agreement of your own free will?"
    d.   "The charge(s) in the agreement is/are _____." [*Read the charge(s) from the McLaughlin Agreement, NOT the charging document.*]
    e.   "Do you understand that you pled no-contest to (this charge/these charges) at Juvenile Intake?"
    f.   "Defense counsel, are you satisfied that the defendant knowingly and willingly signed the agreement with a full understanding of its content and the jurisdiction of Anchorage Youth Court, and that this was his/her own free will?"

6.   "__[Defendant's name]__, having knowingly, willingly and voluntarily signed the agreement with Anchorage Youth Court and agreeing to plead no contest at Juvenile Intake to the charge(s) of _____, it is hereby ordered that the agreement between __[defendant's name]__ and the Anchorage Youth Court is made a part of the record of this proceeding."

7.   "Mr./Ms. __[defendant's last name]__, please rise for the reading of the charging document. Count I . . ." [*Read the charging document.*] "Mr./Ms. __[defendant's last name]__, do you agree that (this is/these are) the same charge(s) you pled no contest to at Juvenile Intake?"

8.   [*If the charge in the charging document is different from what the defendant pled no-contest to at Juvenile Intake, look in the file for a "Change of Charge" form. If there is a "Change of Charge" form, State:* "The charge has been changed from _____ to _____. The effect of this change is __[from the "Change of Charge" form]__. Do you understand this change and do you agree to plead no-contest to __[the new charge]__?" [*If the defendant says no, recess court and call the legal advisor.*]]

9.   "Will the prosecution team please present to the court the probable cause statement, the elements of the charge(s) and the evidence you would bring against the defendant if this case went to trial."

Figure 10.3   Anchorage Youth Court No-Contest Script (Cont.)

10.   "Mr./Ms. ___[defendant's last name]___ , do you understand the case the prosecution has against you?" [*If the defendant says no, ask defense counsel what the defendant doesn't understand so that you can explain it.*]

11.   "Since the defendant has pled no-contest, we will go immediately into a sentencing hearing."
    a.   "Will the prosecution team please present its sentencing recommendation, including any aggravating and mitigating factors, <u>any recommendation from the probation officer</u> and <u>any statement written by the victim</u>."
    b.   "Will the defense team please present its sentencing recommendation. This includes information about the defendant, any mitigating factors and information from the probation officer reports."
    c.   [*Ask any questions needed for clarification.*]

12.   [*If a sentencing agreement has been presented,*
    a.   "Mr./Ms. __[defendant's last name]__ , do you understand the sentencing agreement?"
    b.   "Did you voluntarily sign this agreement?"
    c.   "Were any promises made to you which are not included in the agreement?"
    d.   "Do you understand that, if we follow this agreement, you do <u>not</u> have a right to appeal the sentence?"]

13.   "Mr./Ms. [defendant's last name], at this time you have the right to address the court on your own behalf. This is purely optional and we will not hold it against you if you choose not to do so. Keep in mind that your words are the last thing we will hear before deliberating your sentence. Would you like to take advantage of this opportunity?" [*If you return to the courtroom for any reason prior to reading the sentence, repeat this step, allowing the defendant to have the last word.*]

14.   "We will now adjourn to chambers for deliberation of sentence. Court is in recess."

15.   [*The judges' decision must be unanimous. Completely fill out the sentencing order prior to returning to the courtroom. Give the sentence and reasons behind it. Be sure to state what aggravating and mitigating factors you accepted and why.*] "You have the right to immediately move for reconsideration of this sentence. You also have the right to file a written appeal within 5 working days. Please consult with your attorneys now and then us know whether you accept this sentence or seek immediate reconsideration of the sentence."

16.   [*If the defendant moves for reconsideration, listen to the argument and give the prosecution a chance to respond. You do <u>not</u> have to allow unlimited responses to responses. You do <u>not</u> have to allow the defendant to address the court again. You do not have to adjourn to chambers to decide a motion for reconsideration, but you may and you should if your deliberation will take more than a minute or if you disagree among yourselves. <u>If you change the sentencing order, initial the changes.</u> A defendant <u>still</u> has the right to appeal even if he/she moves for reconsideration.*]

Hand the sentencing order to the clerk or bailiff before leaving the courtroom.

12/30/03 C:\MyDocuments\AYC Cases\Case File Forms\AYC-judge_script

Figure 10.3   Anchorage Youth Court No-Contest Script (Cont.)

ANCHORAGE YOUTH COURT SENTENCING MATRIX

Class B felony and all firearm offenses	*48 CWS hours*
Class C felony	*40 CWS hours*
Class A misdemeanor	32 CWS hours
Class B misdemeanor	24 CWS hours
Theft of $15 or less	12 CWS hours

Add 5 hours for an official misdemeanor prior. Add 10 hours for an official felony prior.
Add 10% for each aggravating factor. Subtract 10% for each mitigating factor.
Matrix and the listed factors are suggested, not mandatory, guidelines.

AGGRAVATING FACTORS

1. A person suffered physical injury as a result of defendant's conduct.
2. The defendant was the leader of a group which committed the crime.
3. The defendant possessed a dangerous instrument during the commission of the crime.
4. The defendant committed an assault offense against someone physically weaker.
5. The defendant's conduct created a risk of injury to three or more persons.
6. The defendant has committed an unreported crime (misdemeanor or felony-level crime) in the past.
7. The offense has more that one victim. (A company, store or business only counts as one victim.)
8. The conduct was the most serious type of offense within its class, approaching the next most serious class of offense. (**Example:** Theft of $49 in merchandise is the most serious in its class, since theft in the fourth degree is defined as theft of less than $50. The crime is close to the next class, theft in the third degree). If the crime is theft in the second degree, the AYC guidelines for determining "most serious" are from $500-$3000, regardless of the official definition of theft in the second degree.
9. The crime was committed against someone:
   within the defendant's household (someone who regularly resides in the house);
   who s/he is related to;
   who lives in the neighborhood; or
   to whom s/he owes a duty, has a special relationship with, or who has specifically entrusted him/her.
     (E.g., robbing a family the defendant baby-sits for).
10. The defendant targeted the victim because of the victim's race, religion, or other discriminatory factor.
11. The defendant was 16 years or older at the time of the crime.
12. The defendant was accompanied by, or influenced by one or more persons younger than s/he during the commission of the crime.
13. If the crime is burglary or criminal trespass, the building was occupied.
14. The crime was committed at night (between sunset and sunrise) or, in the summer months, between the hours of 9 P.M. and 6 A.M.
15. The defendant used drugs and/or alcohol before committing the crime, or possessed drugs and/or alcohol, or committed the crime in order to buy drugs and/or alcohol, or if a theft crime, stole something which was illegal for the defendant to possess (e.g., cigarettes).

MITIGATING FACTORS

1. The defendant has no history of trouble, reported or unreported, with the authorities or police.
2. The defendant fully admitted upon initial confrontation by police, parents, school, authorities, or anyone the defendant could reasonably anticipate would promptly inform authorities.
3. The crime was principally committed by another person.
4. The defendant was accompanied, influenced, or pressured by an older person to commit the crime.
5. The defendant was less than 15 years of age at the time of the crime.
6. In an assault case, the defendant was provoked by the victim.
7. The conduct was among the least serious in its class. (Example: Theft of $52 in merchandise is the least serious in its class, since theft in the third degree is defined as a theft between $50 and $500. The crime is close to the next lower class, theft in the fourth degree.)
8. The defendant made restitution to a victim before the defendant knew the crime had been reported to authorities.
9. The defendant assisted authorities to discover the identity and role of others who participated in the crime.

Revised 7/10/2002

Source: Reprinted with permission from the State of Alaska Juvenile Court.

Figure 10.4   Anchorage Youth Court Sentencing Matrix

HOW TO DETERMINE COMMUNITY WORK SERVICE HOURS

The following guidelines explain how to determine community work service hours in each case. These are only <u>GUIDELINES</u>. The attorneys may deviate from the guidelines as the individual case requires.

AYC SENTENCING GUIDELINE PROCEDURES

The intent of the AYC guidelines is to establish some degree of uniformity in sentencing offenders who commit similar crimes to similar sentences. However, sentencing must be an individualized process. No two crimes are ever the same. No two offenders are ever the same. The sentencing judges have the ultimate duty to balance the factors, the impact on the victim, the need to express community condemnation, and impose a fair and just sentence. Justice rarely can be achieved by rigid application of mathematical formulae. The intent of these guidelines is to **establish a range** within which sentencing judges may balance the variables that may be present in a case. The benchmark will be expressed in terms of hours of community work service.

A.   Duties of attorneys.

At the sentencing hearing, the prosecution and defense will present their sentencing recommendations to the court, including the amount of community work service (CWS) hours.

The prosecution team must also present to the judges the aggravating factors that it believes apply to the case. (The prosecution team may present mitigating factors that it finds, if it is advantageous to do so.) The defense team must present mitigating factors that it believes apply to the case. The written list of aggravating and mitigating factors is **not an exclusive list**. If the attorneys believe that factors which are not listed should be considered, they are free to bring them to the court's attention. The attorneys may present witnesses during the sentencing hearing, if they choose.

Finally, the prosecution and defense teams should present any McLaughlin Juvenile Intake probation officer recommendations and argue the merits of the recommendations. (Probation officer recommendations are not binding on the court.)

B.   Court Procedures.

The sentencing court shall first determine the applicable benchmark sentence for the given crime by referring to the sentencing matrix. The court shall next determine the number of aggravating and mitigating factors only if they are supported by **clear and convincing evidence**.

1.   How To Determine Aggravating and Mitigating Factors.

The court shall determine the number of aggravating and mitigating factors which apply to the case by subtracting the mitigating factors from the aggravating factors. Should the result of this subtraction yield a net number of aggravating factors, the court may, but need not, aggravate the sentence by 10%, expressed in number of CWS hours, for each net aggravating factor. Should the result of subtraction yield a net number of mitigating factors, the court may, but need not, mitigate the sentence by 10% for each net mitigating factor. In no case should the sentence be adjusted by more than 50% from the benchmark sentence as a result of aggravating or mitigating factor adjustment.

<u>EXAMPLE:</u>   Assume that a defendant is to be sentenced for a crime for which the benchmark is 40 CWS hours. The court finds three aggravating factors and one mitigating factor. The result is two net aggravating factors. The court may, but need not, aggravate the sentence by 20%. Therefore, the court may, but need not, sentence the defendant to a total of 48 hours. However, the precise sentence is within the discretion of the sentencing judges.

In each case, whether to aggravate or mitigate a sentence from the benchmark sentence is within the discretion of the sentencing judges.

In each case, the sentencing judges shall announce whether the sentencing court has found aggravating or mitigating factors, and what those factors are. In addition, the court shall

Figure 10.4   Anchorage Youth Court Sentencing Matrix (Cont.)

announce whether the finding of such factors has provided the court with reason to depart from a benchmark sentence.

The judges may, but need not, subtract hours for classes or court viewing. No hours may be subtracted for an essay or letter of apology. **Full monetary restitution must be ordered in all appropriate cases.**

2.   More Than One Count.

In the event that the defendant is charged with more than one count, the judges should determine whether the counts are related to the same crime or two or more crimes. If the two counts are related to the same crime, 100% of the CWS hours for the most serious count are used, and only 50% of the CWS hours for the second and subsequent related counts are used. For example, if a person is charged with a class A misdemeanor and a class B misdemeanor from related crimes, the hours counted would be 32 for class A misdemeanor, and for class B misdemeanor only 12 (usually it is counted at 24 hours). If, however, the defendant is charged with two or more counts which are not related, 100% of the hours for each count is used. An example of related crimes would be a vehicle tampering and a theft from the same vehicle, or a burglary of a house and a theft from the same house. The crimes are not related, for example, if a person vandalized a vehicle and a few hours later shoplifted some candy.

3.   Upper Limit Of Hours.

The cap for actual CWS hours served is 150. In order for a defendant to be sentenced to more than 100 hours, special circumstances must be found. More than 100 hours should be reserved for the most serious cases.

4.   Theft Of $15 Or Less.

If the crime charged is a theft of $15 or less, the benchmark used is 12 CWS hours. Theft is defined as a charge of theft in the fourth degree or concealment of merchandise. If the 12 hour benchmark is used, the judges should assign a JASP class (or adult sentencing, arraignment, or jail tour if the defendant has already been to JASP), and an essay. If it is appropriate, the judges may sentence the defendant to write an apology letter to the defendant's family. With the 12 CWS hours, the mitigating factor of "least serious in the class" does not apply, since that factor was taken into account when the benchmark was reduced. Mitigators or aggravators are calculated as one hour each.

5.   Suspended Hours.

Judges may use suspended CWS hours in a sentence. The CWS hours suspended would **not** be served by the defendant, but would show the defendant what they could have been sentenced for the crime. The suspended CWS hours will be taken into consideration by the McLaughlin probation officer in the future if the defendant ever commits another crime. Actual hours to be served may not exceed the cap of 150.

6.   Optional Sentences.

Judges may sentence a defendant to an "optional" sentence if drug screening or counseling is appropriate. "Optional" means that the defendant has the choice whether to serve the whole amount of CWS hours or serve a lesser amount and present proof of counseling or drug screening. Counseling may only be requested or ordered upon the recommendation of a probation officer.

7.   Prior Record

If a defendant has an official prior record as recorded by Juvenile Intake, the community work service **base rate** will raise in the following manner.

One **misdemeanor** prior add **5** hours of community work service.

One **felony** prior add **10** hours of community work service.

<u>Each</u> prior recorded by Juvenile Intake will be added **separately**.

Figure 10.4   Anchorage Youth Court Sentencing Matrix (Cont.)

Example: A defendant commits a class B misdemeanor, normally 24 hours of community work service. One prior misdemeanor reported by Juvenile Intake will increase the community work service hours by 5 hours. The <u>new</u> base rate is 29 hours.

Example: A defendant commits a class B misdemeanor, normally 24 hours of community work service. One prior felony reported by Juvenile Intake will increase the community work service hours by 10 hours. The <u>new</u> base rate is 34 hours.

The amount of community work service added for each aggravating or mitigating factor will be based on the total amount after the hours for a prior record have been added. The normal 10% for each aggravating and mitigating factor is figured on the new hour number.

<u>These guidelines DO NOT apply to informal priors</u>. For example: a mother may report that the defendant was suspended from school for fighting, or that the defendant was caught shoplifting but was let go with just a warning. Informal priors may **still** be counted as an aggravating factor separate from the prior record as recorded by Juvenile Intake.

Benchmark Community Work Service Hours	10%	20%	30%	40%
12	1.2	2.4	3.6	4.8
17	1.7	3.4	5.1	6.8
22	2.2	4.4	6.6	8.8
24	2.4	4.8	7.2	9.6
29	2.9	5.8	8.7	11.6
32	3.2	6.4	9.6	12.8
34	3.4	6.8	10.2	13.6
37	3.7	7.4	11.1	14.8
40	4	8	12	16
42	4.2	8.4	12.6	16.8
45	4.5	9	13.5	18
48	4.8	9.6	14.4	19.2
50	5	10	15	20
53	5.3	10.6	15.9	21.2
55	5.5	11	16.5	22
58	5.8	11.6	17.4	23.2
60	6	12	18	24

3/22/04

Source: Reprinted with permission from the State of Alaska Juvenile Court.

Figure 10.5   Defense's Sentencing Recommendation

Calculation

1.   Community Work Service Hours:

    a.   Class of crime from charging document (A misd., etc.)   _____

    b.   Benchmark CWS hours for this class of crime: _____

    c.   Does the defendant have any formal prior charges on his/her record? If yes, add 5 CWS hours for each prior misdemeanor; 10 CWS hours for each prior felony. If no, add 0.   _____

    d.   Subtotal of CWS hours prior to mitigators   _____

    e.   Review the list of mitigators. How many apply?   _____
        List them: 1. _____
                    2. _____
                    3. _____
                    4. _____
                    5. _____

    f.   To the CWS subtotal in subpart d, subtract 10% for each mitigator from the CWS subtotal in subpart d. The resulting number is the number of CWS hours you recommend. [DO NO FORGET: DEFENSE DOES NOT INCLUDE AGGRAVATORS.]   _____

2.   Essay. How old is the defendant? Is there any evidence that the defendant has learning disabilities? Ask for an essay between 1000 and 1500 words.   _____ wd essay

3.   Restitution. Is restitution necessary? If the amount is known, state it: _____.
    If the amount is not known, ask that it be determined by the sentencing coordinator.

4.   Classes. JASP / weapons class / anger management class / VOA drug & alcohol assessment, etc.   _____

5.   Other sentencing options. Do any other sentencing options make sense in this case? Jail tour, etc.   _____

Often, one or more victims are likely involved. Their opinions are solicited in written form. Figure 10.7 is a form letter sent to one or more victims of the defendant. This letter advises the victim(s) that the defendant has agreed to participate in AYC and will appear at some future date.

Information about the crime and damage or injuries to the victim(s) is solicited. Thus, victims have an opportunity to verbalize how the crime committed by the defendant affected them. An open-ended form is attached to the letter, and it is recommended that the material be returned to the AYC at the victim's earliest opportunity.

Figure 10.5   Defense's Sentencing Recommendation (Cont.)

<u>Recommendation to Judges</u>

1.   We found _____ mitigators.

   a.   The mitigators are:
   1. _____
   2. _____
   3. _____
   4. _____
   5. _____

   This results in a recommendation of _____ community work service hours.

2.   We recommend a _____ word essay.

3.   *[If restitution if needed]*, we recommend restitution [in the amount of $_____]/ an amount to be determined by the sentencing coordinator].

4.   We recommend that the defendant attend _____ *[appropriate class such as JASP]* _____.

5.   *[If any other sentencing recommendations, state them and the reason for the recommendation.]* _____
   _____
   _____

To summarize, we recommend: _____CWS hours,
   a _____ word essay
   [restitution of $ _____/an amount to be determined by the sentencing coordinator]
   the _____ class
   _____
   _____

Thank you, your honors.

Source: Reprinted with permission from the State of Alaska Juvenile Court.

Victims may indicate how the crime affected them, whether financial losses were sustained, and whether any other comments should be considered by AYC judges. This information is delivered to the AYC for their consideration.

Oral Arguments to the AYC. Both the prosecution and the defense make oral arguments that essentially reflect what their written recommendations to the court contain. Similar to criminal court plea bargain agreements, prosecutors must outline

Figure 10.6   Prosecution's Sentencing Recommendation

<u>Calculation</u>

1. Community Work Service Hours:

   a. Class of crime from charging document (A misd., etc.) _____

   b. Benchmark CWS hours for this class of crime: _____

   c. Does the defendant have any formal prior charges on his/her record? If yes, add 5 CWS hours for each prior misdemeanor; 10 CWS hours for each prior felony. If no, add 0. _____

   d. Subtotal of CWS hours prior to aggravators & mitigators _____

   e. Review the list of aggravators. How many apply? _____
      List them: 1. _____
                    2. _____
                    3. _____
                    4. _____
                    5. _____

   f. Review the list of mitigators. How many apply? _____
      List them: 1. _____
                    2. _____
                    3. _____
                    4. _____
                    5. _____

   g. Subtract the number of mitigators from the number of aggravators. If the result is a positive number, add 10% for each net aggravator to the CWS subtotal in subpart d. If the result is a negative number, subtract 10% for each net mitigator from the CWS subtotal in subpart d. The resulting number is the number of CWS hours you recommend. _____

2. Essay. How old is the defendant? Is there any evidence that the defendant has learning disabilities? Ask for an essay between 500 and 1500 words. _____ wd essay

3. Restitution. Is restitution necessary? If the amount is known, state it: _____.
   If the amount is not known, ask that it be determined by the sentencing coordinator.

4. Classes. JASP / weapons class / anger management class / VOA drug & alcohol assessment, etc. _____

5. Other sentencing options. Do any other sentencing options make sense in this case? Jail tour, etc. _____

3/22/04

Figure 10.6   Prosecution's Sentencing Recommendation (Cont.)

Recommendation of Judges

1.   *If there is recommendation from the probation officer, read the recommendation to the judges. If there is a victim impact statement, read the victim impact statement to the judges. If there is neither a probation officer recommendation nor a victim impact statement, tell the judges:* "There is no recommendation from the probation officer and there is no victim impact statement."

2.   *If the defendant has a formal prior:* "The defendant has <u>number</u> formal prior(s)." *State the charge and the date(s) of the offenses. Inform the judges whether the prior(s) is/are misdemeanors or felonies and how many hours you added for the prior(s).*

3.   We found _____ aggravators and _____ mitigators.

    a.   The aggravators are
        1. _____
        2. _____
        3. _____
        4. _____
        5. _____

    b.   The mitigators are:
        1. _____
        2. _____
        3. _____
        4. _____
        5. _____

This results in a recommendation of _____ community work service hours. These community work service hours will allow the defendant to pay back his/her debt to society.

4.   We recommend a _____ word essay. The essay will allow the defendant to reflect on what he/she has learned through this experience.

5.   *[If restitution if needed]*, we recommend restitution [in the amount of $ _____/ an amount to be determined by the sentencing coordinator] or compensate the victim for _____

6.   We recommend that the defendant attend _____ *[appropriate class such as JASP]* _____ _____ so the defendant can learn _____ _____

7.   *[If any other sentencing recommendations, state them and the reason for the recommendation.]* _____ _____

To summarize, we recommend: _____ CWS hours,
    a _____ word essay
    [restitution of $ _____/an amount to be determined by the sentencing coordinator]
    the _____ class
    _____
    _____

Thank you, your honors.

Source: Reprinted with permission from the State of Alaska Juvenile Court.

Figure 10.7   Letter and Victim Impact Statement

Anchorage Youth Court
PO Box 102735
Anchorage, AK 99510
Phone: (907) 274-5986 • Fax: (907) 272-0491
Email: ayc@alaska.net

Dear (victim name),   February 1, 2005

APD Case # 04-__ was referred to McLaughlin Juvenile Intake regarding a case in which you were a victim.   The juvenile defendant has agreed to attend Anchorage Youth Court for sentencing as a consequence of his/her crime.

The attached form is your opportunity to explain the effect of the crime to the Anchorage Youth Court judges who will sentence the defendant.   You may fill out the form if you wish but are under no obligation to do so.   If your property was damaged or you were injured and incurred medical bills as a result of this crime, please provide details on the form and attach any receipts. If full or partial restitution is ordered, you will be contacted when the money order is collected from the defendant.

Defendants usually appear in Anchorage Youth Court within a couple of weeks of the crime occurring.   For the Anchorage Youth Court judges to consider your comments, we must receive the completed form by _____.   You may bring the completed form to our office at 838 W. 4th Avenue, mail it to us as P.O. Box 102735, or fax it to us at 272-0491.

Anchorage Youth Court is a non-profit 501(c)(3) educational organization which trains youth in grades 7-12 to represent and judge their peers in actual criminal cases.   Members volunteer to serve as prosecuting and defense attorneys, judges, clerks, bailiffs and jurors for juvenile offenders who have committed misdemeanors and minor felonies.   89% of the defendants who complete the program do not commit another crime.

The sentencing options used at Anchorage Youth Court include community work service, a mandatory essay, educational classes about specific crimes, viewing an adult sentencing hearing or jail tour, and restitution for property damage or medical bills for physical injury.   Anchorage Youth Court holds the defendant himself/herself responsible for earning the money to pay for the Anchorage Youth Court service fee ($50), educational class fee(s) ($30-$125) and any restitution amount.

If you have any questions, please call me at 274-5986.

Sincerely,

_____
Denise Wike, AYC Legal Advisor

"A New Generation for Justice"

the factual basis for the crime admitted by the defendant. In short, they must show the AYC judges what they would have presented as evidence of defendant guilt. This portion of the proceeding is scripted to a degree and is illustrated in Figure 10.8.

Defendant's Statement to the AYC.
Defendants are permitted to address the AYC judges on their own behalf. This is their right, and they may or may not choose to exercise it. It is important to note that like criminal defendants, youthful offenders may take this opportunity to accept responsibility for their crime(s), to show remorse, and to perhaps argue for leniency. However, AYC judges admonish them that their words are the last thing these judges will hear before they deliberate and determine the sentence. As an integral part of the defense prep document, defense counsels can advise their clients that they may want to tell judges that they

Youths may be required to write letters of apology to victims in peer courts as a part of their punishment.

are sorry; what they've done to make things right; how they are going to win back the trust of the people they have harmed; and what they will do differently if they are in a similar situation in the future.

Judicial Adjournment and Sentence Determination.
AYC judges retire to their chambers where they deliberate and eventually produce a sentencing document. The sentencing document is a unanimous decision by the judges, outlining the sentencing order and the reasons for it. The aggravating and mitigating factors considered by the judges are listed, and a rationale is given for why these factors were considered important. At that time, they must advise the defendant that he/she has the right to a reconsideration of the sentence by filing a written appeal within five working days. They are then asked to consult with their attorneys and determine whether the sentence is accepted or whether they will file an appeal. In a limited number of cases, judges may revise their original sentencing recommendations, but even these reconsidered sentences may be appealed. In most cases, however, defendants agree to the AYC judicial sentencing terms.

The Successfulness of the AYC.
As is the case with many intervention programs, effectiveness is measured by recidivism. For the AYC, a low recidivism rate of 11 percent has been exhibited by those processed. This means that there is nearly a 90 percent success rate and that most sentenced offenders will not commit future crimes. A majority of youth or teen courts in the United States have reported similar success results, which attests to their growing popularity.

The Holland Teen Court (HTC)

Michigan, in 1988, several juvenile justice officials began to examine alternative procedures to more formalized juvenile courts for processing less-serious juvenile offenders. Teen courts operating in Texas and several other states were studied. In 1991, the Holland City Council authorized the appointment of a Teen Court Advisory Board, consisting of several community representatives, student members, and other key community officials. Officially in Holland, a new teen court was launched. Since its inception, the **Holland Teen Court (HTC)** has been operating largely with volunteers. In close collaboration with the Holland Police Department, area schools, the sheriff's department, juvenile court judges, and other relevant personnel, the HTC has been a very successful

Holland Teen Court (HTC)
Holland, Michigan, youth court program commenced in 1991 involving juveniles who have committed less serious misdemeanor offenses; jurors consist of high-school students with general training in jury deliberations and sentencing matters; limitations on sentencing restricted to community service and restitution; very successful program with recidivism of less than 5 percent.

Figure 10.8   Evidence of Offense and Victim Impact

Anchorage Youth Court
PO Box 102735
Anchorage, AK. 99510
Phone: (907) 274-5986 • Fax: (907) 272-0491

Please return this form to Anchorage Youth Court by 3:00 p.m.

Anchorage Police Department Case # 04-   AYC Case # 04-

1. How did the crime affect you and/or your family?

2. Did you or your family have any financial loss because of this crime?
   If so, describe any loss not covered by insurance and attach copies of receipts for repairing or replacing the damaged items, or your medical bills.

3. Please add any other comments you want the judges to hear.

_____   _____

Signature   Date

Source: Reprinted with permission from the State of Alaska Juvenile Court.

project that has expanded and has been emulated by other cities throughout Michigan and elsewhere.

The goals of the HTC are to (1) interrupt developing patterns of criminal behavior, (2) promote self-improvement, and (3) educate peer jurors about the legal system and local authority processes. The underlying philosophy of HTC is that a youthful law violator does not continue to be an offender whenever a jury of his/her peers decides sentencing.

Acceptance into the HTC Program.
Acceptance into the HTC is restricted to juvenile first-offenders between the ages of 10 and 17. They must plead guilty initially to a range of misdemeanors. Then they must accept the sentence imposed by a teen court and perform whatever is demanded of the sentence. Once they successfully complete the process, they are free of the system and the charges against them are dismissed. The types of offenses considered for HTC resolution are (1) curfew violation, (2) littering, (3) retail fraud (shoplifting), (4) larceny under $100, (5) smoking/possession of cigarettes, (6) fireworks possession, (7) city ordinance violations, (8) disorderly conduct, (9) trespassing, (10) loud music, (11) alcohol possession, (12) minor assault, (13) obstructing police, and (14) driving offenses. Acceptance into the HTC for processing begins through a referral and signing a consent form illustrated in Figure 10.9. If a juvenile does not wish to participate after being referred to the HTC, he/she may sign a "refusal to participate" form shown in Figure 10.10.

Holland Teen Court, Michigan, convenes to hear cases.

Peer Jury Composition.
The HTC peer jury consists of trained high-school students who are given general instructions on how they should proceed. They practice with fictitious scenarios and are evaluated by local judges and other court personnel, including attorneys who monitor them. Judges for these courts are local attorneys, judges, and other court personnel who volunteer to preside whenever a case is heard. One of the offender's parents is required to attend all teen court hearings. The same respect and protocol of a courtroom are observed in the HTC at all times whenever the HTC is in session. A teen court coordinator holds a pre-hearing meeting with the offender and one or both parents. A thorough overview of HTC is explained, as well as its purposes and intended objectives. Offenders and their parents are invited to ask questions. Once this process is concluded, a court clerk announces commencement of an HTC session. The session is made up of a judge, court clerk, bailiff, and foreperson, who is the jury leader. Jury voting must be unanimous. All jury questioning and deliberations are secret and hidden from public view. This is to reduce the adverse effects of labeling that might otherwise occur if a juvenile were processed through traditional juvenile courts. Teen jurors sign a statement swearing that they will keep the proceedings secret. This statement is shown in Figure 10.11.

The defendant is sworn in and the jury questioning begins. The jury is trained to ask fair questions and seek the truth relating to the offense(s). A strong focus is placed on the defendant's feelings about the incident, the offender's perspective regarding consequences for the misdemeanor, and the effect it has had on his/her life, his/her family, and the life of the victim. Once the judge and jury are satisfied with the round of questions posed, the jury deliberates and decides the punishment to be imposed. Due dates are given for concluding whatever punishments are decided. A copy of the jury verdict and sentence requirements is given to the offender and the offender's parents. The completion of all sentencing requirements eventually results in a dismissal of all original charges against a defendant. This information is summarized on an HTC Sentencing Guidelines Jury Verdict form as shown in Figure 10.12.

Figure 10.9   Holland Teen Court Consent Form

HOLLAND TEEN COURT
CONSENT FORM

JUVENILE NAME: _____

ADDRESS: _____

CHARGE: _____

HOLLAND TEEN COURT IS A VOLUNTARY PROGRAM THAT HAS BEEN EXPLAINED TO ME. I ADMIT THAT I AM GUILTY OF THE OFFENSE THAT I HAVE BEEN CHARGED WITH. I UNDERSTAND THAT I HAVE A RIGHT TO SEEK LEGAL COUNSEL. I UNDERSTAND THAT A JURY OF MY PEERS WILL HEAR MY CASE AND ASSIGN THE CONSEQUENCES THEY DEEM APPROPRIATE. THE CONSEQUENCES MAY INCLUDE, BUT ARE NOT LIMITED TO, COMMUNITY SERVICE, RESTITUTION, AN APOLOGY, COUNSELING, OR OTHER ALTERNATIVE OPPORTUNITIES PROGRAM. I UNDERSTAND THAT IF I FAIL TO APPEAR OR COMPLETE THE ASSIGNED CONSEQUENCES WITHIN A SPECIFIED TIME, MY CASE WILL BE REFERRED TO THE OTTAWA COUNTY PROBATE DEPARTMENT FOR CRIMINAL PROSECUTION. I UNDERSTAND THAT IF I SUCCESSFULLY COMPLETE THE CONSEQUENCES THAT THE TEEN COURT JURY ASSIGNS, THIS CHARGE WILL NOT BE HELD AGAINST ME IN ANY FUTURE PROCEEDINGS.

I AGREE TO THESE TERMS: _____   _____
                                                    NAME   DATE

PARENT/GUARDIAN CONSENT

THE HOLLAND TEEN COURT PROGRAM, AND THE CHARGE AGAINST MY CHILD, HAVE BEEN EXPLAINED TO ME. I UNDERSTAND THAT THIS IS A VOLUNTARY PROGRAM AND I HEREBY AUTHORIZE MY CHILD TO PARTICIPATE.

PARENT/GUARDIAN _____

Sentences and Punishments. The following sentences are possible choices for the HTC peer jury: (1) community service hours (varying from 8 to 24 hours, depending on offense seriousness), (2) restitution (jury selects dollar amount), (3) essay (a written document specifying due date and topic), (4) victim apology (proof required), and (5) others (includes miscellaneous assignments). Compliance with the sentence requirements imposed is overseen by various persons associated with the HTC, and the

Figure 10.10 Refusal to Participate Form

REFUSAL TO PARTICIPATE

After being informed of my rights and the requirements of this program, I hereby refuse the services of this court, and ask that my case be referred back to the referring agency. I understand that by this act my case enters into the judicial system and may result in a court hearing.

Date: _____

_____
Signature of Juvenile

_____
Signature of Parent or Guardian

_____
Referring Officer

_____
Teen Court Coordinator/Staff

result is the completion of a Docket Sheet as shown in Figure 10.13. A date is provided to indicate that all sentencing requirements have been fulfilled. This document is filed with the juvenile court.

Successfulness of the HTC. By 2008, the HTC had processed nearly 4,000 teens. Recidivism rates among these sentenced teens were quite low, less than 5 percent. Compared with the informal success standard of intervention programs for other types of offenders of 30 percent or less, the HTC is considered very successful (Holland Teen Court, 2008).

Teen Court Variations

Several variations of teen courts have been described (Butts and Buck, 2002). Four courtroom models of teen courts include (1) adult judge, (2) youth judge, (3) peer jury, and (4) tribunal.

Adult Judge Teen Court Model.
Adult judge teen courts use adult judges to preside over all actions. The judge is responsible for managing all courtroom dynamics. Generally, a youth volunteer acting as the prosecutor presents each case against a juvenile to a jury comprised of one's peers. This is similar to a prosecutor in the adult system presenting a case against a defendant in a grand jury action. A juvenile defense counsel offers mitigating evidence, if any, which the jury may consider. The jury is permitted to

Figure 10.11   Oath of Confidentiality

TEEN COURT

CITY OF HOLLAND

HOLLAND, MICHIGAN
270 SOUTH RIVER AVENUE

Oath of Confidentiality

I solemnly swear or avow that I will not divulge, either by words or signs, any information which comes to my knowledge in the course of a Teen Court case presentation, and that I will keep secret all said proceedings which may be held in my presence, so help me God.

_____

Signature of volunteer or observer

_____

Date

_____

Signature of HTC Teacher or HTC Coordinator

Figure 10.12   Holland Teen Court Sentencing Guidelines Verdict Form

HOLLAND TEEN COURT
SENTENCING GUIDELINES
JURY VERDICT

Defendant: _____   Charge: _____

1. _____ Community Service (Specify in Hours)_____
Level 1: 8-12 hours (Curfew Violation, Smoking/Possessing Cigarettes;
Trespassing; Littering; Fireworks Possession; City Ordinance Violation;
Retail Fraud >.$25; Loud Music).

Level 2: 12-24 hours (Retail Fraud <$25; MDP <$100; Larceny <$200;
Disorderly Conduct; Receiving and Concealing <$200).

To be completed by: (specify date) _____

For Level 1 offenses, please allow 30 days to complete community service. For Level 2 offenses, please allow
45 to 60 days to complete community service.

2. _____ Restitution (specify amounts) $ _____

3. _____ Essay (specify number of words) _____
Topic: _____
To be completed by (specify date): _____

4. _____ Apology to _____ with written proof to the court
within two weeks.

5. _____ Other (specify) _____

Date: _____ Jury foreperson: _____

Figure 10.13   Holland Teen Court Docket Sheet (Holland Teen Court)

HOLLAND TEEN COURT
DOCKET SHEET

NAME _____ DATE OF BIRTH _____

ADDRESS _____

PHONE _____ SCHOOL _____

NAME OF PARENT/GUARDIAN _____

DATE OF OFFENSE _____ CHARGE _____

ESSENTIAL DETAILS OF OFFENSE _____

_____

_____

DATE OF TEEN COURT SENTENCING _____

DETAILS OF SENTENCE _____

_____

_____

DATE SENTENCE REQUIREMENTS COMPLETED _____

---

youth judge model
Youth court model where a juvenile sits as the judge and where juveniles also play the roles of prosecutors and defense counsel; very similar to the tribunal model where an adult judge performs the role of judge.

peer jury model
A peer jury is composed of one's equals or schoolmates who sit on the jury and decide one's punishment.

ask the youthful defendant any question in an effort to determine why the offense was committed and any circumstances surrounding its occurrence. Subsequently, the jury deliberates and determines the most fitting punishment. This is a recommendation only. The suitability of the recommended punishment, which is most often some form of community service and/or victim compensation or restitution, is decided by the judge. About half of all teen courts in the United States use the adult judge model.

Youth Judge Model. The youth judge variation of teen courts uses a juvenile judge instead of an adult judge. Youths are used as prosecutors and defense counsel as well. This teen court variation functions much like the adult judge teen court model. Again, a sentence is recommended by a jury, and the appropriateness of the sentence is determined by the juvenile judge. About a third of all teen courts use this model.

Peer Jury Model. In the **peer jury model**, an adult judge presides, while a jury hears the case against the defendant. There are no youth prosecutors or defense counsels

10.3   Focus on Delinquency

It happened in Texas. At a middle school in a large city, a 12-year-old boy, O.M., was ordered by a teen court to 50 hours of community service following threats he made at school. The youth allegedly pointed a toy gun at the head of another student, J.G., and made terroristic threats against two other students. The parents of the threatened students filed complaints with the police and with the school district. Police came to the school and an investigation followed. Subsequently, a teen court convened and heard the case and decided that it was in O.M.'s best interest to perform the extensive community service. In the courtroom were the boy's mother, as well as the mothers and fathers of the threatened children. O.M. was also obligated to write a letter of apology to each of the students as well as the school. No further action was taken in the incident. Should youths be able to escape juvenile court punishment for threatening other students, even if toy guns are used? What punishment would you recommend? [Source: Adapted from the Associated Press, "Boy Gets 50 Hours of Community Service for Threatening Other Youths with Toy Pistol at School," May 20, 2008.]

present. After hearing the case, which is usually determined through jury questioning of the defendant directly, the jury deliberates and decides the sentence, which the judge must approve.

Tribunal Model. Under the **tribunal model**, one or more youths act as judges, while other youths are designated as prosecutors and defense counsels. The prosecution and defense present their side of the case against the youthful defendant to the judges who subsequently deliberate and return with a sentence. All sentences may be appealed. Again, the sentences usually involve restitution or some form of victim compensation, community service, or a combination of punishments depending upon the circumstances. This tribunal model is the one featured in the AYC example earlier.

Each of these models is summarized below:

> **tribunal model**
> The tribunal model is similar to a peer jury model in that one's peers judge one's actions and determine punishments.

	Judge	Youth Attorneys	Jury/Role of Jury
Adult Judge Model	Adult	Yes	Recommend sentence
Youth Judge Model	Youth	Yes	Recommend sentence
Peer Jury Model	Adult	No	Question defendant, recommend sentence
Tribunal	Youths (1–3)	Yes	No jury present

The Successfulness of Teen Courts

The growing popularity of teen courts as alternatives to formal juvenile court actions attests to their successfulness in sanctioning first-time, low-risk youthful offenders. Being judged by one's peers seems to be an effective method of imposing sanctions. Youths who function as judges, prosecutors, and defense counsels usually receive a certain number of hours of training to perform these important roles. In New York, for instance, an average of 16–20 hours of training is required of youth court juvenile officials (Butts and Buck, 2002). In some instances, written tests are administered following one's training. These are the equivalent of bar exams for youths, to ensure that they understand some basic or fundamental legal principles.

Several national youth court guidelines have been articulated. These guidelines have been developed for (1) program planning and community mobilization, (2) program staffing and funding, (3) legal issues, (4) identified respondent population and referral process, (5) volunteer recruitment and sentencing options, (6) volunteer training, (7) youth court operations and case management, and (8) program evaluation.

Recidivism rates of teen courts have not been studied consistently throughout all jurisdictions. However, available information suggests that the recidivism rates among youthful defendants who have gone through the teen court process are very low, less than 20 percent. One positive consequence that is reported in many jurisdictions is that processed youth emerge with a greater appreciation for the law, a greater understanding of it, and a greater respect for authority figures. They appear to be more law-abiding compared with youths adjudicated in more traditional ways through juvenile courts. A majority of states have adopted teen court models of one type or another, and many are in the process of considering legislation to establish them (Chapman, 2005).

States vary in terms of the eligibility age limits and types of offenses that youth courts may consider. Mostly first-offense, low-level misdemeanors, or status offenses, are included. More serious offenses are usually passed along to the juvenile court beyond the intake stage. The accountability of participating youths is heightened considerably inasmuch as youths must admit guilt before participating in teen courts (Butts and Buck, 2002). Furthermore, they must waive their confidentiality rights in most jurisdictions.

Day Reporting Centers

Goals and Functions of Day Reporting Centers

day reporting centers
Established in England in 1974 to provide intensive supervision for low-risk offenders who lived in neighborhoods; continued in various U.S. jurisdictions today to manage treatment programs, supervise fee collection, and other responsibilities, such as drug-testing and counseling.

Some jurisdictions have day treatment program centers, following a day treatment model. **Day reporting centers** were established first in England in 1974 to provide intensive supervision for offenders who would otherwise be incarcerated (Roy, 2004). Offenders in English day treatment centers typically lived at home while remaining under the supervision of a correctional administrator. Inmates would either work or attend school, regularly participate in treatment programming, devote at least four hours a week to community service, and observe a strict curfew.

A variation on day treatment programs in England has been attempted in the United States for juvenile offenders. The first American day reporting centers were established in Connecticut and Massachusetts in the mid-1980s. During that period, there were 13 day treatment centers operating. By 2007, there were over 500 day treatment centers in 39 states (Office of Juvenile Justice and Delinquency Prevention, 2007).

Both male and female clients benefit from day treatment services. Since the mid-1970s, these programs have helped to expand the continuum of services available to at-risk and delinquent youths. These programs have been developed through the collaborative efforts of educators, judiciary, and social service professionals, and provide an effective alternative to out-of-home placements. Many day treatment programs are operated on a year-round basis, offering community-based non-residential services to at-risk and delinquent youths.

These centers offer offenders a variety of treatments and services. Offenders report to these centers frequently, usually once or twice a day, and treatment and services are provided on site in most instances. For more serious types of problems or illnesses, personnel at these centers will refer clients to the appropriate community services where they can receive necessary specialized treatments. The types of services provided by 60 percent or more of these day reporting centers include the acquisition of job-seeking skills, drug-abuse education, group counseling, job placement services, education, drug treatment, life skills training, individual counseling, transitional housing, and recreation and leisure activities (Henry and Kobus, 2007).

The goals of day treatment centers are to provide access to treatment and services, reduce prison and jail overcrowding, protect the public, and build political support. Eligibility requirements are that offenders should be low-risk delinquents or criminals, with a good chance of succeeding while free in the community. Those with serious and violent prior records are usually excluded. Surveillance of day reporting center clients consists of on-site and off-site contacts. On-site contacts average 18 hours per week, where clients must be at these day reporting centers for treatment and special programming during the most intensive phases. Off-site surveillance includes site visits to one's home or dwelling, telephonic contact, and visits to one's place of work or school. Not all day treatment programs are operated for low-risk offenders. In some jurisdictions, day reporting centers are operated as intermediate sanctions for more serious offenders. Furthermore, some of these day treatment programs are offense-specific, such as day treatment for drug offenders.

Some Examples of Day Reporting Centers

The Moore County Day Reporting Center.
The Moore County Day Reporting Center, North Carolina, is a state-funded program that involves youths of ages 7–16 who have been adjudicated delinquent or undisciplined. The juveniles come to the center every day after school hours to receive various services. Particularly targeted are youths who are nonviolent, who have a substance-abuse history, and who need to develop living skills (Dubowitz, Pitts, and Black, 2004).

Participation in the day reporting center is approved, provided that clients meet the following eligibility requirements:

1. A Moore County resident.
2. Not charged with a serious or violent crime.
3. Have an approved residence.
4. Have access to a telephone.
5. Agree to abide by the conditions of the contract with the day reporting center.
6. Meet the requirements for intermediate punishment under the Structured Sentencing Act of 1994.

Youths who come to the center acquire valuable employment skills; participate in general education development (GED) classes; undergo life skills training; participate in random drug testing; have access to a variety of mental health services, including group or individual counseling; participate in vocational rehabilitation programs; participate in health education courses; and undergo cognitive behavioral interventions. The cognitive behavioral interventions program is a 36-session program designed to change a person's thought processes to more law-abiding orientations. Numerous youths have been assisted by this day reporting program. The recidivism rate is quite low, less than 30 percent (Moore County Government, 2002).

The Englewood Evening Reporting Center.
Some day reporting centers are operated during evening hours. This is true of the Englewood Evening Reporting Center, operated between the hours of 4:00 and 8:00 P.M. weekdays in Englewood, Illinois, a Chicago suburb. The Englewood center is an alternative detention site to serve local juvenile offenders who would otherwise be ordered held in the Juvenile Temporary Detention Center. The center was opened in 1995. Subsequently, the center has received numerous state awards for the services it provides to participating Illinois youths.

A part of the court's Juvenile Alternative Detention initiative, evening reporting centers such as the Englewood center are community-based facilities that operate through partnerships between sponsoring social service organizations and the court. Under the program, the juvenile court judge can order nonviolent juvenile offenders awaiting disposition on a warrant or probation violation to report to the evening reporting center as an alternative to being held in detention. Youths are required to report to the center between the hours of 4:00 and 8:00 P.M. daily. At these centers, they meet with professional staff who consist of educational specialists, recreational specialists, and three group workers who provide programs, activities, and workshops for a maximum of 25 youths. Transportation to and from the Englewood center and an evening meal are provided.

Chief Judge Donald P. O'Connell of the Cook County Court has said that

> The purpose of the Circuit Court's support for establishing evening reporting centers is two-fold. First, we are helping at-risk kids avoid the possibility of being rearrested and sent to detention centers by getting them off the street and offering them positive, structured programming. We are able to do this through a low staff-to-client ratio of five to one which ensures the personal attention that is simply not possible at the detention center.

The expectation is that stronger, safer neighborhoods are fostered by reducing the likelihood of criminal activity and by providing various jobs to community residents.

The average daily cost per client at the Englewood center is $33 per day, which is significantly less than the $100 per day it would cost to hold the juvenile in detention facilities. Funding is provided by the Cook County Court. The Englewood center is operated by the Reach Out and Touch Someone, Inc., Treatment Alternatives for Safer Communities (TASC), Aunt Martha's Youth Service Center, and the Circuit Court of Cook County Juvenile Department's Probation and Court Service Division. This particular evening reporting center is in a community that has one of the highest rates of juvenile arrests and referrals to detention (Cook County Court, 2002).

The Day Reporting Center for Juvenile Firearms Offenses. In McLean County, Illinois, a day reporting center is operated for juveniles who have possessed firearms during the commission of delinquent acts. It is called the Day Reporting Center for Juvenile Firearms Offenses. The purpose of this program is to provide the juvenile court with meaningful sanctions for juveniles possessing firearms. Three components of the program include mandatory public service, public health education addressing the risks of firearms and their possession, and psychological evaluation and appropriate referrals.

Community service is a mandatory component of the program. The purpose of the community service is to assist the juvenile in learning how to assume responsibility for himself/herself and for the community in which he/she lives. Service to the local public will enable the youth to form attachments and commitments that promote civility and safety within the community. Mandatory public health education is designed to instill in the juvenile participants a more complete understanding of the personal and public health risks associated with the unlawful use of firearms. And an exhaustive psychological evaluation is required prior to a juvenile's acceptance into the program. All files are meticulously maintained during the juvenile's participation. Referrals to psychological and/or counseling services are made where appropriate.

Each juvenile spends between 1 and 60 days in the program. Juveniles receive tutoring, especially those in need of assistance with school work. Tutoring time can also be used for the completion of homework. The main goal of this portion of the program is to teach the juvenile how to use his/her study time effectively. Group therapy is also included. Group therapy includes presentations by informed authorities on positive peer relationships, drug education, handgun education, esteem building, and understanding of the juvenile court system. Individual therapy is sometimes conducted on a one-to-one basis, depending upon the youth's needs. Basic life skills are imparted in an instructional component of the program, which includes personal hygiene, meal planning, preparation, and cleanup. The goal of this part of the program is to heighten the juvenile's awareness of himself/herself and family members. The program runs Mondays through Fridays, after normal school hours. Juveniles are expected to attend school and keep up with their studies.

There is strong parental input in this day reporting center. The parent's role in rehabilitating the juvenile is large, as they can reinforce the program's message. Parents are responsible for transporting their children to the program, and they have an opportunity to become integrated into the actual program. Program officials maintain daily case notes on each juvenile in the program. Attainment of and progress toward the juvenile's goals would also be noted. When the juvenile successfully completes the program, a full report of the juvenile's progress is made to the court. The cost of maintaining each child in the day reporting program is $50 per day compared with $92 per day if the juvenile were placed in secure detention in the McLean County Juvenile Detention Center. The recidivism rate of youths who have successfully completed the program is about 25 percent (McLean County Court Services, 2002).

The Predispositional Supervision Program. The Predispositional Supervision (PDS) Program is operated in Geary County, Kansas, through the local community corrections office. The original purpose of the program was to reduce juvenile crime and recidivism. Local law enforcement officials in Geary County believed that the juvenile crime rate was directly related to the high incidence of substance abuse among its youth. Therefore, early assessments and treatments of juveniles arrested for drug-related offenses were believed to be an effective means of decreasing the crime rate.

The predispositional nature of the program is such that juvenile court judges in Geary County are provided with additional information about a youth's suitability for probation prior to disposition. Prior to the program, juvenile court judges were often unaware of a particular juvenile offender's needs and other problems, including behavioral/emotional problems. The predispositional day reporting program operating in Geary County commenced operations in September 1996.

Eligible offenders are restricted to adjudicated youths who have not as yet been disposed (sentenced) by juvenile court judges. Prior to the dispositional hearing, the court can order the juvenile detained or released on bond. As a condition of the bond, the court can order the juvenile to PDS. The local community corrections department offers PDS. Juvenile offenders must report to the community corrections day reporting center for an assessment. The day reporting staff conducts a needs assessment as well as a substance-abuse assessment, including a urinalysis. Services are provided as needed. A local provider supplies substance-abuse assessment and treatment.

The juvenile offender must report to the day reporting center from 8:30 A.M. to 5:00 P.M. daily. During this time, the juvenile participates in academic sessions, job skills training, social skills training, anger management, conflict resolution, and community service for a maximum of 20 hours. All predispositional-ordered youth meet in one classroom and are supervised by two staff members. The staff may utilize electronic monitoring for noncompliant youths. Curfews are generally ordered from 6:00 P.M. to 6:00 A.M., and clients are randomly monitored by the community corrections surveillance officers.

The maximum capacity is 30 clients at any given time, based upon staff and space limitations. The average length of supervision varies between 30 and 60 days. The staff consists of the director and a life skills instructor. The typical length of time clients remain in the predispositional program is four weeks, and the average cost of this experience is $155 per offender. The expenditures include staffing, alcohol and drug evaluations, urinalyses, electronic monitoring, books, and software. The successfulness of this program is reflected by the low 6 percent rate of recidivism among all clientele (Geary County Community Corrections, 2002).

Alternative Dispute Resolution (ADR)

Alternative Dispute Resolution (ADR)

Procedure whereby a criminal case is rendered civil by using an impartial arbiter, where perpetrators and victims reconcile their disputes; usually reserved for minor offenses.

In most U.S. jurisdictions, youths are subject to **Alternative Dispute Resolution (ADR)** or mediation to resolve school problems (Bannan, 2008). The mediation process allows people to resolve conflicts in a nonthreatening and nonpunitive atmosphere. Mediators are third-party neutrals who help people in a dispute to express their points of view, identify their needs, clarify issues, explore solutions, and negotiate satisfactory agreements.

Mediation centers generally train students in different grade levels to serve as mediators to intervene in school-based disputes among students. Several common components of these centers include (1) a conflict resolution curriculum that can be taught in either academic or residential settings, (2) a mediation program that trains residents and staff to help resolve conflicts among themselves, and (3) a reintegration component involving parents and residents developing terms of daily living for when the residents return home. The rationale for such programming is that by giving students a model for positive expression and conflict resolution, it can teach them alternatives to violent and self-destructive behavior. By using these skills within the institutional setting, students can be assisted to interact successfully with their peers and adults. A voluntary program, this mediation effort has seemingly reduced juvenile deviance in the jurisdiction. Thus, it may be viewed as an early intervention for preventing juvenile delinquency.

Victim–offender mediation is now established as an important and growing part of ADR. For juveniles who have committed property offenses, it is often beneficial for them to face their victims and learn how they have been affected by their losses. It is believed that their accountability is heightened and that they are more inclined to accept responsibility for whatever they have done (Bannan, 2008).

Some victim–offender mediation sessions may involve all parties, including family members, the child's attorney, social service agencies, and others involved in the case. The goal is to work toward an agreement and a restitution plan that everyone approves. This agreement is submitted to the juvenile court judge for approval. It is believed that the family-centered nature of the mediation process provides the social support youths need for long-term behavioral change associated with the mediation. No single victim–offender mediation model is workable in all situations, however. Individual factors and circumstances must be considered to configure the best mediation plan (Bannan, 2008).

South Carolina has been operating juvenile arbitration programs since 1983. One such program is the Lexington County Juvenile Arbitration Program. Some of the conditions of this program include waiving rights to legal representation and permitting impartial arbitrators to make a determination of guilt at the beginning of the hearing. The juvenile admits guilt and the hearing proceeds to a mutually satisfactory conclusion between the offender and the victim. If the juvenile does not admit guilt, then the arbitration proceedings are terminated and the juvenile is sent to the juvenile court. Arbitrators are chosen from the community on the basis of their skill and expertise, and they are given over 20 hours of arbitration training prior to conducting arbitration sessions. During 1995–1996, for instance, 370 juveniles were referred to the Lexington County Juvenile Arbitration Program, with a success rate of 94 percent. Total hours of community service generated by these sessions were 4,666, while the restitution amount collected was $5,038. The future of juvenile arbitration in South Carolina is bright and is designed to promote successful prevention/intervention strategies for at-risk juvenile offenders (Alford, 1998:28, 34). Similar programs have been conducted in other jurisdictions, such as Cook County, Illinois, with similar successful results (Bannan, 2008).

The prevailing correctional philosophy applied to juvenile corrections today as well as to programs for adults is punishment/control rather than treatment/rehabilitation

(Sinclair, 2005). But like adults, not all juvenile offenders are the same according to their emotional needs, offense seriousness, educational levels, vocational skills, and honesty. Therefore, it is difficult for judges to prescribe meaningful, categorical punishments for aggregates of youthful offenders facing similar charges. Even if specific predictor variables could be identified, they are not always foolproof for effective program placement decision making (Salinas, 2008).

Summary

Half of all juveniles who enter the juvenile justice system annually are low-risk first-offenders. For many first-offenders, judges use diversion as the means for keeping these youths from the formal trappings of juvenile courts. Several types of diversion programs were described. Not everyone qualifies for diversion, and judges must exercise their best judgment in determining who does and who does not receive it.

Overall, diversion programs appear effective in reducing recidivism among low-risk youths or first-offenders. Adverse labeling is avoided, and youths acquire greater self-esteem and individual coping skills and have better school adjustment following their diversion experiences. Not all citizens approve of diversion, however. They often perceive it as excessive leniency. More credibility is associated with those diversion programs incorporating elements of restitution, heightened accountability, and community service, with some attention given to victims and the losses they have incurred.

Teen courts are used increasingly as an alternative to formal juvenile court action. Teen courts, peer courts, or youth courts consist of youths who function as prosecutors, defense counsels, and juries, and judge other youths who have committed minor offenses. Teen courts, originally established in Washington and Oregon, have proliferated such that by late 2008, there were over 1,300 teen courts operating in different U.S. jurisdictions. Teen courts are considered effective because one's peers, rather than adults, impose punishments. Punishments imposed by teen courts almost always involve community service and restitution. Teen court effectiveness at reducing recidivism among affected youths is especially strong and was described. The general purpose of teen courts is rehabilitation.

Another nominal option is day reporting centers, where day treatments for youthful clients are provided in their own neighborhoods. Youths receive various treatments and assistance, including job placement services, individual counseling, life skills training, drug-abuse education, education, drug treatment, and some amount of recreation. The goals of day reporting centers are reducing prison and jail overcrowding, protecting the public, providing youths access to necessary services, and building public support for their operations. Juveniles may also participate in ADR. ADR is a mediation program where victims and youthful offenders can meet and resolve their conflicts. Parental and community involvement in ADR programs improves their effectiveness. Several ADR programs were described.

Key Terms

Alternative Dispute Resolution (ADR), 344
Anchorage Youth Court (AYC), 318
day reporting centers, 340
diversion, 308
Diversion Plus Program, 311
Holland Teen Court (HTC), 331
mediation, 312

mediator, 312
peer jury model, 338
Reparative Probation Program, 312
See Our Side (SOS) Program, 311
teen courts, 315
tribunal model, 339
youth judge model, 338

Questions for Review

1. How are nominal dispositions distinguished from conditional and custodial dispositions? What are some variations of nominal dispositions? How effective are they at reducing recidivism of disposed juveniles?

2. What is diversion? What are some of the eligibility requirements of prospective divertees?

3. What are some of the functions and dysfunctions of diversion?

4. How is diversion relevant to net-widening? How can judges be influenced to impose diversion in lieu of outright dismissals of cases that otherwise would not come before juvenile courts? Explain.

5. How does the Diversion Plus Program compare with the SOS Program? What are the basic components of each?

6. What is meant by the PINS Diversion Program? Is it effective? Why or why not? Who are CHINS? How are such youths amenable to diversion programs? Explain.

7. What are teen courts? What types of juvenile offenders are the best types of clients for teen courts? How do teen courts function? What are the success rates of teen courts for reducing youth recidivism?

8. What are day reporting centers? What are some of their goals and functions?

9. What are two examples of day reporting centers? What are some of their characteristics and which types of juveniles are served by them?

10. What is meant by ADR? Do you think it is an effective way of settling disputes between victims and youthful offenders? Why or why not?

Internet Connections

Drug Reform Coordination Network
http://www.drcnet.org/

DrugSense
http://www.drugsense.org/

Drug War Chronicle
http://www.stopthedrugwar.org/home

Gangs in the Schools
http://www.ericdigests.org/1995-1/gangs.htm

HandsNet
http://www.handsnet.org/

Idaho Youth Ranch
http://www.youthranch.org/

Resources for Youth
http://www.preventviolence.org/

Teen Court
http://www.teen-court.org

Teens, Crime, and the Community
http://www.ncpc.org/programs/tcc/

Youth Change (problem-youth problem solving)
http://www.youthchg.com

Youth Defense Counsels
http://www.juveniledefense.com

chapter **11**

Chapter outline

Juvenile Probation and Community-Based Corrections

As the result of reading this chapter, you will accomplish the following objectives:

1. Understand what is meant by juvenile probation and parole, as well as the extent to which these sanctions are used in juvenile cases.
2. Become familiar with several important types of probation programs for juveniles.
3. Learn about different dispositional options as conditions of probation, including restitution, fines, community service, and victim compensation.
4. Understand what is meant by home confinement and electronic monitoring for juveniles and how often such options are used in their conditional supervision.
5. Understand what is meant by intermediate punishments for juveniles.
6. Learn about several important intensive supervised probation programs for juveniles, including their weaknesses and strengths.

 ## Case Study

Six youths were charged with assaulting two minority youths one evening in September 2006 as they walked home from Knight High School in Lancaster, California. Technically a hate crime, the assault involved two Latino victims and 15–20 black youths ranging in age from 15 to 22. Of six youths apprehended later, a 15-year-old, Mark Broussard, pleaded no contest to the hate-crime charge. On the basis of the *nolo contendere* plea, the juvenile court judge disposed Broussard to a term of three years of probation. If Broussard violates his probation orders, he faces up to eight years in prison. A second codefendant was sentenced earlier to six months in a probation camp. A third was being sought on an arrest warrant, while the remaining three perpetrators were awaiting trial in juvenile court. [Source: Adapted from the Associated Press, "Teen Sentenced to Probation in Racial Beatings," January 11, 2008.]

 ## Case Study

A tragic incident unfolded in Lauderhill, Florida, when a 12-year-old boy beat to death his second cousin, a 17-month-old toddler, Shaloh Joseph, with a baseball bat. Joseph was beat in the head several times with the bat. All blows were fatal. The boy, unidentified because of his age, confessed and explained to police that he was angered while babysitting his 10-year-old brother and Shaloh Joseph, because she was crying while he was trying to watch cartoons on television. Shaloh's parents asked the juvenile court not to prosecute the boy. They begged the court to allow the boy to remain in juvenile court where he would be tried as a juvenile and not an adult. They also asked the court to treat the youth, placing him on probation, rather than imprison him. They were absolutely devastated by what happened. [Source: Adapted from Paula McMahon and the *Sun-Sentinel,* January 15, 2008.]

Introduction

A 15-year-old black youth assaults two Latino youths and inflicts serious physical injuries as part of a racially motivated hate crime. A 12-year-old boy bludgeons his 17-month-old cousin to death for crying and interrupting his television cartoon show. Are either of these cases deserving of probation?

This chapter describes juvenile probation and a variety of other community-based programs. Probation is the most frequently used sanction by juvenile court judges. Over two-thirds of all youths adjudicated delinquent are placed on probation annually. The chapter opens with a definition of standard probation. All probation is conditional, although there are several common features among most juvenile court jurisdictions that describe standard probation. These features will be described.

Next, the chapter defines standard probation with conditions and describes such programs. Additional requirements of probation orders include community service, restitution, home confinement, and electronic monitoring (EM), or youths may be required to engage in other activities, including school attendance, vocational/educational training, or counseling. Several advantages and disadvantages of probation are described, including evaluations of the successfulness of different types of probation programs.

Next described are juvenile intensive supervised probations (JISPs). JISP is an intermediate punishment. Intermediate punishments range between standard probation and secure confinement. The goals of intermediate punishment programs, all of which are community based, are listed and described. The eligibility requirements of several JISP programs are featured. The strengths and weaknesses of JISP programs are discussed.

Supervising youths more or less intensively are juvenile probation officers (POs). These POs are assigned different caseloads, depending upon their jurisdiction and the total number of juvenile offenders. Increasing numbers of juvenile probation departments are adopting the balanced approach, which seeks to ensure public safety, heighten offender accountability, and individualize one's needs. The relation between juvenile POs and their clients will be explored.

Enabling legislation in most jurisdictions has established various community corrections agencies and services over the years. Community corrections acts (CCAs) in different cities and counties offer a wide variety of services to meet offender needs. Different types of community corrections initiatives will be highlighted, together with their purposes, goals, strengths, weaknesses, and effectiveness.

EM programs and home confinement are described and evaluated. Different types of EM programs are identified, defined, and explained. Frequently used concurrently with EM is home confinement or house arrest. These monitoring and supervisory methods have been very effective in verifying an offender's whereabouts at particular times. The functions, advantages, disadvantages, and usefulness of both EM and home confinement will be examined and discussed.

The chapter concludes with an examination of various conditions that accompany probation programs. These conditions are fines, victim compensation or restitution, victim–offender mediation, and community service. Each condition is imposed on a case-by-case basis, depending on the nature of one's offense and suitability for such punishments and behavioral requirements. All of these conditions are intended to heighten offender accountability and ensure that the ends of juvenile justice are fulfilled. Evaluations of these sanctions will be made in terms of offender recidivism and other criteria.

Standard Probation for Juveniles

Standard Probation Defined

Standard juvenile probation is fairly simple to understand and considered a routine disposition for most juvenile court judges. Of all dispositional options available to juvenile court judges, standard probation is the one most frequently used. The first probation law was enacted in Massachusetts in 1878, although probation was used much earlier.

standard probation
Probationers conform to all terms of their probation program, but their contact with POs is minimal; often, their contact is by telephone or letter once or twice a month.

unconditional probation, unconditional standard probation
Form of conditional release without special restrictions or requirements placed on offender's behavior other than standard probation agreement terms; no formal controls operate to control or monitor divertee's behavior.

conditional probation
Program where divertee is involved in some degree of local monitoring by POs or personnel affiliated with local probation departments.

special conditions of probation
Extra requirements written into a standard probation agreement, including possible vocational or educational training, counseling, drug or alcohol treatment, attendance at meetings, restitution, and community service.

John Augustus invented probation in Boston in 1841. **Standard probation** is either a conditional or an unconditional nonincarcerative disposition for a specified period following an adjudication of delinquency.

There are several types of standard probation programs. Like their diversion program counterparts, probation programs for juveniles are either **unconditional probation** or **conditional probation**. Again, there are many similarities between probation programs devised for adults and those structured for juvenile offenders. **Unconditional standard probation**, another term for unconditional probation, basically involves complete freedom of movement for juveniles within their communities, perhaps accompanied by periodic reports by telephone or mail with a PO or the probation department. Because a PO's caseload is often large, with several hundred juvenile clients who must be managed, individualized attention cannot be given to most juveniles on standard probation. The period of unsupervised probation varies among jurisdictions depending upon offense seriousness and other circumstances (Champion, 2008b).

Conditional probation programs may include optional conditions and program requirements, such as performing a certain number of hours of public or community service, providing restitution to victims, payment of fines, employment, and/or participation in specific vocational, educational, or therapeutic programs. It is crucial to any probation program that an effective classification system is in place so that juvenile court judges can dispose offenders accordingly. It is common practice for conditional probation programs to contain special conditions and provisions that address different youth needs. These special conditions are usually added by the juvenile court judge on the basis of information provided by juvenile POs.

The terms of standard probation are outlined in Figure 11.1 in a General Conditions of Supervision agreement. The probationer signs the form, consenting to the probation conditions. A witness also signs to attest to the probationer's signature. Although these terms may be accompanied by special conditions, known as **special conditions of probation**, more often than not, no special conditions are attached. Thus, youths disposed to standard probation experience little change in their social routines. Whenever special conditions of probation are attached, they usually mean additional work for POs. Some of these conditions might include medical treatments for drug or alcohol dependencies, individual or group therapy or counseling, or participation in a driver's safety course. In some instances involving theft, burglary, or vandalism, restitution provisions may be included, where youths must repay victims for their financial losses. Most standard probation programs in the United States require little, if any, direct contact with the probation office. Logistically, this works out well for POs, who are frequently overworked and have enormous client caseloads of 300 or more youths. However, greater caseloads means less individualized attention devoted to youths by POs, and some of these youths require more supervision than others while on standard probation. Item 12 of the juvenile probation form used by many juvenile probation offices as shown in Figure 11.1, specifies which, if any, special conditions apply for particular juveniles.

Community-service orders are increasingly used, although in some states, juvenile probation departments have found it difficult to find personnel to supervise youthful probationers. For instance, a North Dakota delinquent was ordered to perform 200 hours of community service. The community had about 500 residents, and the work ordered involved park maintenance and general cleanup duties. However, the youth never performed any of this community service, since the probation department did not have the money to pay a juvenile PO to monitor the youth for the full 200 hours. Despite these occasional limitations, most probation program conditions today are geared toward heightening offender accountability by having him/her do something constructive. In a growing number of jurisdictions, drug courts are being established to deal more effectively with youthful substance abusers (Whiteacre, 2007).

Figure 11.1   General Conditions of Supervision

PROBATIONER: _____ COUNTY

GENERAL: The court may sentence the defendant to probation, which shall be subject to the following general conditions unless specifically deleted by the court. The probationer shall:

1. Pay supervision fees, fines, restitution or other fees ordered by the court.

2. Not use or possess controlled substances except pursuant to a medical prescription.

3. Submit to testing of breath or urine for controlled substance or alcohol use if the probationer has a history of substance abuse or if there is a reasonable suspicion that the probationer has illegally used controlled substances.

4. Participate in a substance abuse evaluation as directed by the supervising officer and follow the recommendations of the evaluator if there are reasonable grounds to believe there is a history of substance abuse.

5. Remain in the State of _____ until written permission to leave is granted by the Department of Corrections or a county community corrections agency.

6. If physically able, find and maintain gainful full-time employment, approved schooling, or a full-time combination of both. Any waiver of this requirement must be based on a finding by the court starting the reasons for the waiver.

7. Change neither employment nor residence without prior permission from the Department of Corrections or a county community corrections agency.

8. Permit the probation officer to visit the probationer or the probationer's work site or residence and to conduct a walk-through of the common areas and of the rooms in the residence occupied by or under the control of the probationer.

9. Consent to the search of person, vehicle or premises upon the request of a representative of the supervision officer if the supervising officer has reasonable grounds to believe that evidence of a violation will be found, and submit to fingerprinting or photographing, or both, when requested by the Department of Corrections or a county community corrections agency for supervision purpose.

10. Obey all laws, municipal, county, state and federal.

11. Promptly and truthfully answer all reasonable inquiries by the Department of Corrections or a county community corrections agency.

12. Not possess weapons, firearms or dangerous animals.

13. Reports as required and abide by the direction of the supervising officer.

14. If under supervision for, previously convicted of, a sex offense _____, and if recommended by the supervising officer, successfully complete a sex offender treatment program approved by the supervising officer and submit to polygraph examinations at the direction of the supervising officer.

15. Participate in a mental health evaluation as directed by the supervising officer and follow the recommendation of the evaluator.

16. If required to report to as a sex offender under _____, report with the Department of State Police, a chief of police, a county sheriff or the supervising agency: (A) When supervision begins; (B) Within 10 days of a change in residence; and (C) Once each year within 10 days or the probationer's date of birth.

_____   _____
Probationer Signature   Date

_____   _____
Witness/Title   Date

Parental Responsibilities for a Juvenile's Delinquent Conduct. In more than a few instances, parents of juveniles can be held financially liable for the actions of their delinquent children (Lee, 2008). For instance, D.D.H. was a Texas juvenile who committed burglary and larceny (*Matter of D.D.H.,* 2004). Following D.D.H.'s apprehension and adjudication, the court determined that the damages accruing to the victim amounted to $5,400, which included $4,500 to repair the property at the point where the burglary occurred, as well as $900 for unrecovered stolen property resulting from the burglary. The juvenile court judge ordered D.D.H.'s parents to pay $5,000 restitution to the victim for their son's delinquent acts as a special condition of the youth's probation orders. Although the parents appealed, a Texas appellate court upheld the juvenile court judge's restitution orders for the parents of the youth.

Juvenile Probationer Recidivism. In view of the fact that little or no monitoring of juvenile conduct exists in many state probation agencies, standard probation has fairly high rates of recidivism, ranging from 40 to 75 percent. Even certain youth camps operated in various California counties, where some degree of supervision over youths exists, have reported recidivism rates as high as 76 percent among their youthful clientele (Palmer, 1994). Therefore, it is often difficult to forecast which juveniles will have the greatest likelihood of reoffending, regardless of the program we are examining.

The following steps have been recommended for a reformed type of juvenile probation:

1. Research should drive policy. All too often, the field becomes enthralled in the latest fad and rushes to adopt it. Any and all new initiatives should include an evaluation component. Smart programs should be developed, especially programs that emphasize restitution.

2. Early intervention should be emphasized. Interventions occurring in one's early years are far more effective than those attempted when one is in his/her mid-teens.

3. Paying just debts should receive priority. Just deserts and justice should be emphasized in part to change the coddling image persons presently have of juvenile courts. Restitution and community service do much to heighten offender accountability, and they can easily be integrated into one's probation or parole program.

4. Character building should be an integral part of probation programming. Many delinquents lack character, or good habits of thought and action, as well as self-control. Programs that include psychoeducational strategies are better at character building than those that are strictly punishment-centered.

5. Violence prevention should be given high priority in program development. Juvenile probation must focus on efforts to suppress violent behavior. Programs that are educational in nature are more profitable in the long run compared with punishment-centered programs. These educational programs are geared to enable youths to learn how to cope more effectively with their environment. Such programs would include anger management training, acquiring skills (social and emotional), improving moral reasoning, and instilling heightened self-esteem (Rosky, 2008).

Mission-Driven Probation versus Outcome-Focused Probation. More effective juvenile probation appears to be both mission-driven and outcome-focused. Good juvenile probation is outcome-focused. For both individual offenders and entire juvenile PO caseloads, outcome-focused probation systematically measures the tangible results of its interventions, compares those results to its goals, and makes itself publicly accountable for any differences. Organizations tend to become whatever they measure. Departments must measure more than their failures (recidivism) and the sanctions they have imposed. Outcome measures assess whether goals have been achieved. They provide evidence of the degree to which probation supervision goals have or have not been achieved, in essence measuring the department's performance in meeting system goals. Long-term outcomes measure the degree to which probation supervision has impacted youthful offenders after their release, in terms of changing their thinking, behaviors, and attitudes (Parker, 2005).

Mission-driven juvenile probation is that the work of probation must be directed at achieving clearly articulated and widely shared goals. Getting there requires a commitment to a strategic planning or focus-group process that gives a representative cross-section of staff a chance to define their values about the juvenile justice system and juvenile probation in particular, and to translate them into action and results. Such an effort will increase staff buy-in and provide a basis for continuous feedback, evaluation, and improvement at the policy program and individual employee levels. Mission statements provide an organizational compass that points in the direction of an agreed-upon destination, and they are central to the operations and activities of any organization. What does juvenile probation stand for in the community? What is it attempting to accomplish? Ultimately, mission statements should be broken down into individual goals that are directed at protecting the public, holding the juvenile accountable for repairing harm caused to victims and the community, and engaging offenders in rehabilitative activities designed to address their most pressing problems and needs.

The Youth-to-Victim Restitution Project

One factor associated with significant reductions in recidivism is restitution. Programs that use restitution and enforce it seem to have lower recidivism rates associated with their youthful clientele. This is because offenders are required to repay victims for damages they inflict and take some responsibility for their actions. Restitution is a powerful deterrent to further offending. At least a financial connection is made between what the youthful offenders did and how much it cost to compensate victims for their losses. Therefore, these tangible punishments were considered most effective as delinquency deterrents (Taxman, 2005).

Juvenile Probation Camps

In the early 1980s, California experimented with several types of **juvenile probation camps (JPCs)** (Watson et al., 2003). These camps were county-operated and included physical activities, community contacts, and academic training. These nonincarcerative camps were designed as dispositional alternatives to secure custody for youthful offenders. Eligibility requirements included first-offender status and nonviolent behaviors. Counselors worked with youth who were carefully screened before entering the program. Groups of youths were deliberately small to maximize individualized attention for each youth. Older juveniles who participated in these probation camps had lower rates of recidivism compared with younger youths. Overall, the camps were viewed as successful in minimizing recidivism and maximizing rehabilitation of participants. One reason for the lower rates of recidivism among youthful clients was greater direct supervision by camp personnel. This circumstance is not unlike that found in communities where various methods of formal social control, including police and PO surveillance, are employed to supervise juvenile probationers and parolees.

The Intensive Aftercare Program

Between 1988 and 1990, the **Intensive Aftercare Program (IAP)** was designed in Philadelphia and targeted serious youthful offenders (Altschuler and Armstrong, 2001). A sample of 46 youths committed to the Bensalem Youth Development Center

juvenile probation camps (JPCs) California county-operated camps for delinquent youth placed on probation in early 1980s, including physical activities, community contacts, and academic training.

Intensive Aftercare Program (IAP) Philadelphia-based intervention for serious youthful offenders involving intensive counseling and training for acquiring self-help skills; recidivism of participants greatly reduced during study period of 1980–1990.

11.1   Career Snapshot

Myra Ann Welborn-Weeks

Program Coordinator, Wichita County Teen Court

Background

It was never my intention to work with juveniles. I made the decision to go into the criminal justice field; however, my focus was to be on adults. Blame it on divine intervention or trends in the criminal justice system. No matter, the case in 1992, I began working with juvenile offenders and have been involved with juveniles to date.

My current position is Program Coordinator with the Wichita County Teen Court. This is a program designed to allow first-offender youth the opportunity to satisfy misdemeanors or minor offenses utilizing a peer judicial system. There are several examples of peer justice dating back to the early 1970s, so the first actual Teen Court is unknown. What is known is that one of the first documented Teen Court programs in the United States began in Grand Prairie, Texas, in the early 1980s, soon to be followed by several other programs. It is estimated that there are over 1,200 peer courts currently operating throughout the United States. There are additional programs sprouting up in Canada, Australia, and the United Kingdom.

Experiences

Peer courts or teen courts were programs that I had heard about but really was unaware of what they were for or how they functioned. I was aware that they were designed for first-offenders. I knew that we did not utilize their services through juvenile probation and that was the extent of my teen court knowledge. But a resignation by the director of the existing teen court program operated by the state afforded me an unanticipated opportunity to become better acquainted with it. After minimal research on my part about teen courts, my attraction to such a program was forged. This program was the epitome of early intervention. Youth with offenses in teen court were receiving sentences more involved and proactive than serious felony offenders in the probation field. I was hooked. I was offered the job and was at my new career within a month. Prior to this, I had never been involved

with a program greater than a 50 percent recidivism rate. Teen courts on the average have an 85 percent success rate. I was and still am "hooked" on teen court as a proactive approach to intervention for youth who have committed a criminal offense.

The teen court model used in Texas is called the Adult Judge Model. In Texas, teen court trials are sentencing trials, so a plea of guilty or no contest is entered. At the time of trial, a volunteer attorney or judge presides over the proceedings, which are conducted by youth volunteers trained in both prosecution and defense. The cases referred to teen court in Texas are class "c" misdemeanors or nonjailable offenses. These offenses include status or children in need of supervision (CHINS) offenses as well as petty crimes. Cases are distributed to the youth attorneys in a variety of ways, but most commonly, they are given printed materials a few days down to a few minutes before court begins. Defense attorneys meet with their client and prepare the case to be presented. Because of confidentiality issues and time constraints, prosecutors rarely have a witness or evidence to present. Sentences include community service, jury duty, and any other sentencing option that emphasizes restorative justice while educating the offender of consequences associated with criminal behavior. Many courts also utilize sentencing options such as letters of apology, essays, workshops, counseling tools, and tours of participating agencies. Most often, youth are afforded 30–90 days to complete the requirements of their sentence at which time their offense is dismissed leaving them with a clean slate. An adult volunteer with the Wichita County Teen Court and a victim of a tragic drunk driving accident has coined the phrase "erasable mistake." Youth are offered the chance to erase their criminal record and start fresh as they enter adulthood.

Although it was never my intention to work with juvenile offenders, I am so thoroughly convinced that teen court and peer justice is such an effective tool for working with youth that I have given much of my time helping administer the Teen Court Association of Texas and the newly formed National Association of Youth Courts. Networking among coordinators is the most effective way of developing new courts and enhancing existing programs. Youth court coordinators are primarily innovative people in tune with thinking outside the box. Program development is an ongoing process with input and idea sharing the driving force for establishment and enhancement.

Advice to Students

It takes the entire community to nurture a child to adulthood. As a part of any community, be involved. Whether you chose to contribute as an educator, volunteer, parent, or citizen, youth need you. More than ever, we have absentee parents and over-scheduled children. With technology enhancing lives, personal involvement decreases. Parents increasingly communicate in sound bites versus conversations. Kids learn to type rather than converse. As we discover ever-efficient ways to live our lives, the quantity of time spent with youth and children

cannot become one more convenience. They need to hear and believe that adults are there for support and guidance. Parents are responsible for the development of their youth, but communities have a duty to facilitate the parents in every way possible.

I also want to emphasize the need to be patient with youth and specifically teens. Part of adolescence is trying on various personalities until finding one that fits. This may include hideous wardrobes and unbelievable forms of self-expression. Be confident that most teens will outgrow the offending behavior and overnight become an intelligent person that you thought would never appear.

Although never my intention to work with teens, it has been one of the most rewarding experiences I could have ever wished for. I have experienced the gamut of emotions through my involvement with youth. I have helped young people choose a college and I have been present as young people were sentenced to life incarcerated. It has never been easy, but as it has been said, nothing worthwhile is ever easy.

---

was compared with a control group of 46 youths who received traditional aftercare probation services. While the IAP participants exhibited lower rates of recidivism compared with those subject to conventional aftercare probation, the differences were not significant. It was reported, however, that IAP officers believed that their interventions with IAP youth were both rapid and positive. Thus, some officials believed that they were able to assist some of these IAP participants from incurring subsequent rearrests. The successfulness of IAP in any particular jurisdiction often depends on the nature and quality of supervision received by clients (Meisel, 2001).

The Sexual Offender Treatment Program

Not all specialized programs for juvenile probationers are successful. For example, an assessment was made of the **Sexual Offender Treatment (SOT) Program** established by a juvenile probation department of a large midwestern U.S. metropolitan county in January 1988 (Lab, Shields, and Schondel, 1993). The program consisted of 20 peer-group meetings with psychosocioeducational intervention focus, supplemented by individual family counseling sessions with youths who had been adjudicated delinquent for assorted sex offenses. Subsequently, an experimental program was conducted for 46 youths referred to the SOT program and compared with a control group of 109 youths assigned to nonsexually specific interventions during the same period. Data sources included juvenile court and program records. Essentially, youths handled by the SOT program fared no better than youths processed through normal, nonoffense-specific programming. Thus, these researchers concluded that simply knowing one's symptoms and problems and designing specific interventions for those problems are not always workable. Additional study is needed to identify appropriate treatment factors that might make a difference in reducing their recidivism rates for sexual offending.

> **Sexual Offender Treatment (SOT) Program**
> Treatment program for juvenile offenders adjudicated delinquent on sex charges: includes psychosocioeducational interventions, therapies, and counseling.

The Successfulness of Standard Juvenile Probation

recidivism rate

Proportion of offenders who, when released from probation or parole, commit further crimes.

intensive supervised probation

A method of supervising offenders more intensively compared with standard probation; usually involves more face-to-face contacts with clients, more frequent drug/alcohol checks, electronic monitoring, home confinement, and other restrictions. May also be known as IPS or intensive probation supervision.

recidivists

Offenders who have committed previous offenses.

The successfulness of standard juvenile probation as well as other probation and parole programs is measured according to the **recidivism rate** accompanying these program alternatives. Recidivism is measured in various ways, including rearrests, reconvictions, new adjudications, return to secure confinement, movement from standard probation to **intensive supervised probation (ISP)**, and simple probation program condition violations, such as drug use or alcohol and curfew violation (Clinkinbeard and Murray, 2008; Pires and Jenkins, 2007). **Recidivists** are persons who commit new crimes or delinquent acts after having been convicted or adjudicated for previous offenses.

The most popular meaning of recidivism is a new adjudication as delinquent for reoffending (Champion, 2008a). It is generally the case that, with exceptions, intensive supervision programs have less recidivism associated with them than standard probation. Over the years, a recidivism standard of 30 percent has been established among researchers as the cutting point between a successful probation program and an unsuccessful one. Programs with recidivism rates of 30 percent or less are considered successful, while those programs with more than 30 percent recidivism are not particularly successful. This figure is arbitrary, although it is most often used as a success standard. No program presently has zero percent recidivism (Champion, 2008a).

Probation and Recidivism

Standard probation, which means little or no direct and regular supervision of offenders by POs, has a fairly high rate of recidivism among the various state jurisdictions. Recidivism rates for juveniles on standard probation range from 30 to 70 percent, depending upon the nature of their offenses and prior records. The following elements appear to be predictive of future criminal activity and reoffending by juveniles: one's age at first adjudication, a prior criminal record (a combined measure of the number and severity of priors), the number of prior commitments to juvenile facilities, drug/chemical abuse, alcohol abuse, family relationships (parental control), school problems, and peer relationships (Schaffner, 2006).

At the beginning of the twentieth century, when probation began to be used for juvenile supervision, a report was issued entitled "Juvenile Courts and Probation" in 1914 (Flexner and Baldwin, 1914). Writing seven years following the establishment of the National Probation Association in 1907, Flexner and Baldwin described three important aspects of probation as it applied to juvenile offenders: (1) the period of probation should always be indeterminate because judges cannot possibly fix the period of treatment in advance, (2) to be effective, probation work must be performed by full-time, professionally trained POs, and (3) probation is not a judicial function.

It is interesting to see how Flexner and Baldwin discounted the value of the judiciary in fixing one's term of probation and performing supervisory functions. They were adamant in the belief that only professional POs should engage in such supervisory tasks and that the judicial function should be minimal. The strong treatment orientation of probation is apparent as well, suggesting their belief that probationer treatment programs should be tailored to fit the probationer's needs. Further, they underscored the power originally assigned to POs and the leverage that POs could exert upon their clients, including possible probation revocation action if program infractions occurred.

An effective probation program is one where POs have an awareness of the juvenile offender's needs and weaknesses. One problem in many existing probation programs is that POs find it hard to establish a rapport between themselves and their juvenile clients. A high degree of mistrust exists, in large part because of the age differential between the PO and the offender.

Focus on Delinquency 11.2

It happened in Omaha, Nebraska. An animal shelter was broken into late at night and 16 cats were bludgeoned to death with baseball bats. No one knew who might have committed such an act. The act itself was especially heinous even though these were animals. The culprits turned out to be X.L. and D.P., both 15 and from Omaha. They bragged about killing the cats to others and were reported. Someone called the police who investigated. Later in juvenile court, X.L. and D.P. confessed to the judge. They gave no explanation for killing the cats, only that they just thought it up when they got inside. They brought the baseball bats for self-protection, according to their later statements.

When their case came before the juvenile court judge, the judge ordered them to pay $5,000 for the cats. He also placed them on probation for three years. Animal rights activists were outraged and letters were written to the newspaper. What sentence would you have imposed? How serious is the death of 14 cats? How should the youths have been treated? Was probation sufficient? What do you think? [Source: Adapted from the Associated Press, "Youths Given Probation in Cat Deaths," October 13, 2007.]

Some POs have suggested an approach normally practiced by psychological counselors in developing a rapport between themselves and their clients. It has been suggested, for instance, that each PO should (1) thoroughly review the youth's case, including family and juvenile interviews and other background information; (2) engage in introspection and attempt to discover his/her own reactions to adolescents and responses to verbal exchanges; (3) attempt to cultivate a relationship of acceptance rather than rejection and punitiveness; (4) react favorably to a "critical incident," where the juvenile may "screw up" and expect reprimand or punishment but where acceptance and understanding are reflected instead; and (5) follow through with continued support that bolsters juvenile confidence in the PO (Sweet, 1985:90). When juveniles fail to comply with one or more terms of their standard probation, they run the risk of being in contempt of court, since the juvenile court originally imposed their probation orders. In Dougherty County, Georgia, for example, a PO may believe that a juvenile court judge should review a particular juvenile's behavior where it is believed that he/she has not been in compliance with the terms of the probation orders. A motion is made for a judicial review of the juvenile to determine whether the allegations against him/her are true. Figure 11.2 shows a motion for judicial review, where one or more particulars are noted that indicate what the PO believes are probation violations. The motion also contains a notice of a hearing where these allegations may be aired. Figure 11.3 shows the actual judicial review, where the judge's findings are articulated.

As the result of the judicial review, if the allegations are supported, the judge will make a determination about what should be done to the juvenile as a punishment for noncompliance. Judges have an array of options, including intensifying one's supervision by POs, imposing restitution, community service, fines, or participation in one or more kinds of counseling programs. Or the judge can simply continue the youth's probation with a verbal reprimand or warning.

Some juveniles are unreachable through any kind of effective exchange. Chronic offenders, hard-core offenders, or psychologically disturbed juveniles frequently reject

Figure II.2   Motion for Judicial Review, Dougherty County, GA

IN THE JUVENILE COURT
OF
DOUGHERTY COUNTY, GEORGIA

In The Interest Of:

_____
Name   Race/Sex   DOB

File Number: _____
Referral Number/s: _____
                        _____

MOTION FOR JUDICIAL REVIEW

Now comes _____ and moves the Court to judicially review the
            Name

probation status of the above-named juvenile.

Movant is of the opinion and belief that the juvenile and or parent are not cooperating with the

juvenile's case manager and are not complying with the Court's Order of probation dated

_____ in the following particulars:

1. _____
2. _____
3. _____
4. _____
5. _____

This _____ day of _____, 20___.

                                    _____
                                    Signature of Movant

NOTICE OF HEARING

The within and foregoing motion filed and said matter to come on for a review in the Juvenile

Court of Dougherty County, Georgia, on _____ at _____ a.m. / p.m.,

all interested parties should be present in Court to show cause, if any, why the conditions of

probation have not been complied with, or why the conditions should not be enforced.

This _____ day of _____, 20___.

shared files\probation\motion for judicial review

Figure 11.3   Judicial Review, Dougherty County, GA

**IN THE JUVENILE COURT
OF
DOUGHERTY COUNTY, GEORGIA**

Judicial Review

In The Interest Of:

_____

DOB: _____   **Age:** _____

Hearing Date: _____
File Number: _____

Issue/s:
1. _____
_____
2. _____
_____
3. _____
_____

Juvenile's comments and explanations:_____

_____
_____
_____
_____
_____
_____

Judge's findings:_____

_____
_____
_____
_____
_____
_____
_____
_____
_____
_____

shared files\probation\judicial review form

any attempts by authorities to understand them or assist them in any task (Cauffman, Steinberg, and Piquero, 2005). If some youths are chemically dependent, the fact of substance abuse may interfere with effective interventions of any kind. Where standard probation is not feasible, an **intensive supervision program** is required for certain types of offenders.

Intermediate Punishments for Juvenile Offenders

Intermediate Punishments Defined

Intermediate punishments are community-based sanctions that range from **intensive probation supervision (IPS)** to nonsecure custodial programs. These programs include more intensive monitoring or management of juvenile behaviors through more intensive supervision. They may include home confinement, EM, or both. Other community-based services are included, where the goal is to maintain fairly close supervision over youthful offenders (Abrams, 2006). The most successful ISP programs seem to be those that emphasize the social structural causes of delinquency and use greater community participation and agency networking rather than focus upon individual youths' problems. Cognitive-behavioral interventions and participatory problem-solving activities are used as a part of probation department programs designed to reduce offender recidivism and promote long-term law-abiding behaviors (Bernberg and Thorlindsson, 2007).

Intermediate punishment programs are presently operated in all states for both juvenile and adult offenders. They are sometimes referred to as **creative sentencing**, since they are somewhere between standard probationary dispositions and traditional incarcerative terms that might be imposed by judges. These alternatives to incarceration are regarded as positive interventions for a majority of today's youth who are brought to the attention of the juvenile justice system (Champion, 2008a).

The Goals of Intermediate Punishment Programs

There is considerable variation among intermediate punishment programs, although they tend to exhibit similar goals or objectives. These include, but are not limited to:

1. provision of less-expensive sanctions compared with secure confinement;
2. achievement of lower rates of recidivism compared with standard probation;
3. greater emphasis on reintegration into communities as the primary correctional goal;
4. provision of a greater range of community services and organizations in a cooperative effort to assist youthful offenders;
5. minimization of adverse influence of labeling that might stem from secure confinement; and
6. improvement in personal educational and vocational skills of individual offenders, together with acquisition of better self-concepts and greater acceptance of responsibility for one's actions.

Classification Criteria for Placement in ISP Programs

One problem for juvenile court judges is deciding which juveniles should be assigned to which programs. This is a classification problem, and the level of accuracy associated with juvenile risk prediction instruments is about as poor as adult risk prediction devices. This problem is considered one of correction's greatest challenges (Clinkin-beard and Murray, 2008). Nevertheless, judges attempt to make secure or nonsecure confinement decisions on the basis of the following elements: (1) risk of continued criminal activity and the offender's need for services as an important component for classification; (2) assisting probation and parole officers in developing better case plans and selecting appropriate casework strategies for a more effective case-management system; (3) a management information system designed to enhance planning, moni-toring, evaluation, and accountability for a better management information system; and (4) allowances for agencies to effectively and efficiently allocate their limited resources for a better workload deployment system.

Chronic recidivists and serious offenders are most often designated for secure con-finement. However, an increasing number of community-based programs are being designed to supervise such offenders closely and offer them needed services and treat-ments. It is helpful to review briefly some of the issues relating to the effectiveness of such instrumentation (Latessa, 2005). Depending upon the scores received by vari-ous juvenile clients when classified, they may or may not be entitled to assignment to ISP or to a community-based program. Theoretically, those youthful offenders who are considered dangerous and violent are poor candidates for inclusion, because it is predicted that they might harm themselves or others, including agency staff or POs. Also, those considered not dangerous would be predicted to be good candidates as program clients. However, the flaws of our instrumentation do not always discrimi-nate effectively.

Juvenile Intensive Supervised Probation (JISP)

ISP programs, also known as **JISP**, have become increasingly popular for managing nonincarcerated offender populations. JISP will be used to describe the programs developed in different jurisdictions, regardless of whether the JISP designation is used by individual programs. Since the mid-1960s, these programs have been aimed primar-ily at supervising adult offenders closely, and in recent years, JISP programs have been designed for juvenile offenders as well. JISP is a highly structured and conditional supervision program for either adult or juvenile offenders that serves as an alternative to incarceration and provides for an acceptable level of public safety. For administra-tors of secure facilities for juveniles, community-based options such as ISP are desir-able, since overcrowding is reduced (Parker, 2005).

JISP
Ohio-operated program for youthful offenders, including home confinement, electronic monitoring, and other IPS methods.

Juvenile court judges impose ISP for those juveniles who are believed to be in need of greater monitoring or supervision by POs. Because POs who supervise these youths must meet with and monitor them frequently, their caseloads are reduced substantially. Thus, JISP is more expensive than traditional standard probation. Figure 11.4 shows an order for IPS used by the juvenile court in Dougherty County, Georgia. It is important to note that the juvenile and the parents must sign this order, signifying their intent to comply with it. A violation of one or more of these intensive supervision conditions may result in a judicial review at the request of the supervising PO.

Characteristics of JISP Programs

JISP programs for juveniles have been developed and are currently operating in about half of all U.S. jurisdictions. It is important to note that many of these JISP programs are operated on a countywide or citywide basis, rather than on a statewide basis. Thus, it is difficult to find a state jurisdiction with a uniform policy and program information about JISPs that apply to all local agencies within the state. One example of a JISP pro-gram operated by a county is the Johnson County Department of Corrections, Kansas. The JISP conditions and guidelines for Johnson County are provided following.

Figure 11.4   Order for Intensive Supervision, Dougherty County, GA

ORDER FOR INTENSIVE SUPERVISION

IN THE JUVENILE COURT OF
«COUNTYNAME» COUNTY, GEORGIA

In the interest of

«JUVENILENAMEALL»
A child under 17 years of age

FILE #:	«juvenileFilenbr»
CASE #:	«CASENUMBER»
SEX:	«JUVENILESEX»
DOB:	«JUVENILEDOB»

A petition having been filed and a hearing regarding the allegations contained therein having been held, the Court hereby finds as follows:

1.

The filing of a petition and all proceedings therein, including the hearing, has been held in compliance with the Juvenile Court Code.

2.

Testimony was received (and the child admitted) the allegations as set forth in the complaint (petition).

3.

Based upon said testimony (and admission) the Court hereby finds that the child is hereby adjudicated delinquent (and unruly).

4.

The Court then held its dispositional hearing immediately thereafter with the consent of all parties and hereby finds that said youth is in need of INTENSIVE SUPERVISION, treatment, and rehabilitation, but that commitment is not necessary at this time and the child is therefore placed in the INTENSIVE SUPERVISION PROGRAM until released by order of the Court.

5.

Said child is subject to the terms and conditions of the INTENSIVE SUPERVISION PROGRAM which are attached hereto and made a part hereof.

SO ORDERED this «FORMALDATE».

_____
«HEARINGOFFICER»,

«HEARINGOFFICERTITLE»

«COUNTYNAME» County Juvenile Court

The Johnson County, Kansas Juvenile Intensive Supervision Program.
The court grants probation for a set period of time with the specific conditions of each supervision set out in the "Probation Plan" or Conditional Release Contract. Each client must abide by the written rules and regulations of the program, which will be reviewed by the Intensive Supervision Officer (ISO) assigned.

There are levels in the Intensive Supervision Program. Listed below are some of the minimum requirements of each level:

Level I
1. Thirty days in length.
2. Three face-to-face contacts with the ISO per week.
3. Four random urinalyses/breath analyses per month as directed by the ISO.
4. Twenty hours of community service.
5. Curfew as directed.

Level II
1. Sixty days in length.
2. Two face-to-face contacts with the ISO per week.
3. Three random urinalyses/breath analyses per month as directed by the ISO.
4. Curfew as directed.

Level III
1. Sixty days in length.
2. One face-to-face contact with the ISO per week.
3. Two random urinalyses/breath analyses per month as directed by the ISO.
4. Curfew as directed.

Level IV
1. No specified minimum length.
2. One face-to-face contact with the ISO per week for the first 30 days.
3. One face-to-face contact every other week after a minimum of 30 days.
4. One random urinalysis/breath analysis per month as directed by the ISO.

ISOs are also required to have frequent contact with those individuals who play a significant role in the life of the youth, such as family, friends, treatment providers, and sponsors.

A face-to-face contact may include:

1. visits to the probation office,
2. visits at employment sites,
3. home visits,
4. meetings at other designated places.

The curfew is monitored on a random basis.

Compliance with the previously stated requirements, and any other requirements, will allow the individual to progress through the ISP (Johnson County Department of Corrections, 2002).

Similar to their adult ISP program counterparts, JISP programs are ideally designed for secure incarceration-bound youths and are considered as acceptable alternatives to incarceration. JISP programs are different from other forms of standard probation in terms of the differences in the amount of officer/client contact during the course of the probationary period. For example, standard probation is considered no more than two face-to-face officer/client contacts per month. JISP programs might differ from standard probation according to the following face-to-face criteria: (1) two or three times per week versus once per month, (2) once per week versus twice per month, or (3) four times per week versus once per week (the latter figure being unusually high for standard probation contact).

The brokerage nature of PO dispositions toward their work is evident in the different types of services provided by different JISP programs. Services brokered by various POs in different jurisdictions may include (1) mental health counseling; (2) drug and alcohol counseling; (3) academic achievement and aptitude testing; (4) vocational and employment training; (5) individual, group, and family counseling; (6) job search and placement programs; (7) alternative education programs; (8) foster grandparents programs; and (9) Big Brother/Big Sister programs. Not all JISP programs are alike, but many JISP programs share certain similarities. Some of these include (1) recognition of the shortcomings of traditional responses to serious and/or chronic offenders (e.g., incarceration or out-of-home placement); (2) severe resource constraints within jurisdictions that compel many probation departments to adopt agency-wide classification and workload deployment systems for targeting a disproportionate share of resources for the most problematic juvenile offenders; (3) program hopes to reduce the incidence of incarceration in juvenile secure confinement facilities and reduce overcrowding; (4) programs tend to include aggressive supervision and control elements as a part of the get-tough movement; and (5) all programs have a vested interest in rehabilitation of youthful offenders (Armstrong, 1991).

From these analyses of ISP program content, generally, we can glean the following as basic characteristics of ISP programs:

1. Low officer/client caseloads (i.e., 30 or fewer probationers).
2. High levels of offender accountability (e.g., victim restitution, community service, payment of fines, partial defrayment of program expenses).
3. High levels of offender responsibility.
4. High levels of offender control (home confinement, EM, frequent face-to-face visits by POs).
5. Frequent checks for arrests, drug and/or alcohol use, and employment/school attendance (drug/alcohol screening, coordination with police departments and juvenile halls, teachers, family) (Fagan and Reinarman, 1991).

Strengths and Weaknesses of JISP Programs

A strength of JISP programs is that they are substantially less expensive compared with the costs of incarcerating juvenile offenders. For instance, the Texas Youth Commission reports that juvenile incarceration represents the most expensive criminal justice option, averaging $124 as the daily expenditure per juvenile (Texas Youth Commission, 2005). Alternatively, juvenile probation programs manage youths at the rate of $10.50 per day. Various ISP programs in Texas average $30 per day per juvenile.

Another strength is that JISP programs generally report lower rates of recidivism compared with standardized probation and other more conventional nonincarcerative options. One reason is that JISP clients are more closely monitored and thus are given less opportunity to reoffend. Another reason is that prospective clients for JISP programs are more closely screened. More serious offenders are usually excluded, which increases the success rates of included clients (Gordon and Malmsjo, 2005).

A weakness of most JISP programs is that local demands and needs vary to such an extent among jurisdictions that after 25 years, we have yet to devise a standard definition of what is meant by ISP (Corbett, 2000). Thus, the dominant themes of current JISP programs appear to be (1) those that are designed as front-end alternatives to secure confinement, (2) those that combine incarceration with some degree of community supervision (shock probation), and (3) those that follow secure confinement.

Terminating One's Probation Program

At some point, almost all juveniles placed on standard probation or JISP will complete their programs, more or less successfully. Those who don't complete them will have other dispositions imposed, such as secure confinement or placement in some alternative

Figure 11.5   Termination of Probation, Dougherty County, GA

DOUGHERTY COUNTY JUVENILE COURT
Room 302
225 Pine Avenue
Albany, Georgia 31701

In the Interest of

Date of Birth: **Sex:**   **Race:**

ORDER

TERMINATION OF PROBATION

It appearing to the Court that the above-named juvenile, having been placed on probation under the supervision of the Court, has made satisfactory adjustment while on probation. It is further Ordered and Decreed that said child is hereby dismissed from probation and the Jurisdiction of this Court terminated.

ORDERED AND DECREED THIS

The _____ day of _____ 2004

_____

Judge/Associate Judge

Dougherty County Juvenile Court

setting, such as a group home, foster care, boot camp, or wilderness experience. Again, judges are most often responsible for issuing orders terminating one's probation program. In Dougherty County, Georgia, for example, an order for termination of probation is issued by the juvenile court judge. This form is shown in Figure 11.5. Bonnie Farr, a juvenile PO for the Dougherty County Juvenile Court, has provided a form that

Figure 11.5   Termination of Probation, Dougherty County, GA (Cont.)

Request for Termination

Date:

Childs Name:
Age:

Probation Officer:

Date of Probation:

Offense:

**The above named juvenile is   years of age and has completed all conditions of
probation as ordered by the Court. I am requesting to terminate from probation.**

This juvenile is attending

This juvenile has paid a

This juvenile has completed

Probation Officer's Comments:

her department uses for these types of actions. Figure 11.5 shows a request for termination of probation filed by Officer Farr. She has the option of including any relevant comments for the judge's consideration that are often favorable for the probationer.

On her form, Farr notes when the probation was imposed, the nature of the adjudication offense, the fact that the juvenile has completed all of the terms required by the original probation orders, the fact that the youth is attending school or some vocational program, and whether the youth paid a fine or made restitution to one or more victims. Her recommendation for the youth's termination from probation is usually granted by the juvenile court judge unless there are compelling reasons for not doing so.

Case Supervision Planning

Caseload Assignments

A popular strategy for assigning caseloads to POs and which is used extensively by probation departments is the numbers game reshuffling of **caseloads**, where reduced caseloads for POs are given to improve officer/client interpersonal contact. Reduced caseloads for POs arguably should intensify their supervision as well as their supervisory quality in relation to client/offenders. Several recent studies have experimented with varying degrees of officer/client contact and recidivism rates. PO caseload reductions were mandated by one of the recommendations of the Task Force on Corrections appointed by the President's Commission on Law Enforcement and the Administration of Justice in 1967 (Sturgeon, 2005).

Models of Case Supervision Planning

Case supervision planning makes more sense if we consider several alternative case assignment strategies that are presently used by different probation departments. The most popular model is the **conventional model**, which is the random assignment of probationers to POs on the basis of one's present caseload in relation to others. This is much like the **numbers game model**, where total probationers are divided by the total POs in a given department, and each PO is allocated an equal share of the supervisory task. Thus, POs may supervise both very dangerous and nondangerous probationers. Another model is the **conventional model with geographic considerations**. Simply, this is assigning probationers to POs who live in a common geographic area. The intent is to shorten PO travel between clients. Again, little or no consideration is given to an offender's needs or dangerousness in relation to PO skills. The **specialized caseloads model** is the model used for case supervision planning, where offender assignments are made on the basis of client risks and needs and PO skills and interests in dealing with those offender risks and needs. Some POs may have special training and education in psychology or social work or chemical dependency. Thus, if certain clients have psychological problems or chemical dependencies, it is believed that these POs with special skills and education might be more effective in relating to them (Sturgeon, 2005).

The Balanced Approach

Some of the problems of JISP have been attributable to different caseload assignment models or to other organizational peculiarities and conflicting organizational goals that interfere with the performance of juvenile PO roles. One solution is referred to as the **balanced approach** (Seyko, 2001). The balanced approach to juvenile probation is neither a wholly punitive nor a rehabilitative formulation, but rather it is a more broadbased, constructive approach. It operates on the assumption that decision making must take into consideration the converging interests of all involved parties in the juvenile justice process, including offenders, victims, the community-at-large, and the system itself. No party to the decision making should benefit at the expense of another party; rather, a balancing of interests should be sought. The balanced approach, therefore, simultaneously emphasizes community protection, offender accountability, individualization of treatments, and competency assessment and development (Abatiello, 2005).

The balanced approach obligates community leaders and juvenile justice system actors to consider their individual juvenile codes and determine whether a balance exists between offender needs and community interests (Seyko, 2001). Punitive provisions of these codes should address victim needs as well as the needs of juvenile offenders,

caseloads
Number of cases that a probation or parole officer is assigned according to some standard such as a week, month, or year; caseloads vary among jurisdictions.

case supervision planning
A means whereby a probation or parole department makes assignments of probationers or parolees to POs or parole officers.

conventional model
Caseload assignment model where probation or parole officers are assigned clients randomly.

numbers game model
Caseload assignment model for probation or parole officers where total number of offender/clients is divided by number of officers.

conventional model with geographic considerations
Similar to conventional model; caseload assignment model is based upon the travel time required for POs to meet with offender-clients regularly.

specialized caseloads model
Case assignment method based on POs' unique skills and knowledge relative to offender drug or alcohol problems; some POs are assigned particular clients with unique problems that require more than average PO expertise.

balanced approach
Probation orientation that simultaneously emphasizes community protection, offender accountability, individualization of treatments, and competency assessment and development.

to the extent that restitution and victim compensation are a part of improving an offender's accountability and acceptance of responsibility. The fairness of the juvenile justice system should be assessed by key community leaders, and a mission statement should be drafted that has the broad support of diverse community organizations. Training programs can be created through the close coordination of chief POs in different jurisdictions, where offender needs may be targeted and addressed. All facets of the community and the juvenile justice process should be involved, including juvenile court judges. The high level of community involvement will help to ensure a positive juvenile probation program that will maximize a youth's rehabilitative benefits (Ayers-Schlosser, 2005).

Some ISP programs fail because they often neglect to address many of the problems that include those suggested by the balanced approach. Some of the reasons for why case supervision planning is often unsuccessful are the following:

1. Purpose: The purposes of case supervision planning have not been thought out carefully.
2. Perceptual differences: Offenders often change only when they find it necessary to change, not because we want them to change.
3. Resistance: We don't always recognize that resistance to change is normal; sometimes we prematurely shift emphasis to an enforcement orientation and rules of probation; case planning starts to look more like the probation order whenever this occurs.
4. Expectation: Desired change is sought too quickly; we sometimes expect too much from offenders or expect unrealistic changes to be made.
5. Focus: There is a tendency to focus on lesser problems to gain "success."
6. Involvement: We often fail to involve offenders in the case-planning process.
7. Stereotyping: Case supervision planning is equated with treatment and rehabilitation, and thus, it is often rejected without an adequate consideration of its strengths.
8. Getting too close: Sometimes POs are perceived as getting too close to offenders.
9. Perceptions of accountability: Nonspecific case plans cannot be criticized by supervisors.
10. Use of resources: There is tendency to "burn out" community resources by referring involuntary offenders, those who are not ready to work on their problems.
11. Measurement: Probation successes or failures are not measured according to some case plan, but rather, according to arrests, convictions, or numbers of technical violations; how should success be evaluated or measured?
12. Management: There is a general lack of understanding or support for case supervision planning by management; POs are considered exclusively officers of the court, and judges don't particularly expect offenders to change because of officer "treatments," only that someone shares the blame or accountability whenever offenders commit new crimes or violate one or more of their probationary conditions.
13. Training: Staff members have not been adequately trained in the development, implementation, and evaluation of case plans (Ellsworth, 1988:29–30).

The principles of JISP programs are sound. Basically, implementation problems of one type or another have hindered their successfulness in various jurisdictions. It is apparent that juvenile probation services will need to coordinate their activities and align their departmental and individual PO performance objectives with those of community-based agencies that are a part of the referral network of services and treatments, to maximize goal attainment. Consistent with the balanced approach to managing offenders, it has been recommended that in order for ISP programs to maximize their effectiveness, they should be individualized to a high degree, so that a proper balance of punishment/deterrence and rehabilitation/community protection may be attained (Ayers-Schlosser, 2005). Public safety remains a key goal of any community-based program responsible for serious and violent juvenile offenders (Kennedy, 2005).

An offender's constitutional rights should be recognized, but at the same time, accountability to victims and the community must be ensured. In the next section, we will examine several specific ISP programs that are considered community-based alternatives in contrast with state- or locally-operated public programs.

Community-Based Alternatives

Community Corrections Acts (CCAs)

Community-based corrections agencies and organizations are not new. Originally, these programs were intended to alleviate prison and jail overcrowding by establishing community-based organizations that could accommodate some of the overflow of prison-bound offenders. However, corrections officials soon realized that the potential of such programs was great for offender rehabilitation and reintegration and that juveniles as well as adult offenders could profit from involvement in them. Many states subsequently passed **CCAs** that were aimed at funding local government units to create community facilities that could provide services and other resources to juveniles (Clear and Dammer, 2003).

The overall objective of community corrections agencies is to develop and deliver front-end solutions and alternative sanctions in lieu of state incarceration (Burrell, 2005). In 1984, the **American Correctional Association (ACA)** Task Force on Community Corrections Legislation recommended that CCAs should not target violent offenders. Rather, the states should be selective about who meets their program requirements. It was recommended that (1) states should continue to house violent juvenile offenders in secure facilities, (2) judges and prosecutors should continue to explore various punishment options in lieu of incarceration, and (3) local communities should develop programs with additional funding from state appropriations (Huskey, 1984:45). The ACA Task Force identified the following elements as essential to the success of any CCA:

1. There should be restrictions on funding high-cost capital projects as well as conventional probation services.
2. Local communities should participate on a voluntary basis and may withdraw at any time.
3. Advisory boards should submit annual criminal justice plans to local governments.
4. There should be a logical formula in place for allocating community corrections funds.
5. Incarceration-bound juveniles should be targeted, rather than adding additional punishments for those who otherwise would remain in their communities (in short, avoid "net-widening").
6. Financial subsidies should be provided to local government and community-based corrections agencies.
7. Local advisory boards in each community should function to assess program needs and effectiveness, to propose improvements in the local juvenile justice system, and to educate the general public about the benefits of intermediate punishments.
8. A performance factor should be implemented to ensure that funds are used to achieve specific goals of the act.

Shawnee County Community Corrections. A good example of a contemporary view of CCAs in action within specific cities and counties is the Shawnee County, Kansas, community corrections program (Shawnee County Department of Community Corrections, 2002:1). Originally in Kansas, a CCA was passed in 1978, and Shawnee County was one of the first counties to join in the CCA and begin programming. At first, there were only nine counties involved. In 1989, Kansas mandated that all

Community Corrections Acts (CCAs)
Enabling legislation by individual states to fund local government units to provide community facilities, services, and resources to juveniles who are considered at risk of becoming delinquent or who are already delinquent and need treatment/services.

American Correctional Association (ACA)
Established in 1870 to disseminate information about correctional programs and correctional training; designed to foster professionalism throughout correctional community.

counties should have community corrections services. In 1994, juvenile services were included. And during 1996–1997, juvenile offender services were transferred from the Kansas Department of Corrections to the Juvenile Justice Authority (JJA).

One original purpose of the Kansas CCA was the diversion of prison-bound offenders from institutions to community-based intermediate sanction programs. With the changes brought about by the implementation of sentencing guidelines, offenders are formally sentenced to probation pursuant to the guidelines' computation of sentence. In 2002, the Department of Community Corrections supervised chronic or violent offenders within the community. Effective community-based programming involves intensive supervision of these clients, together with solution-focused case-management services that assist offenders in becoming productive members of society.

When Shawnee County Community Corrections (SCCC) was established, it was one of three units within the Shawnee County Department of Corrections. The Department of Corrections included the jail, a juvenile detention center, and community corrections. In 2000, community corrections became a separate department. Presently, the mission of the SCCC is to (1) provide highly structured community supervision to felony offenders, (2) hold offenders accountable to their victims and to the community, and (3) improve the offenders' ability to live productively and lawfully.

The juvenile community corrections program is a state and local partnership. It is designed to (1) promote public safety, (2) hold juvenile offenders accountable for their behavior, and (3) improve the ability of youth to live productively and responsibly in their communities. In this respect, the juvenile program reflects the basic elements of the balanced approach.

Program goals are attained in the following manner. For the goal of public safety, manageable caseloads are maintained, allowing staff to closely supervise offenders in the community. For the goal of enforcing court-ordered sanctions, supervision plans are devised that meet the requirements of the court and provide structure, which will improve the offender's ability to successfully complete the terms of his/her probation program. For the aim of restoring losses to crime victims, payment of restitution by offenders is overseen, including the collection of court costs and supervision of community service work. Finally, for the aim of assisting offenders to change their behaviors, offender participation in services provided by community corrections or community resources is enforced through close offender monitoring to ensure their compliance. Services include drug treatment, job search and maintenance skills, literacy enhancement, and life skills.

Several supervisory options are available, depending upon the juvenile offender's needs. For example, a JISP program includes intensive monitoring and provides an intermediate sanction between standard probation and placement in a juvenile correctional facility for adjudicated juvenile offenders. The juvenile offender community case-management program consists of services provided for juvenile offenders who have been placed by the court in the care and custody of the JJA. The court may order out-of-home placement for certain juvenile offenders after all other reasonable efforts have been made to address the problems that caused their illegal behavior. Case-management services are provided to assist juveniles and their caregivers to find resources that will meet their needs. Finally, the juvenile conditional release supervision program provides monitoring of juveniles who have been released from one of four JJA-operated juvenile correctional facilities and returned to the community. Community corrections officers monitor these juveniles so that they comply with the conditions of their release. These officers also assist juveniles in accomplishing their aftercare plans.

The juvenile justice process followed in Shawnee County is as follows:

Arrest
Juvenile Detention Center (if danger to self or others during court process)
Adjudication (court determines juvenile committed offense; juvenile is adjudicated a delinquent offender)

Sentencing alternatives:

1. Place juvenile offender in parent's custody (to follow terms and conditions of the court, including making restitution).
2. Place juvenile offender on probation through court services for a fixed period (to follow terms and conditions of the court, including making restitution).
3. Place juvenile offender on ISP for a fixed period through community corrections (to follow terms and conditions of the court, including making restitution; reporting to the ISO as required; submit to drug screens; use no alcohol or illegal drugs; follow mental health or drug treatment plan; perform community service work—20 hours; attend school; employment, if not enrolled in school; no firearms; other conditions as ordered by the court).
4. Place juvenile offender in custody of JJA (case management through community corrections) once reasonable efforts have been met for juveniles requiring more services (supervision plan may include similar items as ISP and may require placement out of the home).
5. Commit juvenile offender to a juvenile correctional facility (incarceration).
6. Conditional release supervision (follow conditional release requirements; similar requirements as outlined under ISP).

On any given day in Topeka and the Shawnee area, there are about 465 juvenile misdemeanors or felony offenders on probation supervised by court services. Approximately 35 juvenile misdemeanors or felony offenders are on ISP, while 90 juvenile misdemeanors or felony offenders are on community case-management supervision. About 15 juvenile offenders are on conditional release and are supervised by community corrections, while 40 juvenile offenders are in a state juvenile correctional facility supervised by community corrections for reintegration planning. Overall, 645 juveniles from Shawnee County are on some type of supervision for a criminal offense. Shawnee County has approximately 165,000 people.

Approximately 2,915 adults and juveniles are in the county criminal or juvenile justice system each day. This figure does not include ex-offenders or alleged offenders. The cost of having an offender on ISP is about $2,650 per year compared with $18,775 per year in a Kansas correctional facility. All offenders are screened and evaluated according to their risk to reoffend. A risk assessment form is the instrument used for this evaluation. The higher one's score is, the more intense their supervision. Offenders are reassessed at different time intervals to allow for progress in their individual programs. This reassessment may reduce the intensity of their future supervision if they are doing well. Besides frequent meetings with each offender, the ISO will have contact with the offenders' employers, counselors, teachers, families, and law enforcement agencies. Random drug/alcohol screens are also conducted (Shawnee County Department of Community Corrections, 2002:1–4). The successfulness of this community corrections program has been assessed in recent years. Between 1999 and 2002, the amount of recidivism among juvenile clients has been approximately 12 percent. This low recidivism rate suggests that at least in Shawnee County, the community corrections program is fulfilling its diverse objectives.

In the following section, we will examine three increasingly important intermediate punishments that seem to be working well with adult and juvenile offenders alike. These include (1) EM, (2) home confinement, and (3) shock probation.

Electronic Monitoring (EM)

EM Defined

EM or **tagging** is the use of telemetry devices to verify that an offender is at a specified location during specified times. EM is also a system of home confinement aimed at monitoring, controlling, and modifying the behavior of defendants or offenders. The

---

Electronic Monitoring (EM)

Use of electronic devices that emit electronic signals; these devices, anklets or wristlets, are worn by offenders, probationers, and parolees; the purpose of such monitoring is to monitor an offender's presence in a given environment where the offender is required to remain or to verify the offender's whereabouts.

tagging

Being equipped with an electronic wristlet or anklet for the purpose of monitoring one's whereabouts.

offender wears an electronic bracelet/anklet or other electronic device in accordance with conditions set by the courts. The tagged person is monitored by computer for 24 hours a day and is supervised by a private company or a combination of a company and the criminal justice authority, usually a probation department. The person must remain in the home under surveillance, unless authorized to leave for employment, school, participation in community treatment programs, or similar activities. EM tends to be used for less serious, nonviolent offenders who are identified by a risk formula.

EM Origins.

EM devices were first used in 1964 as an alternative to incarcerating certain mental patients and parolees. Subsequently, EM was extended to include monitoring office work, employee testing for security clearances, and many other applications. Other countries are currently experimenting with EM. For instance, England and Germany use EM for managing certain adult and youthful offenders.

Second Judicial District Judge Jack Love of New Mexico is credited with implementing a pilot EM project in 1983 for persons convicted of drunk driving and certain white-collar offenses, such as embezzlement (Houk, 1984). Subsequent to its use for probationers, the New Mexico State Supreme Court approved the program, since it required the voluntariness and consent of probationers as a condition of their probation programs. Judge Love directed that certain probationers should wear either anklets or bracelets that emitted electronic signals that could be intercepted by their POs who conducted surveillance operations. After a short period of such judicial experimentation, other jurisdictions decided to conduct their own experiments for offender monitoring with electronic devices. Eventually, experiments were underway, not only for probationers but also for parolees and inmates of jails and prisons.

How Much EM Is There in the United States?

Accurate statistical information about the extent and use of EM in the United States for either juveniles or adults is difficult to obtain. Most of this information is based on estimated usage rather than actual usage. Some of this information is derived from sales figures reported by firms that manufacture EM equipment, such as BI, Inc. Sales figures are often misleading, since jurisdictions that order EM equipment may replace older equipment, or they may only use some of this equipment rather than all of it at any given time. The numbers of electronically monitored clients fluctuate daily, and there are great variations in the amount of time clients spend being monitored. However, the amount of time spent on EM averages about 12–15 weeks (Office of Juvenile Justice and Delinquency Prevention, 2007).

Contemporary surveys that seek accurate information about EM usage throughout the United States only obtain such information from about 25 percent of the jurisdictions canvassed (Seiter and West, 2003). Considering all of these limitations, virtually every report about EM shows that its frequency is increasing annually. For instance, in 1997, a report was issued showing that 31,236 probationers and parolees were being electronically monitored (Schmidt, 1998:11). In 1998, over 95,000 clients were being electronically monitored. By 2004, over 150,000 persons were on EM and/or house arrest (Office of Juvenile Justice and Delinquency Prevention, 2007). Over 28,000 youths were involved in EM programs by 2007 (American Correctional Association, 2007). The average cost of using this equipment in different probation and parole departments ranges from $5 to $25 per day, depending upon the intensity of the surveillance by POs. This is at least half of the cost of maintaining a juvenile or adult under some type of detention per day.

Types of Signaling Devices

There are at least four types of **EM signaling devices**. First, a continuous-signal device consists of a miniature transmitter that is strapped to the probationer's wrist. The

EM signaling devices
Apparatuses worn about the wrist or leg that are designed to monitor an offender's presence in a given environment where the offender is required to remain.

transmitter broadcasts an encoded signal that is received by a receiver-dialer in the offender's home. The signal is relayed to a central receiver over the telephone lines. A second type of monitor is the programmed contact device, which is similar to the continuous-signal device. However, in this case, a central computer from the probation office is programmed to call the offender's home at random hours to verify the probationer's whereabouts. Offenders must answer their telephones, insert the wristlet transmitter into the telephone device, and their voices and signal emissions are verified by computer (Cadigan, 2001).

A third monitor is a cellular device. This is a transmitter worn by offenders and emits a radio signal that may be received by a local area monitoring system. Up to 25 probationers may be monitored simultaneously with such a system. The fourth type of monitor is the continuous signaling transmitter that is also worn by the offender. These also send out continuous signals that may be intercepted by portable receiving units in the possession of POs. These are quite popular, since POs may conduct drive-bys and verify whether offenders are at home during curfew hours when they are supposed to be.

These wristlet anklet transmitters are certainly not tamperproof. They are similar in plastic construction to the wristlet ID tags given patients at the time of hospital admissions. However, these electronic devices are somewhat sturdier. Nevertheless, the plastic is such that it is easy to remove. It is easily seen whether the device has been tampered with (e.g., stretched, burned, mutilated), since it is impossible to reattach without special equipment in the possession of the probation department. If tampering has occurred and probationers have attempted to defeat the intent of the device, they may be subject to probation revocation. This offense may be punished by incarceration.

Types of Offenders on EM

The types of offenders placed on EM are selected because of their low likelihood of reoffending and the fact that their crimes are less serious, usually property offenses. Thus, there is a certain amount of creaming that occurs, where those most likely to succeed are selected. This is one reason why EM exhibits low recidivism rates among its clientele in numerous jurisdictions. However, in recent years, EM has been extended to include more violent types of juvenile offenders, such as violent juvenile parolees (Kubena, 2008). One reason is that juvenile correctional facilities are increasingly overcrowded to the point where more dangerous juveniles must be released short of serving their full terms. The public is increasingly concerned about community safety. One result is the greater use of EM equipment for such offenders to verify their whereabouts and exert a minimum amount of behavioral control. Usually, juveniles are ordered to be electronically monitored for a specified period. The period varies by jurisdiction, anywhere from 30 to 120 days. Figure 11.6 shows electronic monitor conditions that may be imposed by juvenile courts.

When the alternative to EM is jail, most offenders—juveniles or otherwise—prefer EM to confinement in a jail cell. There are significant punitive dimensions of EM, including both physical and psychological. One's presence is required in a particular place at a particular time, and computer checks of one's whereabouts are frequent enough to cause some clients stress. Being confined to one's house as a punishment is more serious than it sounds. Many electronically monitored clients point out that the EM program is in many ways equivalent to a jail sentence and is very much a punishment (Gainey and Payne, 2003).

The SpeakerID Program

Some jurisdictions, such as the Dane County Sheriff's Office, Wisconsin, have implemented a **SpeakerID Program** (Listug, 1996:85). SpeakerID is a voice verification monitoring system allowing law enforcement and criminal justice agencies to monitor

SpeakerID Program
Electronic voice verification system used as a part of EM to verify the identity of the person called by the probation or parole agency.

Figure 11.6   Electronic Monitor Conditions, Glynn County, GA

<u>**ELECTRONIC MONITOR CONDITIONS**</u>

Pursuant to the within and foregoing order, you have been conditionally released from secure detention on an electronic monitor pending a hearing, placement or as sanction. If you are to remain free of secure detention, you shall comply with the following terms and conditions of your release:

1. I realize that Secure Alert will monitor my compliance throughout my sentence.

2. I agree to remain at my residence at all times except for time allowed for school, work, medical treatment, or other types of evaluations or counseling as set forth in the curfew schedule. Furthermore, I understand that only my case manager can grant me a pass.

3. I understand that I will immediately notify my probation officer if I must leave my home because of an emergency. <u>This notification does not necessarily constitute acceptance of the claimed emergency.</u> Such determination will be made by the probation officer.

4. I know that my curfew restrictions will be enforced by the use of computer and satellite technology. I will wear a tamper proof, non-removable ankle bracelet 24 hours a day during the entire monitoring period.

5. I understand that I am responsible for keeping the batteries for the electronic monitor charged and attached to the ankle monitor device.

6. I understand that I will be held responsible for any damage, other than normal wear of the equipment. If I do not return the equipment, or do not return it in good working condition, or tamper with the equipment, I am subject to felony prosecution.

7. I agree that Glynn County Juvenile Court and Secure Alert are not liable for any damage incurred as the result of my wearing or tampering with the monitor device and that any damages associated with my wearing or tampering with the monitoring device are a result of my own negligence.

8. I understand that failure to comply with these terms constitutes violation of this electronic monitor agreement and may subject me to secure detention.

<u>**ACKNOWLEDGEMENT AND AGREEMENT**</u>

By my signature, I certify that I have read and understand the terms of conditional release as set forth above and I agree to abide by them

_____   _____
Youth signature   Date

_____   _____
Parent Signature   Date

_____   _____
Court Officer Signature   Date

_____   _____
Judge signature   Date

low-risk offenders under probation or house arrest. Implemented in October 1994, the SpeakerID program is a completely automated system that calls clients at their authorized locations at random times. Prior to using SpeakerID, the Dade County Sheriff's Office used traditional ankle bracelets and wristlets as described earlier. The SpeakerID system started out with only 8–12 offenders. In 1996, there were between 30 and 35 offenders participating in this system. When offenders answer their telephones, they are asked specific questions. Voice matches are verified perfectly, and thus there is little likelihood that any particular offender can fool the system with a previously recorded tape or some other device. Because of the automated nature of the system, SpeakerID is cost-effective. Apart from initial start-up costs, the SpeakerID system costs about $3 per day per monitored offender. This compares very favorably with jail and prison costs of $40 and $49 per prisoner per day in Wisconsin.

Some Criticisms of EM

Some limitations of EM programs are that they are quite expensive to implement initially. The direct costs associated with their purchase or lease are seemingly prohibitive to local jurisdictions that are used to incarcerating juveniles and defraying their maintenance costs over an extended period. However, once a given jurisdiction has installed such equipment, it eventually pays for itself and functions to reduce overall incarcerative expenses that otherwise would have been incurred had these same youths been placed in secure confinement.

Also, EM programs require some training on the part of the users. While those using such systems do not need to be computer geniuses, some computer training is helpful. EM is a delinquency deterrent for many offenders. However, it is not foolproof. In spite of the fact that they may be easily tampered with, electronic wristlets and anklets only help to verify an offender's whereabouts. They do not provide television images of these persons and whatever they may be doing. One federal PO has reported that one of his federal probationers on EM was running a successful stolen property business out of his own home. Thus, he was able to continue his criminal activity unabated, despite the home confinement constraints imposed by electronics.

EM has also been criticized as possibly violative of the Fourth Amendment search-and-seizure provision, where, it is alleged by some critics, electronic eavesdropping might be conducted within one's home or bedroom. This argument is without serious constitutional merit, since the primary function of such monitoring is to verify an offender's whereabouts. Some sophisticated types of monitoring systems are equipped with closed-circuit television transmissions, such as those advertised by the Bell Telephone Company as viewer-phones of the future. But even if such monitoring were so equipped, this additional feature would only intrude where offenders wished it to intrude, such as their living rooms or kitchens.

The fact is that many offenders may be inexpensively tracked through these monitoring systems and their whereabouts can be verified without time-consuming face-to-face checks. For instance, a single juvenile PO may conduct drive-bys of client residences during evening hours and receive their transmitted signals with a portable unit. This silent means of detection is intended only to enforce one program element; namely, observance of curfews. Other checks, such as those conducted for illegal drug or alcohol use, must be verified directly, through proper testing and expert confirmation. EM is increasingly used in tandem with another sentencing option—home confinement.

Summarizing the arguments for and against EM, proponents of EM say that it (1) assists offenders in avoiding the criminogenic atmosphere of prisons or jails and helps reintegrate them into their communities, (2) permits offenders to retain jobs and support families, (3) assists POs in their monitoring activities and has potential for easing their caseload responsibilities, (4) gives judges and other officials considerable flexibility in sentencing offenders, (5) has the potential of reducing recidivism rates more

Figure 11.7   Supervision Fee Requirement

SUPERVISION FEE REQUIREMENT

As a Condition of Supervision, you are required to pay _____ a month to the Parole and Probation Division.

The _____ County Parole and Probation Division has an automated billing system. Our system automatically bills _____ on the first day of each month. Billing begins the first day of the month following the month of conviction. Example: If you were convicted on _____ the first billing would be September 1, _____ for the month of August.

Supervision fee payments are due by the 5th of each month.

At times other fees may be imposed such as Electronic Home Detention Fees, DUII Evaluation Fee, Polygraph Fees and Treatment Fees. Your Parole/Probation Officer will let you know if any of these fees apply to you. If so, you may make these payments at the above address.

PLEASE NOTE THE FOLLOWING:

1. Checks or Money Order's are to be make out _____ **County Parole and Probation Division** or **LCPP.** Do not make check or money order payable to a PO or Evaluator, otherwise your payment will be returned.
2. Our office does not take any payments for the Court such as fines and restitution. These need to be sent to:
    _____
3. **If you fail to pay your fees** you may be **ordered to do Work Crew, be returned to Court, or be directed to appear before a Hearings Officer.**
4. In order to leave the State on a temporary basis you are required to have a Travel Permit. **Travel Permits will not be issued unless supervision fees are current.**
5. In order to apply for **Early Termination** you will have to be **current on all fees.**

I have read or have had read to me the above information regarding fees, and I understand my obligation regarding fees.

_____   _____
Offender Signature   Date

_____   _____
Parent or Guardian Signature   Date

cc: white-offender yellow-file

than existing probationary alternatives, (6) is potentially useful for decreasing jail and prison populations, (7) is more cost-effective in relation to incarceration, and (8) allows for pre-trial release monitoring as well as for special treatment cases such as substance abusers, the mentally retarded, women who are pregnant, and juveniles. A form outlining supervisory fees is shown in Figure 11.7.

Those against EM say that (1) some potential exists for race, ethnic, or socioeconomic bias by requiring offenders to have telephones or to pay for expensive monitoring equipment and/or fees (ironically, some jurisdictions report that many offenders enjoy better living conditions in jail or prison custody compared with their residences outside of prison); (2) public safety may be compromised through the failure of these programs to guarantee that offenders will go straight and not endanger citizens by committing new offenses while free in the community; (3) it may be too coercive, and it may be unrealistic for officials to expect full offender compliance with such a stringent system; (4) little consistent information exists about the impact of EM on recidivism rates compared with other probationary alternatives; (5) persons frequently selected for participation are persons who probably don't need to be monitored anyway; (6) technological problems exist, making EM somewhat unreliable; (7) it may result in widening the net by being prescribed for offenders who otherwise would receive less costly standard probation; (8) it raises right to privacy, civil liberties, and other constitutional issues such as Fourth Amendment search and seizure concerns; (9) much of the public interprets this option as going easy on offenders and perceives EM as a nonpunitive alternative; and (10) the costs of EM may be more than published estimates. Figure 11.7 illustrates a supervision fee requirement that may be imposed by various jurisdictions. These fees are intended to offset the costs of EM and other ancillary expenses.

Home Confinement or House Arrest

The use of one's home as the principal place of confinement is not new. In biblical times, St. Paul was sentenced in Rome to house arrest for two years, where he performed tent-maker services for others. **Home confinement** is a program of intermediate punishment involving the use of the offender's residence for mandatory incarceration during evening hours, after a curfew, and on weekends (Cadigan, 2001).

Florida introduced the contemporary use of home confinement in 1983 (Boone, 1996). At that time, corrections officials considered the use of homes as incarcerative facilities as acceptable alternatives to prisons or jails for certain low-risk offenders. Home confinement was a very inexpensive way of maintaining supervisory control over those offenders who were deemed not in need of costly incarceration. When Florida began its home confinement program, it was established under the Correctional Reform Act of 1983. This Act provided that the home could be used as a form of intensive supervised custody in the community. This highly individualized program is intended primarily to restrict offender movement within the community, home, or nonresidential placement, together with specific sanctions such as curfew, payment of fines, community service, and other requirements. When Florida started to use home confinement as a punishment, prison costs averaged $30 per inmate per day, while home confinement required an expenditure of about $3 per offender per day. In the late 1990s, prison maintenance costs per prisoner were in excess of $75 per day in most jurisdictions, while home confinement costs stabilized at about $5 per day (Tonry, 1997). Although Florida officials consider **home incarceration** or **house arrest** punitive, some persons disagree. They believe that incarceration should be in a jail or prison, if it is meaningful incarceration (Landreville, 1999).

home confinement
Program intended to house offenders in their own homes with or without electronic devices; reduces prison overcrowding and prisoner costs; intermediate punishment involving the use of offender residences for mandatory incarceration during evening hours, after a curfew, and on weekends.

home incarceration, house arrest
See home confinement.

Functions and Goals of Home Confinement Programs

The functions and goals of home confinement programs include the following:

1. To continue the offender's punishment while permitting the offender to live in his/her dwelling under general or close supervision.
2. To enable offenders to perform jobs in their communities to support themselves and their families.
3. To reduce jail and prison overcrowding.

4. To maximize public safety by ensuring that only the most qualified clients enter home confinement programs and are properly supervised.
5. To reduce the costs of offender supervision.
6. To promote rehabilitation and reintegration by permitting offenders to live under appropriate supervision within their communities.

In many jurisdictions, including U.S. federal probation, home confinement is used together with EM. Relatively little is known about the extent to which home confinement is used as a sentencing alternative for juvenile offenders. Since probation is so widely used as the sanction of choice except for the most chronic recidivists, home confinement is most often applied as an accompanying condition of EM. However, this type of sentencing may be redundant, since curfew for juvenile offenders means home confinement anyway, especially during evening hours. As a day disposition, home confinement for juveniles would probably be counterproductive, since juveniles are often obligated to finish their schooling as a probation program condition. Again, since school hours are during the daytime, it would not make sense to deprive juveniles of school opportunities through some type of home confinement.

Home confinement is also useful for certain types of offenders who are drug- or alcohol-dependent. POs can visit the homes of certain drug-dependent clients and perform instant checks to determine whether they have used alcohol or drugs in the recent past. While access to drugs or alcohol is relatively easy when a client is confined to his/her home, the threat of a random drug/alcohol test by a PO is often a sufficient deterrent. Needs assessments for certain offenders can determine which services they require, and they are relatively mobile to seek these services with probation department approval.

Advantages and Disadvantages of Home Confinement

Among the advantages of home confinement are that (1) it is cost-effective, (2) it has social benefits, (3) it is responsive to local citizen and offender needs, and (4) it is easily implemented and is timely in view of jail and prison overcrowding. Some of the disadvantages of home confinement are that (1) it may actually widen the net of social control, (2) it may be viewed by the public as not being a sufficiently severe sentence, (3) it focuses primarily upon offender surveillance, (4) it is intrusive and possibly illegal, (5) race and class bias may enter into participant selection, and (6) it may compromise public safety. Some of these advantages and disadvantages will be addressed at length following as issues concerning home confinement where EM is also used.

Other ISP Program Conditions

Briefly reviewing judicial dispositional options, at one end of the sentencing spectrum, they may adjudicate youths as delinquent, impose nominal sanctions, and take no further action other than to record the event. Therefore, if the same juveniles reappear before the same judge in the future, sterner measures may be taken in imposing new dispositions. Or the judge may divert juveniles to particular community agencies for special treatment. Juveniles with psychological problems or who are emotionally disturbed, sex offenders, or those with drug and/or alcohol dependencies may be targeted for special community treatments. At the other end of the spectrum of punishments are the most drastic alternatives of custodial sanctions, ranging from the placement of juveniles in nonsecure foster homes and camp ranches, or secure facilities, such as reform schools and industrial schools. These nonsecure and secure forms of placement and/or incarceration are usually reserved for the most-serious offenders.

In many jurisdictions, such as Dougherty County, Georgia, a PO assigned to a juvenile's case will conduct a home evaluation prior to judicial actions imposing EM,

Figure 11.8   Home Evaluation Report, Dougherty County, GA

HOME EVALUATION REPORT

Sending State:_____ Receiving State:_____

Juvenile's Name:_____ DOB:_____

Placement Investigated:

Parent/Guardian:_____
Address:_____
Work Phone: _____ Home Phone #: _____

HOME/NEIGHBORHOOD/PEERS (Physical description, criminal/gang activity,etc.):_____
_____
_____
_____

FAMILY STATUS (composition, interactions, at-risk family members, attitude):
_____
_____
_____
_____

LEGAL HISTORY OF FAMILY (current charges, probation or parole status):
_____
_____

PROPOSED PLAN (school/employment, court ordered conditions,
_____
_____
_____

OTHER COMMENTS
_____
_____
_____
_____
_____

Probation Officer:_____

home confinement, or any other alternative condition. In Dougherty County, POs conduct home evaluations and report the results of these evaluations to juvenile court judges who can then make a more informed decision about the most appropriate disposition to impose. Figure 11.8 is an example of a home evaluation report that might be prepared. This document contains much valuable information about one's neighborhood; neighbors; gang presence, if any; family status; legal history of the family; the proposed plan for the juvenile; and any other comments believed important to include by the investigating PO.

Also helpful in juvenile court judge decision making are regular reports filed by POs in different jurisdictions, outlining the socio-demographic characteristics of youths under supervision, their numbers, number of terminations, transfers, commitments, court-ordered fines and their payment or nonpayment, and other factors. In some instances, psychological evaluations have been ordered. Some juveniles have been ordered to boot camps or to counseling or to participation in youth clubs or other activities. Community service orders have been issued as well. Regular documentation of this and other relevant information enables judges to see whether their dispositional orders are effective or in need of modification. Figure 11.9 shows a juvenile PO monthly report used by the Dougherty County Juvenile Court in Georgia.

Probation is the most commonly used sentencing option. Probation is either unconditional or conditional. This chapter has examined several conditional intermediate punishments, including IPS and community-based programs. A youth's assignment to any of these programs may or may not include conditions. Apart from the more intensive monitoring and supervision by POs, juveniles may be expected to comply with one or more conditions, including restitution, if financial loss was suffered by one or more victims in cases of vandalism, property damage, or physical injury. Also, fines may be imposed. Or the judge may specify some form of community service. All of these conditions may be an integral part of a juvenile's probation program. Violation of or failure to comply with one or more of these conditions may result in a probation revocation action. POs function as the link between juvenile offenders and the courts regarding a youth's compliance with these program conditions.

Restitution, Fines, Victim Compensation, and Victim–Offender Mediation

Restitution.   An increasingly important feature of probation programs is **restitution**. Several models of restitution include

1. the financial/community service model, which stresses the offender's financial accountability and community service to pay for damages;
2. the victim/offender mediation model, which focuses upon victim–offender reconciliation; and
3. the victim/reparations model, where juveniles compensate their victims directly for their offenses.

The potential significance of restitution, coupled with probation, is that it may reduce recidivism among juvenile offenders. Restitution orders impact juveniles directly, and having to repay someone for damages they caused means that they learn the actual cost of the damages they inflicted. This strategy may be very rehabilitative for some youths.

Fines and Victim Compensation.   Beyond reductions in recidivism, restitution, payment of **fines,** and **victim compensation** also increase offender accountability. Given the present philosophical direction of juvenile courts, this condition is consistent with enhancing a youth's acceptance of responsibility for wrongful actions committed against others and the financial harm it has caused. Many of these programs include restitution as a part of their program requirements. Restitution orders may be imposed by juvenile court judges with or without accompanying dispositions of secure confinement.

Victim–Offender Mediation.   There is growing interest in programs for juvenile offenders that heighten their accountability, especially toward their victims. Since 1980, there has been growing awareness of and interest in **victim–offender mediation** as

---

restitution
Stipulation by court that offenders must compensate victims for their financial losses resulting from crime; compensation for psychological, physical, or financial loss by victim; may be imposed as a part of an incarcerative sentence.

fines
Financial penalties imposed at the time of sentencing convicted offenders; most criminal statutes contain provisions for the imposition of monetary penalties as sentencing options.

victim compensation
Financial restitution payable to victims by either the state or the convicted offenders.

victim–offender mediation
Third-party intervention mechanism whereby perpetrator and victim work out civil solution to otherwise criminal or delinquent action.

Figure II.9   Dougherty Juvenile Probation Officer Report, Dougherty County, GA

MONTH OF _____2009

I. **TOTAL NUMBER OF JUVENILES RECEIVED FOR SUPERVISION_____**

   Number of White Males_____   Number of Black Males_____
   Number of White Females_____   Number of Black Females_____

2. **TOTAL NUMBER OF NEW PROBATIONERS THAT REPORTED IN FOR THAT MONTH:____**

   Number of White Males_____ Number of Black Males_____
   Number of White Females_____ Number of Black Females_____

3. **TOTAL NUMBER OF JUVENILES REQUIRING INTENSIVE SUPERVISION_____**

   Number of White Males_____ Number of Black Males_____
   Number of White Females_____ Number of Black Females_____

4. **TOTAL NUMBER OF JUVENILES THAT REPORTED IN FOR THE MONTH_____**

   Number of White Males_____ Number of Black Males_____
   Number of White Females_____ Number of Black Females_____

5. **TOTAL NUMBER OF JUVENILES TERMINATED, TRANSFERRED, COMMITTED OR CLOSED DURING THE MONTH_____**

   Number of White Males_____ Number of Black Males_____
   Number of White Females_____ Number of Black Females_____

6. **TOTAL NUMBER OF JUVENILES BEING SUPERVISED AT THE END OF THE MONTH____**

   Number of White Males_____ Number of Black Males_____
   Number of White Females_____ Number of Black Females_____

I. **TOTAL NUMBER OF JUVENILES THAT OWE SUPERVISION FEES: _____**

   Number of White Males_____ Number of Black Males_____
   Number of White Females_____ Number of Black Females_____

2. **TOTAL NUMBER OF JUVENILES THAT OWE RESTITUTION & FINES_____**

   Number of White Males_____ Number of Black Males_____
   Number of White Females_____ Number of Black Females_____

3. **TOTAL NUMBER OF JUVENILES THAT WERE ORDERED PSYCHOL. EVALUATIONS _____**

NAMES:_____
_____

DOUGHERTY JUVENILE PROBATION OFFICER MONTHLY REPORT
PAGE 2

4. **TOTAL NUMBER OF JUVENILES OVER 17 YEARS OF AGE BEING SUPERVISED_____**

Number of White Males_____ Number of Black Males_____
Number of White Females_____ Number of Black Females_____

_____
_____

l. **TOTAL NUMBER OF JUVENILES THAT ARE IN BOYS CLUB PROGRAM_____**

Number of White Males_____ Number of Black Males_____
Number of White Females_____ Number of Black Females_____

2. **TOTAL NUMBER OF JUVENILES THAT ARE IN A COUNSELING PROGRAM:_____**

Number of White Males_____ Number of Black Males_____
Number of White Females_____ Number of Black Females_____

3. **TOTAL NUMBER OF JUVENILES THAT ARE IN JAG PROGRAM_____**

Number of White Males_____ Number of Black Males_____
Number of White Females_____ Number of Black Females_____

4. **TOTAL NUMBER OF JUVENILES THAT ARE IN BOOT CAMP OR WAITING TO GO_____**

Number of White Males_____ Number of Black Males_____
Number of White Females_____ Number of Black Females_____

5. **TOTAL NUMBER OF JUVENILES RELEASED FROM BOOT CAMP DURING MONTH_____**

Names:_____
_____

TOTAL NUMBER OF JUVENILES THAT WERE ORDERED TO COMPLETE COMMUNITY SERVICE HOURS_____

Number of White Males_____   Number of Black Males_____
Number of White Females_____   Number of Black Females_____

a means of resolving disputes between the juvenile perpetrator and his/her victim. Victim–offender mediation is bringing together victims, offenders, and other members of the community to hold offenders accountable not only for their crimes but for the harm they caused to victims (Sinclair, 2005). These programs provide an opportunity for crime victims and offenders to meet face-to-face to talk about the impact of the crime on their lives and to develop a plan for repairing the harm. Most of these programs work with juvenile offenders, although a growing number are involving adult offenders (Gregorie, 2005). Sometimes referred to as restorative justice, victim–offender mediation was quite prevalent throughout the world in 2004, with over 1,500 programs in 22 countries (Lightfoot and Umbreit, 2004). In 2005, there were 700 victim–offender mediation programs in the United States. One unique feature of such programs is that they are dialogue-driven rather than settlement-driven. While not all victims are totally satisfied with the outcomes of such programs, most report being satisfied with having the opportunity of sharing their stories and their pain resulting from the crime event. Many juveniles report being surprised at learning about the impact their actions had on various victims they confront.

Community Service

Associated with restitution orders is **community service**. Community service may be performed in different ways, ranging from cutting courthouse lawns and cleaning up public parks to painting homes for the elderly or repairing fences on private farms. Youths typically earn wages for this service, and these wages are usually donated to a victim compensation fund. The different types of community service activities are limited only by the imagination of the juvenile court and community leaders. Similar to restitution, community service orders are intended to increase offender accountability and individual responsibility (Sinclair, 2005).

community service
Any activity imposed on a probationer or parolee involving work in one's neighborhood or city; performed in part to repay victims and the city for injuries or damages caused by one's unlawful actions.

Summary

Probation is a conditional nonincarcerative punishment where probationers are supervised by juvenile POs for various periods. It is the punishment most often imposed by juvenile court judges. Standard probation includes conditions such as reporting to POs in person at regular times and submitting written reports, obeying all laws, observing curfew, attending school, avoiding alcohol and drugs, not frequenting places where delinquent juveniles may be present or having any association with them, seeking counseling if directed by the court, not possessing firearms or any dangerous weapons, and participating in designated programs required by juvenile court judges. Probation is intended to be rehabilitative and reintegrative. Heightened accountability is also emphasized, including restitution requirements and compulsory hours of community service. The successfulness of any probation program is most often evaluated by recidivism rates. Risk and needs assessments are often used to determine individual offender needs and prescribe specific treatments to improve one's chances of remaining delinquency-free.

A broad class of intermediate punishments for juveniles has been identified. Intermediate punishments include any sanctions that lie between standard probation and secure confinement. Also known as creative sentencing, intermediate punishments have several goals, such as providing less costly sanctions compared with secure confinement; achieving lower recidivism rates compared with standard probation programs; providing a greater range of community services for juvenile clients; minimizing the adverse effects of labeling by reducing one's contact with the juvenile justice system; improving one's personal educational and vocational skills, which help to improve one's self-concept; and greater acceptance of responsibility.

JISP programs are also used and include EM, house arrest, and other requirements. Eligibility standards for entry into JISPs are strict. JISP effectiveness depends upon factors that heighten offender accountability through increasing offender responsibility; promoting greater offender control through more frequent curfew, drug and alcohol, school, and employment checks.

Strengths and weaknesses of JISPs are that they are more expensive than standard probation programs. More successful JISPs emphasize a balanced approach, which is based on achieving three fundamental goals: improving community protection through close offender surveillance and supervision, using activities and engaging youths in programs that heighten their accountability, and individualizing treatments delivered to juveniles with special problems.

Several caseload assignment models were described. Each community has evolved different community-based programs based on the nature and types of juvenile offenders. The goals of many community-based programs are to promote public safety, hold youths accountable for their behavior, and improve a youth's ability to live productively in the community by providing educational, vocational, and counseling services. The balanced approach is apparent in this program.

EM are used to monitor offender whereabouts. Precise numbers of youths on EM are difficult to determine because of poor record-keeping. The benefits, weaknesses, and strengths of EM were described. Home confinement or house arrest was also described. The goals of home confinement are to enable offenders to remain in their communities and attend school or jobs at regular times, reduce the cost of offender supervision, promote rehabilitation and reintegration, reduce jail and prison overcrowding, and maximize public safety by using one's home as a place of confinement where compliance can be strictly enforced. Other JISP conditions were described, such as restitution, fines, victim compensation, victim–offender mediation, and alternative dispute resolution. The succcessfulness of these programs was discussed.

Key Terms

Questions for Review

1. What is standard probation? What are some of its characteristics? What are some of the conditions of standard probation?

2. How does standard probation differ from probation with special conditions? What are some of the types of special conditions usually included in such probation orders?

3. What are JPCs? What is meant by intensive aftercare? Are such alternative sanctions effective at reducing recidivism? Why or why not?

4. What are intermediate punishments? How do intermediate punishments differ from standard probation?

5. What are some goals of intermediate punishments? What are some of the criteria for placement in ISP programs?

6. What are four types of caseload models? Describe each?

7. What is case supervision planning? Is there an ideal caseload for probation/ parole officers?

8. What is meant by the balanced approach? What are some of its important elements? Is it successful in dealing with delinquent offenders? Why or why not?

9. What are home confinement and EM? Are home confinement and EM used together in many jurisdictions? Who are the juvenile clients who are disposed to EM and/or home confinement? What are the goals and functions of these respective programs?

10. What is victim–offender mediation? What sorts of juveniles are eligible for participating in such mediation? How successful are such programs at resolving disputes between juveniles and their victims?

Internet Connections

CompassPoint Nonprofit Services
http://www.compasspoint.org/

IMPACT Boot Camps
http://www.corrections.state.la.us/Programs/IMPACT.htm

Texas Juvenile Probation Commission
http://www.tjpc.state.tx.us/

Victim-Offender Mediation Association
http://www.igc.org/voma

Victims of Crime with Disabilities Resource Guide
http://wind.uwyo.edu/resourceguide/resources/assistance.asp

Wilderness Programs, Inc.
http://www.wildernessprogramsetc.com

Youth on Trial: A Developmental Perspective on Juvenile Justice
http://www.jlc.org/index.php/research/alternativestodetention/28

chapter **12**

Juvenile Corrections
Custodial Sanctions and Parole

chapter objectives

As the result of reading this chapter, you will realize the following objectives:

1. Understand the different components and goals of juvenile corrections.
2. Differentiate between nonsecure and secure confinement, as well as examine some of the programs associated with nonsecure treatment of juvenile offenders.
3. Learn about various types of custodial facilities for juveniles and their relative success in fostering juvenile rehabilitation and reintegration.
4. Learn about several important correctional issues as they apply to juvenile offenders.
5. Learn about juvenile parole and the characteristics of parole programs.
6. Understand the process of juvenile probation and parole revocation.
7. Learn about some of the important U.S. Supreme Court cases that apply to juvenile probation and parole as well as the revocation process.

 ## Case Study

A youth on parole in Louisiana, Mychal Bell, 17, was ordered back to prison for 18 months following numerous parole violations. He had been placed on probation on four previous occasions for violent incidents. Bell was a former member of the "Jena 6," a group of six black teens who had beaten a white student, Justin Barker, in December 2006. The incident was a culmination of a fight between blacks and whites. Various religious leaders, including Rev. Al Sharpton, called Bell's reimprisonment "revenge" by the judge and called upon the governor, Kathleen Bianco, to intervene. [Source: Adapted from the Associated Press, "Mychal Bell of 'Jena 6' Ordered to Juvenile Facility," October 12, 2007.]

 ## Case Study

Not all is well in juvenile corrections. Some youths escape, others are sexually assaulted. In Baltimore, Maryland, 15-year-old Justin Russell and 16-year-old Davon Julius escaped from the Charles Hickey School in Carney, a Baltimore suburb. The teens were among four inmates being taken to a medical building when they escaped. In an unrelated incident, a 17-year-old youth, J.H., alleged that a staff member, 24-year-old Monet Mason, had lured him into sexual acts by offering cigarettes, pornographic magazines, and cognac. He went along, he said, because he feared Mason would make up complaints against him otherwise. The Mercer County Detention Center, Trenton, New Jersey, may be held liable for the sexual assaults if substantiated. [Sources: Adapted from the Associated Press, "Police Identify Juveniles Who Escaped from Hickey," August 7, 2007; adapted from the Associated Press, "Ruling Puts Kids' Safety First in Juvenile Lockup," August 29, 2007.]

Introduction

Just how effective is juvenile parole for controlling youth behavior after a period of incarceration? How much supervision is required to enforce compliance with parole orders? How well are juvenile custodial facilities operated? Do they rehabilitate offenders? This chapter examines juvenile corrections, particularly institutional corrections. The first section describes various goals of juvenile corrections, including deterrence, rehabilitation, reintegration, prevention, punishment and retribution, and isolation and control.

Custodial alternatives are subsequently described and discussed. The institutionalization of juvenile offenders may be either nonsecure or secure. Nonsecure custody options include foster home placements, group homes, halfway houses, camps, ranches, experience programs, and wilderness projects. The goals of these nonsecure options are examined, together with an evaluation of their respective effectiveness for rehabilitating and reintegrating youthful offenders. Several programs are featured as examples of how these options function and how certain goals are achieved.

Next described is secure confinement for youths. Some youths are placed in boot camps, or military-like facilities with many rules and regulations. Boot camps are described and defined. Their characteristics, their primary goals and rationale, and a profile of boot camp clientele are highlighted.

Juvenile parole is examined. Many states have juvenile parole boards that function in ways similar to parole boards for adults. Juvenile parole is defined and its purposes discussed. General juvenile parole policies in various state jurisdictions are discussed, and juvenile parolees are profiled. Some of the criteria for deciding which juveniles to parole are listed and described. The next section examines the juvenile probation and parole revocation process. Several key U.S. Supreme Court probation and parole revocation cases are presented, and a sampling of state cases involving juvenile probation and parole revocation actions are described. Several important issues are addressed upon which juvenile probation and parole revocation actions are based.

Several important issues in juvenile corrections conclude this chapter. Should the private sector operate juvenile facilities, especially secure facilities? How should juvenile offenders be classified? Is there too much or too little use of secure confinement for juveniles? How can authorities distinguish clearly between those juveniles who deserve to be locked up from those who don't deserve such a punishment? Another issue pertains to detaining juveniles, even for brief periods, in adult lock-ups or jails. Every year, attempts are made to avoid juvenile incarcerations in adult facilities. But every year, a certain proportion of those incarcerated in adult jails are juveniles. There are several reasons for these incarcerations. These issues will be examined in some detail.

Goals of Juvenile Corrections

The goals of juvenile corrections are (1) deterrence, (2) rehabilitation and reintegration, (3) prevention, (4) punishment and retribution, and (5) isolation and control. These goals may at times appear to be in conflict. For instance, some jurisdictions stress delinquency prevention by keeping juveniles away from the juvenile justice system through diversions and warnings. However, other jurisdictions get tough with juveniles by providing more certain and stringent penalties for their offenses. A middle ground would be to stress both discipline and reform.

Deterrence

Significant deterrent elements of juvenile correctional programs include clearly stated rules and formal sanctions, anticriminal modeling and reinforcement, and a high degree of empathy and trust between the juvenile client and staff (Campbell and Gonzalez, 2007). Traditional counseling, institutionalization, and diversion, which are integral features of many community corrections programs, are considered largely ineffective (Burrell, 2005). A natural intervention may occur apart from any particular program designed to deter. As youths grow older, their rate of offending reaches a plateau and then begins to decline. Thus, many youths simply outgrow delinquency as they become older.

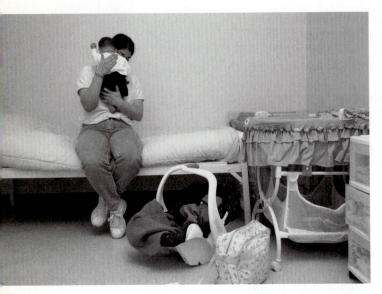

Juvenile correctional systems are confronting more complex problems such as children having children.

Rehabilitation and Reintegration

Various juvenile correctional programs stress internalizing responsibilities for one's actions, while other programs attempt to inculcate youths with social and motor skills. Other programs attempt to diagnose and treat youths who are emotionally disturbed. Alternative medical and social therapies are often used. Group homes are becoming increasingly popular as alternatives to incarceration, since a broader array of services can be extended to juveniles with special needs (Abrams, 2006).

Prevention

Delinquency prevention seems to be a function of many factors. It is believed that the threat of incarceration in a secure facility, even for a brief period, might prevent many juveniles from committing delinquent acts. However, like for many adults, the idea of such a punishment doesn't seem to be much of a deterrent for juveniles.

Punishment and Retribution

Some persons want to see youths, especially violent ones, punished rather than rehabilitated. One major impact of the get-tough-on-crime policy adopted by many jurisdictions is that the juvenile justice system seems to be diverting a larger portion of its serious offenders to criminal courts where they may conceivably receive harsher punishments (Wilson and Petersilia, 2002). This may be one reaction to widespread allegations that the juvenile courts are too lenient in their sentencing of violent offenders, or that the punishment options available to juvenile court judges are not sufficiently severe. For those juveniles who remain within the juvenile justice system for processing, secure confinement for longer periods seems to be the court's primary response to citizen allegations of excessive leniency.

Isolation and Control

Apprehension and incarceration of juvenile offenders, especially chronic recidivists, is believed important to isolating them and limiting their opportunities to reoffend (Gordon and Malmsjo, 2005). In principle, this philosophy is similar to selective incapacitation. However, the average length of juvenile incarcerative terms in public facilities in the United States is less than 10 months (Office of Juvenile Justice and Delinquency Prevention, 2007). Thus, incarceration by itself may be of limited value in controlling the amount of juvenile delinquency.

Current Juvenile Custodial Alternatives

The custodial options available to juvenile court judges are of two general types: (1) nonsecure and (2) secure. Nonsecure custodial facilities are those that permit youths freedom of movement within the community. Youths are generally free to leave the premises of their facilities, although they are compelled to observe various rules, such as curfew, avoidance of alcoholic beverages and drugs, and participation in specific programs that are tailored to their particular needs. These types of nonsecure facilities include foster homes, group homes and halfway houses, and camps, ranches, experience programs, and wilderness projects.

Secure custodial facilities are the juvenile counterpart to adult prisons or penitentiaries. Such institutions are known by different names among the states. For example, secure, long-term confinement facilities might be called youth centers or youth facilities (Alaska, California, Colorado, District of Columbia, Illinois, Kansas, Maine, Missouri), juvenile institutions (Arkansas), schools (California, Connecticut, New Mexico), schools for boys (Delaware), training schools or centers (Florida, Indiana, Iowa, Oregon), youth development centers (Georgia, Nebraska), youth services centers (Idaho), secure centers (New York), industry schools (New York), and youth development centers (Tennessee). This listing is not intended to be comprehensive, but it illustrates the variety of designations states use to refer to their long-term, secure confinement facilities.

Nonsecure Confinement

Nonsecure confinement involves placing certain youths in (1) foster homes; (2) group homes and halfway houses; and (3) camps, ranches, experience programs, and wilderness projects.

Foster Homes.
If the juvenile's natural parents are considered unfit, or if the juvenile is abandoned or orphaned, **foster homes** are often used for temporary placement. Those youths placed in foster homes are not necessarily law violators. They may be children in need of supervision (CHINS) or at-risk youths (Lee, 2008). Foster home placement provides youths with a substitute family. A stable family environment is believed by the courts to be beneficial in many cases where youths have no consistent adult supervision or are unmanageable or unruly in their own households. In 2007, an estimated 26,000 youths were under the supervision of foster homes in state-operated public placement programs (American Correctional Association, 2007). In addition to state-operated facilities, approximately 513,000 youths were in the private foster care system in 2005, as a comparison (Adoption and Foster Care Analysis and Reporting System, 2008).

Foster home placements are useful in many cases where youths have been apprehended for status offenses or other noncrime infractions. A significant portion of youths placed in foster homes have mental, developmental, emotional, or disability issues (National Council on Disability, 2008). Most families who accept youths into their homes have been investigated by state or local authorities in advance to determine their fitness as foster parents. Socioeconomic factors and home stability are considered important for child placements (Loukas, Suizzo, and Prelow, 2007).

Foster parents are typically middle-aged, middle-class citizens with above-average educational backgrounds. Despite these positive features, it is unlikely that foster homes are able to provide the high intensity of adult supervision required by more hard-core juvenile offenders. Further, it is unlikely that these parents can furnish the quality of special treatments that might prove effective in the youth's possible rehabilitation or societal reintegration. Most foster parents simply are not trained as counselors, social workers, or psychologists. For many youths who have committed nonserious offenses, however, a home environment, particularly a stable one, has certain therapeutic benefits (National Council on Disability, 2008).

The intent of foster home programs is not to furnish permanent housing for youths. Rather, foster homes are considered temporary. However, the question of how temporary these foster homes are remains. In 2005, for instance, out of the 513,000 youths in the foster care system, approximately 10 percent, or 55,000 youths, were adopted and placed with permanent families. Relatives of these youths adopted 25 percent of them, foster parents adopted 60 percent, and nonrelatives adopted the remaining 15 percent. The average length of stay in foster homes by these 513,000 youths was 29 months. Approximately 20 percent waited 1–5 months for permanent placement,

foster homes
Facility for temporary placement of youths in need of supervision or control; usually families volunteer to act as foster parents and maintain placed youths for short-term care.

17 percent waited 6–11 months, 12 percent waited 12–17 months, and 14 percent waited 5 years or longer (Adoption and Foster Care Analysis and Reporting System, 2008).

Group Homes and Halfway Houses.

One nonsecure option for juvenile court judges is placing juveniles in **group homes** and **halfway houses**. Group home placement for youths is considered an intermediate alternative available to juvenile court judges. Group homes or halfway houses are community-based operations that may be either publicly or privately administered (Spigel, 2008). Usually, group homes will have counselors or residents to act as parental figures for youths in groups of 10 to 20. Certain group homes, referred to as family group homes, are actually family-operated, and thus, in a sense, they are an extension of foster homes for larger numbers of youths. In most group homes, nonsecure supervision of juvenile clients is practiced. About 12,500 youths were in group homes during 2007 (American Correctional Association, 2007).

Since most group homes are located in residential areas together with other traditional family units, some local residents may react negatively to their presence. Being in close proximity to a group home may cause some residents to feel unsafe and fear that group home clients may pose risks or dangers for them or their children. But if the numbers of youths accommodated by these group homes are limited, few, if any, zoning restrictions can be imposed to bar their community presence.

For instance, in Connecticut, state laws provide that any state or private agency must notify town officials or residents before establishing a group home, and the types of clients served must be identified. However, Connecticut state law prohibits local zoning regulations that might bar a group home from treating six or fewer youths with mental retardation, mental illness or physical disabilities, or substance abuse disorders. Thus, at least in Connecticut, group homes treating six or fewer youths with problems are not required to notify anyone of their existence or to report their operation to town officials. Such homes may be operated, and they may be treated like any other home in the neighborhood. Several lower federal appellate courts have ruled that such notice requirements are discriminatory under the federal Fair Housing Act, because they treat people with mental or physical disabilities living in group homes differently from other people living in similar housing (Spigel, 2008:1). However, group homes cannot be clustered in any particular area. Local zoning authorities must be advised if a second or third group home is planned within 1,000 feet of an existing group home. In such cases, citizens can petition local authorities to bar the establishment of proposed group homes that violate this 1,000-foot rule.

No model or ideal group home exists in the United States to be emulated by all jurisdictions, and what works well for youths in some communities may not work similarly for youths in other jurisdictions. However, most successful group homes have strong structural components, where all residents are obligated to participate in relevant program components, where predictable consequences for rule violations are rigorously enforced, and where constant monitoring by staff workers occurs. Thus, juveniles have the best of both worlds—they can live in a home-like environment and visit with family and friends in a home setting. Yet, they must comply with strict rules governing curfew, program participation, and other court-imposed conditions.

Whether privately or publicly operated, group homes require juvenile clients to observe the rights of others, participate in various vocational or educational training programs, attend school, participate in therapy or receive prescribed medical treatment, and observe curfew. Urinalyses or other tests may be conducted randomly to check whether juveniles are taking drugs or consuming alcohol contrary to group home policy. If one or more program violations occur, group home officials may report these infractions to juvenile court judges, who retain dispositional control over the youths. Assignment to a group home or any other type of confinement is usually for a determinate period.

Positively, group homes provide youths with the companionship of other juveniles. Problem-sharing often occurs through planned group discussions, where the

group homes

Also known as group centers or foster homes, these are facilities for juveniles that provide limited supervision and support; juveniles live in a home-like environment with other juveniles and participate in therapeutic programs and counseling; considered nonsecure custodial.

halfway houses

Nonconfining residential facilities intended to provide an alternative to incarceration as a period of readjustment to the community for offenders after confinement.

subjects might vary from peer relations in school to suicide prevention. Staff are available to assist youths to secure employment, work certain difficult school problems, and absorb emotional burdens arising from difficult interpersonal relationships. However, these homes are sometimes staffed by community volunteers with little training or experience with a youth's problems. There are certain risks and legal liabilities that may be incurred as the result of well-intentioned but bad advice or inadequate assistance. Currently, there are limited regulations among states for how group homes are established and operated. Training programs for group home staff are scarce in most jurisdictions, and few standards exist relating to staff preparation and qualifications. Therefore, considerable variation exists among group homes relating to the quality of services they can extend to the juveniles they serve (Corwin, 2005).

Halfway houses generally refer to community homes used by adult parolees recently released from prison. These halfway houses provide a temporary base of operations for parolees as they seek employment and readjustment within their communities. Therefore, they are perceived as transitional residences halfway between incarceration and full freedom of life "on the outside." For many ex-inmates, exposure to unregulated community life is a traumatic transition from the rigidity of prison culture. Many ex-inmates need time to readjust. The rules of halfway houses provide limited structure as well as freedom of access to the outside during the transitory stage.

For juveniles, halfway houses operate similarly as transitional residences. Thus, for juveniles who have served time in secure facilities because of delinquency adjudications, halfway houses frequently assist them in achieving a higher life quality and in acquiring strategies for a more successful independent living. For example, the Virginia Department of Juvenile Justice operated three halfway houses for youths in 2008. These were (1) the Abraxas House, (2) the Discovery House, and (3) Hampton Place.

Abraxas House. Abraxas House is located in Staunton, Virginia. It is a structured transitional program for male juveniles aged 16–20 who have been released from juvenile correctional centers. The program emphasis is upon independent living skills, employment opportunities, educational services, and character development. Treatment services are also provided to assist adolescents with family issues, substance abuse issues, and sex offender issues, on an as-needed basis.

Discovery House. Discovery House is located in Roanoke, Virginia. Again, like Abraxas House, the age range of youthful offenders is from 16 to 20. The average length of placement in Discovery House is 4–6 months, with the program emphasis on independent living in the community. Discovery House includes three residential phases and one outreach phase. Privileges and freedom are earned incrementally by demonstrating responsible behavior, self-control, and task achievement. Youths learn to acquire law-abiding behaviors in a stable, secure, nonthreatening environment.

Hampton Place. Hampton Place is located in Norfolk, Virginia. It is designed for males aged 17–20 who have been committed there for direct care on a type of parole status. More closely supervised than youths are in Abraxas House or Discovery House, Hampton Place residents are held accountable for their actions and are assisted in significant ways for community reentry to live independently in the community (Virginia Department of Juvenile Justice, 2008).

Aftercare Programs for Juveniles. Professionals in the field agree that the ultimate measure of success for residential or institutional treatment programs is the assurance that youths exiting such facilities maintain positive gains and refrain from reoffending or engaging in otherwise problematic behaviors upon return to the community.

Camps, Ranches, Experience Programs, and Wilderness Projects. Camps, ranches, or camp ranches are nonsecure facilities that are sometimes referred to as

wilderness experiments

Experience programs that include a wide array of outdoor programs designed to improve a juvenile's self-worth, self-concept, pride, and trust in others.

shock probation, shock parole

Intermediate punishment where offenders are initially sentenced to terms of secure detention; after a period of time, between 90 and 180 days, youths are removed from detention and sentenced to serve the remainder of their sentences on probation; the term, "shock probation," was coined by Ohio authorities in 1964.

combination sentences, split sentences

Occur whenever judges sentence offenders to a term, a portion of which includes incarceration and a portion of which includes probation.

intermittent sentences

Occur whenever judges sentence offenders to terms such as weekend confinement only.

mixed sentences

Punishments imposed whenever offenders have been convicted of two or more offenses and judges sentence them to separate sentences for each convicted offense.

jail as a condition of probation

Sentence where judge imposes some jail time to be served before probation commences; also known as shock probation.

wilderness experiments or experience programs. A less expensive alternative to the incarceration of juvenile offenders, even those considered chronic, is their participation in experience programs. Experience programs include a wide array of outdoor programs designed to improve a juvenile's self-worth, self-concept, pride, and trust in others. One example is the Rawhide Boys Ranch (RBR).

The Rawhide Boys Ranch. The RBR is a faith-based residential care center in Wisconsin for at-risk teenage boys that commenced in 1960. It is based on a traditional family home model around which a cluster of youth homes is structured. Both public and private agencies can refer youths to RBR. Juvenile courts are also a source of youth referrals. Families and relatives of youthful offenders can also apply to have RBR accommodate their youths who have gotten into trouble with the law. RBR can accommodate up to 60 boys at any given time. There are strict screening requirements. Psychologically disturbed youths, or youths who suffer from severe mental illnesses, are typically referred to other places where better services for them exist.

Several living units have been established, with each being staffed by 2–4 resident instructors, a housekeeper, and a social worker. There are additional social workers, work experience job trainers, family counselors, and instructors who assist in helping RBR youth. Youths are placed in the RBR program for an indeterminate period, depending upon their individual progress in achieving programming goals. Activities are focused upon family services, social services and case management, academic education, employment training, foster care services, and transitional services. These are the principal program components, although other components may be offered to youthful clients.

Program evaluations of RBR have been conducted since 2003, disclosing a 73 percent success rate among RBR-discharged youth. That figure translates into a recidivism rate of 27 percent in a six-month follow-up, which is fairly low. Informal recidivism measures of different intervention programs over the past few decades, for both adults and juveniles, suggest acceptable recidivism standards to be 30 percent or less. Thus, utilizing this unofficial recidivism standard, RBR appears to be successful in achieving its goals of enabling discharged youth to reenter society and live independent, law-abiding lives. The tool used to evaluate the recidivism and effectiveness of RBR was the Youth Outcomes Questionnaire (YOQ), which measures numerous dimensions, including behaviors, moods, situations, and interpersonal relations that commonly are found among troubled teens. The conclusion reached by Dr. Frank Cummings, a clinical psychologist who conducted the RBR evaluation, was that RBR had produced sustained positive outcomes in the lives of most court-referred youths following their discharge (Rawhide Boys Ranch, 2008).

Secure Confinement: Variations

Shock Probation. **Shock probation** is an intermediate punishment where offenders are initially disposed to incarcerative terms; after a period of time, between 90 and 180 days, the youths are removed from secure confinement and obligated to serve the remainder of their disposition on probation. The actual term, "shock probation," was coined by Ohio authorities in 1964. Shock probation is also known as **shock parole**, because it technically involves a release from jail or prison after serving some amount of time in incarceration.

Sometimes, shock probation is used synonymously with **combination sentences** or **split sentences**. Other terms, such as **intermittent sentences**, **mixed sentences**, or **jail as a condition of probation**, are also used interchangeably with shock probation, although they have somewhat different meanings. Combination sentences or split sentences occur whenever judges sentence offenders to a term, a portion of which includes incarceration and a portion of which includes probation. Mixed sentences occur whenever offenders have been convicted of two or more offenses and judges sentence them to separate sentences for each convicted offense. Intermittent sentences occur whenever judges sentence offenders to terms such as weekend confinement only. Jail as a condition of probation is a sentence that prescribes a specified amount of jail incarceration prior to serving the remainder of the sentence on probation.

Technically, shock probation is none of these. Youths disposed to shock probation don't know they have received such dispositions. The judge disposes them to incarceration. The youths have no way of knowing that within three or four months, they will be yanked out of incarceration, brought before the same judge, and disposed to probation. This new probationary disposition is contingent upon their good behavior during their incarceration. Thus, they are shocked or traumatized by their incarceration. When they are redisposed to probation later, they should be sufficiently shocked to avoid further offending. But recidivism figures suggest it doesn't always work that way.

Nonsecure placements may involve boot camps employing organized activities.

Shock probation is a misnomer in a sense. If we recall that probation is a disposition in lieu of incarceration, then it seems peculiar to incarcerate these offenders first, and then release them later and call them probationers. This practice is more accurately called shock parole, since these are previously incarcerated offenders who are resentenced to a supervised release program. But also, since a parole board does not grant them parole, we are uncertain about what they should be called other than shock probationers. In any case, the intended effect of incarceration is to scare offenders sufficiently so that they refrain from reoffending. Simply, their incarcerative experiences are so shocking that they don't want to face further incarceration.

Boot Camps. The juvenile version of shock probation or **shock incarceration** is perhaps best exemplified by juvenile **boot camps** (Parent, 2003). Also known as the **Army Model**, boot camp programs are patterned after basic training for new military recruits. Juvenile offenders are given a taste of hard military life, and such regimented activities and structure for up to 180 days are often sufficient to shock them into giving up their lives of delinquency or crime and staying out of jail (Gover and MacKenzie, 2003). Boot camp programs in various states have been established, including the Regimented Inmate Discipline program in Mississippi, the **About Face** program in Georgia, and the shock incarceration program in Georgia. These are paramilitary-type programs that emphasize strict military discipline and physical training.

What Are Boot Camps? Boot camps are highly regimented, military-like, short-term correctional programs (90–180 days) where offenders are provided with strict discipline, physical training, and hard labor resembling some aspects of military basic training; when successfully completed, boot camps provide for transfers of participants to community-based facilities for nonsecure supervision. By 1993, boot camps had been formally established in over half of the states.

By 2007, there were over 100 residential boot camps for adjudicated juveniles operating in 35 states (Office of Juvenile Justice and Delinquency Prevention, 2007). Many jurisdictions throughout the United States issue boot camp orders for juveniles who are believed to be unruly and in need of discipline. In Glynn County, Georgia, for instance, boot camp orders are issued by juvenile court judges. Figure 12.1 shows a short-term boot camp order for those juveniles targeted for involvement in such programs.

Boot camps have been perceived as the latest correctional reform (Office of Juvenile Justice and Delinquency Prevention, 2007). Other professionals are skeptical about

shock incarceration
See shock probation.

boot camps, Army Model
Boot camp programs are patterned after basic training for new military recruits. Juvenile offenders are given a taste of hard military life, and such regimented activities and structure for up to 180 days are often sufficient to "shock" them into giving up their lives of delinquency or crime and staying out of jail.

About Face
Louisiana boot camp program.

Figure 12.1   Short-Term Boot Camp Program Order

IN THE JUVENILE COURT OF GLYNN COUNTY
STATE OF GEORGIA

IN THE INTEREST OF: CASE #:_____

_____
A Child
ORDER
SHORT TERM/ BOOT CAMP PROGRAM

Petition(s) having been filed in this Court and after hearing evidence, this Court has determined that the above named child is subject to the jurisdiction and protection of this Court as provided by law; and

After hearing evidence, the Court finds that the child committed the act(s) alleged in said petition(s), to wit:

_____
_____
_____and that said child is hereby found to be in a state of delinquency/unruliness and in need of treatment or rehabilitation.

It is Ordered that said child be and is hereby detained by the Department of Juvenile Justice for care, supervision, and planning as provided by O.C.G.A. Section 15-11-35(b) and 49-4A-8, and that the child be detained for a period of _____days.

THE CHILD WILL/WILL NOT BE GIVEN CREDIT FOR THE TIME SPENT IN DETENTION BOTH PRIOR TO ADJUDICATION AND WHILE AWAITING ENTRY INTO THE PROGRAM.

SAID CHILD SHALL NOT BE GRANTED CREDIT FOR ANY TIME SPENT IN DISCIPLINARY ISOLATION OR DETENTION, FOR REFUSING TO PARTICIPATE IN THE PROGRAM, OR FOR FAILURE TO ABIDE BY THE RULES OF THE FACILITY.

The Department of Juvenile Justice is authorized to provide such emergency psychological evaluation or treatment, medical treatment, hospitalization, or surgery as is considered necessary by competent medical authorities for said child. The Department of Juvenile Justice is authorized to apprehend such child if such child shall have escaped from a facility or institution operated or under the supervision of the Department.

CONSIDERED, ORDERED, AND ADJUDGED this the _____day of _____,_____.

_____
Juvenile Court of Glynn County

Source: Juvenile Court of Glynn County, GA.

their success potential (Zachariah, 2002). Much depends upon how particular boot camps are operated and for how long. Boot camp programs are operated for as short a time as 30 days or as long as 180 days. While boot camps were officially established in 1983 by the Georgia Department of Corrections Special Alternative Incarceration (SAI), the general idea for boot camps originated some time earlier in the late 1970s, also in Georgia (MacKenzie et al., 2001).

The Rationale for Boot Camps. Boot camps have been established as an alternative to long-term traditional incarceration. Austin, Jones, and Bolyard (1993) outline a brief rationale for boot camps:

1. A substantial number of youthful first-offenders now incarcerated will respond to a short but intensive period of confinement followed by a longer period of intensive community supervision.

2. These youthful offenders will benefit from a military-type atmosphere that instills self-discipline and physical conditioning, which was lacking in their lives.

3. The same youths need exposure to relevant educational training, vocational training, drug treatment, and general counseling services to develop more positive and law-abiding values and become better prepared to secure legitimate future employment.

4. The costs involved will be less than a traditional criminal justice sanction that imprisons the offender for a substantially longer period of time (Austin, Jones, and Bolyard, 1993:1).

Boot Camp Goals. Boot camps have several general goals, including (1) rehabilitation/reintegration; (2) discipline; (3) deterrence; (4) easing prison/jail overcrowding; and (5) vocational, educational, and rehabilitative services.

1. To provide rehabilitation and reintegration. Boot camps often seek to improve one's sense of purpose, self-discipline, self-control, and self-confidence through physical conditioning, educational programs, and social skills training, all within the framework of strict military discipline.

2. To inculcate discipline. Boot camps are designed to improve one's discipline. Certain boot camps, especially those aimed at younger offenders, must deal with adjudicated juvenile offenders who usually resist authority and refuse to listen or learn in traditional classroom or treatment environments. Physical conditioning and structure are most frequently stressed in these programs. But most boot camp programs also include educational elements pertaining to literacy, academic and vocational education, intensive value clarification, and resocialization (Styve et al., 2000).

3. To promote deterrence. The sudden immersion into a military-like atmosphere is a frightening experience for many participants. The rigorous approach to formal rules and authority is a challenging dimension of boot camp programs for most participants.

4. To ease prison and jail overcrowding. Boot camps are believed to have a long-term impact on jail and prison overcrowding. Theoretically, this is possible because of the low recidivism rates among boot camp participants. The short-term nature of confinement in boot camp programs with the participant's subsequent return to the community helps to ease the overcrowding problem in correctional settings. It is believed that boot camp experiences are significant in creating more positive attitudes among participants (Gover and MacKenzie, 2003).

5. To provide vocational and rehabilitative services. An integral feature of most boot camp programs is the inclusion of some form of educational and/or vocational training. Educational training is also a key feature of **Intensive Motivational Program of Alternative Correctional Treatment (IMPACT)** in Louisiana jurisdictions.

Intensive Motivational Program of Alternative Correctional Treatment (IMPACT)
Boot camp program operated in Louisiana; incorporates educational training with strict physical and behavioral requirements.

12.1   Career Snapshot

Herbert C. Covey

Vice-Chair, Colorado State Juvenile Parole Board

Statistics:
B.A. (sociology), Colorado State University;
M.A. (sociology), University of Nebraska at Omaha;
Ph.D. (sociology), University of Colorado at Boulder

Background

I serve as the Vice-Chair of the State Juvenile Parole Board and as a part-time instructor at the University of Colorado on juvenile delinquency. My main occupation is being a field administrator with the Colorado Department of Human Services. I provide management support to nine counties' departments of social services and five agencies working with aging populations. My serving on the board is a part-time activity.

Before I joined the board, I had a conversation with an office mate regarding his service on the board and how I could not imagine how he could do it given the responsibility and stress of making such important life-altering decisions. I recall stating, "I don't know how you do it." Two years later, I replaced him and have served over 10 years on the board. It has been one of the richest experiences I have had in my life.

I was asked to serve on the board because Colorado Law required my employer, the Department of Human Services, to have a representative. In addition, I had co-authored a book on youth street gangs and was teaching juvenile delinquency. To become a member of the board, the candidate must apply, be appointed by the governor, be approved by the Senate Judiciary Committee, and then confirmed by the full senate. I remember my confirmation hearing as being more interesting than stressful. The committee essentially wanted to know how I would respond to pressure from juvenile corrections to parole youths that I felt were not ready. In other words, would I succumb to pressure to parole youths for the purpose of freeing up beds in state facilities. For me, the answer was an obvious "no"; community safety should come first. A second set of questions focused on my values relative to parole. I stated that after safety, the best interests of the youth and family should be considered.

I also added that the sentiments of the victims have to be considered. Too often after trial, victims are excluded from the judicial process. Finally, I indicated that it was better to send out youth with transitional services, than to simply let them burn time and turn them loose on the community.

I was attracted to the board because I view parole hearings as being an important rite-of-passage for youth and their families. I wanted to be part of that important passage. For many youth, the parole hearing is similar to a graduation ceremony for their return to the community. For others, it is a wake-up call when they are denied parole and returned to facilities to work on their issues. Finally, I believe that if someone needed to take the responsibility of making parole decisions, it might as well be me because I deeply care about youth, families, victims, and communities.

Work Experiences

There are many pros and a few cons to serving on the board. One pro is that I have served on many committees, work groups, and boards, none of which comes close to offering the kinds of rich experiences I have had serving on the Juvenile Parole Board. It has been my ticket to the "reality of it all." Over the course of about one hour, I get to delve into the human experience in ways not available to most other people. In my 10 years of service, I can honestly say that I have just about seen and heard it all. In saying this, I realize that my next hearing will offer new experiences and little about it will be routine. It can be very humbling at times. A second pro is that although little can occur in a one-hour hearing to turn a youth's life around, sometimes I get a sense that a youth may have been influenced in a positive direction. By being tough, supportive, honest, emphatic, holding the youth accountable, and otherwise appropriately addressing each case, I believe I am playing an important role in the system.

I cannot really think of many cons to serving on the board. If anything, I consider it a privilege to serve the citizens of Colorado. It does take a considerable amount of personal time to prepare for hearings. I believe sometimes it is very difficult to not dwell on specific hearings and what life courses youth have taken. I find myself being haunted by some of the human tragedies that are sometimes summarized over the course of a hearing for the victims as well as the families, and offenders. However, there are also many success stories to counterbalance the negative.

As to the basic question of predicting how well youth do on parole, one must take into account that a one-hour parole hearing is not likely to tell a board member enough about the youth to be 100 percent sure how well the individual will do on parole. The old adage, "you can't judge a book by its cover," is also true for youth. Board members learn that they cannot stereotype youth and predict with 100 percent accuracy how they will behave on parole. Each parole candidate has to be considered on a case-by-case basis.

This is not to suggest that it is total guesswork. I learned early that prior behavior is a good predictor of future behavior. If a youth has a lengthy history of serious offending and started at an early age, then the risk of reoffending increases. Property offenders are more likely to reoffend than violent offenders. If a youth does well in rehabilitation programs, shows victim empathy, has a positive attitude, has positive peers in the community, has bonded with positive adult role models, takes accountability for actions, has developed tools to keep from relapsing, and has good support systems, the chances for success on parole are better. If the youth returns to the same crime-infested neighborhood, begins associating with negative peers, and other systems such as school and family have not changed, then the chances are higher the youth will not succeed on parole.

I have many positive memories of parolees and parole hearings. For instance, one sex offender attempted to reoffend within two weeks of being paroled. Because all the family members had been trained by a multisystemic therapist, he was caught early in his offense cycle and never reoffended. In another hearing, I witnessed a mother of a physical assault victim heal her anger by seeing the offending youth show genuine remorse for what he had done and had changed for the better. Without that hearing, she would have never healed her anger.

Once, we revoked parole of a drug-using youth because he was not complying with parole and we thought he was a danger to himself. He reeked of drugs and had an enabling and argumentative mother. Two weeks after she called us every name in the book, the revoked youth attempted suicide. After much work by youth corrections and an insightful client manager, I paroled a dramatically changed youth who successfully completed parole and finished college. I'd like to think the board played a role in turning this youth around.

Advice to Students

As a board member, I come into contact with many professionals working with youth offenders. I believe the common characteristics of those who are successful are that they really care about helping youth, have the ability to accept failure and success with grace, are forthright with youth and families, and get to know their cases in detail. They never become friends with their clients but are sources of authority and direction. I also offer that being able to work as a member of a multidisciplinary team is important. Many of today's delinquent youth have multiple and confounding issues, such as mental health and substance abuse, and this requires teamwork to address. If you do not have these qualities, along with dedication, then you need to find something else to do with your life. If you possess these qualities and want a meaningful career, this is a great area to pursue.

My advice to students interested in parole and aftercare services, or parole boards, is to contact people working in these areas and conduct informational interviews on how they developed their careers. Students should ask them what they like and dislike about their jobs and why they do what they do. How do they deal with parole successes and failures? What do they believe works and does not work for what types of youth? Many professionals are willing to share their thoughts and help students.

I am convinced that in the juvenile justice system, considerable time and resources are wasted by well-intentioned people who apply ineffective treatments to youth based on feelings and emotions rather than evidence-based practice. Students will do well to become familiar with what research evidence shows works rather than the latest fad or what their feelings suggest. Evidence of effectiveness should drive treatment decisions, not program marketing or false assumptions about effectiveness. While our interventions may not always work for all youth, we want to at least ensure that our efforts are not making them worse.

As an alternative to traditional incarceration, boot camps do much to promote greater social and educational adjustment for clients reentering their communities (Office of Juvenile Justice and Delinquency Prevention, 2007).

Profiling Boot Camp Participants. Who can participate in boot camps or shock incarceration programs? Participants may or may not be able to enter or withdraw from boot camps voluntarily. It depends on the particular program. Most boot camp participants are prison-bound youthful offenders convicted of less serious, nonviolent crimes, and who have never been previously incarcerated (Zachariah, 2002).

Representative Boot Camps. The boot camps described below are indicative of the general nature of boot camps in the various states that have them.

The Camp Monterey Shock Incarceration Facility. New York State has a major boot camp project with the following features:

(a) It accommodates 250 participants in a minimum-security institution.
(b) It has 131 staff (83 custody positions).
(c) Participants are screened and must meet statutory criteria; three-fourths of volunteers and one-third of applicants are rejected.
(d) Inmates form platoons and live in open dormitories.
(e) Successful program completion leads to parole board releases to an intensive probation supervision program called "aftershock."
(f) It includes physical training, drill, and eight hours daily of hard labor.
(g) Inmates must participate in therapeutic community meetings, compulsory adult basic education courses, mandatory individual counseling, and mandatory recreation.
(h) All must attend alcohol and substance abuse treatment.
(i) Training in job-seeking skills and reentry planning is provided.

The Oklahoma Regimented Inmate Discipline Program (RID). Oklahoma has a **Regimented Inmate Discipline Program (RID)** with the following features:

Regimented Inmate Discipline Program (RID)
Oklahoma Department of Corrections program operated in Lexington, Oklahoma, for juveniles; program stresses military-type discipline and accountability; facilities are secure and privately operated.

(a) A 145-bed facility at the Lexington Assessment and Reception Center; also houses 600 long-term general population inmates as medium security.
(b) Offenders screened according to statutory criteria and may volunteer.
(c) Inmates live in single- or double-bunk cells.
(d) Strict discipline, drill, physical training; housekeeping and institutional maintenance.
(e) Six hours of educational/vocational programs daily.
(f) Drug abuse programs, and individual and group counseling.
(g) Subsequently, participants resentenced by judges to intensive supervised probation or "community custody," perhaps commencing at a halfway house.

The Georgia Special Alternative Program:

(a) Program is for male offenders.
(b) Judges control selection process, and SAI is a "condition of probation"; if successful, boot camp graduates are released, since judges do not ordinarily resentence them to probation.
(c) Program includes physical training, drill, hard work; two exercise and drill periods daily, with eight-hour hard labor periods in between.
(d) Participants perform limited community services.
(e) There is little emphasis on counseling or treatment.
(f) Inmates do receive drug abuse education and information about sexually transmitted diseases.

(g) Inmates are double-bunked in two 25-cell units at Dodge; and at Burris, 100 inmates are single-bunked in four 25-cell units (MacKenzie, Shaw, and Gowdy, 1993). Because many of these boot camp programs were established in the late 1980s and early 1990s, evaluation research about general boot camp program effectiveness has not been abundant (Zachariah, 2002). However, indications from available research are that boot camps generally are effective at reducing recidivism among participants. Currently, some states, such as Georgia, report relatively high rates of recidivism among boot camp clientele, whereas New York and Oklahoma have much lower recidivism rates. Besides reducing recidivism, boot camps might also be effective at saving taxpayers money over time. For various states, operating boot camps is considerably cheaper than using traditional incarceration for particular offenders. In some instances, the cost savings is considerable.

Industrial Schools and Other Juvenile Institutions.

In the 1960s and earlier, particularly troublesome youths were sent to reform schools. These were prison-like facilities with few amenities. Juveniles were assigned various menial tasks, and educational opportunities were limited. Some more affluent jurisdictions with reform schools offered various types of counseling and vocational and educational programs. But for most youths sent to reform schools, their prospects for learning useful skills and emerging as law-abiding young adults were bleak. If anything, many youths emerged from these institutions as more hard-core offenders compared with when they entered. More than a few youths went on to commit crimes as adults.

During the period 1950–1970, a concerted effort was made by the Federal Bureau of Investigation and other agencies to intervene in various ways to interrupt those social patterns believed responsible for generating youthful offenders or delinquents. J. Edgar Hoover, the director of the FBI during that period, was a firm believer in delinquency interventions and their relationship to general adult crime prevention. The FBI would send teachers and professors useful teaching materials, articles, and other information that could be used in educational programs to advise and inform. Much of this information was descriptive and informed readers about ongoing interventions in various jurisdictions and their successfulness. In turn, these federal efforts prompted many communities throughout the United States to develop strategies for dealing with delinquent offenders. Different types of treatments and punishments were the subject of experimentation for selected groups of juveniles.

Today there is a wide variety of intervention programs for juveniles operating in virtually every major city in the United States and in most communities. These programs generally emphasize vocational training, acquisition of social and coping skills, education, substance abuse counseling, mental health counseling, and a wide variety of other activities. But it is clear that almost all of these interventions have been limited in their effectiveness at deterring youths from committing delinquent offenses (Cauffman et al., 2007). The growing influence of gangs, the greater use of drugs and other substances, and pervasive family disunity and fragmentation have combined with other factors, such as higher unemployment rates, hard economic times, and pressures for higher standards in education, to frustrate the most well-intentioned intervention programs (Proctor and Mullings, 2008).

Delinquency and violent youthful offending appeared to peak during the mid-1990s, although there continues to be an unacceptable level of violent offending among juveniles. Citizen response to such violence, much of it gang-related, has been to get tough with juveniles. The get-tough movement generally equates with incarceration or institutionalization as the harshest measure to apply as a juvenile punishment for delinquency.

As we have seen, locking up juveniles is generally an unpopular response to juvenile offending. In many jurisdictions, it is considered as a last resort. In Tennessee, for instance, juvenile corrections personnel will place juveniles on electronic monitoring and/or home confinement for 30, 60, or 90 days to see if they can remain law-abiding.

If they cannot remain law-abiding while on these programs, then secure confinement is ordered.

Today institutionalized juveniles in all states are held in facilities most frequently known as **industrial schools**. The use of the term "reform school" has been abandoned. Also, no juvenile facility is called a prison, even though most secure juvenile facilities are prison-like in their construction and operation. Industrial schools are not new. The term has been used for over 60 years in different jurisdictions. In the 1950s, for instance, the Utah State Industrial School was the juvenile prison and also the place where most hard-core juvenile offenders were sent by juvenile court judges. In the 1960s, the Arizona State Industrial School was where Gerald Gault was housed for allegedly making obscene telephone calls (*In re Gault,* 1967). Industrial schools now exist in most states and are operated either publicly or privately or both (Office of Juvenile Justice and Delinquency Prevention, 2007). Youths sent to industrial schools are considered **commitment placements**, where they are held for longer terms compared with youths placed in detention.

Numbers and Types of Juveniles Held in Secure Facilities. There are few precise figures about how many juveniles are held in secure facilities each year. Given the rate of discharges and admissions, the numbers are fluid from one day to the next. However, it is apparent from available information that the number of confined youths in secure facilities is growing each year. Between 1999 and 2007, for instance, the number of youths committed to secure facilities almost doubled from 110,000 to nearly 200,000 (Office of Juvenile Justice and Delinquency Prevention, 2007). In 2007, it was reported that 175,781 youths were assigned beds in 3,621 secure facilities nationwide (Office of Juvenile Justice and Delinquency Prevention, 2007). At the time of this writing, more recent information was unavailable to report. However, extrapolating from previous information and trends suggests that there were over 180,000 youths in secure confinement by 2008 (Champion, 2008a).

Youths are committed either to short- or long-term detention or secure confinement, depending upon the particular stage of juvenile offender processing (Sabol, Minton, and Harrison, 2007). Prior to a formal adjudicatory hearing, juveniles may be detained in the custody of juvenile authorities pending the outcome of a subsequent adjudicatory hearing. Figure 12.2 shows an order for detention for Glynn County, Georgia. The reasons for detention are outlined. These usually pertain to protecting others from the juvenile; protecting the juvenile from himself/herself while awaiting a formal adjudicatory hearing; the absence of parents or legal guardians; or some other valid reason.

Typically, reported figures include all youths under age 21 who are housed in either public or private secure facilities; who have been adjudicated delinquent by the juvenile court; who are in residential placement because of that offense; and who have been assigned a bed by a given date. The American Correctional Association (ACA) reports that in September 2006, there were 44,896 youths under age 18 in 41 reporting jurisdictions (American Correctional Association, 2007). Of these, about 14 percent were female. Also, of those incarcerated, about 36 percent were white, while 64 percent were racial and/or ethnic minorities.

It is not necessarily true that a majority of youths who are incarcerated in secure facilities are violent offenders. About 50 percent of all committed are for nonviolent property, drug, public order, or status offenses. Figure 12.3 shows an order of commitment used by Glynn County, Georgia, for juveniles who are to be placed for long terms in secure confinement. It is interesting to note in these commitment orders that the reasons for commitment are related closely to the need for the youth's rehabilitation or treatment under close supervision. The length of any particular commitment varies according to one's offense or the nature of the unruly behavior.

industrial schools

Institutions that resemble prisons; secure facilities where some juveniles are held for up to one year or longer; such institutions usually have different types of programming to aid in the rehabilitation and reintegration of youthful offenders, consisting of vocational and educational courses or programs, counseling for different types of youth needs, and other services; these facilities are largely self-contained like prisons, and they offer a limited range of medical and health services.

commitment placements

Confinement in a secure juvenile facility, usually for a term such as one year or longer.

Figure 12.2   Order for Detention

ORDER FOR DETENTION

IN THE JUVENILE COURT OF GLYNN COUNTY, GEORGIA

IN THE MATTER OF: **CASE NO.:**
                              SEX:
                              DOB:
A CHILD   **AGE:**

WHEREAS a complaint has been made to the Court concerning the above-named child and the Court finding from information brought before it that it is necessary for the protection of said child and/or society that he or she be detained.

It is therefore ordered that said child be detained in the custody of the Court until further order of the Court or until released by a person duly authorized by the Court.

Said child is being detained pursuant to Official Code of Georgia Ann. 15-11-46 for the following reason(s):

( ) to protect the person or property of others or of the child;
( ) the child may abscond or be removed from the justification of the Court;
( ) because he has no parent, guardian or legal custodian or other person able to provide supervision and care for him and return him to the Court when required;
( ) an order for his detention or shelter care has been made by the Court pursuant to the Juvenile Proceedings Code.

It is further ordered that the place of detention shall be the _____
_____

ORDERED AND ADJUDGED, this the ____ day of _____, 2004.

_____

Source: Juvenile Court of Glynn County, GA.

Figure 12.3   Order of Commitment

ORDER OF COMMITMENT

IN THE JUVENILE COURT OF GLYNN COUNTY, GEORGIA

In the interest of: **CASE NO.**

                                                           SEX:
                                                           DOB: **AGE:**

Petition(s) having been filed in this court and after hearing evidence in this court, this court has determined that the above-named child is subject to the jurisdiction and protection of this court as provided by law; and

After hearing evidence or upon the recommendation of the judge, no appeal having been timely filed, the court finds that the child committed the act(s) alleged in said petition(s), to wit:

_____

And that said child is hereby found to be in a state of: (place an "X" in appropriate space)

_____   delinquency and in need of treatment of rehabilitation.

_____   unruliness and in need of treatment, rehabilitation, or
           supervision. The court also finds that the child is not
           amenable to treatment or rehabilitation pursuant to
           O.C.G.A. §15-11-66(a)(1)(3).

The Court also finds that reasonable efforts have been made to prevent the unnecessary removal of the child from the child's home, and that removal is in the best interest of the child at this time.

It is further ordered that said child be and hereby is committed to the Department of Juvenile Justice, for care, supervision and planning as provided in O.C.G.A. §49-4A-8. The undersigned judge hereby recommends that the child be:

COMMITTED TO THE DEPARTMENT OF JUVENILE JUSTICE

The said Department of Juvenile Justice is authorized to provide such medical treatment, hospitalization and/or surgery as is considered necessary by competent medical authorities for said child.

It is further ordered that said child be released into the custody of _____
_____. Detained in the _____ pending placement by the Department of Juvenile Justice.

Considered, Ordered and Adjudged this the _____ day of _____, 2004.

                                        _____
                                        Juvenile Court of Glynn County

Source: Juvenile Court of Glynn County, GA

Persistent Problems of Nonsecure and Secure Confinement

Secure juvenile incarcerative facilities in the United States are known by various names. Further, not all of these are alike. While many institutions provide only custodial services for chronic or more serious juvenile offenders, other incarcerative facilities offer an array of services and treatments, depending upon the diverse needs of the juveniles confined, such as mental health services. Clarifying the mission and goals of corrections agencies helps staff to do a better job supervising youthful clientele. Institutional rules tend to be couched in a more meaningful context, and incarcerated youth are able to cope more effectively with their confinement (Cauffman et al., 2007).

Architectural Improvements and Officer Training Reforms

In recent years, however, numerous improvements have been made generally in the overall quality of juvenile secure confinement facilities throughout the United States. Evidence of improvement in juvenile corrections is the massive efforts made by authorities in numerous jurisdictions to design and build more adequately equipped juvenile facilities that minimize youthful inmate problems of idle time and overcrowding. Private interests, including the Corrections Corporation of America, have assisted as well in providing more modern designs and plant operations for secure juvenile facilities in various states such as California and Tennessee (Mendel, 2001).

Both male and female correctional officers are targeted for additional training to cope with inmate problems. Formerly, it has been alleged by some critics that female correctional officers tend to lack the degree of authority their male counterparts have when dealing with inmates. However, programs such as on-the-job training and self-improvement courses sponsored and conducted by the ACA have done much to improve correctional officer credibility and performance. According to ACA standards, correctional officers should have at least 160 hours of orientation and training during their first year of employment. Certification is awarded after satisfactorily completing the ACA training course (American Correctional Association, 2007).

Juvenile Detention Resource Centers

The U.S. Department of Justice's Office of Juvenile Justice and Delinquency Prevention (OJJDP) promulgated specific guidelines for all juvenile detention facilities in the early 1980s. These guidelines were published as *Guidelines for the Development of Policies and Procedures for Juvenile Detention Facilities*. The goal of the OJJDP was to establish national juvenile detention resource centers across the United States in various jurisdictions that would provide information, technical assistance, and training to juvenile detention professionals who wished to participate (King, 2005). The ultimate aim of these juvenile detention centers was to provide juveniles with better and more adequate services and assistance (Teske, 2005).

Such **detention centers** have done much to improve juvenile incarceration standards throughout the nation. The ACA has been actively involved in assisting different jurisdictions in their efforts to establish juvenile detention resource centers and operate them successfully (Watson, 2008). The educational dimension of such centers can assist in transmitting knowledge about communicable diseases, such as AIDS, and inform adolescents about the risks of sexual misconduct. Other positive contributions of these centers might be in assisting youths in managing their anger and providing them with opportunities to improve their general mental health (Cauffman et al., 2007).

detention centers
Juvenile secure facilities used for serious and violent juveniles who are awaiting an adjudication hearing.

Short- and Long-Term Facilities

Secure juvenile confinement facilities in the United States are either short term or long term. Short-term confinement facilities are designed to accommodate on a temporary basis those juveniles who are either awaiting a juvenile court adjudication, subsequent foster home or group home placement, or a transfer to criminal court. Whether a juvenile is held for a period of time in detention depends upon the outcome of a **detention hearing**, where the appropriateness of the detention is determined.

Sometimes youths will be placed in short-term confinement because their identity is unknown and it is desirable that they should not be confined in adult lockups or jails. Other youths are violent and must be detained temporarily until more appropriate placements may be made. The designations "short term" and "long term" may range from a few days to several years, although the average duration of **long-term detention** across all offender categories nationally is about six to seven months. The average short-term incarceration in public facilities for juveniles is about 30 days (Office of Juvenile Justice and Delinquency Prevention, 2007).

Some **short-term confinement** is preventive detention or pretrial detention, where juveniles are awaiting formal adjudicatory proceedings (Caudill and Hayslett-McCall, 2008). While some authorities question the legality of jailing juveniles or holding them in detention centers prior to their cases being heard by juvenile court judges, the U.S. Supreme Court has upheld the constitutionality of pretrial or preventive detention of juveniles, especially dangerous ones, in the case of *Schall v. Martin* (1984). One objective of pretrial detention is to prevent certain dangerous juveniles from committing new pretrial crimes (King, 2005). Juvenile court judges must make a determination of whether certain juveniles should be held in pretrial detention or released into the custody of parents or guardians (Lee, 2008). While their discretion is not perfect, many juvenile court judges exercise good judgment in determining which juveniles should be temporarily detained. It is often difficult to determine the future behaviors of adjudicated youths, especially in probation or parole contexts (Xiaoying, 2005).

Some Criticisms of Incarcerating Juveniles

There are numerous proponents and opponents of juvenile secure confinement of any kind (Anderson and Rancer, 2007). Those favoring incarceration cite the disruption of one's lifestyle and separation from other delinquent youths as a positive dimension. For example, youths who have been involved with delinquent gangs or friends who engage in frequent law-breaking would probably benefit from incarceration, since these unfavorable associations would be interrupted or terminated (Taylor et al., 2008). Of course, juveniles can always return to their old ways when released from incarceration. There is nothing the juvenile justice system can do to prevent these reunions. But at least the existing pattern of interaction that contributed to the delinquent behavior initially is temporarily interrupted (Dembo, Turner, and Jainchill, 2007).

Another argument favoring incarceration of juveniles is that long-term secure confinement is a deserved punishment for their actions. This is consistent with the just-deserts philosophy that seems to typify contemporary thinking about juvenile punishment. There is a noticeable trend away from thinking about the best interests of youths and toward thinking about ways to make them more accountable for their actions. This shift has prompted debate among juvenile justice scholars about the true functions of juvenile courts and the ultimate aims of the sanctions they impose (King, 2005).

In some states, such as Texas, juvenile court judges have considerable power over juveniles and their secure confinement. In the case of *Matter of D.L.* (2006), for instance, D.L. was a juvenile charged with aggravated assault. The juvenile court judge ordered him to serve a six-year determinate sentence in a Texas Youth Commission secure facility. When the juvenile reached the age of majority in Texas and was short of the six-year determinate term, the trial court recommended that D.L. be sent to an adult prison where

---

detention hearing
Judicial or quasi-judicial proceeding held to determine whether or not it is appropriate to continue to hold or detain a juvenile in a shelter facility.

long-term detention
Period of incarceration of juvenile offenders in secure facilities that averages 180 days in the United States.

short-term confinement
Placement in any incarcerative institution of either adults or juveniles where the period of confinement is less than one year; jails are considered short-term facilities.

he should serve the remainder of his sentence. D.L. appealed, arguing that the Youth Commission agent who testified in his hearing, asking that he be transferred to a prison, was testifying based on hearsay or reports from others about his prior record and institutional conduct. However, his objections were overruled by a state appellate court and he was remanded to a Texas prison for the remainder of his original sentence.

Opponents of long-term secure confinement of juveniles believe, among other things, that there are possibly adverse labeling effects from confinement with other offenders. Thus, juveniles might acquire labels of themselves as juvenile delinquents and persist in reoffending when released from incarceration later. However, it might be maintained that if they are incarcerated, they know they are delinquents anyway. Will they necessarily acquire stronger self-definitions of delinquents beyond those they already possess? In some respects, it is status-enhancing for youthful offenders to have been confined in some joint or juvenile secure confinement facility, so that they may brag to others about their experiences later. No doubt, confinement of any kind will add at least one dimension to one's reputation as a delinquent offender among other offenders in the community.

Most of the successful incarcerative programs for juveniles have built-in educational and vocational components, many of which are voluntary. It seems to make a difference when confined juveniles are forced to take vocational or educational courses compared to when they can enroll in such programs on a voluntary basis. In recent years, organizations such as the ACA have promulgated standards for juvenile correctional facilities that provide educational and vocational goals for juvenile inmates of these institutions. Presently, educational programming is mandatory for all juvenile offenders, and educational programs in juvenile correctional facilities are required to follow the same laws and practices as their public school counterparts. These standards also are applicable to privately operated secure juvenile facilities (Kupchik, 2007).

Juvenile facilities may seek accreditation from various organizations such as the Correctional Education Association (CEA). In October 2004, the Standards Commission of the CEA approved a set of standards for accrediting correctional educational programs in juvenile facilities. Actually, CEA began accrediting juvenile corrections educational programming in 1988. Both adult and juvenile institutions are now subject to CEA accreditation and the standards established by it. The accreditation process is a dynamic one, with constant improvements and assessment plans being devised. The more corrections professionals learn through the accreditation process, the more valuable they can be in assisting juveniles to achieve their educational and vocational training goals (Corwin, 2005).

It may be that the effects of imprisonment may influence positively a juvenile's self-image and decrease his/her propensity to commit new offenses. However, incarceration as a punishment may be the primary result, without any tangible, long-range benefits such as self-improvement or reduction in recidivism (Dembo, Turner, and Jainchill, 2007). At least there does not appear to be any consistent or reliable evidence that detaining juveniles automatically causes them to escalate to more serious offenses or to become adult criminals. According to some analysts, the peak ages of juvenile criminality fall between the 16th and 20th birthdays, with participation rates falling off rapidly. Thus, incarceration for a fixed period may naturally ease the delinquency rate, at least for some of the more chronic offenders. Some opponents note that racial, ethnic, and gender factors are more operative in secure confinement decisions than legal factors (King, 2005; Merianos, 2005).

Disproportionate Minority Confinement

Considerable attention has been directed in recent years toward the issue of disproportionate minority confinement, especially in secure juvenile facilities (Pope, Lovell, and Hsia, 2002:1). A far greater proportionate number of arrests of juveniles, for instance, involves racial and ethnic minorities. In 2007, the racial composition of the 10–17 population in the United States was 76 percent white, 18 percent black, 4 percent Asian/Pacific Islander, and 2 percent American Indian (American Correctional Association,

2007). However, that same year, of all juvenile arrests for violent crimes, 59 percent of the arrestees were white, 38 percent black, and 3 percent other. For juvenile property offending in 2007, 66 percent of arrests involved white youths, blacks accounted for 28 percent, and 4 percent consisted of Asians and others. Thus, at the point of entry into the juvenile justice system, there were disproportionately larger numbers of minority youths compared with white juveniles.

It is beyond the scope of this book to explore the many reasons or explanations for such disproportionate representations of minorities in these arrest figures. Interestingly, arrest figures for adult offenders mirror those of youthful offenders each year. One plausible explanation, however, is that minority youths are often from the lower socioeconomic levels, and thus, they generally have more limited opportunities for success in school and other activities. Thus, the mere fact of socioeconomic deprivation might account for more frequent property crime among such youths, such as burglary, larceny, and vehicular theft. Violent crimes such as robbery, which are related closely to socioeconomic factors, might also reflect disproportionate numbers of minority offenders. In fact, in 2007, 62 percent of all youths arrested for robbery were black.

Is there pervasive racism throughout law enforcement in cities and towns? Do police officers single out minority youths for arrests and overlook crimes committed by white youths? There have been numerous investigations of the impact of race and minority status generally on the likelihood of arrest. While most of these studies are inconclusive, an indirect bias has been detected in more than a few investigations, indicating that nonwhite juveniles are more likely to be arrested compared with white juveniles when the victim is white rather than nonwhite (Owens-Sabir, 2007). However, no direct evidence presently exists to show that police arrests of juveniles are race-based or biased. Essentially, what the research literature suggests is that whenever youths commit violent crimes and police are aware of these acts, the juveniles will be arrested whether they are white or nonwhite (Zhang, 2008).

Various events transpire between a juvenile's arrest and subsequent disposition in juvenile court. Both legal and extralegal factors are at work to influence decision making at various stages of the juvenile justice process. Ideally, only legal factors should be relevant to all decision making, but there is compelling evidence showing that extralegal factors are operating as well. The pervasiveness of the disproportionality of minority confinement in the United States is underscored further by the fact that minorities make up the majority of those confined in secure institutions in most states (Zhang, 2008).

Presently the issue of race/ethnicity and differential juvenile justice processing is unresolved. Clear evidence of racial and ethnic bias exists and is reported in more than a few studies. No single stage of the juvenile justice process can be singled out as especially discriminatory, however. It may be that white youths use private counsel to defend them to a greater degree, whereas minority youths may have to rely more on public defenders. Therefore, the plea bargaining prospects of minorities might be adversely affected because of the general quality of their defense counsels. Do private counsels do a better job generally in representing their clients compared with public defenders or publicly appointed counsel for indigents? Probably. This particular differential has been explored extensively, but with mixed results in the research literature (Champion, 2005).

It is likely that one's lower socioeconomic status becomes a contributing factor to the quality of defense one receives as well as how one is treated by the juvenile justice system. And the relation between socioeconomic status and race/ethnicity is fairly strong. Therefore, in view of these associations and other related factors, we can understand why there is disproportionality in minority confinement in the United States. It is unknown at present precisely which factors influence this disproportionality. Furthermore, even if such factors could be identified, it would remain unknown as to precisely what could be done to rectify any problems of disproportionality attributable to racial or ethnic factors. This obvious problem continues to be examined and explored, and alternative explanations are being tested by many investigators (Loukas, Suizzo, and Prelow, 2007).

Example of Residential Failure

Not all residential programs for juveniles are successful. One such program was operated for a brief period in Kane County, Illinois, under the direction of the Court Services Department. The Kane County Youth Home was established and designed to house up to nine male delinquents, aged 13–17, who had been previously adjudicated delinquent and deemed in need of intensive services that could not be provided otherwise on an outpatient basis (Kearney, 1994). The program failed because the essential balance between safety and trust could not be achieved. Staff workers could not be hired, trained, or evaluated primarily as residential treatment workers. The program director, court service hierarchy, and child care workers' theory and philosophy of change contrasted dramatically with the therapists' philosophy. Thus, the program philosophy itself was self-contradictory. Through no fault of their own, the youths served by the program were destined to "fail," simply because the administrators and practitioners could not agree on which philosophy should govern the youths' treatment. Kearney has observed that in order to be successful, such programs should have the following three essential components: (1) they must have a consistent philosophy of management shared by all participants; (2) persons should be hired and trained according to that philosophy; and (3) administration of the program should be consonant with the program philosophy, including any changes introduced into program operations. Thus, the program itself was probably workable. However, staff disagreements about how best to implement the program led to its demise.

Example of Program Success

Kent State University's Department of Criminal Justice established a Juvenile Justice Assistants Program in December 1990 (Babb and Kratcoski, 1994). The goals of the program were to maximize the community-based treatment potential for unruly, delinquent, or victimized youths. To ensure the effectiveness of this program, program coordinators screened prospective employees in recruitment, training, and placement over a one-year period. About 45 juvenile justice assistants were hired and devoted a minimum of 200 hours to juvenile courts and justice agencies in a five-county area.

During the first 18 months of the program, 69 assistants were assigned to placement agencies for further training, together with service to the agency and its clients. Ultimately, more than 11,400 hours of training and service were completed in approximately 25 agencies. Students involved in the program were able to assist numerous clientele during this same period. Thus, a successful internship/field experience was converted into a meaningful assistance program with juvenile justice assistants. A director oversaw the project and ensured that all program goals were consistent and implemented evenly. Any staff–client problems were dealt with immediately. Equitable solutions were found. The study yielded little recidivism among participating clientele during a follow-up period.

Juvenile Parole

Juvenile Parole Defined

parolees
Offender who has served some time in jail or prison, but has been released prior to serving entire sentence imposed upon conviction.

Parole for juveniles is similar to parole for adult offenders. Those juveniles who have been detained in various institutions for long periods may be released prior to serving their full sentences. Generally, parole is a conditional supervised release from incarceration granted to youths who have served a portion of their original sentences (Champion, 2008a). They are known as **parolees**.

Purposes of Parole for Juveniles

The general purposes of parole are the following:

1. To reward youths for good behavior during their detention.
2. To alleviate overcrowding.
3. To permit youths to become reintegrated back into their communities and enhance their rehabilitation potential.
4. To deter youths from future offending by ensuring their continued supervision under juvenile parole officers.

It is believed that the prospect of earning parole might induce greater compliance with institutional rules among incarcerated youths. Also, parole is seen by some persons as a continuation of the juvenile's punishment, since parole programs are most often conditional in nature (e.g., observance of curfew, school attendance, staying out of trouble, periodic drug and alcohol urinalyses, participation in counseling programs, and vocational and educational training). Many juvenile justice professionals agree that early-release decision making should not necessarily be automatic. Rather, releases should be based upon a well-defined mission, strategy, and a matching continuum of care which might also include assorted aftercare enhancements. Considerable attention must also be given to community safety as well as offender rehabilitation (Parker, 2005).

A standard parole agreement from a state department of corrections for juveniles is shown in Figure 12.4. Notice that this agreement specifies that the particular juvenile must remain in the legal custody and control of the Commissioner of Corrections "subject to the rules, regulations, and conditions of this parole as set forth on the reverse side of this agreement." The reverse side of this agreement (not shown here) provides sufficient space for the juvenile parole board to specify one or more program conditions, such as mandatory attendance at vocational/educational training schools, therapy or counseling, community service, restitution orders, or fine payments and maintenance fees. The parole plan is actually a continuation of the youth's punishment.

Often, the public thinks that if the youth is free from custody, she/he is completely unrestricted. This is not true. Both probation and parole are considered punishments. The behavioral conditions specified under either parole or probation may be very restrictive. Also, it is ordinarily the case that juvenile probation/parole officers have unlimited access to the premises where the youth is located. This intrusion by parole officers is unrestricted so that if youths are using drugs or in possession of illegal contraband, it can be detected by surprise, through an unannounced visit from an officer at any time of the day or night.

How Many Juveniles Are on Parole?

The American Correctional Association (2007) estimates that over 32,000 juveniles were in nonsecure, state-operated halfway houses and other community-based facilities in 2007. Also, there were over 120,000 youths in secure institutions and training schools. It has been estimated that approximately 11,000 youths were under other forms of state-controlled supervision as parolees, although no precise figures are available.

juvenile offender laws
Regulations providing for automatic transfer of juveniles of certain ages to criminal courts for processing, provided they have committed especially serious crimes.

Characteristics of Juvenile Parolees

Selected studies of juvenile parolees indicate that a majority are male, black, and between 17 and 19 years of age (Office of Juvenile Justice and Delinquency Prevention, 2007). Some jurisdictions, such as New York, have **juvenile offender laws**. These laws define 13-, 14-, 15-, and 16-year-olds as adults under certain conditions, whenever they are charged with committing specified felonies. They may be tried as adults and convicted. When they are subsequently released from institutionalization, they are placed under adult parole

Figure 12.4   Juvenile Parole Agreement

JUVENILE PAROLE AGREEMENT

WHEREAS, it appears to the Commissioner of Corrections that

_____

(NAME)

❑ presently in custody at _____, and
❑ presently on parole, and

   WHEREAS, the said Commissioner, after careful consideration, believes that parole at

this time is in the best interests of this said individual and the public.

   Now, THEREFORE, be it known that the Commissioner of Corrections, under authority

vested by law,   ❑ grants parole to,
                  ❑ continues parole for, _____
                                          (NAME)

and does authorize his/her release from the institution with the parole plan which has been

approved. Upon being paroled and released he/she shall be and remain in legal custody and

under the control of the Commissioner of Corrections subject to the rules, regulations, and

conditions of this parole as set forth on the reverse side of this agreement.

   Signed this _____ day of _____19_____.

                                          COMMISSIONER OF CORRECTIONS
                                          BY:

                                          _____
                                          (HEARING OFFICER)

                                          ❑ New Parole Agreement
                                          ❑ Restructured Parole Agreement

Source: Prepared by author.

supervision. Many other jurisdictions do not have such juvenile offender laws but have waiver or transfer provisions for particularly serious juvenile offenders. Juvenile parolees share many of the same programs used to supervise youthful probationers. Intensive supervised probation programs are used for both probationers and parolees in many jurisdictions. Further, juvenile parole officers often perform dual roles as they supervise both juvenile parole parolees and probationers.

Juveniles as well as adults on parole must report regularly to parole offices in different communities.

Juvenile Parole Policy

Between November 1987 and November 1988, Ashford and LeCroy (1993:186) undertook an investigation of the various state juvenile parole programs and provisions. They sent letters and questionnaires to all state juvenile jurisdictions, soliciting any available information on their juvenile paroling policies. Their response rate was 94 percent, with 47 of the 50 states responding. One interesting result of their survey was the development of a typology of juvenile parole. Ashford and LeCroy discovered eight different kinds of juvenile parole used more or less frequently among the states. These were listed as follows:

1. Determinate parole (length of parole is linked closely with the period of commitment specified by the court; paroling authorities cannot extend confinement period of juvenile beyond original commitment length prescribed by judge; juvenile can be released short of serving the full sentence).

2. Determinate parole set by administrative agency (parole release date is set immediately following youth's arrival at secure facility).

3. Presumptive minimum with limits on the extension of the supervision period for a fixed or determinate length of time (minimum confinement period is specified, and youth must be paroled after that date unless there is a showing of bad conduct).

4. Presumptive minimum with limits on the extension of supervision for an indeterminate period (parole should terminate after fixed period of time; parole period is indeterminate, where PO has the discretion to extend parole period with justification; parole length can extend until youth reaches age of majority and leaves juvenile court jurisdiction).

5. Presumptive minimum with discretionary extension of supervision for an indeterminate period (same as point 4 except PO has the discretion to extend parole length of juvenile with no explicit upper age limit; lacks explicit standards limiting the extension of parole).

6. Indeterminate parole with a specified maximum and a discretionary minimum length of supervision (follows Model Juvenile Court Act of 1968, providing limits for confinement but allows parole board authority to specify length of confinement and period of supervised release within these limits).

7. Indeterminate parole with legal minimum and maximum periods of supervision (parole board is vested with vast power to parole youths at any time with minimum and maximum confinement periods; more liberal than point 1 and point 2).

8. Indeterminate or purely discretionary parole (length of parole unspecified; may maintain youths on parole until youths reach the age of majority; at this time, parole is discontinued; may release youths from parole at any time during this period) (Ashford and LeCroy, 1993:187–191). The most popular parole type is point 8; the least popular is point 1.

Deciding Who Should Be Paroled

The decision to parole particular juveniles is left to different agencies and bodies, depending upon the jurisdiction. In most state jurisdictions, the dispositions imposed are indeterminate (Archwamety and Katsiyannis, 2000). In 32 states, early-release decisions are left up to the particular juvenile correction agency, whereas 6 states use parole boards exclusively, and 5 other states depend upon the original sentencing judge's decision. Only a few states had determinate sentencing schemes for youthful offenders, and therefore, their early release would be established by statute in much the same way as for adult offenders.

In New Jersey, for instance, a seven-member parole board appointed by the governor grants early release to both adult and juvenile inmates. In Utah, a Youth Parole Authority exists, which is a part-time board consisting of three citizens and four staff members from the Utah Division of Youth Corrections. Ideally, paroling authorities utilize objective decision-making criteria in determining which youths should be released short of serving their full incarcerative terms. Often discrepancies exist between what the paroling authority actually does and what it is supposed to do. Thus, some criticisms have been to the effect that the primary early-release criteria are related to one's former institutional behavior rather than to other factors, such as one's prospects for successful adaptation to community life, employment, and participation in educational or vocational programs (American Correctional Association, 2007).

Many parole boards for both adults and juveniles are comprised of persons who make subjective judgments about inmates on the basis of many factors beyond so-called objective criteria. Predispositional reports prepared by juvenile probation officers, records of institutional behavior, a youth's appearance and demeanor during the parole hearing, and the presence of witnesses or victims may exert unknown impacts upon individual parole board members. Parole decision making is not an exact science. Where elements of subjectivity intrude into the decision-making process, a juvenile's rights are seemingly undermined. Thus, parole board decision-making profiles in various jurisdictions may exhibit evidence of early-release disparities attributable to racial, ethnic, gender, or socioeconomic factors.

Recidivism and Parole Revocation

Parole revocation is the termination of one's parole program, usually for one or more program violations. When one's parole is terminated, regardless of who does the terminating, there are several possible outcomes. One is that the offender will be returned to secure confinement. This is the most severe result. A less harsh alternative is to shift offenders to a different kind of parole program. For instance, if a juvenile is assigned to a halfway house as part of the parole program, the rules of the halfway house must be observed. If one or more rules are violated, such as failing to observe curfew, failing drug or alcohol urinalyses, or committing new offenses, a report is filed with the court or the juvenile corrections authority for possible revocation action. If it is decided that the juvenile's parole should be terminated, the result may be that the offender is placed under house arrest or home confinement, coupled with electronic monitoring. Thus, the juvenile would be required to wear an electronic wristlet or anklet and remain on the premises for specified periods. Other program conditions would be applied as well. The fact is that one is not automatically returned to incarceration following a **parole revocation hearing**.

Usually, if a return to incarceration is not indicated, the options available to judges, parole boards, or others are limited only by the array of supervisory resources in the given jurisdiction. These options ordinarily involve more intensive supervision or monitoring of offender behaviors. Severe overcrowding in many juvenile incarcerative facilities discourages revocation action, which would return large numbers of offenders to industrial schools or youth centers.

The process of parole revocation for juveniles is not as clear-cut as it is for adult offenders. The U.S. Supreme Court has not ruled thus far concerning how juvenile parole revocation actions should be completed. Furthermore, very little is known about

parole revocation
Two-stage proceeding that may result from a parolee's reincarceration in jail or prison; the first stage is a preliminary hearing to determine whether the parolee violated any specific parole condition; the second stage is to determine whether parole should be cancelled and the offender reincarcerated.

parole revocation hearing
Formal proceeding where a parole board decides whether a parolee's parole program should be terminated or changed because of one or more program infractions.

Juvenile parole violators may be arrested and brought before juvenile court judges for new dispositions.

the actual numbers of juveniles who are paroled annually. Reliable statistical information about the extent of juvenile parole revocation throughout the United States simply does not exist.

Prior to several significant U.S. Supreme Court decisions, either parole or probation revocation could be accomplished for adult offenders on the basis of reports filed by probation or parole officers that offenders were in violation of one or more conditions of their programs. Criminal court judges, those ordinarily in charge of determining whether to terminate an offender's probationary status, could decide this issue on the basis of available evidence against the offender. For adult parolees, prior decision making about terminating their parole could be made by parole boards without much publicity or complaints from offenders. In short, parole officers and others might simply present evidence that one or more infractions or violations of probation or parole conditions had been committed. These infractions, then, could become the basis for revoking probation or parole as well as a justification for these decisions.

A probationer's or parolee's right to due process in any probation or parole revocation action was largely ignored prior to 1967. Thus, technical violations, such as failing to submit monthly reports, violating curfew, filing a falsified report, or drinking alcoholic beverages "to excess," might result in a recommendation from one's PO that the probation or parole program should be terminated. Popular television shows sometimes portray parole officers as threatening their clients with parole revocation: "Do this or else I'll have you back in the joint!," meaning a return to prison for adult offenders. Currently, it is not so easy to accomplish either type of revocation.

For adult parolees as well as for adult probationers, revocations are currently two-stage proceedings. The landmark cases that have directly affected parolees and probationers and their rights are *Mempa v. Rhay* (1967), *Morrissey v. Brewer* (1972), and *Gagnon v. Scarpelli* (1973). Although these landmark cases pertain to adult probationers and parolees, they are significant for juvenile probationers and parolees also. The significance is that juvenile justice policies are often formulated or influenced on the basis of U.S. Supreme Court decisions about the rights of inmates, parolees, or probationers, and the procedures involved in their processing throughout the criminal justice system. Thus, these cases are not binding on juvenile court judges or juvenile paroling authorities. But they provide a legal basis for specific actions in pertinent juvenile cases, if the juvenile justice system chooses to recognize them as precedent setting.

Mempa v. Rhay (1967)

probation revocation hearing
Proceeding wherein it is determined whether to revoke a probationer's probation program because of one or more violations.

Jerry Mempa was convicted in criminal court of "joyriding" in a stolen vehicle on June 17, 1959, in Spokane, Washington. The judge placed him on probation for two years. A few months later, on September 15, 1959, Mempa was involved in a burglary. The county prosecutor in Spokane requested that Mempa's probation be revoked. Mempa admitted to the police that he had committed the burglary. At a **probation revocation hearing** conducted later, the sole testimony for his involvement in the burglary came from his probation officer, who obtained his information largely from police reports. Mempa, an indigent, was not permitted to offer statements in his own behalf, nor was he provided counsel, nor was he asked if he wanted counsel, nor was he permitted to cross-examine the probation officer about the officer's incriminating statements. The judge revoked Mempa's probation and sentenced him to 10 years in the Washington State Penitentiary.

A short time later, Mempa filed a writ of habeas corpus, which essentially challenges the fact of his confinement and the nature of it. He alleged that he had been denied the right to counsel in his probation revocation hearing, and thus, he claimed, his due process rights had been violated in part. The Washington Supreme Court denied his petition, but the U.S. Supreme Court elected to hear it on appeal. The U.S. Supreme Court overturned the Washington Supreme Court and ruled in Mempa's favor. Specifically, the U.S. Supreme Court ruled that Mempa was entitled to an attorney but was denied one. Furthermore, and perhaps most importantly, the court declared that a probation revocation hearing is a "critical stage" that falls within the due process provisions of the Fourteenth Amendment. Critical stages refer to any stages of the criminal justice process where a defendant is in jeopardy. If defendants are accused of crimes, or arraigned, or prosecuted, their due process rights "attach" or become relevant. Thus, they are entitled to attorneys at any of these critical stages, since they are in jeopardy of losing their freedom. This ruling did not mean that Mempa would be entirely free from further court action. However, it did provide for a rehearing, and his 10-year sentence in the Washington State Penitentiary was set aside.

Morrissey v. Brewer (1972)

In 1967, John Morrissey was convicted in an Iowa court for falsely drawing checks. He was sentenced to "not more than seven years" in the Iowa State Prison. Subsequently, he was paroled in June 1968. Seven months later, his parole officer learned that Morrissey had bought an automobile under an assumed name and operated it without permission, had obtained credit cards giving false information, and had given false information to an insurance company when he became involved in an automobile accident. Further, Morrissey had given his PO a false address for his residence. After interviewing Morrissey, his PO filed a report recommending that Morrissey's parole be revoked. The parole violations involved all of the infractions and false information noted above. In his own defense, Morrissey claimed to be "sick" and that he had been prevented from maintaining continuous contact with his PO during the car-buying, credit-card accumulating, and automobile accident period. The PO countered by alleging that Morrissey was "continually violating the rules." The Iowa Parole Board revoked Morrissey's parole and he was returned to the Iowa State Prison to serve the remainder of his sentence.

During his parole revocation hearing, he was not represented by counsel, nor was he permitted to testify in his own behalf, nor was he permitted to cross-examine witnesses against him, nor was he advised in writing of the charges against him, nor was there any disclosure of the evidence against him. Further, the Iowa Parole Board gave no reasons to Morrissey for their revocation action. Morrissey appealed to the Iowa Supreme Court who rejected his appeal. The U.S. Supreme Court decided to hear his appeal, however, and overturned the Iowa Supreme Court and Iowa Parole Board actions. The court did not specifically address the issue of whether Morrissey should have been represented by counsel, but it did establish the foundation for a two-stage parole revocation proceeding. The first or preliminary stage or hearing would be conducted at the time of arrest or confinement, and its purpose would be to determine whether probable cause exists that the parolee actually committed the alleged parole violations. The second stage or hearing would be more involved and designed to establish the parolee's guilt or innocence concerning the alleged violations. Currently, all parolees in all states must be extended the following rights relating to **minimum due process rights**:

1. The right to have written notice of the alleged violations of parole conditions.
2. The right to have disclosed to the parolee any evidence of the alleged violation.
3. The right of the parolee to be heard in person and to present exculpatory evidence as well as witnesses in his behalf.

minimum due process rights
See due process.

4. The right to confront and cross-examine adverse witnesses, unless cause exists why they should not be cross-examined.
5. The right to a judgment by a neutral and detached body, such as the parole board itself.
6. The right to a written statement of the reasons for the parole revocation.

Thus, the primary significance of the Morrissey case was that it established minimum due process rights for all parolees and created a two-stage proceeding where alleged infractions of parole conditions could be examined objectively and where a full hearing could be conducted to determine the most appropriate offender disposition.

Gagnon v. Scarpelli (1973)

Because the matter of representation by counsel was not specifically addressed in the *Morrissey* case, the U.S. Supreme Court heard yet another parolee's case concerning a parole revocation action and where court-appointed counsel had not been provided. Gerald Scarpelli was convicted of robbery in July 1965 in a Wisconsin court. On August 5, 1965, Scarpelli was sentenced to 15 years in prison, but the judge suspended the sentence and placed him on probation for seven years. Incredibly, the following day, August 6, 1965, Gerald Scarpelli was arrested and charged with burglary. The judge immediately revoked his probation and ordered Scarpelli placed in the Wisconsin State Reformatory for a 15-year term.

At this point, Scarpelli's case becomes a little complicated. During his early stay in prison, Scarpelli filed a habeas corpus petition with the court, alleging that his due process rights had been violated when his probation was revoked. He was not represented by counsel and he was not permitted a hearing. However, Scarpelli was paroled from prison in 1968. Nevertheless, the U.S. Supreme Court acted on his original habeas corpus petition filed earlier and ruled in his favor. The U.S. Supreme Court held that Scarpelli was indeed denied the right to counsel and had not been given a hearing in the probation revocation action. While this might seem to be a hollow victory, since Scarpelli was already free on parole, the case had a profound impact on subsequent parole and probation revocation actions. The U.S. Supreme Court, referring to the *Morrissey* case that it had heard the previous year (1972), said that

> a probation revocation, like parole revocation, is not a stage of a criminal prosecution, but does result in loss of liberty...We hold that a probationer, like a parolee, is entitled to a preliminary hearing and a final revocation hearing in the conditions specified in *Morrissey v. Brewer*.

The significance of the Scarpelli case is that it equated probation with parole regarding revocation hearings. While the court did not say that all probationers and parolees have a right to be represented by counsel in all probation and parole revocation hearings, it did say that counsel should be provided in cases where the parolee or probationer makes a timely claim contesting the allegations. This U.S. Supreme Court decision has been liberally interpreted by the courts and parole boards in all jurisdictions. Thus, while no constitutional basis currently exists for providing counsel in all probation or parole revocation proceedings, most of these proceedings usually involve defense counsel if legitimate requests are made in advance by probationers or parolees.

Some persons are understandably perplexed by the seemingly excessive time interval between when questioned events occur, such as probation revocation actions which may be unconstitutionally conducted, and when the U.S. Supreme Court gets around to hearing such petitions or claims and deciding cases. It is not unusual for these time intervals to be five or six years, or even longer. The wheels of justice move slowly, especially those of the U.S. Supreme Court. Interestingly, of the more than 3,500 cases that are presented to the U.S. Supreme Court annually for hearing, only about 150 to 175 are heard where decisions are written. Four or more justices must agree to hear any specific case, and even then, their convening time may expire before certain cases are heard. It is beyond the scope of this text to discuss the process by which U.S. Supreme Court cases are initiated and processed, but this short discussion serves to explain the apparent slowness in rendering significant opinions in landmark cases.

For juveniles, these three cases are important because they provide juvenile courts and paroling authorities within juvenile corrections with certain guidelines to follow. These guidelines are not mandatory or binding, since these U.S. Supreme Court rulings pertain to adults rather than to juveniles. However, the law is not always abundantly clear regarding its application in a wide variety of different cases. While it may be anticipated that the U.S. Supreme Court will eventually address probation and parole revocation issues pertaining to juvenile offenders, we can only use adult guidelines for the present.

Currently, probation and parole revocation proceedings for juveniles differ widely among jurisdictions. There is a strong *parens patriae* factor that is pervasive in most juvenile matters. In many jurisdictions, explicit criteria exist for determining court or parole board actions relating to juvenile parolees who violate program rules or commit new offenses. Statutory constraints may or may not be in place to regulate judicial or parole board decision making in these situations. Again, the cases of *Morrissey*, *Scarpelli*, and *Mempa* are not binding on juvenile probation or parole revocation boards in any state jurisdiction.

Examples of Probation and Parole Revocation for Juveniles

Since there is no federal law governing juvenile probation or parole revocation, we must examine state statutes and decisions to determine the types of situations and circumstances where the probation or parole programs of juveniles have been revoked. This will give us some indication of what practices are prevalent among the states, as well as the grounds used in such revocation actions. Since federal adult probation and parole revocation cases are not binding on juvenile courts or juvenile parole boards, it is certain that both juvenile courts and parole boards seek guidance from the U.S. Supreme Court or lower appellate courts in their own decision making pertaining to juvenile probation and parole.

Juvenile Probation and Parole Revocation Cases

Several cases involving revocations of juvenile probation and parole have been reported (see following). Probation revocation cases outnumber parole revocation cases by as much as 20 to 1. Thus, most of the cases below are probation revocation cases. It is important to note, however, that the same grounds used to revoke a probation program are also used to revoke a parole program. Thus, for all practical purposes, every jurisdiction can use the same grounds for both probation and parole revocation actions.

Can CHINS and nondelinquents be placed on electronic monitoring for a period of time if the judge orders such electronic monitoring? Yes.

***In re Kristian* CC (2005).** Kristian CC was a child in need of supervision, a nondelinquent. A family court judge ordered Kristian CC to wear an electronic

The Colorado Juvenile Parole Board.

wristlet as a means of keeping track of Kristian CC's whereabouts. Kristian CC appealed, contending that such orders were for delinquents, not CHINS. A higher court disagreed and ruled that it was entirely proper under the circumstances for family court judges to use nonintrusive means to monitor the whereabouts of CHINS.

Are oral pronouncements of standard probation conditions by the juvenile court judge necessary to make them enforceable? No.

D.P.B. v. State (2004).

D.P.B. is a Florida juvenile who was adjudicated delinquent. One of the standard conditions of D.P.B.'s probation was that he should live and remain at liberty without violating the law and that he refrain from conduct proscribed by statute. Following D.P.B.'s adjudicatory hearing and disposition of probation, the court failed to provide D.P.B. with a copy of the formal written probation orders. Subsequently, D.P.B. violated one or more probation conditions and the juvenile court moved to revoke his probation. D.P.B. countered by arguing that the judge failed to orally advise him of the statutory conditions contained in the probation orders that he never received. Thus, according to D.P.B., his due process rights had been violated. The appellate court disagreed and held that the judge was not obligated to articulate verbally the statutory language of D.P.B.'s standard probation orders, which D.P.B. had been required to read and sign prior to the probation disposition. Under the Florida Juvenile Code, the punishment for juveniles who violated one or more conditions of their probation was to be increased. The juvenile was on constructive notice that a new criminal charge could result in the revocation of his probation supervision.

Can new probation violations result in more restrictive probation conditions and a longer probationary term within the maximum limits of one's original statutory probation requirements? Yes.

John L. v. Superior Court (2004).

John L. is a California juvenile and gang member who was adjudicated delinquent on various charges. During his probationary term, John L. committed new probation violations. The juvenile court conducted a probation revocation hearing, and on the basis of a preponderance of the evidence, extended John L.'s probationary term to the maximum term and intensified the nature of his probation supervision. John L. contested the court's decision, arguing that the "beyond a reasonable doubt" standard should be used. He also alleged that his due process rights were violated because of the judge's decision. The appellate court disagreed and allowed the judge's ruling to stand. Under current California juvenile law, if a probation violation occurs, the violator could at most receive more restrictive placement within the original

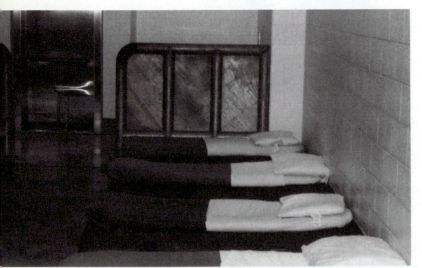

Secure confinement for juveniles is not pleasant.

maximum term. In John L.'s case, the court held that the preponderance of evidence standard was sufficient to establish John L.'s guilt for the probation violations. Further, new criminal charges are treated like probation violations and the judge may impose appropriate punishments within the limits of one's original probationary term.

Can juveniles have their probationary terms extended by committing new offenses? Yes and no.

G.L.C. v. State (2005).

In Alabama, G.L.C. was placed on probation for a delinquent offense. However, G.L.C. violated his probation conditions and committed new offenses. Eventually G.L.C. served three years of probation. By that time, G.L.C. had reached adulthood. The juvenile court judge sought to extend his probation and issued such an order. However, the order was overturned, because the judge no longer had jurisdiction over

G.L.C. and it passed to the criminal court, due to his new adult status. At this point, adult rules apply, and G.L.C. may either be incarcerated or placed on probation for the new offenses committed.

Can a juvenile's probation be terminated as the result of achieving adulthood? Yes and no.

In re Jaime P. (2005). In Illinois, a minor becomes an adult at age 21. Ordinarily, a juvenile court judge loses jurisdiction over the juvenile when the juvenile reaches this age. In the case of Jaime P., a Class X felony, murder, had been committed. Under other circumstances, terms of probation in Illinois for juveniles extend for a maximum of five years or until the juvenile reaches the age of majority. For Class X felonies, however, the term of probation may be extended beyond age 21. Jaime P. argued that his probation should be terminated when he reached age 21, but the court overruled him, indicating that the five-year probationary rule did not apply in his case.

Can a juvenile court judge order a continuation of sex offender therapy for a juvenile following a favorable recommendation for the termination of probation after a successful term of therapy? No.

In re M.O.R. (2004). M.O.R. is a juvenile in the District of Columbia who was placed on probation after he admitted to two counts of simple sexual assault. One of his probation conditions was that he participate in a sex offender counseling program. During his probation supervision, the probation officer reported M.O.R.'s progress to the juvenile court. These reports were consistently favorable to the juvenile. Toward the end of M.O.R.'s probationary period, a review was conducted wherein the probation officer recommended that M.O.R.'s probation be allowed to expire since M.O.R. had responded positively to the counseling program. However, the judge refused the probation termination based on a therapist's report that M.O.R.'s disorder could not be cured. Thus, the stage was set for continued counseling and treatment without end. M.O.R. appealed, and the appellate court reversed the juvenile court's decision, thus terminating M.O.R.'s probation program. Under District of Columbia law, the Director of Social Services is granted the sole authority to decide whether to seek an extension of a probationary period. Any juvenile who is subject to an extension must receive proper notice and a hearing to determine that such an extension is warranted. The juvenile court has the authority to review and decide whether to continue a dispositional order if the recommendation by the director is to continue probation. However, if the director decides not to seek an extension of probation, the juvenile court may inquire into but not review the director's reasons for not doing so. The decision to not seek an extension of probation is solely with the director, not the juvenile court.

If juveniles are ordered to probation and to make restitution, can both probation and restitution be continued beyond the age of their majority? No.

Matter of K.D.K. (2006). K.D.K. is a Montana juvenile who was ordered to probation and to make restitution until age 18. When he reached his eighteenth birthday, the court sought to extend his restitution and probation orders to age 21, so that more restitution could be paid to K.D.K.'s victim. The order was refused. The original order of payment of restitution and probation to age 18 had been fulfilled. It was improper to seek to extend such orders when restitution and probation orders had been fulfilled faithfully by K.D.K. until his eighteenth birthday.

Can weekend detention be ordered by juvenile court judges for juveniles who violate diversion conditions prior to a formal disposition for delinquency? Yes.

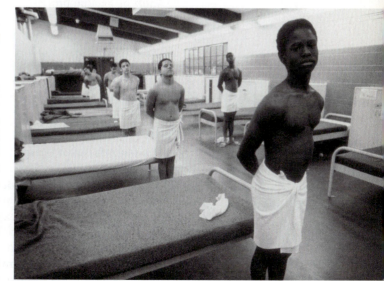

A small proportion of youths are actually confined in secure facilities.

12.2   F o c u s   o n   D e l i n q u e n c y

It happened in St. Paul, Minnesota. D.D., 17, set out to burglarize a neighbor's house. When he entered, he didn't hear any noises. Later, when he heard a few sounds, he became scared and ran into the woods, where he grabbed a large stick. He returned to the house and discovered a 12-year-old female, R.J., babysitting several children. D.D. repeatedly struck her with the stick. He carried R.J.'s body to the basement and raped her repeatedly, while the children slept nearby. D.D. left R.J. for dead. The returning family found her in a critical condition the next morning and took her to the hospital. She had considerable brain injuries but muttered the name of her attacker while awake. She lapsed into a coma. D.D. was arrested and questioned. He had walked away from a juvenile halfway house in the neighborhood a day earlier. He had been diagnosed as retarded, and he had a history of minor crimes but no record of violence. He was charged with rape, attempted murder, and three counts of burglary and was scheduled to be tried as an adult. The juvenile court judge decided to hear his case and placed him on indefinite probation, subject to a thorough mental examination and stay in a mental hospital. Should D.D. have been committed to secure confinement instead of probation? Should he have been placed in a halfway house initially, given his mental problems and prior behaviors? What do you think?

Source: Adapted from the Associated Press, "Minneapolis Boy Gets Probation for Attempted Murder," July 12, 2008.

State v. Steven B. (2004).   Steven B. was a New Mexico juvenile who was adjudicated delinquent but placed on diversion pending completion of a diversion program that required completion of school and other conditions. The actual disposition was deferred pending the successful completion of "Grade Court," an educational course of study. Steven B. subsequently violated a condition of the "Grade Court" and the juvenile court judge placed him in weekend detention as a punishment. Steven B. appealed, arguing that detention was excessive and not consistent with rehabilitation. Furthermore, no formal disposition had been entered yet, and thus the detention was a violation of his due process rights. The appellate court disagreed and upheld the judge's detention orders. The New Mexico juvenile code authorizes judges to detain children who are adjudicated but not yet disposed and who fail to comply with conditions of release. The court found that the juvenile court had the authority to order detention under this statutory provision.

Can juveniles have their probation revoked for associating with persons disapproved by their probation officer without knowing who these disapproved persons are? No.

In re Sheena K. (2004).   Sheena K. is a California juvenile who was placed on probation with the order to avoid associating with any disapproved persons at the discretion of the probation officer. However, Sheena K. was not advised as to which persons she should avoid associating with. Subsequently she associated with one or more persons deemed disapproved by the probation officer, and the officer sought Sheena K.'s probation program revocation. Sheena K. appealed, arguing that the condition imposed was unconstitutionally vague. The appellate court agreed and reversed Sheena K.'s probation revocation. The appellate court noted that, although the condition prohibited the juvenile from associating with any person disapproved by the probation officer, the condition failed to include the requirement that the juvenile know which persons are disapproved. Under these circumstances, the court held that the condition was unconstitutional.

Can a juvenile court judge extend the term of a youth's probation beyond an original period of probation pursuant to an adjudication of delinquency and a probation disposition? Yes.

In re A.N.A. (2004).
A.N.A., a Texas juvenile probationer, violated one or more terms of his original probation orders. The judge had placed A.N.A. on a 12-month probationary term according to A.N.A.'s original conditional disposition. Based on the probation violations, a modification order was entered to redispose A.N.A. to an additional probationary term. In the meantime, the 12-month probationary term for A.N.A. expired. Subsequently, the juvenile court judge imposed an additional 12-month probationary period on A.N.A., and A.N.A. appealed. The Texas appeals court upheld the 12-month probationary extension ordered by the juvenile court judge, because the order to modify A.N.A.'s probation had been entered prior to the expiration of A.N.A.'s original probationary term, and A.N.A. had been found guilty of violating the original probationary terms. Compare with *G.L.C. v. State* (2005).

Can a juvenile's record be expunged following the completion of a probationary disposition, even if the adjudication offense is a felony? Yes.

State v. Sanchez (2004).
Sanchez was an Arizona juvenile who was adjudicated delinquent on a serious felony charge. Although secure confinement was recommended, the judge placed Sanchez on probation. When the probationary term was completed, Sanchez moved to have his record of the felony offense expunged, but the state opposed this motion. The expungement order was entered and the state appealed. An appellate court upheld the juvenile court judge's decision and permitted the expungement order. If the juvenile successfully completes the terms and conditions of probation, the court may set aside the judgment of guilt, dismiss the information or indictment, expunge the juvenile's record, and order the juvenile to be released from all penalties and disabilities resulting from the adjudication.

Can an oral admission by a probationer that he visited his probation officer once in 18 months be grounds for revoking his probation? Yes.

J.W. v. State (2004).
J.W. was a Florida juvenile who was placed on probation. As one condition of J.W.'s probation, he was required to meet with his probation officer once a month. Following an 18-month period, J.W.'s probation officer sought to revoke J.W.'s probation for failure to abide by the original probation conditions, since he had appeared at the probation office only once. J.W. countered by contending that he was never asked by the probation officer to appear at the probation office monthly. Rather, J.W. had showed up once during the 18-month period to "check in" with the probation officer. This was a sufficient self-admission that he had failed to comply with his original probation orders. His probation was revoked and an appellate court upheld the revocation order. Written orders for probationers to appear monthly and meet with the probation officers must be obeyed explicitly.

Can juveniles be placed in out-of-state facilities if those same facilities do not exist in the originating state? Yes.

State v. Steven H. (2004).
Steven H. was a West Virginia juvenile who was adjudicated as a status offender and ordered committed to an out-of-home institution. Since there was no institution in West Virginia to house Steven H., he was sent to a comparable facility in neighboring Virginia. He appealed, contending that the juvenile court had no authority to send him out-of-state to another facility. The appellate court upheld the judge's ruling of placing Steven H. out-of-state in Virginia. The appellate court noted that (1) there was a specific finding that institutional care was in the juvenile's best interests; (2) the institutional care would not produce undue hardship for Steven H.; and (3) there was evidence that all reasonable efforts had been made to provide appropriate services for Steven H. prior to the out-of-state placement order.

Can juvenile court judges impose restitution orders on juvenile probationers as compensation for offenses for which they were not adjudicated delinquent? Yes.

Com. v. Palmer P. (2004). Palmer P. was a Massachusetts juvenile who was charged with burglary and larceny. Subsequently Palmer P. was adjudicated delinquent on the burglary or "breaking and entering" charge although he was acquitted of the larceny charge. However, the juvenile court judge imposed a restitution order requiring Palmer P. to make restitution for property stolen as the result of the burglary. Palmer P. appealed, contending that he should not be required to make restitution if he had been acquitted of the larceny. However, the appellate court disagreed and upheld the juvenile court judge's restitution orders. The court held that juveniles may be ordered to pay restitution even where they are acquitted of the charge in question, so long as the restitution is significantly related to their adjudication offense, in this case, burglary. In the present case, Palmer P.'s burglary or breaking and entering facilitated the taking of the victim's property. Thus, restitution was warranted as a part of Palmer P.'s disposition and conditions of probation.

Can juvenile parole boards terminate a juvenile's commitment to an institution and grant parole despite a judge's order to continue the juvenile's commitment for a period of time until the juvenile is 21? No.

In re Ruben D. (2001). Ruben D., a juvenile, was committed to an industrial school for a period of years. From time to time, the juvenile court judge would review Ruben D.'s institutional behavior and progress. On the basis of these reports, the judge would decide to extend Ruben D.'s commitment to the institution for additional one-year periods. Following one such order, the juvenile parole board convened and acknowledged that Ruben D.'s original commitment order had expired. The parole board did not acknowledge the extension of the commitment order by the juvenile court judge. Ruben D. appealed, contending that he should be paroled because of the juvenile parole board's acknowledgement that his commitment term had expired. The appellate court upheld the juvenile court judge's authority to extend Ruben D.'s commitment by one-year periods until Ruben D. reached 21 years of age. The order that extended the commitment of Ruben D. was affirmed.

Can a juvenile have his parole program revoked for violating an implied rather than written order requiring him to participate in a particular aftercare program following his release from commitment? No.

K.G. v. State (2000). K.G., a female juvenile, was adjudicated delinquent and committed to a juvenile secure facility. Subsequently K.G. was paroled. The parole board implied that it would be a good idea for K.G. to participate in a particular aftercare program involving treatment for substance abuse, which was a problem K.G. had had prior to being committed. K.G. did not participate in the aftercare program, and the parole board sought to revoke her parole program. K.G. appealed, contending that there were no specific orders requiring her to participate in the aftercare program following the completion of the term of commitment. The appellate court reversed the parole board, holding that there was no showing that K.G. had been properly transferred to the aftercare program following the term of commitment. In order for a violation of a parole program to be upheld, a valid written order by the parole board must have been violated. Since no written orders had been violated, K.G. was reinstated into her parole program.

Selected Issues in Juvenile Corrections

Investigations of the rate of secure confinement of juveniles during the past two centuries have disclosed that the rate of juvenile institutionalization has increased, especially during the most recent decades (Office of Juvenile Justice and Delinquency Prevention, 2007).

Many of the youths detained for fairly long periods of 30 days or longer are less serious misdemeanants and status offenders. For this and other reasons, juvenile corrections has been under attack from various sectors for years. This attack comes from many quarters, and it coincides with a general attack on the criminal justice system for its apparent failure to stem the increasing wave of crime in the United States. Sentencing reforms, correctional reforms, experiments with probation and parole alternatives, and a host of other options have been attempted in an apparent effort to cure or control delinquents and criminals.

In 1985, the United Nations and National Council of Juvenile and Family Court Judges adopted policy statements about the juvenile justice system that bear directly on juvenile corrections. The issues to be discussed in this final section may be better understood in the context of these statements. Several recommendations have been made by Dwyer and McNally (1987:50–51). These are the following:

1. Primary dispositions of juvenile courts should be to have a flexible range for restricting freedom, with the primary goal focused on the restoration to full liberty rather than let the punishment fit the crime; that no case dispositions should be of a mandatory nature, but rather, they should be left to the discretion of the judge based on predetermined dispositional guidelines; that in no case should a juvenile under 18 years of age be subject to capital punishment.

2. Individualized treatment of juveniles should be continued, including the development of medical, psychiatric, and educational programs that range from least to most restrictive, according to individual need.

3. While being held accountable, chronic, serious juvenile offenders should be retained within the jurisdiction of the juvenile court. As a resource, specialized programs and facilities need to be developed that focus on restorations rather than punishment.

4. Policy makers, reformers, and researchers should continue to strive for a greater understanding as to the causes and most desired response to juvenile crime; that research should be broad-based rather than limited to management, control, and punishment strategies.

5. Where the juvenile court judge believes that the juvenile under consideration is nonamenable to the services of the court and based on the youth's present charges, past record in court, and his or her age and mental status, the judge may waive jurisdiction; that in all juvenile cases, the court of original jurisdiction be that of the juvenile court; that the discretion to waive be left to the juvenile court judge; that the proportionality of punishment would be appropriate with these cases, but the most high-risk offenders should be treated in small, but secure, facilities.

Each of the issues discussed following are affected directly by these recommendations and policy statements. While these statements are not obligatory for any jurisdiction, they do suggest opinions and positions of a relevant segment of concerned citizens—juvenile court judges and juvenile corrections personnel. These issues include (1) the privatization of juvenile corrections; (2) the classification of juvenile offenders; and (3) the incarceration of juveniles in adult jails and lockups.

The Privatization of Juvenile Corrections

Juvenile corrections has many of the same problems as adult corrections. Chronic overcrowding in secure confinement facilities is extensive among jurisdictions. The existing facilities in many states are deteriorating rapidly. Furthermore, there are disproportionate representations of black, Hispanic, and Native American youths (American Correctional Association, 2007). With the current emphasis on more punitive juvenile sentencing policies, it is unlikely that there will be significant improvements in the quality of juvenile incarcerative facilities in the near future. **Privatization** is believed by

privatization
Trend in prison and jail management and correctional operations where private interests are becoming increasingly involved in the management and operations of correctional institutions.

some authorities to be one solution to overcrowded publicly operated facilities. Privatization is the establishment and operation of correctional services and institutions by nongovernmental interests, including private corporations and businesspersons (Armstrong, 2001).

Nonsecure and secure facilities are both publicly and privately operated. Florida is one of several states experimenting with various forms of private juvenile secure confinement. Historically, Florida sought to rehabilitate youths through incarceration, including placement of serious offenders in reform or training schools (Rivers, Dembo, and Anwyl, 1998). The first school for male juveniles opened in Florida in 1970, and by 1972, four schools were operating in various jurisdictions throughout the state. But because of serious institutional overcrowding and the ineffectiveness of program treatments, Florida officials decided to shift their incarcerative priorities to the development of less secure, community-based facilities (Pingree, 1984:60). Florida's objectives are to (1) reduce the number of juveniles actually placed in secure confinement facilities and (2) provide juveniles with a broader base of community options that will be instrumental in helping them to acquire vocational training and education. Much emphasis is placed on assisting youths with psychological problems as well. Thus, trained counselors work closely with Florida juvenile offenders to meet their psychological and social needs more effectively. The Florida model has served as an example for other jurisdictions.

Several important issues relating to the privatization of corrections, for both adult and juvenile offenders, have been outlined (Robbins, 1986:29):

1. What standards will govern the operation of the institution?
2. Who will monitor the implementation of the standards?
3. Will the public still have access to the facility?
4. What recourse will members of the public have if they do not approve of how the institution is operated?
5. Who will be responsible for maintaining security and using force at the institution?
6. Who will be responsible for maintaining security if the private personnel go on strike?
7. Where will the responsibility for [incarcerative] disciplinary procedures lie?
8. Will the company be able to refuse to accept certain inmates, such as those with AIDS?
9. What options will be available to the government if the corporation substantially raises its fees?
10. What safeguards will prevent a private contractor from making a low initial bid to obtain a contract, and then raising the price after the government is no longer immediately able to reassume the task of operating the facility?
11. What will happen if the company declares bankruptcy?
12. What safeguards will prevent private vendors, after gaining a foothold in the corrections field, from lobbying for philosophical changes for their greater profit?
13. What options will the public have if they do not approve of how the institution is operated?

Currently, juvenile corrections forms a large share of the privatization business. The Corrections Corporation of America (CCA), headquartered in Nashville, Tennessee, currently operates numerous facilities for both adults and juveniles throughout the United States. The CCA began operating several juvenile facilities in Tennessee in 1985, although there have been continuing debates and controversies over the years about the effectiveness of private corrections for the state (Kyle, 1998:88,158). Other private interests are increasingly entering these correctional areas to provide services and supervisory tasks, often at less cost to taxpayers than government-operated facilities.

Favorably for privatization, private interests can often cut the red tape associated with secure confinement operations. The private sector can work cooperatively with the public sector in providing the best of both worlds for offenders. Private sector operations can reward employees more quickly for excellent service performed, and new operational ideas may be implemented more quickly in private operations compared with government organizations. Further, many of those involved in private corrections operations have formerly been employed in administrative and staff capacities in public corrections agencies and institutions. Thus, they possess experience to do the job and do it well.

The profit issue is often raised by opponents of privatization of corrections: that private interests will keep inmates confined for longer periods to maximize profits. However, it is apparent that the current state of chronic overcrowding in both adult and juvenile incarcerative facilities will continue, regardless of whether these institutions are privately or publicly operated. Also, if private interests can make a profit while providing quality services to inmates at less cost to government, this seems to be a compelling argument in favor of greater privatization.

The Classification of Juvenile Offenders

Classification of any offender is made difficult by the fact that the state of the art is such in predictions of risk and dangerousness that little future behavior can be accurately forecasted (Lusignan and Marleau, 2007). This holds for juveniles as well as for adults. For instance, we know that youthful sex offenders are highly unpredictable regarding their future conduct. There is intense disagreement over whether they recidivate at higher or lower rates, compared with other offender categories (Steen, 2007). Fully effective classification schemes have not yet been devised for these and other types of juvenile offenders, although we know that on the basis of descriptions of existing aggregates of offenders, factors such as gender, age, nature of offense, seriousness of offense, race or ethnicity, and socioeconomic status are more or less correlated (Loukas, Suizzo, and Prelow, 2007).

Flaws in various classification schemes are made more apparent when program failures are detected in large numbers (McGhee and Waterhouse, 2007). Juvenile court judges make the wrong judgments and decisions about juvenile placements. Intake officers make similar errors of classification when conducting initial screenings of juveniles. The issue of false positives and false negatives is raised here, because some youths may be unfairly penalized for what authorities believe are valid predictive criteria of future dangerousness. By the same token, some youths are underpenalized, because it is believed, wrongly, that they will not pose risks or commit serious offenses in the future. But these same offenders do pose risks (Lusignan and Marleau, 2007).

Juveniles Held in Adult Jails or LockUps

The most apparent problems with placing juveniles in adult lockups or jails are that (1) youths are subject to potential sexual assault from older inmates, and (2) youths are often traumatized by the jailing experience. The latter problem leads to another problem that is even more serious—jail suicides. Juveniles are especially suicide prone during the first 24 hours of their incarceration in jails. Thus, it is little consolation that states such as Illinois pass laws prohibiting a juvenile's confinement in adult jails for periods longer than six hours. Currently, there are organized movements in many jurisdictions to mandate the permanent removal of juveniles from adult jails, including even those on temporary bases. Civil rights suits as well as class action claims are being filed by and on behalf of many juveniles currently detained in adult facilities (Gallagher and Dobrin, 2007). In the Iowa case of *Hendrickson v. Griggs* (1987), a federal district judge, Donald E. O'Brien, ruled that the Juvenile Justice and Delinquency Prevention Act could be used as the basis for a lawsuit seeking the permanent removal of juveniles from adult jails. Much remains to be done to rectify a situation that seems more within the purview of the juvenile justice system than the criminal justice system.

Summary

Several million youths are under correctional supervision in the United States annually. Juvenile corrections encompasses all of the agencies, personnel, organizations, and institutions that supervise youthful offenders. Both juvenile probationers and parolees, as well as divertees and other youths, are under the general supervisory control of one or more community corrections agencies. The goals of juvenile corrections include deterrence, rehabilitation and reintegration, prevention, punishment and retribution, and isolation and control. These goals were described and discussed.

Institutional corrections for juveniles include both nonsecure and secure facilities. Nonsecure options include foster home placement, halfway houses, group homes, placement in camps and ranches, and wilderness experiences. Camps, ranches, experience programs, and wilderness experiences were described. These programs provide youths with skills and self-sufficiency and make them less dependent on adverse influences, such as other delinquents and gang members.

Boot camps and their operations were described. These are highly regimented, military-like facilities that use strict discipline, hard work, and physical training to provide unmanageable youths greater structure in their lives. Both male and female juveniles who lack discipline may be involved in boot camp programs. The goals of boot camps are rehabilitation and reintegration; reductions in prison/jail overcrowding; inculcation of discipline; promotion of deterrence; and the provision of educational and vocational training. Most youths who participate in boot camps are prison-bound offenders who are carefully screened and scrutinized for inclusion.

Secure confinement for juveniles consists of industrial schools and detention centers for both long-term and short-term confinement for those most likely to require it. Short-term detentions of juveniles average 30 days, while long-term confinement is about 180 days. Those youths adjudicated for the most serious offenses, such as murder, aggravated assault, rape, or robbery, usually serve terms that average two years.

Juvenile parole was examined. The goals and purposes of juvenile parole are designed to alleviate industrial school and detention center overcrowding; permit youths to become reintegrated into their communities; reward good conduct while youths are in confinement; and deter youths from future offending by exercising a high degree of parolee control. Little if any U.S. Supreme Court case law exists concerning the conditions under which juvenile probation or parole can be revoked. Instead, juvenile court judges and parole boards have relied on the decisions of several key adult cases since the late 1960s. U.S. Supreme Court cases decided for adult probationers and parolees are not binding on juvenile authorities. But revocation policies for juveniles closely parallel the criteria used in the adult probation/parole revocation process. Several state-level cases involving probation and parole revocation proceedings for juveniles were examined.

Several juvenile corrections issues were discussed, including the privatization of juvenile corrections, the classification of juveniles, and the issue of holding juveniles in adult jails or lock-ups. Another issue involves the classification of juvenile offenders according to different criteria. A third issue is the jail-removal initiative, which has been in effect for over three decades. The jail-removal initiative was described and explained.

Key Terms

About Face, 397

Army Model, 397

boot camps, 397

combination sentences, 396

commitment placements, 404

detention centers, 407

detention hearing, 408

foster homes, 393

group homes, 394

halfway houses, 394

Questions for Review

1. What are five goals of juvenile corrections? How effectively are these goals achieved?

2. What are foster homes? How do they differ from group homes?

3. What are halfway houses? What are their functions and goals?

4. What are wilderness experiences and what are their functions?

5. What is meant by shock probation? What are different types of shock probation? What are some major differences among them?

6. What is a boot camp? What are some specific goals and features of boot camps? Are they effective? Why or why not?

7. What are some major differences between short- and long-term secure juvenile facilities?

8. What is meant by juvenile parole? How much juvenile parole is there? Is juvenile parole successful? Why or why not?

9. What are three key adult probation and parole revocation cases that have guided state juvenile probation and parole revocation decision making?

10. What are three examples of probation and parole revocation cases for juveniles?

Internet Connections

Boot Camps
http://www.boot-camps-info.com

Boot Camp Information
http://www.ncjrs.org/txtfiles/evalboot.txt

California Youth Authority
http://www.cya.ca.gov/

Close Cheltenham Now!
http://www.citypaper.com/news/story.asp?id=4674

Corrections Education
http://www.doe.state.la.us/slrc/links/corrections.htm

Corrections Connection
http://www.corrections.com

Council of Juvenile Correctional Administrators
http://www.jlc.org/index.php/research/conditionsofconfinement/42

Death of Innocents
http://www.deathofinnocents.net/MoratoriumDonations.html

Engaged Zen Foundation
http://www.engaged-zen.org/

Families Against Mandatory Minimums
http://www.bapd.org/afamms-1.html

Families and Corrections Network
http://www.fcnetwork.org/

Federal Bureau of Prisons
http://www.bop.gov/

Juvenile Boot Camps
http://www.bootcamps.com

Juvenile Intensive Probation Supervision
http://www.nal.usda.gov/pavnet/yf/yfjuvpro.htm

Prison Industry
http://www.pia.ca.gov/

Prison Issues Desk
http://www.prisonactivist.org/

Prison Activist Resource Center
http://www.realjustice.org/

Youthful Offenders Parole Board
http://www.cdcr.ca.gov/ReportsResearch/docs/research/IA2002.pdf

About Face Georgia boot camp program. See also boot camps.

Acceptance of responsibility Genuine admission or acknowledgment of wrongdoing; in federal presentence investigation reports, for example, convicted offenders may write an explanation and apology for the crime(s) they committed; a provision that may be considered in deciding whether leniency should be extended to offenders during the sentencing phase of their processing.

Act to Regulate the Treatment and Control of Dependent, Neglected, and Delinquent Children Delinquency Act passed by Illinois legislature in 1899; established first juvenile court among states.

Actuarial justice Means that the traditional orientation of juvenile justice, rehabilitation, and individualized treatment has been supplanted by the goal of efficient offender processing.

Actuarial prediction The traditional orientation of juvenile justice, rehabilitation, and individualized treatment has been supplanted by the goal of efficient offender processing.

Addams, Jane Established Hull House in Chicago in 1889; assisted wayward and homeless youths.

Adjudication Judgment or action on a petition filed with the juvenile court by others.

Adjudication hearing Formal proceeding involving a prosecuting attorney and a defense attorney where evidence is presented and the juvenile's guilt or innocence is determined by the juvenile judge; about one-fifth of all jurisdictions permit jury trials for juveniles under certain circumstances, with or without judicial approval.

Adversarial proceedings Opponent-driven court litigation, where one side opposes the other; prosecution

seeks to convict or find defendants guilty, while defense counsel seeks to defend their clients and seek their acquittal.

Aftercare Describes a wide variety of programs and services available to both adult and juvenile probationers and parolees; includes halfway houses, psychological counseling services, community-based correctional agencies, employment assistance, and medical treatment for offenders or ex-offenders.

Age of majority Time when one reaches adulthood, usually either 18 or 21; when juveniles are no longer under the jurisdiction of the juvenile courts but rather the criminal courts; also age of consent.

Aggravating circumstances Factors that may enhance the severity of one's sentence; these include brutality of act, whether serious bodily injury or death occurred to a victim during crime commission and whether offender was on probation or parole when crime was committed.

Alternative dispute resolution (ADR) Procedure whereby a criminal case is redefined as a civil one and the case is decided by an impartial arbiter, where both parties agree to amicable settlement; criminal court is not used for resolving such matters; usually reserved for minor offenses; court-approved mediation programs where civilians are selected from community to help resolve minor delinquency, status offense, and abuse/neglect cases without formal judicial hearings.

American Correctional Association (ACA) Established in 1870 to disseminate information about correctional programs and correctional training; designed to foster professionalism throughout correctional community.

Anamnestic prediction Projection of inmate behavior according to past circumstances.

Anchorage Youth Court Teen court established in Anchorage, Alaska, in 1999; cases include minor misdemeanor offenders; juries of one's peers decide punishments after defendants admit guilt in advance of trial proceedings; sanctions include restitution and community service.

Anomie Condition of feelings of helplessness and normlessness.

Anomie theory Robert Merton's theory, influenced by Emile Durkheim, alleging that persons acquire desires for culturally approved goals to strive to achieve, but they adopt innovative, sometimes deviant, means to achieve these goals (e.g., someone may desire a nice home but lack or reject the institutionalized means to achieve this goal, instead using bank robbery, an innovative mean, to obtain money to realize the culturally approved goal). Implies normlessness.

Appearance One's apparent socioeconomic status on the basis of one's clothing and general demeanor; unreliable criterion of socioeconomic status.

Army Model See boot camps.

Arraignment Following booking, a critical stage of the criminal justice process where defendants are asked to enter a plea to criminal charges, a trial date is established, and a formal list of charges is provided.

Arrest Taking persons into custody and restraining them until they can be brought before court to answer the charges against them.

Assessment centers Organizations selecting entry-level officers for correctional work; assessment centers hire correctional officers and probation or parole officers.

Assumptions Statements of fact about the real world or events; examples of assumptions might be, "all societies have laws," or "the greater the deviant conduct, the greater the group pressure on the deviant to conform to group norms."

Atavism Positivist school of thought arguing that a biological condition renders a person incapable of living within the social constraints of a society; the idea that physical characteristics can distinguish criminals from the general population and are evolutionary throwbacks to animals or primitive people.

At-risk youths Any juveniles who are considered more susceptible to the influence of gangs and delinquent peers; tend to be characterized as having less-developed reading skills, greater immaturity, lower socioeconomic status, parental dysfunction, and who are otherwise disadvantaged by their socioeconomic and environmental circumstances.

Automatic transfer laws Jurisdictional laws that provide for automatic waivers of juveniles to criminal court for processing; legislatively prescribed directive to transfer juveniles of specified ages who have committed especially serious offenses to jurisdiction of criminal courts.

Bail Surety provided by defendants or others to guarantee their subsequent appearance in court to face criminal charges; bail is available to anyone entitled to bail; it is denied when suspects are considered dangerous or likely to flee.

Bail bond Written guarantee, often accompanied by money or other securities, that the person charged with an offense will remain within the court's jurisdiction to face trial at a time in the future.

Balanced approach Probation orientation that simultaneously emphasizes community protection, offender accountability, individualization of treatments, and competency assessment and development.

Banishment Sanction used to punish offenders by barring them from a specified number of miles from settlements or towns; often a capital punishment, since those banished could not obtain food or water to survive the isolation.

Barker balancing test Speedy trial standard, where delays are considered in terms of the reason, length, existence of prejudice against the defendant by the prosecutor, and the assertion of the defendant's speedy trial rights [from the case of *Barker v. Wingo*, 407 U.S. 514 (1972)].

Beats Patrol areas assigned to police officers in neighborhoods.

Beccaria, Cesare (1738–1794) Developed classical school of criminology; considered "father of classical criminology;" wrote *Essays on Crimes and Punishments;* believed corporal punishment unjust and ineffective; believed that crime could be prevented by plain legal codes specifying prohibited behaviors and punishments; promoted "just-deserts" philosophy; also endorsed a *utilitarianism* approach to criminal conduct and its punishment by suggesting that useful, purposeful, and reasonable punishments ought to be formulated and applied; also viewed criminal conduct as pleasurable to criminals, and that they sought pleasure and avoided pain; thus, pain might function as a deterrent to criminal behavior.

Bench trials Proceedings where guilt or innocence of defendant is determined by the judge rather than a jury.

Beyond a reasonable doubt Evidentiary standard used in criminal courts to establish guilt or innocence of criminal defendant.

Big Brothers/Big Sisters Program Federation of over 500 agencies to serve children and adolescents; adults relate on a one-to-one basis with youths to promote their self-esteem and self-sufficiency; utilizes volunteers who attempt to instill responsibility, excellence, and leadership among assisted youths.

Biological determinism View in criminology holding that criminal behavior has physiological basis; genes, foods and food additives, hormones, and inheritance are all believed to play a role in determining individual behavior; one's genetic makeup causes certain behaviors to become manifest, such as criminality.

Blended sentencing Any type of sentencing procedure where either a criminal or juvenile court judge can impose *both* juvenile and/or adult incarcerative penalties.

Bonding theory A key concept in a number of theoretical formulations. Emile Durkheim's notion that deviant behavior is controlled to the degree that group members feel morally bound to one another, are committed to common goals, and share a collective conscience; in social control theory, the elements of attachment, commitment, involvement, and belief; explanation of criminal behavior implying that criminality is the result of a loosening of bonds or attachments with society; builds on differential association theory. Primarily designed to account for juvenile delinquency.

Booking Process of making written report of arrest, including name and address of arrested persons, the alleged crimes, arresting officers, place and time of arrest, physical description of suspect, photographs, sometimes called "mug shots," and fingerprints.

Boot camps Also known as the Army Model, boot camp programs are patterned after basic training for new military recruits. Juvenile offenders are given a taste of hard military life, and such regimented activities and structure for up to 180 days are often sufficient to "shock" them into giving up their lives of delinquency or crime and staying out of jail.

Boston Offender Project (BOP) Experimental program in Boston, targeted for violent juveniles; program goals include reducing recidivism, enhancing public protection by increasing accountability for major violators, and improving the likelihood of successful reintegration of juveniles into society by focusing upon these offenders' academic and vocational skills.

Bridewell Workhouse Sixteenth-century London jail (sometimes gaol) established in 1557; known for providing cheap labor to business and mercantile interests; jailers and sheriffs profited from prisoner exploitation.

Bullying Prevention Program Targets bullies in elementary, middle, and high schools; vests school authorities with intervention powers to establish class rules for disciplining bullies and bullying behavior through student committees.

Capital punishment Imposition of the death penalty for the most-serious crimes; may be administered by electrocution, lethal injection, gas, hanging, or shooting.

Career escalation Moving as a juvenile offender to progressively more serious offenses as new offenses are committed; committing new violent offenses after adjudications for property offenses would be career escalation; committing progressively more serious offenses.

CASASTART Program Targets high-risk youths who are exposed to drugs and delinquent activity; decreases risk factors by greater community involvement.

Caseloads Number of cases that a probation or parole officer is assigned according to some standard such as a week, month, or year; caseloads vary among jurisdictions.

Case supervision planning A means whereby a probation or parole department makes assignments of probationers or parolees to POs or parole officers.

Certification Similar to waivers or transfers; in some jurisdictions, juveniles are certified or designated as adults for the purpose of pursuing a criminal prosecution against them.

Chancellors Civil servants who acted on behalf of the King of England during the Middle Ages; chancellors held court and settled property disputes, trespass cases, and minor property offenses; thievery, vagrancy, and public drunkenness.

Chancery courts Court of equity rooted in early English common law where civil disputes are resolved; also responsible for juvenile matters and adjudicating family matters such as divorce; has jurisdiction over contract disputes, property boundary claims, and exchanges of goods disputes.

Children at risk See at-risk youths.

Children in need of supervision (CHINS) Any children determined by the juvenile court and other agencies to be in need of community care or supervision.

Children's tribunals Informal court mechanisms originating in Massachusetts to deal with children charged with crimes apart from the system of criminal courts for adults.

Child savers, child-saving movement Organized effort during early 1800s in United States, comprised primarily of upper- and middle-class interests who sought to provide assistance to wayward youths; assistance was often food and shelter, although social, educational, and religious values were introduced to children later in compulsory schooling.

Chronic offenders Habitual offenders; repeat offenders; persistent offenders; youths who commit frequent delinquent acts.

Citizen action model Youth Services Bureau model using community volunteers to actively intervene and assist in the lives of delinquency-prone youths.

Civil tribunals See children's tribunals.

Classical school Line of thought that assumes that people are rational beings who choose between good and evil.

Classical theory A criminological perspective indicating that people have free will to choose either criminal or conventional behavior; people choose to commit crime for reasons of greed or personal need; crime can be controlled by criminal sanctions, which should be proportionate to the guilt of the perpetrator.

Classification Means used by prisons and probation/parole agencies to separate offenders according to offense seriousness, type of offense, and other criteria; no classification system has been demonstrably successful at effective prisoner or client placements.

Cleared by arrest Term used by FBI in the *Uniform Crime Reports* to indicate that someone has been arrested for a reported crime; does not necessarily mean that the crime has been solved or that the actual criminals who committed the crime have been apprehended or convicted.

Clinical prediction Forecast of inmate behavior based upon professionals' expert training and working directly with offenders.

Combination sentences Occurs whenever judges sentence offenders to a term, a portion of which includes incarceration and a portion of which includes probation.

Commitment placement Confinement in a secure juvenile facility, usually for a term such as one year or longer.

Common law Authority based on court decrees and judgments that recognize, affirm, and enforce certain usages and customs of the people; laws determined by judges in accordance with their rulings.

Community Board Program Civil mediation mechanism utilizing volunteers to mediate between victims and offenders.

Community corrections acts Enabling legislation by individual states to fund local government units to provide community facilities, services, and resources to juveniles who are considered at risk of becoming delinquent or who are already delinquent and need treatment/services.

Community organization model Youth Service Bureau model that uses citizens on a voluntary basis to assist delinquency-prone youth.

Community policing Major police reform that broadens the police mission from a narrow focus on crime to a mandate that encourages the police to explore creative solutions for a host of community concerns, including crime, fear of crime, disorder, and neighborhood decay; rests on belief that only by working together will citizens and police be able to improve the quality of life in their communities, with the police not only as enforcers, but also as advisors, facilitators, and supporters of new community—based police—supervised initiatives.

Community reintegration model Operating theory whereby offender who has been incarcerated is able to live in community under some supervision and gradually adjust to life outside of prison or jail.

Community service Any activity imposed on a probationer or parolee involving work in one's neighborhood or city; performed in part to repay victims and the city for injuries or damages caused by one's unlawful actions.

Community Service Program, Inc. (CSP, Inc.) Established in Orange County, California; designed to instill self-confidence in youths, reduce parental and familial dysfunction, and establish self-reliance and esteem through family counseling therapy and sessions.

Compulsory School Act Passed in 1899 by Colorado, this act targeted those youths who were habitually absent from school; it encompassed youths who wandered the streets during school hours; originally designed to enforce truancy laws; erroneously regarded as first juvenile court act, which was actually passed in Illinois in 1899.

Concentric zone hypothesis Series of rings originating from a city center, such as Chicago, and emanating outward, forming various zones characterized by different socioeconomic conditions; believed to contain areas of high delinquency and crime.

Concurrent jurisdiction Power to file charges against juveniles in either criminal courts or juvenile courts.

Conditional dispositions Results of a delinquency adjudication that obligate youths to comply with one or more conditions of a probation program, such as restitution, community service, work study, therapy, educational participation, or victim compensation.

Conditional probation Program where divertee is involved in some degree of local monitoring by POs or personnel affiliated with local probation departments.

Confidentiality privilege Right between defendant and his/her attorney where certain information cannot be disclosed to prosecutors or others because of the attorney–client relation; for juveniles, records have been maintained under secure circumstances with limited access, and accessed only by those in authority with a clear law enforcement purpose.

Conformity Robert K. Merton's mode of adaptation characterized by persons who accept institutionalized means to achieve culturally approved goals.

Consent decrees Formal agreements that involve children, their parents, and the juvenile court, where youths are placed under the court's supervision without an official finding of delinquency, with judicial approval.

Containment theory Explanation elaborated by Walter Reckless and others that positive self-image enables persons otherwise disposed toward criminal behavior to avoid criminal conduct and conform to societal values. Every person is a part of an external structure and has a protective internal structure providing defense, protection, and/or insulation against one's peers, such as delinquents.

Contempt of court A citation by a judge against anyone in court who disrupts the proceedings or does anything to interfere with judicial decrees or pronouncements.

Conventional model Caseload assignment model where probation or parole officers are assigned clients randomly.

Conventional model with geographic considerations Similar to conventional model; caseload assignment model is based upon the travel time required for POs to meet with offender-clients regularly.

Convictions Judgments of a court, based on a jury or judicial verdict, or on the guilty pleas of defendants, that the defendants are guilty of the offenses alleged.

Cooperating agencies model Youth Services Bureau model where several agencies act as a team to provide delinquency-prone youths with needed services.

C.O.P.Y. Kids (Community Opportunities Program for Youth) Spokane, Washington, program for disadvantaged youth commenced in 1992; youth participated in arts and crafts and learned valuable work skills.

Corporate gangs Juvenile gangs emulating organized crime; profit-motivated gangs that rely on illicit activities, such as drug trafficking, to further their profits.

Corrections Aggregate of programs, services, facilities, and organizations responsible for the management of people who have been accused or convicted of criminal offenses.

Court of record Any court where a written record is kept of court proceedings.

Court reporters Court officials who keep a written word-for-word and/or tape-recorded record of court proceedings.

Courts Public judiciary bodies that apply the law to controversies and oversee the administration of justice.

Courts of equity See chancery courts.

Court unification Proposal that seeks to centralize and integrate the diverse functions of all courts of general, concurrent, and exclusive jurisdiction into a more simplified and uncomplicated scheme.

Creative sentencing Broad class of punishments as alternatives to incarceration that are designed to fit the particular crimes; may involve community service, restitution, fines, becoming involved in educational or vocational training programs, or becoming affiliated with other "good works" activity.

Crime control model Criminal justice program that emphasizes containment of dangerous offenders and societal protection; a way of controlling delinquency by incapacitating juvenile offenders through some secure detention or through intensive supervision programs operated by community-based agencies.

Criminal-exclusive blend Form of sentencing by a criminal court judge where either juvenile or adult sentences of incarceration can be imposed, but not both.

Criminal-inclusive blend Form of sentencing by a criminal court judge where both juvenile and adult sentences can be imposed simultaneously.

Criminal informations Charges filed by prosecutors directly against defendants; usually involve minor crimes.

Criminal justice An interdisciplinary field studying nature and operations of organizations providing justice services to society; consists of lawmaking bodies including state legislatures and Congress, local, state, and federal agencies that try to enforce the law.

Criminal justice professional Anyone interested in studying the criminal justice system; may have a Ph.D. or master's degree in criminal justice or a related field; may be a practitioner, such as a police officer, corrections officer, probation or parole officer, prosecutor, or judge.

Criminal justice system, criminal justice process Interrelated set of agencies and organizations designed to control criminal behavior, to detect crime, and to apprehend, process, prosecute, punish, and/or rehabilitate criminal offenders.

Criminogenic environment Setting where juveniles may feel like criminals or may acquire the characteristics or labels of criminals; settings include courtrooms and prisons.

Criminologists Persons who study crime, the science of crime and criminal behavior, the forms of criminal behavior, the causes of crime, the definition of criminality, and the societal reaction to crime.

Criminology The study of crime, the science of crime and criminal behavior, the forms of criminal behavior, the causes of crime, the definition of criminality, and the societal reaction to crime; an empirical social-behavioral science that investigates crime, criminals, and criminal justice.

Cultural transmission theory Explanation emphasizing transmission of criminal behavior through socialization. Views delinquency as socially learned behavior transmitted from one generation to the next in disorganized urban areas.

Curfew violators Youths who violate laws and ordinances of communities prohibiting youths on the streets after certain evening hours, such as 10:00 P.M.; curfew itself is a delinquency prevention strategy.

Custodial dispositions Either nonsecure or secure options resulting from a delinquency adjudication; juveniles may be placed in foster homes, group homes, community-based correctional facilities, or secure detention facilities that are either publicly or privately operated.

Dangerousness Defined differently in several jurisdictions; prior record of violent offenses; potential to commit future violent crimes if released; propensity to inflict injury; predicted risk of convicted offender or prison or jail inmate; likelihood of inflicting harm upon others.

D.A.R.E. (Drug Abuse Resistance Education) Intervention program sponsored and implemented by the Los Angeles Police Department; utilizes officers familiar with drugs and drug laws who visit schools in their precincts and speak to youths about how to say "no" to drugs; children are taught how to recognize illegal drugs, different types of drugs, as well as their adverse effects.

Day reporting centers Established in England in 1974 to provide intensive supervision for low-risk offenders who lived in neighborhoods; continued in various U.S. jurisdictions today to manage treatment programs, supervise fee collection, and other responsibilities, such as drug-testing and counseling.

Death penalty Sentence that terminates the life of an offender, either through lethal gas, electrocution, lethal injection, hanging, or by firing squad.

Decarceration Type of deinstitutionalization where juveniles charged with status offenses are still under court jurisdiction and subject to filing of petitions; detention of youths is prohibited; youths may be removed from their homes and placed in nonsecure facilities, put on probation, required to attend treatment or service programs, and subjected to other behavioral restraints.

Defendants Anyone charged with one or more crimes.

Defense attorneys Advocates for juvenile defendants; represent the interests and defend the rights of juveniles in either juvenile or criminal courts.

Deinstitutionalization of status offenses (DSO) Eliminating status offenses from the broad category of delinquent acts and removing juveniles from or precluding their confinement in juvenile correctional facilities; the process of removing status offenses from jurisdiction of juvenile court so that status offenders cannot be subject to secure confinement.

Delinquency Act committed by an infant of not more than a specified age who has violated criminal laws or engages in disobedient, indecent, or immoral conduct, and is in need of treatment, rehabilitation, or supervision; status acquired through an adjudicatory proceeding by juvenile court.

Delinquent child Infant of not more than a specified age who has violated criminal laws or engages in disobedient, indecent, or immoral conduct, and is in need of treatment, rehabilitation, or supervision.

Demand waiver Requests by juveniles to have their cases transferred from juvenile courts to criminal courts.

Dependent and neglected children Youths considered by social services or the juvenile court to be in need of some type of adult supervision.

Detention Confining youths for short terms in secure facilities, usually to await a juvenile court adjudicatory hearing or some other proceeding; some youths are placed in secure settings for short terms as a punishment for delinquent offending.

Detention centers Juvenile secure facilities used for serious and violent juveniles who are awaiting an adjudication hearing.

Detention hearing Judicial or quasi-judicial proceeding held to determine whether or not it is appropriate to continue to hold or detain a juvenile in a shelter facility.

Determinism Concept holding that persons do not have a free will but rather are subject to the influence of various forces over which they have little or no control.

Dickerson's Rangers Antidrug program in the San Fernando Valley of southern California; targets children ages 7–13, and it operates in various city parks and recreational centers; children meet weekly and discuss drug abuse in their schools and communities; police officers advise them how to resist overtures made by drug dealers or their peers who might use drugs; field trips are also sponsored that include speakers whose specialties include drug abuse and illicit drug prevention.

Differential association theory Edwin Sutherland's theory of deviance and criminality through associations with others who are deviant or criminal; theory includes dimensions of frequency, duration, priority, and intensity; persons become criminal or delinquent because of a preponderance of learned definitions that are favorable to violating the law over learned definitions unfavorable to it.

Differential reinforcement theory Explanation that combines elements of labeling theory and a psychological phenomenon known as conditioning; persons are rewarded for engaging in desirable behavior and punished for deviant conduct.

Direct file Prosecutorial waiver of jurisdiction to a criminal court; an action taken against a juvenile who has committed an especially serious offense, where that juvenile's case is transferred to criminal court for the purpose of a criminal prosecution.

Discretionary powers Relating to the police role, police discretion is the distribution of nonnegotiable coercive force employed in accordance with the dictates of an intuitive grasp of situational exigencies; police have authority to use force to enforce the law, if, in the officer's opinion, the situation demands it.

Discretionary waivers Transfers of juveniles to criminal courts by judges, at their discretion or in their judgment; also known as judicial waivers.

Dispose To decide the punishment to be imposed on a juvenile following an adjudication hearing.

Dispositions Punishments resulting from a delinquency adjudication; may be nominal, conditional, or custodial.

Diversion Official halting or suspension of legal proceedings against criminal defendants after a recorded justice system entry, and possible referral of those persons to treatment or care programs administered by a nonjustice or private agency.

Diversion Plus Program Established in Lexington, Kentucky, in 1991, designed to reduce recidivism and promote conformity to the law without stigmatization; youths targeted included first-offenders, low-risk delinquent offenders, and any youth without a prior juvenile record; consists of a series of weekly meetings and self-help sessions, stressing self-esteem and self-control, substance-abuse prevention, independent living, one-on-one counseling, and small-group interaction.

Divestiture Strategy for deinstitutionalizing status offenders, where juvenile courts cannot detain, petition, adjudicate, or place youths on probation for any status offense; according to legislatively created statutes, juvenile court does not accept most, if not all, status offense cases.

Double jeopardy Subjecting persons to prosecution more than once in the same jurisdiction for the same offense, usually without new or vital evidence. Prohibited by the Fifth Amendment.

Drift theory David Matza's term denoting a state of limbo in which youths move in and out of delinquency and in which their lifestyles embrace both conventional and deviant values.

Due process Basic constitutional right to a fair trial, presumption of innocence until guilt is proven beyond a reasonable doubt, the opportunity to be heard, to be aware of a matter that is pending, to make an informed choice whether to acquiesce or contest, and to provide the reasons for such a choice before a judicial official.

Due process model Treatment model based upon one's constitutional right to a fair trial, to have an opportunity to be heard, to be aware of matters that are pending, to a presumption of innocence until guilt has been established beyond a reasonable doubt, to make an informed choice whether to acquiesce or contest, and to provide the reasons for such a choice before a judicial officer.

Ectomorphs Body type described by Sheldon; persons are thin, sensitive, delicate.

Electronic monitoring Use of electronic devices that emit electronic signals; these devices, anklets, or wristlets are worn by offenders, probationers, and parolees; the purpose of such monitoring is to monitor an offender's presence in a given environment where the offender is required to remain or to verify the offender's whereabouts.

Electronic monitoring signaling devices Apparatuses worn about the wrist or leg that are designed to monitor an offender's presence in a given environment where the offender is required to remain.

Endomorphs Body type described by Sheldon; persons are fat, soft, plump, jolly.

Exculpatory evidence Information considered beneficial to defendants, tending to show their innocence.

Expungement orders Deletion of one's arrest record from official sources; in most jurisdictions, juvenile delinquency records are expunged when one reaches the age of majority or adulthood.

Extralegal factors Characteristics influencing intake decisions, such as juvenile offender attitudes, school grades and standing, gender, race, ethnicity, SES, and age.

Faith in Families Multi-Systematic Therapy Program (MST) Operated by the Henry and Rilla White Foundation in Bronson, Florida; attempts to modify youth behaviors by working with their interpersonal environment, including family, therapists, and peer groups; subjects taught include self-control, anger management, self-reflectiveness, and problem-solving skills.

False negatives Offenders predicted not to be dangerous who turn out to be dangerous.

False positives Offenders predicted to be dangerous who turn out not to be dangerous.

Family model Established under the Juvenile Law of 1948, exists in all Japanese jurisdictions and hears any matters pertaining to juvenile delinquency, child abuse and neglect, and child custody matters; both status offenders and delinquents appear before Family Court judges; similar to juvenile court judges in U.S. jurisdictions, Family Court judges have considerable discretionary authority; decide cases within the *parens patriae* context.

FAST Track Program Rural and urban intervention program targeting girls and boys of many ethnicities; designed to provide solutions for severe and chronic misconduct problems among high-risk.

Felonies Crimes punishable by imprisonment in prison for a term of one or more years; major crimes; any index offense.

Fines Financial penalties imposed at the time of sentencing convicted offenders; most criminal statutes contain provisions for the imposition of monetary penalties as sentencing options.

First-offender Criminals who have no previous criminal records; these persons may have committed crimes, but they have only been caught for the instant offense.

Flat time Frequently known as hard time, meaning the actual amount of time one must serve while incarcerated.

Foster homes Facility for temporary placement of youths in need of supervision or control; usually families volunteer to act as foster parents and maintain placed youths for short-term care.

Friends for the Love of Reading Project Self-help program and offshoot of District of Columbia Book Buddies Program designed to assist youths with poor reading abilities to improve their reading skills; involves parents and volunteers on a one-to-one basis with youths.

Gangs Groups who form an allegiance for a common purpose and engage in unlawful or criminal activity; any group gathered together on a continuing basis to engage in or commit antisocial behavior.

Gemeinschaft Term created by Ferdinand Tonnies, a social theorist, to describe small, traditional communities where informal punishments were used to punish those who violated community laws.

Gesellschaft Term created by Ferdinand Tonnies, a social theorist, to describe more formalized, larger communities and cities that relied on written documents and laws to regulate social conduct.

Get-tough movement View toward criminals and delinquents favoring maximum penalties and punishments for crimes or delinquent act; any action toward toughening or strengthening sentencing provisions or dispositions involving adults or juveniles.

Graffiti Removal Initiative Program Community program designed as condition of probation in cases of vandalism, where youths must remove graffiti from public buildings or houses; used in conjunction with other program conditions.

Grand juries Investigative bodies whose numbers vary among states; duties include determining probable cause regarding commission of a crime and returning formal charges against suspects. See also true bill and no bill.

G.R.E.A.T. (Gang Resistance Education and Training) Established in Phoenix, Arizona; police officers visit schools and help youths understand how to cope with peer pressure to commit delinquent acts; topics of educational programs include victim rights, drugs and neighborhoods, conflict resolution, and need fulfillment.

Group homes Also known as group centers or foster homes, these are facilities for juveniles that provide limited supervision and support; juveniles live in a home-like environment with other juveniles and participate in therapeutic programs and counseling; considered nonsecure custodial.

Guardians ad litem Special authorities appointed by the court in which particular litigation is pending to represent a youth, ward, or unborn person in that particular litigation.

Habeas corpus Writ meaning "produce the body;" used by prisoners to challenge the nature and length of their confinement.

Halfway houses Nonconfining residential facilities intended to provide an alternative to incarceration as a period of readjustment to the community for offenders after confinement.

Hands-off doctrine Policy practiced by the federal courts, where official court policy was not to intervene in matters relating to adult corrections; belief that correctional superintendents and wardens and departments of corrections are in best position to make decisions about welfare of inmates; applied to juvenile corrections and juvenile courts similarly.

Hard time Also known as flat time, actual amount of secure confinement juveniles must serve as the result of a custodial disposition from a juvenile court judge.

Hedonism Jeremy Bentham's term indicating that people avoid pain and pursue pleasure.

Hidden delinquency Infractions reported by surveys of high-school youths; considered "hidden" because it most often is undetected by police officers; disclosed delinquency through self-report surveys.

Holland Teen Court (HTC) Holland, Michigan, youth court program commenced in 1991 involving juveniles who have committed less serious misdemeanor offenses; jurors consist of high-school students with general training in jury deliberations and sentencing matters; limitations on sentencing restricted to community service and restitution; very successful program with recidivism of less than 5 percent.

Home confinement Program intended to house offenders in their own homes with or without electronic devices; reduces prison overcrowding and prisoner costs; intermediate punishment involving the use of offender residences for mandatory incarceration during evening hours after a curfew and on weekends.

Home incarceration See home confinement.

Homeward Bound Established in Massachusetts in 1970; designed to provide juveniles with mature responsibilities through the acquisition of survival skills and wilderness experiences. A six-week training program subjected

32 youths to endurance training, physical fitness, and performing community service.

Hospital of Saint Michael Custodial institution established at request of Pope in Rome in 1704; provided for unruly youths and others who violated the law; youths were assigned tasks, including semi-skilled and skilled labor, which enabled them to get jobs when released.

House arrest See home confinement.

Houses of refuge Workhouses, the first of which was established in 1824 as a means of separating juveniles from the adult correctional process.

Id Sigmund Freud's term to depict that part of personality concerned with individual gratification; the "I want" part of a person, formed in one's early years.

Illinois Juvenile Court Act Legislation passed by Illinois legislature in 1899 providing for the first juvenile court and treatment programs for various types of juvenile offenders.

IMPACT (Intensive Motivational Program of Alternative Correctional Treatment) Boot camp program operated in Louisiana; incorporates educational training with strict physical and behavioral requirements.

Incident Specific criminal act involving one crime and one or more victims.

Inculpatory evidence Information considered adverse to defendants or tending to show their guilt.

Indentured servants, indentured servant system Voluntary slave pattern where persons without money for passage from England entered into a contract with merchants or businessmen, usually for seven years, wherein merchants would pay for their voyage fare to the American colonies from England in exchange for their labor.

Index crimes Any violations of the law listed by the *Uniform Crime Reports* under index offenses (e.g., homicide, rape, aggravated assault, robbery, burglary, larceny, arson).

Index offenses Specific felonies used by the Federal Bureau of Investigation in the *Uniform Crime Reports* to chart crime trends; there are eight index offenses listed prior to 1988 (includes aggravated assault, larceny, burglary, vehicular theft, arson, robbery, forcible rape, murder).

Indictments Charges or written accusations found and presented by a grand jury that a particular defendant probably committed a crime.

Industrial schools Institutions that resemble prisons; secure facilities where some juveniles are held for up to one year or longer; such institutions usually have different types of programming to aid in the rehabilitation and reintegration of youthful offenders, consisting of vocational and educational courses or programs, counseling for different types of youth needs, and other services; these facilities are largely self-contained like prisons, and they offer a limited range of medical and health services.

Infants Legal term applicable to juveniles who have not attained the age of majority (in most states it is 18).

Informations Sometimes called criminal informations; written accusations made by a public prosecutor against a person for some criminal offense, without an indictment; usually restricted to minor crimes or misdemeanors.

Initial appearance Formal proceeding during which the judge advises defendants of the charges against them.

Innovation Robert K. Merton's mode of adaptation where persons reject institutionalized means to achieve culturally approved goals; instead, they engage in illegal acts, considered innovative, to achieve their goals.

Intake Critical phase where a determination is made by a juvenile probation officer or other official whether to release juveniles to their parent's custody, detain juveniles in formal detention facilities for a later court appearance, or release them to parents pending a later court appearance.

Intake hearings, intake screenings Proceedings where juvenile official, such as juvenile probation officer, conducts an interview with a youth charged with a delinquent or status offense.

Intake officer Juvenile probation officer who conducts screenings and preliminary interviews with alleged juvenile delinquents or status offenders and their families.

Intensive Aftercare Program (IAP) Philadelphia-based intervention for serious youthful offenders involving intensive counseling and training for acquiring self-help skills; recidivism of participants greatly reduced during study period of 1980–1990.

Intensive supervised probation (ISP) Controlled probation overseen by probation officer; involves close monitoring of offender activities by various means (also known as "Intensive Probation Supervision" or IPS).

Intensive probation supervision (IPS) See intensive supervised probation; may also stand for intensive parole supervision.

Intensive supervision program (ISP) Offender supervision program with following characteristics: (1) low officer/client caseloads (i.e., 30 or fewer probationers); (2) high levels of offender accountability (e.g., victim restitution, community service, payment of fines, partial defrayment of program expenses); (3) high levels of offender responsibility; (4) high levels of offender control (home confinement, EM, frequent face-to-face visits by POs); and (5) frequent checks for arrests, drug and/or alcohol use, and employment/school attendance (drug/alcohol screening, coordination with police departments and juvenile halls, teachers, family).

Interagency Agreement Plan Early intervention plan instituted in San Diego, California, in 1982, for the purpose of reducing delinquency; graduated sanctions used for repeat offenders; youths held accountable for their actions; gradual increase of services and punishments for repeat offenders.

Intermediate punishments Sanctions involving sanctions existing somewhere between incarceration and probation on a continuum of criminal penalties; may include home incarceration and electronic monitoring.

Intermittent sentences Occur whenever judges sentence offenders to terms such as weekend confinement only.

Interstitial area In concentric zone hypothesis, area nearest the center of a city undergoing change, such as urban renewal; characterized by high rates of crime.

Jail as a condition of probation Sentence where judge imposes some jail time to be served before probation commences; also known as shock probation.

Jail removal initiative Action sponsored by the Office of Juvenile Justice and Delinquency Prevention and the Juvenile Justice and Delinquency Prevention Act of 1974 to deinstitutionalize juveniles from secure facilities, such as jails.

Jails City or county operated and financed facilities to contain those offenders who are serving short sentences; jails also house more serious prisoners from state or federal prisons through contracts to alleviate overcrowding; jails also house pretrial detainees, witnesses, juveniles, vagrants, and others.

Judicial waivers Decision by juvenile judge to waive juvenile to jurisdiction of criminal court.

Judicious nonintervention Use of minimal intervention in a youth's behavior and environment to effect changes in behavior.

Jurisdiction Power of a court to hear and determine a particular type of case; also, territory within which a court may exercise authority such as a city, county, or state.

Jury See petit jury.

Jury trials Proceeding where guilt or innocence of defendant is determined by jury instead of by the judge.

Just-deserts/justice model Stresses offender accountability as a means to punish youthful offenders; uses victim compensation plans, restitution, and community services as ways of making offenders pay for their offenses; philosophy which emphasizes punishment as a primary objective of sentencing, fixed sentences, abolition of parole, and an abandonment of the rehabilitative ideal; rehabilitation is functional to the extent that offenders join rehabilitative programs voluntarily.

Juvenile court records Formal or informal statements concerning an adjudication hearing involving sustained allegations against a juvenile; a written document of a juvenile's prior delinquency or status offending.

Juvenile courts Formal proceeding with jurisdiction over juveniles, juvenile delinquents, status offenders, dependent or neglected children, children in need of supervision, or infants.

Juvenile-contiguous blend Form of sentencing by a juvenile court judge where the judge can impose a disposition beyond the normal jurisdictional range for juvenile offenders; e.g., a judge may impose a 30-year term on a 14-year-old offender, but the juvenile is entitled to a hearing when he/she reaches the age of majority to determine whether the remainder of the sentence shall be served.

Juvenile delinquency Violation of the law by a person prior to his/her eighteenth birthday; any illegal behavior committed by someone within a given age range punishable by juvenile court jurisdiction; whatever the juvenile court believes should be brought within its jurisdiction; violation of any state or local law or ordinance by anyone who has not as yet achieved the age of their majority.

juvenile delinquent Anyone, who, under the age of his/her majority has committed one or more acts that would be crimes if adults committed them.

Juvenile delinquents See delinquent child.

Juvenile-exclusive blend Sentencing form where a juvenile court judge can impose either adult or juvenile incarceration as a disposition and sentence but not both.

Juvenile-inclusive blend Form of sentencing where a juvenile court judge can impose *both* adult and juvenile incarceration simultaneously.

Juvenile intensive supervised probation (JISP) Ohio-operated program for youthful offenders, including home confinement, electronic monitoring, and other IPS methods.

JJDPA (Juvenile Justice and Delinquency Prevention Act) of 1974 Legislation recommending various alternatives to incarcerating youths, including deinstitutionalization of status offending, removal of youths from secure confinement, and other rehabilitative treatments.

Juvenile justice system Stages through which juveniles are processed, sentenced, and corrected after arrests for juvenile delinquency.

Juvenile Mentoring Program (JUMP) Federally funded program administered by the Office of Juvenile Justice and Delinquency Prevention; promotes bonding between an adult and a juvenile relating on a one-to-one basis over time; designed to improve school performance and decrease gang participation and delinquency.

Juvenile offenders Any infant or child who has violated juvenile laws.

Juvenile offender laws Regulations providing for automatic transfer of juveniles of certain ages to criminal courts for processing, provided they have committed especially serious crimes.

Juvenile Probation Camps (JPCs) California county-operated camps for delinquent youth placed on probation in early 1980s, including physical activities, community contacts, and academic training.

Juveniles Persons who have not reached the age of majority or adulthood.

Labeling Process whereby persons acquire self-definitions that are deviant or criminal; process occurs through labels applied to them by others.

Labeling theory Explanation of deviant conduct attributed to Edwin Lemert whereby persons acquire self-definitions that are deviant or criminal; persons perceive themselves as deviant or criminal through labels applied to them by others; the more people are involved in the criminal justice system, the more they acquire self-definitions consistent with the criminal label.

Law enforcement agencies, law enforcement Any organization whose purpose is to enforce criminal laws; the activities of various public and private agencies at local, state, and federal levels that are designed to insure compliance with formal rules of society that regulate social conduct.

Law enforcement officers Any persons sworn to uphold and enforce local, state, or federal laws.

Legal factors Variables influencing the intake decision relating to the factual information about delinquent acts; crime seriousness, type of crime committed, prior record of delinquency adjudications, and evidence of inculpatory or exculpatory nature.

Legislative waiver Provision that compels juvenile court to remand certain youths to criminal courts because of specific offenses that have been committed or alleged.

Libido Sigmund Freud's term describing the sex drive he believed innate in everyone.

Life-without-parole Penalty imposed as maximum punishment in states that do not have death penalty; provides for permanent incarceration of offenders in prisons, without parole eligibility; early release may be attained through accumulation of good time credits.

Litigation explosion Rapid escalation of case filings before appellate courts, often based upon a landmark case extending rights to particular segments of the population, such as jail or prison inmates or juveniles.

Lockups Small rooms or buildings designed for confining arrested adults and/or juveniles for short periods, such as 24 hours or less.

Lombroso, Cesare (1835–1909) His school of thought linked criminal behavior with abnormal, unusual physical characteristics.

Long-term detention Period of incarceration of juvenile offenders in secure facilities that averages 180 days in the United States.

Looking-glass self Concept originated by Charles Horton Cooley where persons learn appropriate ways of behaving by paying attention to how others view and react to them.

Mandatory waiver Automatic transfer of certain juveniles to criminal court on the basis of (1) their age and (2) the seriousness of their offense; e.g., a 17-year-old in Illinois who allegedly committed homicide would be subject to mandatory transfer to criminal court for the purpose of a criminal prosecution.

Mediation A process whereby a third party intervenes between a perpetrator and a victim to work out a noncriminal or civil resolution to a problem that might otherwise result in a delinquency adjudication or criminal conviction.

Mediator Third-party arbiter in ADR.

Medical model Known as the treatment model, this model considers criminal behavior as an illness to be treated; delinquency is also a disease subject to treatment.

Mesomorphs Body type described by Sheldon; persons are strong, muscular, aggressive, tough.

Midwestern Prevention Project Multifaceted program for adolescent drug abuse prevention; targets middle and late adolescents; assists youths to recognize pressures to use drugs and to avoid such pressures.

Minimum due process rights See due process.

Miranda warning Sanction given to suspects by police officers advising suspects of their legal rights to counsel, to refuse to answer questions, to avoid self-incrimination, and other privileges.

Misdemeanor Crime punishable by confinement in city or county jail for a period of less than one year; a lesser offense.

Mistrial Trial ending before defendant's guilt or innocence can be established; usually results from hung jury where jurors unable to reach agreement on one's guilt or innocence; also occurs because of substantial irregularities in trial conduct.

Mitigating circumstances Factors that lessen the severity of the crime and/or sentence; such factors include old age, cooperation with police in apprehending other offenders, and lack of intent to inflict injury.

Mixed sentences Punishments imposed whenever offenders have been convicted of two or more offenses and judges sentence them to separate sentences for each convicted offense.

Mode of adaptation A way that persons who occupy a particular social position adjust to cultural goals and the institutionalized means to reach those goals.

Monitoring the Future Survey Study of 3,000 high-school students annually by Institute for Social Research at University of Michigan; attempts to discover hidden delinquency not ordinarily disclosed by published public reports.

National Crime Victimization Survey (NCVS) Published in cooperation with the United States Bureau of the Census, a random survey of 60,000 households, including 127,000 persons 12 years of age or older; includes 50,000 businesses; measures crime committed against specific victims interviewed and not necessarily reported to law enforcement officers.

National Juvenile Court Data Archive Compendium of national statistical information and data bases about juvenile delinquency available through the National Center for Juvenile Justice, under the sponsorship of the Office of Juvenile Justice and Delinquency Prevention (OJJDP); involves acquisition of court dispositional records and publishing periodic reports of juvenile offenses and adjudicatory outcomes from different jurisdictions.

National Youth Gang Survey (NYGS) Conducted annually since 1995; purpose of survey is to identify and describe critical gang components and characteristics.

National Youth Survey Study of large numbers of youths annually or at other intervals to assess hidden delinquency among high school students.

Needs assessment See risk/needs assessment instruments.

Net-widening Pulling juveniles into the juvenile justice system who wouldn't otherwise be involved in delinquent activity; applies to many status offenders (also known as "widening the net").

Neutralization theory Holds that delinquents experience guilt when involved in delinquent activities and that they respect leaders of the legitimate social order; their delinquency is episodic rather than chronic, and they adhere to conventional values while "drifting" into periods of illegal behavior. In order to drift, the delinquent must first neutralize legal and moral values.

New York House of Refuge Established in New York City in 1825 by the Society for the Prevention of Pauperism; school managed largely status offenders; compulsory education provided; strict prison-like regimen was considered detrimental to youthful clientele.

No bill, no true bill Decision issued by grand jury indicating no basis exists for charges against defendant; charges are usually dropped or dismissed later by judge.

Nolle prosequi Decision by prosecution to decline to pursue criminal case against defendant.

Nominal dispositions Adjudicatory disposition resulting in lenient penalties such as warnings and/or probation.

Noninterventionist model Philosophy of juvenile delinquent treatment meaning the absence of any direct intervention with certain juveniles who have been taken into custody.

Nonsecure custody, nonsecure confinement Custodial disposition where a juvenile is placed in a group home, foster care, or other arrangement where he/she is permitted to leave with permission of parents, guardians, or supervisors.

Numbers game model Caseload assignment model for probation or parole officers where total number of offender/clients is divided by number of officers.

Office of Juvenile Justice and Delinquency Prevention (OJJDP) Agency established by Congress under the JJDPA of 1974; designed to remove status offenders from jurisdiction of juvenile courts and dispose of their cases less formally.

Ohio experience Program for juvenile delinquents in various Ohio counties where home confinement, electronic monitoring, and other forms of intensive supervised probation are used; emphasis is upon public safety, offender accountability, and offender rehabilitation.

Once an adult/always an adult provision Ruling that once a juvenile has been transferred to criminal court to be prosecuted as an adult, regardless of the criminal court outcome, the juvenile can never be subject to the jurisdiction of juvenile courts in the future; in short, the juvenile, once transferred, will always be treated as an adult if future crimes are committed, even though the youth is still not of adult age.

Orange County Peer Court Established in Orange County, California, teen court consists of high-school students who volunteer for different court positions, including prosecutors, defense counsel, and jurors; intent is to vest youths with responsibility and accountability in deciding whether other youths charged with delinquency or status offenses are guilty or innocent through jury process; judge presides, together with community volunteers.

Overrides Actions by an authority in an institution or agency that overrules a score or assessment made of a client or inmate; raw scores or assessments or recommendations can be overruled; the function of override is to upgrade the seriousness of offense status or downgrade the seriousness of offense status, thus changing the level of custody at which one is maintained in secure confinement; may also affect the type and nature of community programming for particular offenders.

Parens patriae Literally "parent of the country" and refers to doctrine where the state oversees the welfare of youth; originally established by the King of England and administered through chancellors.

Parole Status of offenders conditionally released from a confinement facility prior to expiration of their sentences, placed under supervision of a parole agency.

Parole board Committee of persons who determine whether or not prisoners should be released prior to serving their full terms prescribed by original sentences in court.

Parolees Offender who has served some time in jail or prison, but has been released prior to serving entire sentence imposed upon conviction.

Parole revocation Two-stage proceeding that may result from a parolee's reincarceration in jail or prison; the first stage is a preliminary hearing to determine whether the parolee violated any specific parole condition; the second stage is to determine whether parole should be cancelled and the offender reincarcerated.

Parole revocation hearing Formal proceeding where a parole board decides whether a parolee's parole program should be terminated or changed because of one or more program infractions.

PATHS Program Promoting Alternative Thinking Strategies program aimed to promote emotional and social competencies and to reduce aggression and related emotional and behavioral problems among elementary school children.

Pathways Developmental sequences over the course of one's adolescence which are associated with serious, chronic, and violent offenders.

Peer jury model A peer jury is composed of one's equals or schoolmates who sit on the jury and decide one's punishment.

Perry Preschool Program Provides high-level, early childhood education to disadvantaged children in order to improve their later school life and performance.

Petitions Official documents filed in juvenile courts on juvenile's behalf, specifying reasons for the youth's court appearance; document asserts that juveniles fall within the categories of dependent or neglected, status offender, or delinquent, and the reasons for such assertions are usually provided.

Petit juries Traditional jury that hears evidence of crime in jury trial and decides a defendant's guilt or innocence.

Philadelphia Society for Alleviating the Miseries of Public Prisons Philanthropic society established by the Quakers in Pennsylvania in 1787; attempted to establish prison reforms to improve living conditions of inmates; brought food, clothing, and religious instruction to inmates.

PINS Diversion Program New York program established in 1987 to divert youths in need of supervision to out-of-home placements, such as foster care.

Pittsburgh Youth Study (PYS) Longitudinal investigation of 1,517 inner-city boys between 1986–1996; studied factors involved in what caused delinquency among some youths and why others did not become delinquent.

Placed Judicial disposition where juvenile is disposed to a group or foster home, or other type of out-of-home care; may also include secure confinement in an industrial school or comparable facility.

Placement One of several optional dispositions available to juvenile court judges following formal or informal proceedings against juveniles where either delinquent or status offenses have been alleged; adjudication proceedings yield a court decision about whether facts alleged in petition are true; if so, a disposition is imposed which may be placement in a foster or group home, wilderness experience, camp, ranch, or secure institution.

Plea bargains, plea bargaining Preconviction agreement between the defendant and the state whereby the defendant pleads guilty with the expectation of either a reduction in the charges, a promise of sentencing leniency, or some other government concession short of the maximum penalties that could be imposed under the law.

Police discretion Range of behavioral choices available to police officers within the limits of their power.

Poor Laws Regulations in English Middle Ages designed to punish debtors by imprisoning them until they could pay their debts; imprisonment was for life, or until someone could pay the debtor's debts for them.

Positive school of criminology School of criminological thought emphasizing analysis of criminal behaviors through empirical indicators such as physical features compared with biochemical explanations. Postulates that human behavior is a product of social, biological, psychological, or economic forces. Also known as the "Italian School."

Positivism Branch of social science that uses the scientific method of the natural sciences and that suggests that human behavior is a product of social, biological, psychological, or economic factors.

Prediction Assessment of some expected future behavior of a person, including criminal acts, arrests, or convictions.

Predictors of dangerousness and risk Assessment devices that attempt to forecast one's potential for violence or risk to others; any factors that are used in such instruments.

Predisposition reports Documents prepared by juvenile intake officer for juvenile judge; purpose of report is to furnish the judge with background about juveniles to make a more informed sentencing decision; similar to the PSI report.

Preliminary hearing, preliminary examination Proceeding where both prosecutor and defense counsel present some evidence against and on behalf of defendants; proceeding to determine whether probable cause exists to believe that a crime was committed and that the particular defendant committed the crime.

Preponderance of the evidence Standard used in civil courts to determine defendant or plaintiff liability and where the result does not involve incarceration.

Presentence investigation reports (PSI) Inquiry conducted about a convicted defendant at the request of the judge; purpose of inquiry is to determine worthiness of defendant for parole or sentencing leniency.

Presentments Charge brought against a defendant by grand jury acting on its own authority.

Presumptive waiver Requirement that shifts the burden to the juvenile for defending against their transfer to criminal court by showing that they are capable of being rehabilitated; following automatic or legislative waiver, juveniles can challenge the waiver in a hearing where they must demonstrate to the court's satisfaction their capability of becoming reformed.

Pretrial detention Holding delinquent or criminal suspects in incarcerative facilities pending their forthcoming adjudicatory hearing or trial.

Prevention/control model Attempts to repress or prevent delinquency by using early intervention strategies, including wilderness programs, elementary school interventions.

Preventive detention Constitutional right of police to detain suspects prior to trial without bail, where suspects are likely to flee from the jurisdiction or pose serious risks to others.

Primary deviation Part of labeling process whenever youths engage in occasional pranks and not especially serious violations of the law.

Prisons Incarcerative facilities designed to house long-term serious offenders; operated by state or federal government; houses inmates for terms longer than one year.

Privatization Trend in prison and jail management and correctional operations where private interests are becoming increasingly involved in the management and operations of correctional institutions.

Proactive units Police youth squad units assigned special duties of aggressively patrolling high-delinquency areas in an effort to deter gangs from operating.

Probable cause Reasonable belief that a crime has been committed and that person accused of crime committed it.

Probation Sentence not involving confinement that imposes conditions and retains authority in sentencing court to modify conditions of sentence or resentence offender for probation violations.

Probation revocation hearing Proceeding wherein it is determined whether to revoke a probationer's probation program because of one or more violations.

Project New Pride One of the most popular probation programs established in Denver, Colorado, in 1973; a blend of education, counseling, employment, and cultural education directed at those more serious offenders between the ages of 14 and 17; juveniles eligible for the New Pride program must have at least two prior convictions for serious misdemeanors and/or felonies; goals include (1) reintegrating participants into their communities through school participation or employment, and (2) reducing recidivism rates among offenders.

Project Outward Bound See wilderness experiments.

Propositions Statements about the real world that lack the high degree of certainty associated with assumptions; examples of propositions are, "Burnout among probation officers may be mitigated or lessened through job enlargement and giving officers greater input in organizational decision making," or "Two-officer patrol units are less susceptible to misconduct and corruption than one-officer patrol units."

Prosecution and the courts Organizations that pursue cases against criminal suspects and determine whether they are guilty or innocent of crimes alleged.

Prosecutors Court officials who commence civil and criminal proceedings against defendants. Represent state or government interest, prosecuting defendants on behalf of state or government.

Psychoanalytic theory Sigmund Freud's theory of personality formation through the id, ego, and superego at various stages of childhood. Maintains that early life experiences influence adult behavior.

Psychological theories Explanations linking criminal behavior with mental states or conditions, antisocial personality traits, and early psychological moral development.

Radical nonintervention Similar to a "do-nothing" policy of delinquency nonintervention.

Reactive units Police youth squad units that respond to calls for service whenever gangs are terrorizing neighborhoods.

Reality therapy model Equivalent of shock probation, where short incarcerative sentences are believed to provide "shock" value for juvenile offenders and scare them from reoffending behaviors.

Rebellion Mode of adaptation suggested by Robert K. Merton where persons reject institutional means to achieve culturally approved goals and create their own goals and means to use and seek.

Recidivism New crime committed by an offender who has served time or was placed on probation for previous offense; tendency to repeat crimes.

Recidivism rate Proportion of offenders who, when released from probation or parole, commit further crimes.

Recidivists Offenders who have committed previous offenses.

Reeve Chief law enforcement officer of English counties, known as shires.

Referrals Any citation of a juvenile to juvenile court by a law enforcement officer, interested citizen, family member, or school official; usually based upon law violations, delinquency, or unruly conduct.

Reform schools Different types of vocational institutions designed to both punish and rehabilitate youthful offenders; operated much like prisons as total institutions.

Regimented Inmate Discipline Program (RID) Oklahoma Department of Corrections program operated in Lexington, Oklahoma, for juveniles; program stresses military-type discipline and accountability; facilities are secure and privately operated.

Rehabilitation model Concept of youth management similar to medical model, where juvenile delinquents are believed to be suffering from social and psychological handicaps; provides experiences to build self-concept; experiences stress educational and social remedies.

Relabeling Redefinition of juvenile behaviors as more or less serious than previously defined; example would be police officers who relabel or redefine certain juvenile behaviors, such as curfew violation, as loitering for purposes of committing a felony, such as burglary or robbery; relabeling is associated with political jurisdictions which have deinstitutionalized status offenders or have divested juvenile courts of their authority over specific types of juvenile offenders; as one result, police officers lose power, or their discretionary authority, to warn such juveniles or take them into custody; new law may mandate removing such juveniles to community social services rather than to jails; in retaliation, some officers may relabel status behaviors as criminal ones, in order to preserve their discretionary authority over juveniles.

Released on own recognizance (ROR) Arrangement where a defendant is able to be set free temporarily to await a later trial without having to post a bail bond; persons released on ROR are usually well-known or have strong ties to the community and have not been charged with serious crimes.

Reparative Probation Program Reparative Probation Program is a voluntary civil mediation agenda involving minor offenders, where mediators determine fair compensation to victims through a series of meetings.

Repeat offender Any juvenile or adult with a prior record of delinquency or criminality.

Restitution Stipulation by court that offenders must compensate victims for their financial losses resulting from crime; compensation for psychological, physical, or financial loss by victim; may be imposed as a part of an incarcerative sentence.

Restorative justice Mediation between victims and offenders whereby offenders accept responsibility for their actions and agree to reimburse victims for their losses; may involve community service and other penalties agreeable to both parties in a form of arbitration with a neutral third party acting as arbiter.

Restorative policing Police-based family group conferencing uses police, victims, youths, and their families to discuss the harm caused by the youth and creates an agreement to repair the harm; similar to restorative justice.

Retreatism Mode of adaptation suggested by Robert K. Merton where persons reject culturally approved goals and institutionalized means and do little or nothing to achieve; homeless persons, bag ladies, vagrants, and others sometimes fit the retreatist profile.

Reverse waiver Motion to transfer juvenile's case from criminal court to juvenile court following a legislative or automatic waiver action.

Reverse waiver hearings, reverse waiver actions Formal proceedings to contest automatic transfer of juveniles to jurisdiction of criminal courts; used in jurisdictions with automatic transfer laws.

Risk Potential likelihood for someone to engage in further delinquency or criminality.

Risk/needs assessment instruments Predictive device intended to forecast offender propensity to commit new offenses or recidivate.

Ritualism Mode of adaptation suggested by Robert K. Merton where persons reject culturally approved goals but work toward lesser goals through institutionalized means.

Runaways Juveniles who leave their home for long-term periods without parental consent or supervision; unruly youths who cannot be controlled or managed by parents or guardians.

San Francisco Project Compared recidivism rates of probationers supervised by POs with caseloads of 20 and 40, respectively, and found no significant differences in recidivism rates of probationers were reported between "intensive" and "ideal" caseload scenarios.

Scared Straight Juvenile delinquency prevention program that sought to frighten samples of hard-core delinquent youths by having them confront inmates in a Rahway, New Jersey, prison; inmates would yell at and belittle them, calling them names, cursing, and yelling; inmates would tell them about sexual assaults and other prison unpleasantries in an attempt to get them to refrain from reoffending.

Scavenger gangs Groups formed primarily as a means of socializing and for mutual protection.

Screening Procedure used by prosecutor to define which cases have prosecutive merit and which ones don't; some screening bureaus are made up of police and lawyers with trial experience.

Sealing records of juveniles See expungement orders.

Second Chance Program Probation program operated in Iowa in the early 1990s to provide delinquent youths with opportunities to acquire skills, vocational and educational training, pre-employment training, and job placement services.

Secondary deviation Part of labeling theory which suggests that violations of the law become a part of one's normal behavior rather than just occasional pranks.

Secure custody, secure confinement Incarceration of juvenile offender in facility which restricts movement in community; similar to adult penal facility involving total incarceration.

See Our Side (SOS) Program Juvenile aversion program in Prince George's County, Maryland, designed to prevent delinquency.

Selective incapacitation Incarcerating individuals who show a high likelihood of repeating their previous offenses; based on forecasts of potential for recidivism; includes but not limited to dangerousness.

Self-reports, self-report information Surveys of youths (or adults) based upon disclosures these persons might make about the types of offenses they have committed and how frequently they have committed them; considered more accurate than official estimates.

Sentencing hearing Formal proceeding where convicted offender receives a punishment by the court.

Sexual Offender Treatment Program (SOT) Treatment program for juvenile offenders adjudicated delinquent on sex charges; includes psychosocioeducational interventions, therapies, and counseling.

Shires Early English counties.

Shock incarceration See shock probation.

Shock parole See shock probation.

Shock probation Intermediate punishment where offenders are initially sentenced to terms of secure detention; after a period of time between 90 and 180 days, youths are removed from detention and sentenced to serve the remainder of their sentences on probation; the term "shock probation" was coined by Ohio authorities in 1964.

Short-term confinement Placement in any incarcerative institution of either adults or juveniles where the period of confinement is less than one year; jails are considered short-term facilities.

Situationally-based discretion Confronting crime in the streets on the basis of immediate situational factors, time of night, presence of weapons, numbers of offenders; requires extensive personal judgments by police officers.

Smart sentencing See creative sentencing.

Social control theory Explanation of criminal behavior which focuses upon control mechanisms, techniques and strategies for regulating human behavior, leading to conformity or obedience to society's rules, and which posits that deviance results when social controls are weakened or break down, so that individuals are not motivated to conform to them.

Social learning theory Applied to criminal behavior, theory stressing importance of learning through modeling others who are criminal; criminal behavior is a function of copying or learning criminal conduct from others.

Society for the Prevention of Pauperism Philanthropic society that established first public reformatory in New York in 1825, the New York House of Refuge.

Sociobiology Scientific study of causal relation between genetic structure and social behavior.

Socioeconomic status (SES) Station or level of economic attainment one enjoys through work; acquisition of wealth; the divisions between various levels of society according to material goods acquired.

Sociological theories Explanations of criminal conduct that emphasize social conditions that bear upon the individual as the causes of criminal behavior.

Solitary confinement Segregation of prisoners into individual cells; originally used at Walnut Street Jail in Philadelphia, Pennsylvania, in 1790.

Sourcebook of Criminal Justice Statistics Compendium of statistical information about juvenile and adult offenders; court facts, statistics, and trends; probation and parole figures; and considerable additional information; published annually by the Hindelang Criminal Justice Research Center at the University of Albany, SUNY; funded by grant from the U.S. Department of Justice, Bureau of Justice Statistics.

SpeakerID Program Electronic voice verification system used as a part of EM to verify the identity of the person called by the probation or parole agency.

Special conditions of probation Extra requirements written into a standard probation agreement, including possible vocational or educational training, counseling, drug or alcohol treatment, attendance at meetings, restitution, and community service.

Specialized caseloads model Case assignment method based on POs' unique skills and knowledge relative to offender drug or alcohol problems; some POs are assigned particular clients with unique problems that require more than average PO expertise.

Split sentences See combination sentences.

Standard of proof Norms used by courts to determine validity of claims or allegations of wrongdoing against offenders; civil standards of proof are "clear and convincing evidence" and "preponderance of evidence," while criminal standard is "beyond a reasonable doubt."

Standard probation Probationers conform to all terms of their probation program, but their contact with POs is minimal; often, their contact is by telephone or letter once or twice a month.

Stationhouse adjustments Decisions made by police officers about certain juveniles taken into custody and brought to police stations for processing and investigation; adjustments often result in verbal reprimands and release to custody of parents.

Status offenders Anyone committing a status offense, including runaway behavior, truancy, curfew violation, loitering.

Status offenses Violation of statute or ordinance by minor, which, if committed by adult, would not be considered either a felony or a misdemeanor; also any acts committed by juveniles which would (1) bring them to the attention of juvenile courts and (2) not be crimes if committed by adults.

Statute of limitations Maximum time period within which a prosecution can be brought against a defendant for a particular offense; many criminal statutes have three- or six-year statute of limitations periods; there is no statute of limitations on homicide charges.

Statutory exclusion Provisions that automatically exclude certain juveniles and offenses from the jurisdiction of the juvenile courts; e.g., murder, rape, armed robbery.

Stigmas, stigmatize, stigmatization Social process whereby offenders acquire undesirable characteristics as the result of imprisonment or court appearances; undesirable criminal or delinquent labels are assigned those who are processed through the criminal and juvenile justice systems.

Stop Assaultive Children (SAC) Program Activity started in Phoenix, Arizona, in the late 1980s and designed for those youths who have committed serious family violence; children are detained in a juvenile facility for a short time, and their release is contingent upon being law-abiding, observing curfew, and other conditions; their prosecution is deferred; they must participate in counseling; may include volunteer work.

Strain theory A criminological theory positing that a gap between culturally approved goals and legitimate means of achieving them causes frustration which leads to criminal behavior.

Strategic leniency Less harsh dispositions meted out to certain offenders believed to be nonviolent and least likely to reoffend.

Street outreach model Youth Services Bureau model establishing neighborhood centers for youths who are delinquency-prone, where youths can have things to do other than hang out on the streets.

Subculture of delinquency A culture within a culture where the use of violence in certain social situations is commonplace and normative; Marvin Wolfgang and Franco Ferracuti devised this concept to depict a set of norms apart from mainstream conventional society, in which the theme of violence is pervasive and dominant. Learned through socialization with others as an alternative lifestyle.

Superego Sigmund Freud's label for that part of personality concerned with moral values.

Sustained petitions Adjudications resulting in a finding that the facts alleged in a petition are true; a finding that the juvenile committed the offenses alleged, which resulted in an adjudication and disposition.

Sweat shops Exploitative businesses and industries that employed child labor and demanded long work hours for low pay.

Systems modification model Youth Services Bureau model involving the establishment of community-based facilities for delinquency-prone youths; associations of churches, schools, and neighborhood businesses organizing to assist youths.

Tagging Being equipped with an electronic wristlet or anklet for the purpose of monitoring one's whereabouts.

Taken into custody For juveniles, not technically an arrest; law enforcement officers may pick up juvenile hitchhikers or runaways and take them into custody, meaning that the juveniles are taken to a care facility where their parents or legal guardians can be located.

Teen courts Tribunals consisting of teenagers who judge other teenagers charged with minor offenses, much like regular juries in criminal courts, where juvenile prosecutors and defense counsel argue cases against specific juvenile offenders; juries decide punishment with judicial approval.

Territorial gangs Groups of youths organized to defend a fixed amount of territory, such as several city blocks.

Theory A set of propositions from which a large number of new observations can be deduced. An integrated body of definitions, assumptions, and propositions related in such a way to explain and predict relations between two or more variables.

Totality of circumstances Sometimes used as the standard whereby offender guilt is determined or where search and seizure warrants may be obtained; officers consider entire set of circumstances surrounding apparently illegal event and act accordingly.

Traditional model Juvenile court proceedings characterized by less formal adjudications, greater use of detention.

Transfer hearings Proceeding to determine whether juveniles should be certified as adults for purposes of being subjected to jurisdiction of adult criminal courts where more severe penalties may be imposed.

Transfers Proceedings where juveniles are remanded to the jurisdiction of criminal courts; also known as certifications and waivers.

Transportation Early British practice of sending undesirables, misfits, and convicted offenders to remote territories and islands controlled by England.

Treatment model See medical model.

Tribunal model The tribunal model is similar to a peer jury model in that one's peers judge one's actions and determine punishments.

Truancy courts Special bodies that convene to determine punishments for youths who absent themselves from school.

Truants Juveniles who are habitually absent from school without excuse.

True bills Indictments or charges against defendants brought by grand juries after considering inculpatory evidence presented by prosecutor.

Unconditional probation, unconditional standard probation Form of conditional release without special restrictions or requirements placed on offender's behavior other than standard probation agreement terms; no formal controls operate to control or monitor divertee's behavior.

Uniform Crime Reports (UCR) Official source of crime information published by Federal Bureau of Investigation annually; accepts information from reporting law enforcement agencies about criminal arrests; classifies crimes according to various index criteria; tabulates information about offender age, gender, race, and other attributes.

Victim compensation Financial restitution payable to victims by either the state or the convicted offenders.

Victim-impact statement Appendage to a predisposition report or PSI that addresses the effect of the defendant's actions against victims or anyone harmed by the crime or delinquent act; usually compiled by the victim.

Victimization Basic measure of the occurrence of a crime. A specific criminal act affecting a specific victim.

Victim-offender mediation Third-party intervention mechanism whereby perpetrator and victim work out civil solution to otherwise criminal or delinquent action.

Violent Juvenile Offender Programs (VJOP) Procedures designed to provide positive interventions and treatments; reintegrative programs, including transitional residential programs for those youths who have been subject to long-term detention; provides for social networking, provision of educational opportunities for youths, social learning, and goal-oriented behavioral skills.

VisionQuest Carefully regulated, intensive supervision program designed to improve the social and psychological experiences of juveniles; reintegrative program to improve one's educational and social skills; wilderness program.

Waiver See transfer.

Waiver hearing Request by prosecutor to transfer juvenile charged with various offenses to a criminal or adult court for prosecution; waiver motions make it possible to sustain adult criminal penalties.

Waiver motion Formal request by prosecutor to send juvenile's case from juvenile court to criminal court.

Walnut Street Jail Reconstructed from earlier Philadelphia Jail in 1790; first real attempt by jail officials to classify and segregate prisoners according to age, gender, and crime seriousness; introduced idea of solitary confinement.

Wilderness experiments Experience programs that include a wide array of outdoor programs designed to improve a juvenile's self-worth, self-concept, pride, and trust in others.

With prejudice To dismiss charges, but those same charges cannot be brought again later against the same defendant.

Without prejudice To dismiss charges, but those same charges can be brought again later against the same defendant.

Workhouses Early penal facilities designed to use prison labor for profit by private interests; operated in shires in mid-sixteenth century and later.

XYY theory Explanation of criminal behavior suggesting that some criminals are born with an extra Y chromosome, characterized as the "aggressive" chromosome compared with the passive X chromosome; an extra Y chromosome produces greater agitation, greater aggressiveness, and criminal propensities.

Youth Judge Model Youth Judge Model Version of teen court where juveniles perform the role of judges as well as prosecutors and defense counsel; some teen court moels use adult judges to regulate proceedings.

Youth Services Bureaus (YSBs) Various types of diversion programs operated in the United States for delinquency-prone youth.

Youth Services/Diversion (YS/D) Program Established in Orange County, California, with the goals of reducing family dysfunction and teaching youth responsibility; instilling self-esteem and self-confidence through family counseling sessions.

Youth squads Teams of police officers in police departments whose responsibility it is to focus upon particular delinquency problems and resolve them.

Youth-to-Victim Restitution Project Program operated by the juvenile court in Lincoln, Nebraska, based on the principle that youths must repay whatever damages they inflicted on victims; enforcement of restitution orders decreased recidivism among delinquent offenders.

Zone of transition An area nearest center of city center undergoing rapid social change; believed to contain high rates of crime and delinquency.

Abatiello, Jennifer D. (2005). "Juvenile Competency and Culpability: What the Public Deserves." Unpublished paper presented at the annual meeting of the Academy of Criminal Justice Sciences, Chicago (March).

Abbott-Chapman, J., C. Denholm, and C. Wyld (2007). "Pre-Service Professionals' Constructs of Adolescent Risk-Taking and Approaches to Risk Management." *Journal of Sociology* 11:241–261.

Abrams, L.S. (2006). "From Corrections to Community: Youth Offenders' Perceptions of the Challenges of Transition." *Journal of Offender Rehabilitation* 44:31–53.

Adoption and Foster Care Analysis and Reporting System (2008). *Adoption and Foster Care Analysis and Reporting System Report*. Washington, DC: Adoption and Foster Care Analysis and Reporting System.

Aisenberg, E., et al. (2007). "Maternal Depression and Adolescent Behavior Problems: An Examination of Mediation among Immigrant Latino Mothers and Their Adolescent Children Exposed to Community Violence." *Journal of Interpersonal Violence* 22:1227–1349.

Alford, Susan (1998). "The Effectiveness of Juvenile Arbitration in South Carolina." *APPA Perspectives* 22:28–34.

Altschuler, David M., and Troy L. Armstrong (2001). "Reintegrating High-Risk Juvenile Offenders into Communities: Experiences and Prospects." *Corrections Management Quarterly* 5:72–88.

American Correctional Association (2007). *2007 Directory*. College Park, MD: American Correctional Association.

Anchorage Youth Court (2005). "Youth Courts Strive for Sustainability." *Gavel* 16:1–4.

Anderson, C.M., and A.S. Rancer (2007). "The Relationship between Argumentativeness, Verbal Aggressiveness, and Communication Satisfaction in Incarcerated Male Youth." *The Prison Journal* 87:328–343.

Anderson, James F., and Laronistine Dyson (2001). *Legal Rights of Prisoners: Cases and Comments*. Lanham, MD: University Press of America.

Apel, R., et al. (2007). "Unpacking the Relationship between Adolescent Employment and Antisocial Behavior: A Matched Samples Comparison." *Criminology* 45:67–97.

APPA Perspectives (2004). "APPA Resolves Support for Youth Courts." *APPA Perspectives* 28:8.

Archwamety, Teara, and Antonis Katsiyannis (2000). "Academic Remediation, Parole Violations, and Recidivism Rates among Delinquent Youths." *Remedial and Special Education* 21:161–170.

Armour, S., and D.L. Haynie (2007). "Adolescent Sexual Debut and Later Delinquency." *Journal of Youth and Adolescence* 36:141–152.

Armstrong, Edward G. (2008). "Critiques of Drug Courts: Rhetoric and Reality." Unpublished paper presented at the annual meeting of the Academy of Criminal Justice Sciences, Cincinnati, OH (March).

Armstrong, Gaylene (2001). *Private vs. Public Operation of Juvenile Correctional Facilities*. New York: LFB Scholarly Publishing.

Armstrong, Troy L. (1991). *Intensive Interventions with High-Risk Youths: Promising Approaches in Juvenile Probation and Parole*. Monsey, NY: Criminal Justice Press.

Ashford, Jose B., and Craig Winston LeCroy (1988). "Decision-Making for Juvenile Offenders in Aftercare." *Juvenile and Family Court Journal* 39:45–58.

Ashford, Jose B., and Craig Winston LeCroy (1993). "Juvenile Parole Policy in the United States: Determinate Versus Indeterminate Models." *Justice Quarterly* 10:179–195.

Austin, Andrew (2003). "Does Forced Sexual Contact Have Criminogenic Effects? An Empirical Test of Derailment Theory." *Journal of Aggression, Maltreatment, and Trauma* 8:41–66.

Austin, James, Michael Jones, and Melissa Bolyard (1993). *The Growing Use of Jail Boot Camps*. Washington, DC: U.S. Department of Justice, Office of Justice Programs.

Ayers-Schlosser, Lee (2005). "2004 Juvenile Justice Summit: The Oregon Update." Unpublished paper presented at the annual meeting of the Academy of Criminal Justice Sciences, Chicago (March).

Babb, Susan, and Peter C. Kratcoski (1994). "The Juvenile Justice Assistants Program." *Juvenile and Family Court Journal* **45:**43–49.

Bannan, Rosemary (2008). "Tracking Resilience and Recidivism Mediation of Cook County Youth, 1999–2007." Unpublished paper presented at the annual meeting of the Academy of Criminal Justice Sciences, Cincinnati, OH.

Barfeind, James (2008). *Predisposition Report Writing.* Missoula, MT: University of Montana.

Barnes, Allan R. (2005). "Weed and Seed Initiative: An Evaluation Using a Pre/Post Community Survey Approach." Unpublished paper presented at the annual meeting of the Academy of Criminal Justice Sciences, Chicago (March).

Baron, S.W. (2007). "Street Youth, Gender, Financial Strain, and Crime: Exploring Broidy and Agnew's Extension to General Strain Theory." *Deviant Behavior* **28:**273–302.

Baron, S.W., and D.R. Forde (2007). "Street Youth Crime: A Test of Control Balance Theory." *Justice Quarterly* **24:**335–350.

Beaver, K.M., Matt Delisi, and Michael G. Vaughn (2008). "The Intersection of Genes and Neuropsychological Deficits in the Prediction of Adolescent Delinquency and Self-Control." Unpublished paper presented at the annual meeting of the Academy of Criminal Justice Sciences, Cincinnati, OH.

Beaver, K.M., J.P. Wright, and M. Delisi (2007). "Self-Control as an Executive Function: Reformulating Gottfredson's and Hirshi's Parental Socialization Thesis." *Criminal Justice and Behavior* **34:**1345–1361.

Beccaria, Cesare Bonesana (1764). *On Crimes and Punishments.* Indianapolis, IN: Bobbs-Merrill, 1963, reprinted edition.

Becker, Howard S. (1963). *Outsiders: Studies in the Sociology of Deviance.* New York: Free Press.

Belshaw, Scott H., and Dean Lanham (2008). "OC Pepper Spray and the Juvenile Justice System in Texas: A Review of the Recent Changes and Policy Recommendations." Unpublished paper presented at the annual meeting of the Academy of Criminal Justice Sciences, Cincinnati, OH.

Bentham, Jeremy (1790). *An Introduction to the Principles of Morals and Legislation.* New York: Hafner, 1948, reprinted edition.

Bernat, Frances P. (2005). "Evaluating Schools at Hope: Alternative Paradigm to Kids at Risk." Unpublished paper presented at the annual meeting of the Academy of Criminal Justice Sciences, Chicago (March).

Bernberg, J.G., and T. Thorlindsson (2007). "Community Structure and Adolescent Delinquency in Iceland: A Contextual Analysis." *Criminology* **45:**415–444.

Bilchik, Shay (1996). *State Responses to Serious and Violent Juvenile Crime.* Pittsburgh, PA: National Center for Juvenile Justice.

Billings, F.J., et al. (2007). "Can Reinforcement Induce Children to Falsely Incriminate Themselves?" *Law and Human Behavior* **31:**125–139.

Bjerk, D. (2007). "Measuring the Relationship between Youth Criminal Participation and Household Economic Resources." *Journal of Quantitative Criminology* **23:**1573–1579.

Blevins, Kristie R. (2005). "The Correctional Orientation of 'Child Savers': The Level, Sources, and Impact of Support for Juvenile Correctional Workers." Unpublished paper presented at the annual meeting of the Academy of Criminal Justice Sciences, Chicago (March).

Bonczar, Thomas P., and Tracy L. Snell (2004). *Capital Punishment, 2003.* Washington, DC: U.S. Department of Justice, Bureau of Justice Statistics (November).

Boone, Harry N., Jr. (1996). "Electronic Home Confinement: Judicial and Legislative Perspectives." *APPA Perspectives* **20:**18–25.

Bouhours, B., and K. Daly (2007). "Youth Sex Offenders in Court: An Analysis of Judicial Sentencing Remarks." *Punishment and Society* **9:**371–394.

Bowman, Cathy (2005). "Involvement of Probation and Parole in Project Safe Neighborhoods." Unpublished paper presented at the annual meeting of the American Probation and Parole Association, New York (July).

Bowman, M.A., H.M. Prelow, and S.R. Weaver (2007). "Parenting Behaviors, Association with Deviant Peers, and Delinquency in African American Adolescents." *Journal of Youth and Adolescence* **36:**517–527.

Boyd, Rebecca J., and David L. Myers (2005). "Impact of Risk and Protective Factors for Alcohol Use among a Rural Youth Sample." Unpublished paper presented at the annual meeting of the Academy of Criminal Justice Sciences, Chicago (March).

Bradley, Tracey (2005). "Holistic Representation: Identifying Success." Unpublished paper presented at the annual training institute of the American Probation and Parole Association, New York (July).

Brandau, Timothy J. (1992). *An Alternative to Incarceration for Juvenile Delinquents: The Delaware Bay Marine Institute.* Ann Arbor, MI: University Microfilms International.

Bratina, Michele P. (2008). "ADHD and School-Related Behavioral Problems: A Futile Mix?" Unpublished paper presented at the annual meeting of the Academy of Criminal Justice Sciences, Cincinnati, OH.

Brewer, Steven L. (2008). "In the Yard: Bullying in School and Prison Systems." Unpublished paper presented at the annual meeting of the Academy of Criminal Justice Sciences, Cincinnati, OH.

Brookbanks, Warren (2002). "Public Policy, Moral Panics, and the Lure of Anticipatory Containment." *Psychiatry, Psychology, and the Law* **9**:127–135.

Brown, Joe M. (2005). "The Future of Juvenile Justice: Does Determinate Sentencing in Juvenile Court Serve the Same Purpose as Certification to Criminal Court?" Unpublished paper presented at the annual meeting of the Academy of Criminal Justice Sciences, Chicago (March).

Browning, Katharine, and Rolf Loeber (1999). *Highlights of Findings from the Pittsburgh Youth Study*. Washington, DC: Office of Juvenile Justice and Delinquency Prevention Programs.

Buckler, Kevin G., et al. (2008). "Public Support of Capital Punishment: Assessing the Importance of Core Values and Racial Sentiment." Unpublished paper presented at the annual meeting of the Academy of Criminal Justice Sciences, Cincinnati, OH.

Buffington-Vollum, Jackqueline, John F. Edens, and Andrea Keilen (2008). "Institutional Violence among Capital Inmates: The Impact of Changing Death Row." Unpublished paper presented at the annual meeting of the Academy of Criminal Justice Sciences, Cincinnati, OH.

Bureau of Justice Statistics (2008). *Annual Reports*. Washington, DC: U.S. Department of Justice, Bureau of Justice Statistics.

Burek, Melissa, et al. (2008). "Minority Juvenile Arrests: Mitigated or Instigated by Policing Practices?" Unpublished paper presented at the annual meeting of the Academy of Criminal Justice Sciences, Cincinnati, OH.

Burgess, Robert, and Ronald Akers (1966). "Differential Association-Reinforcement Theory of Criminal Behavior." *Social Problems* **14**:128–147.

Burke, Alison (2008). "Gender Specific Delinquency Prevention: The Unique Needs of Girls." Unpublished paper presented at the annual meeting of the Academy of Criminal Justice Sciences, Cincinnati, OH.

Burrell, William D. (2005). "Leaders for the Future: Two Views of Leadership Development." Unpublished paper presented at the annual meeting of the American Probation and Parole Association, New York (July).

Busseri, M.A., T. Willoughby, and H. Chalmers (2007). "A Rationale and Method for Examining Reasons for Linkages among Adolescent Risk Behaviors." *Journal of Youth and Adolescence* **36**:279–289.

Butts, Jeffrey A. (1996a). *Offenders in Juvenile Court*. Washington, DC: Office of Juvenile Justice and Delinquency Prevention.

Butts, Jeffrey A. (1996b). "Speedy Trial in Juvenile Court." *American Journal of Criminal Law* **23**:515–561.

Butts, Jeffrey A., and Janeen Buck (2002). *The Sudden Popularity of Teen Courts*. Washington, DC: Urban Institute.

Butts, Jeffrey A., and Gregory J. Halemba (1996). *Waiting for Justice: Moving Young Offenders Through the Juvenile Court Process*. Pittsburgh, PA: National Center for Juvenile Justice.

Butts, Jeffrey A., et al. (1996). *Juvenile Court Statistics 1993: Statistics Report*. Washington, DC: Office of Juvenile Justice and Delinquency Prevention.

Bynum, Tim (2005). "Evaluating Project Safe Neighborhoods in the Eastern District of Michigan." Unpublished paper presented at the annual meeting of the Academy of Criminal Justice Sciences, Chicago (March).

Cadigan, Timothy P. (2001). "PACTS." *Federal Probation* **65**:25–30.

California Youth Authority (2008). *Predictions of Risk*. Sacramento, CA: California Youth Authority.

Campbell, Jacob, and Brian Gonzalez (2007). *Juveniles Involved in the Juvenile Justice System*. Spokane, WA: Eastern Washington University, School of Social Work.

Cary, Pauline L. (2005). "ADHD and Juvenile Delinquency: A Review of the Literature." Unpublished paper presented at the annual meeting of the Academy of Criminal Justice Sciences, Chicago (March).

Case, S. (2007). "Questioning the 'Evidence' of Risk that Underpins Evidence-Led Youth Justice." *Youth Justice* **7**:91–105.

Caudill, Jonathan, and Karen Hayslet-McCall (2008). "Short-Term Stay at the Gray Door Hotel: Assessment of Juvenile Pre-Trial Detention on Future Recidivism." Unpublished paper presented at the annual meeting of the Academy of Criminal Justice Sciences, Cincinnati, OH.

Cauffman, Elizabeth, Laurence Steinberg, and Alex R. Piquero (2005). "Psychological, Neuropsychological, and Physiological Correlates of Serious Antisocial Behavior in Adolescence: The Role of Self-Control." *Criminology* **43**:133–176.

Cauffman, Elizabeth, et al. (2007). "Gender Differences in Mental Health Symptoms among Delinquent and Community Youth." *Youth Violence and Juvenile Justice* **5**:297–307.

Champion, Dean J. (1994). *Measuring Offender Risk: A Criminal Justice Sourcebook*. Westport, CT: Greenwood Press.

Champion, Dean J. (2005). *Probation, Parole, and Community Corrections*, 5th ed. Upper Saddle River, NJ: Prentice Hall.

Champion, Dean J. (2008a). *Probation, Parole, and Community Corrections*, 6th ed. Upper Saddle River, NJ: Prentice Hall.

Champion, Dean J. (2008b). "Sentencing Differentials According to Private vs. Court-Appointed Counsel." Unpublished paper presented at the annual meeting of the Academy of Criminal Justice Sciences, Cincinnati, OH (March).

Champion, Dean J. (2009). *Leading U.S. Supreme Court Cases: Briefs and Key Terms*. Upper Saddle River, NJ: Pearson/Prentice Hall.

Champion, Dean J., and G. Larry Mays (1991). *Juvenile Transfer Hearings: Some Trends and Implications for Juvenile Justice*. New York: Praeger.

Chapman, Yvonne K. (2005). "Teen Courts and Restorative Justice." Unpublished paper presented at the annual meeting of the Academy of Criminal Justice Sciences, Chicago (March).

Chapple, Constance L. (2005). "Self-Control, Peer Relations, and Delinquency." *Justice Quarterly* **22**:89–106.

Chapple, Constance L., and K.A. Johnson (2007). "Gender Differences in Impulsivity." *Youth Violence and Family Justice* **5**:221–234.

Chen, X., et al. (2007). "Onset of Conduct Disorder, Use of Delinquent Subsistence Strategies, and Street Victimization among Homeless and Runaway Adolescents in the Midwest." *Journal of Interpersonal Violence* **22**:1156–1183.

Chiang, S., et al. (2007). "Heroin Use among Youths Incarcerated for Illicit Drug Use: Psychosocial Environment, Substance Use History, Psychiatric Comorbidity, and Route of Administration." *American Journal of Addictions* **15**:233–241.

Choi, Y. (2007). "Academic Achievement and Problem Behaviors among Asian Pacific Islander American Adolescents." *Journal of Youth and Adolescence* **36**:403–415.

Choi, Alfred, and Wing T. Lo (2002). *Fighting Youth Crime: Success and Failure of Two Little Dragons*. Singapore: Times Academic Press.

Clear, Todd R., and Harry R. Dammer (2003). *The Offender in the Community,* 2nd ed. Belmont, CA: Wadsworth/Thomson Learning.

Clinkinbeard, Samantha, and Colleen Murray (2008). "Treatment Belonging and Support as Predictors of Future-Oriented Planning among Incarcerated Offenders." Unpublished paper presented at the annual meeting of the Academy of Criminal Justice Sciences, Cincinnati, OH.

Coalition for Juvenile Justice (2007). *History and Current Strategy*. Washington, DC: Coalition for Juvenile Justice.

Cohen, Albert K. (1955). *Delinquent Boys*. New York: Free Press.

Congressional Research Service (2007). *Juvenile Justice: Legislative History and Current Legislative Issues*. Washington, DC: Congressional Research Service.

Cook County Court (2002). *The Englewood Evening Reporting Center*. Chicago: Cook County Court.

Copes, H., and J.P. Williams (2007). "Techniques of Alienation: Deviant Behavior, Moral Commitment, and Subcultural Identity." *Deviant Behavior* **28**:247–272.

Corbett, Ronald P. (2000). "Juvenile Probation on the Eve of the Next Millennium." *APPA Perspectives* **24**:22–30.

Corwin, Joe-Anne (2005). "Juvenile Correctional Education Standards Approved." *Corrections Today* **67**:83.

Crawford, Kim (2007). "Grant to 'Supercharge' Local Efforts to Fight Guns, Gangs." *The Flit Journal First Edition*, September 20.

Crawley, William R., et al. (2005). "Exploring the Experience of Collective Identity and Conflict in Schooling." Unpublished paper presented at the annual meeting of the Academy of Criminal Justice Sciences, Chicago (March).

Crooks, C.V., et al. (2007). "Understanding the Link between Childhood Maltreatment and Violent Delinquency: What Do Schools Have to Add?" *Child Maltreatment* **12**:269–280.

Dahlgren, Daniel C. (2005). "Emotional Sociology and Juvenile Delinquency: The Value of Interpreting Emotional Subculture of Gangs." Unpublished paper presented at the annual meeting of the Academy of Criminal Justice Sciences, Chicago (March).

Daigle, L.E., Francis T. Cullen, and J.P. Wright (2007). "Gender Differences in the Predictors of Juvenile Delinquency: Assessing the Generality-Specificity Debate." *Youth Violence and Juvenile Justice* **5**:254–286.

D'Angelo, Jill M., and Michael P. Brown (2005). "Missouri Juvenile Justice Reform Act: Comparison of Case Outcomes from 1994 and 2000." Unpublished paper presented at the annual meeting of the Academy of Criminal Justice Sciences, Chicago (March).

Dario, Lisa, and David Holleran (2008). "A Re-Examination of Christian Fundamentalism and Support for the Death Penalty." Unpublished paper presented at the annual meeting of the Academy of Criminal Justice Sciences, Cincinnati, OH.

Davidson-Methot, David G. (2004). "Calibrating the Compass: Using Quality Improvement Data for Outcome Evaluation, Cost Control, and Creating Quality Organizational Cultures." *Residential Treatment for Children and Youth* **21**:45–68.

Death Penalty Information Center (2008). *The Death Penalty in the United States*. Washington, DC: Death Penalty Information Center.

Decker, Scott H. (2005). "Evaluating Project Safe Neighborhoods in the Eastern District of Missouri." Unpublished paper presented at the annual meeting of the Academy of Criminal Justice Sciences, Chicago (March).

Dembo, Richard, and James Schmeidler (2003). "A Classification of High-Risk Youths." *Crime and Delinquency* **49**:201–230.

Dembo, Richard, C.W. Turner, and N. Jainchill (2007). "An Assessment of Criminal Thinking among Incarcerated Youths in Three States." *Criminal Justice and Behavior* **34**:1157–1167.

Dembo, Richard, et al. (2000a). "A Longitudinal Study of the Impact of a Family Empowerment Intervention on Juvenile Offender Psychosocial Functioning: An Expanded Assessment." *Journal of Child and Adolescent Substance Abuse* **10**:1–7.

Dembo, Richard, et al. (2000b). "Youth Recidivism Twelve Months after a Family Empowerment Intervention." *Journal of Offender Rehabilitation* **31**:29–65.

Dembo, Richard, et al. (2006). "Special Issue on Arbitration Intervention Worker Service." *Journal of Offender Rehabilitation* **43**:1–131.

Dimmick, Susan (2005). "Holistic Representation: Identifying Success." Unpublished paper presented at the annual training institute of the American Probation and Parole Association, New York (July).

Dubowitz, H., S.C. Pitts, and M.M. Black (2004). "Measurement of Three Major Subtypes of Child Neglect." *Child Maltreatment* **9**:344–356.

Duran, Robert (2005). "Manufacturing Gang Fears: A Critique of the Police Suppression Industry." Unpublished paper presented at the annual meeting of the Academy of Criminal Justice Sciences, Chicago (March).

Dussich, J.P., and C. Maekoya (2007). "Physical Child Harm and Bullying-Related Behaviors: A Comparative Study in Japan, South Africa, and the United States." *International Journal of Offender Therapy and Comparative Criminology* **51**:495–509.

Dwyer, Diane C., and Roger B. McNally (1987). "Juvenile Justice: Reform, Retain, and Reaffirm." *Federal Probation* **51**:47–51.

Eitle, David, Lisa Stolzenberg, and Stewart D'Alessio (2005). "Police Organizational Factors, the Racial Composition of the Police, and the Probability of Arrest." *Justice Quarterly* **22**:30–56.

Ellsworth, Thomas (1988). "Case Supervision Planning: The Forgotten Component of Intensive Probation Supervision." *Federal Probation* **52**:28–33.

Ellsworth, Thomas, Michelle T. Kinsella, and Kimberlee Massin (1992). "Prosecuting Juveniles: *Parens Patriae* and Due Process in the 1990's." *Justice Professional* **7**:53–67.

Ellwanger, S.J. (2007). "Strain, Attribution, and Traffic Delinquency among Young Drivers: Measuring and Testing General Strain Theory in the Context of Driving." *Crime and Delinquency* **53**:523–551.

Empey, Lamar T., and Jerome Rabow (1961). "The Provo Experiment in Delinquency Rehabilitation." *American Sociological Review* **26**:679–695.

Erez, Edna, and Kathy Laster (1999). "Neutralizing Victim Reform." *Crime and Delinquency* **45**:530–553.

Estell, D.B., T.W. Farmer, and B.D. Cairns (2007). "Bullies and Victims in Rural African-American Youth: Behavioral Characteristics and Social Network Placement." *Aggressive Behavior* **33**:145–159.

Estell, D.B., et al. (2007). "Patterns of Middle School Adjustment and Ninth Grade Adaptation of Rural African-American Youth: Grades and Substance Use." *Journal of Youth and Adolescence* **36**:477–487.

Fagan, Jeffrey A. (1990). "Treatment and Reintegration of Violent Juvenile Offenders: Experimental Results." *Justice Quarterly* **7**:233–263.

Fagan, Jeffrey A., and Craig Reinarman (1991). "The Social Context of Intensive Supervision: Organizational and Ecological Influences on Community Treatment." In *Intensive Interventions with High-Risk Youths: Promising Approaches in Juvenile Probation and Parole,* Troy L. Armstrong (ed.). Monsey, NY: Criminal Justice Press.

Feiring, C., S. Miller-Johnson, and C.M. Cleland (2007). "Potential Pathways from Stigmatization and Internalizing Symptoms to Delinquency in Sexually Abused Youth." *Child Maltreatment* **12**:220–232.

Feld, Barry C. (2007). "Final Results from Investigation of Blended Sentencing in Ohio and Vermont." Unpublished paper presented at the annual meeting of the American Society of Criminology, Atlanta, GA (November).

Ferri, Enrico (1901). *Criminal Sociology.* Boston: Little, Brown.

Ferzan, Ibrahim Halil (2008). "Comparison of Juvenile Justice System and Delinquency in the United States and Turkey." Unpublished paper presented at the annual meeting of the Academy of Criminal Justice Sciences, Cincinnati, OH (March).

Flexner, Bernard, and Roger N. Baldwin (1914). *Juvenile Courts and Probation.* New York: Harcourt.

Foley, Roger P. (2008). "Disposition and Post-Disposition: Predisposition Reports." Ft. Lauderdale, FL. Unpublished paper.

Free Press (2007). "Operation Proves How Team Work Beats Crime." *Free Press,* August 10.

Friday, Paul C., and X. Ren (2006). *Delinquency and Juvenile Justice Systems in the Non-Western World.* Monsey, NY: Criminal Justice Press.

Frisher, M., et al. (2007). *Predicted Factors for Illicit Drug Use among Young People.* London: Home Office Research, Development and Statistics Directorate.

Gainey, Randy R., and Brian K. Payne (2003). "Changing Attitudes Toward House Arrest with Electronic

Monitoring." *International Journal of Offender Therapy and Comparative Criminology* **47**:196–209.

Gallagher, C.A., and A. Dobrin (2007). "Risk of Suicide in Juvenile Justice Facilities: The Problem of Rate Calculations in High-Turnover Populations." *Criminal Justice and Behavior* **34**:1362–1376.

Gavazzi, Stephen M., et al. (2000). "The Growing Up FAST Diversion Program." *Aggression and Violent Behavior* **5**:159–175.

Geary County Community Corrections (2002). *Pre-Dispositional Supervision Program.* Geary County, KS: Geary County Community Corrections.

Gelber, Seymour (1990). "The Juvenile Justice System: Vision for the Future." *Juvenile and Family Court Journal* **41**:15–18.

George, Rani, and George Thomas (2008). "Ethnic Identity and Self-Esteem as Protective Factors from Violence Risk among Minority Youth." Unpublished paper presented at the annual meeting of the Academy of Criminal Justice Sciences, Cincinnati, OH.

Glueck, Sheldon, and Eleanor Glueck (1950). *Unraveling Juvenile Delinquency.* New York: Commonwealth Fund.

Goffman, Erving (1961). *Asylums.* Garden City, NY: Anchor Press.

Gomez, Fernando, and Juan Jose Ganuza (2002). "Civil and Criminal Sanctions Against Blackmail: An Economic Analysis." *International Review of Law and Economics* **21**:475–498.

Gordon, Jill A., and Page Malmsjo (2005). "The Impact of Offender Characteristics on Recidivism: An Evaluation of Barrett Juvenile Correctional Center." Unpublished paper presented at the annual meeting of the Academy of Criminal Justice Sciences, Chicago (March).

Goring, Charles (1913). *The English Convict.* London: His Majesty's Stationery Office.

Gover, Angela R., and Doris Layton MacKenzie (2003). "Child Maltreatment and Adjustment in Juvenile Correctional Institutions." *Criminal Justice and Behavior* **30**:374–396.

Grant, Lorna Elaine (2008). "The Recent Development of Jamaican Gangs in Schools." Unpublished paper presented at the annual meeting of the Academy of Criminal Justice Sciences, Cincinnati, OH.

Graves, K.N. (2007). "Not Always Sugar and Spice: Expanding Theoretical and Functional Explanations for Why Females Aggress." *Aggression and Violent Behavior: A Review Journal* **12**:131–140.

Greenleaf, Richard G. (2005). "A Survey of Gang and Non-Gang Members Regarding Their Attitudes Toward the Police, Community, and Crime: A Chicago Study." Unpublished paper presented at the annual meeting of the Academy of Criminal Justice Sciences, Chicago (March).

Gregorie, Trudy (2005). "Victims' Rights and Issues: Educating Judicial and Court Personnel." Unpublished paper presented at the annual training institute of the American Probation and Parole Association, New York (July).

Grisso, Thomas (1998). *Forensic Evaluation of Juveniles.* Sarasota, FL: Professional Resource Press.

Haraway, Daniel Scott (2008). "The Juvenile Waiver: The Perfect Solution for Serious Juvenile Offenders?" Unpublished paper presented at the annual meeting of the Academy of Criminal Justice Sciences, Cincinnati, OH.

Hart, Likisha (2005). "Learning Disabilities and Juvenile Delinquency: Examining the Correlation between Labeling and Delinquent Behavior." Unpublished paper presented at the annual meeting of the Academy of Criminal Justice Sciences, Chicago (March).

Haynie, Dana L., D. Steffensmeier, and K.E. Bell (2007). "Gender and Serious Violence: Untangling the Role of Friendship Sex Composition and Peer Violence." *Youth Violence and Juvenile Justice* **5**:235–253.

Haynie, Dana L., et al. (2005). "Adolescent Romantic Relationships and Delinquency Involvement." *Criminology* **43**:177–210.

Henderson, Thomas A., et al. (1984). *The Significance of Judicial Structure: The Effect of Unification on Trial Court Operations.* Washington, DC: U.S. Government Printing Office.

Henry, D.B., and K. Kobus (2007). "Early Adolescent Social Networks and Substance Use." *The Journal of Early Adolescence* **27**:346–362.

Hensley, Christopher, et al. (2005). "Exploring the Possible Link between Childhood and Adolescent Bestiality and Interpersonal Violence." Unpublished paper presented at the annual meeting of the Academy of Criminal Justice Sciences, Chicago (March).

Herman, Susan, and Cressida Wasserman (2001). "A Role for Victims in Offender Reentry." *Crime and Delinquency* **47**:428–445.

Hill, M., et al. (2007). "More Haste, Less Speed? An Evaluation of Fast Track Policies to Tackle Persistent Youth Offending in Scotland." *Youth Justice* **7**:121–137.

Hinduja, Sameer, Justin W. Patchin, and Trevor Lippman (2008). "Cyberbullying among Middle Schoolers: Focusing in on the Causes and Consequences." Unpublished paper presented at the annual meeting of the Academy of Criminal Justice Sciences, Cincinnati, OH.

Hirschi, Travis (1969). *Causes of Delinquency.* Berkeley, CA: University of California Press.

Holland Teen Court (2008). *The Holland Teen Court.* Holland, MI: Holland Teen Court.

Holsinger, Alex M., and Edward J. Latessa (1999). "An Empirical Evaluation of a Sanction Continuum:

Pathways Through the Juvenile Justice System." *Journal of Criminal Justice* **27**:155–172.

Hooton, Earnest A. (1939). *Crime and the Man*. Cambridge, MA: Harvard University Press.

Houk, Julie M. (1984). "Electronic Monitoring of Probationers: A Step Toward Big Brother?" *Golden Gate University Law Review* **14**:431–446.

Huskey, Bobbie L. (1984). "Community Corrections Acts." *Corrections Today* **46**:45.

Ingram, Jason R., et al. (2005). "Family Environment, Peers, and Delinquency: A Path Analysis." Unpublished paper presented at the annual meeting of the Academy of Criminal Justice Sciences, Chicago (March).

Ingram, Jefferson (2008). "The Future of Death Penalty Litigation: The End of the Road with *Baez v. Rees*." Unpublished paper presented at the annual meeting of the Academy of Criminal Justice Sciences, Cincinnati, OH.

Jarjoura, Roger, et al. (2008). "An Assessment of the Punitive Nature of Juvenile Court Dispositions." Unpublished paper presented at the annual meeting of the Academy of Criminal Justice Sciences, Cincinnati, OH.

Johnson County Department of Corrections (2002). *Juvenile ISP Conditions & Guidelines*. Johnson County, KS: Johnson County Department of Corrections.

Johnson, Kay (2005). "Trauma and Substance Abuse Treatment for Women Offenders." Unpublished paper presented at the annual meeting of the American Probation and Parole Association, New York (July).

Kammer, James J., Kevin I. Minor, and James B. Wells (1997). "An Outcome Study of the Diversion Plus Program for Juvenile Offenders." *Federal Probation* **61**:51–56.

Karp, David R. (2001). "Harm and Repair: Observing Restorative Justice in Vermont." *Justice Quarterly* **18**:727–757.

Karp, David R. (2004). "Teen Courts." *APPA Perspectives* **28**:18–20.

Katz, Charles M., Vincent J. Webb, and Scott H. Decker (2005). "Using the Arrestee Drug Abuse Monitoring (ADAM) Program to Further Understand the Relationship between Drug Use and Gang Membership." *Justice Quarterly* **22**:58–88.

Kearney, Edmund M. (1994). "A Clinical Corrections Approach: The Failure of a Residential Juvenile Delinquency Treatment Center." *Juvenile and Family Court Journal* **45**:33–41.

Kelly, Katharine (2005). "Auto Theft and Youth Culture: A Nexus of Masculinities, Femininities, and Car Culture." Unpublished paper presented at the annual meeting of the Academy of Criminal Justice Sciences, Chicago (March).

Kempf-Leonard, Kimberly, and P. Johansson (2007). "Gender and Runaways: Risk Factors, Delinquency, and Juvenile Justice Experiences." *Youth Violence and Juvenile Justice* **5**:308–327.

Kennedy, Sharon (2005). "Increasing the Effectiveness of Probation and Parole Through Research." Unpublished paper presented at the annual training institute of the American Probation and Parole Association, New York (July).

Khalili, Ahmad (2008). "Neighborhood Quality of Life and Delinquency: A Contextual Explanation of Juvenile Delinquency." Unpublished paper presented at the annual meeting of the Academy of Criminal Justice Sciences, Cincinnati, OH.

Kidd, S.A. (2007). "Youth Homelessness and Social Stigma." *Journal of Youth and Adolescence* **36**:291–299.

King, Tammy (2005). "Juvenile Detention: A Descriptive Study of Rule Infractions." Unpublished paper presented at the annual meeting of the Academy of Criminal Justice Sciences, Chicago (March).

King, Tammy, Kelly Melvin, and Jennifer Biederman (2008). "Juvenile Detention Facilities: Challenges and Changes." Unpublished paper presented at the annual meeting of the Academy of Criminal Justice Sciences, Cincinnati, OH.

Kitsuse, John I. (1962). "Societal Reaction to Deviant Behavior: Problems of Theory and Method." *Social Problems* **9**:247–256.

Klein, Malcolm W., L. Rosenzweig, and M. Bates (1975). "The Ambiguous Juvenile Arrest." *Criminology* **24**:185–194.

Knox, George W., Brad Martin, and Edward D. Tromanhauser (1995). "Preliminary Results of the 1995 National Prosecutor's Survey." *Journal of Gang Research* **2**:59–71.

Kohlberg, L. (1981). *The Philosophy of Moral Development*. New York: Harper and Row.

Konty, Mark (2005). "Microanomie: The Cognitive Foundations of the Relationship between Anomie and Deviance." *Criminology* **43**:107–132.

Kretschmer, Ernest (1936). *Physique and Character*. London: Kegan, Paul, Trench, and Trubner.

Kuanliang, Attapol (2008). "A Comparison of Institutional Violent Misconduct between Juvenile and Adult Prisoners." Unpublished paper presented at the annual meeting of the Academy of Criminal Justice Sciences, Cincinnati, OH.

Kubena, Jiletta (2008). "Juvenile Offender Reentry: An Examination of the Issues." Unpublished paper presented at the annual meeting of the Academy of Criminal Justice Sciences, Cincinnati, OH.

Kuntsche, E., et al. (2007). "Drinking Motives as Mediators of the Link between Alcohol Expectancies and Alcohol Use among Adolescents." *Journal of Studies on Alcohol and Drugs* **68**:76–85.

Kupchik, A. (2007). "The Correctional Experiences of Youth in Adult and Juvenile Prisons." *Justice Quarterly* **24**:247–270.

Kwak, Dae-Hoon, and Seok-Jin Jeong (2008). "Juvenile Justice Decision Making in a Midwestern State: Does Type of Court Matter?" Unpublished paper presented at the annual meeting of the Academy of Criminal Justice Sciences, Cincinnati, OH.

Kyle, Jim (1998). "The Privatization Debate Continues." *Corrections Today* **60**:88–158.

Lab, Steven P., Glenn Shields, and Connie Schondel (1993). "Research Note: An Evaluation of Juvenile Sexual Offender Treatment." *Crime and Delinquency* **39**:543–553.

LaMade, Megan (2008). "Juvenile Courts: Who Receives Punishment?" Unpublished paper presented at the annual meeting of the Academy of Criminal Justice Sciences, Cincinnati, OH.

Landreville, P. (1999). "Electronic Surveillance of Delinquents: A Growing Trend." *Deviance et Societe* **23**:105–121.

Lansford, J.E., et al. (2007). "Early Physical Abuse and Later Violent Delinquency: A Prospective Longitudinal Study." *Child Maltreatment* **12**:233–245.

LaSean, Glenda (2008). "Juvenile Interrogation Techniques: A Law Enforcement Perspective." Unpublished paper presented at the annual meeting of the Academy of Criminal Justice Sciences, Cincinnati, OH.

Latessa, Edward J. (2005). "Increasing the Effectiveness of Probation and Parole Through Research." Unpublished paper presented at the annual training institute of the American Probation and Parole Association, New York (July).

LaTorre, Diana Tecco (2008). "A Closer Look at Child Abuse Laws." Unpublished paper presented at the annual meeting of the Academy of Criminal Justice Sciences, Cincinnati, OH.

Lawrence, Richard A. (1984). "The Role of Legal Counsel in Juveniles' Understanding of Their Rights." *Juvenile and Family Court Journal* **34**:49–58.

Lea, S.R. (2007). *Delinquency and Animal Cruelty: Myths and Realities about Social Pathology*. New York: LFB Scholarly Publishing.

Lee, Byung Hyun (2008). "The Impact of Parental Supervision and Control on Delinquent Behaviors." Unpublished paper presented at the annual meeting of the Academy of Criminal Justice Sciences, Cincinnati, OH.

Lee, V., and P.N. Hoaken (2007). "Cognition, Emotion, and Neurobiological Development: Mediating the Relation between Maltreatment and Aggression." *Child Maltreatment* **12**:281–298.

Leiber, Michael J. (1995). "Toward Clarification of the Concept of 'Minority' Status and Decision Making in Juvenile Court Proceedings." *Journal of Crime and Justice* **18**:79–108.

Lemert, Edwin M. (1951). *Social Pathology*. New York: McGraw-Hill.

Lemert, Edwin M. (1967a). *Human Deviance, Social Problems, and Social Control*. Englewood Cliffs, NJ: Prentice-Hall.

Lemert, Edwin M. (1967b). "The Juvenile Court—Quests and Realities." In *Task Force Report: Juvenile Delinquency and Youth Crime*. Washington, DC: President's Commission on Law Enforcement and the Administration of Justice.

Lemmon, John H., Thomas L. Austin, and Alan Feldberg (2005). "Developing an Index of Child Maltreatment Severity Based on Survey Data of Child and Youth Services Professionals." Unpublished paper presented at the annual meeting of the Academy of Criminal Justice Sciences, Chicago (March).

Lexington Herald Leader (2003). "Governor Commutes Stanford's Sentence." December 9, 2003:B3.

Lewis, T., et al. (2007). "Maltreatment History and Weapon Carrying among Early Adolescents." *Child Maltreatment* **12**:259–267.

Liberman, Akiva, W. Raudenbush, and Robert J. Sampson (2005). "Neighborhood Context, Gang Presence, and Gang Involvement." Unpublished paper presented at the annual meeting of the Academy of Criminal Justice Sciences, Chicago (March).

Lightfoot, E., and Mark Umbreit (2004). "An Analysis of State Statutory Provisions for Victim-Offender Mediation." *Criminal Justice Policy Review* **15**:5–25.

Listug, David (1996). "Wisconsin Sheriff's Office Saves Money and Resources." *American Jails* **10**:85–86.

Lord, George F., Shanhe Jiang, and Sarah Hurley (2005). "Parental Efficacy and Delinquent Behavior: Longitudinal Analysis of At-Risk Adolescents in Treatment." Unpublished paper presented at the annual meeting of the Academy of Criminal Justice Sciences, Chicago (March).

Loukas, A., M. Suizzo, and H.M. Prelow (2007). "Examining Resource and Protective Factors in the Adjustment of Latino Youth in Low Income Families: What Role Does Material Acculturation Play?" *Journal of Youth and Adolescence* **36**:489–501.

Lusignan, R., and J.D. Marleau (2007). "Risk Assessment and Offender-Victim Relationship in Juvenile Offenders." *International Journal of Offender Therapy and Comparative Criminology* **51**:433–443.

Mack, K.Y., et al. (2007). "Reassessing the Family-Delinquency Association: Do Family Type, Family Processes, and Economic Factors Make a Difference?" *Journal of Criminal Justice* **35**:51–67.

MacKenzie, Doris Layton, James W. Shaw, and Voncile B. Gowdy (1993). *An Evaluation of Shock Incarceration in Louisiana*. Washington, DC: U.S. Department of Justice, Office of Justice Programs.

MacKenzie, Doris Layton, et al. (2001). *A National Study Comparing the Environments of Boot Camps with Traditional Facilities for Juvenile Offenders*. Washington, DC: U.S. Department of Justice.

Maloney, Dennis M., Dennis Romig, and Troy Armstrong (1988). "Juvenile Probation: The Balanced Approach." *Juvenile and Family Court Journal* **39:**1–63.

Marriott, S. (2007). "Applying a Psychodynamic Treatment Model to Support an Adolescent Sentenced for Murder to Confront and Manage Feelings of Shame and Remorse." *Journal of Forensic Psychiatry and Psychology* **18:**248–260.

Martin, Richard, et al. (2008). "Alabama Youth Gang Survey." Unpublished paper presented at the annual meeting of the Academy of Criminal Justice Sciences, Cincinnati, OH.

Maruna, Shadd, Amanda Matravers, and Anna King (2004). "Disowning Our Shadow: A Psychoanalytic Approach to Understanding Punitive Public Attitudes." *Deviant Behavior* **25:**277–299.

Massachusetts Statistical Analysis Center (2001). *Implementation of the Juvenile Justice Reform Act*. Boston: Massachusetts Statistical Analysis Center.

Matrix Research and Consultancy (2007). *Evaluation of Drug Intervention Programs*. London: Home Office Online Report, Home Office Research and Development and Statistics Directorate.

Matza, David (1964). *Delinquency and Drift*. New York: Wiley.

Mauro, David M. (2005). "Total Gang Awareness." Unpublished paper presented at the annual training institute of the American Probation and Parole Association, New York (July).

McCartan, L.M., and E. Gunnison (2007). "Examining the Origins and Influence of Low Self-Control." *Journal of Crime and Justice* **30:**35–62.

McCold, Paul, and Benjamin Wachtel (1998). *Restorative Policing Experiment: The Bethlehem Police Family Group Conferencing Project*. Bethlehem, PA: Real Justice.

McDevitt, Jack (2005). "Evaluating Project Safe Neighborhoods in the District of Massachusetts." Unpublished paper presented at the annual meeting of the Academy of Criminal Justice Sciences, Chicago (March).

McGarrell, Edmund (2005). "Comprehensive Examination of the Project Safe Neighborhoods Initiative." Unpublished paper presented at the annual meeting of the Academy of Criminal Justice Sciences, Chicago (March).

McGarrell, Edmund, and N. Kroovand-Hipple (2007). "Family Group Conferencing and Re-Offending among First-Time Juvenile Offenders." *Justice Quarterly* **24:**221–246.

McGhee, J., and L. Waterhouse (2007). "Classification in Youth Justice and Child Welfare: In Search of 'The Child.'" *Youth Justice* **7:**107–120.

McKeesport CASASTART (2008). *The CASASTART Program*. McKeesport, PA: The CASASTART Program.

McLean County Court Services (2002). *Day Reporting Center for Juveniles Possessing Firearms*. McLean County, IL: McLean County Court Services.

McMorris, B.J., et al. (2007). "Prevalence of Substance Use and Delinquent Behavior in Adolescents from Victoria, Australia and Washington State, United States." *Health Education and Behavior* **34:**634–650.

McNamara, Robert (2008). "The Issues Surrounding Juvenile Curfews." Unpublished paper presented at the annual meeting of the Academy of Criminal Justice Sciences, Cincinnati, OH.

McNeill, F., and S. Batchelor (2004). "Persistent Offending by Young People: Developing Practice." In *Issues in Community and Criminal Justice: Monograph 3*. London: Napo.

McSherry, Joseph (2008). "Characteristics and Outcomes of Transferred Youth to Criminal Court." Unpublished paper presented at the annual meeting of the Academy of Criminal Justice Sciences, Cincinnati, OH.

Mears, Daniel P., et al. (2007). "Public Opinion and the Foundation of the Juvenile Court." *Criminology* **45:**223–257.

Meisel, Joshua S. (2001). "Relationships and Juvenile Offenders: The Effects of Intensive Aftercare Supervision." *Prison Journal* **81:**206–245.

Mellins, C.A., et al. (2007). "Predicting the Onset of Sexual and Drug Risk Behaviors in HIV-Negative Youths with HIV-Positive Mothers: The Role of Contextual, Self-Regulation, and Social-Intervention Factors." *Journal of Youth and Adolescence* **36:**265–278.

Mendel, Richard A. (2001). *Less Cost, More Safety: Guiding Lights for Reform in Juvenile Justice*. Washington, DC: American Youth Policy Forum.

Merianos, Dorothy (2005). "Gender Differences in Mental Health Status among Incarcerated Juveniles." Unpublished paper presented at the annual meeting of the Academy of Criminal Justice Sciences, Chicago (March).

Mersky, J.P., and A.J. Reynolds (2007). "Child Maltreatment and Violent Delinquency: Disentangling Main Effects and Subgroup Effects." *Child Maltreatment* **12:**246–258.

Merton, Robert K. (1957). *Social Theory and Social Structure*. New York: Free Press.

Metts, Michelle (2005). "Involvement of Probation and Parole in Project Safe Neighborhoods." Unpublished paper presented at the annual meeting of the American Probation and Parole Association, New York (July).

Miller, J., and J. Lin (2007). "Applying a Generic Juvenile Risk Assessment Instrument to a Local Context: Some Practical and Theoretical Lessons." *Crime and Delinquency* **53:**552–580.

Miller, J. Mitchell, Holly Ventura Miller, and J. Barnes (2007). "The Effect of Demeanor on Drug Court Admission." *Criminal Justice Policy Review* **18:**246–259.

Miller, K. (2007). "Traversing the Spatial Divide: Gender, Place, and Delinquency." *Feminist Criminology* **2:**202–222.

Mitchell, John J., and Sharon A. Williams (1986). "SOS: Reducing Juvenile Recidivism." *Corrections Today* **48:**70–71.

Moore County Government (2002). *Moore County Day Reporting Center.* Moore County, NC: Moore County Government.

Moore, Joan (1993). "Gangs, Drugs, and Violence." In *Gangs: The Origins and Impact of Contemporary Youth Gangs in the United States,* S. Cummings and D.J. Monti (eds). Albany, NY: SUNY Press.

Morris, Sherill, and Camille Gibson (2008). "Impact of Victimization and Trauma on Female Assaultive Behavior." Unpublished paper presented at the annual meeting of the Academy of Criminal Justice Sciences, Cincinnati, OH.

Moseley, IvyAnn (2005). "Exposure to Violence and Its Relation to Problem-Solving Strategies." Unpublished paper presented at the annual meeting of the Academy of Criminal Justice Sciences, Chicago (March).

Mueller, David, and Lisa Hutchison-Wallace (2005). "Verbal Abuse, Self-Esteem, and Peer Victimization." Unpublished paper presented at the annual meeting of the Academy of Criminal Justice Sciences, Chicago (March).

Murrell, Pamela R. (2005). "Advocating for Children in the Juvenile Justice System." Unpublished paper presented at the annual meeting of the Academy of Criminal Justice Sciences, Chicago (March).

Musser, Denise Casamento (2001). "Public Access to Juvenile Records." *Corrections Today* **63:**112–113.

Myers, Bryan (2004). "Victim Impact Statements and Mock Jury Sentencing: The Impact of Dehumanizing Language on a Death Qualified Sample." *American Journal of Forensic Psychology* **22:**39–55.

Myers, Matthew L. (1973). "Legal Rights in a Juvenile Correctional Institution." *Journal of Law Reform* **7:**242–266.

National Council on Disability (2008). *Youth with Disabilities in the Foster Care System: Barriers to Success and Proposed Policy Solutions.* Washington, DC: National Council on Disability.

New Mexico Juvenile Justice Division (2002). *Decision Tree for Juvenile Decision Making.* Santa Fe, NM: New Mexico Juvenile Justice Division.

Norris, Michael, Sarah Twill, and Chigon Kim (2008). "9/11 and Juvenile Court Net-Widening." Unpublished paper presented at the annual meeting of the Academy of Criminal Justice Sciences, Cincinnati, OH (March).

North Carolina Department of Juvenile Justice and Delinquency Prevention (2008). *Support Our Students (SOS).* Raleigh: North Carolina Department of Juvenile Justice and Delinquency Prevention.

Office of Juvenile Justice and Delinquency Prevention (2007). *Juvenile Offenders and Victims: National Report.* Washington, DC: Office of Juvenile Justice and Delinquency Prevention.

Office of Juvenile Justice and Delinquency Prevention (2008). *Female Delinquents: Patterns and Trends.* Washington, DC: U.S. Government Printing Office.

Olivero, J. Michael (2005). "Youth at Risk and Measures of Psychopathy." Unpublished paper presented at the annual meeting of the Academy of Criminal Justice Sciences, Chicago (March).

Ousey, G.C., and P. Wilcox (2007). "The Interaction of Antisocial Personality and Life-Course Predictors of Delinquent Behavior." *Criminology* **45:**313–343.

Owens-Sabir, M.C. (2007). *The Effects of Race and Family Attachment on Self-Esteem, Self-Control, and Delinquency.* New York: LFB Scholarly.

Palmer, Ted (1994). *A Profile of Correctional Effectiveness and New Directions for Research.* Albany: State University of New York Press.

Parent, Dale (2003). *Correctional Boot Camps: Lessons from a Decade of Research.* Washington, DC: U.S. National Institute of Justice.

Park, Suyeon (2005). "The Effect of Age of Onset on Violent Crime." Unpublished paper presented at the annual meeting of the Academy of Criminal Justice Sciences, Chicago (March).

Parker, Chauncey G. (2005). "Expanding the Role of Probation and Parole in Public Safety Partnerships." Unpublished paper presented at the annual training institute of the American Probation and Parole Association, New York (July).

Passetti, Audry, and Alida Merlo (2008). "Comparative Youth Crime Policies: What Is Happening Outside of the United States?" Unpublished paper presented at the annual meeting of the Academy of Criminal Justice Sciences, Cincinnati, OH (March).

Peterson, B. Michelle, Martin D. Ruck, and Christopher J. Koegl (2001). "Youth Court Dispositions: Perceptions of Canadian Juvenile Offenders." *International Journal of Offender Therapy and Comparative Criminology* **45:**593–605.

Peterson, Scott (2005). *The Growth of Teen Courts in the United States.* Washington, DC: Office of Juvenile Justice and Delinquency Prevention.

Pierce, Christine Schnyder, and Stanley L. Brodsky (2002). "Trust and Understanding in the Attorney-Juvenile Relationship." *Behavioral Sciences and the Law* **20**:89–107.

Pingree, David H. (1984). "Florida Youth Services." *Corrections Today* **46**:60–62.

Pires, P., and J.M. Jenkins (2007). "A Growth Curve of the Joint Influences of Parenting Affect, Child Characteristics and Deviant Peers on Adolescent Illicit Drug Use." *Journal of Youth and Adolescence* **36**:169–183.

Platt, Anthony N. (1969). *The Child Savers: The Invention of Delinquency*. Chicago: University of Chicago Press.

Pope, Carl E., Rick Lovell, and Heidi Hsia (2002). *Disproportionate Minority Confinement: A Review of the Research Literature from 1989 through 2001*. Washington, DC: U.S. Department of Justice, Bureau of Justice Statistics.

Porterfield, Austin L. (1943). "Delinquency and Its Outcome in Court and College." *American Journal of Sociology* **49**:199–208.

Preston, Frederick W., and Roger I. Roots (eds.) (2004). "When Laws Backfire: Unintended Impacts of Public Policy." *American Behavioral Scientist* **47**:1371–1466.

Proctor, Amy, and Janet Mullings (2008). "Youth Maltreatment and Gang Membership among Youth Incarcerated in Texas." Unpublished paper presented at the annual meeting of the Academy of Criminal Justice Sciences, Cincinnati, OH.

Project Safe Neighborhoods (2005). "Project Safe Neighborhood." Unpublished paper presented at the annual meeting of the Academy of Criminal Justice Sciences, Chicago (March).

Rasmussen, A. (2004). "Teen Court Referral, Sentencing, and Subsequent Recidivism: Two Proportional Hazards Models and a Little Speculation." *Crime and Delinquency* **50**:615–635.

Rawhide Boys Ranch (2008). *Rawhide*. New London, WI: Rawhide Boys Ranch.

Reckless, Walter (1967). *The Crime Problem*. New York: Appleton-Century-Crofts.

Reddington, Frances P. (2005). "The Status of Juvenile Justice in Chicago." Unpublished paper presented at the annual meeting of the Academy of Criminal Justice Sciences, Chicago (March).

Rehling, William R. (2005). "Adult Consultation for Minors in Custody During Interrogation." Unpublished paper presented at the annual meeting of the Academy of Criminal Justice Sciences, Chicago (March).

Rhoades, Philip W., and Kristina M. Zambrano (2005). "Leading Practice to Theory: Data Driven Strategic Delinquency Prevention Planning Goes Regional." Unpublished paper presented at the annual meeting of the Academy of Criminal Justice Sciences, Chicago (March).

Rivers, Anthony L. (2005). "Appropriateness of Juvenile Transfer to Adult Court." Unpublished paper presented at the annual meeting of the Academy of Criminal Justice Sciences, Chicago (March).

Rivers, James E., Richard Dembo, and Robert S. Anwyl (1998). "The Hillsborough County, Florida Juvenile Assessment Center." *Prison Journal* **78**:439–450.

Robbers, Monica (2008). "Examining Race as a Factor in Discretionary Waiver." Unpublished paper presented at the annual meeting of the Academy of Criminal Justice Sciences, Cincinnati, OH.

Robbins, Ira (1986). "Privatization of Corrections: Defining the Issues." *Federal Probation* **50**:24–30.

Rockhill, A., B.L. Green, and C. Furrer (2007). "Is the Adoption and Safe Families Act Influencing Child Welfare Outcomes for Families with Substance Abuse Issues?" *Child Maltreatment* **12**:7–19.

Rosky, Jeffrey W. (2008). "Examining Resiliency Within the Contexts of Self-Control Theory and Life Course Analysis." Unpublished paper presented at the annual meeting of the Academy of Criminal Justice Sciences, Cincinnati, OH.

Ross, James (2008). "Impact of Court Personnel Interpersonal Dynamics on Delinquency and Status Offense Petitions." Unpublished paper presented at the annual meeting of the Academy of Criminal Justice Sciences, Cincinnati, OH.

Roy, Sudipto (2004). "Factors Related to Success and Recidivism in a Day Reporting Center." *Criminal Justice Studies* **17**:3–17.

Sabol, William J., Todd D. Minton, and Paige M. Harrison (2007). *Prison and Jail Inmates at Midyear 2006*. Washington, DC: Bureau of Justice Statistics.

Salinas, Patti Ross (2008). "Juvenile Justice Alternative Education Programs in Texas." Unpublished paper presented at the annual meeting of the Academy of Criminal Justice Sciences, Cincinnati, OH.

Salzinger, S., M. Rosario, and R.S. Feldman (2007). "Physical Child Abuse and Adolescent Violent Delinquency: The Mediating and Moderating Roles of Personal Relationships." *Child Maltreatment* **12**:208–219.

San Miguel, Claudia, and Richard Hartley (2008). "Mental Illness and Gun Ownership among College Students." Unpublished paper presented at the annual meeting of the Academy of Criminal Justice Sciences, Cincinnati, OH.

Santana, Edwin L. (2005). "Total Gang Awareness." Unpublished paper presented at the annual training institute of the American Probation and Parole Association, New York (July).

Sawicki, Donna Rau, Beatrix Schaeffer, and Jeanie Thies (1999). "Predicting Successful Outcomes for Serious and Chronic Juveniles in Residential Placement." *Juvenile and Family Court Journal* **50**:21–31.

Schaefer-McDaniel, N. (2007). "'They Be Doing Illegal Things': Early Adolescents Talk about Their Inner-City Neighborhoods." *Journal of Adolescent Research* **22**:413–436.

Schaffner, Laurie (2005). "Gender Responsive Programs for Girls: Theory into Practice." Unpublished paper presented at the annual meeting of the Academy of Criminal Justice Sciences, Chicago (March).

Schaffner, Laurie (2006). *Girls in Trouble with the Law.* New Brunswick, NJ: Rutgers University Press.

Schexnayder, Vena M. (2008). "Solutions to School Violence." Unpublished paper presented at the annual meeting of the Academy of Criminal Justice Sciences, Cincinnati, OH.

Schmidt, Annesley K. (1998). "Electronic Monitoring: What Does the Literature Tell Us?" *Federal Probation* **62**:10–19.

Schur, Edwin (1973). *Radical Nonintervention: Rethinking the Delinquency Problem.* Englewood Cliffs, NJ: Prentice-Hall.

Sears, H.A., et al. (2007). "The Co-Occurrence of Adolescent Boys' and Girls' Use of Psychologically, Physically, and Sexually Abusive Behaviors in Their Dating Relationships." *Journal of Adolescence* **30**:487–504.

Seiter, Richard P., and Angela D. West (2003). "Supervision Styles in Probation and Parole: An Analysis of Activities." *Journal of Offender Rehabilitation* **38**:57–75.

Seyko, Ronald J. (2001). "Balanced Approach and Restorative Justice Efforts in Allegheny County, Pennsylvania." *Prison Journal* **81**:187–205.

Shafer, Joseph A., David L. Carter, and Andra Katz-Bannister (2004). "Studying Traffic Stop Encounters." *Journal of Criminal Justice* **32**:159–170.

Shaw, Clifford R., and Henry D. McKay (1972). *Juvenile Delinquency and Urban Areas,* rev. ed. Chicago: University of Chicago Press.

Shawnee County Department of Community Corrections (2002). *Shawnee County Community Corrections.* Topeka, KS: Shawnee County Department of Community Corrections.

Sheldon, William H. (1949). *The Varieties of Delinquent Youth.* New York: Harper.

Shine, James, and Dwight Price (1992). "Prosecutors and Juvenile Justice: New Roles and Perspectives." In *Juvenile Justice and Public Policy: Toward a National Agenda,* I.M. Schwartz (ed.). New York: Lexington Books.

Short, James F., Jr., and F. Ivan Nye (1958). "Extent of Unrecorded Juvenile Delinquency: Tentative Conclusions." *Journal of Criminal Law and Police Science* **49**:296–302.

Sinclair, Jim (2005). "Victim's Rights and Issues: Educating Judicial and Court Personnel." Unpublished paper presented at the annual training institute of the American Probation and Parole Association, New York (July).

Slater, M.D., A.F. Hayes, and V.L. Ford (2007). "Examining the Moderating and Mediating Roles of News Exposure and Attention on Adolescent Judgments of Alcohol-Related Risks." *Communication Research* **34**:355–381.

Slesnick, N., et al. (2007). "Treatment Outcome for Street-Living, Homeless Youth." *Addictive Behaviors* **32**:1237–1251.

Song, Juyoung, and Sheila Royo (2008). "An Empirical Test of General Strain Theory: Explaining Delinquency among Korean Youth." Unpublished paper presented at the annual meeting of the Academy of Criminal Justice Sciences, Cincinnati, OH.

Souhami, A. (2007). *Transforming Youth Justice: Occupational Identity and Cultural Change.* Cullompton, UK: Willan.

Spano, R., C. Rivera, and J. Bolland (2006). "The Impact of Timing of Exposure to Violence on Violent Behavior in a High Poverty Sample of Inner City African American Youth." *Journal of Youth and Adolescence* **35**:681–692.

Spencer, R. (2007). "'It's Not What I Expected': A Qualitative Study of Youth Mentoring Relationship Failures." *Journal of Adolescent Research* **22**:331–354.

Spigel, Saul (2008). *Group Home Notice Requirements.* Hartford, CT: Department of Children and Families.

Springer, Nicollette, and Autumn M. Frei (2008). "Propositional Integration of Anomie and Conflict Theories: A Multilevel Examination of School Delinquency." Unpublished paper presented at the annual meeting of the Academy of Criminal Justice Sciences, Cincinnati, OH.

Steen, S. (2007). "Conferring Sameness: Institutional Management of Juvenile Sex Offenders." *Journal of Contemporary Ethnography* **36**:31–49.

Streib, Victor L. (1987). *The Death Penalty for Juveniles.* Bloomington, IN: Indiana University Press.

Sturgeon, Bill (2005). "Case Management of Youthful Offenders in the Community." Unpublished paper presented at the annual training institute of the American Probation and Parole Association, New York (July).

Styve, Gaylene J., et al. (2000). "Perceived Conditions of Confinement: A National Evaluation of Juvenile Boot Camps and Traditional Facilities." *Law and Human Behavior* **24**:297–308.

Sullivan, C.J., et al. (2007). "Reducing Out-of-Community Placement and Recidivism: Diversion of Delinquent Youth with Mental Health and Substance Use Problems from the Justice System." *International Journal of Offender Therapy and Comparative Criminology* **51**:555–577.

Sullivan, T.N., et al. (2007). "Exposure to Violence in Early Adolescence: The Impact of Self-Restraint, Witnessing Violence, and Victimization on Aggression and Drug Use." *The Journal of Early Adolescence* **27**:296–323.

Sungi, Simeon P. (2008). "Preventing Juvenile Delinquency: A Fundamental Human Rights Perspective." Unpublished paper presented at the annual meeting of the Academy of Criminal Justice Sciences, Cincinnati, OH.

Supancic, Michael (2005). "A Back Door Approach to Aggression and Gender Violence in Middle Schools." Unpublished paper presented at the annual meeting of the Academy of Criminal Justice Sciences, Chicago (March).

Sutherland, Edwin H. (1939). *Principles of Criminology.* Philadelphia, PA: Lippincott.

Sutherland, Edwin H. (1951) "Critique of Sheldon's Varieties of Delinquent Youth." *American Sociological Review* **16**:10–13.

Swain, R.C., K.L. Henry, and N.E. Baez (2004). "Risk-Taking, Attitudes Toward Aggression, and Aggressive Behavior among Rural Middle School Youth." *Violence and Victims* **19**:157–170.

Swanson, Cheryl G. (2005). "Incorporating Restorative Justice into the School Resource Officer Model." Unpublished paper presented at the annual meeting of the Academy of Criminal Justice Sciences, Chicago (March).

Sweet, Joseph (1985). "Probation as Therapy." *Corrections Today* **47**:89–90.

Taxman, Faye (2005). "Tools of the Trade: Incorporating Science into Practice." Unpublished paper presented at the annual meeting of the American Probation and Parole Association, New York (July).

Taylor, Terrance, et al. (2008). "Youth Gang Membership and Serious Violent Victimization: The Importance of Lifestyles/Routine Activities." Unpublished paper presented at the annual meeting of the Academy of Criminal Justice Sciences, Cincinnati, OH.

Teske, Steven C. (2005). "Juvenile Detention Reform: Using Collaborative Strategies and Evidence-Based Practices." Unpublished paper presented at the annual training institute of the American Probation and Parole Association, New York (July).

Texas Youth Commission (2005). *Certification Rates in Texas, 1990–1999.* Austin, TX: Texas Youth Commission Department of Research and Planning.

Thurman, Quint C., and Jihong Zhao (2004). *Contemporary Policing: Controversies, Challenges, and Solutions.* Los Angeles: Roxbury.

Titterington, V.B., and V. Grundies (2007). "An Exploratory Analysis of German and U.S. Youthful Homicide Offending." *Homicide Studies* **11**:189–212.

Tonry, Michael (1997). *Intermediate Sanctions in Sentencing Guidelines.* Washington, DC: U.S. National Institute of Justice.

Torbet, Patricia, and Linda Szymanski (1998). *State Legislative Responses to Violent Juvenile Crime: 1996–1997 Update.* Washington, DC: U.S. Department of Justice.

Torbet, Patricia, et al. (1996). *State Responses to Serious and Violent Juvenile Crime.* Washington, DC: Office of Juvenile Justice and Delinquency Prevention.

Toth, Reid C. (2005). "Limiting Discretion at Intake: An Analysis of Intake Data from North Carolina Juvenile Courts." Unpublished paper presented at the annual meeting of the Academy of Criminal Justice Sciences, Chicago (March).

Trester, Harold B. (1981). *Supervision of the Offender.* Englewood Cliffs, NJ: Prentice-Hall.

Trojanowicz, Robert, and Bonnie Bucqueroux (1990). *Community Policing: A Contemporary Perspective.* Cincinnati, OH: Anderson.

Trulson, Chad R., and Darin Haerle (2008). "The Final Chance for Change: Recidivism among a Cohort of the Most Serious State Delinquents." Unpublished paper presented at the annual meeting of the Academy of Criminal Justice Sciences, Cincinnati, OH.

Trulson, Chad R., James W. Marquart, and Janet Mullings (2005). "Towards an Understanding of Juvenile Persistence in the Transition to Young Adulthood." Unpublished paper presented at the annual meeting of the Academy of Criminal Justice Sciences, Chicago (March).

Tubman, J.G., A.G. Gil, and E.F. Wagner (2004). "Co-Occurring Substance Abuse and Delinquent Behavior During Early Adolescence: Emerging Relations and Implications for Intervention Strategies." *Criminal Justice and Behavior* **3**:463–488.

Turner, M.G., J.L. Hartman, and D.M. Bishop (2007). "The Effects of Prenatal Problems, Family Functioning, and Neighborhood Disadvantage in Predicting Life-Course-Persistent Offending." *Criminal Justice and Behavior* **34**:1241–1261.

Urban, Lynn S. (2005). "The Effect of a Curfew Check Program on Juvenile Opportunities for Delinquent Activity." Unpublished paper presented at the annual meeting of the Academy of Criminal Justice Sciences, Chicago (March).

U.S. Code (2009). *U.S. Code Annotated.* St. Paul, MN: West Group.

U.S. General Accounting Office (1995a). *Juvenile Justice: Minimal Gender Bias Occurred in Processing Noncriminal Juveniles.* Washington, DC: U.S. General Accounting Office.

U.S. General Accounting Office (1995b). *Juvenile Justice: Representation Rates Varied as Did Counsel's Impact on Court Outcomes*. Washington, DC: U.S. General Accounting Office.

Valdez, Avelardo (2007). *Mexican American Girls and Gang Violence: Beyond Risk*. New York: Palgrave Macmillan.

van Wijk, A.P., et al. (2007). "Criminal Profiles of Violent Juvenile Sex and Violent Juvenile Non-Sex Offenders: An Explorative Longitudinal Study." *Journal of Interpersonal Violence* **22:**1340–1355.

Vaughn, M.G., et al. (2007). "Psychiatric Symptoms and Substance Abuse among Juvenile Offenders." *Criminal Justice and Behavior* **34:**1296–1312.

Virginia Department of Juvenile Justice (2008). *Halfway Houses*. Richmond, VA: Department of Juvenile Justice.

Vivian, J.P., J.N. Grimes, and S. Vasquez (2007). "Assaults in Juvenile Correctional Facilities: An Exploratory Study." *Journal of Crime and Justice* **30:**17–34.

Vollman, Brenda, and Karen J. Terry (2005). "Reporting Trends for Sexual Abuse Victims." Unpublished paper presented at the annual meeting of the Academy of Criminal Justice Sciences, Chicago (March).

Wallace, S.A., and C.B. Fisher (2007). "Substance Use Attitudes among Black Adolescents: The Role of Parent, Peer, and Cultural Factors." *Journal of Youth and Adolescence* **36:**441–451.

Wallace, Lisa, Kevin Minor, and James Wells (2005). "Defining the Differential in Differential Oppression Theory: Exploring the Role of Social Learning." Unpublished paper presented at the annual meeting of the Academy of Criminal Justice Sciences, Chicago (March).

Wallenius, M., R. Punamaki, and A. Rimpela (2007). "Digital Game Playing and Direct and Indirect Aggression in Early Adolescence." *Journal of Youth and Adolescence* **36:**325–336.

Walls, M.L., C.L. Chapple, and K.D. Johnson (2007). "Strain, Emotion, and Suicide among American Indian Youth." *Deviant Behavior* **28:**219–246.

Warr, Mark (2005). "Making Delinquent Friends: Adult Supervision and Children's Affiliations." *Criminology* **43:**77–106.

Watson, Karly (2008). "Perceptions of Prohibited Sexual Activity from Staff and Youth in a State Juvenile Facility." Unpublished paper presented at the annual meeting of the Academy of Criminal Justice Sciences, Cincinnati, OH.

Watson, Donnie W., et al. (2003). "Comprehensive Residential Education, Arts, and Substance Abuse Treatment." *Youth Violence and Juvenile Justice* **1:**388–401.

Watts-Farmer, Kalori Niesha (2008). "What Is the Effect of the Juvenile Waiver on the Juvenile Justice System?" Unpublished paper presented at the annual meeting of the Academy of Criminal Justice Sciences, Cincinnati, OH.

West, Angela D. (2005). "Smoke and Mirrors: Measuring Gang Activity with School and Police Data." Unpublished paper presented at the annual meeting of the Academy of Criminal Justice Sciences, Chicago (March).

Whitaker, Ashley (2005). "Children Who Witness Abuse: The Role of an Intern in the Research Process." Unpublished paper presented at the annual meeting of the Academy of Criminal Justice Sciences, Chicago (March).

White, Elvira M. (2008). "The Ethical and Theoretical Orientation of a State Sentencing Commission When Drafting Juvenile Law Recommendations." Unpublished paper presented at the annual meeting of the Academy of Criminal Justice Sciences, Cincinnati, OH.

Whiteacre, K.W. (2007). "Strange Bedfellows: The Tensions of Coerced Treatment." *Criminal Justice Policy Review* **18:**260–273.

Whitehead, Michele (2008). "Juvenile Justice: Delinquency and the Formation of Public Policy." Unpublished paper presented at the annual meeting of the Academy of Criminal Justice Sciences, Cincinnati, OH.

Wilkerson, Dawn (2005). "Organizational Structuring within Juvenile Justice: Why Reform Is Needed." Unpublished paper presented at the annual meeting of the Academy of Criminal Justice Sciences, Chicago (March).

Wilson, E.O. (1975). *Sociobiology: The New Synthesis*. Cambridge, MA: Harvard University Press.

Wilson, James Q., and Richard J. Herrnstein (1985). *Crime and Human Nature*. New York: Simon and Schuster.

Wilson, James Q., and Joan Petersilia (2002). *Crime: Public Policies for Crime Control*. Oakland, CA: Institute for Contemporary Studies Press.

Wilson, John J. (2001). *1998 National Youth Gang Survey*. Washington, DC: Office of Juvenile Justice and Delinquency Prevention.

Wolfgang, Marvin, and Franco Ferracuti (1967). *The Subculture of Violence*. London: Tavistock.

Wolfgang, Marvin, Robert M. Figlio, and Thorsten Sellin (1972). *Delinquency in a Birth Cohort*. Chicago: University of Chicago Press.

Worling, James R. (1995). "Adolescent Sex Offenders Against Females: Differences Based on the Age of Their Victims." *International Journal of Offender Therapy and Comparative Criminology* **39:**276–293.

Xiaoying, Dong (2005). "A Study of Young Offenders Who Desist from Re-Offending." Unpublished paper presented at the annual meeting of the Academy of Criminal Justice Sciences, Chicago (March).

Yalda, Christine A. (2005). "From School Halls to School Walls: Student Perceptions of Effective Campus Security at a Public High School." Unpublished paper presented at the annual meeting of the Academy of Criminal Justice Sciences, Chicago (March).

Yeager, Clay R., John A. Herb, and John H. Lemmon (1989). *The Impact of Court Unification on Juvenile Probation Systems in Pennsylvania.* Shippensburg, PA: Center for Juvenile Justice Training and Research, Shippensburg University.

Zachariah, John K. (2002). *An Overview of Boot Camp Goals, Components, and Results.* Washington, DC: Koch Crime Institute.

Zhang, Yu (2008). "The Effect of Race, Gender, and Family Background on Juvenile Transfer Decisions." Unpublished paper presented at the annual meeting of the Academy of Criminal Justice Sciences, Cincinnati, OH.

Zimmermann, Carol A., and Edmund F. McGarrell (2005). "The Effects of Family Group Conferencing and Family Bonding on Delinquency Desistance." Unpublished paper presented at the annual meeting of the Academy of Criminal Justice Sciences, Chicago (March).

Case Index

Name Index

Subject Index